R. Gupta's®

All About REASONING

Verbal

- Concise Study Material with **2500⁺** Solved Questions
- A Useful Book for All Competitive Examinations

by

RPH Editorial Board

Ramesh Publishing House, New Delhi

Published by
O.P. Gupta *for* Ramesh Publishing House

Admin. Office
12-H, New Daryaganj Road, Opp. Officers' Mess,
New Delhi-110002 ✆ 23261567, 23275224, 23275124

E-mail: info@rameshpublishinghouse.com
For Online Shopping: www.rameshpublishinghouse.com

Showroom
- Balaji Market, Nai Sarak, Delhi-6 ✆ 23253720,23282525
- 4457, Nai Sarak, Delhi-6, ✆ 23918938

Book Code: R-296

ISBN: 978-93-5012-525-0

HSN Code: 49011010

Price: ₹ 380

Printed at: Deepak Offset, Delhi

CONTENTS

SERIES

PART - I

LETTER SERIES

In letter series the letters follow a definite order. The given series of letters can be in natural order or in reverse order or combination of both. The letters may be skipped or repeated or consecutive. The given series may be single or may even comprise of two different series merged at alternate positions. While attempting questions on letter series one should note the pattern of alphabet series.

Alphabets in natural series are :

A B C D E F G H I J K L M N O P Q R S T U V W X Y Z

A ↓ 1st, E ↓ 5th, J ↓ 10th, O ↓ 15th, T ↓ 20th, Y ↓ 25th

Alphabets in reverse series are :

Z Y X W V U T S R Q P O N M L K J I H G F E D C B A

Z ↓ 1st, V ↓ 5th, Q ↓ 10th, L ↓ 15th, G ↓ 20th, B ↓ 25th

Note : On reaching Z, the series restarts from A and on reaching A, it restarts from Z.

SOLVED EXAMPLES

Directions : *Which of the given options will complete the given series?*

1. B D F H J ?

(*a*) L (*b*) O (*c*) M (*d*) K

Ans. (*a*) : The series follows the pattern of moving the letters two steps forward.

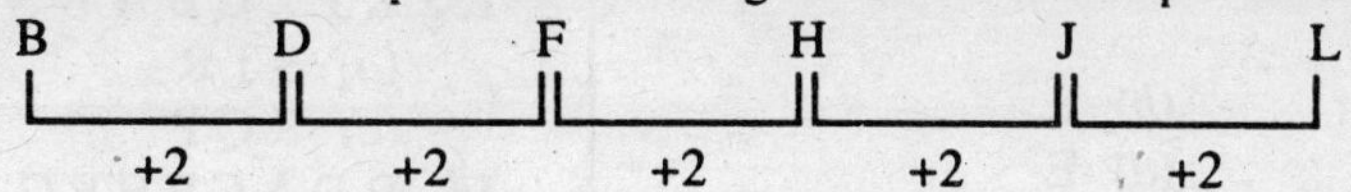

2. A Z B Y C ?

(*a*) D (*b*) X (*c*) U (*d*) E

Ans. (*b*) : There are two alternate series.

Series I : A B C (Consecutive letters in natural series)

Series II : Z Y X (Consecutive letters in reverse series)

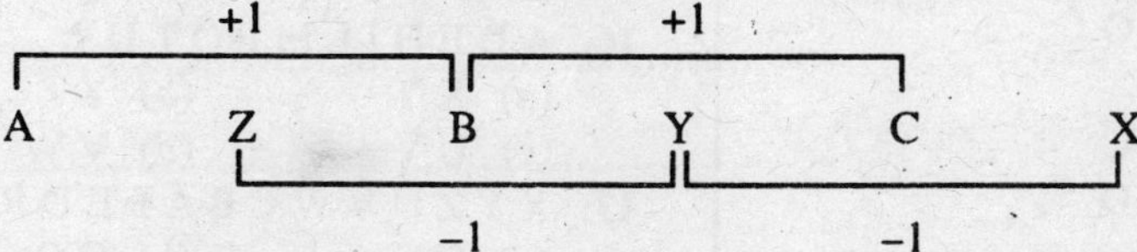

3. A A C D D F G G I ?

(*a*) I (*b*) K (*c*) J (*d*) L

Ans. (*c*) : The first letter is repeated and then moved two steps forward. The consecutive letter follows which is repeated and the above pattern continues.

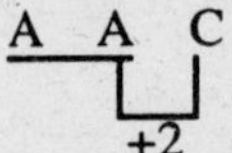

D D F — +2 G G I J — +2

4. Which combination of letters completes the given series : NRJ, PNP, RJV, ?

(*a*) BFT (*b*) TFB (*c*) TBF (*d*) BTF

Ans. (*b*) : The letters in one group correspond to the letters in the next group in the manner two steps forward, four steps backward, six steps forward (+2, –4, +6) respectively, *i.e.*,

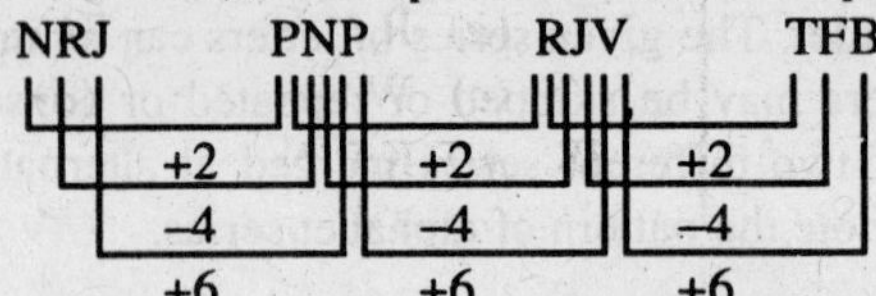

EXERCISE

Directions : *In each of the following series determine the order of the letters. Then from the given options select the one which will complete the given series.*

1. B Y C X D W E ?

(*a*) S (*b*) T (*c*) U (*d*) V

2. A D C G E ?

(*a*) G (*b*) J (*c*) I (*d*) L

3. L N P R T ?

(*a*) U (*b*) V (*c*) W (*d*) Y

4. X O I F ?

(*a*) D (*b*) F (*c*) B (*d*) E

5. D Q G O J M ?

(*a*) K (*b*) P (*c*) M (*d*) L

6. B A F E J I P O ? U

(*a*) V (*b*) T (*c*) S (*d*) Q

7. Z A A Y B B X C ?

(*a*) W (*b*) C (*c*) V (*d*) D

8. B D G K ? V

(*a*) N (*b*) P (*c*) Q (*d*) M

9. V R O K ? D

(*a*) L (*b*) I (*c*) H (*d*) J

10. Z X V T ?

(*a*) Q (*b*) S (*c*) R (*d*) P

11. Z A Y B X C W D V E ?

(*a*) U D (*b*) U C (*c*) T R (*d*) U F

12. B C D B D D B E D B F D B G ?

(*a*) B D (*b*) B F (*c*) H B (*d*) D B

13. Z Y X C B A W V U F E D ?

(*a*) S T R (*b*) T S R (*c*) R Q P (*d*) I H G

14. B D A C F H E G ?

(*a*) J L (*b*) I K (*c*) J K (*d*) K L

15. A Z Y B X W C V U D T S E ?

(*a*) R S (*b*) S T (*c*) R Q (*d*) Q R

16. A D E H I L M P Q T U ?

(*a*) X Y (*b*) Y Z (*c*) U V (*d*) V W

17. X Y Z U V W C B A F E D R S T O ?

(*a*) G E (*b*) O P (*c*) P Q (*d*) G H

18. ZXYWVTUSRPQO?
(*a*) MN (*b*) MK
(*c*) NL (*d*) LN

19. CABFDEIGH?
(*a*) JLK (*b*) JKL
(*c*) LKJ (*d*) LJK

20. MNLOKPJQIRHS?
(*a*) TG (*b*) GT
(*c*) FU (*d*) RH

21. BFKQ?
(*a*) U (*b*) T
(*c*) X (*d*) Y

22. CEFIJLMPQS?
(*a*) TW (*b*) TV
(*c*) WY (*d*) VY

23. EDCHGFKJIN?
(*a*) LM (*b*) OP
(*c*) MO (*d*) ML

24. AEIMQ?
(*a*) T (*b*) U
(*c*) V (*d*) W

25. CEHJMO?
(*a*) Q (*b*) S
(*c*) R (*d*) T

26. AABACA?
(*a*) A (*b*) D
(*c*) B (*d*) C

27. EOISMWQA?
(*a*) UE (*b*) TD
(*c*) VF (*d*) SC

28. ABD?K
(*a*) G (*b*) F
(*c*) H (*d*) I

29. BEIL?S
(*a*) Q (*b*) M
(*c*) P (*d*) N

30. XUROL?
(*a*) J (*b*) G
(*c*) H (*d*) I

31. CGLR?
(*a*) W (*b*) X
(*c*) Y (*d*) Z

32. BADC?HGJI
(*a*) EF (*b*) FE
(*c*) FG (*d*) DF

33. RKF?B
(*a*) D (*b*) C
(*c*) E (*d*) B

34. ZX?NF
(*a*) T (*b*) R
(*c*) Q (*d*) O

35. WSOK?
(*a*) G (*b*) F
(*c*) H (*d*) E

36. TTSRRQPPON?
(*a*) M (*b*) L
(*c*) O (*d*) N

37. DKP?B
(*a*) R (*b*) T
(*c*) W (*d*) Z

38. AFKP?
(*a*) T (*b*) U
(*c*) W (*d*) X

39. CCCCDC?EC
(*a*) D (*b*) C
(*c*) E (*d*) B

40. RZJKSBC?
(*a*) W (*b*) K
(*c*) L (*d*) X

41. ALWBMXCN?
(*a*) V (*b*) W
(*c*) Y (*d*) X

42. DHMS?
(*a*) W (*b*) X
(*c*) Y (*d*) Z

43. URPMK?
(*a*) G (*b*) E
(*c*) H (*d*) F

44. ABFGKL?
(*a*) P (*b*) M
(*c*) R (*d*) O

45. ADG, XVT, BEH, WUS, ?
(*a*) VTR (*b*) CFI
(*c*) DFJ (*d*) STU

46. GMSY, IOUA, KQWC, ?
(*a*) MSYE (*b*) NSYE
(*c*) MTYE (*d*) MSYF

47. ADG, GJM, ?, SVY
(*a*) MPS (*b*) MQR
(*c*) MQS (*d*) SPM

48. KNQ, TWZ, CFI, ?
(*a*) KOR (*b*) LOR
(*c*) MNQ (*d*) JLM

49. AEI, BFJ, CGK, ?
(*a*) DLH (*b*) EGF
(*c*) EFL (*d*) DHL

50. CFI, IKM, OPQ, ?
(*a*) UUU (*b*) UST
(*c*) VUS (*d*) TUV

51. LAZ, NEX, PIV, ?
(*a*) SLS (*b*) QNS
(*c*) RMT (*d*) RMS

52. DED, EFE, FGF, ?
(*a*) HGH (*b*) GHG
(*c*) EFE (*d*) FHF

53. XYZ, UVW, ?, OPQ
(*a*) RST (*b*) STU
(*c*) QRS (*d*) TUV

54. VCL, UEI, TGF, ?
(*a*) SJC (*b*) THI
(*c*) SIC (*d*) RHD

55. ABC, EFG, HIJ, ?
(*a*) IJK (*b*) KLM
(*c*) LMN (*d*) JKL

56. PQR, HIJ, DEF, ?
(*a*) DEF (*b*) CDE
(*c*) ABC (*d*) BCD

57. KNQ, TWZ, CFI, ?
(*a*) MNQ (*b*) LOR
(*c*) LPR (*d*) KOR

58. JOBS, KMEO, LKHK, ?, NGNC
(*a*) MJLH (*b*) LIKG
(*c*) MIKG (*d*) MNGM

59. ABC, ACE, ADG, ?
(*a*) AEG (*b*) AFH
(*c*) AFG (*d*) AEI

60. IOU, JKL, PQR, ?
(*a*) UVW (*b*) XYZ
(*c*) TUV (*d*) VWX

61. AZ, GT, MN, ?, YB
(*a*) KF (*b*) TS
(*c*) RX (*d*) SH

62. BMY, DNW, FOU, ?
(*a*) HPT (*b*) HPS
(*c*) HQS (*d*) GPS

63. ADG, GJM, MPS, ?
(*a*) SVW (*b*) SVY
(*c*) SUW (*d*) SWY

64. AZ, CX, EV, ?
(*a*) HU (*b*) GS
(*c*) GT (*d*) HT

65. DMP, FLN, HKL, JJJ, ?
(*a*) MIH (*b*) III
(*c*) LIH (*d*) MII

66. ECA, JHF, OMK, ?, YWU
(*a*) TRP (*b*) LNP
(*c*) QPN (*d*) RPT

67. ABP, CDQ, EFR, ?
(*a*) GHS (*b*) HGS
(*c*) GHR (*d*) GHT

68. BEH, KNQ, TWZ, ?
(*a*) IJL (*b*) BDF
(*c*) CFI (*d*) ADG

69. DMU, EOT, FQS, ?
(*a*) GRS (*b*) GSQ
(*c*) GRT (*d*) GSR

70. EJOT, DHLP, CFIL, ?
(*a*) BDFH (*b*) DGKL
(*c*) DEIJ (*d*) BLHM

71. BMK, DLM, FKO, HJQ, ?
(*a*) JIR (*b*) JIT
(*c*) JHS (*d*) JIS

72. A, CD, FGH, ?
(*a*) IJKL (*b*) KLMN
(*c*) JKLM (*d*) LMNO

73. BXJ, ETL, HPN, KLP, ?
(*a*) PHR (*b*) NIR
(*c*) NHR (*d*) MHR

74. PUF, QVG, RWH, ?
(*a*) SXI (*b*) SYZ
(*c*) SXJ (*d*) SVI

75. DEF, HIJ, MNO, ?
(*a*) RTV (*b*) STU
(*c*) PTU (*d*) SRU

76. DJT, FIU, HHV, ?
(*a*) IGX (*b*) KGV
(*c*) HHW (*d*) JGW

77. HUA, GTZ, FSY, ERX, ?
(*a*) DRV (*b*) DSW
(*c*) DQW (*d*) DQV

78. ABZ, BCY, CDX, DEW, ?
(*a*) EFV (*b*) EGH
(*c*) EFG (*d*) EGV

79. HKN, PSV, XAD, ?
(*a*) JMN (*b*) FIL
(*c*) JLO (*d*) KLN

80. YCL, MQZ, AEN, ?
(*a*) PUE (*b*) OSB
(*c*) PSE (*d*) OUB

81. QPO, SRQ, UTS, WVU, ?
(*a*) YXW (*b*) AZY
(*c*) XYZ (*d*) YZA

82. KUZ, MOX, OIV, QET, ?
(*a*) SAT (*b*) PAM
(*c*) SAR (*d*) PBR

83. CFL, EIK, GLJ, IOI, ?
(*a*) JRH (*b*) KQH
(*c*) KRH (*d*) KRK

84. EJO, TYD, INS, XCH, ?
(*a*) MRW (*b*) NRV
(*c*) MRV (*d*) NRW

85. ABP, CDQ, EFR,?
(*a*) GHS (*b*) GIS
(*c*) GGS (*d*) GJS

86. NRA, PRC, RRE, TRG, ?
(*a*) USI (*b*) VRI
(*c*) WRJ (*d*) TRI

87. DUW, CVV, BWU, AXT, ?
(*a*) BYS (*b*) CZV
(*c*) XYS (*d*) ZYS

88. FJKP, ILMQ, LNOR, OPQS, ?
(*a*) RQTV (*b*) RQSS
(*c*) RRST (*d*) RTTU

89. DQCP, EPEN, FOGL, GNIJ, ?
(*a*) HNLG (*b*) HLJG
(*c*) HOMI (*d*) HMKH

90. DFST, FSTD, STDF, ?
(*a*) TSFD (*b*) FDTS
(*c*) TDFS (*d*) SFDT

91. RYL, VBN, ZEP, DHR, ?
(*a*) HLK (*b*) HKT
(*c*) HJT (*d*) HKS

92. FAV, KEY, PIB, UME, ?
(*a*) XRH (*b*) ZQH
(*c*) YPG (*d*) WQI

93. AJN, XKK, ULH, RME, ?
(*a*) ROC (*b*) NNC
(*c*) POB (*d*) ONB

94. AGFH, BFGG, CEHF, ?
(*a*) DEIF (*b*) DDIE
(*c*) DCIB (*d*) DEIC

95. WCG, PIB, IOW, ?
(*a*) CVS (*b*) DUQ
(*c*) EVT (*d*) BUR

96. MFJ, PIM, TMQ, ?
(*a*) YRV (*b*) XRV
(*c*) WVR (*d*) VYR

97. IXT, MAV, QDX, ?
(*a*) WGX (*b*) VHY
(*c*) UGZ (*d*) YHZ

98. QYK, ?, ISG, EPE
(*a*) NWJ (*b*) MVI
(*c*) NVI (*d*) MVJ

99. JMC, CLT, KND, ?, LOE, GPX
(*a*) ENV (*b*) DMX
(*c*) EOU (*d*) DRX

100. ZDV, XGS, VJP, ?
(*a*) SNM (*b*) TMM
(*c*) TNR (*d*) SNT

EXPLANATORY ANSWERS

1. (*d*) : There are two alternate series.

+1 +1 +1
B Y C X D W E V
−1 −1 −1

Series I : BCDE (natural order)
Series II : YXWV (reverse order)

2. (*b*) : There are two alternate series.

+2 +2
A D C G E J
+3 +3

Series I : ACE (follows +2 pattern)
Series II : DGJ (follows +3 pattern)

3. (*b*) : The series follows the +2 pattern. *i.e.*

L N P R T V
+2 +2 +2 +2 +2

4. (*b*) : The series follows the sequence of the difference decreasing by 3 *i.e.*

X O I F F
−9 −6 −3 −0

5. (*c*) : There are two alternate series.

Series I : DGJM (follows +3 pattern)
Series II : QOM (follows –2 pattern)

6. (*a*) : Each vowel (AEIOU) is preceded by the letter that comes next to it in the natural alphabetical series.

B A F E J I P O V U

7. (*b*) : There are three alternate series. The second and the third set are the same, *i.e.,*

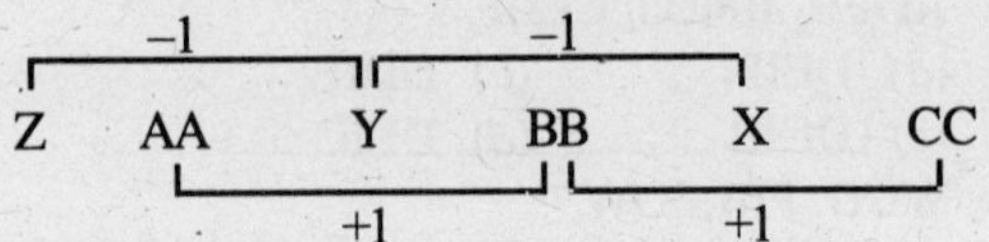

Series I : ZYX (in reverse order)
Series II and *III* : ABC (in natural order)
The letter 'C' needs to be repeated.

8. (*b*) : The difference between the letters increases at each step after beginning with two.

B D G K P V
+2 +3 +4 +5 +6

9. (*c*) : The letters are in reverse series and the difference is four and three alternately.

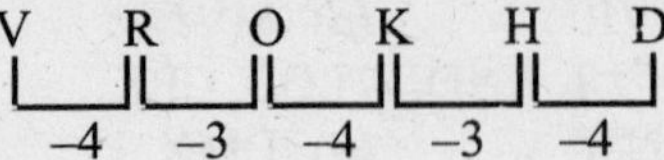

10. (*c*) : The letters in this series are moved two steps backward.

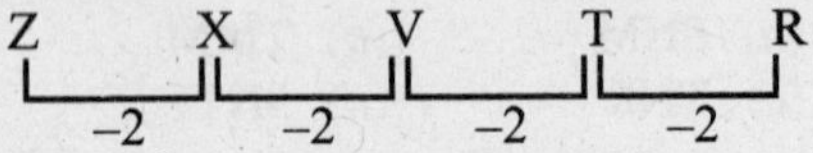

11. (*d*) : There are two alternate series

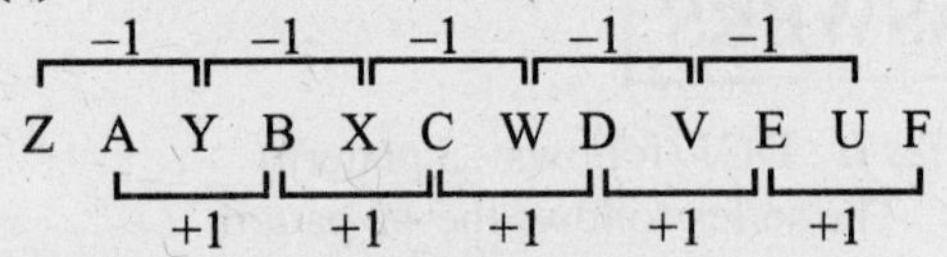

Series I : ZYXWVU (in reverse order)
Series II : ABCDEF (in natural order)

12. (*d*) : The actual letters which are moving one step forward in the series are packed between B and D.

B C D B D D B E D B F D B G D
+1 +1 +1 +1

13. (*b*) : The letters in the series are in group of three. The letters in the groups are in consecutive reverse series and are in two alternate sections.

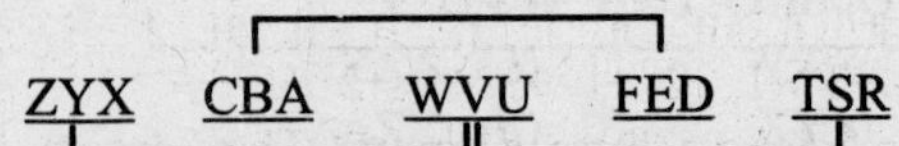

14. (*a*) : The letters in the series are arranged in following order (Four letters are mixed)

A B C D is written as BDAC; and

E F G H as FHEG. Similarly,

I J K L will be JLIK.

The answer option is JL, *i.e.,* (a)

15. (*c*) : There are two alternate series.

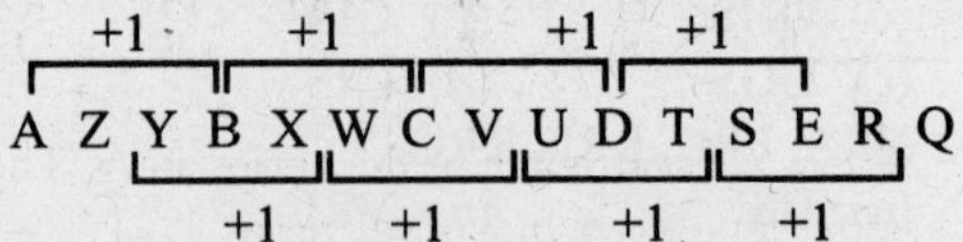

Series I : ABCDE (in natural series)
Series II : ZY XW VU TS RQ (double letter in reverse series)

16. (*a*) : The series is formed by moving the letters three and one steps forward alternately.

A D E H I L M P Q T U X Y
+3 +1 +3 +1 +3 +1 +3 +1 +3 +1 +3 +1

17. (*c*) : Three letters form a section in this manner.

XYZ UVW CBA FED RST OPQ

18. (*a*) : The letters form the sections in the following manner.

ZXYWV TUSR PQO MN

19. (*d*) : Three letters in natural series form a section. The first letter is in the centre, second to its right and the third to its left.

CAB FDE IGH LJK

20. (*b*) : There are two alternate series

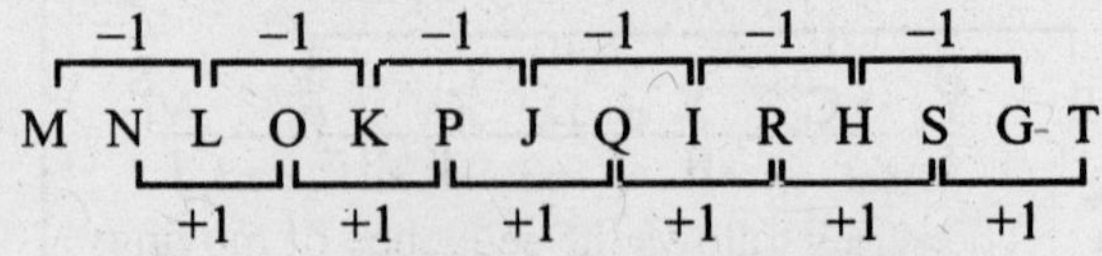

Series I : MLKJIHG (in reverse series)
Series II : NOPQRST (in natural series)

21. (*c*) : The difference between the letters in the series increases by one at each step.

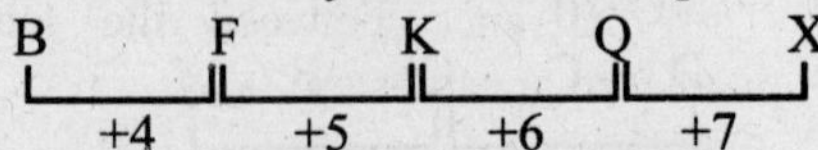

22. (*a*) : The order of difference between the letters is two, one, three and one, which is repeated.

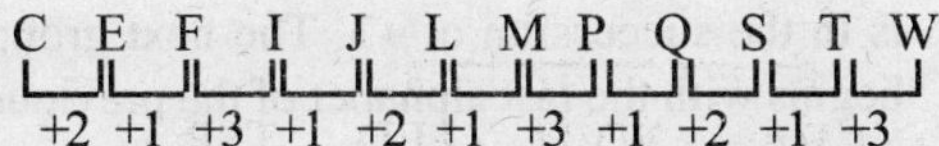

23. (*d*) : Three letters form a group. They are in natural series but the letters in each group are written backwards.

EDC HGF KJI NML

24. (*b*) : The letters in the series are moved four steps forward.

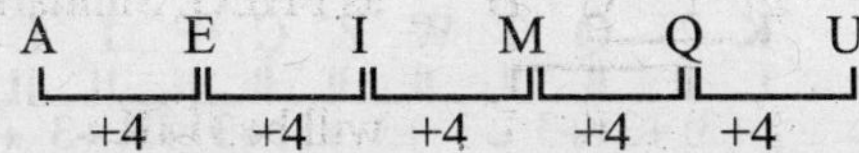

25. (*c*) : The letters are moved two and three steps forward alternately.

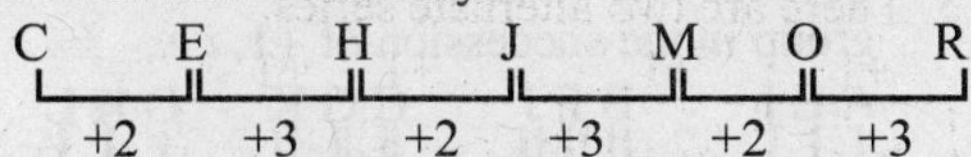

26. (*b*) : Every second letter in the series is A. The other letters are in natural series.

A A B A C A D

+1 +2 +3

27. (*a*) : The two alternate series follow the sequence of moving the letters four steps forward.

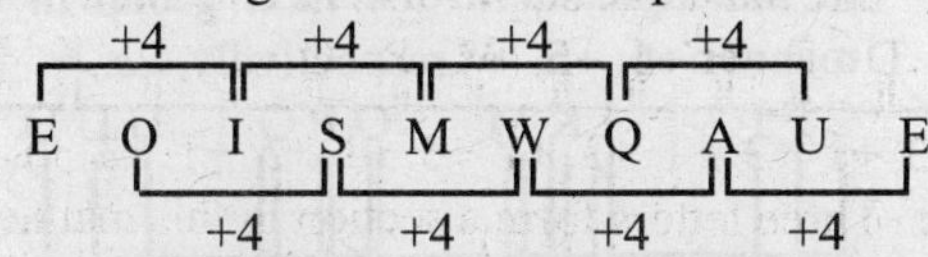

Series I : EIMQU

Series II : OSWAE

(the series restarts from A on reaching Z)

28. (*a*) : The difference between the letters is increased by one at each step.

A B D G K

+1 +2 +3 +4

29. (*c*) : The series follows the pattern +3, +4 which is repeated.

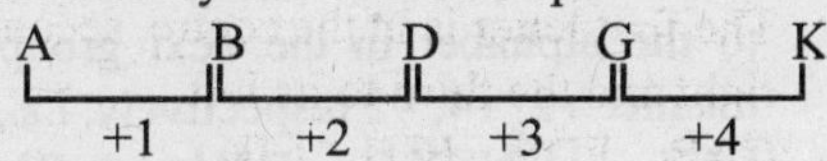

30. (*d*) : The series follows the sequence of moving the letters three steps in this order.

X U R O L I

−3 −3 −3 −3 −3

31. (*c*) : The difference between the letters is increased at each step.

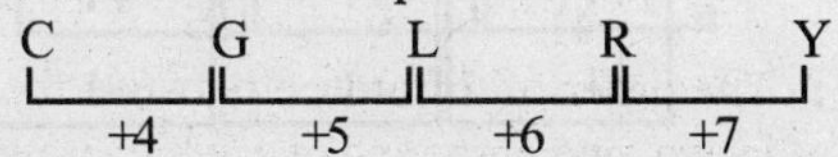

32. (*b*) : The letters in natural series are divided into sections of two letters each. The letters in each section are written backward.

BA DC FE HG JI

33. (*b*) : The difference between the letters is reduced by two at each step.

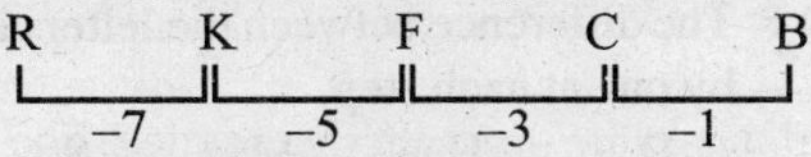

34. (*a*) : The difference between the letters is increased by two at each step

Z X T N F

−2 −4 −6 −8

35. (*a*) : The letters in this series are moved four steps backward.

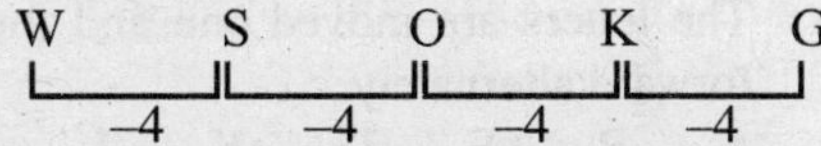

36. (*d*) : The letters at odd positions are repeated.

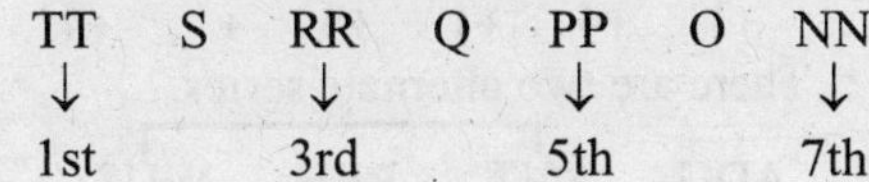

37. (*c*) : The letters in the series follow alternate sequence of +7 and +5.

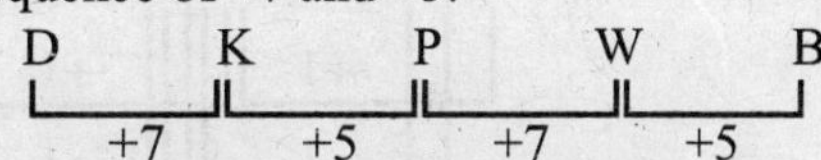

(Series restarts from A on reaching Z)

38. (*b*) : The letters in the series are moved five steps forward.

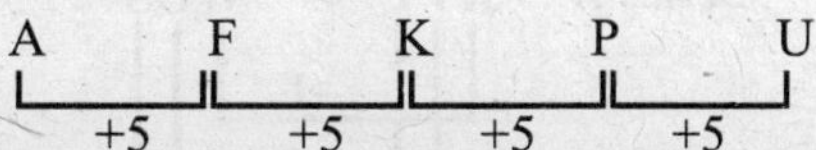

39. (*b*) : The series is in natural order and each letter is enclosed within two C's.

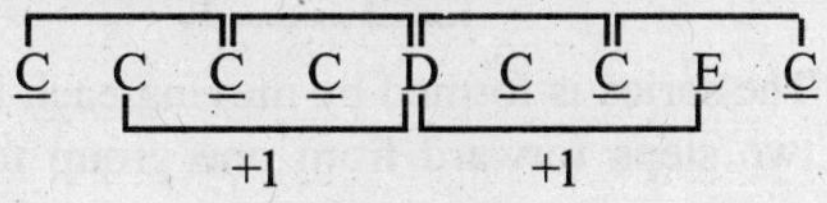

40. (*b*) : Every three letters form a group in this series. The first letter is moved eight steps forward and backward to obtain the second and third letters respectively. The consecutive letter to the third letter is the first letter of the second group of three letters. The above process then continues.

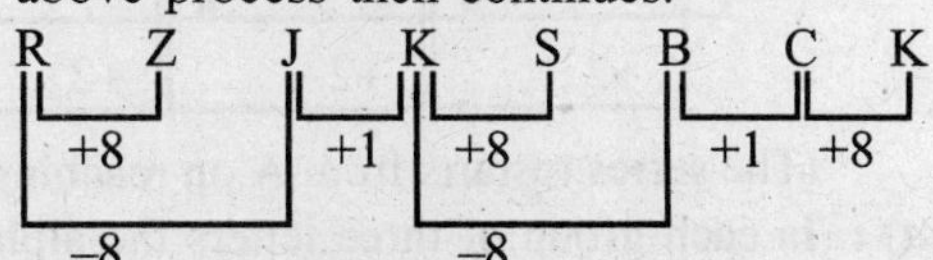

41. (c) : There are three alternate series.

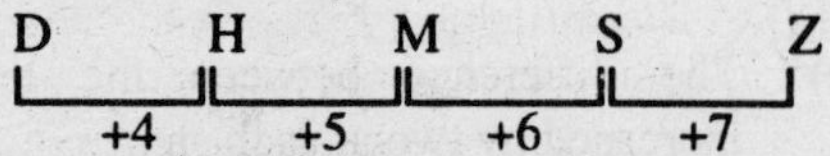

Series I : ABC
Series II : LMN
Series III : WXY

42. (d) : The difference between the letters increases by one at each step.

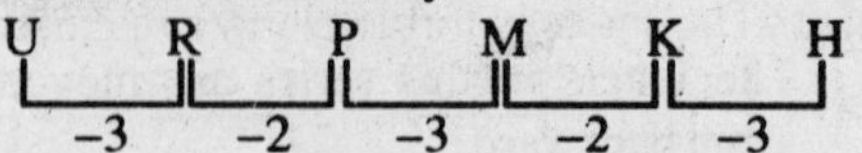

43. (c) : The letters are moved three and two steps backward alternately.

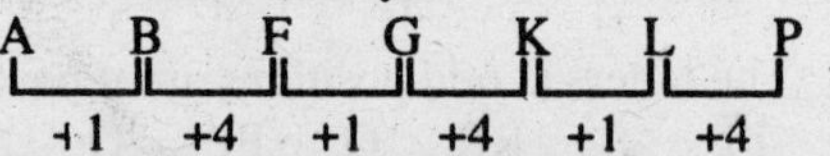

44. (a) : The letters are moved one and four steps forward alternately.

A B F G K L P
+1 +4 +1 +4 +1 +4

45. (b) : There are two alternate series.

ADG XVT BEH WUS CFI

Series I : ADG BEH CFI

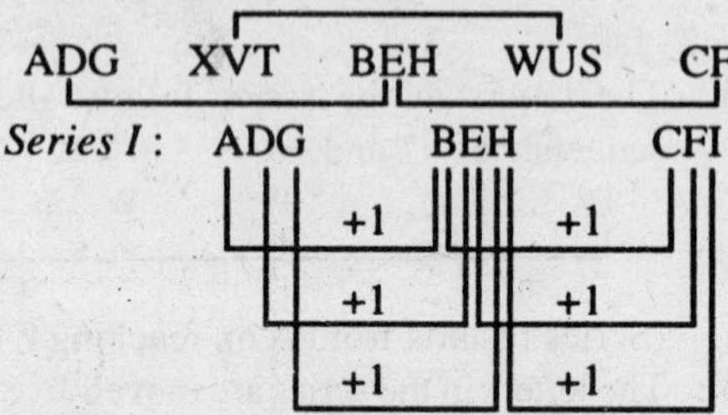

Series II : XVT WUS

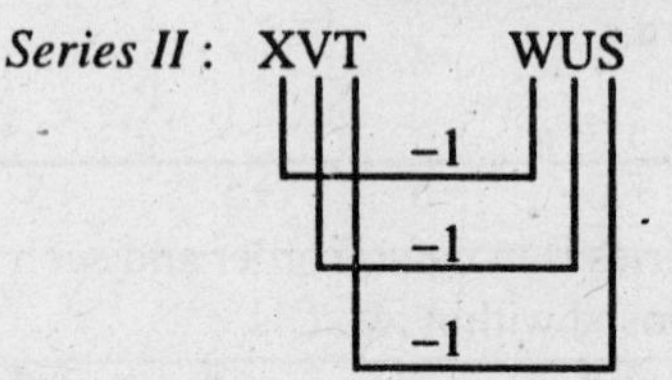

46. (a) : The series is formed by moving each letter two steps forward from one group to the next.

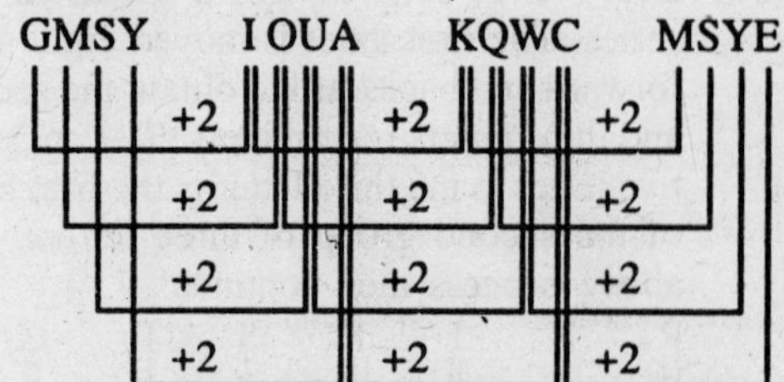

(The series restarts from A on reaching Z)

47. (a) : In each group of three letters the alphabet is in the succession of +3. The next group begins with the last alphabet of the previous group.

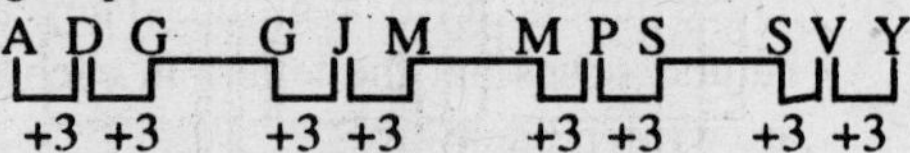

48. (b) : All the alphabet in this group series is in succession of +3. The alphabetical series repeat from 'A' on reaching 'Z'.

K N Q T W Z C F I L O R
+3 +3 +3 +3 +3 +3 +3 +3 +3 +3 +3

49. (d) : Each of the three alphabet in one group corresponds to the alphabet in the next group in the succession of +1, *i.e.*,

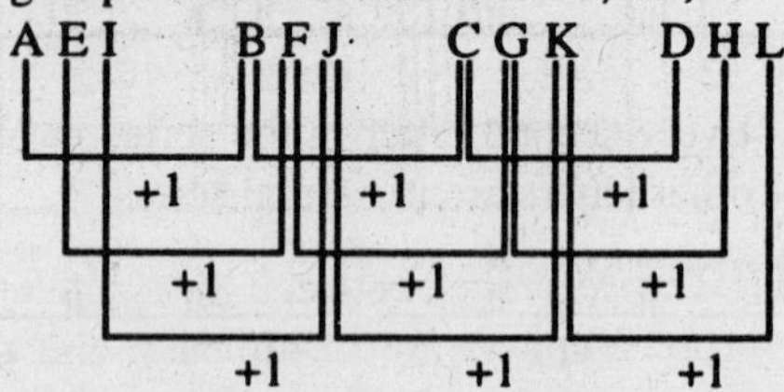

50. (a) : The three alphabet in one group correspond to the alphabet in the next group in the manner +6, +5, +4 respectively, *i.e.*,

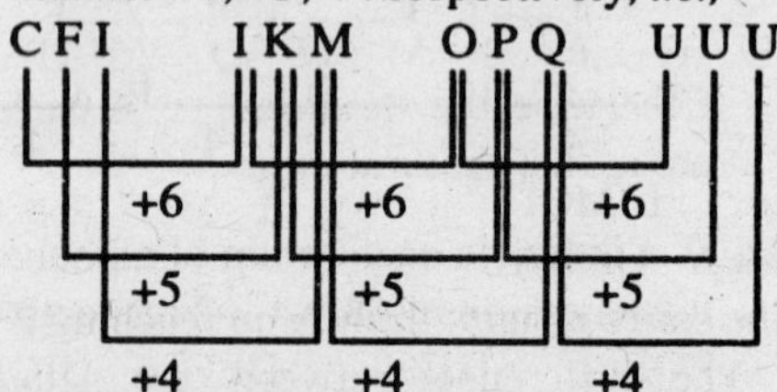

51. (c) : The three alphabet in one group correspond to the alphabet in the next group in the manner +2, +4, −2 respectively, *i.e.*,

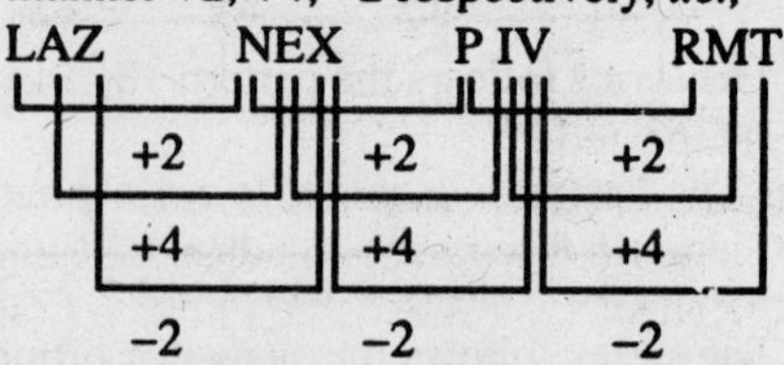

52. (b) : The alphabet from one group to the next are in succession of +1, *i.e.*,

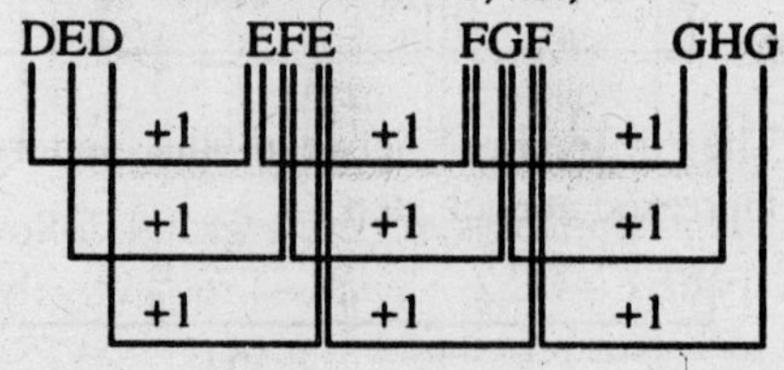

53. (*a*) : The alphabet from one group to the next are in recession of –3, *i.e.*,

XYZ UVW RST OPQ

–3 –3 –3

–3 –3 –3

–3 –3 –3

54. (*c*) : The alphabet in one group correspond to the alphabet in the next group in the manner –1, +2, –3 respectively, *i.e.*,

VCL UEI TGF SIC

–1 –1 –1

+2 +2 +2

–3 –3 –3

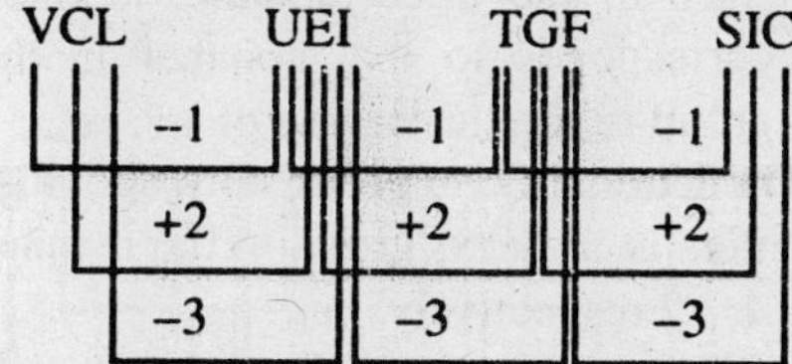

55. (*d*) : The difference between the last letter of the preceding group of alphabet and the first letter of the next group is decreasing by 1, *i.e.*,

ABC EFG HIJ JKL

+2 +1 +0

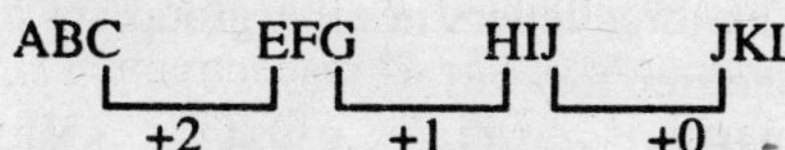

Otherwise the three letters in each group are in their natural order.

56. (*d*) : The letters in each group of alphabet are in the recession of –8, –4, –2 respectively.

PQR HIJ DEF BCD

–8 –4 –2

–8 –4 –2

–8 –4 –2

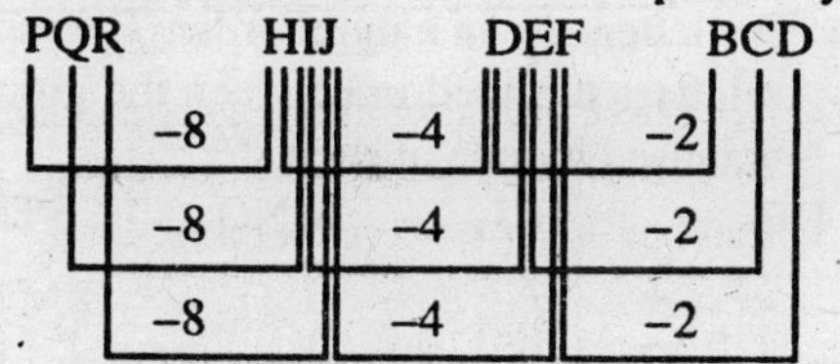

57. (*b*) : The letters in each group correspond to the letter in next group in the succession of +9.

KNQ TWZ CFI LOR

+9 +9 +9

+9 +9 +9

+9 +9 +9

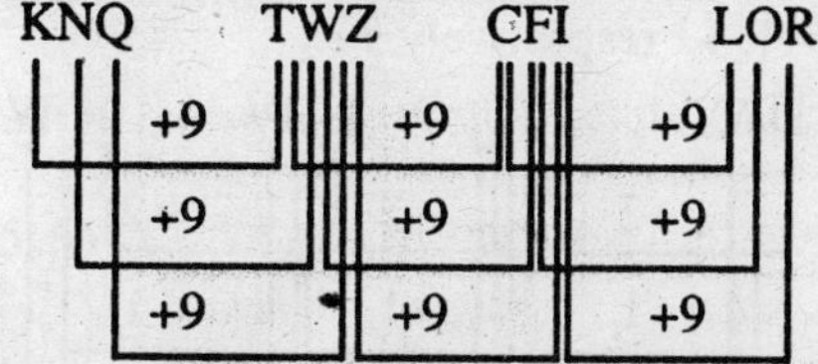

58. (*c*) : The alphabets in each group follow the pattern +1, –2, +3 and –4 respectively from one group to the next group.

JOBS KMEO LKHK MIKG NGNC

+1 +1 +1 +1

–2 –2 –2 –2

+3 +3 +3 +3

–4 –4 –4 –4

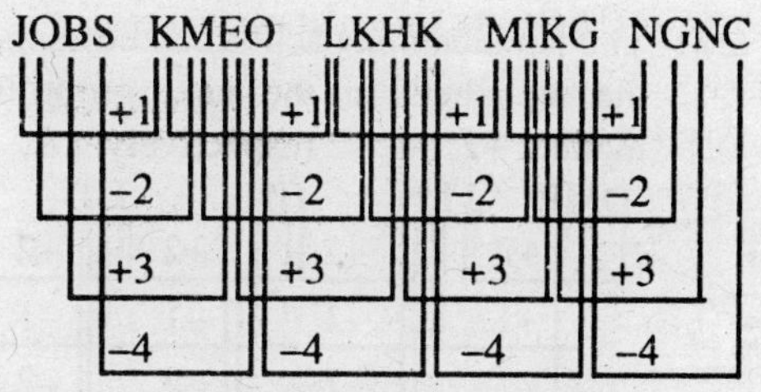

59. (*d*) : The difference between the letters in each group is increased by one.

A B C A C E A D G A E I

+1 +1 +2 +2 +3 +3 +4 +4

60. (*d*) : The series is formed in this manner :

I O U J K L P Q R V W X

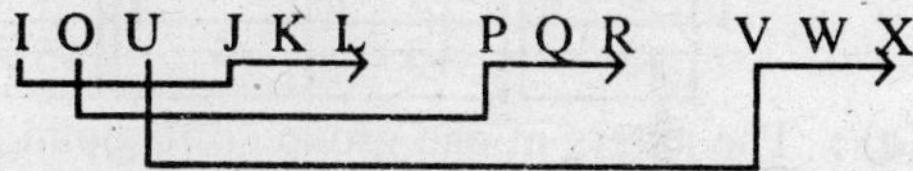

Three consecutive letters to each letter in the first group forms the other groups in the series.

61. (*d*) : The letters in one group correspond to the letters in the next group in the manner +6, –6 respectively, *i.e.*,

AZ GT MN SH YB

+6 +6 +6 +6

–6 –6 –6 –6

62. (*b*) : The letters in one group correspond to the letters in the next group in the manner +2, +1, -2 respectively, *i.e.*,

BMY DNW FOU HPS

+2 +2 +2

+1 +1 +1

–2 –2 –2

63. (*b*) : The letters in each group are moved six steps forward, *i.e.*,

ADG GJM MPS SVY

+6 +6 +6

+6 +6 +6

+6 +6 +6

64. (*c*) : The letters in each group correspond to the letters in the next group in the manner +2, –2 respectively, *i.e.*,

AZ CX EV GT

+2 +2 +2

–2 –2 –2

65. (*c*) : The alphabets in each group correspond to the alphabets in the next group in the manner +2, –1, –2 respectively, *i.e.*,

DMP FLN HKL JJJ LIH

+2 +2 +2 +2
–1 –1 –1 –1
–2 –2 –2 –2

66. (*a*) : The alphabets in each group are moved five steps forward, *i.e.*,

ECA JHF OMK TRP YWU

+5 +5 +5 +5
+5 +5 +5 +5
+5 +5 +5 +5

67. (*a*) : The letters in one group correspond to the letters in the next group in the manner +2, +2, +1 respectively, *i.e.*,

ABP CDQ EFR GHS

+2 +2 +2
+2 +2 +2
+1 +1 +1

68. (*c*) : All the letters in each group are moved nine steps forward.

BEH KNQ TWZ CFI

+9 +9 +9
+9 +9 +9
+9 +9 +9

69. (*d*) : The letters in one group correspond to the letters in the next group in the manner +1, +2, –1 respectively, *i.e.*,

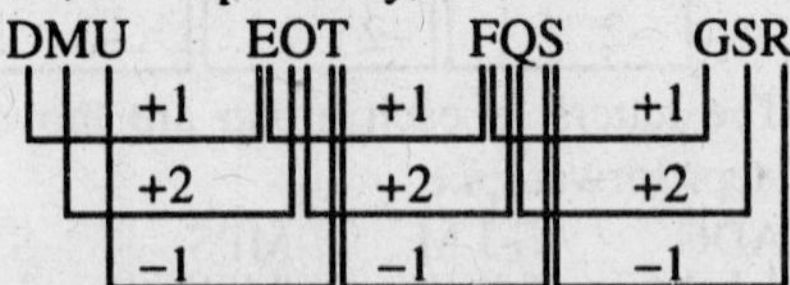

70. (*a*) : The letters in each group correspond to the letters in the next group in the manner –1, –2, –3, –4 respectively.

71. (*d*) : The letters in one group correspond to the letters in the next group in the manner +2, –1, +2 respectively.

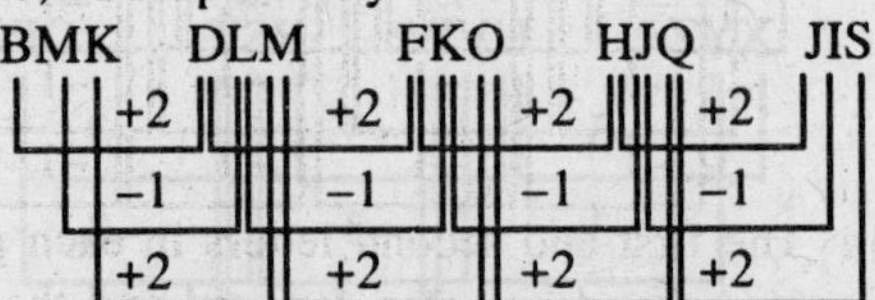

72. (*c*) : The letters are in natural sequence and from one group to the next one letter is dropped. Also the number of letters in groups is increased by one.

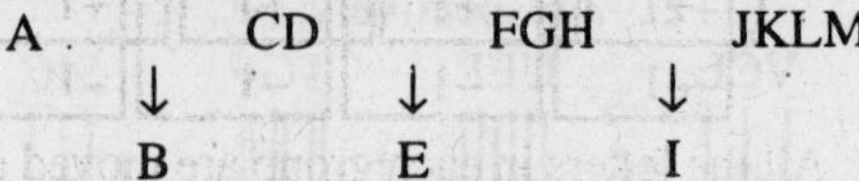

73. (*c*) : The letters in one group correspond to the letters in the next group in the manner +3, – 4, +2 respectively, *i.e.*,

BXJ ETL HPN KLP NHR

+3 +3 +3 +3
–4 –4 –4 –4
+2 +2 +2 +2

74. (*a*) : The three letters in each group are moved one step forward.

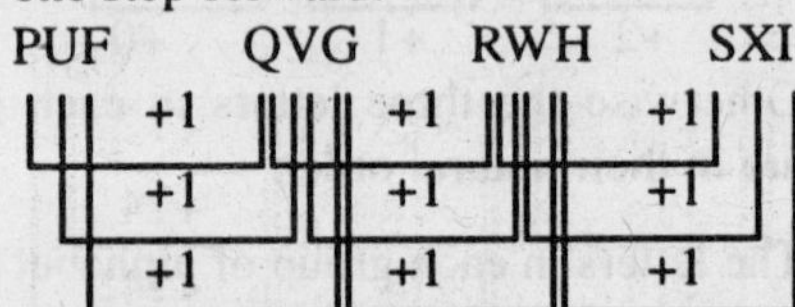

75. (*b*) : The letters are in natural order. The number of letters dropped in between the groups is increased by one at each step.

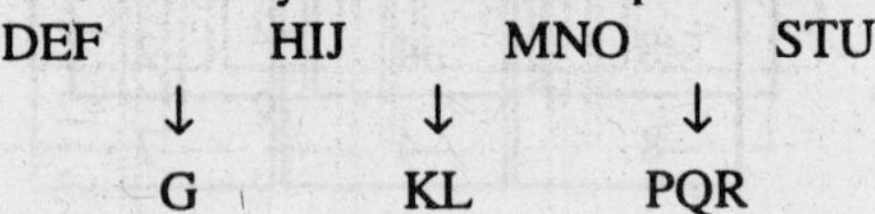

76. (*d*) : The letters in one group correspond to the letters in the next group in the manner +2, –1, +1 respectively, *i.e.*,

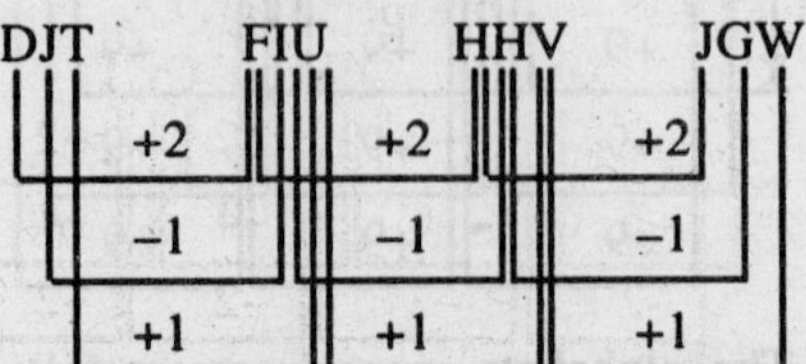

77. (*c*) : The letters in each group are moved one step backward.

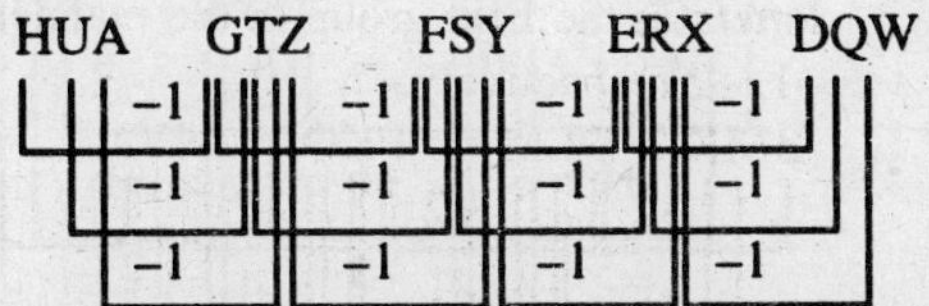

78. (*a*) : The first and second letters in each group are moved one step forward and the third letter is moved one step backward.

ABZ BCY CDX DEW EFV

+1 +1 +1 +1

+1 +1 +1 +1

–1 –1 –1 –1

79. (*b*) : All the letters in each group are moved eight steps forward.

HKN PSV XAD FIL

+8 +8 +8

+8 +8 +8

+8 +8 +8

80. (*b*) : The letters in one group correspond to the letters in the next group in the manner +12, +14, +14 respectively, *i.e.*,

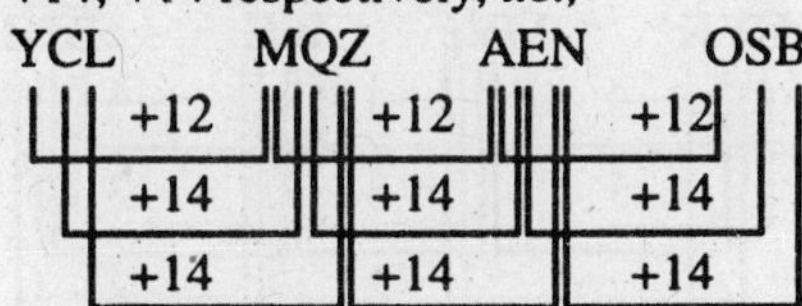

81. (*a*) : All the letters in each group are moved two steps forward, *i.e.*,

QPO SRQ UTS WVU YXW

+2 +2 +2 +2

+2 +2 +2 +2

+2 +2 +2 +2

82. (*c*) : The letters in one group correspond to the letters in the next group in the manner +2, –6, –2 respectively till the third group and then +2, –4, –2 respectively, *i.e.*,

KUZ MOX OIV QET SAR

+2 +2 +2 +2

–6 –6 –4 –4

–2 –2 –2 –2

83. (*c*) : The letters in one group correspond to the letters in the next group in the manner +2, +3, –1 respectively, *i.e.*,

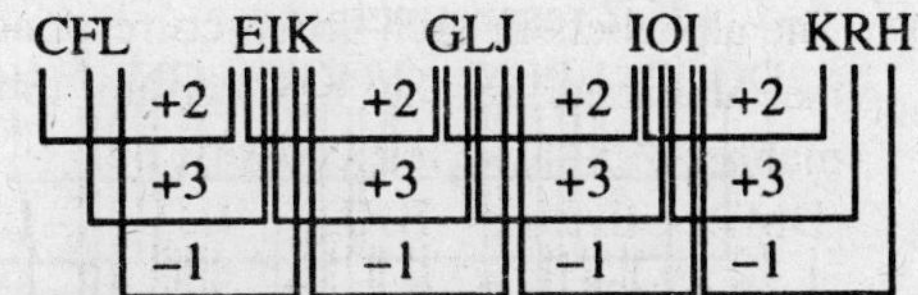

84. (*a*) : There are two alternate series :

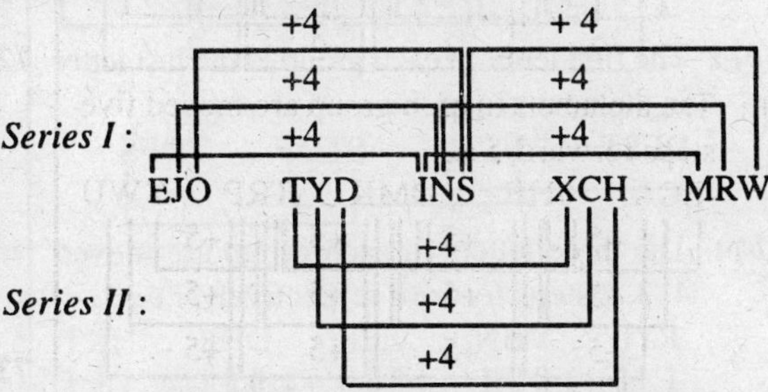

85. (*a*) : The letters in one group correspond to the letters in the next group in the manner +2, +2, +1 respectively, *i.e.*,

ABP CDQ EFR GHS

+2 +2 +2

+2 +2 +2

+1 +1 +1

86. (*b*) : The first and third letters are moved two steps forwards while the middle letter remains unchanged, *i.e.*,

NRA PRC RRE TRG VRI

+2 +2 +2 +2

+2 +2 +2 +2

87. (*d*) : The letters in one group correspond to the letters in the next group in the manner –1, +1, –1, respectively, *i.e.*,

DUW CVV BWU AXT ZYS

–1 –1 –1 –1

+1 +1 +1 +1

–1 –1 –1 –1

88. (*c*) : The four letters are moved 3, 2, 2, 1 steps forward respectively, *i.e.*,

FJKP ILMQ LNOR OPQS RRST

+3 +3 +3 +3

+2 +2 +2 +2

+2 +2 +2 +2

+1 +1 +1 +1

89. (*d*) : The letters in one group correspond to the letters in the next group in the manner, +1,

–1, +2 –2 respectively, *i.e.*,

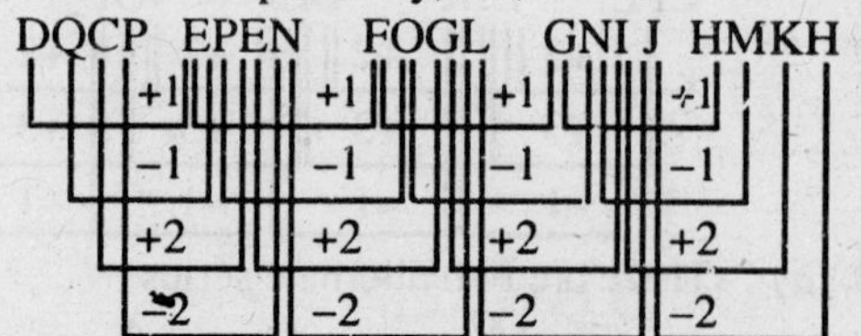

90. (*c*) : The first letter in each group is the last letter in the next group, *i.e.*,

DFST FSTD STDF TDFS

91. (*b*) : The three letters in each group are moved 4, 3, 2 steps forward respectively, *i.e.*,

RYL VBN ZEP DHR HKT

+4 +4 +4 +4

+3 +3 +3 +3

+2 +2 +2 +2

92. (*b*) : The three letters in each group are moved, 5, 4, 3 steps forward respectively, *i.e.*,

FAV KEY PIB UME ZQH

+5 +5 +5 +5

+4 +4 +4 +4

+3 +3 +3 +3

93. (*d*) : The letters in one group correspond to the letters in the next group in the manner –3, +1 –3 respectively, *i.e.*,

AJN XKK ULH RME ONB

–3 –3 –3 –3

+1 +1 +1 +1

–3 –3 –3 –3

94. (*b*) : The first and third letters in each group are moved one step forward and second and fourth letters are moved one step backward, *i.e.*,

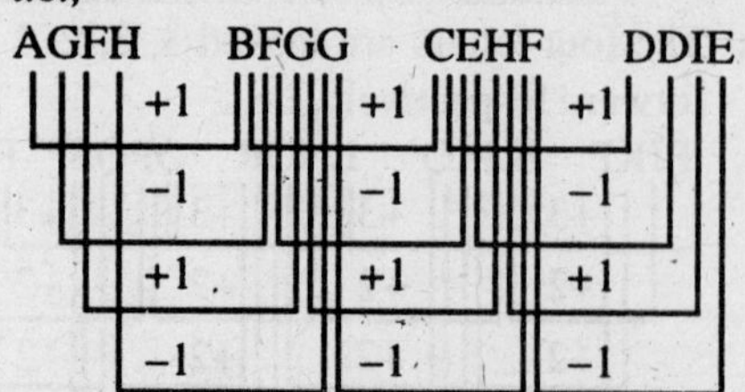

95. (*d*) : The letters in each group correspond to the letters in the next group in the manner –7, +6 –5 respectively, *i.e.*,

WCG PIB I OW BUR

–7 –7 –7

+6 +6 +6

–5 –5 –5

96. (*a*) : From one group to the next the number of steps of moving the letters in increased by one, *i.e.*,

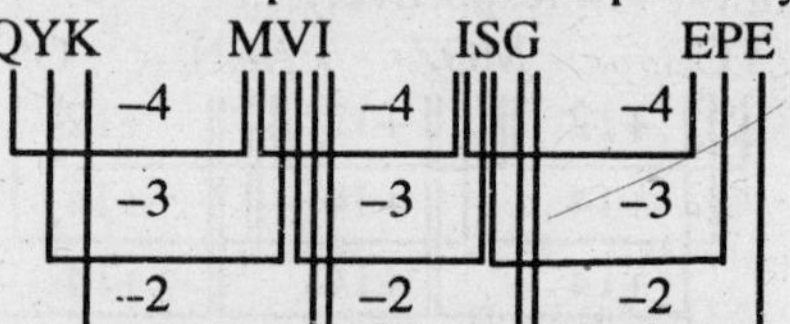

97. (*c*) : The three letters in each group are moved 4, 3 and 2 steps forward respectively, *i.e.*,

IXT MAV QDX UGZ

+4 +4 +4

+3 +3 +3

+2 +2 +2

98. (*b*) : The three letters in each group are moved 4, 3 and 2 steps backward respectively, *i.e.*,

QYK MVI ISG EPE

–4 –4 –4

–3 –3 –3

–2 –2 –2

99. (*a*) : There are two alternate series :

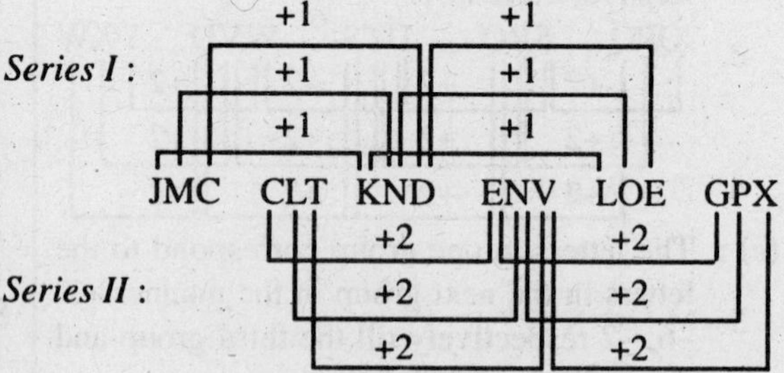

100. (*b*) : The letters in one group correspond to the letters in the next group in the manner –2, +3 –3 respectively, *i.e.*,

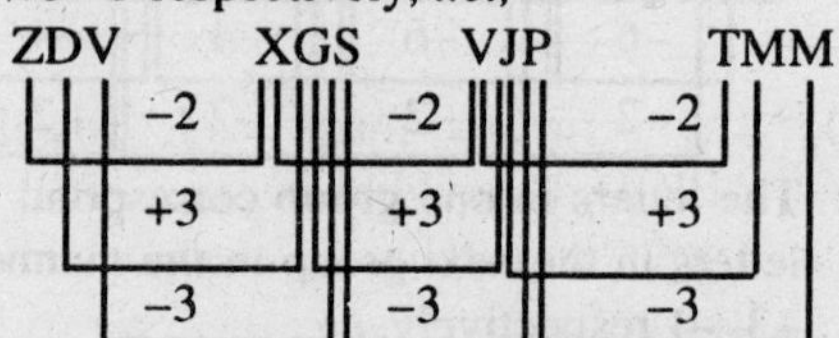

PART - II

WRONG LETTER SERIES

In this type of series the candidates are not required to find the letter or group of letters which will complete the given series but, they have to identify the letter or number which is wrong or misfit in the given series.

SOLVED EXAMPLE

1. Which of the following letters in the given series is wrong?
. J M P T V Y

(*a*) J (*b*) P (*c*) T (*d*) Y

Ans. (*c*) : The letters in this series are moved three steps forward, *i.e.*,

J M P S V Y
+3 +3 +3 +3 +3

Letter 'T' should have been 'S'.

EXERCISE

Directions : *Which letter(s) in each of the following series is wrong or is misfit in the series?*

1. A E H O U
(*a*) U (*b*) O
(*c*) H (*d*) E

2. C H M S W B
(*a*) C (*b*) S
(*c*) B (*d*) W

3. X S N I C Y
(*a*) Y (*b*) C
(*c*) S (*d*) I

4. Z A W B X C
(*a*) D (*b*) C
(*c*) X (*d*) W

5. M L O N Q P R
(*a*) R (*b*) O
(*c*) Q (*d*) L

6. D K R Y F L
(*a*) L (*b*) D
(*c*) R (*d*) Y

7. L N Q T W Z C F
(*a*) C (*b*) Q
(*c*) L (*d*) F

8. XW, DC, CB, NM, PQ
(*a*) NM (*b*) CB
(*c*) PQ (*d*) XW

9. B E I N S A I
(*a*) A (*b*) E
(*c*) S (*d*) I

10. Z T P K H F
(*a*) Z (*b*) P
(*c*) T (*d*) F

EXPLANATORY ANSWERS

1. (*c*) : The series is made with vowels only. AEIOU. I should be in place of H.

2. (*b*) : The letters in the series are moved five steps forward.

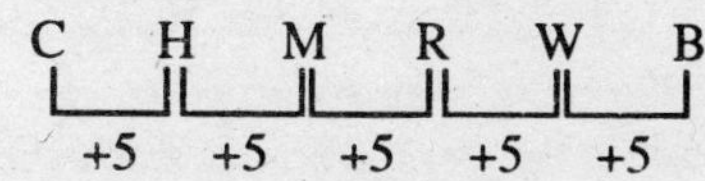

R should be in place of S

(The series restarts from A on reaching Z)

3. (*b*) : The pattern in the series is –5, *i.e.*,

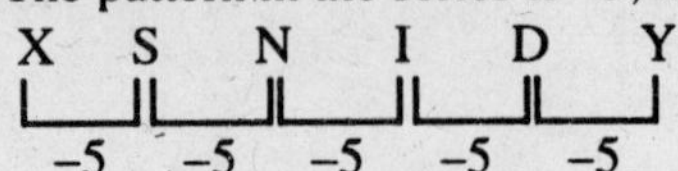

D should be in place of C.

4. (*d*) : There are two alternate series

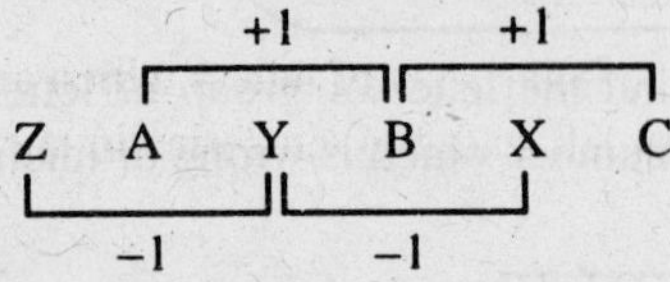

Series I : ZYX (reverse series)

Series II : ABC (natural series)

Y should be in place of W.

5. (*a*) : Two consecutive letters are written backwards.

<u>ML</u> <u>ON</u> <u>QP</u> <u>SR</u>

S should be in place of R.

6. (*a*) : The pattern in this series in moving the letters seven steps forward.

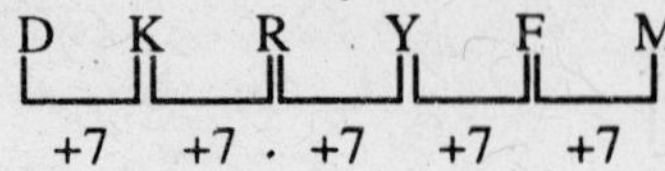

M should be in place of L.

7. (*c*) : The pattern in the series is +3

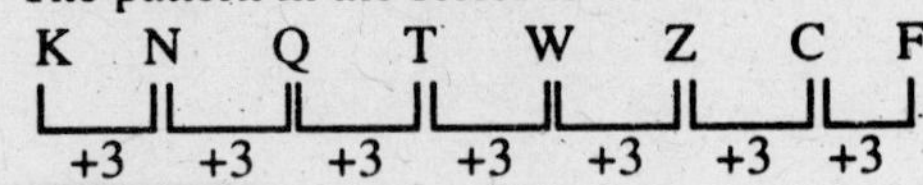

K should be in place of L.

8. (*c*) : The series is made with any two consecutive letters written backwards.

XW DC CB NM QP

← ← ← ← ←

Q should come before P in the series.

9. (*c*) : The difference between the letters is increased by one at each step.

B E I N T A I

+3 +4 +5 +6 +7 +8

T should be in place of S.

10. (*b*) : The difference between the letters is decreased by one at each step.

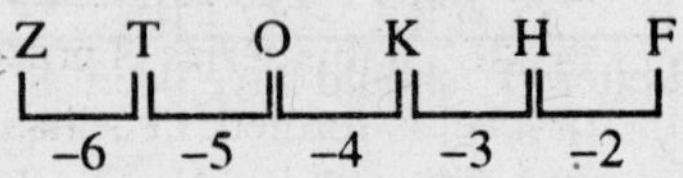

O should be in place of P.

PART - III

REPEAT SERIES

In this type of series small letters of the alphabet are used to make a set of letters which are repeated. The candidate has to find the set of letters which will fit the blanks left in the given series in such a manner that one section of the series is further repeated in the same manner.

SOLVED EXAMPLE

1. Which of the following groups of letters will complete the given series?
   ba-b-aab-a-b
   (*a*) baab (*b*) abba (*c*) abaa (*d*) babb

Ans. (*b*) : The series is baab, baab, baab. Here the section 'baab' is repeated in the series.

Solving steps : The candidate has to look for clues to solve such series pattern. 'aab' in the Series indicates that 'b' in this series is preceded by two 'a' so, the first blank and the last blank will be filled by 'a'. Now the first set is formed, *i.e.*, 'baab' in the beginning. This set is repeated, so the second and third blanks will have 'b' filling them. Now, solve the exercise given below to know the different ways in which these series are formed.

EXERCISE

Directions : *Which of the following groups of letters will complete the given series?*

1. ab---b-bbaa-
   (*a*) babba (*b*) abaab
   (*c*) abbab (*d*) baaab
2. aa-ab--aaa-a
   (*a*) baaa (*b*) abab
   (*c*) aaab (*d*) aabb
3. -baa-aab-a-a
   (*a*) baab (*b*) abab
   (*c*) aaba (*d*) aabb
4. -a cca-ccca-acccc-aaa
   (*a*) ccaa (*b*) acca
   (*c*) caac (*d*) caaa
5. c-bbb--abbbb-abbb-
   (*a*) abccb (*b*) bacbb
   (*c*) aabcb (*d*) abacb
6. ac-cab-baca-aba-acac
   (*a*) bcbb (*b*) aacb
   (*c*) babb (*d*) acbc
7. --aba--ba-ab
   (*a*) abbab (*b*) bbaba
   (*c*) baabb (*d*) abbba
8. --babbba-a--
   (*a*) bbaba (*b*) babbb
   (*c*) baaab (*d*) ababb
9. k-mk-lmkkl-kk-mk
   (*a*) lklm (*b*) lkmk
   (*c*) lkmm (*d*) lkml
10. abc-d-bc-d-b-dd
    (*a*) decdb (*b*) dadac
    (*c*) cdabe (*d*) bacde
11. b-abbc-bbca-bcabb-ab
    (*a*) acba (*b*) acaa
    (*c*) cacc (*d*) cabc
12. aca-ac--a-ac
    (*a*) babc (*b*) aaac
    (*c*) cacc (*d*) caca
13. ba-cb-b-bab-?
    (*a*) acbb (*b*) bcaa

(*c*) cabb (*d*) bacc

14. ab-aa-caab-aab-a
(*a*) bcbc (*b*) bbca
(*c*) cbcc (*d*) caba

15. -bbcaa-bcaa-bc-a-bca
(*a*) bacab (*b*) abbab
(*c*) abcba (*d*) bcaab

16. a-bccb-ca-cca-baab-c
(*a*) accab (*b*) abcaa
(*c*) bacaa (*d*) ababc

17. b-dabbcd-b-c-ab
(*a*) cabd (*b*) bcad
(*c*) dcba (*d*) acbd

18. a-ba-caacb-bc-
(*a*) acbb (*b*) cbab
(*c*) cbaa (*d*) cbba

19. c-baa-aca-cacab-acac-bca
(*a*) acbaa (*b*) cbaac
(*c*) bccab (*d*) bbcaa

20. -bcc-ac-aabb-ab-cc
(*a*) bacab (*b*) abaca
(*c*) aabca (*d*) bcaca

21. ab-ccca-bccc-bbcc-
(*a*) abbc (*b*) bbac
(*c*) bbca (*d*) cabc

22. -cbc-a-bcaac-ca
(*a*) aaba (*b*) caab
(*c*) bcab (*d*) aacb

23. ab-ba--ba-
(*a*) abba (*b*) baab
(*c*) baba (*d*) abab

24. yx-yx-yxz-xzy-zyxz
(*a*) zzyx (*b*) xxzy
(*c*) yyzx (*d*) yzxz

25. xxxy-y-xxy-yxx-
(*a*) xyxy (*b*) yxyx
(*c*) yyxx (*d*) xxyy

26. aa-aabb-b-aa-aabb-bb
(*a*) abbab (*b*) bbbaa
(*c*) babba (*d*) aabbb

27. ab-aabc-abc-
(*a*) aab (*b*) caa
(*c*) bca (*d*) cba

28. c-abca-b-aab
(*a*) bbc (*b*) bca
(*c*) aac (*d*) cab

29. cc-bac-bbacc-baccb-a
(*a*) cbca (*b*) bcbc
(*c*) bcbb (*d*) bbbc

30. aaab-aaaaba-a-abaa
(*a*) baa (*b*) aaa
(*c*) aba (*d*) bba

31. nl-n-mn-m-lm
(*a*) mlnn (*b*) lnnm
(*c*) mlnl (*d*) mlln

32. lm-nnll-mn-llmm-nl
(*a*) lmmn (*b*) lnnm
(*c*) mmnn (*d*) mnll

33. aba-caab-cca-bac-a
(*a*) cbac (*b*) caac
(*c*) bccb (*d*) abcb

34. -cd-bc-ab-dabc-a
(*a*) badcd (*b*) ccddb
(*c*) abccd (*d*) ccbab

35. -cabcc-bc-abcca-
(*a*) babc (*b*) acac
(*c*) cacb (*d*) bacc

36. mn-om-oom-oo-noo
(*a*) onnm (*b*) nmmo
(*c*) mnoo (*d*) nmon

37. -lmn-ll-nol-mno
(*a*) nlmo (*b*) mnoo
(*c*) omlm (*d*) loml

38. xx-zzx-yzz-xyz-
(*a*) xyzx (*b*) zyxx
(*c*) yxxy (*d*) yxxz

39. y-xx-yxx-yyx-xy
(*a*) xyxx (*b*) xxxy
(*c*) yxxy (*d*) xxyx

40. a-bab--b-abb
(*a*) abab (*b*) bbab
(*c*) aabb (*d*) babb

41. aa-bbb-ccaaab-bc-c
(*a*) cabc (*b*) acbc
(*c*) accb (*d*) cbac

42. aba-a-acab-caba-
(*a*) cbac (*b*) bbcc
(*c*) abab (*d*) cacb

43. l-nnlm-nlmn-lmn-
(*a*) lmnn (*b*) nnml
(*c*) mlnm (*d*) mnnn

44. ll-mnnl-mm-nllm-nn
(*a*) nlmn (*b*) mlnm
(*c*) mnln (*d*) lmmn

45. -ba-baa-ab-a
(*a*) babb (*b*) baab
(*c*) abbb (*d*) aaba

46. ab-da-cd-bc-
(*a*) abdc (*b*) cbad
(*c*) bcad (*d*) acbd

47. -yyx-xxyx-yxyx-y
(*a*) yxxy (*b*) xyxy
(*c*) yxyx (*d*) xyyx

48. a-ba-bb-ab-a
(*a*) abab (*b*) baab
(*c*) baba (*d*) abbb

49. x-yyx-y--xyy
(*a*) xyyy (*b*) yyyx
(*c*) xyxy (*d*) xxyx

50. -bcbc-caba--
(*a*) aabc (*b*) abac
(*c*) caab (*d*) baba

EXPLANATORY ANSWERS

1. (*d*) : The series is abbaab, abbaab
2. (*c*) : The series is aaaaba, aaaaba
3. (*b*) : The series is aba, aba, aba, aba
4. (*d*) : The series is c,a,cc,aa, ccc, aaa, cccc, aaaa
5. (*a*) : The series is cabbbb, cabbbb, cabbbb
6. (*b*) : The series is acac, abab, acac, abab, acac
7. (*a*) : The series is ab, ab, ab, ab, ab, ab
8. (*b*) : The series is bababb, bababb
9. (*d*) : The series is klmk, klmk, klmk, klmk
10. (*b*) : The series is abcdd, abcdd, abcdd
11. (*d*) : The series is bcab, bcab, bcab, bcab, bcab
12. (*c*) : The series is ac, ac, ac, ac, ac, ac
13. (*d*) : The series is babc, babc, babc
14. (*c*) : The series is abca, abca, abca, abca
15. (*b*) : The series is abbca, abbca, abbca, abbca
16. (*d*) : The series is aabcc, bbcaa, ccabb, aabcc
17. (*a*) : The series is bcdab, bcdab, bcdab
18. (*c*) : The series is acbabca, acbabca
19. (*a*) : The series is cabaac, acabca, cabaac, acabca
20. (*a*) : The series is bbccaa, ccaabb, aabbcc.
21. (*b*) : The series is abbccc abbccc.
22. (*d*) : The series is acbca acbca acbca.
23. (*d*) : The series is ab ab ab ab ab.
24. (*a*) : The series is yxz yxz yxz yxz yxz yxz.
25. (*b*) : The series is xxx yyy xxx yyy xxx.
26. (*a*) : The series is aaaaa bbbbb aaaaa bbbbb.
27. (*b*) : The series is abca abca abca.
28. (*c*) : The series is caab caab caab.
29. (*c*) : The series is ccbba ccbba ccbba ccbba.
30. (*b*) : The series is aaabaa aaabaa aaabaa.
31. (*d*) : The series is nlm, nlm, nlm, nlm.
32. (*c*) : The series is lmmnnl lmmnnl lmmnnl.
33. (*b*) : The series is abacca abacca abacca.
34. (*a*) : The series is bcda bcda bcda bcda.
35. (*c*) : The series is ccab ccab ccab ccab.
36. (*a*) : The series is mnoo mnoo mnoo mnoo.
37. (*d*) : The series is llmno llmno llmno.
38. (*d*) : The series is xxyzz xxyzz xxyzz.
39. (*a*) : The series is yxxxy yxxxy yxxxy.
40. (*b*) : The series is abb abb abb abb.
41. (*b*) : The series is aaa bbb ccc aaa bbb ccc.
42. (*a*) : The series is abac abac abac abac.
43. (*d*) : The series is lmnn lmnn lmnn lmnn.
44. (*b*) : The series is ll mm nn ll mm nn ll mm nn.
45. (*c*) : The series is ababba ababba.
46. (*b*) : The series is abcd abcd abcd.
47. (*d*) : The series is xyyx yxxy xyyx yxxy.
48. (*b*) : The series is abba abba abba.
49. (*d*) : The series is xxyy xxyy xxyy.
50. (*a*) : The series is abc bca cab abc.

PART - IV

NUMBER SERIES

In this type of series, the set of given numbers in a series are related to one another in a particular pattern or manner. The relationship between the numbers may be (i) consecutive odd/even numbers; (ii) consecutive prime numbers; (iii) squares/cubes of some numbers with/without variation of addition or subtraction of some number; (iv) sum/product/difference of preceding numbers; (v) addition/subtraction/multiplication/division by some number; and (vi) many more combinations of the relationships given above.

SOLVED EXAMPLES

1. Which number will complete the given series?

4, 8, 12, 16, ?

(*a*) 18 (*b*) 20 (*c*) 22 (*d*) 24

Ans. (*b*): The series is made of numbers which are multiples of 4. Other explanation can be that the difference between the two consecutive numbers is 4.

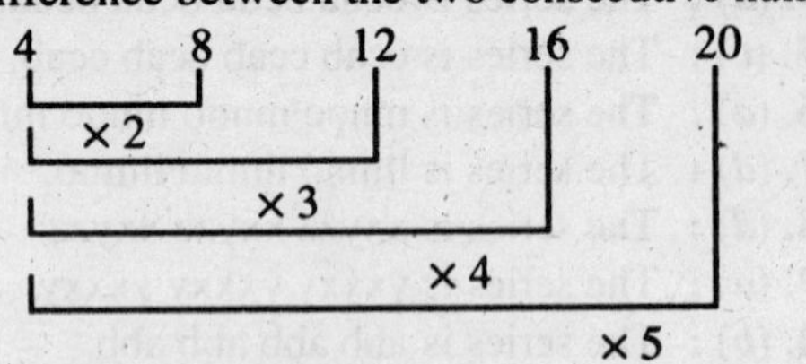

Or

4 8 12 16 20
+4 +4 +4 +4

2. Complete the given series.

2, 14, 98, 686, ?

(*a*) 1976 (*b*) 2548 (*c*) 980 (*d*) 4802

Ans. (*d*) : The numbers are multiplied by 7 to obtain the next numbers.

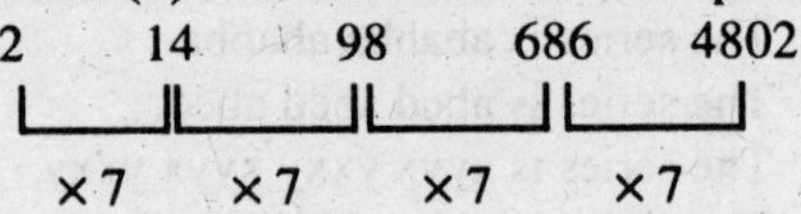

The given series may also comprise of two alternate series merged as one.

3. Find the missing number in the series.

49, 16, 25, 36, 9, ?

(*a*) 64 (*b*) 52 (*c*) 45 (*d*) 43

Ans. (*a*) : In this series the first set comprises of squares of odd numbers in descending order and the second set comprises of squares of even numbers in ascending order.

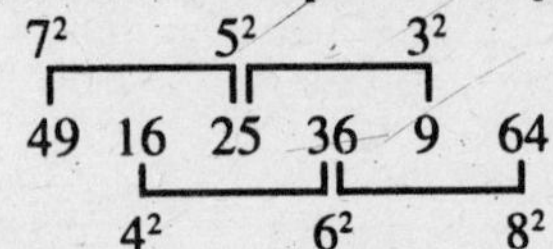

Series I : 49, 25, 9 (Squares of 7, 5, 3)

Series II : 16, 36, 64 (Squares of 4, 6, 8)

EXERCISE

Directions : ***In the following questions, select the number(s) from the given options for completing the given series.***

1. 3, 9, 27, 81, 243, ?
(*a*) 486 (*b*) 729
(*c*) 972 (*d*) 359

2. 1, 6, 12, 19, 27, ?
(*a*) 38 (*b*) 35
(*c*) 36 (*d*) 54

3. 2, 6, 14, 30, 62, ?
(*a*) 126 (*b*) 128
(*c*) 120 (*d*) 130

4. 8, 48, 16, 96, 32, ?
(*a*) 192 (*b*) 150
(*c*) 64 (*d*) 288

5. 2, 8, 14, 24, 34, 48, ?
(*a*) 66 (*b*) 62
(*c*) 58 (*d*) 64

6. 4, 9, 19, 34, 54, ?, 109
(*a*) 89 (*b*) 84
(*c*) 74 (*d*) 79

7. 3, 15, 35, 63, 99, ?
(*a*) 144 (*b*) 143
(*c*) 121 (*d*) 169

8. 2, 3, 6, 18, 108, ?
(*a*) 1944 (*b*) 1658
(*c*) 648 (*d*) 1008

9. 1, 2, 3, 2, 3, 5, 4, 5, ?
(*a*) 9 (*b*) 6
(*c*) 10 (*d*) 7

10. 7776, 1296, 216, 36, 6, ?
(*a*) 6 (*b*) 0
(*c*) 3 (*d*) 1

11. 1, 8, 27, 64, 125, ?
(*a*) 172 (*b*) 176
(*c*) 216 (*d*) 189

12. 2, 3, 5, 7, 11, 13, ?
(*a*) 19 (*b*) 57
(*c*) 31 (*d*) 17

13. 80, 64, 48, 32, 16, ?
(*a*) 4 (*b*) 0
(*c*) 8 (*d*) 1

14. 3, 8, 13, 24, 41, ?
(*a*) 65 (*b*) 75
(*c*) 70 (*d*) 80

15. 9, 81, 90, 810, 819, ?
(*a*) 7371 (*b*) 900
(*c*) 8100 (*d*) 1638

16. 0, 8, 24, 48, 80, ?
(*a*) 110 (*b*) 96
(*c*) 120 (*d*) 140

17. 2, 4, 8, 3, 9, 27, 4, 16, ?
(*a*) 64 (*b*) 32
(*c*) 48 (*d*) 24

18. 27, 28, 25, 25, 23, 22, 21, ?
(*a*) 20 (*b*) 21
(*c*) 19 (*d*) 18

19. 80, 63, 72, 72, 64, 81, 56, ?
(*a*) 96 (*b*) 98
(*c*) 89 (*d*) 90

20. 0, 5, 22, 57, ?, 205
(*a*) 198 (*b*) 116
(*c*) 172 (*d*) 92

21. 19200, 1920, 240, 40, 10, ?
(*a*) 1 (*b*) 0
(*c*) 5 (*d*) 10

22. 1, 2, 1, 3, 2, 7, 13, ?
(*a*) 39 (*b*) 26
(*c*) 92 (*d*) 108

23. 2, 4, 4, 8, 16, 16, 256, ?
(*a*) 64 (*b*) 36
(*c*) 180 (*d*) 32

24. 3, 6, 9, 36, 27, 216, 81, ?
(*a*) 1296 (*b*) 648
(*c*) 243 (*d*) 1944

25. 19, 4, 14, 7, 10, 11, 7, ?
(*a*) 16 (*b*) 15
(*c*) 17 (*d*) 23

26. 1, 2, 3, 5, 8, ?
(*a*) 11 (*b*) 13
(*c*) 15 (*d*) 9

27. 64, 16, 32, 8, ?
(*a*) 24 (*b*) 32
(*c*) 4 (*d*) 16

28. 2, 3, 5, 10, 20, 40, ?
(*a*) 65 (*b*) 75
(*c*) 60 (*d*) 80

29. 3, 15, 90, 630, 5040, ?
(*a*) 35280 (*b*) 40320
(*c*) 45360 (*d*) 10080

30. 1890, 1890, 630, 126, 18, ?
(*a*) 6 (*b*) 9
(*c*) 2 (*d*) 3

31. 138, 115, 92, 69, 46, ?
(*a*) 9 (*b*) 18
(*c*) 21 (*d*) 23

32. 55, 45, 36, 28, 21, ?
(*a*) 11 (*b*) 16
(*c*) 15 (*d*) 17

33. 29282, 2662, 242, 22, ?
(*a*) 1 (*b*) 2
(*c*) 0 (*d*) 11

34. 4, 2, 8, 16, 128, ?
(*a*) 562 (*b*) 1018
(*c*) 2024 (*d*) 2048

35 9, 54, 44, 264, 254, 1524, ?
(*a*) 1514 (*b*) 508
(*c*) 3048 (*d*) 1330

36. 1, 2, 2, 4, 16, ?, 65536
(*a*) 276 (*b*) 64
(*c*) 256 (*d*) 198

37. 186, 115, 71, 44, 27, ?
(*a*) 19 (*b*) 17
(*c*) 13 (*d*) 21

38. 48, ?, 24, 30, 12, 90
(*a*) 56 (*b*) 10
(*c*) 33 (*d*) 16

39. 100, 25, 64, 49, 36, ?, 16
(*a*) 81 (*b*) 64
(*c*) 25 (*d*) 9

40. 128, 64, 32, 16, ?, 4
(*a*) 10 (*b*) 8
(*c*) 6 (*d*) 12

41. 2, 8, 18, 32, 50, 72, ?
(*a*) 132 (*b*) 102
(*c*) 89 (*d*) 98

42. 36, 24, 15, 9, 6 ?
(*a*) 3 (*b*) 6
(*c*) 0 (*d*) 2

43. 1, 1, 2, 8, 64, ?, 65536
(*a*) 1024 (*b*) 2556
(*c*) 4096 (*d*) 1088

44. 3, 5, 9, 15, 23, ?, 45
(*a*) 37 (*b*) 35
(*c*) 31 (*d*) 33

45. 7, 21, 35, 49, 63, ?
(*a*) 70 (*b*) 77
(*c*) 81 (*d*) 108

46. 1, 3, 7, 15, 31, ?
(*a*) 62 (*b*) 46
(*c*) 63 (*d*) 57

47. 1, 2, 4, 8, 16, 32, ?
(*a*) 48 (*b*) 56
(*c*) 64 (*d*) 70

48. 10, 14, 23, 39, 64, ?, 149
(*a*) 78 (*b*) 128
(*c*) 103 (*d*) 100

49. 6, 24, 29, 116, 121, ?, 489
(*a*) 468 (*b*) 484
(*c*) 243 (*d*) 363

50. 5, 50, 45, 450, 445, ?, 4445
(*a*) 4450 (*b*) 4600
(*c*) 4550 (*d*) 4500

51. 57, 87, 50, 81, 45, 77, 42, ?
(*a*) 71 (*b*) 75
(*c*) 53 (*d*) 69

52. 6.25, 9, 12.25, 16, 20.25, 25, 30.25?
(*a*) 36 (*b*) 32
(*c*) 28.25 (*d*) 40.25

53. 243, 5, 81 15, 27, 45, 9, ?
(*a*) 5 (*b*) 15
(*c*) 135 (*d*) 27

54. 2, 7, 14, 23, ?, 47
(*a*) 31 (*b*) 38
(*c*) 28 (*d*) 34

55. 0, 1, 8, 27, 64, ?
(*a*) 125 (*b*) 128
(*c*) 256 (*d*) 121

56. 1, 2, 2, 5, 3, 10, ?
(*a*) 8 (*b*) 4
(*c*) 7 (*d*) 11

57. 17, 27, 37, 56, 66, ?
(*a*) 67 (*b*) 76
(*c*) 82 (*d*) 97

58. 37, 47, 58, ?, 79, 95
(*a*) 71 (*b*) 69
(*c*) 68 (*d*) 67

59. 8, 10, 18, 28, 46, ?
(*a*) 64 (*b*) 68
(*c*) 70 (*d*) 74

60. 4, –8, 14, –22, 32, ?
(*a*) –44 (*b*) 42
(*c*) –42 (*d*) 44

61. 98, 72, 14, ?
(*a*) 8 (*b*) 6
(*c*) 4 (*d*) 2

62. 14, 56, 448, 5376, ?
(*a*) 75264 (*b*) 86016
(*c*) 84816 (*d*) 129024

63. 6, 7, 9, 11, 15, 15, 24, 19, ?
(*a*) 32 (*b*) 34
(*c*) 36 (*d*) 37

64. 2, 6, 12, 20, 30, ?
(*a*) 42 (*b*) 36
(*c*) 41 (*d*) 40

65. 4, 7, 12, 19, 28, ?
(*a*) 35 (*b*) 37
(*c*) 39 (*d*) 41

66. 11, 13, 17, 19, 23, ?
(*a*) 37 (*b*) 31
(*c*) 25 (*d*) 41

67. 0, 2, 10, 30, 68, ?
(*a*) 125 (*b*) 120
(*c*) 175 (*d*) 130

68. 69, 55, 26, 13, ?
(*a*) 3 (*b*) 6.5
(*c*) 13 (*d*) 4

69. 10, 26, 50, 82, 122, ?
(*a*) 160 (*b*) 170
(*c*) 180 (*d*) 150

70. 1, 4, 5, 11, 9, 18, ?, 25
(*a*) 12 (*b*) 13
(*c*) 19 (*d*) 23

71. 2, 5, 10, 17, 26, 37, ?
(*a*) 40 (*b*) 43
(*c*) 50 (*d*) 53

72. 4, 32, 288, ?, 31680
(*a*) 2880 (*b*) 25600
(*c*) 7420 (*d*) 10,000

73. 27, 45, 9,15, 3, 5, ?
(*a*) 1 (*b*) 1/3
(*c*) 1/5 (*d*) 1/9

74. 6, 9, 18, 45, 126, 369, ?
(*a*) 1059 (*b*) 1095
(*c*) 1080 (*d*) 1098

75. 3, 1/3, 14, 1/14, 25, 1/25, ?
(*a*) 1/36 (*b*) 34
(*c*) 35 (*d*) 36

76. 3, 5, 6, 11, 9, 17, 12, ?
(*a*) 20 (*b*) 10
(*c*) 22 (*d*) 23

77. 2, 5, 4, 8, 6, 11, 8, 14, 10, ?
(*a*) 17 (*b*) 16
(*c*) 7 (*d*) 9

78. 2, 7, 11, 8, 13, 17, 14, 19, 23, ?
(*a*) 22 (*b*) 20
(*c*) 18 (*d*) 25

79. 121, 101, ?, 86, 83.5
(*a*) 90.5 (*b*) 89
(*c*) 98 (*d*) 91

80. 9, 17, 19, 27.5, 29, ?, 39
(*a*) 38.5 (*b*) 38
(*c*) 37 (*d*) 37.5

81. 1, 4, 9, 16, 25, ?
(*a*) 35 (*b*) 36
(*c*) 47 (*d*) 48

82. 1/2, 3/4, 5/8, 7/16, ?
(*a*) 10/17 (*b*) 9/32
(*c*) 11/34 (*d*) 12/35

83. 0.5, 1.5, 5.5, 14.5, ?
(*a*) 30.5 (*b*) 39.5
(*c*) 40.5 (*d*) 45.5

84. 3, 5, 8, 12, 17, 23, ?
(*a*) 19 (*b*) 30
(*c*) 33 (*d*) 45

85. 840, 168, 42, 14, 7, ?
(*a*) 12 (*b*) 7
(*c*) 9 (*d*) 3

86. 2, 4, 7, 14, 17, 34, ?
(*a*) 36 (*b*) 68
(*c*) 37 (*d*) 73

87. 11, 12, 17, 18, 23, 24, ?
(*a*) 12 (*b*) 39
(*c*) 32 (*d*) 29

88. 4, 10, 22, 46, ?
(*a*) 56 (*b*) 66
(*c*) 76 (*d*) 94

89. 3, 8, 22, 63, 185, ?
(*a*) 285 (*b*) 295
(*c*) 550 (*d*) 320

90. 12, 32, 72, 152, ?, 632
(*a*) 515 (*b*) 613
(*c*) 815 (*d*) 312

91. 4, 11, 7, 14, 10, 17, ?
(*a*) 13 (*b*) 15
(*c*) 20 (*d*) 23

92. 37, 29, ?, 19, 17
(*a*) 21 (*b*) 17

(c) 19 (d) 23

93. 8, 9, 8, 7, 10, 9, 6, 11, 10, ?, 12
(a) 4 (b) 6
(c) 5 (d) 8

94. 2, 6, 14, 30, 62, ?, 254
(a) 124 (b) 130
(c) 126 (d) 142

95. 2, 6, 12, 20, 30, 42, ?
(a) 50 (b) 54
(c) 56 (d) 64

96. 4, 8, 7, 14, 12, 22, 19, ?, 28
(a) 12 (b) 24
(c) 28 (d) 32

97. 96, 90, 78, ?, 36, 6
(a) 60 (b) 72
(c) 48 (d) 54

98. 5, 7, 11, ?, 35, 67
(a) 19 (b) 24
(c) 28 (d) 32

99. 10, 16, 12, 20, 14, ?
(a) 20 (b) 24
(c) 25 (d) 28

100. 7, 9, 12, 14, 17, 19, ?
(a) 18 (b) 20
(c) 21 (d) 22

101. 20, 19, 17, ?, 10, 5
(a) 12 (b) 15
(c) 14 (d) 13

102. 7, 12, 19, ?, 39
(a) 22 (b) 24
(c) 26 (d) 28

103. 3, 12, 24, 96, 192, ?
(a) 768 (b) 384
(c) 702 (d) 298

104. 6, 3, 11, 8, 18, 15, 27, 24, ?, ?
(a) 36, 33 (b) 36, 35
(c) 38, 35 (d) 38, 34

105. 24, 60, 120, 210, ?
(a) 300 (b) 336
(c) 420 (d) 525

106. 18, 9, 24, 12, 32, 16, 42, ?
(a) 19 (b) 20
(c) 21 (d) 24

107. 2, 5, 9, ?, 20, 27
(a) 14 (b) 16
(c) 18 (d) 24

108. 18, 10, 6, 4, 3, ?
(a) 8 (b) 2
(c) 3.5 (d) 2.5

109. 2, 6, 12, 20, 30, 42, ?
(a) 50 (b) 52
(c) 54 (d) 56

110. 3, 5, 9, 15, 25, 41, 67, ?
(a) 108 (b) 109
(c) 110 (d) 111

111. 1, 6, 15, ?, 45, 66, 91
(a) 25 (b) 26
(c) 27 (d) 28

112. 1, 2, 5, 12, 27, 58, 121, ?
(a) 246 (b) 247
(c) 248 (d) 249

113. 0, 3, 12, 30, ?, 105, 168
(a) 60 (b) 61
(c) 62 (d) 63

114. 1, 3, 7, 13, 21, ?
(a) 27 (b) 29
(c) 31 (d) 33

115. (2,1), (1,5), (5,7), (7,11), (11,13), ?
(a) (13, 15) (b) (13,17)
(c) (13, 19) (d) (15,16)

116. 4, 9, 16, 25, 36, ?
(a) 47 (b) 48
(c) 49 (d) 64

117. 150, 30, 15, 3, ?
(a) 1.5 (b) 2
(c) 0 (d) – 2.5

118. 0, 4, 6, 3, 7, 9, 6, ?, 12
(a) 8 (b) 10
(c) 11 (d) 14

119. 2, 7, 4, 9, 6, 11, 8, 13, 10, 15, 12, ?
(a) 16 (b) 17
(c) 19 (d) 21

120. 1, 1, 3, 9, 6, 36, 10, 100, ?, 225
(a) 15 (b) 16
(c) 20 (d) 22

121. 3, 8, 15, 24, ?, 48, 63
(a) 30 (b) 32
(c) 35 (d) 36

122. 9, 16, 30, 58, ?
(a) 104 (b) 114
(c) 116 (d) 118

123. 5, 14, 41, 86, ?
(*a*) 149 (*b*) 123
(*c*) 157 (*d*) 131

124. 2, 11, 7, 16, 12, ?, 17, 26
(*a*) 21 (*b*) 8
(*c*) 11 (*d*) 76

125. 54, 45, 38, 33, ?
(*a*) 32 (*b*) 31
(*c*) 30 (*d*) 29

EXPLANATORY ANSWERS

1. (*b*) : The numbers in the series are multiplied by 3 to get the next numbers.

2. (*c*) : The difference between the numbers in the series increases by 1, after beginning from 5, *i.e.,*

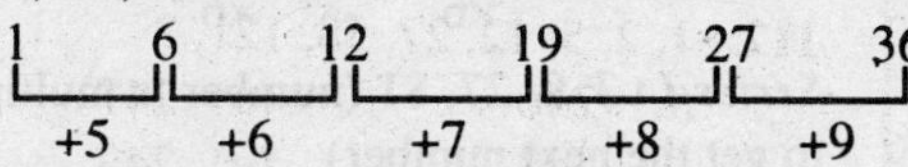

3. (*a*) : The difference between the numbers in the series doubles each time, after beginning from 4, *i.e.,*

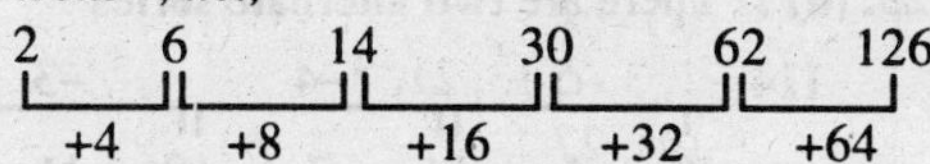

4. (*a*) : *Explanation I* : The sequence in the series is × 6, ÷ 3 which is repeated.

8 48 16 96 32 192
× 6 ÷ 3 × 6 ÷ 3 × 6

Explanation II : There are two alternate series and the numbers are multiplied by 2.

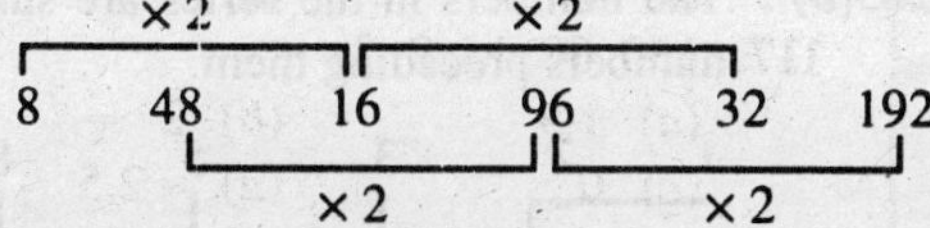

Series I : 8, 16, 32
Series II : 48, 96, 192

5. (*b*) : The sequence in the series is :

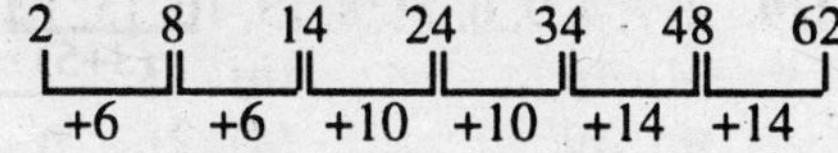

The difference increases by 4 at alternate step.

6. (*d*) : The difference between the numbers increases by 5, after beginning from 5, *i.e.,*

4 9 19 34 54 79 109
+5 +10 +15 +20 +25 +30

7. (*b*) : The series follows the sequence of the squares of even numbers beginning from 2, minus 1.

8. (*a*) : Every third number in the series is the product of previous two numbers.

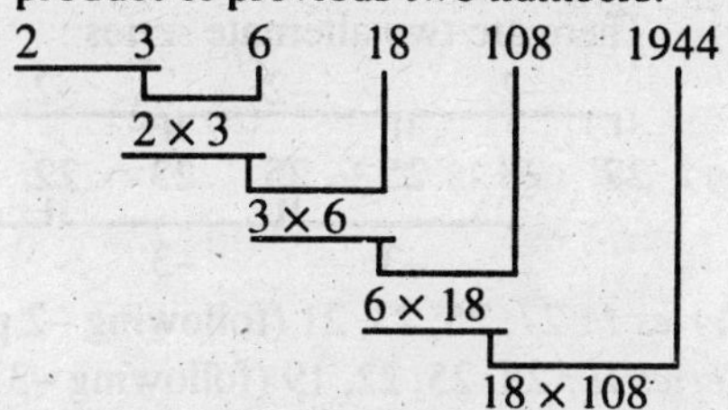

9. (*a*) : In this series three numbers from a set. The first two numbers of each set are in natural order and the third number is the sum of first and second numbers. The first number of the next set begins with double the first number of the previous set.

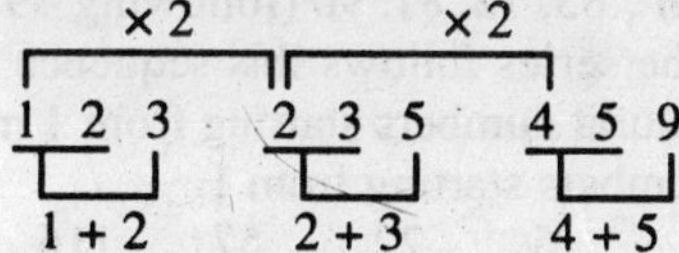

10. (*d*) : The numbers in this sequence are divided by 6 each time.

11. (*c*) : The sequence in the series is cube of numbers in their natural order.

12. (*d*) : The series consists of prime numbers in increasing order.

13. (*b*) : The numbers in the series are decreasing with the difference of 16 at each step.

14. (*c*) : The sequence in the series is (number + next number) + addition of natural number increasing by 1 at each step, after beginning from 2.

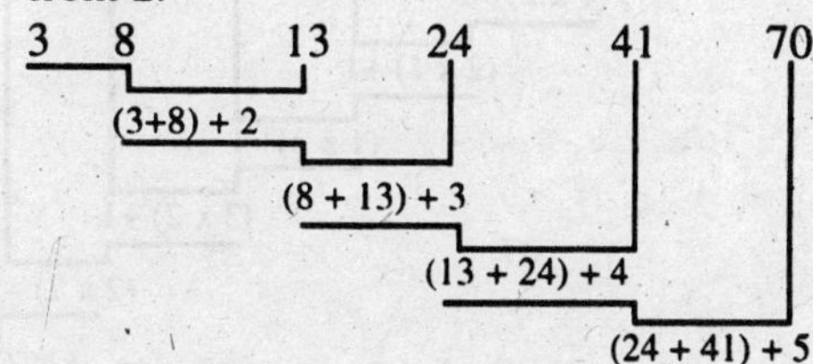

15. (a) : The sequence in the series is × 9, + 9 which is repeated.

16. (c) : The sequence of the series consists of the product of 2 even numbers in natural order, *i.e.*,

0	8	24	48	80	120
↓	↓	↓	↓	↓	↓
(0 × 2)	(2 × 4)	(4 × 6)	(6 × 8)	(8 × 10)	(10 × 12)

17. (a) : In this series 3 numbers form a set. The first number is in natural order. The second number is the square of above number. The third number is the cube of first number.

18. (c) : There are two alternate series :

−2 −2 −2

27 28 25 25 23 22 21 19

−3 −3 −3

Series I : 27, 25, 23, 21 (following −2 pattern)
Series II : 28, 25, 22, 19 (following −3 pattern)

19. (d) : There are two alternate series :

−8 −8 −8

80 63 72 72 64 81 56 90

+9 +9 +9

Series I : 80, 72, 64, 56 (following −8 pattern)
Series II : 63, 72, 81, 90 (following +9 pattern)

20. (b) : The series follows this sequence : cube of natural numbers starting from 1 minus odd numbers starting from 1.

0	5	22	57	116	205
↓	↓	↓	↓	↓	↓
1^3-1	2^3-3	3^3-5	4^3-7	5^3-9	6^3-11

21. (c) : The sequence in the series is divided by even numbers in descending order, starting from 10, *i.e.*,

19200 1920 240 40 10 5

÷10 ÷8 ÷6 ÷4 ÷2

22. (c) : The sequence in the series is the product of previous two numbers −1, +1 alternately, *i.e.*,

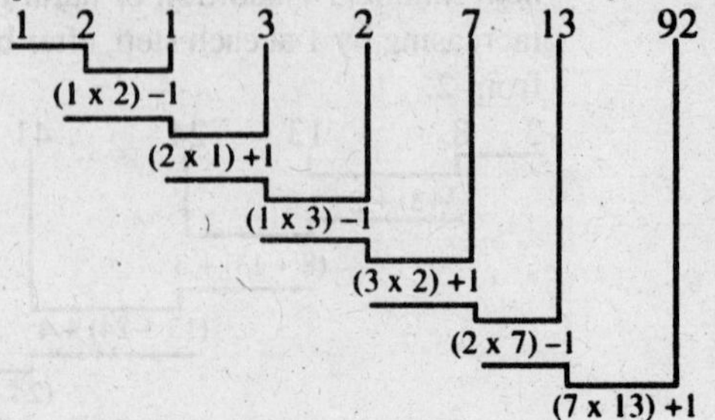

23. (d) : There are two alternate series :

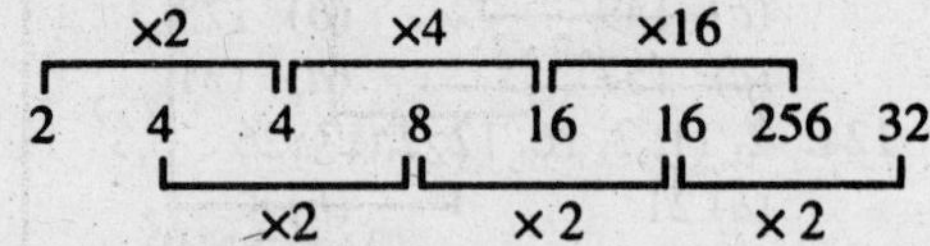

Series I : 2, 4, 16, 256 (next number is the square of previous number)
Series II: 4, 8, 16, 32 (number is multiplied by 2 to get the next number)

24. (a) : There are two alternate series :

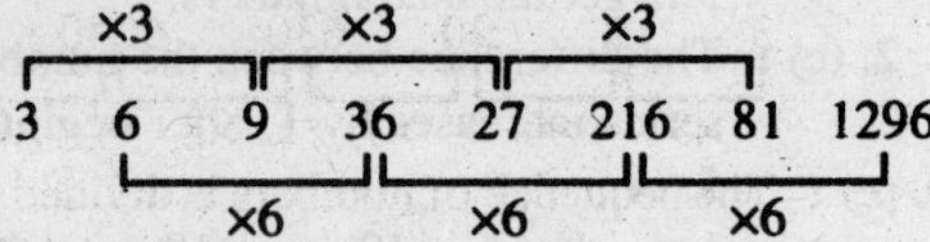

Series I : 3, 9, 27, 81 (number is multiplied by 3 to get the next number)
Series II : 6, 36, 216, 1296 (number is multiplied by 6 to get the next number)

25. (a) : There are two alternate series :

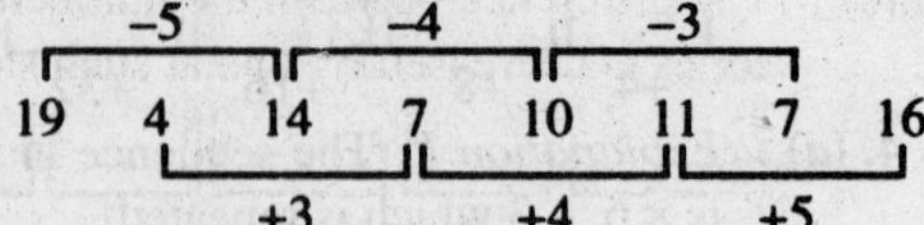

Series I : 19, 14, 10, 7 (The sequence followed is −5, −4, −3)
Series II : 4, 7, 11, 16 (The sequence followed is +3, +4, +5)

26. (b) : The numbers in the series are sum of two numbers preceding them.

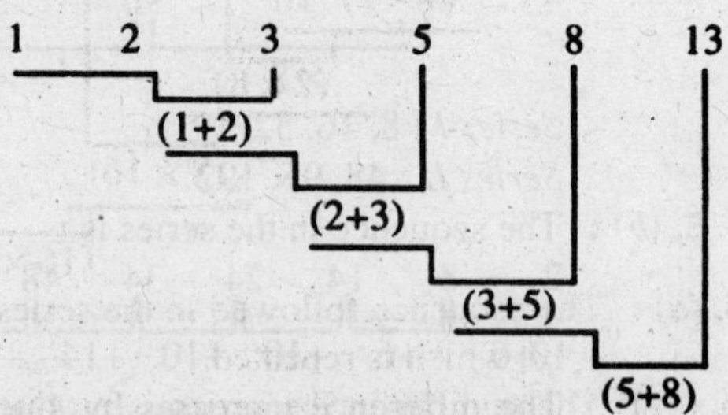

27. (d) : There are two alternate series and the numbers are divided by 2.

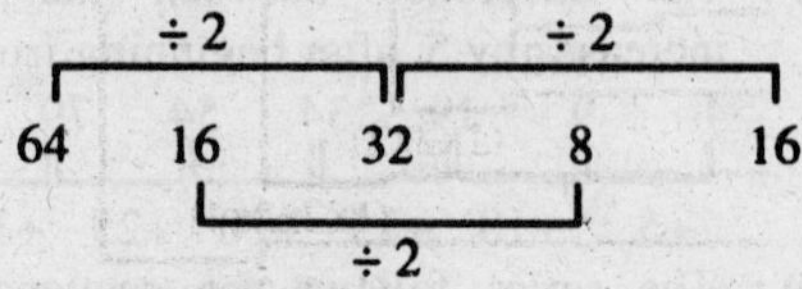

28. (d) : The sequence in the series is that a number is the sum of all the numbers preceding it.

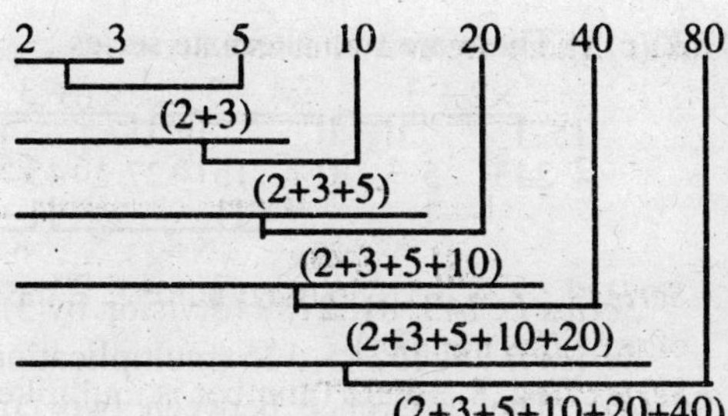

29. (c) : The sequence in the series is ×5, ×6, ×7, ×8, ×9.

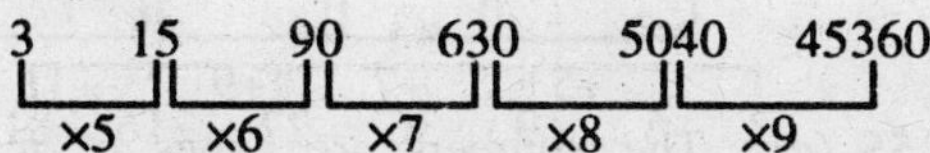

30. (c) : The sequence of numbers is divided by odd numbers in increasing order starting from 1.

1890 1890 630 126 18 2

÷ 1 ÷ 3 ÷ 5 ÷ 7 ÷ 9

31. (d) : The numbers in the series are decreasing by 23.

32. (c) : The difference between the numbers in the series is decreased by one at such step.

55 45 36 28 21 15

–10 –9 –8 –7 –6

33. (b) : The numbers in the series are divided by 11 at each step.

34. (d) : The number in the series is product of two numbers preceding it.

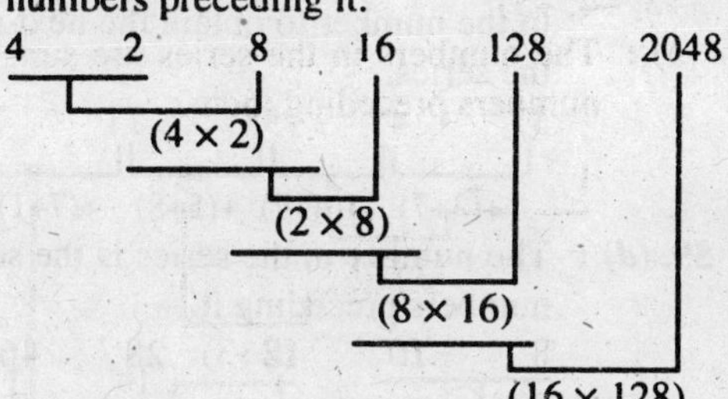

35. (a) : The sequence followed in the series is × 6, – 10, which is repeated.

36. (c) : The number in the series is product of all the numbers preceding it.

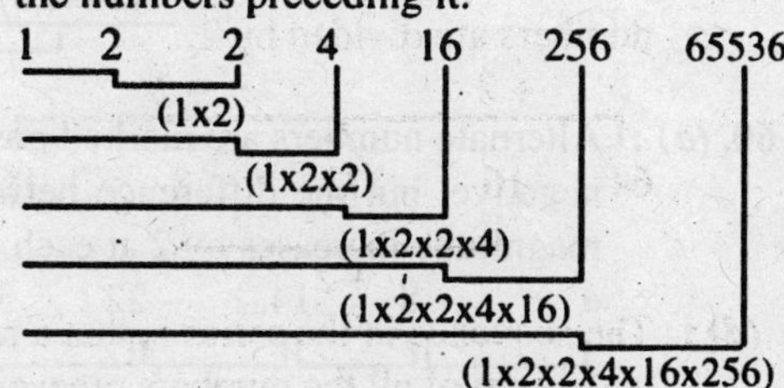

37. (b) : The sequence in the series is that the number subtracted from its previous number gives the next number.

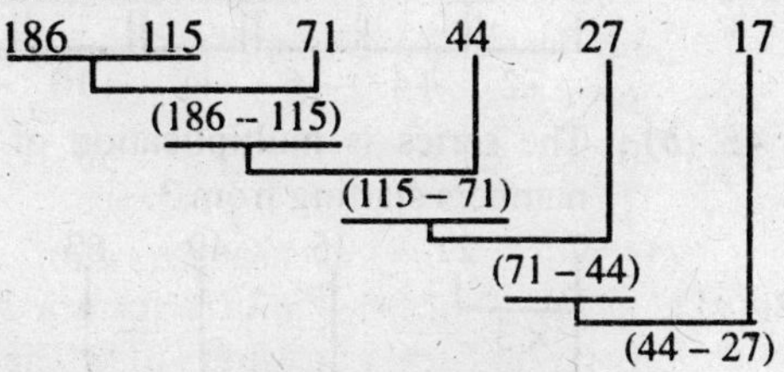

38. (b) : There are two alternate series :

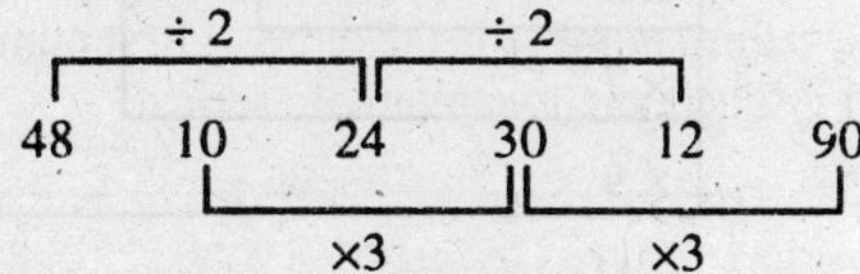

Series I : 48, 24, 12 (division by 2)

Series II : 10, 30, 90 (multiplication by 3)

39. (a) : There are two alternate series :

100	25	64	49	36	81	16
↓	↓	↓	↓	↓	↓	↓
10^2	5^2	8^2	7^2	6^2	9^2	4^2

Series I : 100, 64, 36, 16 (squares of even numbers in decreasing order)

Series II : 25, 49, 81 (squares of odd number in increasing order)

40. (b) : The numbers in the series are divided by 2 at each step.

41. (d) : The sequence in the series is double the square of numbers in their natural order.

$1^2 \times 2 = 2$

$2^2 \times 2 = 8$

$3^2 \times 2 = 18$

$4^2 \times 2 = 32$

$5^2 \times 2 = 50$

$6^2 \times 2 = 72$

$7^2 \times 2 = 98$

42. (b) : The series follows the sequence of subtraction of numbers 12, 9, 6, 3, 0 (reduced by 3 at each step).

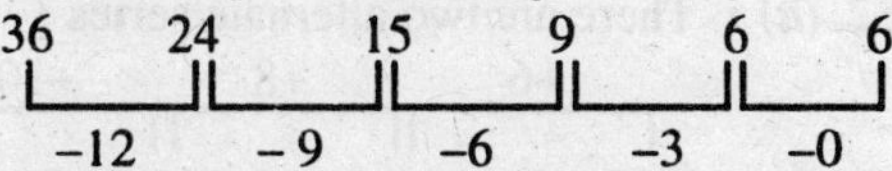

43. (a) : The sequence in the series is × 1, × 2, × 4, × 8, × 16, × 64.

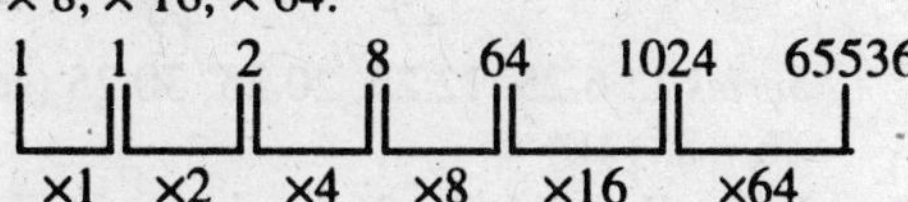

44. (d) : The difference between consecutive numbers increases by 2 at each step.

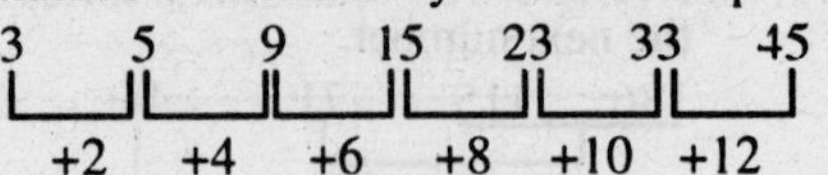

45. (b) : The series is multiplication of 7 by odd numbers starting from 3.

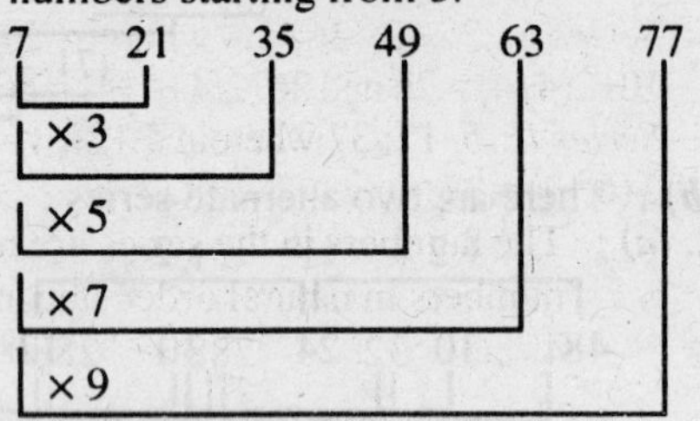

46. (c) : Double the number plus 1 gives the next number in the series.

1 3 7 15 31 63

(1x2) +1 (3x2) +1 (7x2)+1 (15x2)+1 (31x2)+1

47. (c) : The numbers in the series are double the previous number.

48. (d) : The number plus the square of numbers in natural order starting from 2 gives the next number in the series.

10 14 23 39 64 100 149

$+2^2$ $+3^2$ $+4^2$ $+5^2$ $+6^2$ $+7^2$

49. (b) : The sequence in the series is ×4, +5, which is repeated.

50. (a) : The sequence in the series is ×10, –5, which is repeated.

51. (b) : There are two alternate series :

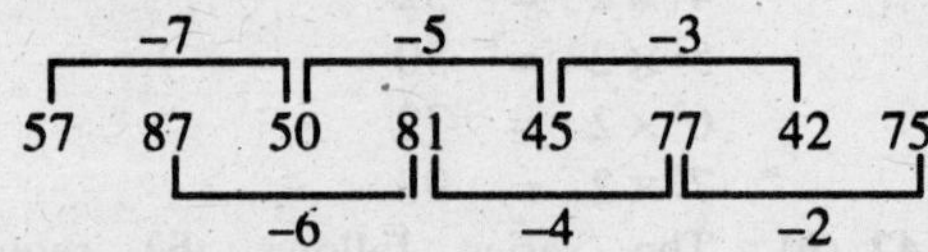

Series I : 57, 50, 45, 42 (sequence is –7, –5, –3)
Series II : 87, 81, 77, 75 (sequence is –6, –4, –2)

52. (a) : There are two alternate series :

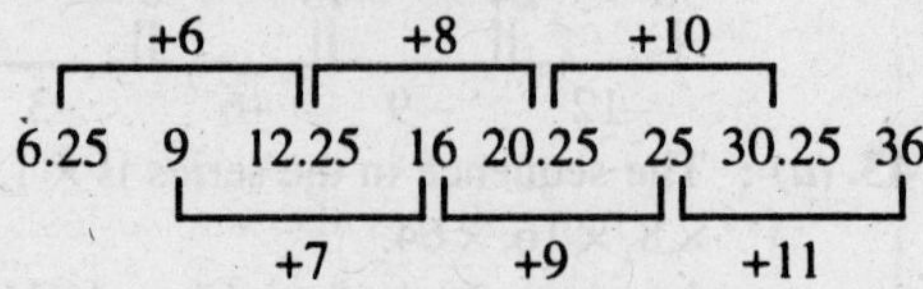

Series I : 6.25, 12.25, 20.25, 30.25 (sequence is +6, +8, +10)
Series II : 9, 16, 25, 36 (sequence is +7, +9, +11)

53. (c) : There are two alternate series :

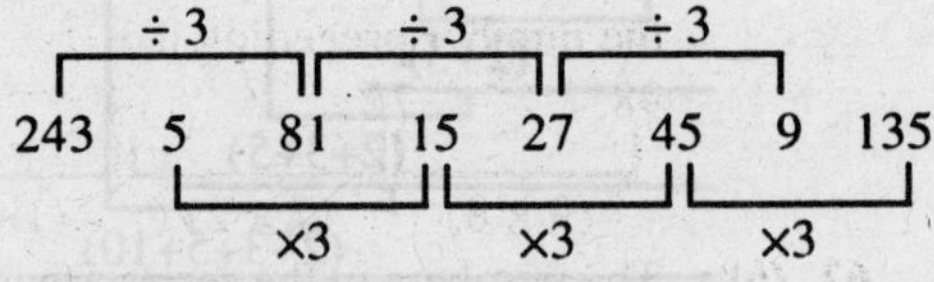

Series I : 243, 81, 27, 9 (division by 3)
Series II : 5, 15, 45, 135 (multiplication by 3)

54. (d) : The difference between two consecutive numbers is increasing by 2 starting from 5.

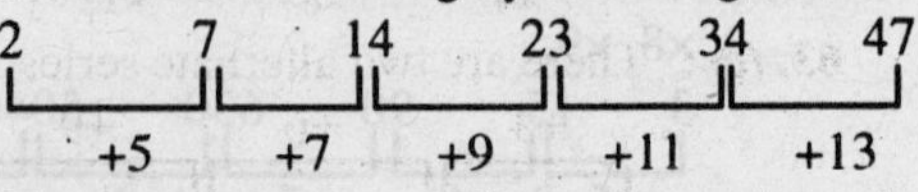

55. (a) : The numbers are cubes of numbers in natural order.

56. (b) : There are two alternate series :

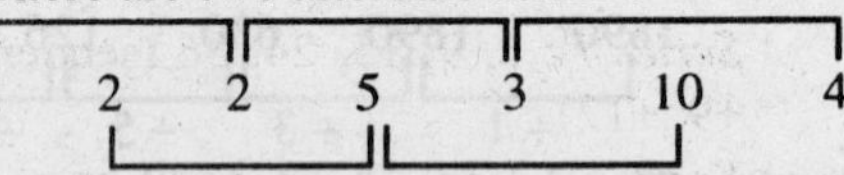

Series I : 1, 2, 3, 4 (numbers are increasing in natural order)
Series II : 2, 5, 10 (third number is product of previous two numbers)

57. (a) : The sum of two digits of the number increases by one at each step.

17 27 37 56 66 67
↓ ↓ ↓ ↓ ↓ ↓
1+7=8 2+7=9 3+7=10 5+6=11 6+6=12 6+7=13

58. (a) : The sum of the digits of the number is added to the number to obtain the next number in the series.

37 47 58 71 79 95

+(3+7) +(4+7) +(5+8) +(7+1) +(7+9)

59. (d) : The number in the series is the sum of two numbers preceding it.

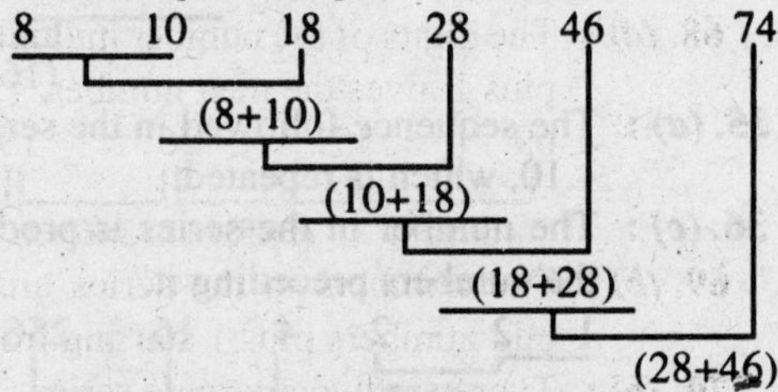

60. (a) : Alternate numbers are marked positive and negative, but the difference between their magnitude increases by 2 at each step.

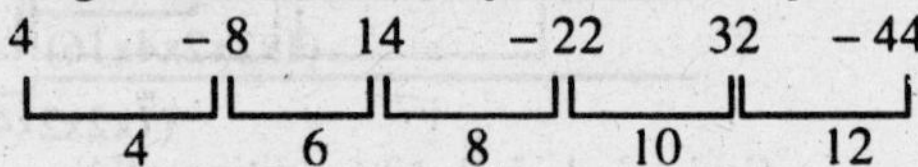

61. (c) : The number is the product of two digits of the number preceding it.

98 72 14 4

(9 × 8) (7 × 2) (1× 4)

62. (b) : The numbers in the series are multiplied by multiples of 4.

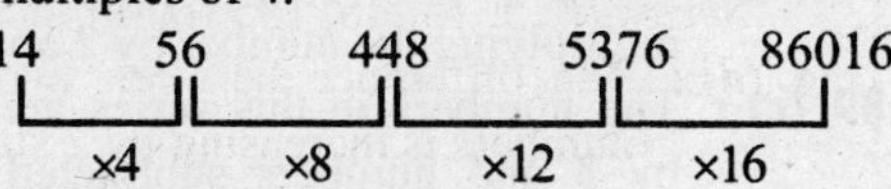

63. (c) : There are two alternate series :

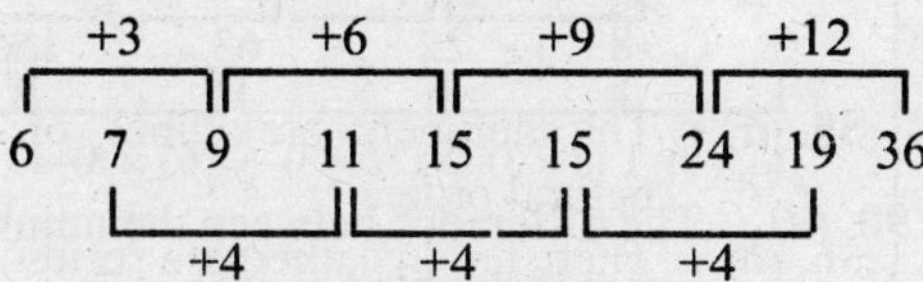

Series I : 6, 9, 15, 24, 36 (sequence is +3, +6, +9, +12)

Series II : 7, 11, 15, 19 (addition of 4 at each step)

64. (a) : The difference between the consecutive numbers in the series increases by 2 at each step.

2 6 12 20 30 42

+4 +6 +8 +10 +12

65. (c) : The difference between the consecutive numbers in the series increases by 2 at each step.

4 7 12 19 28 39

+3 +5 +7 +9 +11

66. (c) : The difference between the numbers follows the pattern +2, +4 which is repeated.

67. (d) : The numbers in the series are cubes of numbers in natural order plus the number itself.

68. (d) : The digits of the number multiplied together plus 1 gives the next number.

69 55 26 13 4

(6×9)+1 (5×5)+1 (2×6)+1 (1×3)+1

69. (b) : The numbers in the series are squares of odd numbers plus 1 starting from 3.

70. (b) : There are two alternate series :

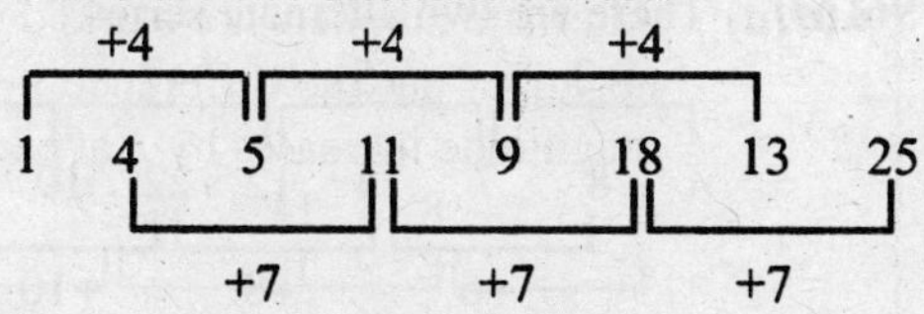

Series I : 1, 5, 9, 13 (addition of 4)

Series II : 4, 11, 18, 25 (addition of 7)

71. (c) : There are two alternate series :

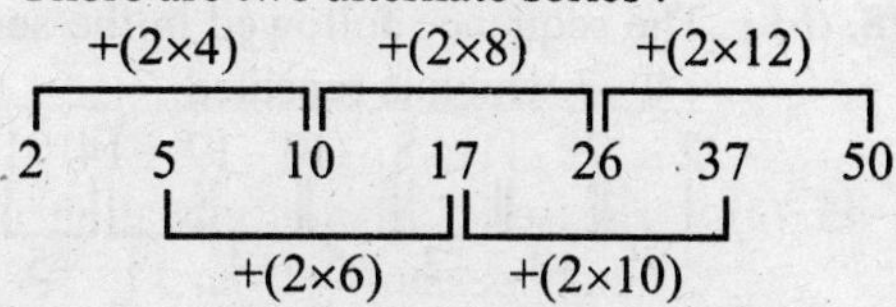

Series I : 2, 10, 26, 50 wherein 2+2 (4) = 10; 10+2(4+4) = 26 and 26+2(4+4+4) = 50

Series II: 5, 17, 37 wherein 5 +2(6) = 17 and 17 + 2 (6 +4) = 37

72. (a) : The numbers in the series are multiplied by numbers in natural order starting from 8.

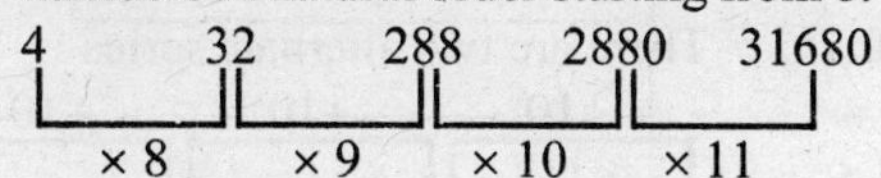

73. (a) : There are two alternate series :

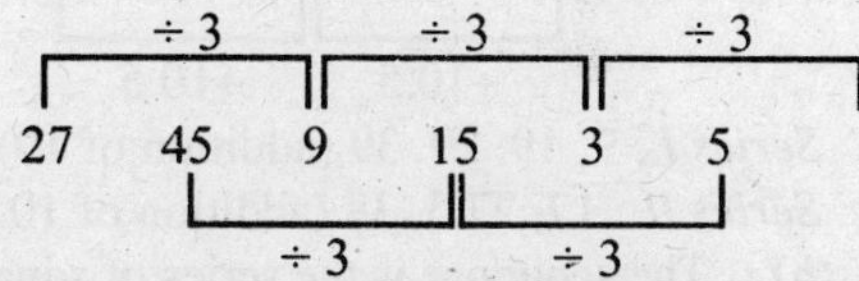

Series I : 27, 9, 3, 1 (division by 3)

Series II : 45, 15, 5 (division by 3)

74. (c) : The difference between the numbers increases with the increasing power of 3.

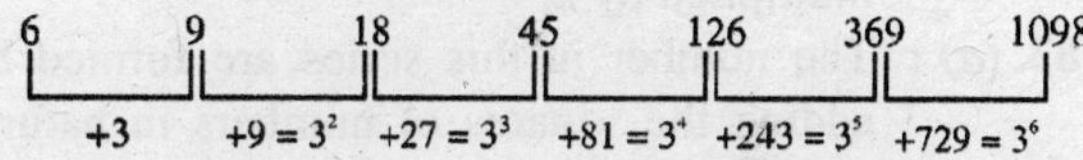

75. (d) : Two consecutive numbers form a pair. The difference between the numbers placed at odd places increases by 11 and the second number is the fraction part of the number.

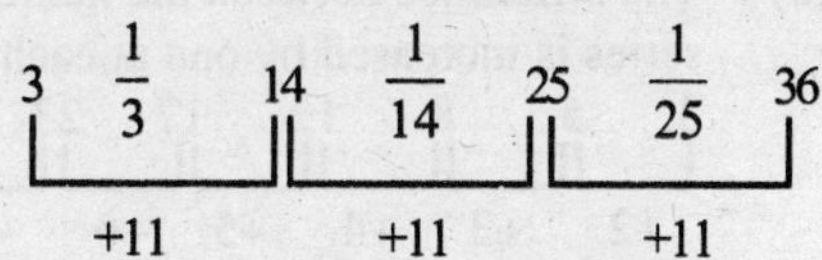

76. (d) : There are two alternate series :

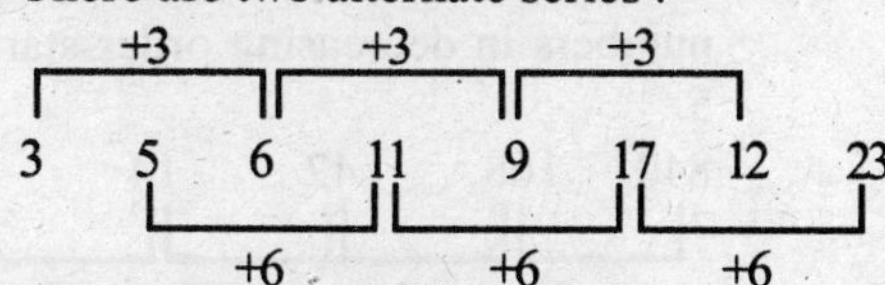

Series I : 3, 6, 9, 12 (addition of 3)

Series II : 5, 11, 17, 23 (addition of 6)

77. (a) : There are two alternate series :

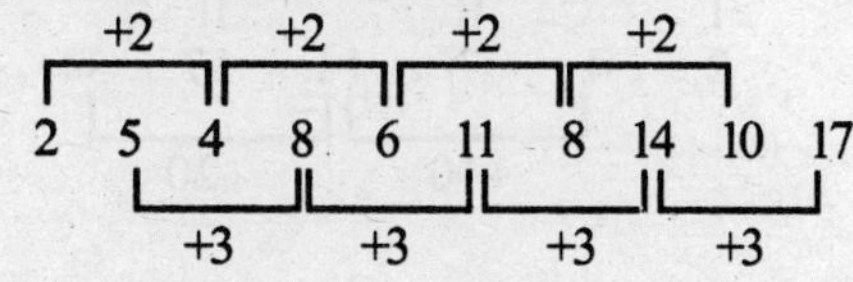

Series I : 2, 4, 6, 8, 10 (addition of 2)
Series II : 5, 8, 11, 14, 17 (addition of 3)

78. (*b*) : The sequence followed in the series is +5, +4, –3 which is repeated.

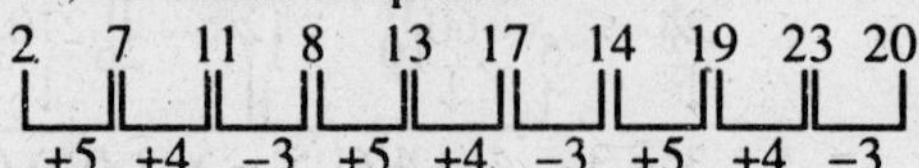

79. (*d*) : The difference between the consecutive numbers is reduced to half at each step starting from 20.

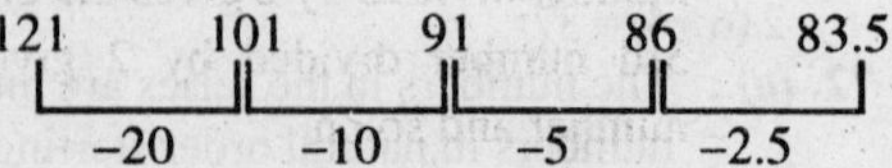

80. (*b*) : There are two alternate series :

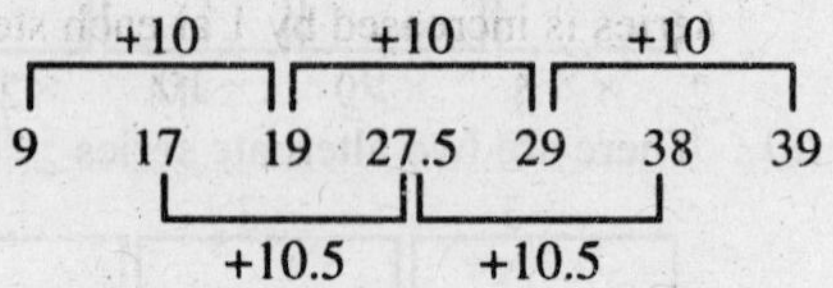

Series I : 9, 19, 29, 39 (addition of 10)
Series II : 17, 27.5, 38 (addition of 10.5)

81. (*b*) : The sequence is the series of squares of the numbers in natural order.

82. (*b*) : In this fraction series the numbers on the top are increased by ? and at the bottom, multiplied by 2.

83. (*a*) : The number in this series are formed by adding the squares of numbers in natural order.

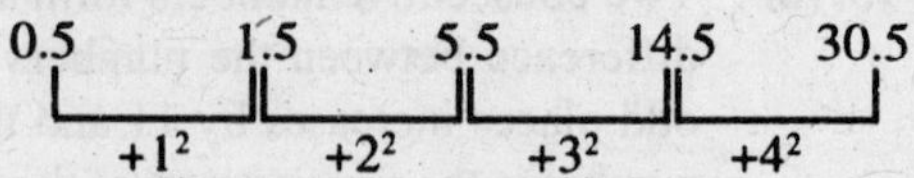

84. (*b*) : The difference between the numbers in this series is increased by one at each step.

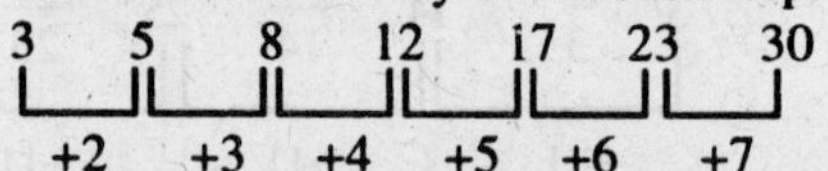

85. (*b*) : The numbers in this series are divided by numbers in decreasing order starting from 5.

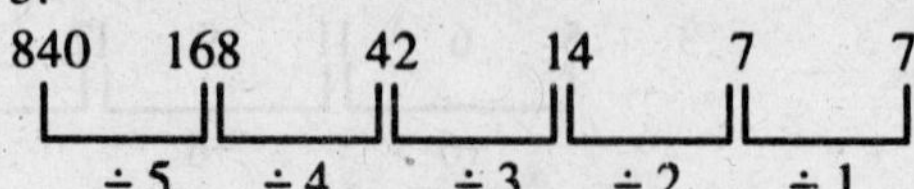

86. (*c*) : There are two alternate series :

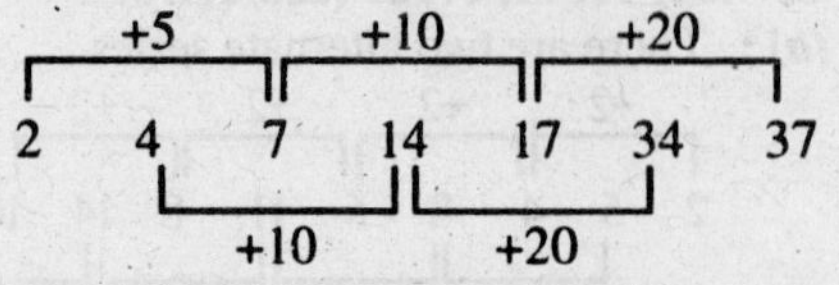

Series I : 2, 7, 17, 37
Series II : 4, 14, 34
(both series are following the pattern of doubling the difference at each step)

87. (*d*) : The sequence in the series is +1, +5 which is repeated.

88. (*d*) : The sequence in the series is formed by multiplying the number by 2 and adding 2.

89. (*c*) : The numbers in this series are multiplied by 3 and numbers subtracted in natural order starting from 1.

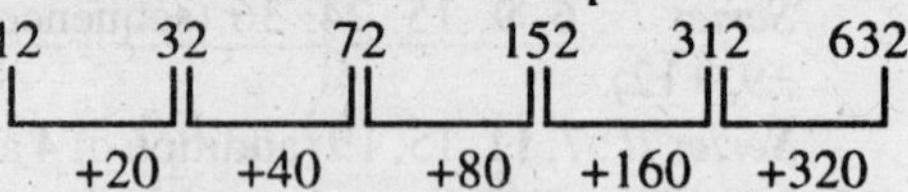

90. (*d*) : The difference between the numbers in this series is doubled at each step.

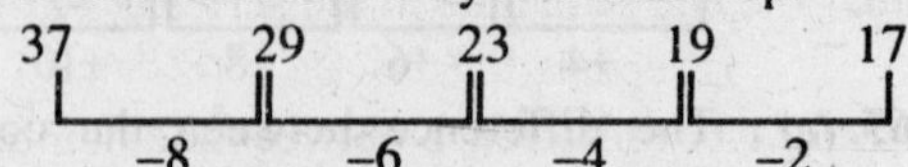

91. (*a*) : The sequence in the series is +7, –4 which is repeated.

92. (*d*) : The difference between the numbers in the series is decreased by 2 at each step.

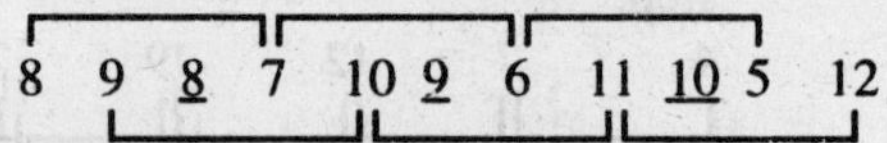

93. (*c*) : There are three alternate series :

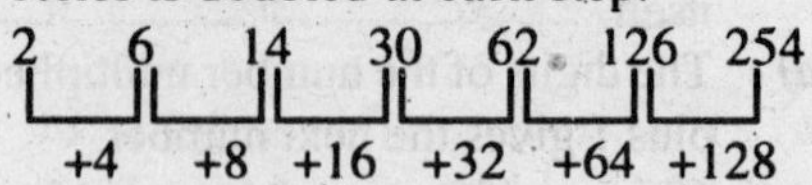

Series I : 8, 7, 6, 5 (following –1 pattern)
Series II : 9, 10, 11, 12 (following +1 pattern)
Series III : 8, 9, 10 (following +1 pattern)

94. (*c*) : The difference between the numbers in the series is doubled at each step.

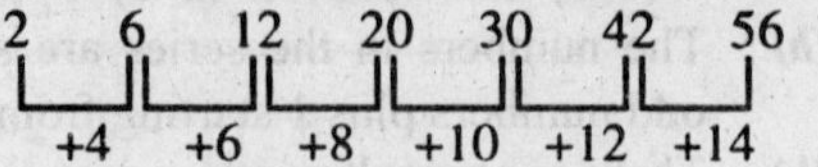

95. (*c*) : The series is formed by adding the even numbers in natural series starting from 4.

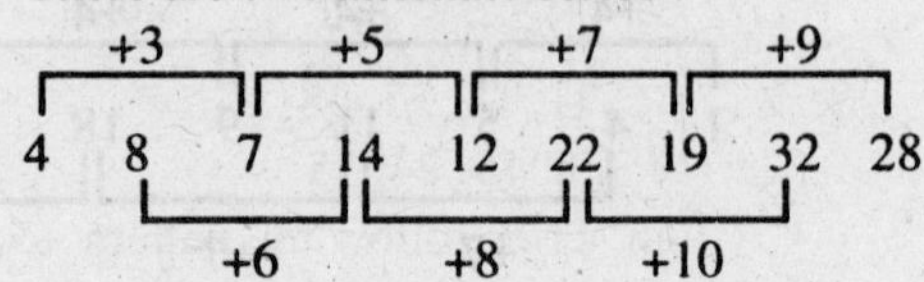

96. (*d*) : There are two alternate series :

Series I : 4, 7, 12, 19, 28 (sequence is +3, +5, +7, +9)

Series II : 8, 14, 22, 32 (sequence is +6, +8, +10)

97. (a) : The series is formed by multiples of 6 in this manner :

6 × 16 = 96
6 × 15 = 90 (16 – 1) = 15
6 × 13 = 78 (15 – 2) = 13
6 × 10 = 60 (13 – 3) = 10
6 × 6 = 36 (10 – 4) = 6
6 × 1 = 6 (6 – 5) = 1

98. (a) : This sequence pattern is – double the number minus 3 to get the next number.

99. (b) : There are two alternate series :

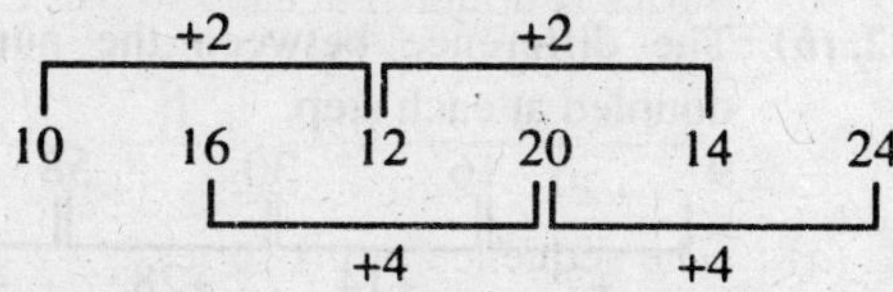

Series I : 10, 12, 14 (following +2 pattern)

Series II : 16, 20, 24 (following +4 pattern)

100. (d) : The sequence in the series is +2, +3 which is repeated.

101. (c) : The difference between the numbers in the series is the natural order of numbers starting from 1.

20 19 17 14 10 5
–1 –2 –3 –4 –5

102. (d) : The difference between the numbers in the series is increased by 2 at each step.

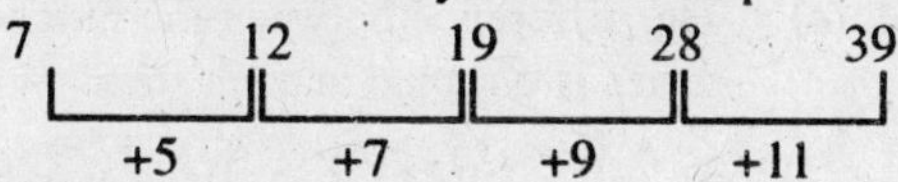

103. (a) : The sequence in the series is ×4, ×2 which is repeated.

104. (c) : There are two alternate series :

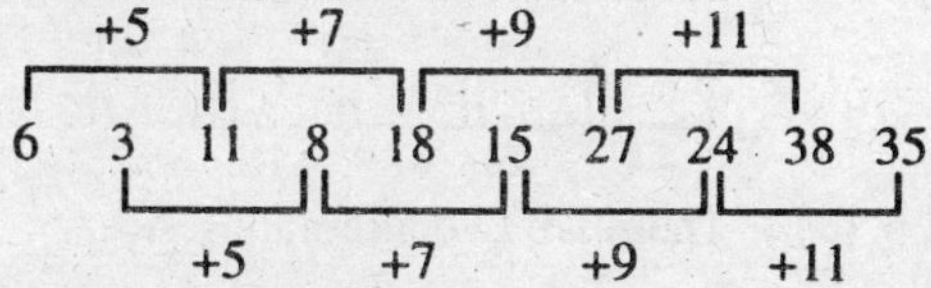

Series I : 6, 11, 18, 27, 38

Series II : 3, 8, 15, 24, 35

(Both series follow the pattern +5, +7, +9, +11)

105. (b) : The numbers in this series are the cubes of natural numbers starting from 3 minus the number itself.

24	60	120	210	336
↓	↓	↓	↓	↓
$3^3 - 3$	$4^3 - 4$	$5^3 - 5$	$6^3 - 6$	$7^3 - 7$
27 – 3	64 – 4	125 – 5	216 – 6	343 – 7

106. (c) : The pattern in this series is that the 1st number divided by 2 gives the 2nd number, 3rd number divided by 2 gives the 4th number and so on.

107. (a) : The difference between the numbers in this series is increased by 1 at each step.

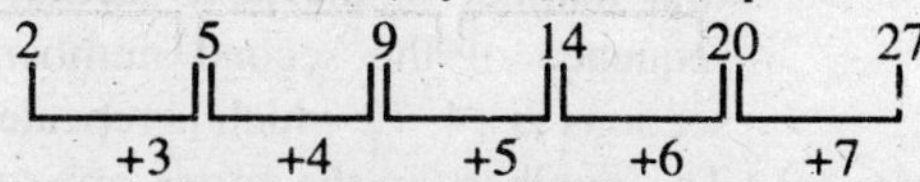

108. (d) : The difference between the numbers is reduced by half at each step.

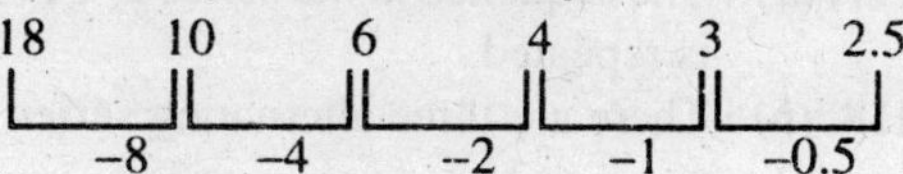

109. (d) : The difference between the numbers in this series is increased by 2 at each step.

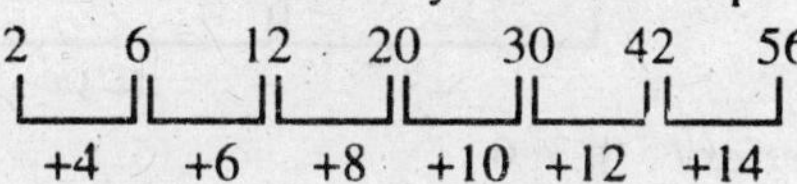

110. (b) : The difference between the numbers in this series is the sum of two previous differences.

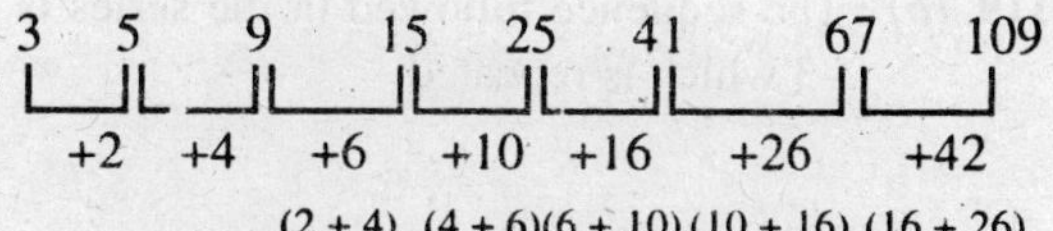

111. (d) : The difference between the numbers in this series is increased by 4 at each step.

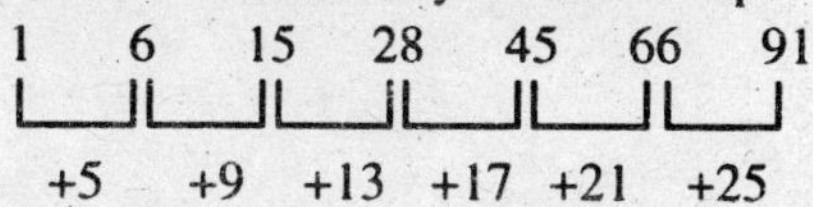

112. (c) : The sequence in this series is number into 2 plus the numbers in natural order starting from 0.

1 2 5 12 27 58 121 248

(1 x 2)+0 (2 x 2)+1 (5 x 2)+2 (12 x 2)+3 (27 x 2)+4 (58 x 2)+5 (121 x 2)+6

113. (a) : The sequence in this pattern is of multiples

of 3. The pattern is :

$3 \times 0 = 0$
$3 \times 1 = 3$ $(1 + 3 = 4)$ > difference of 3 (6 – 3)
$3 \times 4 = 12$ $(4 + 6 = 10)$ > difference of 4 (10 – 6)
$3 \times 10 = 30$ $(10 + 10 = 20)$ > difference of 5 (15 – 10)
$3 \times 20 = 60$ $(20 + 15 = 35)$ > difference of 6 (21 – 15)
$3 \times 35 = 105$ $(35 + 21 = 56)$
$3 \times 56 = 168$

114. *(c)* : The difference between the numbers in this series is increased by 2 at each step.

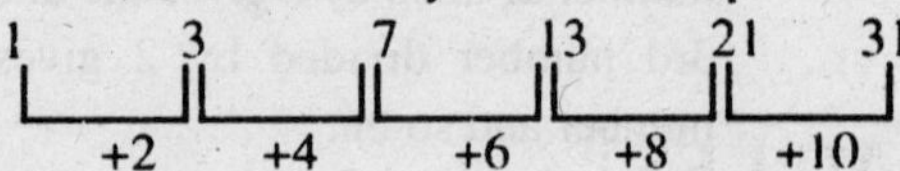

115. (b) : The second number in one section is the first number in the next section and the sequence of the second numbers in the sections is +4, +2 which is repeated.

116. *(c)* : The numbers in the series are squares of numbers in natural order starting from 2.

117. *(a)* : The sequence in the series is ÷ 5, ÷ 2 which is repeated.

118. *(b)* : There are three alternating series :

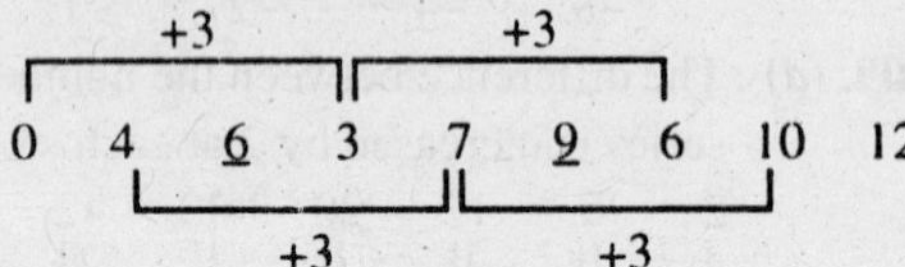

Series I : 0, 3, 6
Series II : 4, 7, 10
Series III : 6, 9, 12
(All series follow the pattern +3)

119. *(b)* : The sequence followed in the series is +5, –3 which is repeated.

120. *(a)* : Two consecutive numbers form a pair. The difference between the first number increases in the manner +2, +3, +4, +5 and the second number is the square of the number.

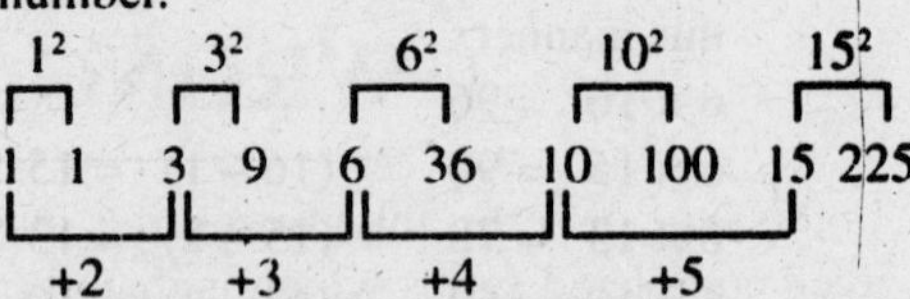

121. *(c)* : The numbers in this series are the squares of number in natural order minus 1 starting from 2.

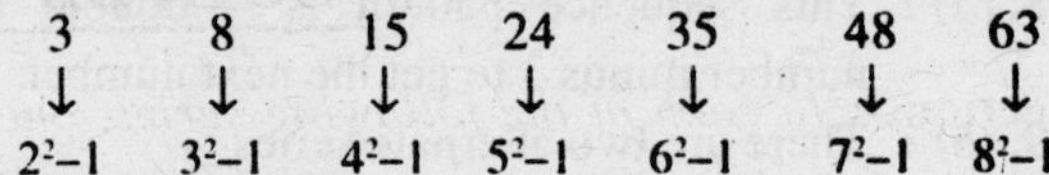

122. *(b)* : The difference between the numbers is doubled at each step.

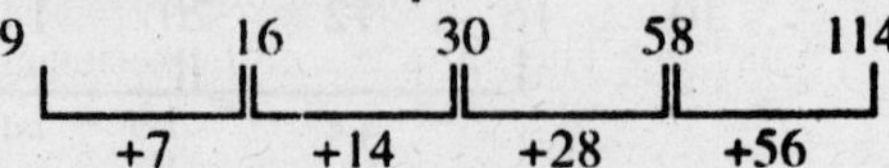

123. *(a)* : The difference between the numbers is the multiple of 9 with odd numbers.

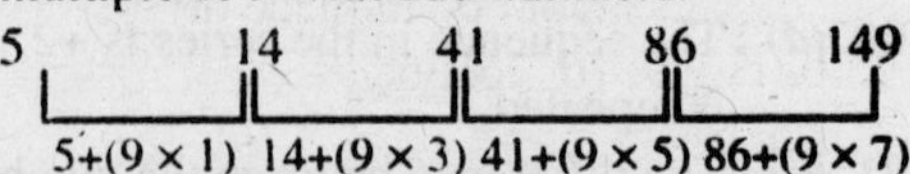

124. *(a)* : The sequence in the series is +9, – 4 which is repeated.

125. *(c)* : The difference between the numbers in the series is decreased by 2 at each step.

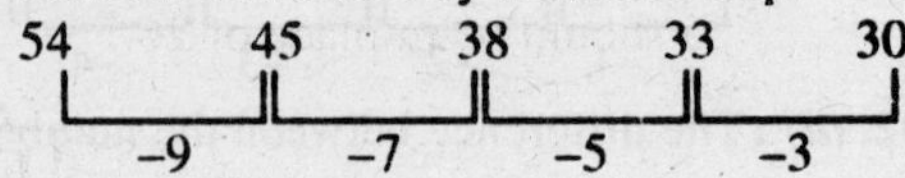

PART - V

WRONG NUMBER SERIES

In this type of series the given series may be complete but what needs to be identified is the number in the given completed series which is disturbing the sequential pattern of that series and does not fit in with the relationship shared between the other numbers.

SOLVED EXAMPLES

Directions : *In each of the following series, one number is wrong. Select the answer from the given options.*

1. 2, 4, 8, 16, 30, 64, 128

(*a*) 8 (*b*) 128 (*c*) 30 (*d*) 4

Ans. (*c*) : The numbers in the series are multiplied by 2.

2 → 4 → 8 → 16 → 32 → 64 → 128 (each ×2)

∴ 32 should be in place of 30.

2. 0, 1, 4, 9, 16, 26, 36, 49

(*a*) 26 (*b*) 9 (*c*) 49 (*d*) 16

Ans. (*a*) : The numbers in the series are squares of numbers in their natural order.

0	1	4	9	16	25	36	49
↓	↓	↓	↓	↓	↓	↓	↓
0^2	1^2	2^2	3^2	4^2	5^2	6^2	7^2

∴ 25 should be in place of 26.

EXERCISE

Directions : *In the given series find the number which is wrong.*

1. 5, 25, 120, 625, 3125, 15625

(*a*) 15625 (*b*) 625
(*c*) 120 (*d*) 5

2. 4, 8, 11, 22, 18, 36, 24, 50

(*a*) 8 (*b*) 22
(*c*) 36 (*d*) 24

3. 2, 4, 12, 24, 72, 142, 432

(*a*) 432 (*b*) 12
(*c*) 142 (*d*) 72

4. 2, 3, 4, 4, 6, 8, 9, 12, 16

(*a*) 3 (*b*) 9
(*c*) 6 (*d*) 12

5. 97, 91, 86, 83, 79, 77, 76, 76

(*a*) 86 (*b*) 76
(*c*) 91 (*d*) 83

6. 7, 11, 11, 9, 15, 7, 19, 5, 23, 1

(*a*) 5 (*b*) 7
(*c*) 1 (*d*) 9

7. 3, 7, 12, 28, 48, 118, 192, 448

(*a*) 12 (*b*) 118
(*c*) 28 (*d*) 7

8. 10, 100, 1100, 11000, 111000, 1210000

(*a*) 1210000 (*b*) 11000
(*c*) 100 (*d*) 111000

9. 24576, 6144, 1536, 386, 96, 24

(*a*) 386 (*b*) 6144

(c) 96 (d) 1536

10. 11, 13, 15, 17, 19, 23, 29, 31, 37
(a) 13 (b) 23
(c) 15 (d) 31

11. 36, 43, 49, 54, 60, 61, 63, 64
(a) 60 (b) 63
(c) 54 (d) 43

12. 3, 10, 41, 206, 1236, 8660
(a) 10 (b) 41
(c) 206 (d) 1236

13. 17, 25, 37, 50, 65, 82, 101
(a) 25 (b) 17
(c) 101 (d) 65

14. 12, 20, 38, 42, 56, 72
(a) 20 (b) 38
(c) 56 (d) 72

15. 5, 6, 11, 22, 42, 88, 176
(a) 5 (b) 42
(c) 176 (d) 11

16. 905, 180, 175, 35, 30, 6, 1
(a) 6 (b) 1
(c) 175 (d) 905

17. 5040, 840, 160, 42, 14, 7
(a) 7 (b) 160
(c) 14 (d) 840

18. 3, 32, 363, 3993, 43923
(a) 363 (b) 3
(c) 32 (d) 43923

19. 3, 18, 38, 78, 123, 178, 243
(a) 78 (b) 3
(c) 123 (d) 18

20. 0, 1, 2, 2, 4, 4, 6, 8, 8, 10
(a) 6 (b) 0
(c) 1 (d) 10

21. 5, 12, 16, 24, 27
(a) 12 (b) 16
(c) 24 (d) 27

22. 27, 36, 45, 60, 71, 99
(a) 27 (b) 45
(c) 60 (d) 71

23. 81, 64, 49, 35, 25, 16
(a) 64 (b) 35
(c) 25 (d) 16

24. 625, 125, 25, 5, 0
(a) 0 (b) 125
(c) 5 (d) 625

25. 25, 19, 17, 13, 11, 7
(a) 25 (b) 17
(c) 13 (d) 7

26. 3, 10, 27, 4, 16, 64, 5, 25, 125
(a) 25 (b) 16
(c) 10 (d) 3

27. 301, 244, 186, 130, 73, 16
(a) 301 (b) 186
(c) 130 (d) 73

28. 4, 5, 9, 14, 22, 37, 60
(a) 5 (b) 9
(c) 14 (d) 22

29. 13, 39, 195, 1363, 12285
(a) 13 (b) 1363
(c) 39 (d) 195

30. 215, 28, 63, 126, 7, 343
(a) 215 (b) 28
(c) 126 (d) 343

31. 1, 5, 5, 9, 7, 11, 11, 15, 12, 17
(a) 11 (b) 15
(c) 17 (d) 12

32. 99, 79, 88, 70, 77, 59, 66, 48
(a) 79 (b) 88
(c) 54 (d) 66

33. 72, 75, 80, 83, 84, 87, 88, 89
(a) 72 (b) 83
(c) 88 (d) 89

34. 2, 3, 4, 5, 6, 8, 10, 13, 16, 22
(a) 22 (b) 8
(c) 13 (d) 4

35. 2, 3, 6, 18, 108, 1942
(a) 6 (b) 18
(c) 1942 (d) 3

EXPLANATORY ANSWERS

1. (c) : The numbers in the series are multiplied by 5 to get the next number.
∴ 125 should be in place of 120.

2. (d) : Two numbers form a pair. The first number increases by 7 for the next pair and the second number is the double of first number.

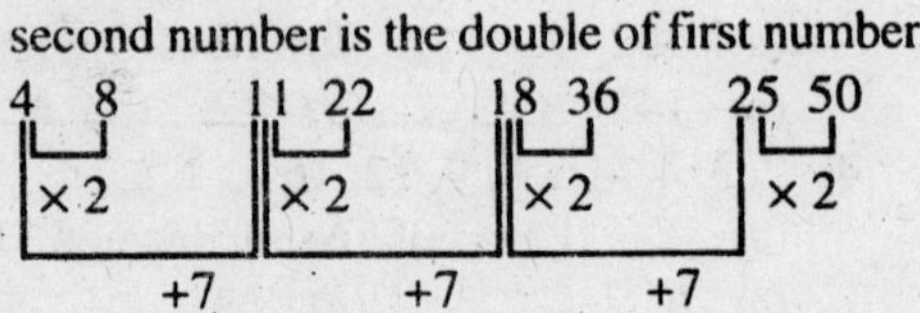

∴ 25 should be in place of 24.

3. (*c*) : There are two alternate series and in each series, the numbers are multiplied by 6 to get the next number.

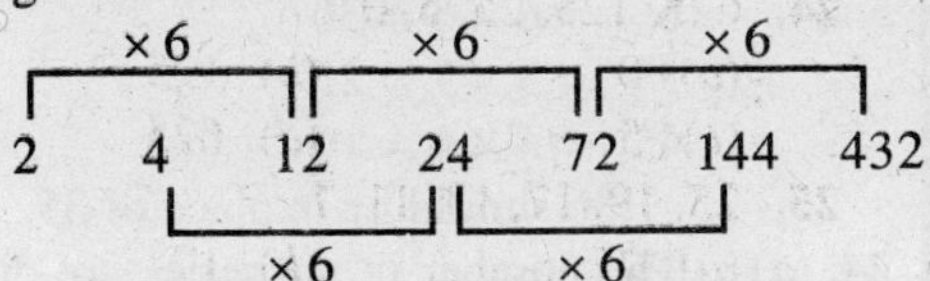

∴ 144 should be in place of 142.

4. (*b*) : There are three alternate series and in each series, the numbers are multiplied by 2 to get the next number.

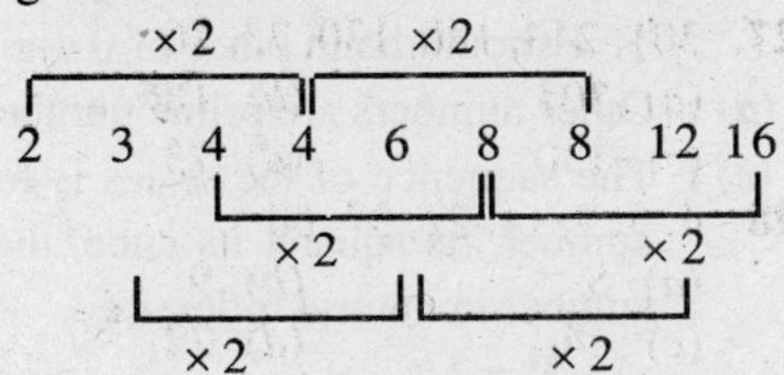

Series I : 2, 4, 8
Series II : 3, 6, 12
Series III : 4, 8, 16
∴ 8 should be in place of 9.

5. (*d*) : The difference between the consecutive numbers in the series decreases by 1 at each step.

97 91 86 82 79 77 76 76
–6 –5 –4 –3 –2 –1 –0

∴ 82 should be in place of 83.

6. (*c*) : There are two alternate series :

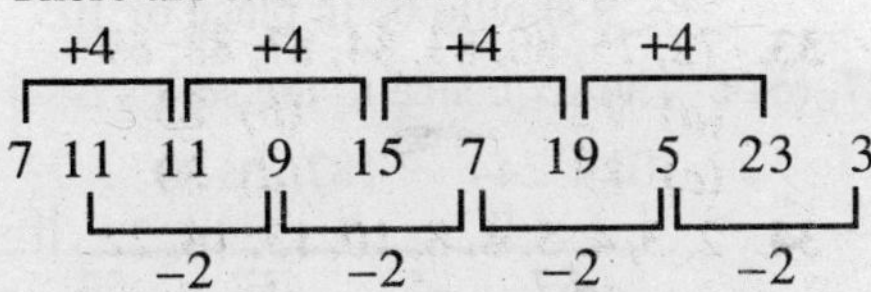

Series I : 7, 11, 15, 19, 23 (addition of 4)
Series II : 11, 9, 7, 5, 3 (subtraction of 2)
∴ 3 should be in place of 1.

7. (*b*) : There are two alternate series and in each series, the numbers are multiplied by 4 to get the next number.

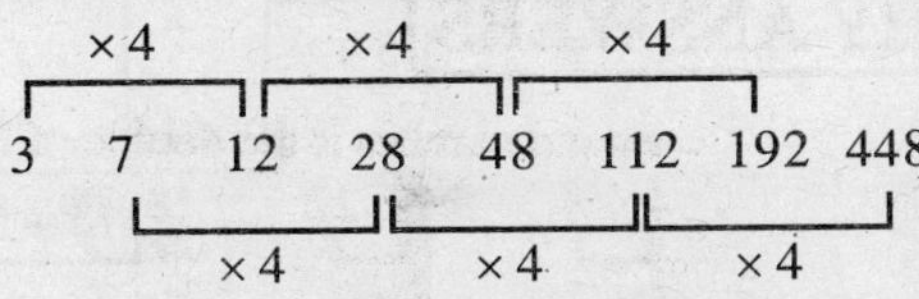

∴ 112 should be in place of 118.

8. (*d*) : The numbers in this series are multiplied by 10 and 11 alternately is, *i.e.*, × 10, × 11.

10 100 1100 11000 121000 1210000
× 10 × 11 × 10 × 11 × 10

∴ 121000 should be in place of 111000.

9. (*a*) : The numbers in this series are divided by 4 to get the next number.

24576 6144 1536 384 96 24
÷ 4 ÷ 4 ÷ 4 ÷ 4 ÷ 4

∴ 384 should be in place of 386.

10. (*c*) : The series comprises of prime numbers in increasing order. Only 15 is an exception.

11. (*a*) : The difference between two consecutive numbers is decreasing by 1 at each step.

36 43 49 54 58 61 63 64
+7 +6 +5 +4 +3 +2 +1

∴ 58 should be in place of 60.

12. (*d*) : The sequence followed in this series is :

$3 \times 3 + 1 = 10$
$10 \times 4 + 1 = 41$
$41 \times 5 + 1 = 206$
$206 \times 6 + 1 = 1237$; and
$1237 \times 7 + 1 = 8660$

∴ 1237 should be in place of 1236.

13. (*a*) : The numbers in the series are 1 plus the squares of numbers in natural order starting from 4.

17 26 37 50 65 82 101
↓ ↓ ↓ ↓ ↓ ↓ ↓
4^2+1 5^2+1 6^2+1 7^2+1 8^2+1 9^2+1 10^2+1

∴ 26 should be in place of 25.

14. (*b*) : The sequence followed in this series is :

$3 \times 4 = 12$
$4 \times 5 = 20$
$5 \times 6 = 30$
$6 \times 7 = 42$
$7 \times 8 = 56$
$8 \times 9 = 72$

∴ 30 should be in place of 38.

15. (*b*) : The numbers in the series are the sum of all the numbers preceding them.

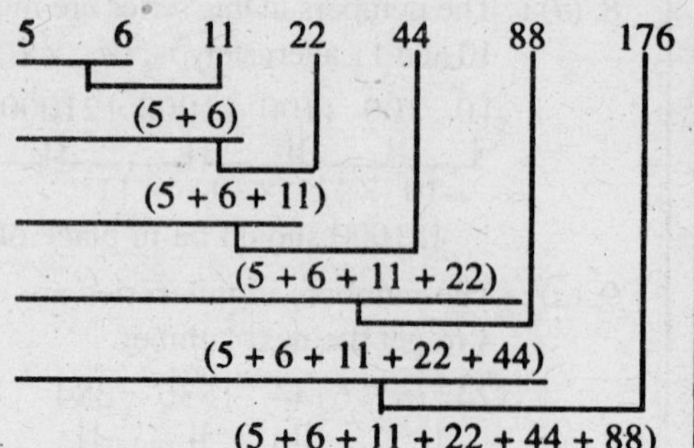

∴ 44 should be in place of 42.

16. (*d*) : The sequence followed in the series is ÷ 5, – 5 which is repeated.

900 180 175 35 30 6 1

÷ 5 – 5 ÷ 5 – 5 ÷ 5 – 5

∴ 900 should be in place of 905.

17. (*b*) : The numbers in the series are divided by numbers in reverse order starting from 6 to get the next number.

5040 840 168 42 14 7

÷ 6 ÷ 5 ÷ 4 ÷ 3 ÷ 2

∴ 168 should be in place of 160.

18. (*c*) : The numbers in this series are multiplied by 11 to get the next number.

3 33 363 3993 43923

× 11 × 11 × 11 × 11

∴ 33 should be in place of 32.

19. (*b*) : 3 is the only prime number in the series.

20. (*d*) : There are two alternate series :

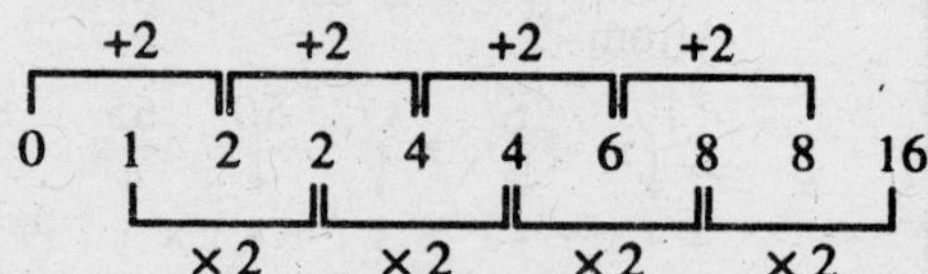

Series I : 0, 2, 4, 6, 8, (addition of 2)

Series II : 1, 2, 4, 8, 16 (multiplication by 2)

∴ 16 should be in place of 10.

21. (*c*) : The sequence in the series is +7, +4 which is repeated, *i.e.*,

5 12 16 23 27

+7 +4 +7 +4

∴ 23 should be in place of 24.

22. (*d*) : All other numbers are divisible by 3.

23. (*b*) : The sequence is the square of the number in decreasing order starting from 9, *i.e.*,

$9^2 = 9 \times 9 = 81$

$8^2 = 8 \times 8 = 64$

$7^2 = 7 \times 7 = 49$

$6^2 = 6 \times 6 = 36$

$5^2 = 5 \times 5 = 25$

$4^2 = 4 \times 4 = 16$

∴ 36 should be in place of 35.

24. (*a*) : The number in the series are divided by 5 to get the next number

625 125 25 5 1

÷ 5 ÷ 5 ÷ 5 ÷ 5

∴ 1 should be in place of 0 digit.

25. (*a*) : Other numbers are prime numbers.

26. (*c*) : The sequence of the series is formed by a number, its square, its cube, then the next number in natural order, *i.e.*,

$3^1 = 3$

$3^2 = 3 \times 3 = 9$

$3^3 = 3 \times 3 \times 3 = 27$

next number :

$4^1 = 4$

$4^2 = 4 \times 4 = 16$

$4^3 = 4 \times 4 \times 4 = 64$

next number :

$5^1 = 5$

$5^2 = 5 \times 5 = 25$

$5^3 = 5 \times 5 \times 5 = 125$

∴ 9 should be in place of 10.

27. (*b*) : The sequence in the series is –57, *i.e.*,

301 244 187 130 73 16

–57 –57 –57 –57 –57

∴ 187 should be in place of 186.

28. (*d*) : In this series a number is the sum of two numbers preceding it, *i.e.*,

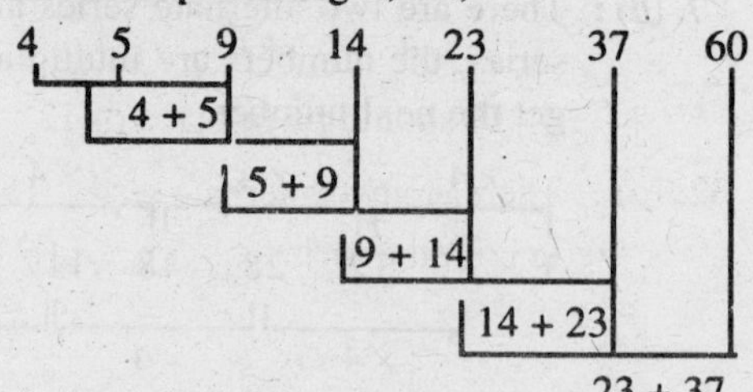

∴ 23 should be in place of 22.

29. (*b*) : In this series the numbers are multiplied by odd numbers in natural order starting from 3, *i.e.*,

13 39 195 1365 12285

×3 ×5 ×7 ×9

∴ 1365 should be in place of 1363.

30. (*d*) : There are two alternate series :

$6^3 - 1$ $4^3 - 1$ $2^3 - 1$

215 28 63 126 7 344

$3^3 + 1$ $5^3 + 1$ $7^3 + 1$

The 1st series consists of cubes of even numbers (starting from 6) in decreasing order minus 1.

$6^3 - 1 = (6 \times 6 \times 6) - 1 = 216 - 1 = 215$

$4^3 - 1 = (4 \times 4 \times 4) - 1 = 64 - 1 = 63$

$2^3 - 1 = (2 \times 2 \times 2) - 1 = 8 - 1 = 7$

The 2nd series consists of cubes of odd numbers (starting from 3) in ascending order plus 1.

$3^3 + 1 = (3 \times 3 \times 3) + 1 = 27 + 1 = 28$

$5^3 + 1 = (5 \times 5 \times 5) + 1 = 125 + 1 = 126$

$7^3 + 1 = (7 \times 7 \times 7) + 1 = 343 + 1 = 344$

∴ 344 should be in place of 343.

31. (*d*) : There are two alternate series. In each series the sequence is +4, +2 which is repeated, *i.e.*,

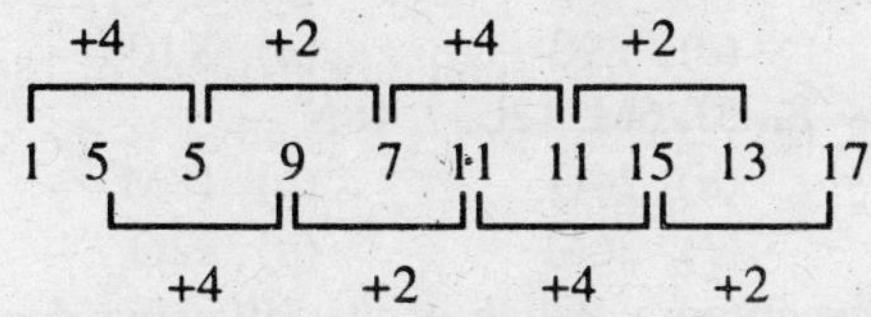

∴ 13 should be in place of 12.

32. (*a*) : There are two alternate series. The sequence in both the series is – 11, *i.e.*,

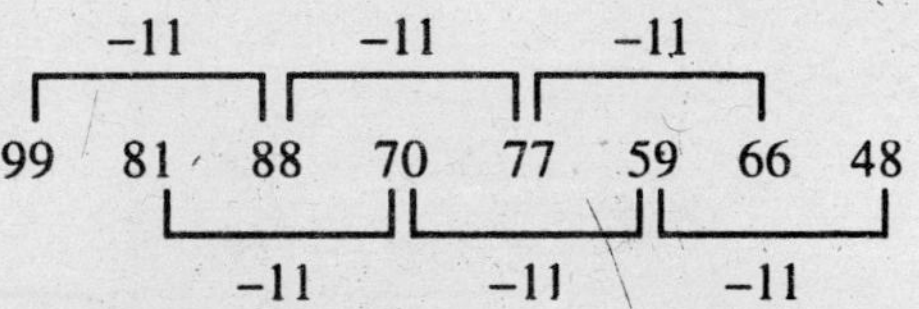

∴ 81 should be in place of 79.

33. (*c*) : There are two alternate series. The sequence in both the series is +8, +4, +2, *i.e.*,

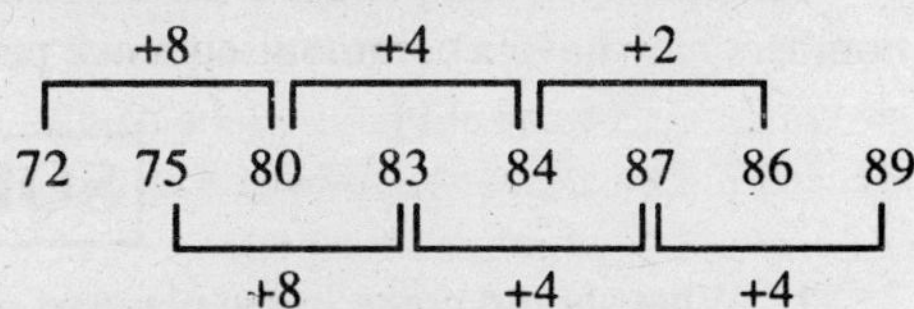

∴ 86 should be in place of 88.

34. (*a*) : There are two alternate series. In each series a number is the sum of two numbers preceding it, *i.e.*,

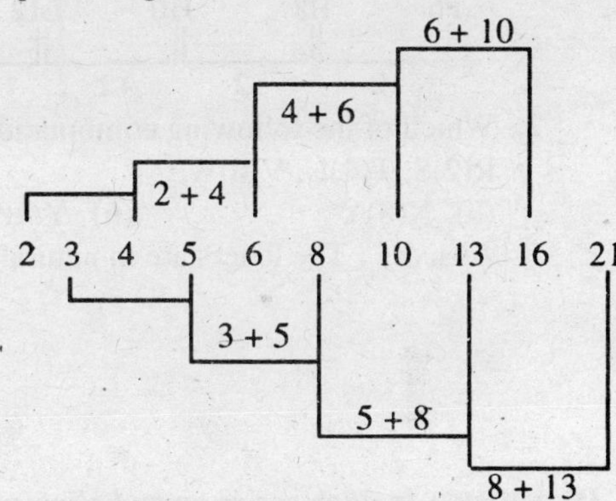

∴ 21 should be in place of 22.

35. (*c*) : The numbers in the series are the product of two numbers preceding it, *i.e.*,

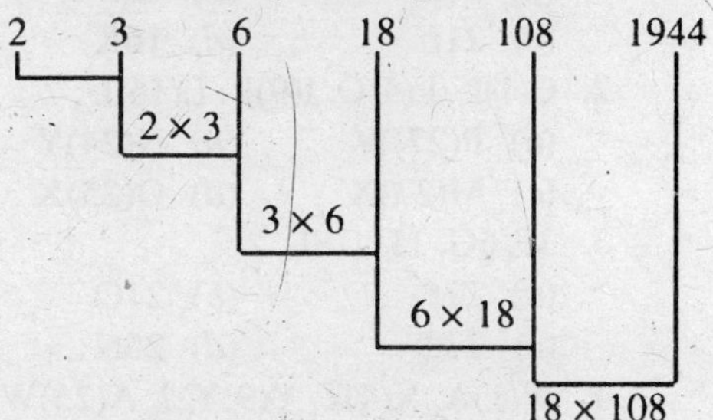

∴ 1944 should be in place of 1942.

PART - VI

MIXED SERIES

Mixed series comprises of the combination of letters and numbers. In this type of series the letters and numbers may have a common sequence pattern or may have separate sequence patterns.

SOLVED EXAMPLES

1. What should come in the place of question mark in the following letter-number combination?
F6, H8, J10, L12, ?
(*a*) N15 (*b*) O14 (*c*) N14 (*d*) O13

Ans. (*c*) : The letters are moved two steps forward and the number indicates the position of the letter in the alphabet series.

F6 → H8 → J10 → L12 → N14
+2 +2 +2 +2

2. Which of the following combinations will complete the given series?
R(2)S, T(4)U, V(6)W, ?
(*a*) X(8)Y (*b*) Y(10)Z (*c*) Z(8)A (*d*) Y(6)Z

Ans. (*a*) : The letters are in natural order, whereas the numbers are regular multiples of two.

EXERCISE

Directions : *In each series given below, what would come in place of the question-mark?*

1. 2B, 4C, 8E, 14H, ?
(*a*) 20L (*b*) 22L
(*c*) 21I (*d*) 16K

2. C(1)L, F(4)O, I(9)R, L(16)U, ?
(*a*) P(27)W (*b*) N(24)Y
(*c*) M(23)X (*d*) O(25)X

3. 3F, 6G, 11I, 18L, ?
(*a*) 27P (*b*) 21O
(*c*) 27Q (*d*) 25N

4. W(1)A, X(4)Z, Y(9)Y, ?, A(25)W
(*a*) X(11)Z (*b*) Z(21)A
(*c*) Z(16)X (*d*) Z(14)X

5. 81Y, 27S, 9N, 3J, ?
(*a*) 0H (*b*) 1G
(*c*) 0F (*d*) 1E

6. E5, K11, Q17, ?
(*a*) X20 (*b*) Y24
(*c*) V22 (*d*) W25

7. D2, I3, N6, S18, ?
(*a*) V72 (*b*) W36
(*c*) Y90 (*d*) X108

8. 3J, 6M, 12L, ?, 48N
(*a*) 24O (*b*) 18M
(*c*) 26M (*d*) 22O

Directions : *Which of the following does not fit in the letter number series given below?*

9. G4T, J10R, M20P, P43N, S90L
(*a*) J10R (*b*) S90L
(*c*) M20P (*d*) G4T

10. B0R, G3U, E3P, J7S, H9N
(*a*) E3P (*b*) J7S
(*c*) H9N (*d*) G3U

EXPLANATORY ANSWERS

1. (*b*) : The sequence of numbers is +2, +4, +6 +8 and sequence of letters is +1, +2, +3, +4.

2. (*d*) : The corresponding letters are moved 3 steps forward and the sequence of numbers is +3, +5, +7, +9.

3. (*a*) : The sequence of numbers is +3, +5, +7, +9 and the letters are moved 1,2,3,4 steps forward.

4. (*c*) : The letters on the left are in reverse series, the letters on the right are in natural series, and the numbers are squares of numbers in natural order starting from 1.

5. (*b*) : The numbers are divided by 3 at each step and the letters are moved 6,5,4,3 steps backward.

6. (*c*) : The series comprises of random letters and numbers indicate the position of the letter in alphabet series.

7. (*d*) : The letters are moved five steps forward and every third number is the product of two preceding numbers.

8. (*a*) : Every number is double the previous number and the sequence of letters is +3, –1 (3 steps forward, 1 step backward) which is repeated.

9. (*a*) : The letters on the left are moved 3 steps forward, the letters on the right are moved 2 steps backward and the sequence of numbers is $(4 \times 2) + 1$, $(9 \times 2) + 2$, $(20 \times 2) + 3$, $(43 \times 2) + 4$. So, J9R should be in place of J10R.

10. (*b*) : The sequence of letters on the left is +5, –2 (5 steps forward, 2 steps backward) which is repeated, the sequence of letters on the right is +3, –5 (3 steps forward, 5 steps backward) which is repeated, and the numbers are the sum of two preceeding numbers. So J6S should be in place of J7S.

ANALOGIES OR RELATIONSHIPS

PART - I

WORD ANALOGY

In Analogy Tests the relationship between two given words is established and then applied to the other words. The type of relationship may vary, so while attempting such questions the first step is to identify the type of relationship, which can be any one of the following.

SOLVED EXAMPLES

1. **Action Object Relationship**
   Example : Shoot is to Gun as Eat is to.....
   (*a*) Hunger (*b*) Thirst (*c*) Dinner (*d*) Fruit
   Ans. (*d*) : The relationship between the given words is that 'shoot' is the action and 'Gun' is the specified object of action. Similarly 'eat' is the action and 'fruit' is the specified object.
2. **Association Relationship**
   Example : Glamour is to Stardom as Colour is to.....
   (*a*) Rainbow (*b*) Shades (*c*) Art (*d*) Painting
   Ans. (*d*) : As glamour is associated with stardom so is colour with painting.
3. **Antonym Relationship**
   Example : INTROVERT : EXTROVERT
   (*a*) ANGLE : TANGENT (*b*) EXTREME : INTERIM
   (*c*) AGAINST : FAVOUR (*d*) ACTION : LAW
   Ans. (*c*) : The related words are opposite in meaning.
4. **Cause and Effect Relationship**
   Example : INJURY : PAIN
   (*a*) GRADES : MERIT (*b*) THUNDER : LIGHTNING
   (*c*) ROTATE : CHURNING (*d*) MATTER : LABOUR
   Ans. (*b*) : Injury is the cause of pain and so is thunder the cause of lightning.
5. **Degree Relationship**
   Example : Tepid is to Hot as... is to Wail.
   (*a*) Sob (*b*) Shout (*c*) Smile (*d*) Calm
   Ans. (*a*) : Tepid is less hot and so also the lower degree of wail is sob.
6. **Grammatical Relationship**
   Example: Clever is to Beautiful as Sour is to ...
   (*a*) Lemon (*b*) Cunning (*c*) Loathing (*d*) Taste
   Ans. (*b*) : The related words are Adjectives.
7. **Obvious Relationship**
   Example : Mt. EVEREST : NEPAL

(*a*) MEXICO : SOUTH AMERICA (*b*) K2 : CHINA
(*c*) BIG BEN : RUSSIA (*d*) AHMEDABAD : GUJARAT

Ans. (*d*) : Mt. Everest is in Nepal and so is Ahmedabad in Gujarat.

8. Part Whole Relationship

Example : MAN : MAMMAL
(*a*) HAIL : SNOW (*b*) NATIVE : INHABITANT
(*c*) OFFSPRING : FAMILY (*d*) LIBERTY : LITERATE

Ans. (*c*) : Man is a part of the whole species of mammal so is an offspring of the whole family.

9. Purpose Relationship

Example : INSTITUTION : EDUCATION
(*a*) WAR : PEACE (*b*) HEALTH : OBESITY
(*c*) MEDICATION : RECUPERATION (*d*) BUILDING : URBANISM

Ans. (*c*) : The purpose of institution is to impart education and the purpose of medication is quick recuperation (recovery).

10. Sequence Relationship

Example : .... is to Dusk as Summer is to Monsoon.
(*a*) Evening (*b*) Dawn (*c*) Night (*d*) Noon

Ans. (*a*) : Summer season is immediately followed by monsoon (rainy season) and evening is immediately followed by dusk.

11. Synonym Relationship

Example : INDENT : REQUEST
(*a*) REPLICA : CHEAT (*b*) DOLE : ALMS (*c*) DISMAL : DUNCE (*d*) EXACT : CHECK

Ans. (*b*) : The related words have the same meaning.

12. Volume Relationship

Example : GALLONS : SWIMMING POOL
(*a*) SPECTATORS : AUDITORIUM (*b*) CURRENCY : SHARES
(*c*) DUST : MOUNTAIN (*d*) BOOKS : CATALOGUE

Ans. (*a*) : Gallons of water is needed to fill a swimming pool and large number of spectators can be admitted into an auditorium.

EXERCISE

Directions : *In the questions given below establish the relationship between the two words. Then from the given options select one which has the same relationship as of the given two words.*

1. *Mania* is to *Craze* as *Phobia* is to .....
(*a*) Desires (*b*) Hobbies
(*c*) Want (*d*) Fear
(*e*) Favourites

2. *Stammering* is to *Speech* as *Deafness* is to.....
(*a*) Ear (*b*) Hearing
(*c*) Noise (*d*) Silence
(*e*) Commotion

3. *Secretive* is to *Open* as *Snide* is to.....
(*a*) Forthright (*b*) Hidden
(*c*) Outcome (*d*) Forward
(*e*) Advanced

4. *Leash* is to *Pet* as *Handcuffs* is to.....
(*a*) Cunning (*b*) Dacoits
(*c*) Criminals (*d*) Robbers
(*e*) Accused

5. *Ride* is to *Horse* as *Smoke* is to.....
(*a*) Chimney (*b*) Sparkling
(*c*) Pipe (*d*) Ashes
(*e*) Fire

6. *Squander* is to *Money* as *Dissipate* is to....
(*a*) Light (*b*) Finance
(*c*) Savings (*d*) Energy
(*e*) Banking

7. *Tipsy* is to *Drunken* as *Walk* is to.......
(*a*) Stroll (*b*) Exercise

(c) Stride (d) Tired
(e) Run

8. *Sphere* is to *Circle* as *Cone* is to.........
(a) Prism (b) Cylinder
(c) Triangle (d) Trapezium
(e) None of these

9. *Leader* is to *Follower* as ..... is to *Soldier*.
(a) Captain (b) Unit
(c) Army (d) Barrack
(e) Cavalry

10. *Guilt* is to *Past* as *Hope* is to.....
(a) Present (b) Future
(c) Today (d) Despair
(e) Hopeless

11. .... is to *Liquid* as *Mile* is to *Distance*.
(a) Unit (b) Kilo
(c) Scale (d) Litre
(e) Mercury

12. *Gum* is to.... as *Socket* is to *Eye*.
(a) Tree (b) Paper
(c) Tooth (d) Stick
(e) None of these

13. *Bench* is to *Judges* as *Chair* is to.......
(a) Attorney (b) President
(c) Lawyer (d) Ruler
(e) Administrator

14. *Stars* are to *Night* as *Sun* is to....
(a) Noon (b) Dawn
(c) Day (d) Light
(e) Dusk

15. ..... is to *Nose* as *Skin* is to *Touch*.
(a) Smell (b) Face
(c) Breath (d) Perfume
(e) Nostril

16. *Spasm* is to *Pain* as *Flash* is to.....
(a) Wind (b) Light
(c) Signal (d) Fire
(e) Rain

17. *War* is to..... as *Smoke* is to *Pollution*.
(a) Alliance (b) Peace
(c) Victory (d) Treaty
(e) Destruction

18. *Treatment* is to ...... as *Education* is to *Teacher*.
(a) Doctor (b) Matron
(c) Hospital (d) Clinic
(e) Chemist

19. *Mammals* is to *Man* as *Aves* is to.....
(a) Aeroplanes (b) Birds
(c) Pigeons (d) Fruit
(e) Winds

20. *Mango* is to *Fruit* as ... is to *Monument*.
(a) Remains (b) Tombs
(c) Red Fort (d) History
(e) Pillars

21. *Statue* is to *Shape* as *Song* is to.....
(a) Singer (b) Lyrics
(c) Composer (d) Poetry
(e) Tune

22. *Train* is to *Track* as *Bullet* is to....
(a) Barrel (b) Kill
(c) Firing (d) Ammunition
(e) Weapon

23. *Psychology* is to *Emotions* as *Philosophy* is to.....
(a) Knowledge (b) Scholar
(c) Research (d) Wisdom
(e) Learning

24. *Mermaid* is to *Fish* as *Centaur* is to.....
(a) Pegasus (b) Unicorn
(c) Deer (d) Cat
(e) Horse

25. *Punishment* is to *Imprisonment* as *Reward* is to......
(a) Prize (b) Remand
(c) Money (d) Rebuke
(e) Award

26. *Surgeon* is to *Scalpel* as *Sculptor* is to....
(a) Pastle (b) Chisel
(c) Pallet (d) Engraving
(e) Hammer

27. *Backbone* is to *Back* as ... is to *Belly*.
(a) Stomach (b) Navel
(c) Ribs (d) Femur
(e) Abdomen

28. *Star* is to......as *Drop* is to *Ocean*.
(a) Sky (b) Shine
(c) Earth (d) Twinkle
(e) None of these

29. .... is to *Strike* as *Whisper* is to *Shout*.
(a) Slap (b) Touch
(c) Anger (d) Noisy
(e) Kill

30. .... is to *Dumb* as *Light* is to *Blind*.
(*a*) Voice (*b*) Language
(*c*) Speech (*d*) Tongue
(*e*) None of these

31. *Physicist* is to *Physics* as .... is to *Anatomy*.
(*a*) Botany (*b*) Botanist
(*c*) Body (*d*) Biologist
(*e*) Medicine

32. *Love* is to *Hate* as *Friend* is to.......
(*a*) Trust (*b*) Companion
(*c*) Enemy (*d*) Despise
(*e*) Adore

33. *Flower* is to *Petal* as ... is to *Arm*.
(*a*) Hand (*b*) Weapon
(*c*) Clock (*d*) Law
(*e*) Body

34. *Sweep* is to ...... as *Wash* is to *Soap*.
(*a*) Broom (*b*) Dust
(*c*) Floor (*d*) Water
(*e*) Clean

35. *Dull* is to..... as *Intelligent* is to *Clever*.
(*a*) Bright (*b*) Foolish
(*c*) Insane (*d*) Idiot
(*e*) Slow

36. *Scales* is to *Fish* as *Feathers* is to.....
(*a*) Hat (*b*) Birds
(*c*) Prune (*d*) Fly
(*e*) Light

37. *Burn* is to *Ointment* as *Grief* is to.....
(*a*) Sorrow (*b*) Adversity
(*c*) Consolation (*d*) Pity
(*e*) Sympathy

38. *Frequently* is to *Always* as *Seldom* is to......
(*a*) Often (*b*) Rarely
(*c*) Occasionally (*d*) Never
(*e*) None of these

39. *Mine* is to *I* as *His* is to......
(*a*) Him (*b*) Their
(*c*) Them (*d*) Me
(*e*) He

40. *Delhi* is to *Haryana* as *Orissa* is to ....
(*a*) Jammu & Kashmir
(*b*) Andhra Pradesh
(*c*) Tamil Nadu
(*d*) Nagaland
(*e*) Punjab

41. *Pen* is related to *Stationery* in the same way as *Chair* is related to.....
(*a*) Wood (*b*) Rest
(*c*) Room (*d*) Position
(*e*) Furniture

42. *Tailor* is related to *Cloth* in the same way as *Cobbler* is related to ....
(*a*) Machine (*b*) Leather
(*c*) Stiching (*d*) Mending
(*e*) Making

43. As *Dam* is to *Mad* so also *Drab* is to....
(*a*) Barb (*b*) Brab
(*c*) Bard (*d*) Badr
(*e*) Brda

44. As *Cassock* is to *Priest* so also .... is to *Graduate*.
(*a*) Gown (*b*) Cap
(*c*) Tie (*d*) Coat
(*e*) Degree

45. As *Dilatory* is to *Expeditious* so also *Direct* is to....
(*a*) Straight (*b*) Tortuous
(*c*) Curved (*d*) Circumlocutory
(*e*) Perfect

46. *Intelligent* is related to *Clever* in the same way as *Dull* is related to.......
(*a*) Idiot (*b*) Cunning
(*c*) Slow (*d*) Foolish
(*e*) Bright

47. As *Boat* is to *Sails* so also *Balloon* is to...
(*a*) Rubber (*b*) Nylon
(*c*) Rope (*d*) Hot air
(*e*) Wind

48. As *Horse* is to *Grass* so also *Automobile* is to.......
(*a*) Smoke (*b*) Petrol
(*c*) Brake oil (*d*) Mobil oil
(*e*) Water

49. *Crime* is related to *Court* in the same way as *Disease* is related to.....
(*a*) Lawyer (*b*) Punishment
(*c*) Hospital (*d*) Doctor
(*e*) Medicine

50. *Millionaire* is related to *Wealth* in the same way as *Genius* is related to........
(*a*) Capability (*b*) Smartness
(*c*) Intelligence (*d*) Awareness

(*e*) Alertness

51. *Needle* is related to *Thread* in the same way as *Pen* is related to.......
(*a*) Write (*b*) Ink
(*c*) Cap (*d*) Paper
(*e*) Word

52. As *Paw* is to *Cat* so also *Hoof* is to.......
(*a*) Horse (*b*) Lamb
(*c*) Elephant (*d*) Lion
(*e*) Hen

53. *House* is related to *Mason* in the same way as *Chair* is related to.......
(*a*) Wood (*b*) Furniture
(*c*) Table (*d*) Seat
(*e*) Carpenter

54. *Bullet* is to *Rifle* as *Arrow* is to.......
(*a*) Archer (*b*) Bow
(*c*) Target (*d*) Cord
(*e*) Bull's eye

55. *Chapter* is related to *Book* in the same way as *Brick* is related to.......
(*a*) Heap (*b*) Building
(*c*) Clay (*d*) mason
(*e*) Mud

56. *Walk* is related to *Run* in the same way as *Breeze* is related to.......
(*a*) Cold (*b*) Dust
(*c*) Air (*d*) Wind
(*e*) Smoke

57. *Driving* is related to *Bus* in the same way as *Flying* is related to.......
(*a*) Air (*b*) Kite
(*c*) Bird (*d*) Aeroplane
(*e*) Paper

58. What is related to *Elbow* in the same way as *Knee* is related to *Leg*?
(*a*) Palm (*b*) Fingers
(*c*) Shoulder (*d*) Hand
(*e*) Head

59. What is related to *Fruit* in the same way as *Cabbage* is related to *Vegetable*?
(*a*) Ginger (*b*) Orange
(*c*) Carrot (*d*) Capsicum
(*e*) Potato

60. *Centimetre* is related to *Metre* in the same way as *Paisa* is related to.......
(*a*) Capital (*b*) Rupee
(*c*) Coin (*d*) Wealth
(*e*) Money

61. *Top* is related to *Bottom* in the same way as *Sky* is related to.......
(*a*) Cloud (*b*) Air
(*c*) Earth (*d*) Water
(*e*) Land

62. *Yes* is related to *No* in the same way as *Alive* is related to.......
(*a*) Dead (*b*) Life
(*c*) Live (*d*) Funeral
(*e*) Gone

63. *Kathak* is related to *Uttar Pradesh* in the same way as *Odissy* is related to.......
(*a*) Assam (*b*) Gujarat
(*c*) Orissa (*d*) Maharashtra
(*e*) Punjab

64. *Table* is related to *Carpenter* in the same way as *Building* is related to.......
(*a*) Craftsman (*b*) Contractor
(*c*) Mason (*d*) Architect
(*e*) Cobbler

65. *House* is related to *Shelter* in the same way as *Soap* is related to.......
(*a*) Washerman (*b*) Bathroom
(*c*) Water (*d*) Fragrance
(*e*) Cleanliness

66. *Hot* is related to *Oven* in the same way as *Cold* is related to.......
(*a*) Air-conditioner
(*b*) Refrigerator
(*c*) Ice-cream
(*d*) Snow
(*e*) Ice-cube

67. *Swim* is related to *Fish* in the same way as *Walk* is related to.......
(*a*) Man (*b*) Bird
(*c*) Legs (*d*) Foot
(*e*) Athlete

68. *Jungle* is related to *Zoo* in the same way as *Sea* is related to.......
(*a*) Harbour (*b*) Water
(*c*) Aquarium (*d*) Fishery
(*e*) Oceanarium

69. *Metal* is related to *Conduction* in the same way as *Plastic* is related to.......
(*a*) Petro Chemicals

(*b*) Industries
(*c*) Inflammation
(*d*) Insulation
(*e*) Induction

70. *Patient* is related to *Doctor* in the same way as *Student* is related to ....
(*a*) School (*b*) Teacher
(*c*) Book (*d*) Classmates
(*e*) Studies

71. *Water* is to *Draught* as *Energy* is to.......
(*a*) Fatigue (*b*) Jovial
(*c*) Fuel (*d*) Health
(*e*) Coal

72. *Pencil* is to *Write* as *Knife* is to.......
(*a*) Injure (*b*) Peel
(*c*) Prick (*d*) Attack
(*e*) Blade

73. *Mosquito* is to *Malaria* as *Rat* is to......
(*a*) Poison (*b*) Bacteria
(*c*) Plague (*d*) Infection
(*e*) Cholera

74. *Pig* is to *Sty* as an *Aeroplane* is to......
(*a*) Depot (*b*) Kennel
(*c*) Hangar (*d*) Terminal
(*e*) Dock

75. *Army* is to *Soldier* as *Galaxy* is to......
(*a*) Meteors (*b*) Satellites
(*c*) Moon (*d*) Stars
(*e*) Planets

76. HUNGER : FOOD : : THIRST : ?
(*a*) Water (*b*) Drink
(*c*) Tea (*d*) Coffee
(*e*) Juice

77. HUNTER : GUN : : WRITER : ?
(*a*) Book (*b*) Pen
(*c*) Poem (*d*) Page
(*e*) Copy

78. WOOL : SHEEP : : SILK : ?
(*a*) Saree (*b*) String
(*c*) Silkworm (*d*) Moth
(*e*) Fabric

79. FOOD : STOMACH : : FUEL : ?
(*a*) Engine (*b*) Automobile
(*c*) Rail (*d*) Aeroplane
(*e*) Car

80. WATER : SAND : : OCEAN : ?
(*a*) Island (*b*) River
(*c*) Desert (*d*) Waves
(*e*) Pond

81. ADULT : BABY : : FLOWER : ?
(*a*) Seed (*b*) Bud
(*c*) Fruit (*d*) Butterfly
(*e*) Plant

82. WRITER : READER : : PRODUCER : ?
(*a*) Creator (*b*) Contractor
(*c*) Creature (*d*) Consumer
(*e*) Customer

83. ENTRANCE : EXIT : : LOYALTY : ?
(*a*) Treachery (*b*) Patriotism
(*c*) Fidelity (*d*) Reward
(*e*) Clarity

84. MOTHER : MATERNAL : : FATHER : ?
(*a*) Eternal (*b*) Detrimental
(*c*) Paternal (*d*) Formidable
(*e*) Sentimental

85. PEARL : NECKLACE : : FLOWER : ?
(*a*) Plant (*b*) Garden
(*c*) Petal (*d*) Bouquet
(*e*) Tree

86. ALPHABET : WORD : : WORD : ?
(*a*) Sound (*b*) Music
(*c*) Sentence (*d*) Dictionary
(*e*) Speech

87. LIFE : DEATH : : HOPE : ?
(*a*) Cry (*b*) Pain
(*c*) Despair (*d*) Sad
(*e*) Joy

88. GOOD : BAD : : VIRTUE : ?
(*a*) Blame (*b*) Sin
(*c*) Despair (*d*) Vice
(*e*) Scold

89. BIRD : FLY : : SNAKE : ?
(*a*) Timid (*b*) Clatter
(*c*) Crawl (*d*) Hole
(*e*) Run

90. CAT : MOUSE : : BIRD : ?
(*a*) Cage (*b*) Trap
(*c*) Eagle (*d*) Cheese
(*e*) Worm

91. STATE : EXILE
(*a*) Police : Arrest
(*b*) Judge : Convict
(*c*) Constitution : Amendment
(*d*) Church : Excommunicate

(*e*) Doctor : Treatment

92. CAPRICIOUSNESS : RELIABILITY
(*a*) Extemporaneous : Predictability
(*b*) Unreliable : Inhuman
(*c*) Tenacious : Practicality
(*d*) Arbitrary : Whimsical
(*e*) Heated : Boiling.

93. LOATH : COERCION
(*a*) Detest : Caressing
(*b*) Irritate : Caressing
(*c*) Irate : Antagonism
(*d*) Reluctant : Persuasion
(*e*) Contemplative : Meditative.

94. SCALES : FISH
(*a*) Lady : Dress (*b*) Tree : Leaves
(*c*) Bird : Feather (*d*) Skin : Man
(*e*) Bear : Fur

95. TREE : SAPLING
(*a*) Hut : Mansion (*b*) Giant : Dwarf
(*c*) Horse : Foal (*d*) Ant : Elephant
(*e*) Rock : Mountain

96. CHALK : BLACKBOARD
(*a*) Door : Handle (*b*) Table : Chair
(*c*) Ink : Paper (*d*) Type : Paint
(*e*) Jug : Water

97. PRIMEVAL : MEDIEVAL
(*a*) Dinosaur : Dragon
(*b*) Gorilla : Soldier
(*c*) Evolution : Revelation
(*d*) Thorn : Rose
(*e*) Snow : Ice

98. TRILOGY : NOVEL
(*a*) Rice : Husk
(*b*) Milk : Cream
(*c*) Fabric : Weaving
(*d*) Gun : Cartridge
(*e*) Serial : Episode

99. PEDANT : ERUDITION
(*a*) Prude : Modesty
(*b*) Blunt : Politician
(*c*) Diplomats : Tactless
(*d*) Enemy : Friendly
(*e*) Rude : Politeness

100. FURY : IRE
(*a*) Convulsion : Spasm
(*b*) Amusement : Happiness
(*c*) Joke : Laugh
(*d*) Dispassion : Emotion
(*e*) Cry : Whisper

101. INCANDESCENT : GLOWING
(*a*) Indefatigable : Untiring
(*b*) Boor : Oafish
(*c*) Tedious : Bore
(*d*) Flash : Flame
(*e*) Candle : Light

102. ELEVATED : EXALTED
(*a*) Promoted : Excellence
(*b*) Raise : Commensurate
(*c*) Disorderly : Unfaithful
(*d*) Dirty : Filthy
(*e*) Purified : Hygienic

103. COMMANDER : COMMANDS
(*a*) Surgeon : Diagnosis
(*b*) Checks : Teacher
(*c*) Senator : Legislates
(*d*) Aerates : Aviator
(*e*) Specific : Responses

104. HYGROMETER : HUMIDITY
(*a*) Water : Mercury
(*b*) Snow : Rain
(*c*) Barometer : Pressure
(*d*) Temperature : Weather
(*e*) Forecast : Rain

105. DIET : WEIGHT
(*a*) Food : Fat
(*b*) Dinner : Supper
(*c*) Bread : Starchy
(*d*) Drug : Pain
(*e*) Water : Sea

106. VIXEN : SCOLD
(*a*) Wound : Scar (*b*) Hero : Win
(*c*) Burn : Sting (*d*) Pimple : Irritate
(*e*) Exalt : Anger

107. ENCOURAGE : RESTRICT
(*a*) Gain : Success
(*b*) Dearth : Surplus
(*c*) Seeing : Believing
(*d*) Heart : Soul
(*e*) Induce : Raise

108. ERRORS : INEXPERIENCE
(*a*) Skill : Mistake
(*b*) Training : Economy
(*c*) Success: Victory
(*d*) News : Publication

(*e*) Losses : Carelessness

109. ITALY : ROME
(*a*) Paris : Moscow
(*b*) Moscow : Bahrain
(*c*) Spain : Madrid
(*d*) Chicago : New York
(*e*) Vietnam : Oslo

110. CORRESPONDENCE : CLERK
(*a*) Office : Manager
(*b*) Secretary : Stenographer
(*c*) Orders : Accountant
(*d*) Records : Archivist
(*e*) Music : Lyricist

111. CHILD : FAMILY
(*a*) Bird : Nest
(*b*) Mother : Baby
(*c*) Tentacle : Octopus
(*d*) Flower : Tulip
(*e*) Pond : Fish

112. FRAME : PICTURE
(*a*) Cup : Saucer (*b*) Table : Floor
(*c*) Chair : Room (*d*) Roof : Building
(*e*) Wheel : Chair

113. GUN : HOLSTER
(*a*) Shoe : Soldier (*b*) Sword : Warrior
(*c*) Ink : Pen (*d*) Books : School Bag
(*e*) Cannon : Plunder

114. SHOVEL : HOE
(*a*) Eraser : Chalk (*b*) Garden : Gardener
(*c*) Farm : House (*d*) House : Lawn
(*e*) Pen : Writer

115. TEPID : HOT
(*a*) Pat : Slap
(*b*) Winter : Summer
(*c*) Topple : Tumble
(*d*) Bing : Bang
(*e*) Cut : Hit

116. WAR : DEFEAT
(*a*) Arm : Let
(*b*) Contest : Victory
(*c*) Crime : Praise
(*d*) Doctor : Lawyer
(*e*) Action : Caution

117. ATOM : ELECTRON
(*a*) Sun : Earth
(*b*) Constellation : Satellite
(*c*) Sputnik : Satellite
(*d*) Neutron : Proton
(*e*) Moon : Saturn

118. THREAT : INSECURITY
(*a*) Challenge : Fight
(*b*) Reason : Anger
(*c*) Thunder : Lightning
(*d*) Speed : Acceleration
(*e*) Joy : Pain

119. FINGER : HAND
(*a*) Dictionary : Word
(*b*) Toe : Foot
(*c*) Medicine : Doctor
(*d*) Law : Advocate
(*e*) Book : Author

120. THIRST : PARCH
(*a*) Flush : Fever
(*b*) Water : Sink
(*c*) Hunger : Strangle
(*d*) Laughter : Appease
(*e*) Hatred : Reprimand

121. OCTAVO : BINDING
(*a*) Pica : Printing (*b*) Music : Octave
(*c*) Day : Week (*d*) Pamphlet : Book
(*e*) Ruler : Artist

122. COOL : NIGHT
(*a*) Black : Dark
(*b*) Humidity : Sunshine
(*c*) Fear : Fright
(*d*) Smoke : Fire
(*e*) Warm : Day

123 LARGE : ENORMOUS
(*a*) Royal : Regal
(*b*) Cat : Tiger
(*c*) Human : Ferocious
(*d*) Frost : Warmth
(*e*) Plump : Fat

124. COURT : JUSTICE
(*a*) Product : Consumer
(*b*) Hospital : Treatment
(*c*) Government : Policeman
(*d*) Chief : Boss
(*e*) Station : Master

125. SHOE : LEATHER
(*a*) Magnet : Iron
(*b*) Cloth : Texture
(*c*) Gun : Ammunition
(*d*) Mirror : Reflection

(*e*) Honesty : Cruelty

126. SORROW : DEATH
(*a*) Laugh : Tears
(*b*) Fire : Candle
(*c*) Happiness : Birth
(*d*) Hate : Fear
(*e*) Gain : Profit

127. FALL : PAIN
(*a*) Walking : Dieting
(*b*) Laughter : Joy
(*c*) Ample : Rare
(*d*) Mixture : Altercation
(*e*) Disobedience : Punishment

128. STEP : STAIRWAY
(*a*) Staircase : Banister
(*b*) Wood : Carpet
(*c*) House : Roof
(*d*) Rung : Ladder
(*e*) Table : Wood

129. EXPLOSION : DEBRIS
(*a*) Plague : Rats
(*b*) Fire : Ashes
(*c*) Crash : Sorrow
(*d*) Death : Rebirth
(*e*) Famine : Abundance

130. MONUMENT : CENOTAPH
(*a*) Orifice : Opening
(*b*) Guide : Follower
(*c*) Protect : Protocol
(*d*) Sponsor : Cleave
(*e*) Sport : Branch

131. TUNA : FISH
(*a*) Tomato : Fruit
(*b*) Beetroot : Flower
(*c*) Hare : Animal
(*d*) Cricket : Stadium
(*e*) Coffee : Meal

132. SCIENTIST : LABORATORY
(*a*) Research : Home
(*b*) Planning : Resort
(*c*) Teacher : History
(*d*) Major : Country
(*e*) Chef : Kitchen

133. JUDGE : JUDGEMENT
(*a*) Author : Professor
(*b*) Action : Reaction
(*c*) Worker : Workmanship
(*d*) Rotary : Order
(*e*) Doctor : Diagnosis

134. CEREBRUM : BRAIN
(*a*) Aorta : Hand
(*b*) Ligament : Blood
(*c*) Ventricle : Heart
(*d*) Country : Universe
(*e*) Sinew : Fur

135. TABLOID : JOURNAL
(*a*) Discourse : Coup
(*b*) Reproach : Deter
(*c*) Destroy : Gratify
(*d*) Elegy : Requiem
(*e*) Fantasy : Allure

136. PIGEON : PEACE
(*a*) Olive Oil : Enmity
(*b*) Eagle : Friendship
(*c*) Whiteflag : Surrender
(*d*) Roses : Garden
(*e*) Ring : Engagement

137. COFFEE : BEVERAGE
(*a*) Food : Tiffin
(*b*) Crayon : Stationery
(*c*) Invitation : Party
(*d*) Butter : Cosmetic
(*e*) Gift : Present

138. TRAP : PART
(*a*) Here : There (*b*) Liar : Rail
(*c*) Arrive : Went (*d*) Now : Then
(*e*) Nest : Tear

139. INNINGS : CRICKET
(*a*) Punch : Boxing
(*b*) Serve : Hockey
(*c*) Kick : Tennis
(*d*) Deuce : Skiing
(*e*) Goal : Chess

140. RICKETS : BONES
(*a*) Gout : Spleen
(*b*) Malaria : Lungs
(*c*) Jaundice : Eyes
(*d*) Cataract : Throat
(*e*) Eczema : Skin

141. COSMOLOGY : UNIVERSE
(*a*) Ethics : Morals
(*b*) Pathologist : Discipline
(*c*) Plasma : Fossils
(*d*) Nerves : Impulse

(*e*) Hygiene : Development

142. BERNE : SWITZERLAND
(*a*) Tunis : Turkey
(*b*) Bangkok : Thailand
(*c*) Doha : Poland
(*d*) Paris : French
(*e*) Beijing : Cuba

143. OMINOUS : AUSPICIOUS
(*a*) Register : Embody
(*b*) Unusual : Strange
(*c*) Dogma : Notion
(*d*) Feeble : Forceful
(*e*) Chaos : Implore

144. CONFUTE : RETORT
(*a*) Confuse : Edify
(*b*) Sharp : Dainty
(*c*) Tarnish : Corrupt
(*d*) Source : Close
(*e*) Attractive : Garish

145. SYMPATHY : EQUITY
(*a*) Common : Exclusive
(*b*) Certain : Precise
(*c*) Snub : Admire
(*d*) Beloved : Paltry
(*e*) Unity : Strife

146. SKELETON : BODY
(*a*) Cement : Building
(*b*) Grammar : Language
(*c*) Water : River
(*d*) Articles : Market
(*e*) Wood : Furniture

147. MILE : DISTANCE
(*a*) Money : Thousand
(*b*) Quantity : Weight
(*c*) Genius : Award
(*d*) Litre : Liquid
(*e*) Circle : Area

148. NOVICE : SCHOLAR
(*a*) Watch : Detect
(*b*) Kind : Civil
(*c*) Scanty : Scarce
(*d*) Acclaim : Protect
(*e*) Impeach : Defend

149. STAMMERING : SPEECH
(*a*) Dumbness : Nerve
(*b*) Stumbling : Senses
(*c*) Deafness : Ear
(*d*) Shivering : Exposure
(*e*) Anger : Error

150. MERMAID : FISH
(*a*) Unicorn : Goat
(*b*) Centaur : Horse
(*c*) Amadus : Beast
(*d*) Cupid : Nymph
(*e*) Apollo : Man

151. SPHERE : CIRCLE
(*a*) Cone : Triangle
(*b*) Prism : Rectangle
(*c*) Cylinder : Square
(*d*) Cuboid : Arc
(*e*) Pentagon : Octave

152. NATION : FLAG
(*a*) Emblem : Sign
(*b*) School : Uniform
(*c*) House : Child
(*d*) Company : Biscuits
(*e*) Organisation : Location

153. CLOCK : TIME
(*a*) Shop : Boxes
(*b*) People : Way
(*c*) Books : Knowledge
(*d*) Map : Place
(*e*) Principal : Discipline

154. LEMON : ORANGE
(*a*) Ginger : Potato
(*b*) Melon : Apple
(*c*) Tree : Flower
(*d*) Leader : Follower
(*e*) Minister : Worker

155. SISTER : AUNT
(*a*) Cousin : Uncle
(*b*) Mother : Brother
(*c*) Niece : Nephew
(*d*) Father : Son
(*e*) Daughter : Grandson

156. JUPITER : PLANET
(*a*) Earth : Orbit (*b*) Saturn : Sun
(*c*) Cosmos : Star (*d*) Moon : Satellite
(*e*) Milky way : Pole

157. IRELAND : SHAMROCK
(*a*) Canada : Rose
(*b*) Spain : Beach
(*c*) Australia : Kangaroo
(*d*) Italy : Shamrock
(*e*) Iran : Eagle

158. POISON : DEATH
(*a*) Driver : Accident
(*b*) Smoke : Pollution
(*c*) Criminal : Prison
(*d*) Error : Pain
(*e*) Fatigue : Sickness

159. MUCH : MORE
(*a*) Good : Best (*b*) Sweet : Caramel
(*c*) Ugly : Scary (*d*) Few : Least
(*e*) Bad : Worse

160. EVIDENT : REAL
(*a*) Hasty : Cool (*b*) Lapse : Remain
(*c*) Mollify : Vex (*d*) Pallid : Shiny
(*e*) Sober : Sedate

161. CENSURE : PRAISE
(*a*) Deny : Abjure (*b*) Assert : Rebut
(*c*) Ordain : Fix (*d*) Common : Stale
(*e*) Goal : End

162. DYNE : FORCE
(*a*) Knot : Light (*b*) Fathom : Energy
(*c*) Calorie : Fat (*d*) Bar : Pressure
(*e*) Ohm : Distance

163. TIARA : HEAD
(*a*) Watch : Wrist (*b*) Glove : Foot
(*c*) Ring : Toe (*d*) Socks : Hand
(*e*) Scarf : Waist

164. VITAMIN : HEALTH
(*a*) Glory : Progress
(*b*) Building : Construction
(*c*) Loyalty : Friendship
(*d*) Knowledge : Study
(*e*) Power : Furnace

165. COAT : GARMENT
(*a*) Flower : Beauty
(*b*) Jack : Instrument
(*c*) Bangle : Jewellery
(*d*) Periscope : Tool
(*e*) Gas : Air

166. ELT : PIG
(*a*) Foal : Horse (*b*) Cub : Duck
(*c*) Colt : Lion (*d*) Pup : Hen
(*e*) Larve : Frog

167. LECHEROUS : CARNAL
(*a*) Virile : Feeble
(*b*) Diatribe : Abuse
(*c*) Impede : Begin
(*d*) Sunder : Link
(*e*) Beam : Wane

168. ENVOY : MESSENGER
(*a*) Regulate : Muddle
(*b*) Gruff : Polite
(*c*) Adviser : Mentor
(*d*) Pain : Gusto
(*e*) Finite : Eternal

169. NOBLE : HUMBLE
(*a*) Cruelty : Tyranny
(*b*) Soft : Ductile
(*c*) Pomp : Modesty
(*d*) Vile : Sinful
(*e*) Moral : Upright

170. CIRCLE : CIRCUMFERENCE
(*a*) Square : Area
(*b*) Rectangle : Perimeter
(*c*) Triangle : Base
(*d*) Cylinder : Radius
(*e*) Pentagon : Sides

171. ASSERT : DENY
(*a*) Bliss : Mitigate
(*b*) Violent : Placid
(*c*) Mark : Relic
(*d*) Broad : Slack
(*e*) Gale : Blast

172. BLOOD : RED
(*a*) Ink : Faded (*b*) Jelly : Yellow
(*c*) Skin : Pale (*d*) Eyes : Shiny
(*e*) Sky : Blue

173. METAL : COIN
(*a*) Tree : Wood (*b*) Sweets : Sugar
(*c*) Words : Editor (*d*) Pulp : Paper
(*e*) Cup : Pottery

174. COMPASS : DIRECTION
(*a*) Eudiometer : Sound
(*b*) Hygrometer : Liquids
(*c*) Altimeter : Height
(*d*) Lactometer : Eyesight
(*e*) Sextant : Earthquakes

175. PEDAGOGY : TEACHING
(*a*) Telepathy : Emotions
(*b*) Mycology : Fossils
(*c*) Cosmology : Cosmetics
(*d*) Entomology : Insects
(*e*) Radiology : Sound

176. LEARNING : MASTERY
(*a*) Vocabulary : Verbosity

(*b*) Attainment : Rigidity
(*c*) Losses : Crimes
(*d*) Practice : Perfection
(*e*) Nagging : Satisfaction

177. PAST : HISTORY
(*a*) Sand : Lithography
(*b*) Water : Humidity
(*c*) Crust : Cristology
(*d*) Land : Hematology
(*e*) Earth : Geography

178. DISAGREEMENT : DEBATE
(*a*) Unison : Law
(*b*) Acceptance : Discord
(*c*) Punishment : Refinement
(*d*) Group : Chaos
(*e*) Pressure : Fatigue

179. ELECTRICITY : BULB
(*a*) Light : Refrigerator
(*b*) Cell : Torch
(*c*) Power : Consumption
(*d*) Battery : Candle
(*e*) Fuel : Coal

180. NOMAD : ROVER
(*a*) Endure : Halt (*b*) Surface : Edge
(*c*) Display : Hide (*d*) Careful : Discreet
(*e*) Amiable : Cynical

181. ARDUOUS : DIFFICULT
(*a*) Spurn : Prefer
(*b*) Inapt : Facile
(*c*) Cleave : Resign
(*d*) Pest : Genial
(*e*) Pivot : Axis

182. PETAL : FLOWER
(*a*) Leaf : Fruit (*b*) Pupil : Eye
(*c*) Brick : Garden (*d*) Ink : Pencil
(*e*) Elbow : Leg

183. BEE : HIVE
(*a*) Hen : Den (*b*) Lion : Sty
(*c*) Dog : Kennel (*d*) Bus : Hanger
(*e*) Aeroplane : Terminal

184. THAR : DESERT
(*a*) Ural : Ocean (*b*) Nile : River
(*c*) Alps : Plains (*d*) Sahara : Country
(*e*) Russia : Capital

185. WARSAW : POLAND
(*a*) Oslo : Norway
(*b*) Tripoli : Malaysia
(*c*) Dublin : Indonesia
(*d*) Nairobi : Maldives
(*e*) Helsinki : Egypt

186. AVOCADO : FRUIT
(*a*) Shark : Scientist
(*b*) Pallet : Gadget
(*c*) Ewe : Sheep
(*d*) Yatch : Weight
(*e*) Nine : Colour

187. BLOOD : HEART
(*a*) Respiration : Nostrils
(*b*) Digestion : Kidneys
(*c*) Sight : Pancreas
(*d*) Smell : Lungs
(*e*) Nerves : Brain

188. LIBRARY : BOOKS
(*a*) News : Pictures
(*b*) Jungle : Animals
(*c*) Dictionary : Words
(*d*) Jewellery : Rings
(*e*) Hospital : Sick

189. RIVAL : ALLY
(*a*) Press : Jostle
(*b*) Placate : Provoke
(*c*) Venture : Aspire
(*d*) Doleful : Miserable
(*e*) Glide : Cease

190. SNOW : WHITE
(*a*) Money : Coins (*b*) Time : Seconds
(*c*) Water : Cold (*d*) Giraffe : Tall
(*e*) Police : Frightening

191. DIVA : OPERA
(*a*) Thespian : Play
(*b*) Distributor : Acts
(*c*) Producer : Theatre
(*d*) Director : Drama
(*e*) Conductor : Bus

192. BAR : BARMAN
(*a*) Church : Sexton
(*b*) Truck : Trolley
(*c*) Car : Cleaner
(*d*) Ship : Dock
(*e*) Aeroplane : Hangar

193. MEDAL : DECORATION
(*a*) Pearl : Jewellery
(*b*) Scarf : Dress
(*c*) Diamond : Ring

(*d*) Window : Room
(*e*) Necklace : Adornment

194. DOCTOR : DISEASE
(*a*) Paediatrician : Senility
(*b*) Psychiatrist : Maladjustment
(*c*) Cardiologist : Surgery
(*d*) Charlatan : Truth
(*e*) Moron : Imbecility

195. DIPLOMA : KNOWLEDGE
(*a*) House : Security
(*b*) Mace : Majesty
(*c*) Happiness : Birth
(*d*) Sickness : Nurse
(*e*) Acclamation : Pleasure

196. EARTH : PLANET
(*a*) Moon : Satellite
(*b*) Star : Sun
(*c*) Saturn : Universe
(*d*) Mars : Venus
(*e*) Sun : Galaxy

197. ROTATE : GYRATE
(*a*) Accolade : Criticism
(*b*) Absolve : Exonerate
(*c*) Prism : Rainbow
(*d*) Anachronism : Cubism
(*e*) Putrefy : Reject

198. CAT : FELINE
(*a*) Sheep : Bovine
(*b*) Tiger : Carnivorous
(*c*) Man : Masculine
(*d*) Pig : Omnivorous
(*e*) Dog : Canine

199. FISH : SHOAL
(*a*) Shark : School
(*b*) Elephant : Flock
(*c*) Pride : Ants
(*d*) Audience : Theatre
(*e*) Whale : Herd

200. STREPTOCOCCI : PNEUMONIA
(*a*) Quinine : Malaria
(*b*) Asthma : Asphyxiation
(*c*) Malnutrition : Beriberi
(*d*) Cause : Sickness
(*e*) Result : Prevention

201. HOPE : ASPIRES
(*a*) Film : Plan
(*b*) Fake : Ordinary
(*c*) Fib : Lie
(*d*) Spirits : Soar
(*e*) Love : Elevates

202. STETHOSCOPE : PHYSICIAN
(*a*) Drug : Patient
(*b*) Editor : Author
(*c*) Pestle : Pharmacist
(*d*) Canvas : Sculpture
(*e*) Water : Tank

203. PROPENSITY : TENDENCY
(*a*) Virtue : Disobedience
(*b*) Audacity : Impudence
(*c*) Prologue : Epilogue
(*d*) Conduct : Immorality
(*e*) Master : Slave

204. WOOD : TREE
(*a*) Stool : Seat
(*b*) Newspaper : Journalist
(*c*) Grass : Country
(*d*) Intimate : Intimacy
(*e*) Ball : Bullet

205. ICHTHYOLOGIST : MARINE LIFE
(*a*) Ornithologist : Stamps
(*b*) Flower : Horticulture
(*c*) Bible : Psalms
(*d*) Archaeologist : Antiquity
(*e*) Idioms : Dictionary

206. REQUEST : REFUSAL
(*a*) Action : Activity
(*b*) Trial : Failure
(*c*) Struggle : Victory
(*d*) Swim : Sinking
(*e*) Fat : Obesity

207. JEW : RABBI
(*a*) Pagan : Pan
(*b*) Japanese : Samurai
(*c*) Muslim : Mullah
(*d*) Christian : Church
(*e*) Chinese : Mandarin

208. VINDICATE : CONDEMN
(*a*) Judge : Jury
(*b*) Convict : Debar
(*c*) Charge : Accuse
(*d*) Dismiss : Indict
(*e*) Defendent : Plantiff

209. MODESTY : ARROGANCE
(*a*) Debility : Strength

(*b*) Skimmerish : Sluggard
(*c*) Speak : Write
(*d*) Ship : Fleet
(*e*) Obese : Fat

210. FILE : RECORDS
(*a*) Book : Binding
(*b*) Cashier : Cash
(*c*) Needle : Cloth
(*d*) Hammer : Screws
(*e*) Pen : Signature

211. DUSK : DAWN
(*a*) Necromancy : Magic
(*b*) Senility : Childhood
(*c*) Corpulence : Obesity
(*d*) Adolescence : Infancy
(*e*) Shrewd : Clever

212. BEEF : CATTLE
(*a*) Pork : Pig (*b*) Oil : Seeds
(*c*) Sap : Tree (*d*) Wax : Bark
(*e*) Noise : Music

213. CAUTIOUS : CAREFUL
(*a*) Eager : Desire
(*b*) Suspicious : Doubtful
(*c*) Noxious : Fruitful
(*d*) Disease : Contagious
(*e*) Medal : Honour

214. ARMY : LOGISTICS
(*a*) Soldiers : Students
(*b*) Team : Individual
(*c*) Group : Person
(*d*) Business : Strategy
(*e*) War : Logic

215. CLOCK : SECOND
(*a*) Calendar : Month
(*b*) Calendar : Year
(*c*) Calendar : Day
(*d*) Watch : Hour
(*e*) Calendar : Week

216. SENSITIVE : OBSTINATE
(*a*) Emotional : Delicate
(*b*) Weak : Fragile
(*c*) Sentimental : Insensitive
(*d*) Arrogance : Rigid
(*e*) Harsh : Tough

217. NARCOTIC : PHARMACY
(*a*) Somnolent : Sleep
(*b*) Liquid : Solid
(*c*) Weapon : Weaponry
(*d*) Press : Pressure
(*e*) Water : Aqua

218. PROJECTILE : TRAJECTORY
(*a*) Meter : Meteor
(*b*) Satellite : Orbit
(*c*) Catastrophic : Tragedy
(*d*) Cartridge : Rifle
(*e*) Bullet : Weapon

219. OCEAN : BAY
(*a*) Headland : Promontory
(*b*) Continent : Peninsula
(*c*) Salt Water : Sweet Water
(*d*) Beach : Moor
(*e*) Island : Peninsula

220. PEDAGOGUE : LEARNING
(*a*) Coaching : Books
(*b*) Professor : Erudition
(*c*) Student : Teacher
(*d*) Plato : Yedant
(*e*) Lesson : Learning

221. ENCOURAGE : ASSIST
(*a*) Dishearten : Neglect
(*b*) Discourage : Ignore
(*c*) Discourage : Obstruct
(*d*) Dishearten : Cheer
(*e*) Discourage : Obstacle

222. CORPORAL : SPIRITUAL
(*a*) Mesa : Plateau
(*b*) Foreigner : Immigrant
(*c*) Moor : Hillock
(*d*) Moron : Savant
(*e*) Pedagogue : Teacher

223. CONCEALMENT : DIVULGATION
(*a*) Excrete : Excretion
(*b*) Fabrication : Destruction
(*c*) Sensibility : Sensitivity
(*d*) Concord : Agreement
(*e*) Farm : Enclosure

224. RUNG : LADDER
(*a*) Star : Constellation
(*b*) Time : Clock
(*c*) Money : Finance
(*d*) Edge : Blade
(*e*) Dream : Dreamer

225. BUILDING : VERTICAL
(*a*) Road : Narrow

(*b*) Street : Horizontal
(*c*) Lane : Wide
(*d*) Line : Straight
(*e*) Room : Big

226. EROSION : SOIL
(*a*) Heat : Oven
(*b*) Indulgence : Character
(*c*) Crime : Prison
(*d*) Fish : Pond
(*e*) Speech : Speaker

227. AUTHENTIC : GENUINE
(*a*) Pragmatic : Realistic
(*b*) Proper : Rustic
(*c*) Warrant : Demand
(*d*) Truth : Oath
(*e*) Nostalgic : Idiotic

228. BRAIN : NEUROLOGY
(*a*) Biology : Animals
(*b*) Hydrology : Water
(*c*) Horology : Horoscopes
(*d*) Body : Physiology
(*e*) Entomology : Plants

229. FAMILY : CHILD
(*a*) Set : Bird
(*b*) Colony : Sheep
(*c*) Herd : Calf
(*d*) Bunch : Flowers
(*e*) Pond : Fish

230. LAWYER : COURT
(*a*) Librarian : Auditorium
(*b*) Chemist : Laboratory
(*c*) Businessman : Market
(*d*) Labourer : Playground
(*e*) Athlete : Olympics

231. CHEF : KITCHEN
(*a*) Spider : Web
(*b*) Soldier : Gun
(*c*) Admiral : Navy
(*d*) Beer : Brewery
(*e*) Student : Class

232. CLOCK : TIME
(*a*) Altimeter : Weight
(*b*) Speedometer : Height
(*c*) Year : Century
(*d*) Glitter : Diamond
(*e*) Thermometer : Temperature

233. DAYBREAK : BEDSTEAD
(*a*) Earthen : Brazen
(*b*) Fresh : Tired
(*c*) Nocturnal : Diurnal
(*d*) Eyeglass : Landmark
(*e*) Work : Rest

234. ASSAULT : IMPREGNABLE
(*a*) Purchase : Sell
(*b*) Misery : Poverty
(*c*) Insult : Invulnerable
(*d*) Offerings : Charity
(*e*) Achievement : Capability

235. DUNCE : CLEVER
(*a*) Fearful : Courage
(*b*) Moron : Dullhead
(*c*) Charming : Attractive
(*d*) Repel : Loath
(*e*) Appeal : Satisfy

236. CHILD : FIRE
(*a*) Aged : Wisdom
(*b*) Student : Examination
(*c*) Youth : Adolescence
(*d*) Judge : Dishonour
(*e*) Man : Enmity

237. GRAIN : SALT
(*a*) Shred : Wool
(*b*) Cave : Stone
(*c*) Chip : Glass
(*d*) Blades : Grass
(*e*) Shard : Pottery

238. IGNOMINY : DISLOYALTY
(*a*) Death : Victory
(*b*) Martyr : Man
(*c*) Fame : Heroism
(*d*) Destruction : Victory
(*e*) Immortal : Moral

239. GREASE : SLIP
(*a*) Clouds : Rain
(*b*) Water : Boil
(*c*) Butter : Fry
(*d*) Ice : Slide
(*e*) Sand : Scatter

240. EMULATE : MIMIC
(*a*) Express : Copy
(*b*) Aggravate : Promote
(*c*) Initiate : Proceed
(*d*) Slander : Demote
(*e*) Praise : Flatter

241. DEBATE : SOLILOQUY
(*a*) Monologue : Theory
(*b*) Ovation : Silence
(*c*) Sun : Warmth
(*d*) Group : Hermit
(*e*) Elegant : Regal

242. DUBIOUS : INDISPUTABLE
(*a*) Painful : Tormenting
(*b*) Slander : Libel
(*c*) Avaricious : Generous
(*d*) Stammer : Heave
(*e*) Perspicacious : Tenacity

243. AUTHOR : INVENTOR
(*a*) Book : Factory
(*b*) Copyright : Patent
(*c*) Paper : Metal
(*d*) Novel : Literature
(*e*) Plot : Machine

244. FISH : BIRD
(*a*) Submarine : Aeroplane
(*b*) Rifle : Tank
(*c*) Hydra : Ocean
(*d*) Master : Eagle
(*e*) Aquarium : Tree

245. PARASITISM : SYCOPHANCY
(*a*) Celebration : Celebrity
(*b*) Truth : Falsehood
(*c*) Liability : Onus
(*d*) Demos : Democracy
(*e*) Politics : Philosophy

246. TEN : DECIMAL
(*a*) Five : Quince
(*b*) Seventh : Septet
(*c*) Three : Triplet
(*d*) Two : Binary
(*e*) Four : Quadrete

247. JOY : ECSTASY
(*a*) Hatred : Antipathy
(*b*) Strive : Slog
(*c*) Tepid : Hot
(*d*) Jealousy : Envy
(*e*) Unity : Harmony

248. CIRCUITOUS : DIRECT
(*a*) Faulty : Improper
(*b*) Tortuous : Straight
(*c*) Reckless : Winding
(*d*) Alert : Forward
(*e*) Cautious : Straight

249. DUCK : QUACK
(*a*) Dog : Growl
(*b*) Sparrow : Peck
(*c*) Snake : Creep
(*d*) Camel : Desert
(*e*) Fisherman : Net

250. NAIVE : CHEAT
(*a*) Refined : Victory
(*b*) Hurt : Stubborn
(*c*) Gullible : Convince
(*d*) Contentious : Scorn
(*e*) Genius : Merit

EXPLANATORY ANSWERS

1. (*d*) : The related words are synonyms.

2. (*b*) : Defect in speech causes stammering and in hearing causes deafness.

3. (*a*) : The related words are antonyms.

4. (*c*) : Leash is used to tie a pet, handcuffs to tie criminals.

5. (*a*) : Horse is the object of action 'to ride' and Chimney is the object of action 'to smoke'.

6. (*d*) : Squander is misuse of money and dissipate is misuse of energy.

7. (*e*) : As tipsy is lesser degree of drunken so is walk to run.

8. (*c*) : One-dimensional view of a sphere is circle and that of cone a triangle.

9. (*a*) : As followers are guided by their leader so are soldiers by their captain.

10. (*b*) : Feeling of guilt comes with mistakes in past and that of hope for a good future.

11. (*d*) : Liquid is measured in litres and distance in miles.

12. (*c*) : As gum holds the tooth in place so socket holds the eye.

13. (*b*) : The seat of judges is bench and that of President a chair.

14. (*c*) : Stars are seen during the night and sun during day.

15. ***(a)*** **:** Sense organ skin senses the touch and nose senses smell.

16. ***(b)*** **:** A second's spur of pain is spasm and that of light is flash.

17. ***(e)*** **:** Smoke causes pollution and war causes destruction.

18. ***(a)*** **:** Education is sought by the teacher and treatment by doctor.

19. ***(c)*** **:** Species of man is mammals and that of pegions aves.

20. ***(c)*** **:** Mango is a specified fruit; Red Fort a specified monument.

21. ***(e)*** **:** Shape of an object forms the statue and tune of lyrics forms the song.

22. ***(a)*** **:** Track is the path of train, barrel is of bullet.

23. ***(d)*** **:** Psychology is the study of emotions as philosophy is of wisdom.

24. ***(e)*** **:** Mermaid is a mythological fish and centaur a mythological horse.

25. ***(c)*** **:** Imprisonment is the form of punishment, money a kind of reward.

26. ***(b)*** **:** As scalpel is an instrument used by a surgeon so is chisel of a sculptor.

27. ***(c)*** **:** Backbone supports the back and ribs support the belly.

28. ***(a)*** **:** A single drop is a very tiny part in an ocean so is a star in the sky.

29. ***(b)*** **:** The lesser degree of shout is whisper and that of strike is touch.

30. ***(c)*** **:** Blind cannot see the light and dumb cannot give speech.

31. ***(d)*** **:** Physicist deals with the subject Physics and biologist with subject anatomy.

32. ***(c)*** **:** The related words are antonyms.

33. ***(e)*** **:** Petal is a part of flower, arm is a part of body.

34. ***(a)*** **:** Soap is the object of action 'to wash' and broom is 'to sweep'.

35. ***(b)*** **:** One who is clever is intelligent and one who is foolish is dull.

36. ***(b)*** **:** As fish is covered with scales so are birds with feathers.

37. ***(c)*** **:** As ointment soothes the burn, so does consolation to grief.

38. ***(d)*** **:** The related words are near opposites.

39. ***(e)*** **:** The related words are noun–pronoun.

40. ***(b)*** **:** The related words are neighbouring States.

41. ***(e)*** **:** Pen is a type of stationery, chair is a type of furniture.

42. ***(b)*** **:** Tailor makes clothes from cloth, cobbler makes shoes from leather.

43. ***(c)*** **:** Letter of the related words are written backwards.

44. ***(a)*** **:** The dress worn on attaining Priesthood is a cassock, the dress worn on becoming a graduate is a gown.

45. ***(d)*** **:** The related words are opposites.

46. ***(c)*** **:** The related words are synonyms.

47. ***(d)*** **:** Sails are needed to sail a boat, hot air is needed to float a balloon in air.

48. ***(b)*** **:** Horse depends on grass for food and energy, automobile on petrol for energy.

49. ***(c)*** **:** Crime is taken care of in a court by punishment, disease is taken care of in a hospital by treatment.

50. ***(c)*** **:** A millionaire has lots of wealth, a genius has lots of intelligence.

51. ***(b)*** **:** Needle uses thread for sewing, pen uses ink for writing.

52. ***(a)*** **:** Cat's leg is a paw, horse's leg is a hoof.

53. ***(e)*** **:** House is made by a mason, chair is made by a carpenter.

54. ***(b)*** **:** Bullet is shot with a rifle, arrow is shot with a bow.

55. ***(b)*** **:** Chapter is a part of the book, brick is a part of a building.

56. ***(d)*** **:** A 'fast walk' is - 'run', a 'fast breeze' is 'wind'.

57. ***(d)*** **:** Mode of conveyance, bus, is driven and mode of conveyance, aeroplane, is flown.

58. ***(d)*** **:** Knee is a joint in the leg, elbow is a joint in the hand.

59. ***(b)*** **:** Cabbage is a vegetable, orange is a fruit.

60. ***(b)*** **:** Centimetre is one hundred part of a metre, paisa is one hundredth part of a rupee.

61. ***(c)*** **:** The related words are opposites.

62. ***(a)*** **:** The related words are opposites.

63. ***(c)*** **:** Kathak is a dance form of Uttar Pradesh and Oddisi of Orissa.

64. ***(c)*** **:** Table is made by a carpenter, a building is made by a mason.

65. ***(e)*** **:** House provides shelter, soap provides cleanliness.

66. *(b)* : Food remains hot in an oven, and cold in a refrigerator.

67. *(a)* : Fishes swim, man walks.

68. *(a)* : Part of tamed jungle is a zoo, part of sea a harbour.

69. *(d)* : Metal is a good conductor and plastic a good insulator of heat.

70. *(b)* : Problem of patient is attended by a doctor, problem of student is attended by the teacher.

71. *(a)* : Lack of water causes draught, lack of energy causes fatigue.

72. *(b)* : Pencil is used to write, knife is used to peel.

73. *(c)* : Malaria is caused by mosquitoes, plague is caused by rats.

74. *(c)* : Sty is resting place for pigs, hanger is resting place for aeroplanes.

75. *(d)* : Army is a group of soldiers, galaxy is a group of stars.

76. *(a)* : Hunger is satiated by food, thirst by water.

77. *(b)* : Weapon of a hunter is a gun, weapon of a writer is a pen.

78. *(c)* : Wool is obtained from sheep, silk is obtained from silkworm.

79. *(a)* : Food is consumed in stomach, fuel is consumed in engine.

80. *(c)* : The related words are near opposites.

81. *(b)* : The youngone of an adult is a baby and that of a flower is a bud.

82. *(d)* : A writer aims to please the readers by his writings, a producer aims to please the consumers by his products.

83. *(a)* : The related words are opposites.

84. *(c)* : Relations on the mother's side are maternal and on the father's side paternal.

85. *(d)* : Many pearls make a necklace, many flowers make a bouquet.

86. *(c)* : More than one alphabet make a word, more than one word make a sentence.

87. *(c)* : The related words are opposites.

88. *(d)* : The related words are opposites.

89. *(c)* : Birds fly, snakes crawl.

90. *(e)* : Cat chases the mouse, bird chases the worm.

91. *(d)* : Punishment of leaving the State is exile, punishment of leaving the Church is excommunication.

92. *(c)* : The related words are antonyms

93. *(d)* : Loathing is the result of constant coersion, reluctance is the result of constant persuasion.

94. *(d)* : Covering of the fish is scales, covering of man is skin.

95. *(c)* : Young tree is a sapling, young horse is a foal.

96. *(c)* : Chalk is used to write on blackboard, ink is used to write on paper.

97. *(a)* : The related words represent almost the same time period and answer option represents almost the same sized creatures.

98. *(e)* : Trilogy is section of a novel, episode is a section of a serial.

99. *(a)* : The related words are synonyms.

100. *(b)* : Fury causes ire, amusement causes happiness.

101. *(a)* : The related words are synonyms.

102. *(d)* : The related words are synonyms.

103. *(c)* : The work of a commander is to command, the work of a senator is to legislate.

104. *(c)* : Hygrometer is an instrument for measuring humidity, barometer is an instrument for measuring pressure.

105. *(d)* : Diet controls weight, drug controls pain.

106. *(c)* : The related words are synonyms.

107. *(b)* : The related words are antonyms.

108. *(e)* : Errors are the result of inexperience, losses are the result of carelessness.

109. *(c)* : Rome is the capital of Italy, Madrid is the capital of Spain.

110. *(d)* : Correspondence is maintained by a clerk, records are maintained by an archivist.

111. *(c)* : Child is the part of a family, tentacle is the part of an octopus.

112. *(d)* : Frame confines a picture, roof confines a building.

113. *(d)* : Gun is carried in a holster, books are carried in a school bag.

114. *(a)* : Shovel and hoe are kind of tools, eraser and chalk are kind of stationery.

115. *(a)* : Tepid is lower degree of hot, pat is lower degree of slap.

116. *(b)* : In war there is defeat, in contest there is victory.

117. (d) : Atom and electron are particles, so are neutron and proton.

118. (a) : Threat arouses insecurity, challenge arouses fight.

119. (b) : Finger is a part of hand, toe is a part of foot.

120. (a) : Parch causes thirst, fever causes flush.

121. (a) : Octavo is a term used in binding, pica is a term used in printing.

122. (e) : Nights are cool, days are warm.

123. (e) : The related words are synonyms.

124. (b) : Justice is given in court, treatment is given in hospital.

125. (a) : Shoe is made of leather, magnet is made of iron.

126. (c) : Death brings sorrow, birth brings happiness.

127. (e) : When one falls one gets hurt and it pains, when one is disobedient one is punished.

128. (d) : While climbing, a step is a part of stairway, a rung is a part of ladder.

129. (b) : Result of explosion is debris, result of fire is ashes.

130. (a) : The related words are synonyms.

131. (c) : Tuna is a fish, hare is an animal.

132. (e) : Scientist works in a laboratory, chef works in a kitchen.

133. (e) : Judge provides judgement, doctor provides diagnosis.

134. (c) : Cerebrum is a part of brain, ventricle is the part of heart.

135. (d) : The related words are synonyms.

136. (c) : Pigeon is the sign of peace, white flag is the sign of surrender.

137. (b) : Coffee is a kind of beverage, crayon is a kind of stationery.

138. (b) : The letters of the related words are written backwards.

139. (a) : Innings is a term used in cricket, punch is a term used in boxing.

140. (e) : Rickets is a disease of bones, eczema is a disease of skin.

141. (a) : Cosmology is the study of universe, ethics is the study of morals.

142. (b) : Berne is the capital of Switzerland, Bangkok is the capital of Thailand.

143. (d) : The related words are near opposites

144. (c) : The related words are synonyms.

145. (b) : The related words are synonyms.

146. (b) : Skeleton is the mainframe of a body, grammar is of language.

147. (d) : Mile is measure for distance, litre is measure for liquid.

148. (e) : The related words are antonyms.

149. (c) : Stammering is caused by defect in speech, deafness is caused by defect in ear.

150. (b) : Mermaid is a mythological fish, centaur is a mythological horse.

151. (a) : One-dimensional view of a sphere is circle and that of a cone a triangle.

152. (b) : A nation is recognised by its flag, a school is recognised by its uniform.

153. (d) : A clock shows time, map shows the place.

154. (a) : The related words have common property. Lemon and Orange are citrus fruits, ginger and potato are cultivated underground.

155. (d) : The related words have common property. Sister and Aunt are feminine genders, father and son are masculine genders.

156. (d) : Jupiter is a planet, moon is a satellite.

157. (c) : Shamrock is the emblem of Ireland, Kangaroo is of Australia.

158. (b) : Poison causes death, smoke causes pollution.

159. (e) : The related words are positive and comparative degrees.

160. (e) : The related words are synonyms.

161. (b) : The related words are antonyms.

162. (d) : Dyne is a unit of force, bar is a unit of pressure.

163. (a) : Tiara is worn on head, watch is worn on wrist.

164. (c) : Vitamins are needed for good health, loyalty is needed in good friendship.

165. (c) : Coat is a kind of garment, bangle is a kind of jewellery.

166. (a) : Elt is a young pig, foal is a young horse.

167. (b) : The related words are synonyms.

168. (c) : The related words are synonyms.

169. (c) : The related words are antonyms.

170. (b) : The outline of a circle is its circumference and that of a rectangle is perimeter.

171. (b) : The related words are antonyms.

172. (e) : Colour of blood is red, colour of sky is blue.

173. *(d)* : Coins are made of metal, paper is made from pulp.
174. *(c)* : Compass is an instrument that shows direction, altimeter is the instrument that shows height.
175. *(d)* : Pedagogy is the science of teaching, entomology is the science of insects.
176. *(d)* : Constant learning lead to mastery in any subject, constant practice leads to perfection in any activity.
177. *(e)* : History is the study of past, geography is the study of earth.
178. *(c)* : Disagreement causes debate, punishment causes refinement.
179. *(b)* : Electricity is needed to light a bulb, cells are needed to light a torch.
180. *(d)* : The related words are synonyms.
181. *(e)* : The related words are synonyms.
182. *(b)* : Petal is a part of flower, pupil is a part of eye.
183. *(c)* : Bees live in hive, dog lives in kennel.
184. *(b)* : Thar is the name of a desert, Nile is the name of a river.
185. *(a)* : Warsaw is the capital of Poland, Oslo is the capital of Norway.
186. *(c)* : Avocado is a kind of fruit, ewe is a female sheep.
187. *(e)* : In a human body, the circulation of blood is controlled by heart, the nervous system is controlled by brain.
188. *(c)* : Library is collection of books, dictionary is collection of words.
189. *(b)* : The related words are antonyms.
190. *(d)* : Snow is always white, giraffe is always tall.
191. *(a)* : As diva (female singer) is a performer in an opera so is thespian (a tragic actor) in a play.
192. *(a)* : As barman is an attendant in the bar, so is sexton in the church.
193. *(e)* : Medal is a part of decoration, necklace is of adornment.
194. *(b)* : Doctor cures the disease and psychiatrist corrects maladjustment.
195. *(b)* : A knowledgeable person is awarded diploma and a majestic person is honoured with mace.
196. *(a)* : Earth is one of the planets, moon one of the satellites.
197. *(b)* : The related words are synonyms.
198. *(e)* : As the genus of the cat are feline, so are dog's canine.
199. *(a)* : Group of fishes is shoal, group of sharks is school.
200. *(d)* : The related words establish a relation that every sickness has a cause as pneumonia is caused by bacteria streptococci.
201. *(c)* : The related words are synonyms.
202. *(c)* : As Stethoscope is an instrument used by a physician, so is pestle by a pharmacist.
203. *(b)* : The related words are synonyms.
204. *(e)* : As wood gives the shape to a tree, ball gives to the bullet.
205. *(d)* : As Ichthyologist studies about marine life, so does archaeologist about antiquity.
206. *(b)* : The related words are near opposites.
207. *(c)* : As Rabbi is the religious head of Jews, Mullah is of Muslims.
208. *(d)* : The related words are antonyms.
209. *(a)* : The related words are antonyms.
210. *(e)* : File is used for keeping records, pen is used for writing signatures.
211. *(d)* : Dusk comes before dawn, adolescence after infancy.
212. *(a)* : Beef is the meat of cattle, pork is of pig.
213. *(b)* : A cautious person is always careful and a suspicious person is always doubtful.
214. *(d)* : Army functions on logistics and business on its strategy.
215. *(c)* : As second is the smallest reading in the clock so is day in a calendar.
216. *(c)* : The related words are opposite in meaning.
217. *(c)* : As pharmacy deals with narcotics (drugs) so does weaponry with weapons.
218. *(b)* : Every curve (trajectory) has a projection (projectile) and every satellite has its orbit.
219. *(a)* : A semi enclosed part of an ocean is bay and that of headland is promontory.
220. *(b)* : As a pedagogue (instructor/teacher) is nursed with learning so is a professor with erudition (knowledge).
221. *(c)* : Assisting someone in some task causes encouragement while obstructing other's work causes discouragement.
222. *(d)* : The related words are antonyms.

223. *(b)* : The related words have opposite meanings.

224. *(a)* : As rung is a part of ladder, so is star of constellation.

225. *(b)* : A building is extended vertically and street horizontally.

226. *(e)* : As erosion is caused due to loose soil, so is speech delivered by an expert speaker.

227. *(a)* : The related words are synonyms.

228. *(d)* : As neurology is the science that deals with every aspect of brain, so does physiology with body.

229. *(c)* : As child is a young member of the family, so is calf in a herd.

230. *(c)* : As workplace of lawyer is a court, so is of businessman a market.

231. *(c)* : As chef is the head in a kitchen, so is Admiral in Navy.

232. *(e)* : Clock shows time, thermometer shows temperature.

233. *(d)* : At daybreak one sees the bed and its bedstead, on wearing, eyeglasses one sees the land and landmarks.

234. *(c)* : An impregnable person faces less risk of assault, an invulnerable person has less chances of facing insult.

235. *(a)* : The related words are near opposites.

236. *(b)* : As child is scared of fire, so is student of examination.

237. *(c)* : Fraction of salt is grain, tiny pieces of glass are chips.

238. *(c)* : Disloyalty leads to ignominy (public disgrace) as heroism leads to fame.

239. *(d)* : As one slips on the grease so does one slide on ice.

240. *(e)* : The related words have almost same meaning.

241. *(d)* : Debate involves two or more persons and soliloquy means talking to oneself. Similarly, hermit is a single identity and group involves two or more identities.

242. *(c)* : The related words are antonyms.

243. *(b)* : Author and inventor can be bracketed into same category and also copyright and patent.

244. *(a)* : Fish swims in water and bird flies in sky. Similarly, submarine runs under water and aeroplane flies in sky.

245. *(e)* : As sycophancy deals with parasitism, so does philosophy with politics.

246. *(d)* : Decimal denotes base ten and so binary is to base two.

247. *(c)* : As joy is lesser form of ecstasy so is tepid of hot.

248. *(b)* : The related words are near opposite in meaning.

249. *(a)* : As the sound of duck is a quack, so is of dog a growl.

250.*(c)* : A naive person can be easily cheated, and a gullible person can be easily convinced.

PART - II

LETTER ANALOGY

In this type of analogy the relationship between two given set of letters is established and then applied to the other set to obtain the required set of letters as the answer. These letters can be moved some steps backward or forward; reversed in whole or in sections or have some common identity between each other.

SOLVED EXAMPLES

Directions : *Which set of letters will come in the place of question mark?*

1. JILK : KLIJ : : MNPQ : ?

(*a*) QNPM (*b*) MPQN (*c*) QPNM (*d*) PNMQ

Ans. (*c*) : The letters are written in reverse order to get the related set of letters.

JILK : KLIJ : : MNPQ : QPNM

2. FLO : DOL : : RDP : ?

(*a*) PGM (*b*) MGP (*c*) GMP (*d*) MPG

Ans. (*a*) : The first and third letters are moved two and three steps backwards respectively and the second letter three steps forward.

FLO : DOL (−2, +3, −3) : : RDP : PGM (−2, +3, −3)

3. DumB : BonD : : RusT : ?

(*a*) MOst (*b*) TeNt (*c*) PaTH (*d*) WorK

Ans. (*d*) : The two corner letters are capital in each group.

EXERCISE

Directions : *In the questions given below one term is missing. Based on the relationship of the two given words find the missing term from the given options.*

1. GFC : CFG : : RPJ : ?

(*a*) JRP (*b*) JPR
(*c*) PJR (*d*) RJP

2. BCF : DEG : : MNQ : ?

(*a*) OPR (*b*) PQS
(*c*) OPP (*d*) QRT

3. NATION : ANITNO : : HUNGRY : ?

(*a*) HNUGRY (*b*) UNHGYR
(*c*) YRNGUH (*d*) UHGNYR

4. SSTU : MMNO : : AABC : ?

(*a*) GGHH (*b*) IJKK
(*c*) XXYZ (*d*) NOOP

5. ACE : FGH : : LNP : ?

(*a*) QRS (*b*) PQR
(*c*) QST (*d*) MOQ

6. UVW : SXU : : LMN : ?
(*a*) JOL (*b*) KNM
(*c*) JKL (*d*) MLO

7. EIGHTY : GIEYTH : : OUTPUT : ?
(*a*) UTOPTU (*b*) UOTUPT
(*c*) TUOUTP (*d*) TUOTUP

8. TSR : FED : : WVU : ?
(*a*) CAB (*b*) MLK
(*c*) PQS (*d*) GFH

9. CJDL : FMGR : : IKJR : ?
(*a*) OQPT (*b*) RSTU
(*c*) OQRT (*d*) KRMO

10. BOQD : ERTG : : ANPC : ?
(*a*) DQSF (*b*) FSHU
(*c*) SHFU (*d*) DSQF

11. BaBy : TaTa : : LiLy : ?
(*a*) PooL (*b*) ROse
(*c*) HaNd (*d*) DoWN

12. BCDA : STUR : : KLMJ : ?
(*a*) VWXU (*b*) EFHG
(*c*) SRTU (*d*) QSRP

13. AEI : LPT : : CGK : ?
(*a*) OSV (*b*) RUY
(*c*) TXC (*d*) FJN

14. RUX : TRP : : BEH : ?
(*a*) SQN (*b*) QON
(*c*) QOM (*d*) QNL

15. CART : ART : : FOUR : ?
(*a*) RUN (*b*) TWO
(*c*) QUE (*d*) OUR

16. FIK : JGO : : DFR : ?
(*a*) BIO (*b*) HDV
(*c*) GCU (*d*) FLP

17. LJH : KKI : : CIA : ?
(*a*) BJB (*b*) DHB
(*c*) BJC (*d*) BBJ

18. ACE : HIL : : MOQ : ?
(*a*) SVW (*b*) TUX
(*c*) RTW (*d*) WUS

19. BCDE : WVUT : : QRST : ?
(*a*) EFHG (*b*) JIHG
(*c*) POML (*d*) GEDC

20. PNLJ : IGEC : : USQO : ?
(*a*) HJLN (*b*) LNJH
(*c*) NLJH (*d*) JHNL

21. DIMO : DMIO : : JUVR : ?
(*a*) JVRU (*b*) JRVU
(*c*) JVUR (*d*) JUVR

22. RRS : XMW : : ITB : ?
(*a*) PNE (*b*) NOG
(*c*) RSW (*d*) OOF

23. ODRS : OSRD : : PAGJ : ?
(*a*) PJGA (*b*) PJAG
(*c*) PGJA (*d*) PGAJ

24. MEQI : JUOD : : ANIW : ?
(*a*) RUKE (*b*) URIA
(*c*) EUIO (*d*) PTRE

25. AKU : AJS : : CRD : ?
(*a*) BQE (*b*) CQB
(*c*) DSB (*d*) APC

26. LOM : NMK : : PKI : ?
(*a*) RNK (*b*) RSM
(*c*) RMP (*d*) RIG

27. ARQ : DTR : : JNG : ?
(*a*) MPH (*b*) PHJ
(*c*) LPI (*d*) GLE

28. ODL : LOD : : PWN : ?
(*a*) WNP (*b*) NWP
(*c*) NPW (*d*) NMP

29. MAR : RAMP : : INS : ?
(*a*) NEST (*b*) SNIP
(*c*) TINS (*d*) SNAP

30. SUW : RST : : DFH : ?
(*a*) DEF (*b*) FGH
(*c*) CDE (*d*) GHI

31. PYG : OZF : : SBJ : ?
(*a*) QDJ (*b*) PEG
(*c*) OFH (*d*) RCI

32. ABC : ZYX : : IJK : ?
(*a*) RST (*b*) RQP
(*c*) RTS (*d*) RPQ

33. DMT : FNS : : HRJ : ?
(*a*) ISK (*b*) JSI
(*c*) JTK (*d*) JTI

34. ABDH : ZYWS : : EFHL : ?
(*a*) USOV (*b*) VOSU
(*c*) VUSO (*d*) TSUV

35. BYDW : FVHT : : GQIO : ?
(*a*) JLNP (*b*) QSTR
(*c*) KMOL (*d*) KNML

36. CIRCLE : RICELC : : SQUARE : ?
(*a*) UQSERA (*b*) QUSERA
(*c*) QSUERA (*d*) UQSAER

37. PSQR : CFED : : JMKL : ?
(*a*) UXVW (*b*) WZYX
(*c*) YVXZ (*d*) YZWX

38. JKLM : XYZA : : NOPQ : ?
(*a*) BCDE (*b*) RSTU
(*c*) YZAB (*d*) IJKL

39. EGI : NPR : : HJL : ?
(*a*) RTW (*b*) FGI
(*c*) NQT (*d*) TVX

40. TPNX : XNP : : BUCW : ?
(*a*) WUC (*b*) CUW
(*c*) WCU (*d*) COW

41. CNO : FLP : : WHF : ?
(*a*) GFZ (*b*) ADH
(*c*) ZFG (*d*) YGF

42. DUST : BUSY : : JOIN : ?
(*a*) ROIT (*b*) SOON
(*c*) RIOT (*d*) COST

43. FHJL : VTRP : : MOQS : ?
(*a*) JHFD (*b*) IGFD
(*c*) IGED (*d*) JHED

44. SWZ : XTA : : DGM : ?
(*a*) JEO (*b*) IDN
(*c*) HCM (*d*) NDI

45. NBRC : CRAB : : TYDA : ?
(*a*) DRAY (*b*) ADAY
(*c*) DATB (*d*) YDAB

46. BdNf : JnLo : : OrGh : ?
(*a*) GhnM (*b*) WbDq
(*c*) NMoh (*d*) FwbF

47. GNTB : GTNB : : WROX : ?
(*a*) WORX (*b*) RONX
(*c*) WYOX (*d*) RWOX

48. JMP : GOQ : : DBL : ?
(*a*) BCN (*b*) AEN
(*c*) BDN (*d*) ADM

49. UCFH : VEIL : : RXDJ : ?
(*a*) RYFM (*b*) TAHO
(*c*) SZNG (*d*) SZGN

50. ICHQ : HCIT : : PMBK : ?
(*a*) BMYR (*b*) BMPN
(*c*) MBPY (*d*) MPBS

51. RNOI : CANE : : FUIG : ?
(*a*) DURB (*b*) NEMD
(*c*) EPXU (*d*) QSTV

52. HKNQ : CGKO : : SVYB : ?
(*a*) SPVX (*b*) ORVX
(*c*) NRVZ (*d*) RNXZ

53. TXGM : WWJL : : DGMP : ?
(*a*) HHNQ (*b*) GFPO
(*c*) LPMK (*d*) FRNQ

54. CHJR : RHJC : : TARD : ?
(*a*) DART (*b*) ATRD
(*c*) DRAT (*d*) ARDT

55. GaMX : BViH : : FDJo : ?
(*a*) ReJW (*b*) XMVU
(*c*) OrDN (*d*) QSmP

56. ACE : FFF : : JNS : ?
(*a*) UVV (*b*) RRY
(*c*) OQT (*d*) PRU

57. WVUT : NOPQ : : MLKJ : ?
(*a*) CFED (*b*) RSTU
(*c*) HIGJ (*d*) UTSR

58. RCUF : CRFU : : MXBN : ?
(*a*) XMBN (*b*) XMNB
(*c*) MBXN (*d*) NBXM

59. DDFE : DFEE : : JJCR : ?
(*a*) JCRR (*b*) JCCR
(*c*) JRRC (*d*) JJRC

60. DNE : NDE : : FYR : ?
(*a*) YFR (*b*) FRY
(*c*) YRF (*d*) FYY

61. QRST : RSQT : : HUZC : ?
(*a*) HZUC (*b*) UZHC
(*c*) UCZH (*d*) UHZC

62. NNF : PLH : : PTX : ?
(*a*) QQZ (*b*) RRZ
(*c*) ORZ (*d*) ROZ

63. DBRG : ECSH : : NTUJ : ?
(*a*) OVWL (*b*) OWVM
(*c*) OUWN (*d*) OUVK

64. PZQW : NXOU : : FISK : ?
(*a*) EFPJ (*b*) FERI
(*c*) DGQI (*d*) HKUM

65. AXTC : TXAC : : GUMY : ?
(*a*) GMUY (*b*) MUGY
(*c*) MGUY (*d*) YUGM

66. CABD : FDEG : : RTQO : ?
(*a*) VUST (*b*) QTRN
(*c*) UWTR (*d*) WTSR

67. HIBD : GJAE : : MNSD : ?
(*a*) KPRE (*b*) OPUE
(*c*) PRSE (*d*) LORE

68. ZXWV : WVZX : : CRDB : ?
(*a*) BDCR (*b*) BCDR
(*c*) DCBR (*d*) DBCR

69. RQTP : PTQR : : KLNJ : ?
(*a*) JKLN (*b*) NLJK
(*c*) JNLK (*d*) KJLN

70. WBCU : XCBV : : GCBL : ?
(*a*) HCBL (*b*) HBCM
(*c*) FBCL (*d*) FCBL

71. FJNR : PTXB : : MQUY : ?
(*a*) CGKO (*b*) SWZD
(*c*) LQTX (*d*) RVZC

72. ADLC : CLAD : : RGUB : ?
(*a*) RUGB (*b*) GRUB
(*c*) UBRG (*d*) BURG

73. SFYT : TFSY : : BMJX : ?
(*a*) JMBX (*b*) XMBJ
(*c*) XBJM (*d*) XBMJ

74. WXYZ : UYXX : : DEFH : ?
(*a*) EFHH (*b*) BGFF
(*c*) EFEE (*d*) BFEF

75. CUZA : HYCC : : NNJO : ?
(*a*) TURS (*b*) SRMQ
(*c*) TRMP (*d*) SSNR

EXPLANATORY ANSWERS

1. (*b*) : The letters of the first group are reversed.

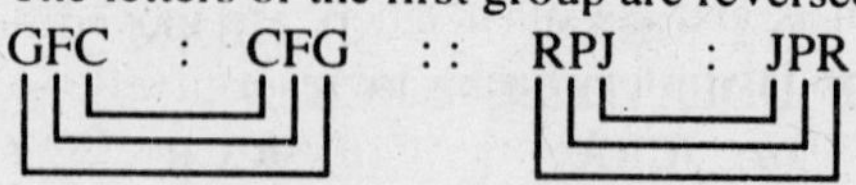

2. (*a*) : The three letters are moved 2, 2 and 1 steps forward respectively.

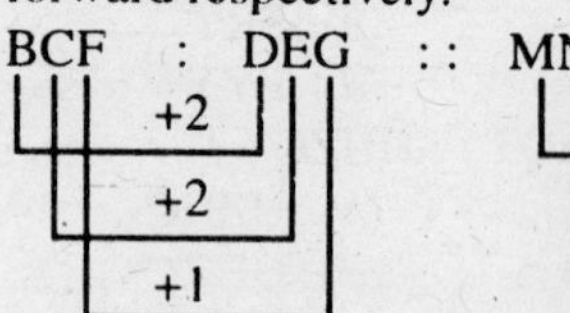

: : MNQ : OPR
+2
+2
+1

3. (*d*) : The word is divided in sections of two letters and the letters are reversed.

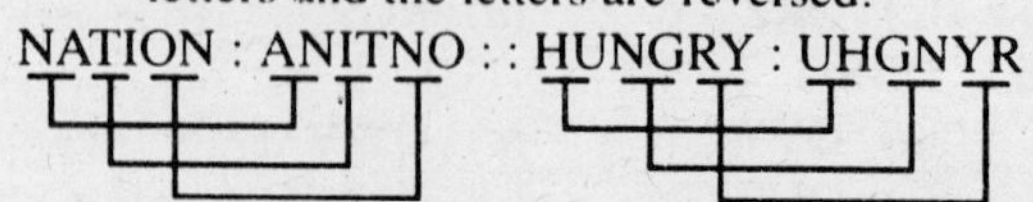

4. (*c*) : The first letter in each group is repeated and followed by two consecutive letters.

5. (*a*) : The three letters are moved 5, 4, and 3 steps forward respectively.

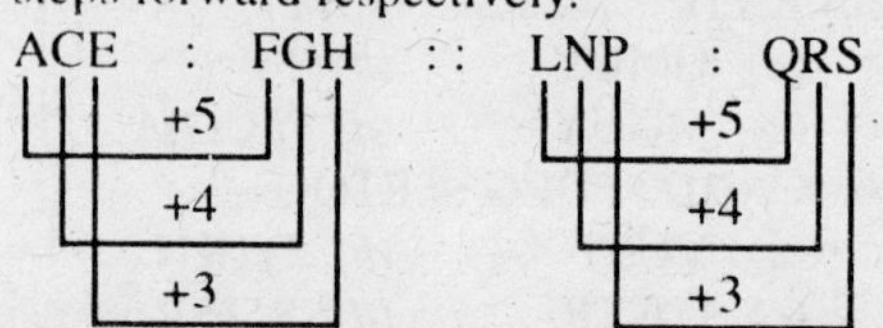

6. (*a*) : The three letters are moved −2, +2 and −2 steps respectively.

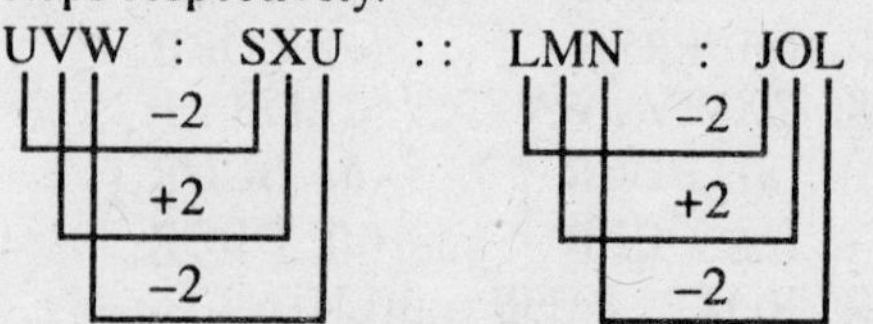

7. (*d*) : The word is divided into two sections and the letters are written backwards.

EIGHTY : GIEYTH : : OUTPUT : TUOTUP

8. (*b*) : The letters are consecutive and written in reverse order.

9. (*a*) : In each set of letters, the 1st and 3rd letters are consecutive.

CJDL : FMGR : : IKJR : OQPT

10. (*a*) : In each group, the first and fourth letters are jumping one letter and the second and third letters are also jumping one letter.

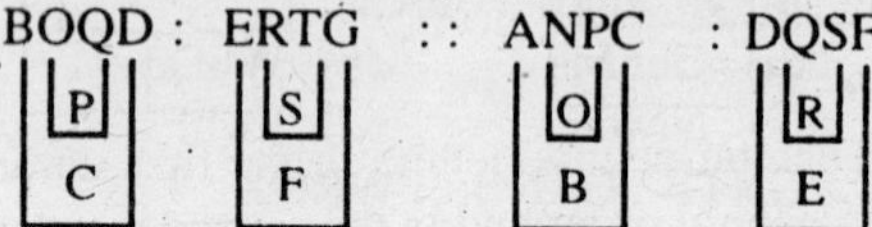

11. (*c*) : In each group the alternate letters are capitals.

12. (*a*) : In each group the first three letters are consecutive and they follow the fourth letter.

ABCD : RSTU : : JKLM : UVWX

13. (*d*) : In each group the letters jump three letters between them, *i.e.*, they are moving to the fourth letter.

A E I : L P T : : C G K : F J N
+4 +4   +4 +4   +4 +4   +4 +4

14. (*c*) : The letters in first set are jumping two letters, *i.e.*, moving three steps forward and in the second they are jumping one letter, *i.e.* moving two steps backward.

R U X : T R P : : B E H : Q O M
+3 +3   −2 −2   +3+3   −2 −2

15. (*d*) : The first set of letters drop the first letter to get the second set.

C A R T : A R T :: F O U R : O U R

16. (*b*) : The three letters in first set are moved +4, −2, and +4 steps respectively.

FIK : JGO :: DFR : HDV

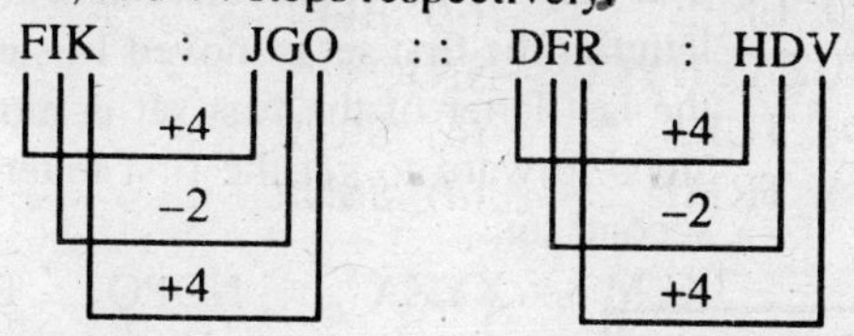

17. (*a*) : The letters in the first set are moved −1, +1 and +1 steps respectively.

LJH : KKI :: CIA : BJB

18. (*b*) : The three letters are moved +7, +6 and +7 steps forward respectively.

ACE : HIL :: MOQ : TUX

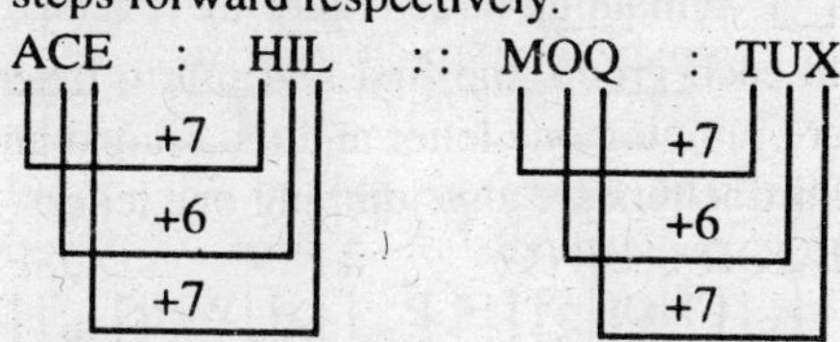

19. (*b*) : The consecutive letters in the first set are in natural order and in the second set, they are in reverse order.

BCDE : WVUT :: QRST : JIHG

20. (*c*) : The letters are moved seven steps backwards.

PNLJ : IGEC :: USQO : NLJH

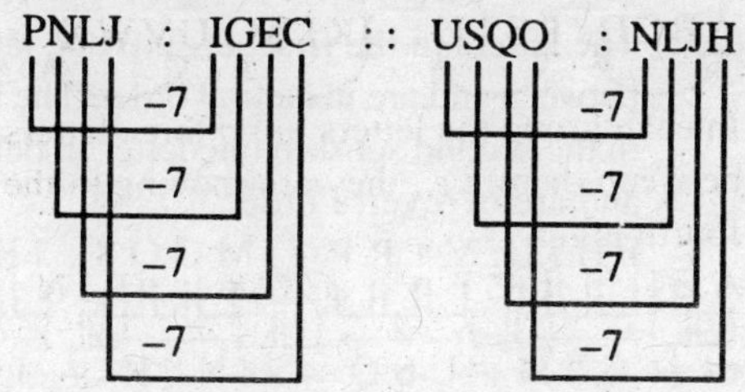

21. (*c*) : Only the middle letters are reversed to obtain the second set of letters.

DIMO : DMIO :: JUVR : JVUR

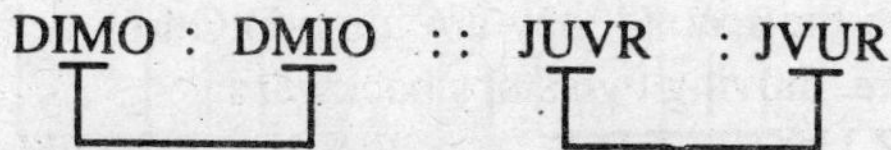

22. (*d*) : The three letters are moved +6, −5 and +4 steps respectively.

RRS : XMW :: ITB : OOF

+6 −5 +4   +6 −5 +4

23. (*a*) : Of the four letters the first letter is left at its place while the other three letters are written in reverse order.

ODRS : OSRD :: PAGJ : PJGA

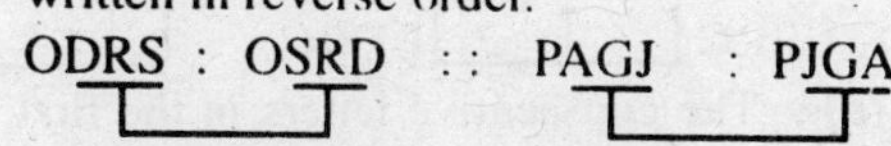

24. (*a*) : Of the four letters in each set the two letters are vowels.

25. (*b*) : Of the three letters the first letter is left as it is and the other letters are moved one and two steps backward respectively.

AKU : AJS :: CRD : CQB

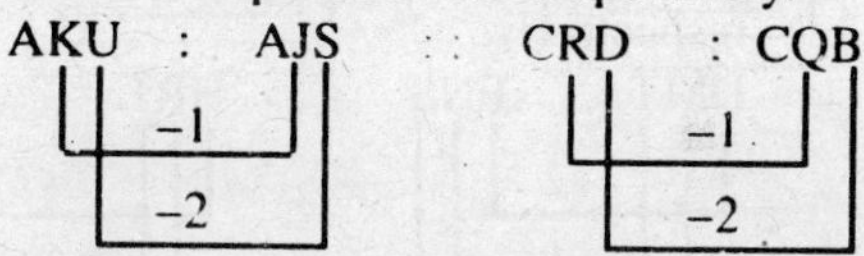

26. (*d*) : The first letter is moved two steps forward and the second and third letters two steps backward.

LOM : NMK :: PKI : RIG

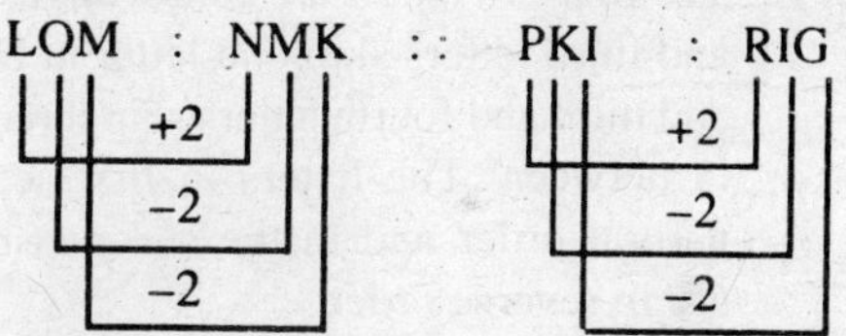

27. (*a*) : The three letters are moved 3, 2 and 1 step forward respectively.

ARQ : DTR :: JNG : MPH

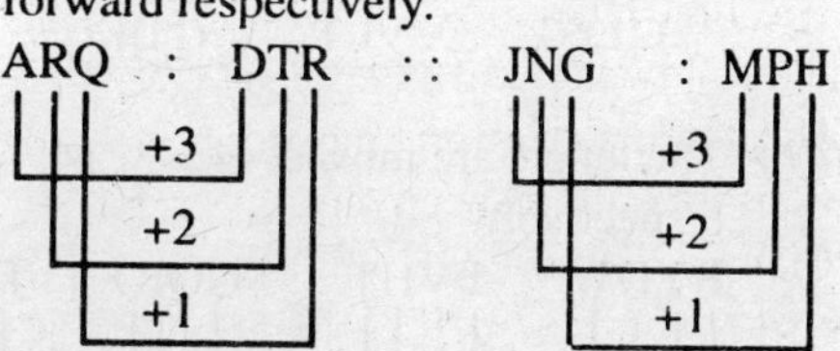

28. (*c*) : The third letter is placed ahead of the first and second letters.

ODL : LOD :: PWN : NPW

29. (*b*) : The letters of the first group are reversed and letter P added in the end.

MAR : RAMP :: INS : SNIP

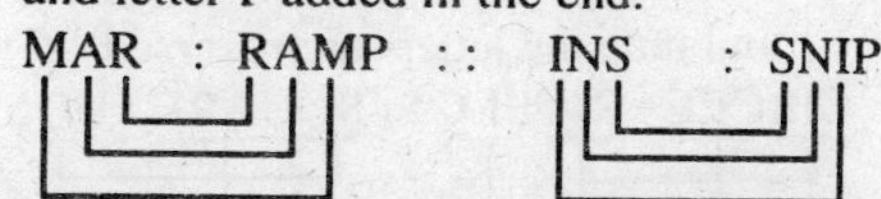

30. (*c*) : The first letter in the first set of letters has its consecutive letters on either side in the second set.

SUW : RST :: DFH : CDE

31. (d) : The three letters are moved –1, +1, –1 steps respectively.

PYG : OZF :: SBJ : RCI

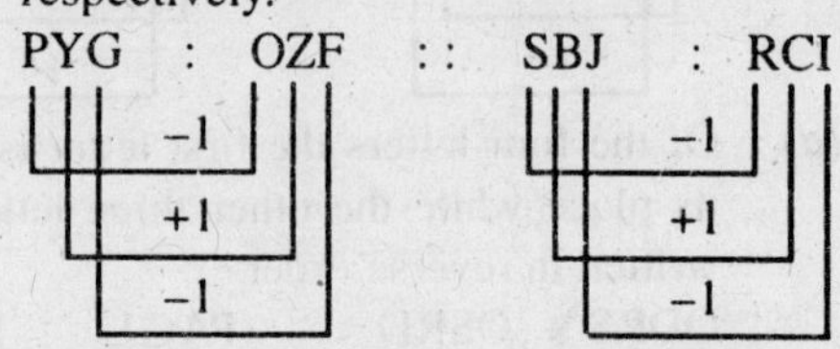

32. (b) : The consecutive letters in the first set are in natural order and in the second set, they are in reverse order.

ABC : ZYX :: IJK : RQP

33. (b) : The three letters are moved +2, +1, –1 steps respectively.

DMT : FNS :: HRJ : JSI

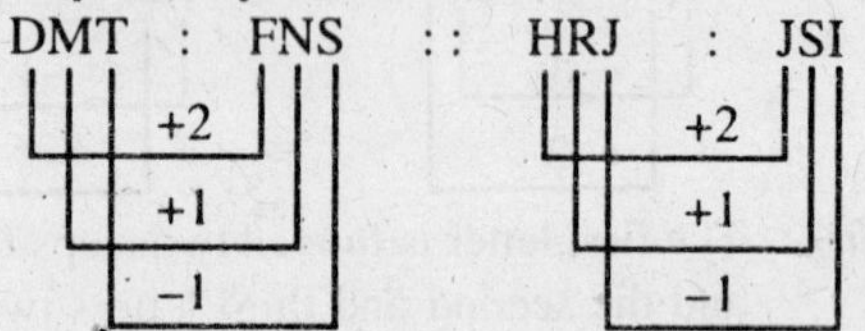

34. (c) : The first two letters are consecutive, second and third letters skip one letter in between and third and fourth letters skip three letters in between. The letters in first set are in natural order and in the second set, they are in reverse order.

A B D H : Z Y W S :: E F H L : V U S O

35. (d) : The letters are moved +4, –3, +4, –3 steps respectively

BYDW : FVHT :: GQIO : KNML

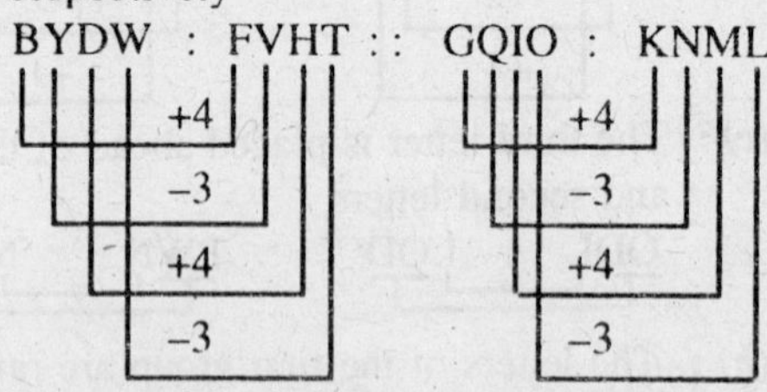

36. (a) : The word is divided into two equal parts and then the letters are reversed.

CIRCLE : RICELC :: SQUARE : UQSERA

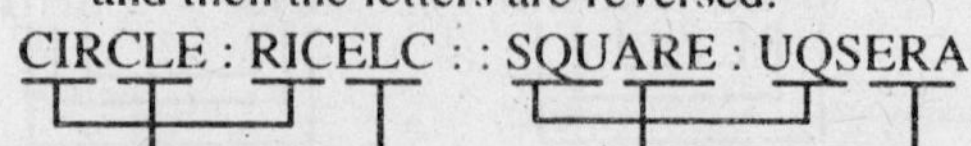

37. (b) : In the first set the first, third, fourth and second positioned letters are in consecutive order. In the second set the first, fourth, third and second positioned letters are in consecutive order.

PSQR : CFED :: JMKI : WZYX

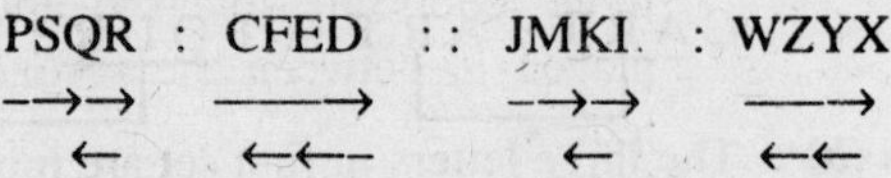

38. (a) : The letters are consecutive and the first letter of the first set is moved 14 steps 'or' the last letter of the first set is moved 11 steps forward to get the first letter of the second set.

JKLM : XYZA :: NOPQ : BCDE

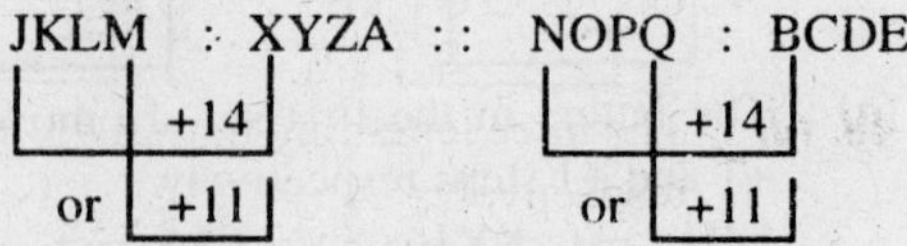

39. (d) : The letters are in natural order and skip one letter in between.

E G I : N P R :: H J L : T V X

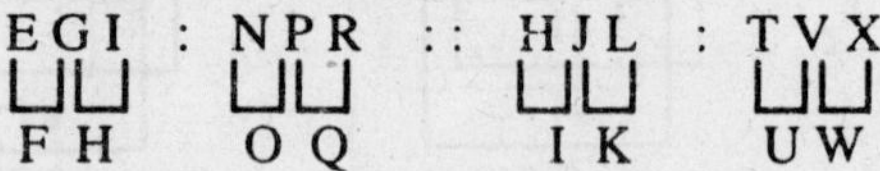

40. (c) : The first letter is dropped and the remaining three letters are reversed.

TPNX : XNP :: BUCW : WCU

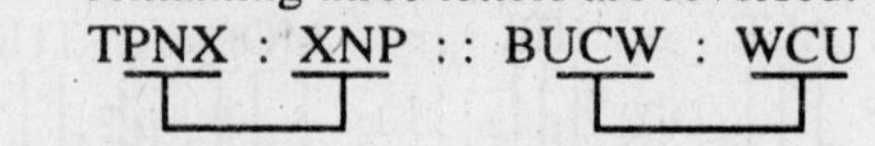

41. (c) : The letters are moved +3, –2, +1, steps respectively.

CNO : FLP :: WHF : ZFG

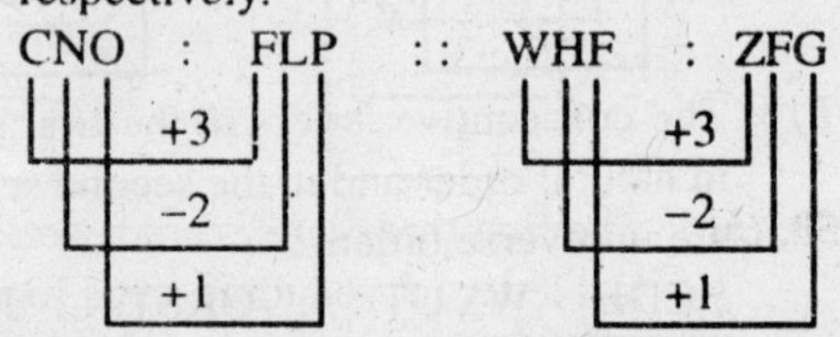

42. (a) : The two letters in the centre remain the same in second set.

DUST : BUSY :: JOIN : ROIT

43. (a) : The letters in the first set skip one letter in between and are in natural order. The letters in the second set skip one letter in between and are in reverse order.

F H J L : V T R P :: M O Q S : J H F D

G I K U S Q N P R I G E

44. (b) : The three letters are moved +5, -3, +1 steps respectively.

S W Z : X T A :: D G M : I D N

45. *(b)* : The first letter is dropped, the remaining three letters are reversed and letter 'A' placed in between the second and third letters.

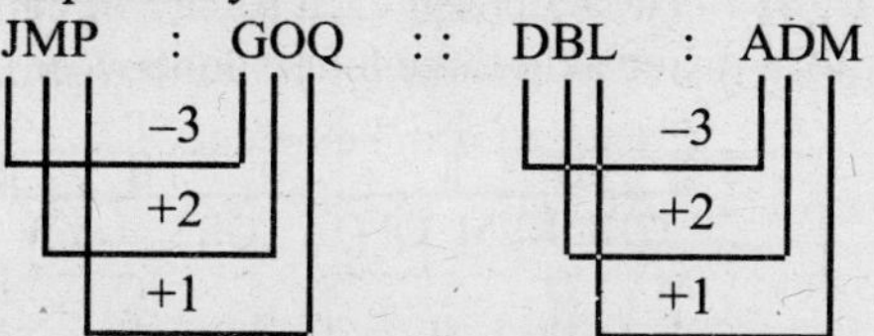

46. *(b)* : The first and the third letters are capital letters.

47. *(a)* : The two letters in the middle are reversed.

GNTB : GTNB :: WROX : WORX

48. *(d)* : The three letters are moved –3, +2, +1 step respectively.

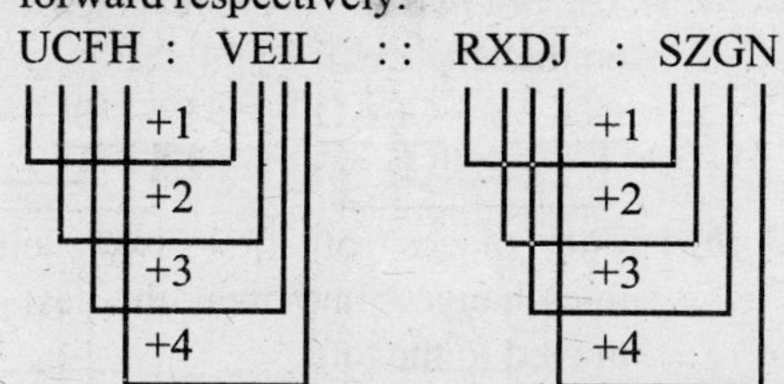

49. *(d)* : The letters are moved 1, 2, 3, 4 steps forward respectively.

UCFH : VEIL :: RXDJ : SZGN

50. *(b)* : The first three letters are reversed and the last letter moved three steps forward.

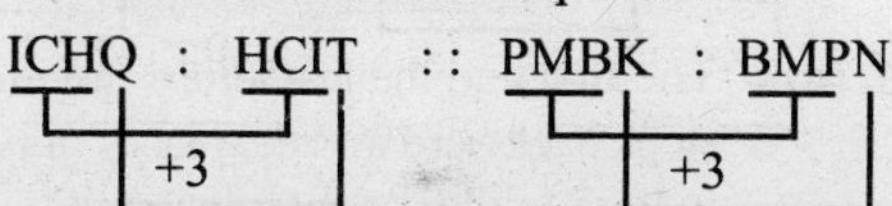

51. *(c)* : There are two vowels in each set.

RNOI : CANE :: FUIG : EPXU

52. *(c)* : The letters are moved 5, 4, 3 and 2 steps backward respectively.

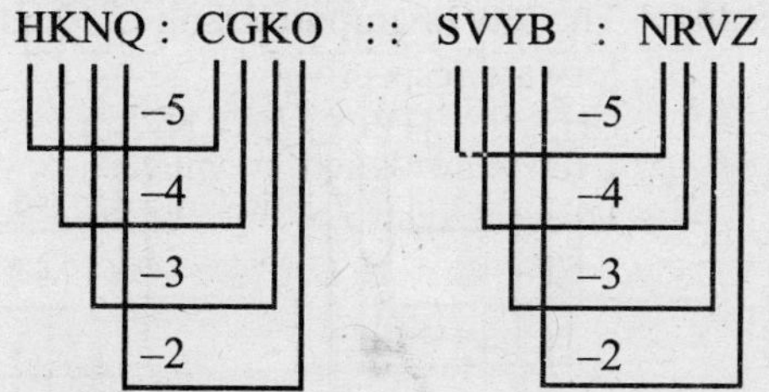

53. *(b)* : The letters are moved +3, –1, +3, –1 steps respectively

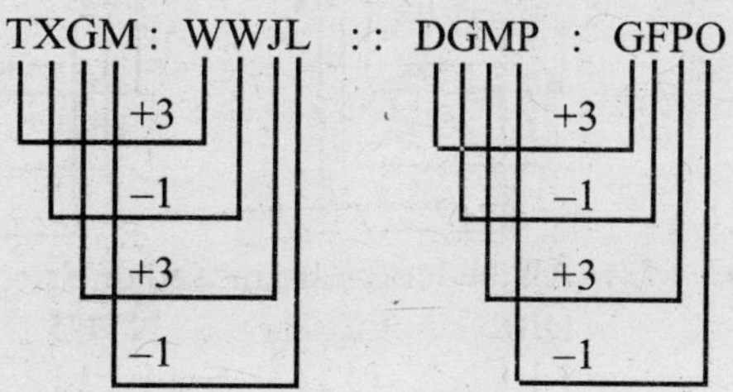

54. *(a)* : Only the places of first and last letters are interchanged.

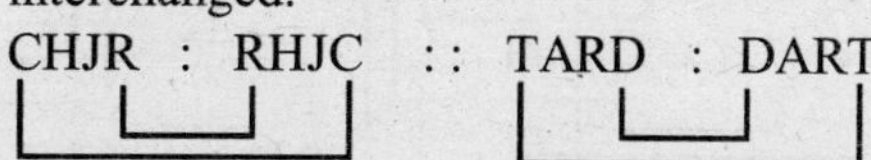

55. *(a)* : There is only one vowel in each set which is a small letter.

56. *(c)* : The letters are moved 5, 3 and 1 step forward respectively

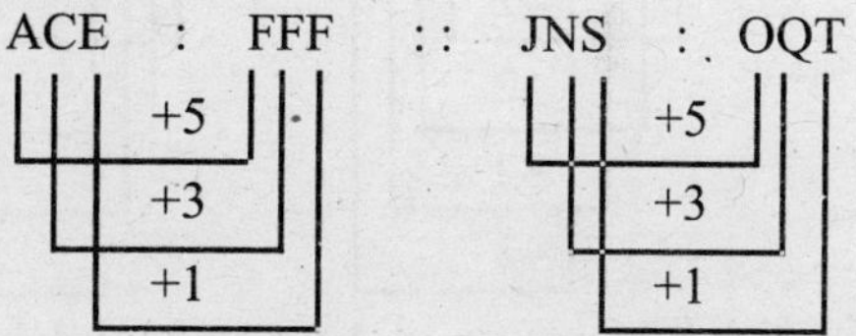

57. *(b)* : The consecutive letters in the first set are in reverse order and in the second set they are in natural order.

58. *(b)* : The letters are divided equally into two parts and letters in each part reversed.

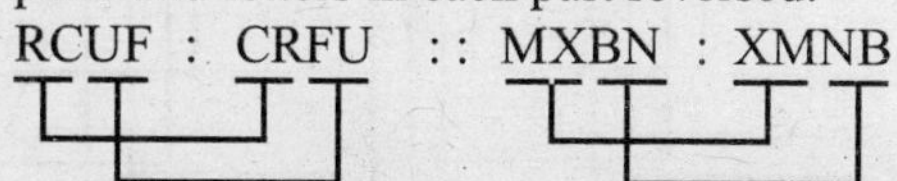

59. *(a)* : In the first set the first letter is repeated and in the second set the last letter is repeated.

60. *(a)* : The first letter is placed in between the second and third letters.

DNE : NDE :: FYR : YFR

61. *(b)* : The two letters in the middle are moved to the left and the first letter is moved to the third place.

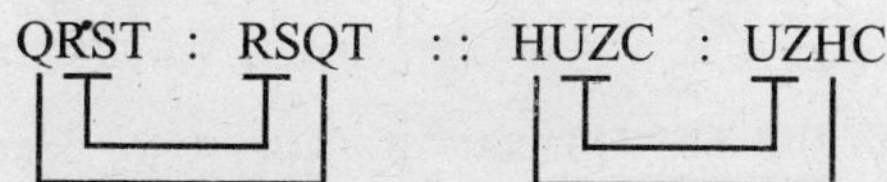

62. *(b)* : The letters are moved +2, –2 and +2 steps respectively.

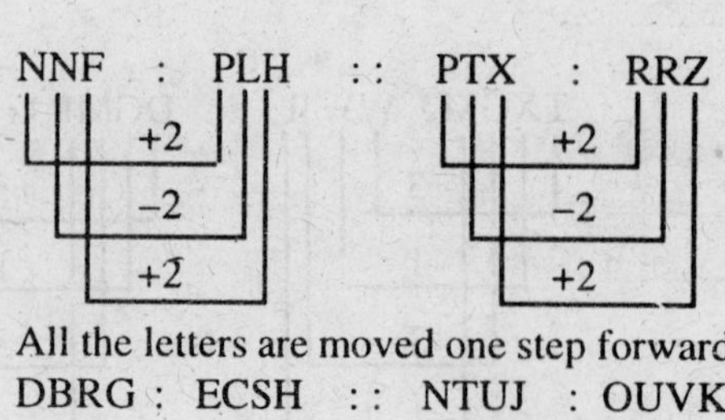

63. (d) : All the letters are moved one step forward.

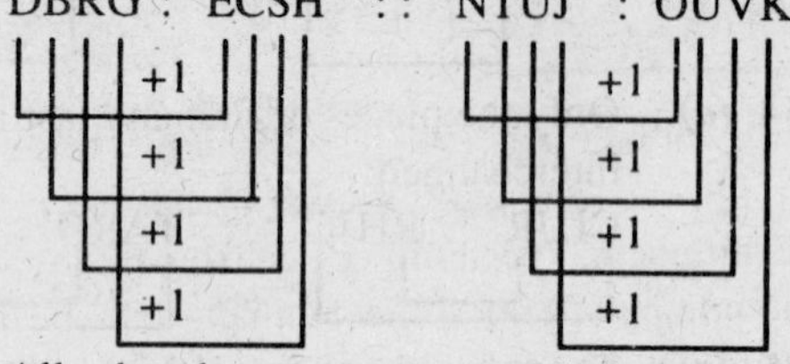

64. (c) : All the letters are moved two steps backward.

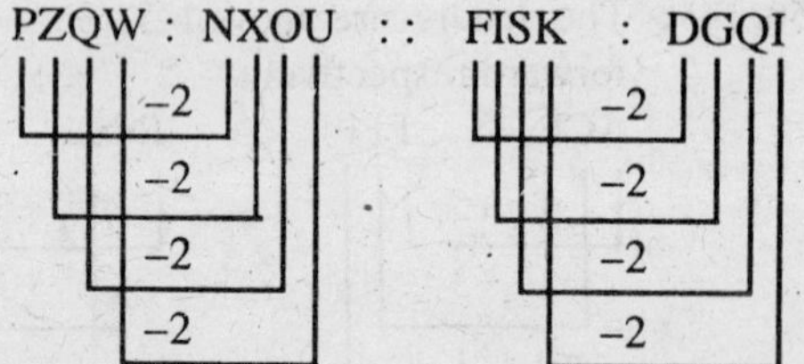

65. (b) : The places of first and third letters are interchanged.

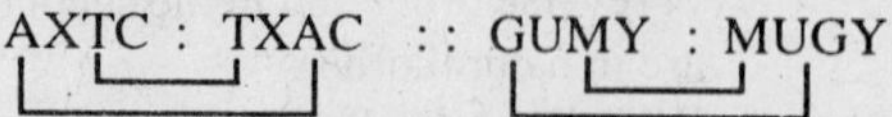

66. (c) : All the letters are moved three steps forward.

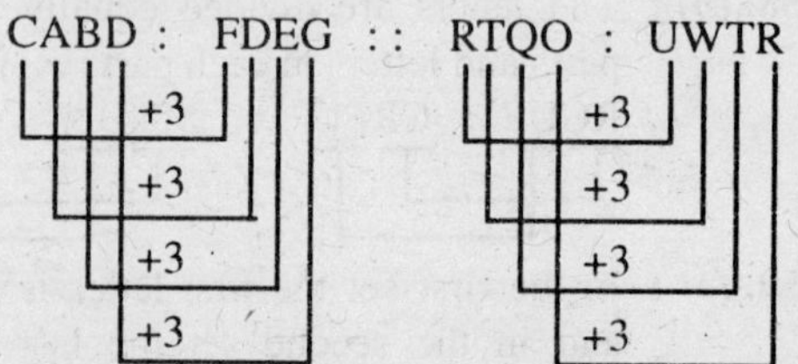

67. (d) : The letters are moved one step backward and one step forward alternately.

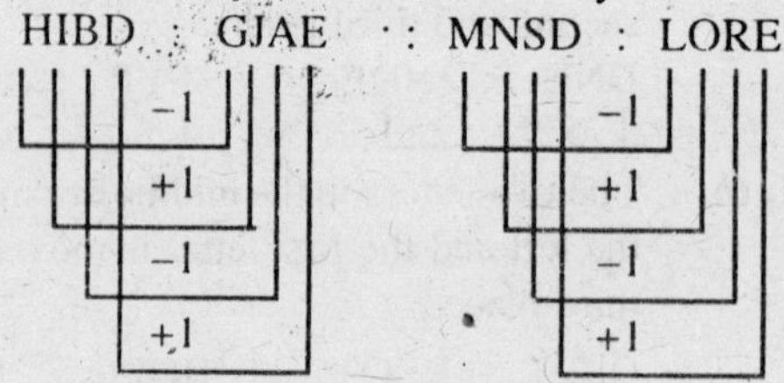

68. (d) : The places of first two letters are interchanged with the last two letters.

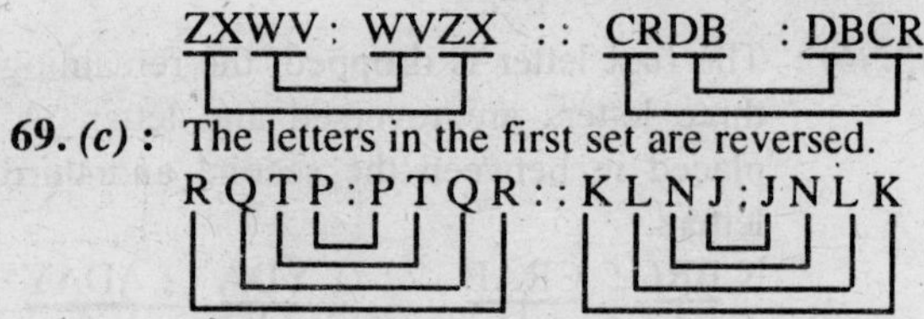

69. (c) : The letters in the first set are reversed.

70. (b) : The first and last letters are moved one step forward and the places of two letters in the middle are interchanged.

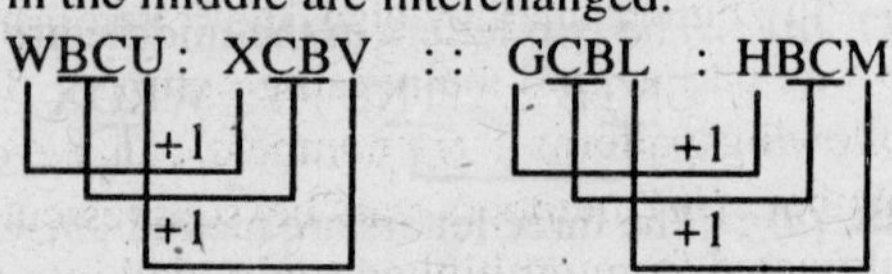

71. (a) : The letters in each set are in natural order and skip three letters inbetween.

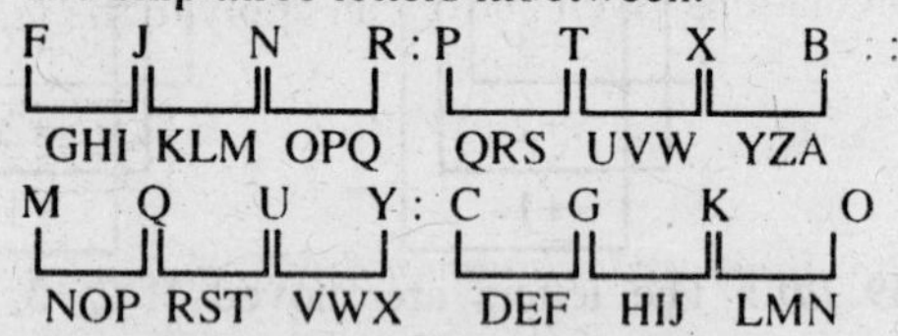

72. (d) : The last two letters are reversed and placed on the left.

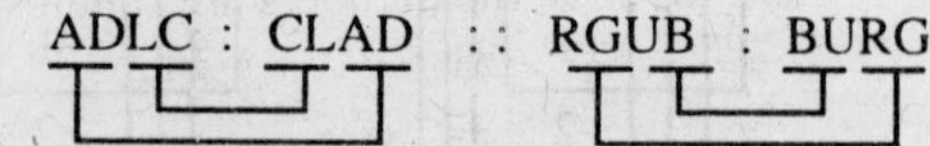

73. (b) : The places of first two letters are interchanged and then the last letter is moved to the left.

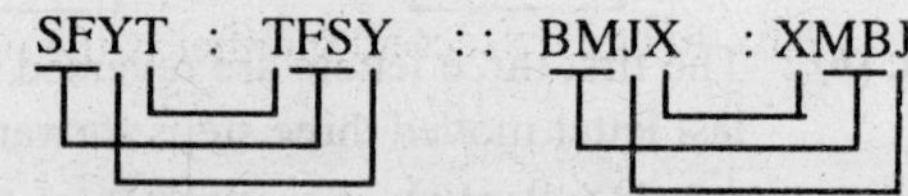

74. (d) : The first and the last letters are moved two steps backward and the places of two letters in the middle are interchanged.

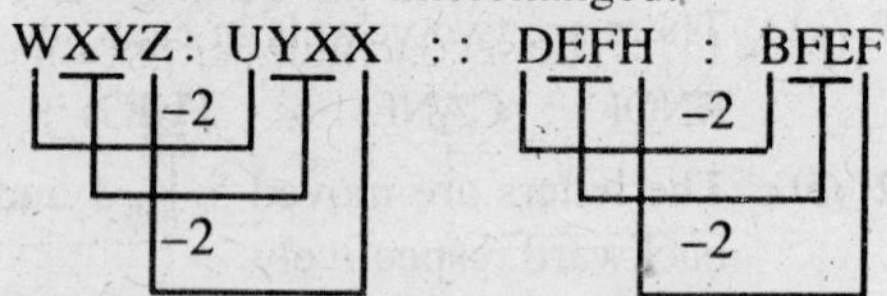

75. (b) : The letters are moved 5, 4, 3 and 2 steps forward respectively.

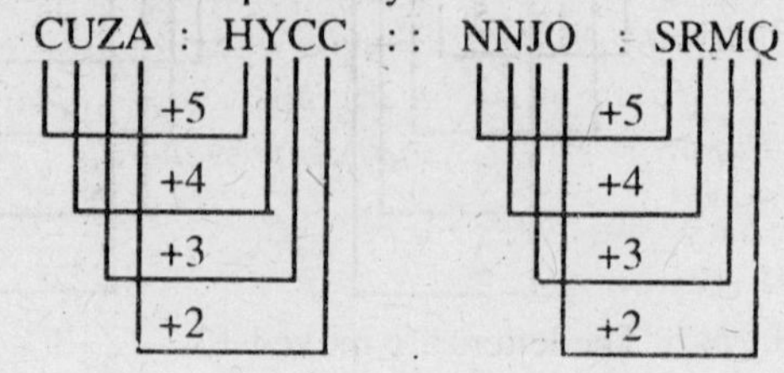

PART - III

NUMBER ANALOGY

In number analogy also, the relationship between the given numbers is detected and then applied to the second part to find the missing numbers. This relationship between the numbers can be based on any of the following patterns : *(i)* numbers can be odd/even/prime numbers; *(ii)* numbers can be multiples of one number; *(iii)* numbers can be squares/cubes of different numbers; *(iv)* some numbers can be added to/ subtracted from/multiplied to/divided into the first number to get the second number; *(v)* the second number can be the sum/product/difference of the digits of first number; and *(vi)* combinations of any mathematical calculations given above can apply to the relationship between the two given numbers.

SOLVED EXAMPLES

Directions : *Which number will come in the place of question mark?*

1. 25 : 81 : : 36 : ?

(*a*) 121 (*b*) 93 (*c*) 65 (*d*) 103

Ans. (*a*) : All the numbers are squares of different numbers.

25 : 81 : : 36 : 121

↓ ↓ ↓ ↓

5^2 9^2 6^2 11^2

2. 36 : 18 : : 72 : ?

(*a*) 164 (*b*) 134 (*c*) 94 (*d*) 14

Ans. (*d*) : The second number is the product of digits of the first number.

36 : 18 : : 72 : 14

3×6 7×2

3. 37 : 23 : : 19 : ?

(*a*) 9 (*b*) 5 (*c*) 6 (*d*) 8

Ans. (*b*) : The second number is 14 less than the first number.

37 : 23 : : 19 : 5

−14 −14

EXERCISE

Directions : *In the following questions, select the number from the given options which follows the same relationship as shared between the first two numbers.*

1. 1 : 11 : : 2 : ?

(*a*) 20 (*b*) 22

(*c*) 24 (*d*) 44

2. 18 : 27 : : 22 : ?

(*a*) 42 (*b*) 39

(*c*) 33 (*d*) 54

3. 14 : 20 : : 16 : ?

(*a*) 23 (*b*) 10

(*c*) 48 (*d*) 32

4. 8 : 27 : : 64 : ?

(*a*) 277 (*b*) 125

(*c*) 250 (*d*) 99

5. $\frac{1}{7} : \frac{1}{14} :: \frac{1}{9} : ?$

(*a*) $\frac{1}{88}$ (*b*) $\frac{1}{80}$

(*c*) $\frac{1}{81}$ (*d*) $\frac{1}{18}$

6. 0.16 : 0.0016 : : 1.02 : ?

(*a*) 10.20 (*b*) 0.102

(*c*) 0.0102 (*d*) 1.020

7. 5 : 24 : : 8 : ?

(*a*) 65 (*b*) 63

(*c*) 62 (*d*) 64

8. 23 : 53 : : 8 : ?

(*a*) 66 (*b*) 57

(*c*) 27 (*d*) 19

9. 6 : 9 : : 7 : ?

(*a*) 4 (*b*) 14

(*c*) 10 (*d*) 28

10. 7 : 28 : : 2 : ?

(*a*) 8 (*b*) 16

(*c*) 24 (*d*) 12

11. 65 : 30 : : 44 : ?

(*a*) 79 (*b*) 62

(*c*) 28 (*d*) 16

12. 99 : 76 : : 24 : ?

(*a*) 1 (*b*) 13

(*c*) 9 (*d*) 7

13. 11 : 35 : : 17 : ?

(*a*) 3 (*b*) 22

(*c*) 58 (*d*) 10

14. 663 : 884 : : 221 : ?

(*a*) 332 (*b*) 554

(*c*) 773 (*d*) 442

15. 16 : 0.16 : : ?

(*a*) 2 : 0.02 (*b*) 7 : 0.007

(*c*) 1.3 : 0.13 (*d*) 0.01 : 0.001

16. $3 : \frac{1}{3}$: : ?

(*a*) 6 : 12 (*b*) 5 : 2/15

(*c*) 8 : 1/8 (*d*) 9 : 27

17. 43 : 34 : : 52 : ?

(*a*) 49 (*b*) 25

(*c*) 36 (*d*) 64

18. 65 : 13 : : 180 : ?

(*a*) 93 (*b*) 36

(*c*) 133 (*d*) 102

19. 882 : 447 : : 881 : ?

(*a*) 444 (*b*) 445

(*c*) 446 (*d*) 447

20. 125 : 27 : : 343 : ?

(*a*) 729 (*b*) 64

(*c*) 216 (*d*) 512

21. 30 : 42 : : 56 : ?

(*a*) 92 (*b*) 21

(*c*) 38 (*d*) 72

22. 190 : 10 : : 102 : ?

(*a*) 4 (*b*) 7

(*c*) 3 (*d*) 5

23. 95 : 38 : : 167 : ?

(*a*) 110 (*b*) 120

(*c*) 113 (*d*) 134

24. 4 : 36 : : 6 : ?

(*a*) 63 (*b*) 54

(*c*) 35 (*d*) 30

25. 6 : 12 : : 20 : ?

(*a*) 50 (*b*) 30

(*c*) 42 (*d*) 38

26. 6 : 18 : : 4 : ?

(*a*) 2 (*b*) 6

(*c*) 8 (*d*) 16

27. 10 : 20 : : 30 : ?

(*a*) 45 (*b*) 60

(*c*) 50 (*d*) 70

28. 92 : 69 : : 46 : ?

(*a*) 57 (*b*) 23

(*c*) 31 (*d*) 19

29. 63 : 9 : : 49 : ?

(*a*) 12 (*b*) 3

(*c*) 36 (*d*) 7

30. 2 : 11 : : ?

(*a*) 6 : 17 (*b*) 8 : 43

(*c*) 5 : 41 (*d*) 7 : 35

31. 357 : 73 : : ?

(*a*) 429 : 94 (*b*) 201 : 21

(*c*) 138 : 38 (*d*) 93 : 39

32. 42 : 63 : : 84 : ?

(*a*) 185 (*b*) 95

(*c*) 142 (*d*) 125

33. 731 : 902 : : 655 : ?

(*a*) 646 (*b*) 800

(*c*) 793 (*d*) 546

34. 89 : 72 : : ?
(*a*) 30 : 0 (*b*) 14 : 5
(*c*) 66 : 12 (*d*) 48 : 36

35. 162 : 9 : : 310 : ?
(*a*) 33 (*b*) 27
(*c*) 16 (*d*) 4

36. 411 : 441 : : 755 : ?
(*a*) 705 (*b*) 775
(*c*) 635 (*d*) 665

37. 13 : 17 : : 15 : ?
(*a*) 19 (*b*) 11
(*c*) 21 (*d*) 16

38. 225 : 15 : : 256 : ?
(*a*) 26 (*b*) 16
(*c*) 20 (*d*) 28

39. 46 : 48 : : 54 : ?
(*a*) 59 (*b*) 40
(*c*) 67 (*d*) 62

40. 33 : 36 : : 21 : ?
(*a*) 9 (*b*) 18
(*c*) 25 (*d*) 32

41. 19 : 39 : : 42 : ?
(*a*) 60 (*b*) 83
(*c*) 85 (*d*) 91

42. 5 : 45 : : 2 : ?
(*a*) 40 (*b*) 36
(*c*) 20 (*d*) 18

43. 123 : 149 : : 201 : ?
(*a*) 202 (*b*) 404
(*c*) 401 (*d*) 227

44. 7 : 105 : : 5 : ?
(*a*) 97 (*b*) 83
(*c*) 75 (*d*) 61

45. 11 : 101 : : 73 : ?
(*a*) 153 (*b*) 330
(*c*) 543 (*d*) 703

46. 4 : 32 : : 8 : ?
(*a*) 34 (*b*) 68
(*c*) 92 (*d*) 128

47. 94 : 26 : : 62 : ?
(*a*) 16 (*b*) 22
(*c*) 39 (*d*) 48

48. 27 : 47 : : 32 : ?
(*a*) 70 (*b*) 92
(*c*) 66 (*d*) 84

49. 6 : 21 : : 14 : ?
(*a*) 82 (*b*) 75
(*c*) 60 (*d*) 41

50. 31 : 124 : : 103 : ?
(*a*) 98 (*b*) 215
(*c*) 412 (*d*) 517

EXPLANATORY ANSWERS

1. (*b*) : The first number is repeated to obtain the second number.

2. (*c*) : In the given set, the numbers are multiples of 9 and in the second set, multiples of 11.

18 : 27 : : 22 : 33
↓ ↓ ↓ ↓
9×2 9×3 11×2 11×3

3. (*a*) : The relationship between the numbers is :

14 : 20 : : 16 : 23
↓ ↓ ↓ ↓
7×2 $(7 \times 3) - 1$ 8×2 $(8 \times 3) - 1$

4. (*b*) : The numbers are cubes of different numbers.

8 : 27 : : 64 : 125
↓ ↓ ↓ ↓
2^3 3^3 4^3 5^3

5. (*d*) : The first fraction is multiplied by half to obtain the second fraction.

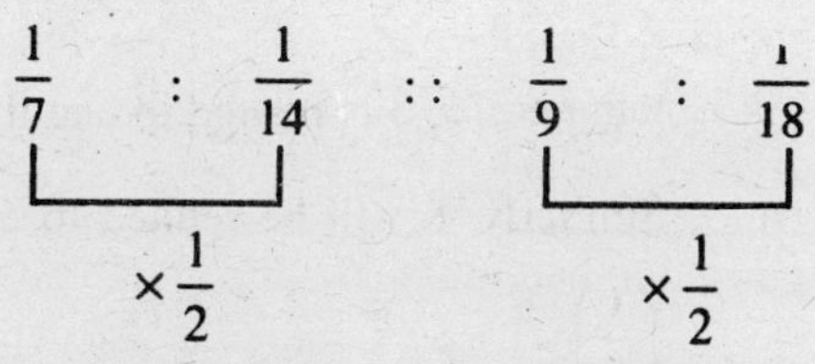

$\frac{1}{7} : \frac{1}{14} :: \frac{1}{9} : \frac{1}{18}$ ($\times \frac{1}{2}$, $\times \frac{1}{2}$)

6. (*c*) : The decimals are divided by 100.

0.16 : 0.0016 : : 1.02 : 0.0102
÷ 100 ÷ 100

7. (*b*) : The second number is square of first number minus 1.

5 : 24 : : 8 : 63
$(5^2) - 1$ $(8^2) - 1$

8. (*d*) : All the numbers are prime numbers.

9. (*c*) : The second number is three more than the first number.

10. (a) : The second number is four times the first.

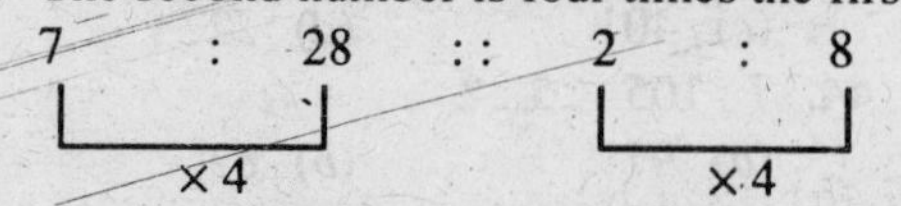

11. (d) : The second number is the product of digits of first number.

$\xrightarrow[(6 \times 5)]{65 : 30}$ :: $\xrightarrow[(4 \times 4)]{44 : 16}$

12. (a) : The second number is 23 less than the first number.

13. (a) : All the numbers are odd numbers.

14. (d) : The digits at tens and hundreds place is same but the digit at the units place is half the other identical digits.

66 3 : 88 4 :: 22 1 : 44 2

15. (a) : Of the two related numbers, the second number is the result of first number divided by 100.

16 : 0.16 :: 2 : 0.02
÷ 100   ÷ 100

16. (c) : Of the two related numbers, the second number is the part fraction of the first number, *i.e.* 3 is related to one-third $\left(\frac{1}{3}\right)$. Similarly, 8 will be related to one-eighth $\left(\frac{1}{8}\right)$.

17. (b) : The digits are written in reverse order in the second number.

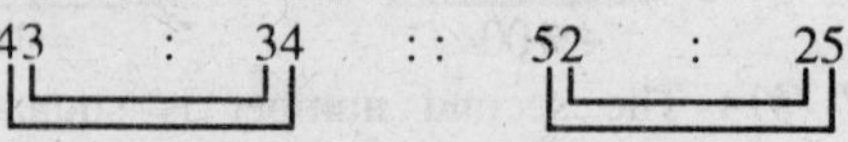

18. (b) : The first number is divided by 5 to get the second number.

65 : 13 :: 180 : 36
÷ 5   ÷ 5

19. (c) : The relationship between two numbers is :

88 2 : 44 7 :: 88 1 : 44 6
÷ 2, +5   ÷ 2, +5

20. (a) : The numbers are cubes of different odd numbers.

125 : 27 :: 343 : 729
↓ ↓ ↓ ↓
5^3 3^3 7^3 9^3

21. (d) : The numbers are squares of different numbers plus the number itself.

30 : 42 :: 56 : 72
↓ ↓ ↓ ↓
$5^2 + 5$ $6^2 + 6$ $7^2 + 7$ $8^2 + 8$

22. (c) : The second number is the sum of digits of first number.

$\xrightarrow[(1+9+0)]{190 : 10}$ :: $\xrightarrow[(1+0+2)]{102 : 3}$

23. (a) : The second number is 57 less than the first number.

95 : 38 :: 167 : 110
−57   −57

24. (b) : The second number is 9 times the first number.

4 : 36 :: 6 : 54
× 9   × 9

25. (b) : The numbers are squares of different numbers minus the number itself.

6 : 12 :: 20 : 30
↓ ↓ ↓ ↓
$3^2 - 3$ $4^2 - 4$ $5^2 - 5$ $6^2 - 6$

26. (c) : Half the square of first number is the second number.

6 : 18 :: 4 : 8
$6^2 \div 2$ $4^2 \div 2$

27. (b) : The second number is double the first number.

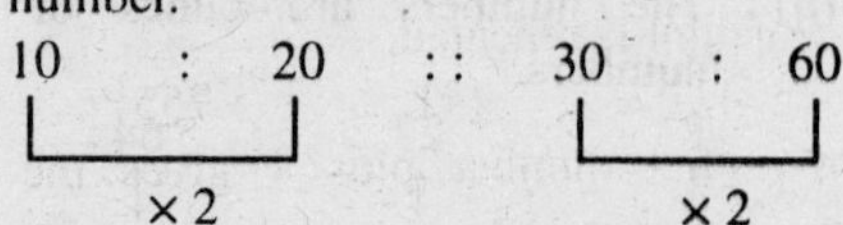

28. (b) : The difference between the two numbers is 23.

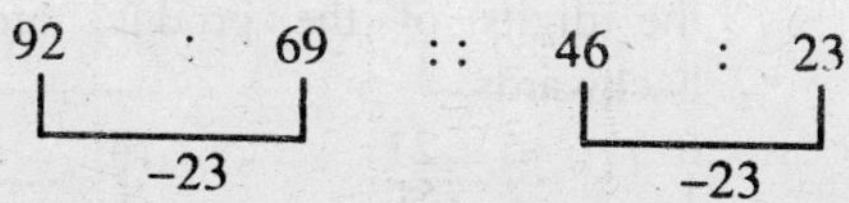

92 : 69 :: 46 : 23

−23 −23

29. (d) : The first number is divided by 7 to get the second number.

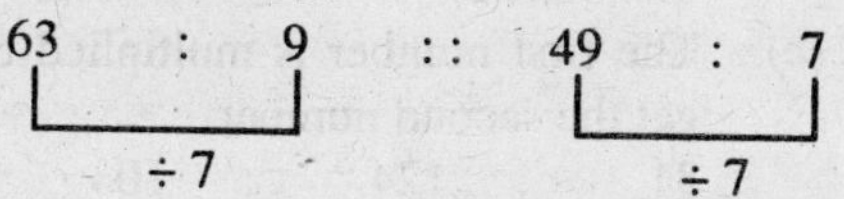

63 : 9 :: 49 : 7

÷ 7 ÷ 7

30. (c) : The sum of the digits of the second number is equal to the first number.

2 : 11 :: 5 : 41

(1 + 1) (4 + 1)

31. (a) : The central digit of the first number is left out and the corner digits written in reverse order to get the second number.

357 : 73 :: 429 : 94

32. (c) : Both the related numbers are divisible by same number.

42 : 63 are divisible by 3

84 : 142 are divisible by 2

33. (a) : The sum of the digits of both the numbers is same.

731 : 902 → 7 + 3 + 1

= 9 + 0 + 2 *i.e.* 11 = 11

655 : 646 → 6 + 5 + 5

= 6 + 4 + 6 *i.e.* 16 = 16

34. (a) : The product of the digits of the first number is the second number.

89 : 72 :: 30 : 0

8 × 9 3 × 0

35. (d) : The sum of the digits of the first number is the second number.

162 : 9 :: 310 : 4

1 + 6 + 2 3 + 1 + 0

36. (b) : In the first number the second digit is repeated and in the second number the first digit is repeated.

4<u>11</u> : <u>44</u>1 :: 7<u>55</u> : <u>77</u>5

37. (a) : First number plus 4 gives the second number.

13 : 17 :: 15 : 19

+4 +4

38. (b) : The root of first number is the second number.

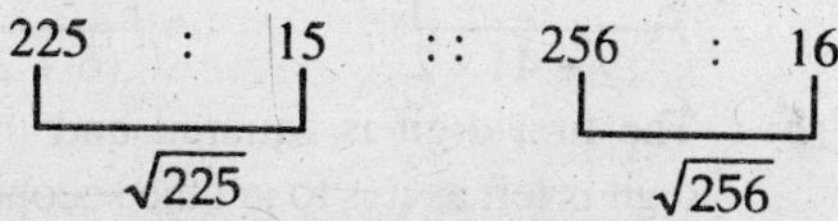

225 : 15 :: 256 : 16

$\sqrt{225}$ $\sqrt{256}$

39. (b) : The product of the digits of first number is multiplied by 2 to get the second number.

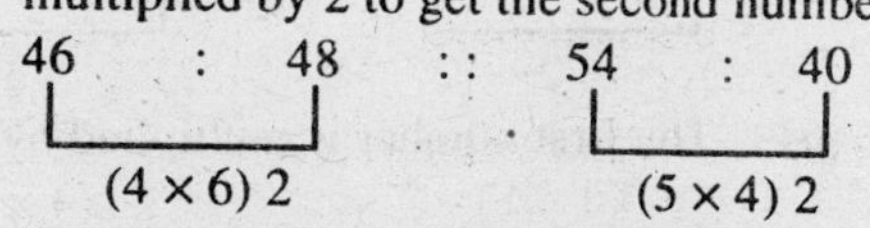

46 : 48 :: 54 : 40

(4 × 6) 2 (5 × 4) 2

40. (a) : The square of the sum of the digits of the first number is the second number.

33 : 36 :: 21 : 9

$(3 + 3)^2$ $(2 + 1)^2$

41. (c) : Double the first number plus one is the second number :

19 : 39 :: 42 : 85

(19 × 2) +1 (42 × 2) +1

42. (d) : The first number is multiplied by nine to get the second number.

5 : 45 :: 2 : 18

× 9 × 9

43. (c) : Each digit of the first number are squared to get the digits of the second number.

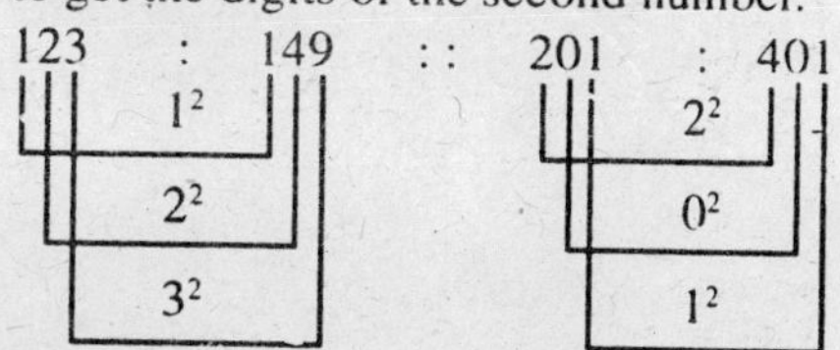

123 : 149 :: 201 : 401

1^2 2^2 3^2 2^2 0^2 1^2

44. (c) : The first number is multiplied by 15 to get the second number.

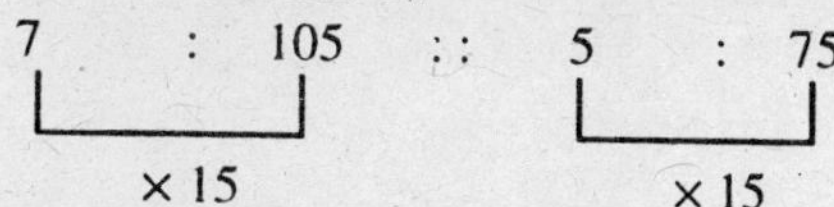

7 : 105 :: 5 : 75

× 15 × 15

45. (d) : Zero is inserted in between the digits of the first number to get the second number.

11 : 1<u>0</u>1 :: 73 : 7<u>0</u>3

46. (d) : Double the first number multiplied by the number itself gives the second number.

4 : 32 :: 8 : 128

(4 × 2) 4 (8 × 2) 8

47. (a) : The sum of the digits of the first number

multiplied by two gives the second number.

94 : 26 :: 62 : 16

$(9 + 4) \times 2$ $(6 + 2) \times 2$

48. *(b)* : The first digit is squared and the second digit is left as it is to get the second number.

27 : 47 :: 32 : 92

2^2 3^2

49. *(a)* : The first number is multiplied by two and the digits of the product are written backwards.

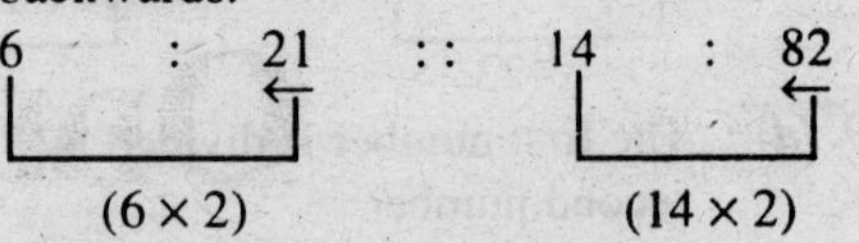

50. *(c)* : The first number is multiplied by four to get the second number.

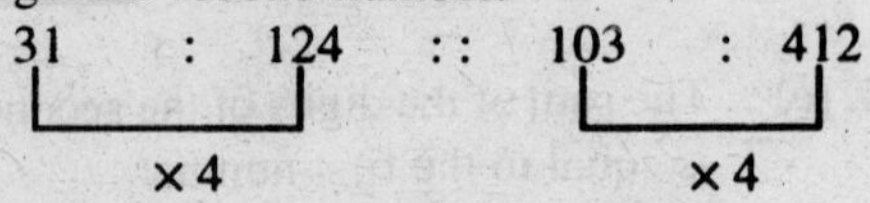

CLASSIFICATION OR ODD ONE OUT

PART - I

ODD ONE OUT—WORDS

In this type of classification, five words are given out of which four are almost same in matter or meaning and only one word is different from the common four. One has to find out the word which is different from the rest.

SOLVED EXAMPLES

Directions : *In the following questions spot the odd one out.*

1. (*a*) Father (*b*) Mother (*c*) Friend (*d*) Brother (*e*) Sister

Ans. (*c*) : All other are blood relations.

2. (*a*) Water (*b*) Jelly (*c*) Lemonade (*d*) Coffee (*e*) Milk

Ans. (*b*) : All other are liquids.

EXERCISE

Directions : *In each of the following questions, four words are alike in some manner. Spot the odd one out.*

1. (*a*) Green (*b*) Red (*c*) Colour (*d*) Orange (*e*) Black

2. (*a*) Stable (*b*) Hole (*c*) Canoe (*d*) Sty (*e*) Nest

3. (*a*) Nose (*b*) Eyes (*c*) Skin (*d*) Tongue (*e*) Teeth

4. (*a*) Venus (*b*) Moon (*c*) Pluto (*d*) Mars (*e*) Earth

5. (*a*) Happy (*b*) Gloomy (*c*) Lively (*d*) Cheerful (*e*) Ecstatic

6. (*a*) Cone (*b*) Circle (*c*) Triangle (*d*) Rectangle (*e*) Square

7. (*a*) Lead (*b*) Mercury (*c*) Copper (*d*) Iron (*e*) Tin

8. (*a*) Kite (*b*) Bird (*c*) Radar (*d*) Jet (*e*) Rocket

9. (*a*) Knee (*b*) Shoulder (*c*) Ankle (*d*) Elbow (*e*) Palm

10. (*a*) Deluge (*b*) Calamity (*c*) Catastrophe (*d*) War (*e*) Disaster

11. (*a*) Cub (*b*) Chicken

(c) Pig (d) Pup
(e) Lamb

12. (a) Rabbit (b) Crocodile
(c) Earthworm (d) Snail
(e) Lizard

13. (a) Tree (b) Leaf
(c) Bush (d) Herb
(e) Creeper

14. (a) Doctor (b) Teacher
(c) Engineer (d) Carpenter
(e) Diver

15. (a) Trot (b) Equestrian
(c) Derby (d) Grunt
(e) Neigh

16. (a) Ornate (b) Pleasant
(c) Decorate (d) Beautify
(e) Adorn

17. (a) Polo (b) Chess
(c) Ludo (d) Squash
(e) Cards

18. (a) Tutor (b) Principal
(c) Pupil (d) Professor
(e) Teacher

19. (a) Pond (b) River
(c) Stream (d) Brook
(e) Spring

20. (a) Quotation (b) Duty
(c) Tax (d) Octroi
(e) Invoice

21. (a) Root (b) Tree
(c) Branch (d) Flower
(e) Fruit

22. (a) Mumbai (b) Chandigarh
(c) Lucknow (d) Hyderabad
(e) Chennai

23. (a) Immortal (b) Eminence
(c) Perpetual (d) Everlasting
(e) Infinite

24. (a) Spinach (b) Potato
(c) Carrot (d) Ginger
(e) Beetroot

25. (a) Van (b) Aeroplane
(c) Helicopter (d) Transport
(e) Scooter

26. (a) Fathom (b) Marine
(c) Deep (d) Nautical
(e) Lacuna

27. (a) Attorney (b) Lawyer
(c) Judge (d) Liquidator
(e) Advocate

28. (a) Sparrow (b) Kingfisher
(c) Kiwi (d) Parrot
(e) Dove

29. (a) Arrow (b) Daggar
(c) Knife (d) Sword
(e) Spear

30. (a) Mathematics (b) Algebra
(c) Trigonometry (d) Geometry
(e) Arithmetic

31. (a) Irish (b) Iranian
(c) Eastern (d) Chinese
(e) German

32. (a) December (b) June
(c) January (d) March
(e) July

33. (a) Boxer (b) Wrestler
(c) Jockey (d) Cricketer
(e) Player

34. (a) Mature (b) Outdo
(c) Ripen (d) Bloom
(e) Mellow

35. (a) Kanpur (b) Haridwar
(c) Varanasi (d) Lucknow
(e) Gaya

36. (a) Adore (b) Like
(c) Love (d) Covet
(e) Admire

37. (a) Greedy (b) Rapacious
(c) Endear (d) Avaricious
(e) Acquisitive

38. (a) Club (b) Heart
(c) Spade (d) Diamond
(e) Ace

39. (a) Permit (b) Allow
(c) Agree (d) Consent
(e) Confess

40. (a) Stool (b) Wood
(c) Table (d) Chair
(e) Bench

41. (a) Foundation (b) Bottom
(c) Bane (d) Base
(e) Pedestal

42. (a) Cheese (b) Milk
(c) Curd (d) Ghee

(*e*) Butter

43. (*a*) Ear (*b*) Hand
(*c*) Nose (*d*) Eye
(*e*) Thumb

44. (*a*) Lower limb (*b*) Cheek
(*c*) Heart (*d*) Lung
(*e*) Kidney

45. (*a*) Cannon (*b*) Gun
(*c*) Pistol (*d*) Sword
(*e*) Rifle

46. (*a*) Guitar (*b*) Sarod
(*c*) Violin (*d*) Tabla
(*e*) Sitar

47. (*a*) Tennis (*b*) Soccer
(*c*) Billiards (*d*) Cricket
(*e*) Hockey

48. (*a*) Dismay (*b*) Bay
(*c*) Say (*d*) Toy
(*e*) Neigh

49. (*a*) Gobi (*b*) Thar
(*c*) Arabian (*d*) Indian
(*e*) Sahara

50. (*a*) M.F. Hussain (*b*) Leonardo da Vinci
(*c*) Birju Maharaj (*d*) Picasso
(*e*) Satish Gujral

51. (*a*) Franc (*b*) Hoity
(*c*) Pound (*d*) Dinar
(*e*) Zloty

52. (*a*) Oblivious (*b*) Colossal
(*c*) Gigantic (*d*) Stupendous
(*e*) Enormous

53. (*a*) Acme (*b*) Pack
(*c*) Zenith (*d*) Summit
(*e*) Crest

54. (*a*) Ozone (*b*) Oxygen
(*c*) Zone (*d*) Helium
(*e*) Hydrogen

55. (*a*) Amsterdam (*b*) Europe
(*c*) Antarctica (*d*) Australia
(*e*) America

56. (*a*) Palace (*b*) Residence
(*c*) Portico (*d*) Villa
(*e*) Bunglow

57. (*a*) Tie (*b*) Pant
(*c*) Shirt (*d*) Umbrella
(*e*) Socks

58. (*a*) Rose (*b*) Pink
(*c*) Red (*d*) Maroon
(*e*) Crimson

59. (*a*) Strength (*b*) Sinew
(*c*) Muscle (*d*) Vagrant
(*e*) Might

60. (*a*) Stag (*b*) Cock
(*c*) Mare (*d*) Horse
(*e*) Rooster

61. (*a*) Myopia (*b*) Cataract
(*c*) Glaucoma (*d*) Conjunctivitis
(*e*) Spondylitis

62. (*a*) Friend (*b*) Mother
(*c*) Brother (*d*) Sister
(*e*) Father

63. (*a*) Grandmother (*b*) Brother
(*c*) Aunt (*d*) Sister-in-law
(*e*) Niece

64. (*a*) Prism (*b*) Hexagon
(*c*) Cone (*d*) Cylinder
(*e*) Cube

65. (*a*) Chemistry (*b*) Geography
(*c*) Subject (*d*) Literature
(*e*) Architecture

66. (*a*) Pencil (*b*) Brush
(*c*) Crayon (*d*) Pen
(*e*) Club

67. (*a*) Nilgiri Hills (*b*) Aravalli Hills
(*c*) Satpura Hills (*d*) Mole Hills
(*e*) Shivalik Hills

68. (*a*) Uncle (*b*) Aunt
(*c*) Mother (*d*) Nephew
(*e*) Niece

69. (*a*) Krishna (*b*) Ganga
(*c*) Beas (*d*) Rawi
(*e*) Sind

70. (*a*) Area (*b*) Height
(*c*) Length (*d*) Breadth
(*e*) Width

71. (*a*) Actor (*b*) Performer
(*c*) Hero (*d*) Artist
(*e*) Director

72. (*a*) Lead (*b*) Marble
(*c*) Ink (*d*) Chalk
(*e*) Crayon

73. (*a*) Look (*b*) Scan
(*c*) View (*d*) Wink
(*e*) See

74. (a) Perfect (b) Interrogative
(c) Present (d) Future
(e) Past

75. (a) Chisel (b) Nail
(c) Axe (d) Scalpel
(e) Hammer

76. (a) Cockroach (b) Fly
(c) Termite (d) Insects
(e) Spider

77. (a) Sulphur (b) Phosphorus
(c) Lead (d) Carbon
(e) Silicon

78. (a) Duck (b) Parrot
(c) Crow (d) Pigeon
(e) Mynah

79. (a) Out (b) Boy
(c) Cow (d) Bow
(e) Duel

80. (a) Here (b) Near
(c) Where (d) There
(e) Nowhere

81. (a) Looks (b) Beauty
(c) Cuteness (d) Character
(e) Graceful

82. (a) Intimacy (b) Attachment
(c) Enmity (d) Friendship
(e) Closeness

83. (a) Holiday
(b) Good Friday
(c) Independence day
(d) Republic day
(e) Christmas

84. (a) Sun (b) Milky way
(c) Moon (d) Earth
(e) Venus

85. (a) Inch (b) Foot
(c) Yard (d) Quart
(e) Meter

86. (a) Mustard oil (b) Cowdung
(c) Petrol (d) Furnace
(e) Coal

87. (a) Zeal (b) Seal
(c) Kneal (d) Meal
(e) Deal

88. (a) July (b) September
(c) October (d) November
(e) December

89. (a) Mature (b) Labour
(c) Digest (d) Ripen
(e) Final

90. (a) Copper (b) Gold
(c) Silver (d) Steel
(e) Radium

91. (a) Apple (b) Mango
(c) Potato (d) Orange
(e) Cherry

92. (a) Guava (b) Apple
(c) Pink (d) Pear
(e) Mango

93. (a) Square (b) Triangle
(c) Cube (d) Rectangle
(e) Circle

94. (a) Door (b) Gate
(c) Table (d) Window
(e) Ventilator

95. (a) Lion (b) Panther
(c) Tiger (d) Wolf
(e) Leopard

96. (a) Poult (b) Pigeon
(c) Owl (d) Sparrow
(e) Chicken

97. (a) Compass (b) Needle
(c) Direction (d) Magnet
(e) Gimbal

98. (a) Graft (b) Branch
(c) Thorn (d) Tumour
(e) Bud

99. (a) Spade (b) Mace
(c) Cinnamon (d) Cassia
(e) Nutmeg

100. (a) Axe (b) Lean
(c) Scissors (d) Shovel
(e) Saw

101. (a) Currant (b) Almond
(c) Tamarind (d) Cashewnut
(e) Chestnut

102. (a) Carrot (b) Clarion
(c) Pear (d) Papaya
(e) Orange

103. (a) Ring (b) Bangle
(c) Chain (d) Cloves
(e) Opal

104. (a) Bronze (b) Silver
(c) Quail (d) Copper
(e) Zink

105. (*a*) Mule (*b*) Drake (*c*) Pony (*d*) Spaniel (*e*) Panther

106. (*a*) Ostrich (*b*) Swan (*c*) Crane (*d*) Parrot (*e*) Ewe

107. (*a*) Leech (*b*) Spider (*c*) Falcon (*d*) Locust (*e*) Cricket

108. (*a*) Hind (*b*) Chamois (*c*) Lamb (*d*) Turtle (*e*) Hyena

109. (*a*) Attic (*b*) Plough (*c*) Tile (*d*) Shed (*e*) Cupola

110. (*a*) Carder (*b*) Golfer (*c*) Antimony (*d*) Weaver (*e*) Baker

111. (*a*) Clarion (*b*) Whistle (*c*) Flute (*d*) Piano (*e*) Clarinet

112. (*a*) Spade (*b*) Pestle (*c*) Shovel (*d*) Hammer (*e*) Adze

113. (*a*) Pillow (*b*) Bedsheet (*c*) Blanket (*d*) Mirror (*e*) Quilt

114. (*a*) Aunt (*b*) Grandmother (*c*) Niece (*d*) Maternal Grandmother (*e*) Nephew

115. (*a*) Dumb (*b*) Lame (*c*) Blind (*d*) Sinus (*e*) Dwarf

116. (*a*) Ear (*b*) Lung (*c*) Kidney (*d*) Tongue (*e*) Intestine

117. (*a*) Finger (*b*) Hand (*c*) Toe (*d*) Thumb (*e*) Arm

118. (*a*) Nose (*b*) Eye (*c*) Lip (*d*) Cheek (*e*) Sole

119. (*a*) Beef (*b*) Mutton (*c*) Venison (*d*) Whey (*e*) Pork

120. (*a*) Banyan (*b*) Myrtle (*c*) Acacia (*d*) Teak (*e*) Pine

121. (*a*) Wheat (*b*) Rice (*c*) Pulse (*d*) Maize (*e*) Pollen

122. (*a*) Onion (*b*) Cabbage (*c*) Brinjal (*d*) Pear (*e*) Bean

123. (*a*) Magnolia (*b*) Beet (*c*) Balsam (*d*) Marigold (*e*) Daisy

124. (*a*) Curd (*b*) Butter (*c*) Cheese (*d*) Cream (*e*) Molasses

125. (*a*) Table (*b*) Chair (*c*) Stool (*d*) Cot (*e*) Pillow

126. (*a*) Shirt (*b*) Stocking (*c*) Tie (*d*) Scarf (*e*) Cap

127. (*a*) Ring (*b*) Watch (*c*) Bangle (*d*) Armlet (*e*) Tiara

128. (*a*) Car (*b*) Train (*c*) Bus (*d*) Scooter (*e*) Ship

129. (*a*) Snail (*b*) Scorpion (*c*) Tadpole (*d*) Fish (*e*) Crocodile

130. (*a*) Horse (*b*) Cow (*c*) Donkey (*d*) Pig (*e*) Turkey

131. (*a*) Swim (*b*) Run (*c*) Sit (*d*) Slide (*e*) Fly

132. (*a*) April (*b*) May (*c*) March (*d*) July (*e*) January

133. (*a*) Volume (*b*) Roasting (*c*) Cooking (*d*) Boiling (*e*) Frying

134. (*a*) Picture (*b*) Poster (*c*) Photograph (*d*) Scenery (*e*) Painting

135. (*a*) Dictionary (*b*) Novel (*c*) Thesis (*d*) Magazine

(e) Periodical

136. (a) Cigarette (b) Tobacco (c) Pipe (d) Bidi (e) Cigar

137. (a) Jaipur (b) Mumbai (c) Lucknow (d) Patna (e) Tripura

138. (a) Boa (b) Cobra (c) Firefly (d) Wall-lizard (e) Chameleon

139. (a) Kite (b) Vulture (c) Hawk (d) Bat (e) Duck

140. (a) Panther (b) Wolf (c) Lion (d) Hyena (e) Buffalo

141. (a) Coriander (b) Cubeb (c) Chilli (d) Garlic (e) Birch

142. (a) Crowd (b) Swarm (c) Flock (d) Team (e) Herd

143. (a) Nausea (b) Coryza (c) Itches (d) Typhus (e) Pine

144. (a) Thigh (b) Chest (c) Limb (d) Palm (e) Stud

145. (a) Cauldron (b) Spoon (c) Sieve (d) Ladle (e) Wrist

146. (a) Tea (b) Coffee (c) Whisky (d) Lemonade (e) Milk

147. (a) Tool (b) Rule (c) Cool (d) Pool (e) Fool

148. (a) Trousers (b) Ribbon (c) Shorts (d) Skirts (e) Pantaloon

149. (a) Yesterday (b) Thursday (c) Monday (d) Sunday (e) Friday

150. (a) Hawaii (b) Lakshadweep (c) Paris (d) Andaman & Nicobar (e) Java

EXPLANATORY ANSWERS

1. (c) : All others are types of colour.

2. (c) : Canoe is a boat. Others are resting places of birds/animals.

3. (e) : All others are sense organs.

4. (b) : All others are planets.

5. (b) : All others are expressions of joy

6. (a) : All others are geometrical figures.

7. (b) : All others are solid metals.

8. (c) : All others are flying objects. Radar traces the objects in sky.

9. (e) : All others are joints in human body.

10. (d) : All others are nature-bound. Only war is man-made.

11. (c) : All others are young ones of animals.

12. (a) : All others are crawling animals.

13. (b) : All others are types of vegetation.

14. (e) : All others are professions, but only Diver's profession comprises of diving under water.

15. (d) : All other terms are related with activities of a horse.

16. (b) : All other words have the same meaning.

17. (a) : All others are indoor games.

18. (c) : All others are instructors. Pupil learns from the instructor.

19. (a) : All others are running forms of water.

20. (a) : All others are forms of taxes.

21. (a) : All others are parts of tree which are above the ground.

22. (b) : All are capitals of single states but Chandigarh is the capital of two states.

23. (b) : All others have the same meaning.

24. (a) : All others are underground vegetables.

25. (d) : All others are means of transport.

26. (e) : All others words are related to sea.

27. (d) : All others are legal professionals.

28. (c) : Only Kiwi is a flightless bird.

29. (a) : Only arrow needs a bow. Others can be used by hand.

30. (a) : All others are branches of mathematics.

31. ***(c)*** **:** All others refer to people from particular country.
32. ***(b)*** **:** All other months have 31 days.
33. ***(e)*** **:** All others are players.
34. ***(b)*** **:** All other words have the same meaning.
35. ***(d)*** **:** Only Lucknow is a capital city.
36. ***(d)*** **:** All other words refer to modes of attachment or liking.
37. ***(c)*** **:** All others are synonyms of greedy.
38. ***(e)*** **:** All others are four kinds of cards in the pack.
39. ***(e)*** **:** All other words convey permission to do something.
40. ***(b)*** **:** All other objects are made of wood.
41. ***(c)*** **:** All other words mean the same.
42. ***(b)*** **:** All others are preparations from milk.
43. ***(c)*** **:** All others are two in number in the human body.
44. ***(c)*** **:** All others are two in number in human body.
45. ***(d)*** **:** All others are used for shooting.
46. ***(d)*** **:** All others are tringed instruments.
47. ***(c)*** **:** All others are outdoor games.
48. ***(d)*** **:** All other words have rhyming end. Pronunciation of 'toy' is different.
49. ***(d)*** **:** All others are deserts.
50. ***(c)*** **:** All others are artists (painting).
51. ***(b)*** **:** All others are currencies.
52. ***(a)*** **:** All other words refer to degree of huge or big object.
53. ***(b)*** **:** All other words are expressions of the topmost position.
54. ***(c)*** **:** All others are gases.
55. ***(a)*** **:** All others are continents.
56. ***(c)*** **:** All others are used to identify the type of houses.
57. ***(d)*** **:** All others are garments.
58. ***(a)*** **:** All others are shades of red.
59. ***(d)*** **:** All other words have the same meaning.
60. ***(c)*** **:** All others are male animals.
61. ***(e)*** **:** All others are diseases of the eye.
62. ***(a)*** **:** All others are relations of the blood—they are members of family.
63. ***(b)*** **:** All others are female relatives.
64. ***(b)*** **:** All others are solid geometric figures.
65. ***(c)*** **:** All others are subjects of study.
66. ***(e)*** **:** All others are used for writing or painting.
67. ***(d)*** **:** All other hills have natural geographic identities.
68. ***(c)*** **:** Only mother is a direct relation. All others are secondary relations.
69. ***(a)*** **:** All others are north Indian rivers.
70. ***(a)*** **:** All others are measurements used to calculate the area.
71. ***(e)*** **:** Director directs the actions of the other four.
72. ***(b)*** **:** All other materials are used for writing.
73. ***(d)*** **:** Wink is a momentary action of the eye.
74. ***(b)*** **:** All others are grammatical tenses.
75. ***(b)*** **:** All others are tools.
76. ***(d)*** **:** All others are types of insects.
77. ***(c)*** **:** All others are non-metallic elements.
78. ***(a)*** **:** All others cannot swim.
79. ***(a)*** **:** All others are nouns, out is an adverb.
80. ***(c)*** **:** 'Where' is an interrogative word.
81. ***(d)*** **:** All others are appearances.
82. ***(c)*** **:** All others are indicative of positive feelings
83. ***(a)*** **:** All others are Gazetted Holidays.
84. ***(b)*** **:** Milky way is a galaxy of stars. All others are single identities.
85. ***(d)*** **:** All others are used to measure ground distance, quart is used to measure liquids.
86. ***(d)*** **:** All others are used as fuel.
87. ***(c)*** **:** All other words are made of four letters with 'ea' in the middle.
88. ***(a)*** **:** All other months have the same ending.
89. ***(b)*** **:** All other words indicate the last stage of any activity or process.
90. ***(d)*** **:** All others are metallic elements.
91. ***(c)*** **:** All others are fruits.
92. ***(c)*** **:** All others are fruits. Pink is colour.
93. ***(c)*** **:** All others are geometrical figures. Cube is an object.
94. ***(c)*** **:** Table is a furniture. All others are parts of a house supported by hinges.
95. ***(d)*** **:** All others are large cats.
96. ***(c)*** **:** Owl is a night bird.
97. ***(c)*** **:** All others are objects.
98. ***(d)*** **:** All others are found on a tree, tumour is a swelling in a body.
99. ***(a)*** **:** Spade is a tool. All others have seasoning properties.
100. ***(b)*** **:** All others are tools.

101. *(c)* : All others are dry fruits.
102. *(b)* : All others are edible items. Clarion is an instrument.
103. *(d)* : All others are jewellery items.
104. *(c)* : All others are metallic elements.
105. *(b)* : All others are animals.
106. *(e)* : All others are birds.
107. *(c)* : Falcon is a bird. All others can hop/crawl.
108. *(d)* : All other animals can gallop and run fast.
109. *(b)* : All other terms are related with a house. Plough is used in fields.
110. *(c)* : All other words are ending with 'er'.
111. *(d)* : All others are played by passing wind through the lips. Piano is played by hands.
112. *(b)* : All others are tools. Pestle is an instrument.
113. *(d)* : All others are items of furnishings.
114. *(e)* : All others are female genders.
115. *(d)* : All others are handicaps or deformities. Sinus is a disease.
116. *(a)* : All others are internal organs.
117. *(c)* : All others are parts of upper arm. Toe is a part of lower arm.
118. *(e)* : All others are visible parts of the face. Sole is the part under the feet.
119. *(d)* : All others are forms of meat. Whey is the watery part of milk separated from curd.
120. *(b)* : All others are trees. Myrtle is a shrub.
121. *(e)* : All others are foodgrains. Pollen is a fine yellow powder found on flowers.
122. *(d)* : All others are vegetables.
123. *(b)* : All others are flowers.
124. *(e)* : All others are milk products. Molasses is obtained from sugar.
125. *(e)* : All others are types of furniture.
126. *(b)* : All others are items of clothing. Stocking here means 'a hoard of savings'.
127. *(e)* : All others are worn on parts of hand. Tiara is worn on the head.
128. *(e)* : All other means of transportation are driven on land. Ship sails on water.
129. *(c)* : Only tadpole is the young one (of a frog).
130. *(e)* : All others are animals who give birth to their young ones. Only turkey lays eggs.
131. *(c)* : All other verbs indicate movement from one place to another. Sitting is confined to a particular place.
132. *(a)* : There are 31 days in all other months.
133. *(a)* : All other terms are used while/for preparing various food items.
134. *(c)* : All other items are hung on a wall. Photograph is kept in an album.
135. *(a)* : A dictionary contains only words. All others contain sentences and paragraphs.
136. *(b)* : All others are means of smoking tobacco.
137. *(e)* : All others are capital cities.
138. *(c)* : All others are reptiles.
139. *(e)* : All others can fly.
140. *(e)* : All others are wild animals.
141. *(e)* : All others are used for flavouring. Birch is a forest-tree.
142. *(d)* : All the terms specify groups but in 'Team' the number of members is calculated.
143. *(e)* : All others are ailments.
144. *(e)* : All others are parts of the body.
145. *(e)* : All others are kitchen utensils.
146. *(c)* : Whisky is an alcoholic drink.
147. *(b)* : All other words end with 'ool'
148. *(b)* : All others are worn on the waist. Ribbon is tied to the hair.
149. *(a)* : All others are weekdays.
150. *(c)* : All others are islands.

PART - II

ODD ONE OUT—LETTERS

In this classification of letters, four groups of letters or a series of letters is given as options. One has to select the option as answer which does not share the commonness of the others.

SOLVED EXAMPLES

Directions : *Find the odd one out in the following letters :*

1. (*a*) NOP (*b*) RTU (*c*) JKL (*d*) EFG

Ans. (*b*) : In each group the letters are consecutive. In this option the first two letters jump one letter (S) inbetween.

2. (*a*) RUX (*b*) CFI (*c*) BDG (*d*) FIL

Ans. (*c*) : In each group, the difference between the letters is same. In this option B and D jump one letter and D and G jump two letters.

EXERCISE

Directions : *Three of the following four in each question are alike in a certain way and so form a group. Select the group of letters that does not belong to that group.*

1. (*a*) ACE (*b*) LOR (*c*) GIK (*d*) VXZ
2. (*a*) TSR (*b*) LKJ (*c*) PQO (*d*) HGF
3. (*a*) EF LM (*b*) KJ SR (*c*) XW HG (*d*) ED YX
4. (*a*) JOPK (*b*) BOPC (*c*) QOPR (*d*) TOPS
5. (*a*) DfH (*b*) MoQ (*c*) UwY (*d*) InO
6. (*a*) JKkL (*b*) OPpQ (*c*) DEEf (*d*) VWwX
7. (*a*) BdfH (*b*) FHJL (*c*) RTvX (*d*) uVwX
8. (*a*) DFHEG (*b*) TWXUV (*c*) OQSPR (*d*) JLNKM
9. (*a*) FEUV (*b*) DCXW (*c*) BAZY (*d*) HGTS
10. (*a*) UTSR (*b*) XYZW (*c*) ONML (*d*) IHGF
11. (*a*) MKGA (*b*) PNID (*c*) RPLF (*d*) VTPJ
12. (*a*) ABJNM (*b*) QRTUZ (*c*) IXYOQ (*d*) WGFPO
13. (*a*) BFJQ (*b*) RUZG (*c*) GJOV (*d*) ILQX
14. (*a*) CS (*b*) OU (*c*) EV (*d*) QO
15. (*a*) EFGH (*b*) IRST (*c*) ULMN (*d*) JKLO
16. (*a*) LNP (*b*) ECA (*c*) JLN (*d*) RTV
17. (*a*) SU (*b*) BD (*c*) PN (*d*) WY
18. (*a*) KI (*b*) SQ (*c*) CA (*d*) VX
19. (*a*) SC (*b*) FT (*c*) MK (*d*) HV
20. (*a*) END (*b*) PUT (*c*) ARM (*d*) OWL
21. (*a*) CFIL (*b*) ABCD (*c*) ACDF (*d*) EFGH
22. (*a*) SPQR (*b*) MKLN (*c*) WUVX (*d*) FDEG

23. (a) HK (b) DG (c) NK (d) UX
24. (a) MLKA (b) HGFA (c) RQPA (d) STUA
25. (a) KNOS (b) QTUY (c) DFGJ (d) BEFJ
26. (a) GEC (b) PRT (c) TVX (d) SUW
27. (a) USNID (b) UPKEA (c) OMIDB (d) VTOJE
28. (a) DF (b) PR (c) FG (d) MQ
29. (a) MLKI (b) PMOL (c) ZWYV (d) TQSP
30. (a) CDFIM (b) ABDGK (c) EFGIK (d) BCEHL
31. (a) USAGE (b) UKASE (c) URINE (d) USUAL
32. (a) TVRG (b) CSRS (c) NPAD (d) CPNT
33. (a) PCDW (b) NTFV (c) QNIS (d) DRKY
34. (a) FKP (b) LPU (c) HMR (d) DIN
35. (a) BAD (b) OFF (c) INN (d) SIS
36. (a) RiGP (b) MoRH (c) FBlP (d) DtJA
37. (a) PQRN (b) GHIS (c) XYZQ (d) STVW
38. (a) ErIc (b) nOtE (c) rUIn (d) TieD
39. (a) FARM (b) TRAY (c) CARD (d) WARN
40. (a) DCBA (b) SRQP (c) IHGF (d) NOPQ
41. (a) TBVD (b) JOKQ (c) AXCZ (d) FRHT
42. (a) QRS (b) CDE (c) KMN (d) GHI
43. (a) SYZ (b) MRS (c) DJK (d) QWX
44. (a) BROW (b) PLAN (c) GRIN (d) THEN
45. (a) ERPT (b) DUXI (c) PAOC (d) XENO
46. (a) PQNO (b) GHXY (c) SUCE (d) UVJK
47. (a) TVL (b) FEH (c) KCW (d) ZNI
48. (a) NCDT (b) BRSF (c) ZGHV (d) AQDM
49. (a) RTWZ (b) GJMP (c) CEHO (d) TWYZ
50. (a) QWNB (b) KCNL (c) EOAF (d) RUIS

EXPLANATORY ANSWERS

1. (b) : The sequence in each group is +2. Only option B has sequence in +3, *i.e.,*

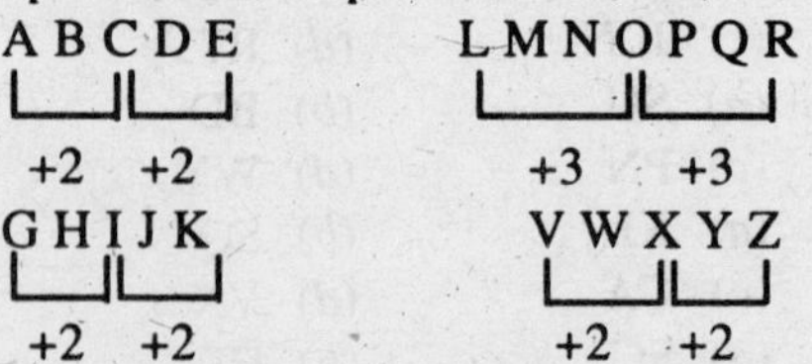

2. (c) : The sequence of alphabet in each group is in reverse order. Only option C has sequence in disturbed order.

3. (a) : Two consecutive alphabet in each group are in reverse sequence (–1), *i.e.,*

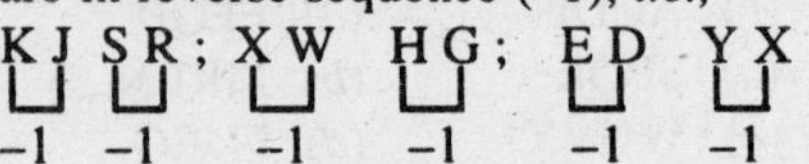

Only in option (a) the sequence is in natural order (+1), *i.e.,*

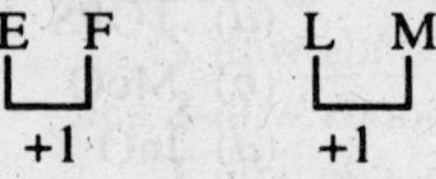

4. (d) : In each group, letters 'OP' are common. The two corner alphabet are in natural order (+1); *i.e.,*

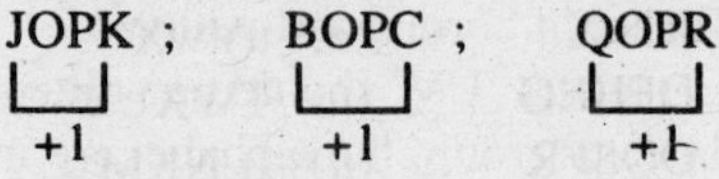

Only in option (d) they are in reverse order (–1); *i.e.,*

5. (d) : In other groups, only the alphabet in the centre is of lower case. In this option letter 'L' on the left is also in lower case.

6. (c) : In other groups, the third letter which is a repeat of the second alphabet is in lower case.

7. (d) : In each group, the sequence of the alphabet, irrespective of the case, is +2; *i.e.*,

B D f H ; F H J L ; R T v X

+2 +2 +2   +2 +2+2   +2 +2 +2

Only in option (d) the sequence is in natural order (+1), *i.e.*,

u V w X

+1 +1 +1

8. (b) : In each group; the alphabet at positions-first, fourth, second, fifth and third, form a natural sequence.

In option (b), the alphabet at positions first, fourth, fifth, second and third, form the natural sequence.

9. (a) : In each group, two alphabets in the corner and two alphabets in the centre correspond to their reverse order positioned alphabet. *i.e.*,

natural order → A B C D E F G H I J K L M
reverse order → Z Y X W V U T S R Q P O N
natural order → N O P Q R S T U V W X Y Z
reverse order → M L K J I H G F E D C B A

As such—

D corresponds with W and
C corresponds with X.
B corresponds with Y and
A corresponds with Z.
H corresponds with S and
G corresponds with T.

Similarly,

F should correspond with U and
E should correspond with V;
i.e. letters 'UV' should be written as 'VU'

10. (b) : In each group, the alphabet are in reverse order.

In option (b), the order is disturbed.

11. (b) : The sequence of alphabet in each group follows the reverse pattern of −2, −4, −6, *i.e.*,

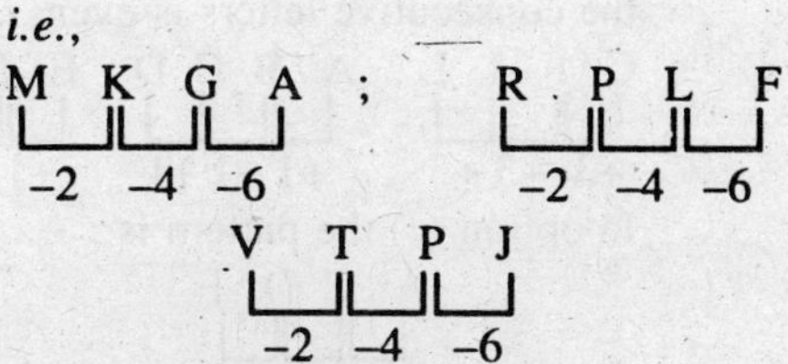

In option (b), the pattern is

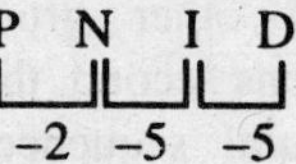

The correct pattern should be→P N J D

−2 −4 −6

12. (c) : In each group at least two pairs of alphabet are in sequence, *i.e.*,

In option (c) only one pair is in sequence

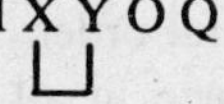

13. (a) : The sequence of alphabet in each group follows the natural pattern of +3, +5, +7, *i.e.*,

Note : The alphabetical series restarts from letter 'A' on reaching letter 'Z'.

In option (a), the pattern is

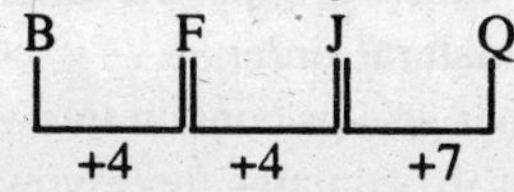

14. (c) : Only this group has letters made by straight lines.

15. (d) : In all other groups the first letter is a vowel followed by three consecutive letters.

16. (b) : In all other groups the alternate letters are in natural alphabet order.

17. (c) : In all other groups the alternate letters are in natural alphabet order.

18. (d) : In all other groups the alternate letters are in reverse alphabet order.

19. (a) : Only this group has letters made by curved lines.

20. (b) : In all other groups the first letter is a vowel.

21. (c) : In all other groups the difference between

the consecutive letters is even, *i.e.*,

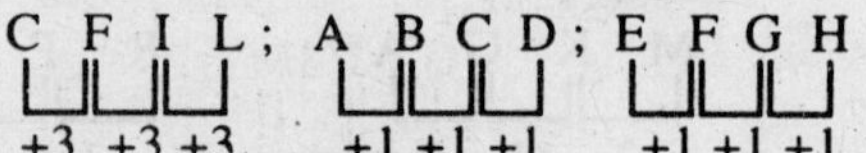

In option (c) the pattern is :

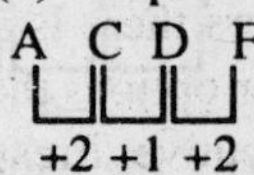

22. *(a)* : In all other groups the alphabet at positions second, third, first and last form a natural sequence. In option (a), the alphabet at positions second, third, fourth and first form the natural sequence.

23. *(c)* : In all other groups the letters skip two letters in between and are in natural order. In option (c) they are in reverse order.

24. *(d)* : In all other groups the first three letters are in reverse order followed by A at the last position. In option (d) the three letters are in natural order.

25. *(c)* : The sequence in all other groups is +3, +1, +4, *i.e.*,

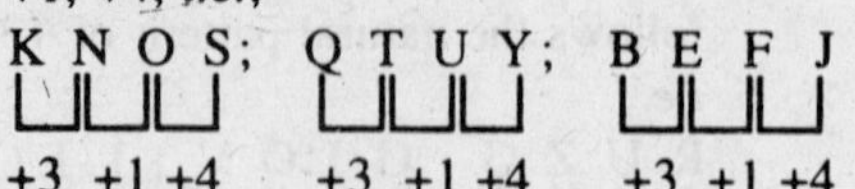

In option (c) the sequence is disturbed, *i.e.*,

26. *(a)* : In all other groups the alternate letters are in natural order.

27. *(b)* : All other groups contain two vowels each. Option (b) contains three vowels.

28. *(c)* : Only this option has two consecutive letters.

29. *(a)* : Only this option has three consecutive letters which are in reverse order 'MLK'.

30. *(c)* : In all other groups the sequence is +1, +2, +3, +4, *i.e.*,

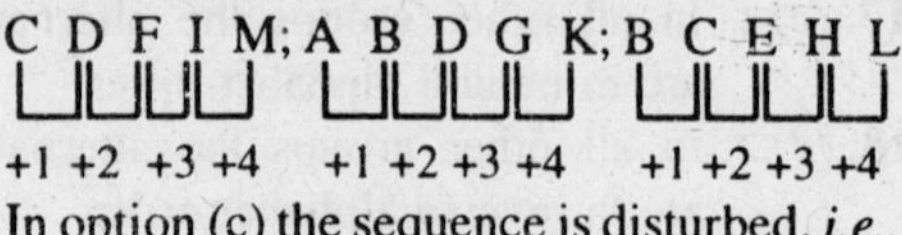

In option (c) the sequence is disturbed, *i.e.*,

31. *(d)* : In all other options the last letter is 'E'.

32. *(b)* : Only this option has one letter (S) which is repeated.

33. *(c)* : Only this option has a vowel (I).

34. *(b)* : The sequence in all other groups is +5, *i.e.*,

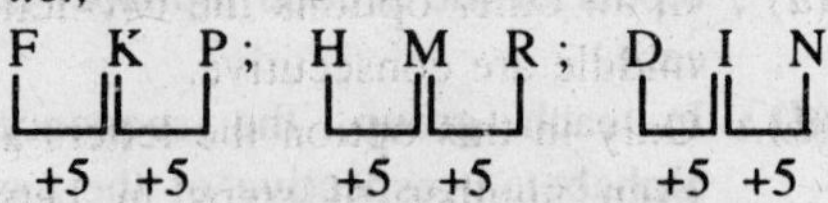

The sequence in option (b) is :

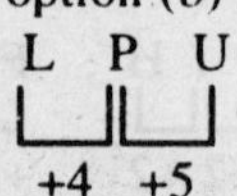

35. *(a)* : In all other groups one alphabet is repeated.

36. *(c)* : In all other groups the second letter is in small case.

37. *(d)* : In all other groups the first three letters are consecutive.

38. *(d)* : Only in this group the vowels are in small case.

39. *(b)* : In all other groups the two letters in the middle are 'AR'. In option (b) they are 'RA'.

40. *(d)* : In all other groups the sequence of letters is in reverse order.

41. *(b)* : In all other groups the first and second letters are moved two steps forward to get the third and fourth letters respectively, *i.e.*,

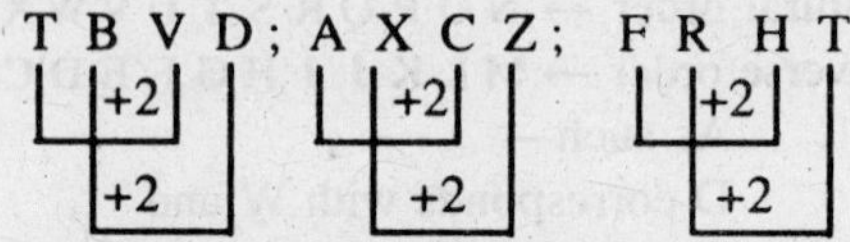

In option (b) the sequence is :

42. *(c)* : In all other groups the sequence of letters is in continuous natural order.

43. *(b)* : In all other groups the first and second letters drop five letters in between. In this option only four letters are dropped.

44. *(a)* : Only this option is not ending with letter 'N'.

45. *(a)* : In all other groups there are two vowels. In this option there is only one.

46. *(c)* : In all other options the first two letters and the last two letters are consecutive.

47. *(c)* : Only this option has one letter made by curved line.

48. *(d)* : In all other options the two letters in the middle are consecutive.

49. *(b)* : Only in this option the letters are moved even number of steps in between two letters, *i.e.*,

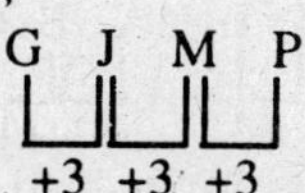

In all others there is no uniformity.

50. *(a)* : In all other options the first and last letters are consecutive, irrespective of the letters in the middle.

PART - III

ODD ONE OUT—NUMBERS

In this type of classification, different numbers are given as options. These numbers have some commonness; except one which is the odd one. One has to identify the similarity and then strike the odd one out as answer option. The number can be odd/even/consecutive, prime numbers, multiple of some number, single, square or cubes of different numbers, plus/minus of some other number or combinations of any mathematical calculation.

SOLVED EXAMPLES

Directions : *Find the odd number from the given options.*

1. (*a*) 62 (*b*) 121 (*c*) 36 (*d*) 256

Ans. (*a*) : The other numbers are squares of :
11, (= 121), 6 (= 36) and 16 (= 256)

2. (*a*) 27 (*b*) 132 (*c*) 93 (*d*) 154

Ans. (*d*) : All other numbers are divisible by 3.

EXERCISE

Directions : *In each of the following questions, there are four options. Three numbers, in these options, are alike in certain manner. Only one number does not fit in. Choose the one which is different from the rest.*

1. (*a*) 1948 (*b*) 2401 (*c*) 966 (*d*) 1449

2. (*a*) 182 (*b*) 169 (*c*) 130 (*d*) 158

3. (*a*) 129 (*b*) 130 (*c*) 131 (*d*) 132

4. (*a*) 3215 (*b*) 9309 (*c*) 4721 (*d*) 2850

5. (*a*) 1776 (*b*) 2364 (*c*) 1976 (*d*) 3776

6. (*a*) 64 (*b*) 34 (*c*) 16 (*d*) 36

7. (*a*) 24 (*b*) 90 (*c*) 54 (*d*) 36

8. (*a*) 7658 (*b*) 1234 (*c*) 9876 (*d*) 6543

9. (*a*) 3 (*b*) 9 (*c*) 5 (*d*) 7

10. (*a*) 6450 (*b*) 1776 (*c*) 2392 (*d*) 3815

11. (*a*) 24 (*b*) 48 (*c*) 42 (*d*) 12

12. (*a*) 616 (*b*) 252 (*c*) 311 (*d*) 707

13. (*a*) 18 (*b*) 12 (*c*) 30 (*d*) 20

14. (*a*) 3730 (*b*) 6820 (*c*) 5568 (*d*) 4604

15. (*a*) 2587 (*b*) 7628 (*c*) 8726 (*d*) 2867

16. (*a*) 63 (*b*) 29 (*c*) 27 (*d*) 25

17. (*a*) 23 (*b*) 37 (*c*) 21 (*d*) 31

18. (*a*) 18 (*b*) 9 (*c*) 21 (*d*) 7

19. (*a*) 9875432 (*b*) 98765 (*c*) 98756 (*d*) 9876543

20. (*a*) 602 (*b*) 431 (*c*) 530 (*d*) 813

21. (*a*) 4 (*b*) 6 (*c*) 7 (*d*) 10

22. (*a*) 3456 (*b*) 2345 (*c*) 5467 (*d*) 5678

23. (*a*) 10 (*b*) 11 (*c*) 15 (*d*) 16

24. (*a*) 336 (*b*) 213 (*c*) 436 (*d*) 819

25. (*a*) 258 (*b*) 326 (*c*) 224 (*d*) 339

26. (*a*) 28751 (*b*) 52638 (*c*) 85362 (*d*) 63852

27. (*a*) 73 (*b*) 43 (*c*) 63 (*d*) 83

28. (*a*) 64 (*b*) 27 (*c*) 125 (*d*) 9

29. (*a*) 63 (*b*) 49 (*c*) 21 (*d*) 81

30. (*a*) 74930 (*b*) 89435 (*c*) 66535 (*d*) 32116

31. (*a*) 7642 (*b*) 9325 (*c*) 5840 (*d*) 6318

32. (*a*) 565 (*b*) 315 (*c*) 275 (*d*) 435

33. (*a*) 28 (*b*) 65 (*c*) 117 (*d*) 91

34. (*a*) 625 (*b*) 225 (*c*) 122 (*d*) 256

35. (*a*) 372164 (*b*) 319416 (*c*) 387315 (*d*) 318963

36. (*a*) 2838 (*b*) 7911 (*c*) 6055 (*d*) 8344

37. (*a*) 5243 (*b*) 9251 (*c*) 4256 (*d*) 3257

38. (*a*) 102 (*b*) 143 (*c*) 51 (*d*) 136

39. (*a*) 2948 (*b*) 2738 (*c*) 4289 (*d*) 9824

40. (*a*) 161 (*b*) 105 (*c*) 103 (*d*) 133

41. (*a*) 3 (*b*) 7 (*c*) 5 (*d*) 9

42. (*a*) 95 (*b*) 57 (*c*) 84 (*d*) 38

43. (*a*) 111 (*b*) 300 (*c*) 201 (*d*) 100

44. (*a*) 54 (*b*) 32 (*c*) 24 (*d*) 48

45. (*a*) 417 (*b*) 255 (*c*) 183 (*d*) 241

46. (*a*) 15 (*b*) 17 (*c*) 23 (*d*) 29

47. (*a*) 2553 (*b*) 1224 (*c*) 7992 (*d*) 3885

48. (*a*) 2762 (*b*) 9489 (*c*) 7651 (*d*) 4374

49. (*a*) 3223 (*b*) 4554 (*c*) 6116 (*d*) 9887

50. (*a*) 92 (*b*) 46 (*c*) 24 (*d*) 69

EXPLANATORY ANSWERS

1. (*a*) : Other numbers are divisible by 7.

2. (*d*) : Other numbers are multiples of 13.

3. (*c*) : 131 is a prime number.

4. (*b*) : In other numbers, no digit is repeated.

5. (*b*) : In other numbers the last two digits are same.

6. (*b*) : All other numbers are perfect squares.

7. (*a*) : In other numbers, the sum of both the digits is 9.

8. (*a*) : In others, the digits are consecutive in natural or reverse series.

9. (*b*) : All others are prime numbers.

10. (*d*) : All other numbers are divisible by 2.

11. (*c*) : All other numbers are multiples of 12.

12. (*c*) : In other numbers, the first and last digits are same.

13. (*a*) : The other numbers are $3^2 + 3 = 12$, $5^2 + 5 = 30$, $4^2 + 4 = 20$

14. (*b*) : In all other numbers, two digits are same.

15. (*a*) : Other numbers are made with digits 2, 6, 7 and 8.

16. (*b*) : 29 is a prime number.

17. (*c*) : All other numbers are prime numbers.

18. (*d*) : All other numbers are divisible by 3.

19. (*c*) : In all other numbers the sequence of digits after 987 is in decreasing order.

20. (d) : In all other numbers the total of digits is 8.
21. (c) : All other numbers are even numbers.
22. (c) : In all other numbers the digits are in increasing order.
23. (b) : 11 is a prime number.
24. (c) : In all other numbers the digit on the right is the sum of two digits on the left.
25. (a) : In all other numbers the digit on the right is the product of two digits on the left.
26. (a) : 28751 is an odd number.
27. (c) : All other numbers are prime numbers.
28. (d) : All other numbers are cubes of natural numbers, 9 is a perfect square.
29. (d) : All other numbers are multiples of 7.
30. (d) : All other numbers are divisible by 5.
31. (b) : In all other numbers the two digits on the right are the product of two digits on the left.
32. (a) : In 565, number 5 is repeated.
33. (a) : All other numbers are multiples of 13.
34. (c) : All other numbers are squares of whole numbers, $25^2 = 625$, $15^2 = 225$, $16^2 = 256$.
35. (a) : All other numbers are divisible by 3.
36. (a) : In all other numbers, the last two digits are same.
37. (a) : In all other numbers 25 is in the middle and the sum of two corner numbers is 10.
38. (b) : All other numbers are multiples of 17.
39. (b) : All other numbers have 2, 4, 8 and 9. This option has 7 and 3 instead of 9 and 4.
40. (c) : All other numbers are divisible by 7.
41. (d) : Only 9 is a perfect square, all others are prime numbers.
42. (c) : All other numbers are multiples of 19.
43. (d) : In all other numbers the sum of digits is 3.
44. (b) : All other numbers are multiples of 6.
45. (d) : All other numbers are divisible by 3.
46. (a) : All other numbers are prime numbers.
47. (b) : In all other numbers the sum of two corner digits is equal to the digit in the middle which is repeated.
48. (c) : In all other numbers the digits on the corners is same.
49. (d) : In all other numbers the first two digits are written backwards to get the last two digits.
50. (c) : All other numbers are multiples of 23.

PART - IV

ODD ONE OUT—WORD GROUPS

Classification of group of words, letters or numbers is not much different from single words, letters or numbers. Here one has to observe the type of relation between the two related words and find out the pair which does not follow the relationship pattern of the other groups. The related words can be opposite or identical in meaning or nature, or can vary in their degrees or representation or can be rhyming words.

SOLVED EXAMPLES

Directions : *Which of the following pair is different from the other three?*

1. (*a*) Good - Better (*b*) Tepid - Hot
(*c*) Gain - Profit (*d*) Whisper - Shout

Ans. (*c*) : Other pairs of words are different in degrees of comparison though having the same meaning.

2. (*a*) Scissors - Cloth (*b*) Knife - Bread
(*c*) Axe - Wood (*d*) Hammer - Nail

Ans. (*d*) : Though the relation between the words is right, yet hammer is not used for cutting nails. The other three pairs indicate the instruments on the left used for cutting the object on the right.

EXERCISE

Directions : *In the following questions select the pair which is different from the other three.*

1. (*a*) Chair - Furniture
(*b*) Shirt - Garment
(*c*) Necklace - Jewellery
(*d*) Bogie - Engine

2. (*a*) Crayon - Paper
(*b*) Pencil - Lead
(*c*) Pen - Ink
(*d*) Brush - Paint

3. (*a*) War - Peace
(*b*) Real - Natural
(*c*) Premiere - First
(*d*) Wrath - Anger

4. (*a*) Finger - Thimble
(*b*) Head - Cap
(*c*) Waist - Tiara
(*d*) Foot - Shoe

5. (*a*) Day - Night
(*b*) Clever - Foolish
(*c*) Clear - Blurred
(*d*) Arrive - Come

6. (*a*) Quintal - Gallon
(*b*) Bouquet - Flowers
(*c*) Book - Pages
(*d*) Parliament - Members

7. (*a*) Birds - Chirp
(*b*) Horses - Hum
(*c*) Lions - Roar
(*d*) Snakes - Hiss

8. (*a*) Niece - Nephew
(*b*) Husband - Wife
(*c*) Brother - Sister
(*d*) Father - Mother

9. (*a*) Petrol - Car
(*b*) Oil - Lamp
(*c*) Diesel - Wood
(*d*) Wax - Candle

10. (*a*) Ganga - Narmada
(*b*) Thar - Gobi
(*c*) Stomach - Hands
(*d*) Everest - Mountain

11. (*a*) Medicine - Doctor
(*b*) Flower - Artist
(*c*) Shoes - Cobbler
(*d*) Skin - Dermatologist

12. (*a*) Authority - Sanction
(*b*) Repel - Attract
(*c*) Finicky - Choosy
(*d*) Breath - Entity

13. (*a*) Polo - Rink
(*b*) Golf - Lawn
(*c*) Tennis - Court
(*d*) Chess - Board

14. (*a*) Ecstacy - Fantasy
(*b*) Price - Thrice
(*c*) Crime - Prune
(*d*) Both - Oath

15. (*a*) Army - General
(*b*) College - Principal
(*c*) Ship - Captain
(*d*) Navy - Lieutenant

16. (*a*) Train - Tracks
(*b*) Birds - Fly
(*c*) Aeroplane - Sky
(*d*) Submarine - Sea

17. (*a*) Jelly - Gentle
(*b*) Stone - Hard
(*c*) Fur - Soft
(*d*) Glass - Smooth

18. (*a*) Branch - Tree
(*b*) Minute - Hour
(*c*) Sentence - Paragraph
(*d*) Student - Teacher

19. (*a*) Sum - Total
(*b*) Now - Present
(*c*) Big - Notion
(*d*) Yes - Agree

20. (*a*) Four - Foursome
(*b*) Three - Triplet
(*c*) Two - Double
(*d*) One - Single

21. (*a*) Brahmaputra - River
(*b*) Sahara - Desert
(*c*) Aravalli - Ocean
(*d*) Europe - Continent

22. (*a*) Much - Most
(*b*) Bad - Worse
(*c*) Simple - Simpler
(*d*) Little - Less

23. (*a*) Ripe - Crude
(*b*) Close - Near
(*c*) Warm - Tender
(*d*) Believe - Trust

24. (*a*) Giraffe - Tall
(*b*) Snail - Heavy
(*c*) Jet - Fast
(*d*) Ant - Industrious

25. (*a*) Nine - Twine
(*b*) Fire - Liar
(*c*) Honey - Money
(*d*) Rust - Crest

26. (*a*) Cattle - Beef
(*b*) Swine - Pork
(*c*) Lamb - Veal
(*d*) Dear - Venison

27 (*a*) Rickets - Bone
(*b*) Insomnia - Blood
(*c*) Myopia - Eye
(*d*) Arthritis - Joints

28. (*a*) Eczema - Vitamin A
(*b*) Beriberi - Vitamin B
(*c*) Anemia - Vitamin E
(*d*) Scurvy - Vitamin C

29. (*a*) Marigold - Lady
(*b*) Hammer - Tool
(*c*) Skirt - Garment
(*d*) Lion - Animal

30. (*a*) Ill - Sick
(*b*) Below - Aloft
(*c*) Aloof - Cold
(*d*) Motive - Cause

31. (*a*) Rust - Rest
(*b*) Most - Must
(*c*) Firm - Film
(*d*) Bard - Bird

32. (*a*) Abundant - Dearth
(*b*) Clean - Tidy
(*c*) Lucid - Difficult
(*d*) Hushed - Noisy

33. (*a*) School - Principal
(*b*) Ship - Captain
(*c*) Army - Director
(*d*) Bus - Driver

34. (*a*) Deny - Accept
(*b*) Strength - Might

(*c*) Lend - Borrow
(*d*) Gentle - Harsh

35. (*a*) Cow - Milk
(*b*) Sheep - Wool
(*c*) Bee - Hive
(*d*) Silkworm - Silk

36. (*a*) Purse - Money
(*b*) Jug - Tools
(*c*) Inkpot - Ink
(*d*) Wardrobe - Clothes

37. (*a*) Blind - Eye
(*b*) Deaf - Ear
(*c*) Lame - Leg
(*d*) Dumb - Lip

38. (*a*) Racing - Court
(*b*) Boxing - Arena
(*c*) Acting - Stage
(*d*) Skating - Rink

39. (*a*) Hay - Stick
(*b*) Flower - Bouquet
(*c*) Branch - Tree
(*d*) Stick - Broom

40. (*a*) Why - Because
(*b*) Who - He
(*c*) Where - If
(*d*) When - Now

41. (*a*) Apple - Fruit
(*b*) Rose - Flower
(*c*) Chair - Furniture
(*d*) Occasion - Festival

42. (*a*) Coal - Black
(*b*) Grass - Grey
(*c*) Sky - Blue
(*d*) Ice - White

43. (*a*) Rain - Grain
(*b*) Cope - Crape
(*c*) Each - Teach
(*d*) Lead - Plead

44. (*a*) Hangar - Aeroplane
(*b*) Dock - Ship
(*c*) Kernel - Dog
(*d*) Sty - Pig

45. (*a*) Wood - Product
(*b*) Grapes - Wine
(*c*) Egg - Omlette
(*d*) Yarn - Fabric

46. (*a*) Mart - Tram
(*b*) Spin - Nips
(*c*) Take - Kent
(*d*) Drab - Bard

47. (*a*) Dog - Pup
(*b*) Sheep - Limb
(*c*) Hen - Chicken
(*d*) Horse - Pony

48. (*a*) Spain - Madison
(*b*) Nepal - Kathmandu
(*c*) USA - Washington DC
(*d*) Pakistan - Islamabad

49. (*a*) Aunt - Niece
(*b*) Husband - Wife
(*c*) Father - Son
(*d*) Uncle - Brother

50. (*a*) Surgeon - Scalpel
(*b*) Farmer - Plough
(*c*) Chef - Knife
(*d*) Author - Book

EXPLANATORY ANSWERS

1. *(d)* : Bogie is a part of train which is a type of conveyance. Chair, Shirt and Necklace are types of furniture, garment and jewellery respectively.

2. *(a)* : The medium used for writing with pencil is lead, with pen it is ink and with brush, it is paint. With crayon it should be wax.

3. *(a)* : The pair of words are opposite. Other pairs are synonyms.

4. *(c)* : Tiara is worn on the head.

5. *(d)* : Other words are opposite to each other.

6. *(a)* : In all other groups the first word is the collection of the second.

7. *(b)* : In all other groups the second word is the sound of the first. Horses neigh.

8. *(a)* : The related pairs are first masculine and then feminine. In (a), it is opposite.

9. *(c)* : Petrol is used to run a car, oil to burn a lamp and wax for candle. Diesel and wood have no relation.

10. *(d)* : The related pairs have same identity. (a) has rivers, (b) deserts and (c) parts of body.

In (d), mountain identifies the first word - Everest.

11. *(b)* : Doctor deals with medicine, cobbler with shoes and dermatologist with skin. Person dealing with flowers should be gardener or a horticulturist.

12. *(b)* : The other pairs of words have same meaning. Repel and attract are opposites.

13. *(a)* : The related words are the games and the places where they are played. Polo is played on ground.

14. *(c)* : The other pairs of words are rhyming words.

15. *(d)* : The head of the Navy is Commander.

16. *(b)* : Birds fly in sky as train runs on its tracks, aeroplane flies in sky and submarine runs under sea. Birds are living objects.

17. *(a)* : The second words shows the quality of the first word. Jelly is tender or wobbly.

18. *(d)* : In other groups the first word is a part of the second.

19. *(c)* : The other pairs share the same meaning.

20. *(b)* : Three is thrice or threesome.

21. *(c)* : Aravallis are Mountains.

22. *(a)* : All other words are combinations of positive and comparative degrees of comparisons. Option (a) has a pair of positive and superlative degree of comparison.

23. *(a)* : All other pair of words have the same meaning.

24. *(b)* : In all other pairs the second word is the characteristic feature of the first. Snail should be slow.

25. *(d)* : The other pair of words are rhyming words.

26. *(c)* : In all other pairs the second word is the flesh of the first. Lamb's flesh is mutton.

27. *(b)* : In all other pairs the first word is the disease of the second. Anemia is the disease of the blood.

28. *(a)* : In all other pairs the first word is the disease caused by the deficiency of the second. Eczema is caused by deficiency of Vitamin B.

29. *(a)* : Marigold is a flower.

30. *(b)* : All other pair of words have the same meaning.

31. *(c)* : In all other pair of words only the vowel of the first word is replaced by another vowel to form a new word.

32. *(b)* : The other pair of words are near opposites.

33. *(c)* : Head of the Army is a General.

34. *(b)* : The other pair of words are opposites.

35. *(c)* : In other pair of words the second is obtained from the first. 'Honey' should be in place of 'Hive'.

36. *(b)* : Water is kept in a jug.

37. *(d)* : In all other pairs of words the first is the deformity of the second.

38. *(a)* : Racing is done on the tracks.

39. *(a)* : Hay is a part of 'stack' not 'stick'.

40. *(c)* : In all other pairs the second word is the answer to the first.

41. *(d)* : In all other pairs the first word is a type of the second word.

42. *(b)* : Colour of grass is green.

43. *(b)* : The second word in other groups is formed by prefixing one letter to the first word.

44. *(c)* : Resting place of dog is kennel.

45. *(a)* : In all other pair of words the second is made from the first.

46. *(c)* : In all other pairs the letters of the first word are written backwards to form the second word.

47. *(b)* : Young one of the sheep is lamb.

48. *(a)* : Capital of Spain is Madrid.

49. *(b)* : All other pair of words share the same gender.

50. *(d)* : In all other pair of words the second is a tool used by the first. Author's tool is a pen.

PART - V

ODD ONE OUT—LETTER GROUPS

The group of letters can be in natural or reverse order, jumping letters, repetitive letters, even combination of capital letters, small letters, vowels or consonants.

SOLVED EXAMPLE

1. *Which one of the following pairs is different from the other groups?*

(*a*) ABC - CBA (*b*) JKL - KLJ
(*c*) XYZ - ZYX (*d*) MNO - ONM

Ans. (*b*) : In all other pair of groups, the letters in the second group are the letters of the first group written backwards.

EXERCISE

Directions : *In the following questions, which of the following pair of letters is different from the other three?*

1. (*a*) FGH - HIJ (*b*) PQR - RST
(*c*) MNO - OPQ (*d*) CDE - DEF

2. (*a*) JuM - jUm (*b*) iLo - Ilo
(*c*) PSa - psA (*d*) ZeX - zEx

3. (*a*) NQT - JMP (*b*) CFI - RUX
(*c*) ADG - FGH (*d*) SVY - ORU

4. (*a*) DXD - XDX (*b*) KUK - UKU
(*c*) FHF - EHE (*d*) RSR - SRS

5. (*a*) AYT - BZU (*b*) FNG - EMF
(*c*) RWO - QVN (*d*) HJD - GIC

6. (*a*) POT - TOP (*b*) TAN - ANT
(*c*) BIN - NIB (*d*) DUB - BUD

7. (*a*) LT - HF (*b*) IN - VA
(*c*) ZE - XM (*d*) RB - SC

8. (*a*) MQU - CGK (*b*) BGL - TYD
(*c*) RWB - FKP (*d*) JOT - DIN

9. (*a*) JLN - KMO (*b*) GIK - HJL
(*c*) DFJ - EGI (*d*) OQS - PRT

10. (*a*) URS - UrS (*b*) JPL - JpL
(*c*) PQM - PqM (*d*) MoN - MON

11. (*a*) PQR - HGF (*b*) RST - ONM
(*c*) IJK - CBE (*d*) WXY - FED

12. (*a*) JM - KL (*b*) QP - RS
(*c*) EH - FG (*d*) MP - NO

13. (*a*) AE - OL (*b*) UI - OE
(*c*) IO - UE (*d*) EA - OU

14. (*a*) VWX - OCU (*b*) IFH - SGQ
(*c*) LAN - BDR (*d*) EJP - ZTY

15. (*a*) MEAL - LAME
(*b*) BARK - KERB
(*c*) SPOT - TOPS
(*d*) RUBY - BURY

EXPLANATORY ANSWERS

1. (*d*) : In all other groups the letters are in natural series and the last letter of first part is the first letter of the second part.

2. (*b*) : In all other groups only the vowel is in lower case in the first part and in second part the case is reversed.

3. (*c*) : In all other groups the letters jump two letters in between them.

4. (*c*) : In all other groups the single letter in first part is repeated in the second and vice versa.

5. (a) : In all other groups the letters in the first part are one step forward than the corresponding letters in the second part.

6. (b) : In all other groups the letters in the first part are written backwards in the second part.

7. (d) : All other groups have letters made by straight lines only.

8. (a) : In all other groups the letters jump four letters in between then.

9. (c) : In all others groups the letters jump one letter between them.

10. (d) : In all other groups the second part is same as first except that the middle letter is changed to small letter.

11. (c) : In all other groups the letters in first part are in natural series and in second part in reverse series.

12. (b) : In all other groups the two letters on the right fit between the two letters on the left.

13. (a) : All other pairs have only vowels.

14. (d) : In other groups, the letters on the left are made with straight lines and the letters on the right have curved lines.

15. (b) : In other groups, the letters on the left are used to form · new word on the right.

PART - VI

ODD ONE OUT—NUMBER GROUPS

The group of numbers can be consecutive numbers in natural or reverse series, multiplication; subtraction; mathematical rules can also be used to frame the groups.

SOLVED EXAMPLE

1. *Which of the following pair of numbers is different from the other three pairs?*

(*a*) 14, 28 (*b*) 40, 80 (*c*) 16, 32 (*d*) 15, 35

Ans. (*d*) : In each pair the second number is double the first number. In option (d), the number 35 should have been 30, the very reason as to why it is the odd one out.

EXERCISE

Directions : *Which of the following pair of numbers is different from the other three pairs?*

1. (*a*) 28, 4 (*b*) 63, 7 (*c*) 56, 8 (*d*) 35, 5

2. (*a*) 3, 11 (*b*) 8, 16 (*c*) 5, 13 (*d*) 14, 24

3. (*a*) 13, 156 (*b*) 12, 144 (*c*) 15, 180 (*d*) 16, 176

4. (*a*) 32, 13 (*b*) 46, 20 (*c*) 51, 24 (*d*) 72, 45

5. (*a*) 5, 25 (*b*) 9, 81 (*c*) 4, 64 (*d*) 6, 36

6. (*a*) 91, 10 (*b*) 57, 12 (*c*) 69, 15 (*d*) 72, 13

7. (*a*) 20, 10 (*b*) 45, 27 (*c*) 15, 12 (*d*) 30, 18

8. (*a*) 7, 3 (*b*) 13, 9 (*c*) 11, 7 (*d*) 17, 8

9. (*a*) 10, 20 (*b*) 40, 50 (*c*) 30, 40 (*d*) 50, 60

10. (*a*) 16, 26 (*b*) 3, 4 (*c*) 26, 24 (*d*) 27, 25

11. (*a*) 39, 13 (*b*) 57, 19 (*c*) 64, 16 (*d*) 72, 26

12. (*a*) 16, 43 (*b*) 29, 56 (*c*) 53, 82 (*d*) 71, 98

13. (*a*) 7, 47 (*b*) 5, 25 (*c*) 3, 9 (*d*) 4, 16

14. (*a*) 92, 46 (*b*) 77, 38.5 (*c*) 30, 16 (*d*) 42, 21

15. (*a*) 13, 65 (*b*) 18, 90 (*c*) 17, 95 (*d*) 24, 120

16. (*a*) 63, 52 (*b*) 75, 64 (*c*) 80, 69 (*d*) 32, 12

17. (*a*) 17, 37 (*b*) 8, 13 (*c*) 5, 13 (*d*) 23, 7

18. (*a*) 55, 10 (*b*) 76, 13 (*c*) 92, 14 (*d*) 83, 11

19. (*a*) 7, 343 (*b*) 8, 514 (*c*) 5, 125 (*d*) 6, 216

20. (*a*) 42, 14 (*b*) 56, 19 (*c*) 69, 23 (*d*) 108, 36

EXPLANATORY ANSWERS

1. (*b*) : In all other pairs 7 times the second number is the first number. In this option 9 times 7 is the first number.

2. (*d*) : In all other groups the difference between the two numbers is 8.

3. (*d*) : In other groups 12 times the first number

is the second number. In this option 11 times the first number is the second number.

4. (a) : 13 is a prime number.

5. (c) : In all other pairs the second number is a perfect square of the first.

6. (d) : In all other pairs the second number is the sum of the digits of the first number.

7. (a) : In all other pairs the numbers are divisible by 3.

8. (d) : In other groups the difference between the numbers is 4.

9. (a) : In this option the second number is double the first number. In other groups the difference between the two numbers is 10.

10. (a) : In other groups the first digits of the two numbers are same (consider 3 and 4 as 03 and 04).

11. (d) : In other pairs the first number is divisible by the second number.

12. (c) : In other pairs the difference between the two numbers is 27.

13. (a) : The second number in other pairs is the square of the first number.

14. (c) : The second number in other pairs is half of the first number.

15. (c) : The second number in other pairs is five times the first number.

16. (d) : The difference in each pair is of 11. In this option, it is 10.

17. (b) : 8 is not a prime number.

18. (c) : The second number in other groups is the sum of digits of the first number.

19. (b) : The second number in other groups is the cube of the first number.

20. (b) : In all other pairs, the first number is divided by 3 to get the second number.

CODING AND DECODING

PART - I

Coding is a secretive language which is used to change the representation of the actual term/word/ value. This coded language can be framed by *(i)* moving the letters one or more steps forward or backward; *(ii)* substituting numbers for letters and vice–versa; *(iii)* writing the letters of the given word in reverse order in part or in whole; and *(iv)* replacing the letters in their natural series by the same positioned letters in their reverse series.

Alphabet in natural series are :

A B C D E F G H I J K L M N O P Q R S T U V W X Y Z

A ↓	E ↓	J ↓	O ↓	T ↓	Y ↓
1st	5th	10th	15th	20th	25th

Alphabet in reverse series are :

Z Y X W V U T S R Q P O N M L K J I H G F E D C B A

Z ↓	V ↓	Q ↓	L ↓	G ↓	B ↓
1st	5th	10th	15th	20th	25th

Note : On reaching Z, the series restarts from A and on reaching A, it restarts from Z.

SOLVED EXAMPLES

1. If FACE is coded as GBDF, then BADE will be coded as :
   (*a*) CBEF (*b*) CEBF (*c*) CFBE (*d*) CBFE
   Ans. *(a)* : The word is coded by moving the letters one step forward.

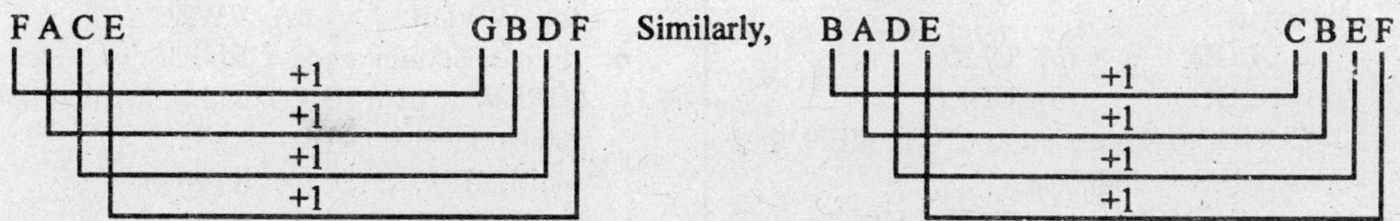

2. If RESULT is coded as 798206, LET will be coded as :
   (*a*) 680 (*b*) 092 (*c*) 096 (*d*) 086
   Ans. *(c)* : The letters are coded by numbers, and to code the given word, select the respective coded numbers.

   R E S U L T → letters
   7 9 8 2 0 6 → code

   So, code for LET will be

   L E T → letters
   0 9 6 → code

Decoding is the reverse of coding. Here the code needs to be deciphered with the help of given words.

3. If ZXV stands for ACE; what will YZW stand for?

(*a*) ABD (*b*) EAC (*c*) SAD (*d*) BAD

Ans. (*d*) : The letters of the word ACE are deciphered by decoding ZXV. The letters are decoded by substituting their represented letters in the natural order. (*i.e.*, 'Z' is 1st in the reverse series and 'A' is 1st in natural series)

Z	X	V	Similarly,	Y	Z	W	⟶	letters in reverse series
A	C	E		B	A	D	⟶	letters is natural series
↓	↓	↓		↓	↓	↓		
1st	3rd	5th		2nd	1st	4th	⟶	position of letters

4. In a certain code MHUSMD stands for LITTLE. What shall NTUD stand for in the same code?

(*a*) MOVE (*b*) MUTE (*c*) MITE (*d*) MATE

Ans. (*b*) : The code is decoded by moving the letters one step backward and one step forward alternately.

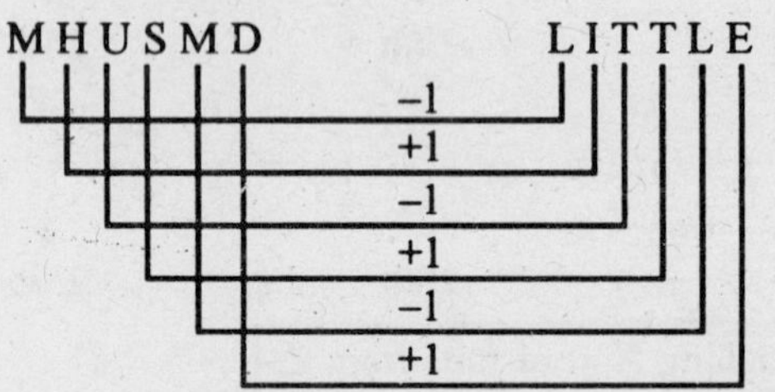

Similarly,

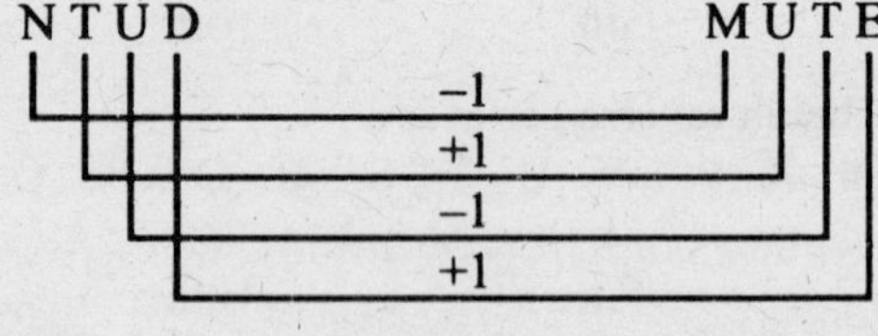

EXERCISE

Directions : *In the following questions select the right option which indicates the correct code for the word or letter given in the question.*

1. If CHAIR is coded as FKDLU then RAID is coded as :

(*a*) ULGD (*b*) ULKG
(*c*) ULDG (*d*) UDLG

2. If CONDEMN is coded as CNODMEN, then TEACHER is coded as :

(*a*) TEACHER (*b*) TAEECHR
(*c*) TCAEEHR (*d*) TAECEHR

3. In a code language COME is written as XLNV and ABLE as ZYOV. How will MOLLY be written in that code?

(*a*) NLOBO (*b*) NLBOO
(*c*) LNOOB (*d*) NLOOB

4. In a certain code PROFESSION is written as EFORPNOISS. In the same code DICTIONARY will be written as :

(*a*) YRANOITCID
(*b*) ITCIDYRANO
(*c*) ITCIDYRNAO
(*d*) ITCDIYARNO

5. JUNE is coded as NXPF, how will STAY be coded in the same manner?

(*a*) WWCZ (*b*) WVCZ
(*c*) WWDB (*d*) VWZC

6. If in a certain code GENIUS is coded as IGPKWU, then IDIOT will be written in the same code as :

(*a*) JEJPU (*b*) KFKQV
(*c*) LGLRW (*d*) HCHNS

7. If ACTION is coded as ZXGRLM, then HEALTH will be coded in the same way as :

(*a*) SVZOGS (*b*) TVZOGT
(*c*) RUZPGR (*d*) QVGOZQ

8. If THOUSAND is coded as SGNTRZMC, then FUMING will be coded as :

(*a*) GVNJOH (*b*) ETHLMF
(*c*) EVLJMH (*d*) ETLHMF

9. If EARTHQUAKE is coded as MOGPENJOSM, then EQUATE will be coded as :

(*a*) MENOPM (*b*) MENOMF

(*c*) MJOGPM (*d*) MNJOPM

10. In a certain code language HJIZT code is deciphered as MONEY, in the same way NOVGZ will be deciphered as :
(*a*) STUMP (*b*) STALE
(*c*) STICK (*d*) SPIRE

11. If in a certain code JOSEPH is coded as FKOALD, then GEORGE will be coded in the same way as :
(*a*) CBJNCA (*b*) CANKCA
(*c*) CAKNCA (*d*) CAKCNA

12. If COUNTRY is coded in a certain way as EMWLVPA, ELECTORATE will be coded in the same manner as :
(*a*) CJCEVQPYWC
(*b*) GJGERQTYVG
(*c*) CNCERQPCRG
(*d*) GJGAVMTYVC

13. In a certain code PORTUGESE is written as ESEGUTROP, MALAYALAM will be written in the same code as :
(*a*) MALAYALAM
(*b*) MALYALAM
(*c*) MALAYALM
(*d*) MALAYLAM

14. If PHILOSOPHY is coded as HPLISOPOYH, ORNAMENTAL will be coded as :
(*a*) ROANEMNTLA
(*b*) ONRAMNEALT
(*c*) ROANEMTNLA
(*d*) ROANEMNATL

15. If SABOTAGE is coded as UADOVAIE, how will EMERGENCY be coded in the same manner?
(*a*) GMGRIEPCA
(*b*) GMGRGEPCA
(*c*) BNBQFDOBZ
(*d*) EOETGGNEY

16. If OPFGBCST stands for NEAR, in the same manner IJVWHI will stand for :
(*a*) HAG (*b*) HUG
(*c*) HUT (*d*) KEG

17. If 'w' is coded as 'a', 's' as 'r' and 'r' as 'w', how will 'answer' be written?
(*a*) wnsaes (*b*) anraew
(*c*) anrwas (*d*) wnraes

18. If m is coded as g, g as o, a as i and i as y, then 'imagination' will be written as :
(*a*) ygagynatyin (*b*) ygioynityog
(*c*) ygioynityon (*d*) ygioyintyon

19. In a certain code PUNCTUAL is written as 16598623, in the same code ACTUPULN will be written as :
(*a*) 29861653 (*b*) 29861635
(*c*) 28916135 (*d*) 29851536

20. If OUT is coded as 152120, IN will be coded as :
(*a*) 1015 (*b*) 819
(*c*) 1813 (*d*) 914

21. If MUSK is coded as 146816, then ZERO will be coded as :
(*a*) 113811 (*b*) 122912
(*c*) 15915 (*d*) 2651815

22. If BAD is coded as 7, HIS as 9, LOW will be coded as :
(*a*) 50 (*b*) 8
(*c*) 23 (*d*) 5

23. In a certain code LIBERATE is written as 56403170, TRIBAL will be written in the same code as :
(*a*) 734615 (*b*) 736415
(*c*) 136475 (*d*) 034615

24. In certain military code, SYSTEM is written as SYSMET, and NEARER as AENRER, what will be the code for FRACTION?
(*a*) CRAFNOIT (*b*) FRCAITNO
(*c*) CARFNOIT (*d*) FRACNOIT

25. If CRUDE is written as BSTED, then MOIST will be coded as :
(*a*) NNJRU (*b*) LNHRS
(*c*) NPJTU (*d*) LPHTS

26. In a certain code ALPACA is written as ACAPLA. How will ANIMAL be written in that code?
(*a*) LAMINA (*b*) ALAMIN
(*c*) LAMNIA (*d*) AAMLIN

27. In a certain code FINGER is written as DGLECP. What will be the code for KIDNEY?
(*a*) IGBLCW (*b*) IGCLBW
(*c*) IBCGLE (*d*) IGBKCV

28. In a certain code QUESTION is written as NXBVQLLQ. How will REPLY be coded?
(*a*) YHMOV (*b*) OBMVI

(*c*) VHSOB (*d*) OHMOV

29. If in a certain code SKEW is coded as PNCY, then what will JXQV will stand for?
(*a*) MUTS (*b*) MUST
(*c*) MTSU (*d*) STUM

30. In a certain code LONDON is written as MPOEPO. What will IVOHSZ mean in the same code?
(*a*) HUNGRY (*b*) HUNDRY
(*c*) GRUNHY (*d*) HONDUS

31. In a certain code language 8514 is a code for HEAD, 3945 for RIDE and 057 for BEG. What will be the code for GRADE?
(*a*) 71345 (*b*) 73415
(*c*) 74135 (*d*) 73145

32. If MOTHERLAND is coded as 9501623748, how will DREAM be coded?
(*a*) 82697 (*b*) 86297
(*c*) 82769 (*d*) 82679

33. If OATH is coded in a certain language as TEYL, then how will WORD be coded?
(*a*) BWRH (*b*) HRWB
(*c*) BSWH (*d*) CSXI

34. If FINANCE is coded as GKQESIL, then how will BANK be coded in the same manner?
(*a*) CBOL (*b*) CDRP
(*c*) CCQO (*d*) CCPN

35. PLANNING is coded in a certain language as UFFHSCSA. How will AUTHORITY be coded in the same language?
(*a*) FOYBTLNND
(*b*) FYOTBNNLT
(*c*) FBOYTLNTN
(*d*) FBOYTNLTN

36. In a certain code ABCD is written as 2468 and EFGH as 1357. How will CAGE be written in that code?
(*a*) 6453 (*b*) 6251
(*c*) 6521 (*d*) 6215

37. If 341782 denotes MONKEY and 0596 denotes RAGS, then 75195044 will denote.
(*a*) KANGAROO (*b*) PALMANTT
(*c*) HANGAMEE (*d*) KARNAGOO

38. If HARD is coded as 1357 and SOFT as 2468, what will 21448 stand for?
(*a*) SHAFT (*b*) SHORT
(*c*) SHOOT (*d*) SHART

39. In a certain code COUNTRY is coded as KVASXUA. How will INDIA be coded in the same manner?
(*a*) PTIMD (*b*) QUJNE
(*c*) QUINE (*d*) RVKOF

40. If GASP is coded as LNPQ and BROW as XABF, then SPARROW will be coded in the same manner as :
(*a*) PQAANBF (*b*) PQANNBF
(*c*) PQNAABF (*d*) PQNBBAF

41. If CORRESPONDENCE is coded as NUTTRAXUPQRPNR in a certain code, how will SCOPE be coded?
(*a*) AUXNR (*b*) ANUXR
(*c*) RNUXA (*d*) XUPAR

42. In a certain code language SECRET is written as UIIZOF. How will MYSTERY be written in the same code?
(*a*) OCYANCN (*b*) OCYBOCM
(*c*) OCYAODM (*d*) OCYBODM

43. In a certain code LOCATE is written as 981265 and SPARK as 47230, CASKET will be coded in the same manner as :
(*a*) 124056 (*b*) 210465
(*c*) 164025 (*d*) 124506

44. If HALT is coded as SZOG in a certain code, how will STOP be coded in the same manner?
(*a*) GFLK (*b*) HGLK
(*c*) HGKJ (*d*) IHML

45. In a certain code language DELAY is coded as ABIXV. In the same code what will BXOIV stand for?
(*a*) EARTH (*b*) EARNS
(*c*) EARLY (*d*) ELDER

46. In a certain code FLOWER is coded as EIJPVG. How will ROSE be coded?
(*a*) QMOW (*b*) QLOX
(*c*) QKNX (*d*) QLNX

47. If SPORTS is coded in a certain manner as TOPQUR, then TENNIS will be coded as :
(*a*) SFMOJT (*b*) UFONHT
(*c*) SDOMJR (*d*) UDOMJR

48. If BROTHER is coded as IYVAOLY, then SISTER will be coded as :
(*a*) ZQZALY (*b*) ZOZBLY
(*c*) ZPZALY (*d*) ZPZLAY

49. In a certain language RESULT is coded as SFTVMU. In that language what does

GJSTU mean?
(*a*) FLIRT (*b*) HURTS
(*c*) FIRST (*d*) FIRED

50. In a certain code APPROACH is coded as CHOAPRAP. How will RESTRICT be coded?
(*a*) CTRISTER (*b*) ERTSIRTC
(*c*) CTRISTRE (*d*) TCIRSTRE

51. If EDUCATION is written as DECUTAOIN, then COLLEGE will be written as :
(*a*) OCLLGEE (*b*) OCLGEEL
(c) COELLEG (d) EOLCGLE

52. In a certain code VILLA is coded as YKOND, then HOUSE will be coded in the same manner as :
(*a*) KQYTG (*b*) KQXUH
(*c*) JPWTG (*d*) LRYVI

53. SCIENTIST is coded in a certain language as ICSTNETSI. AMBULANCE will be coded in the same language as :
(*a*) MBUALNCEA
(*b*) BMAALUECN
(*c*) MAUBALCNE
(*d*) UBMLAECNA

54. In a certain code ELECTION is written as GLGCVIQN, then VOTER will be coded as :
(*a*) XOVET (*b*) VOXET
(*c*) WPUFU (*d*) VQTGR

55. EXCURTION is coded as CXEURTNOI, OUTBURSTS will be coded in the same manner as :
(*a*) UTBTRUTSS (*b*) OUTRUBSTS
(*c*) TUOBURSTS (*d*) TUOBRSUTS

56. If ADD is coded as WOO, SUM as QJM and TOTAL as KPKWX, then TOADS will be coded as :
(*a*) KPOWQ (*b*) KPWQO
(*c*) KPWOQ (*d*) KPWOJ

57. If BOMBAY is coded as GLRYFV, then MADRAS will be coded as :
(*a*) RIXOIP (*b*) RXIOXP
(*c*) RXIOGQ (*d*) RXIOFP

58. If PUNISH is written in a certain code as QVOJTI, what will SFXBSE mean?
(*a*) RETARD (*b*) REWARD
(*c*) ROTARY (*d*) REBUKE

59. If ADMIRE is coded as AIDRME, then ADORES will be coded as :
(*a*) AODRSE (*b*) ARDESO
(*c*) ARDEOS (*d*) AREDOS

60. FAILURE is coded as OHRSDYN, SUCCESS will be coded in the same manner as :
(*a*) BBNNZBB (*b*) BBLJNZB
(*c*) BLNNZZB (*d*) BLNNZBB

61. If PURCHASE is coded as UPCRAHES, then HIRE will be coded in the same manner as :
(*a*) RHIE (*b*) HIER
(*c*) HERI (*d*) IHER

62. If FADE is coded as UZWV, then what does IFHG stand for in the same code?
(*a*) RUST (*b*) PORT
(*c*) QUIT (*d*) ROSE

63. ACTOR is coded in a certain language as EGXSV. How will STAGE be coded in the same language?
(*a*) VWFLJ (*b*) XYFLJ
(*c*) WXEKI (*d*) WYDJH

64. If DRINK is coded as IMNIP, then COKE will be coded as :
(*a*) GIOA (*b*) HJPZ
(*c*) HIOA (*d*) GJPZ

65. HORSE is written in a certain code as BUNGY and CAT as HOW, how will CHEST be written in the same code?
(*a*) OBYGW (*b*) WYGBN
(*c*) UNHBY (*d*) HBYGW

66. If MOTHERLAND is coded as 9206314758, then NORTH will be coded as :
(*a*) 72406 (*b*) 52406
(*c*) 52360 (*d*) 52106

67. If BAD is coded in a certain language as 514, GIVE as 3068 and FOR as 729, then how will VIDEO be written?
(*a*) 60482 (*b*) 03482
(*c*) 30214 (*d*) 60487

68. In a certain code language CHILD is written as IMOQJ. How will BABE be written in the same language?
(*a*) HFHJ (*b*) FGFK
(*c*) FFGJ (*d*) HFGJ

69. QUOTE is coded as OWMVC, how will WRITE be coded?
(*a*) TSFUB (*b*) UTGVC
(*c*) VUHWD (*d*) TUFWC

70. VACATE is coded as YEFEWI, OCCUPY will be coded as :
(*a*) QEEXRB (*b*) SHGZTD
(*c*) SFGXTC (*d*) RGFYSC

71. If CHART stands for GLEVX, then BOARD will stand for :
(*a*) FSEVH (*b*) HVESF
(*c*) VESFH (*d*) SEVHF

72. If BOOK is coded as CNPJ, then MOON will be coded as :
(*a*) MPNN (*b*) NNPM
(*c*) PNMN (*d*) NMPN

73. If PAPER stands for QBQFS, then what will GLASS stand for?
(*a*) MTBHT (*b*) MHTBT
(*c*) HMBTT (*d*) HMTBT

74. If DOWN is coded as FQYP, then the word WITH will be coded as :
(*a*) KYJV (*b*) IJYK
(*c*) YKVJ (*d*) JKVY

75. If CHAIR stands for EJCKT, then TABLE would stand for :
(*a*) NGDC (*b*) VCDNG
(*c*) DCGNV (*d*) GNVCD

76. If the word CLERK is coded as EOIWQ, then how would you code the word TABLE?
(*a*) VCDNG (*b*) VCDGN
(*c*) VDFQK (*d*) VDFOK

77. If the word TRADE is coded as XVEHI, then how should the word PUBLIC be coded?
(*a*) TYFMPG (*b*) SXEOLF
(*c*) TYFPMG (*d*) SXLLOP

78. If the word PENCIL is coded as LICNEP, then how would the word INKPOT be coded?
(*a*) TOPINK (*b*) JOLQPU
(*c*) HMKOPS (*d*) TOPKNI

79. If the word TRAIN is coded as WUDLQ, then how will the word BUS be coded?
(*a*) EXU (*b*) DWU
(*c*) EXV (*d*) VXE

80. If the word UNITED is coded as SLGRCB, then how should the word DISOWN be coded?
(*a*) BGQMUL (*b*) CGRLTK
(*c*) CGRTLK (*d*) BGQLUM

81. In a certain code TRANSMISSION is written as RTANMSISISON. How will COMMUNICATIONS be written in the same code?
(*a*) OCMMUNCIATIONS
(*b*) OCMMNUICTAIONS
(*c*) OCMMNUICTAISNO
(*d*) OCMMNUICTAIOSN

82. In a certain code REGISTRY is written as VAKEWPVU. How will ENTRY be written in the same code?
(*a*) IJXNC (*b*) ARPVW
(*c*) ARPVU (*d*) IJXMC

83. AUSTRALIA is written in a certain code language as 973609429 and CANADA as 591989. How should CRUST be written in the same code?
(*a*) 50763 (*b*) 53076
(*c*) 50376 (*d*) 50736

84. DAZE is written as 41265 in a certain code. How will BOY be written in the same code?
(*a*) 41425 (*b*) 5120
(*c*) 21525 (*d*) 359

85. If MEDAL is coded as XPOLW, then how will CADGE be coded in the same manner?
(*a*) NLORP (*b*) PNQTR
(*c*) LJMPN (*d*) MLOQP

86. The code for certain letters are indicated in the following words: BRAIN–12345, GRADE–72308, DRAIN–02345, STATE–78388. What is the code for 'D'?
(*a*) 3 (*b*) 2
(*c*) 0 (*d*) 4

87. If in a certain code FIRST is represented as 36509, TOP as 154, MORE as 4837 and MERIT as 83579, then what is the code for 'R'?
(*a*) 8 (*b*) 3
(*c*) 9 (*d*) 7

88. Certain letters are coded as : TODAY–45738, WROTE–10542, DATE–7342 and DIRTH–79046, what does the code number '5' stand for?
(*a*) D (*b*) R
(*c*) O (*d*) T

89. In a certain code language certain words are coded as given below : JOKER–29750, TRUMP–45813, PROJECT–1572064. What is the code for 'C'?
(*a*) 6 (*b*) 7

(*c*) 5 (*d*) 0

90. If FACE is coded as 6135, BIG as 297, HAD as 814 and BADGE as 21475, then what is the code for 'A'?

(*a*) 3 (*b*) 1
(*c*) 2 (*d*) 4

91. In a certain code certain words are coded as follows : ACTION–014853, FORCE–25916, REGAIN–967083. Which of the following letters is coded as '7'?

(*a*) A (*b*) N
(*c*) R (*d*) G

92. In a certain code WORK is written as 0918, ROUND as 19354, KIND as 8654, BRING as 71652 and BROOD as 71994. Which of the following is represented by '2'?

(*a*) R (*b*) G
(*c*) N (*d*) B

93. Certain words are coded as follows : BEAR–9218, DRUM–0863, PRY–485 and DOOR–7998. What is the code for 'R'?

(*a*) 9 (*b*) 3
(*c*) 8 (*d*) 4

94. FRANK is coded as 93210, AFTER as 29463, MUFFET as 879964, FERRY as 96335 and REEF as 3669. What is the code for 'F'?

(*a*) 9 (*b*) 3
(*c*) 6 (*d*) 1

95. If SAY is coded as 069, ASK as 608, YES as 930, DYE as 493 and EYE as 393, then what is the code for 'Y'?

(*a*) 0 (*b*) 9
(*c*) 3 (*d*) 6

96. If STABILITY is coded as 321956527 and RESTICATE as 403258120, what is 'I' coded as?

(*a*) 6 (*b*) 2
(*c*) 5 (*d*) 9

97. If EXAMINATION is coded as 83690567045, the codes for 'N' and 'A' are :

(*a*) 7, 5 (*b*) 5, 6
(*c*) 6, 5 (*d*) 5, 7

98. In a certain code BEAUTY is coded as 835247, DEVIL as 03916 and ABIDE as 58103. What does '3' stand for?

(*a*) E (*b*) D
(*c*) B (*d*) A

99. Certain words are coded in the following manner : BARK–0735, DIRT–4927, WAGE–4086, RISK–5718. What is the code for 'R'?

(*a*) 2 (*b*) 7
(*c*) 5 (*d*) 0

100. The code for certain letters are indicated in the following words : TRADE–54321, BADGE–93271, GRADE–74321, QUEUE–80101. What is the code for 'G'?

(*a*) 7 (*b*) 4
(*c*) 2 (*d*) 8

EXPLANATORY ANSWERS

1. (*d*) : The word is coded by moving the letters three steps forward.

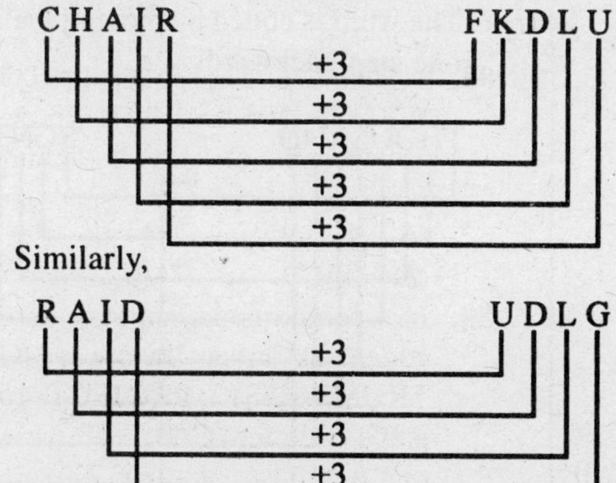

2. (*d*) : In this word, the second and third letters interchange their places and the fifth and sixth letters do the same. Other letters retain their position.

Similarly,

3. (*d*) : The letters of the word are coded by their represented letters in the reverse series.

C	O	M	E	→ letters in natural series
X	L	N	V	→ letters in reverse series
↓	↓	↓	↓	
3rd	15th	13th	5th	→ position of letters

A	B	L	E	→ letters in natural series
Z	Y	O	V	→ letters in reverse series
↓	↓	↓	↓	
1st	2nd	12th	5th	→ position of letters

Similarly,

M	O	L	L	Y	→ letters in natural series
N	L	O	O	B	→ letters in reverse series
↓	↓	↓	↓	↓	
13th	15th	12th	12th	25th	→ position of letters

4. (*b*) : The word is divided into two equal parts and the letters of each part are written backwards.

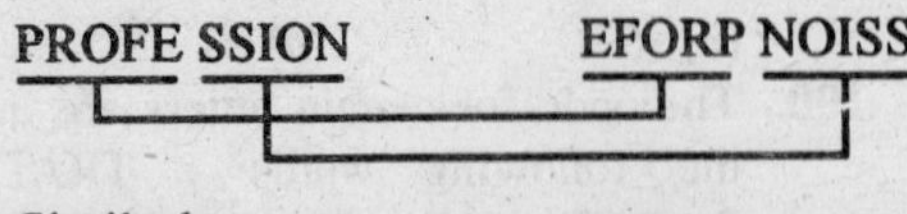

Similarly,

5. (*a*) : The word is coded by moving the letters +4, +3, +2, and +1 steps respectively.

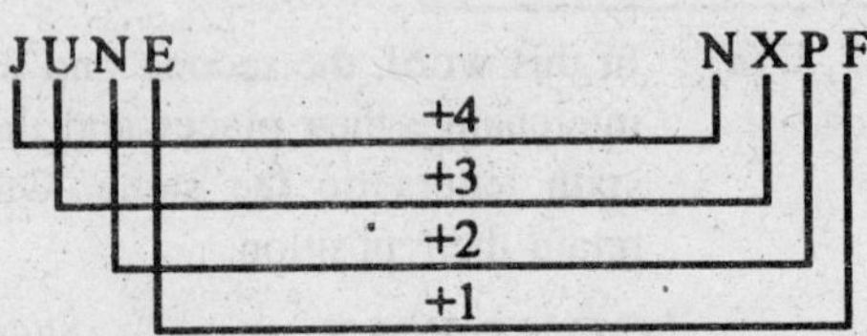

Similarly,

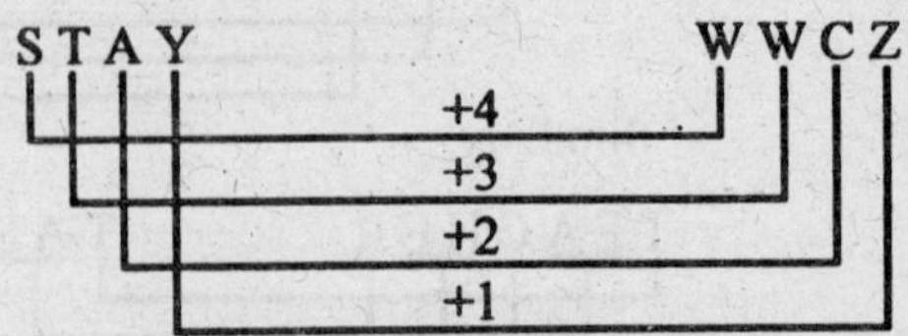

6. (*b*) : The word is coded by moving the letters two steps forward, *i.e.*,

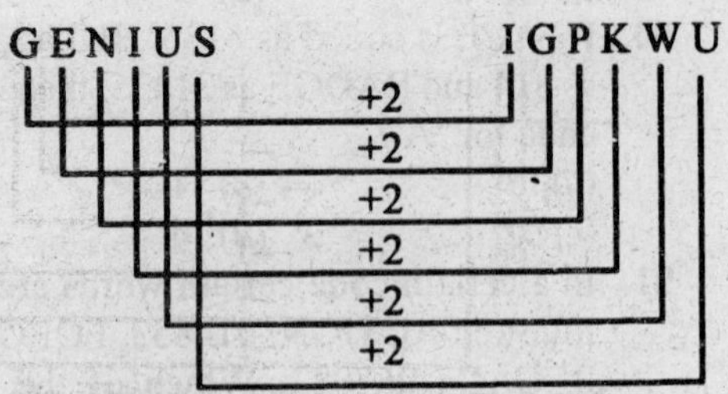

Similarly,

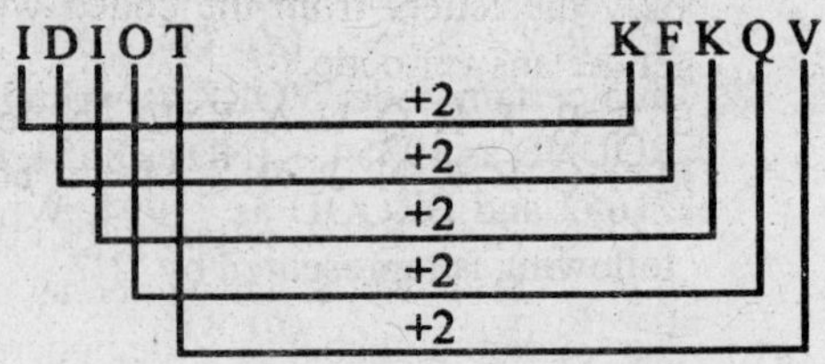

7. (*a*) : The letters of the word are coded by their represented letters in the reverse series.

A	C	T	I	O	N	→ letters in natural series
Z	X	G	R	L	M	→ letters in reverse series
↓	↓	↓	↓	↓	↓	
1st	3rd	20th	9th	15th	14th	position of letters

Similarly,

H	E	A	L	T	H	→ letters in natural series
S	V	Z	O	G	S	→ letters in reverse series
↓	↓	↓	↓	↓	↓	
8th	5th	1st	12th	20th	8th	→ position of letters

8. (*d*) : The word is coded by moving the alphabet one step backwards, *i.e.*,

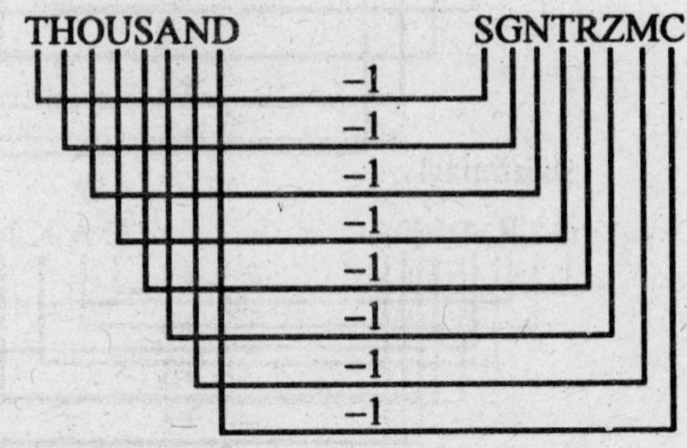

Similarly,

FUMING ETLHMF

–1
–1
–1
–1
–1
–1

9. (*d*) : The alphabet in word EQUATE are taken from the given word EARTHQUAKE. Tally the letters from the coded word to get the answer code.

E A R T H Q U A K E → letters
M O G P E N J O S M → codes
E Q U A T E → letters to be coded
M N J O P M → answer codes

10. (*b*) : The coded alphabet are deciphered by moving five steps forward, *i.e.*,

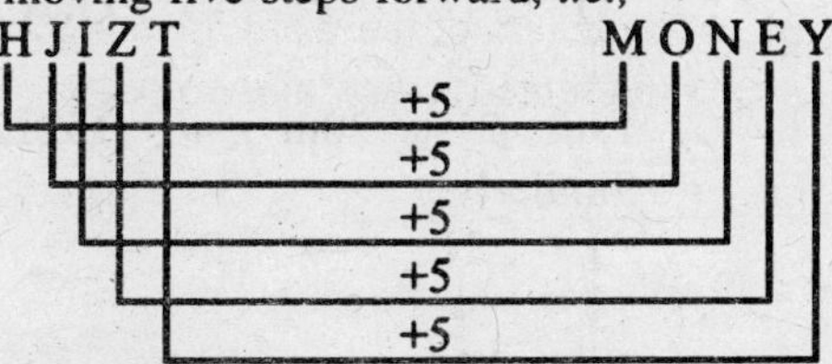

Similarly,

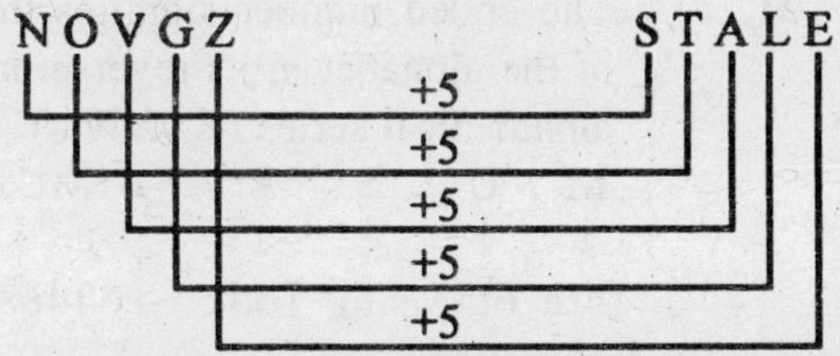

11. (*c*) : The word is coded by moving the alphabet four steps backward, *i.e.*,

Similarly,

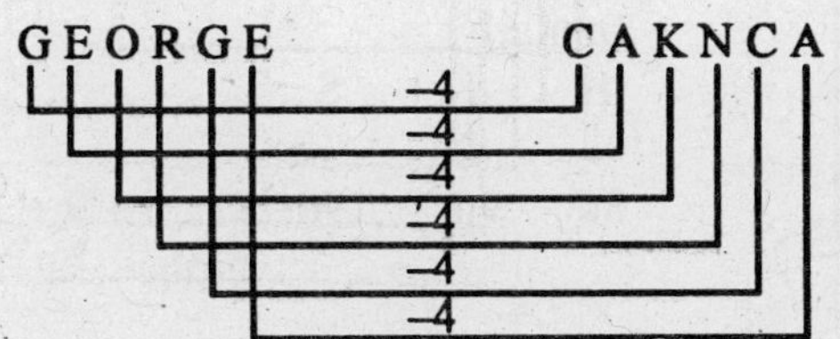

12. (*d*) : The word is coded by moving the alphabet two steps forward and two steps backward alternately, *i.e.*,

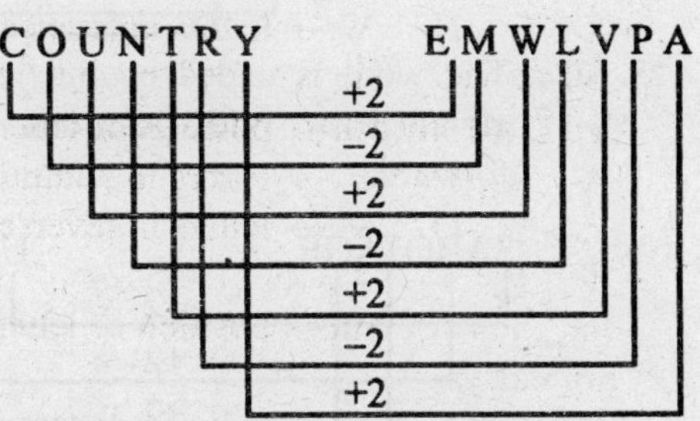

Similarly,

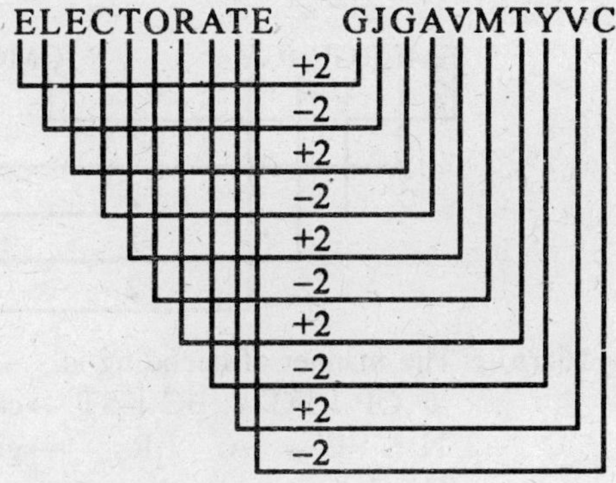

13. (*a*) : The coded word is the alphabet of the word written backwards.

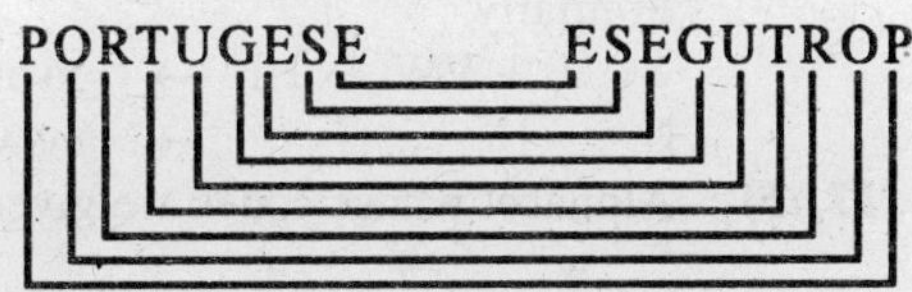

Similarly,

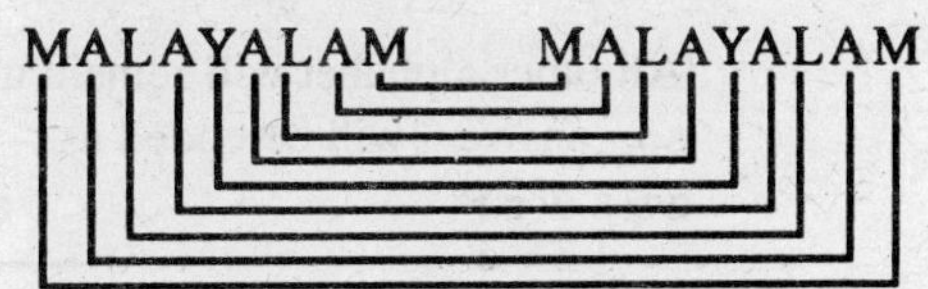

14. (*c*) : The places of two consecutive letters in the word are interchanged to form the coded word.

Similarly,

15. *(a)* : The word is coded by moving only the alphabet at odd positions two steps forward.

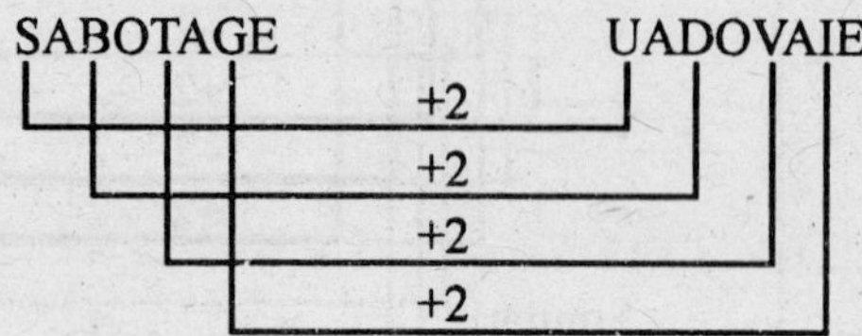

Similarly,

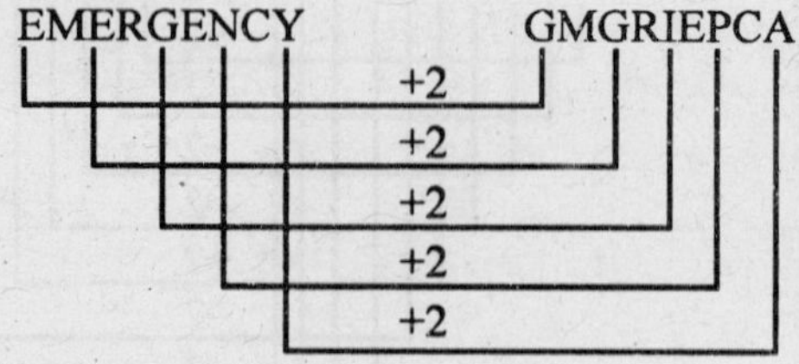

16. *(b)* : The manner of decoding is

↓ OP ↓ FG ↓ BC ↓ ST →codes
N E A R →given word

The letters preceeding two consecutive letters in the alphabetical series are picked to depict the words.

Similarly,

↓ IJ ↓ VW ↓ HI → given codes
H U G → answer word

17. *(b)* : Alphabet whose codes are given

w → a
s → r
r → w

All other alphabet will remain unchanged, so, 'answer' will be coded as :

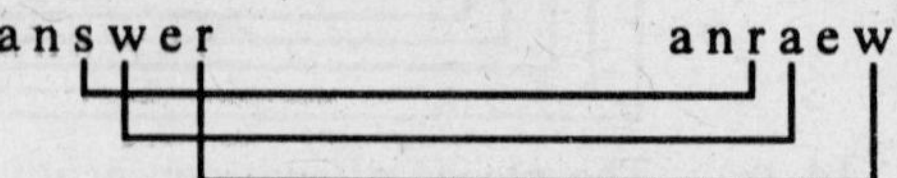

18. *(c)* : Alphabet whose codes are given

m → g
g → o
a → i
i → y

All other alphabet will remain unchanged so, 'imagination' will be coded as :

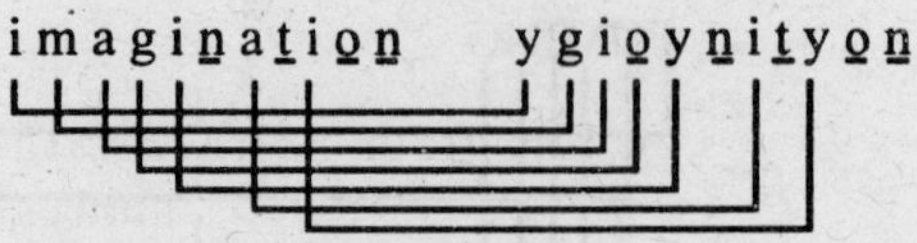

letters n, t and o do not change.

19. *(b)* : The letters in the word PUNCTUAL are jumbled to form ACTUPULN. So will the number code.

P U N C T U A L → given word
1 6 5 9 8 6 2 3 → codes

Similarly,

A C T U P U L N → word to be coded
2 9 8 6 1 6 3 5 → answer codes

20. *(d)* : The coded number signifies the position of the alphabet in its natural alphabetical series (ABCD...)

O U T → OUT
↓ ↓ ↓
15th 21st 20th → 152120.

Similarly,

I N → IN
↓ ↓
9th 14th → 914

21. *(b)* : The coded number signifies the position of the alphabet in its reverse order of the alphabetical series (ZYXW...)

M U S K → MUSK
↓ ↓ ↓ ↓
14th 6th 8th 16th → 146816

Similarly,

Z E R O → ZERO
↓ ↓ ↓ ↓
1st 22nd 9th 12th → 122912

22. *(d)* : The coded number is the sum of number digits signifying the position of the alphabet in the natural order.

B A D
↓ ↓ ↓
2nd 1st 4th *i.e.,* 2 + 1 + 4 = 7

Similarly,

H I S
↓ ↓ ↓
8th 9th 19th *i.e.,* 8 + 9 + 19 = 36
further, 3 + 6 = 9

Also,

L O W
↓ ↓ ↓
12th 15th 23rd *i.e.*, 12 + 15 + 23 = 50
further, 5 + 0 = 0

23. (*b*) : The letters of the word TRIBAL are picked from LIBERATE. So will be the coded numbers.

L I B E R A T E → given word
5 6 4 0 3 1 7 0 → codes

Similarly,

T R I B A L → word to be coded
7 3 6 4 1 5 → answer codes

24. (*c*) : The word is divided into two equal parts and the letters of each part are written in reverse order.

Similarly,

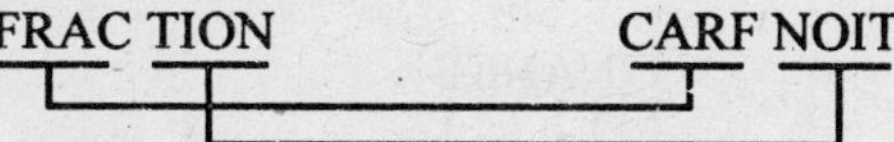

25. (*d*) : The code is formed by moving the letters one step backwards and one step forward alternately.

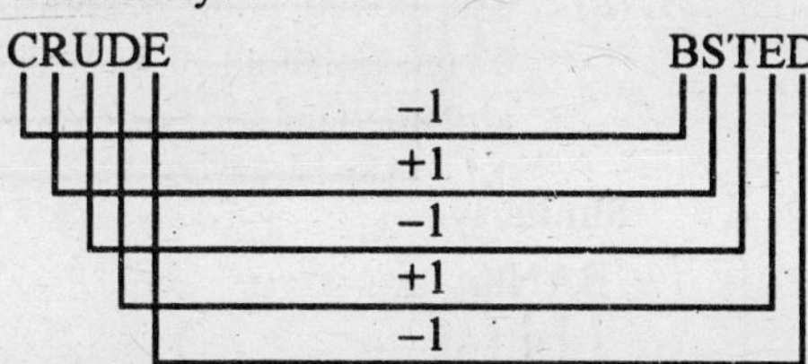

Similarly,

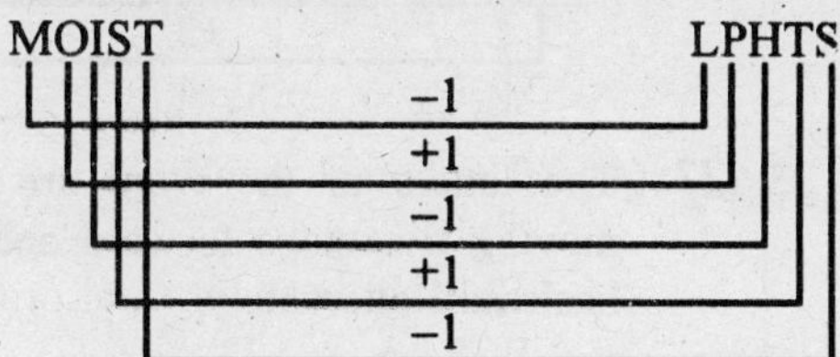

26. (*a*) : The letters of the word are written backwards.

Similarly,

27. (*a*) : The word is coded by moving the letters two steps backwards.

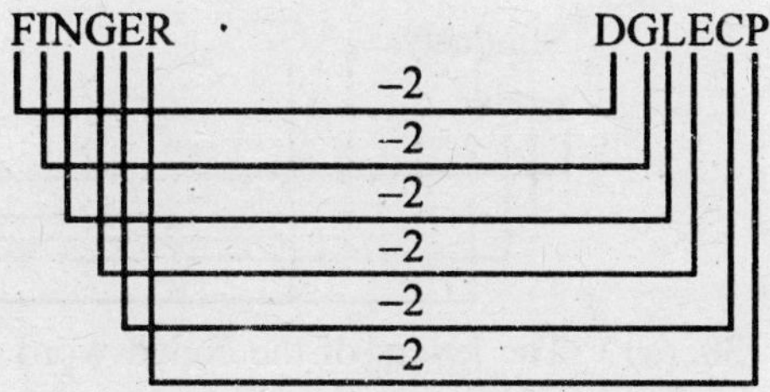

Similarly,

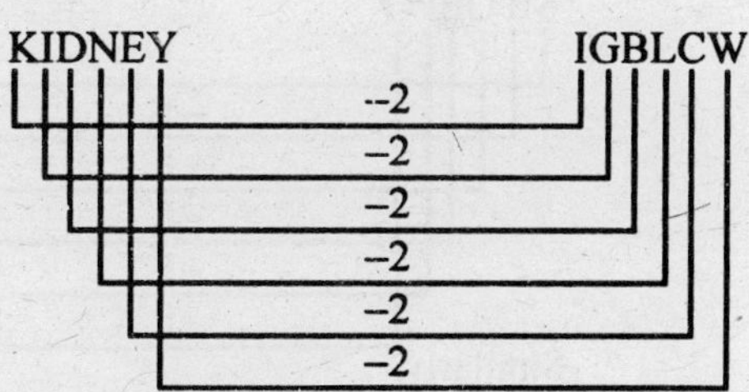

28. (*d*) : The letters of the word are coded by moving three steps backward and three steps forward alternately.

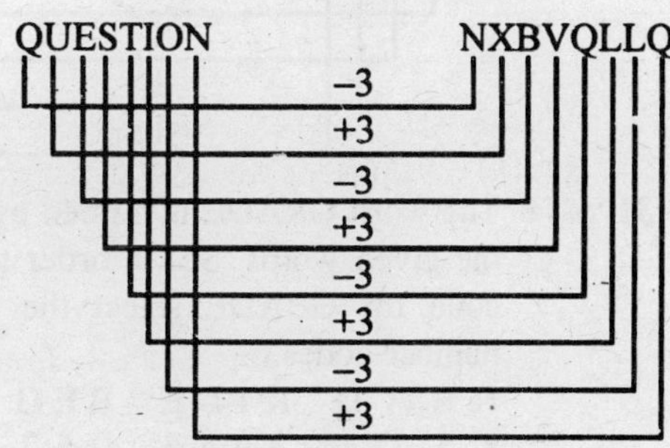

Similarly,

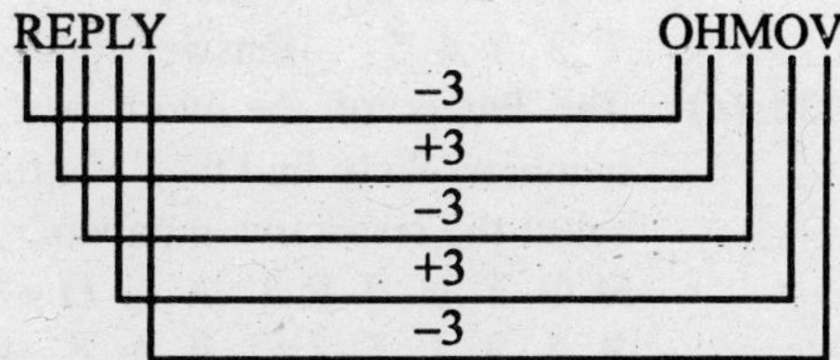

29. ***(b)*** **:** The letters are decoded by moving the letters +3, –3, +2 and –2 steps respectively.

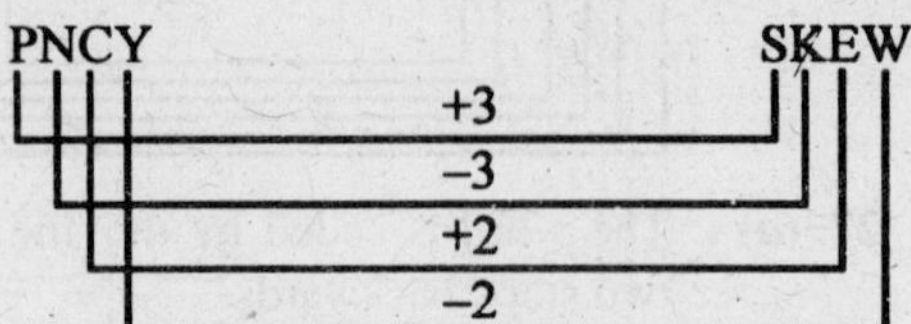

Similarly,

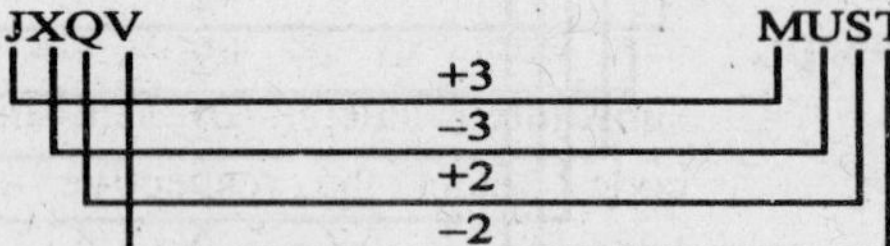

30. ***(a)*** **:** The letters of the coded word are moved one step backward.

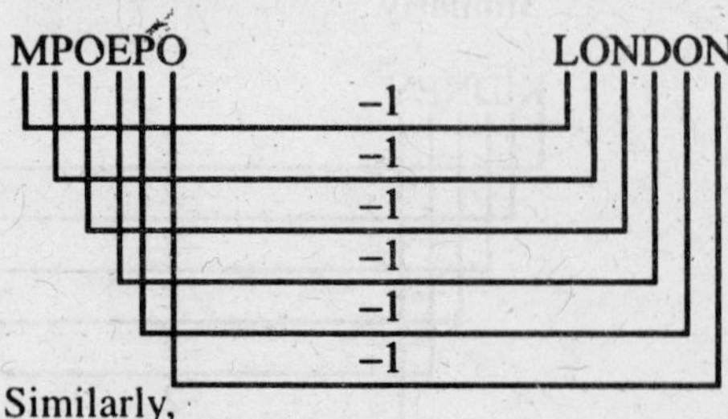

Similarly,

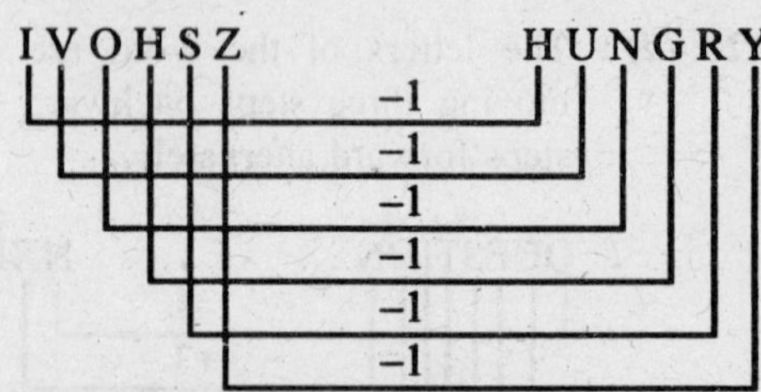

31. ***(d)*** **:** The word GRADE is framed by letters in the given words. So, in order to find the code for GRADE select the respective number codes.

H E A D R I D E B E G → letters
8 5 1 4 3 9 4 5 0 5 7 → codes

So,

G R A D E →letters
7 3 1 4 5 →answer codes

32. ***(d)*** **:** The letters of the word are coded by numbers. So to find the code for DREAM select the respective numbers.

M O T H E R L A N D → letters
9 5 0 1 6 2 3 7 4 8 → codes

So, D R E A M → letters
8 2 6 7 9 → answer codes

33. ***(c)*** **:** The letters are coded by moving five and four steps forward alternately.

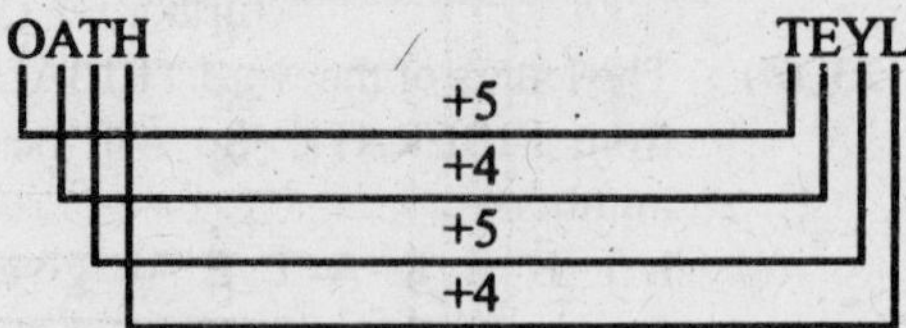

Similarly,

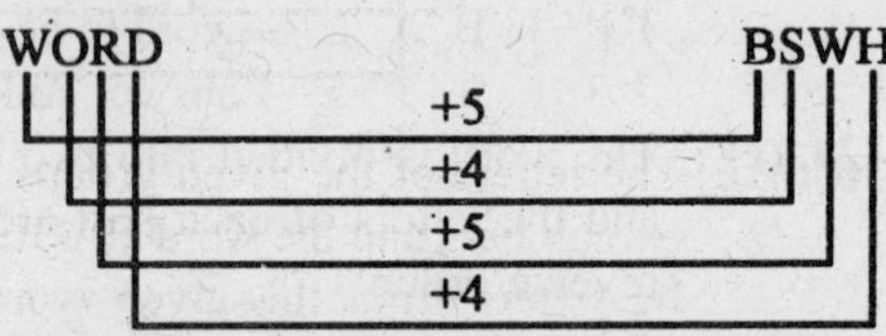

34. ***(c)*** **:** The letters of the word are coded by moving one step ahead and increasing the difference by one.

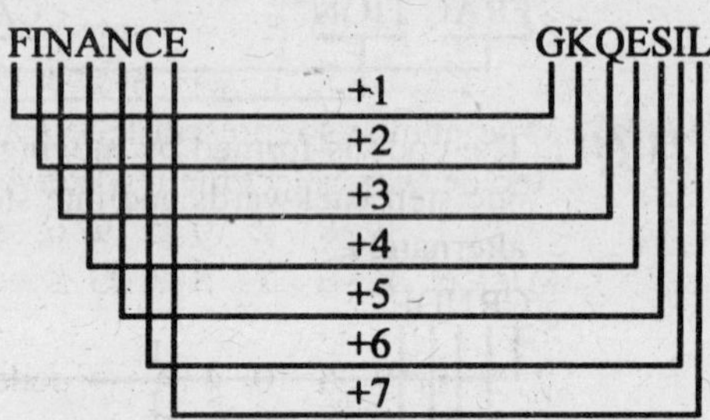

Similarly,

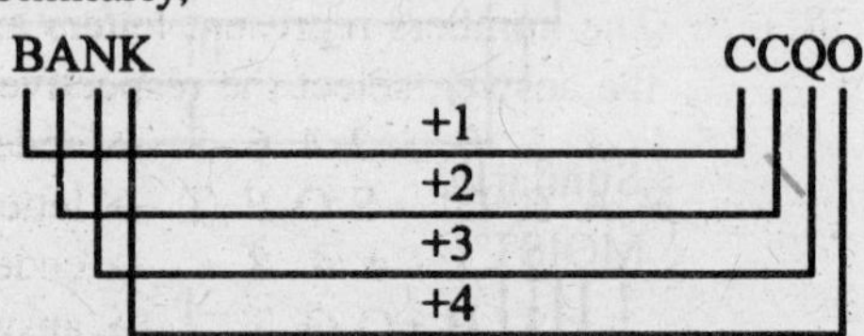

35. ***(a)*** **:** The letters of the word are coded by moving five steps forward and six steps backward alternately.

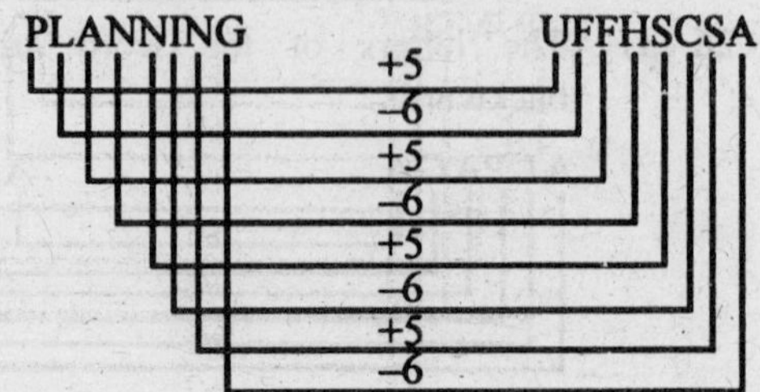

Similarly,

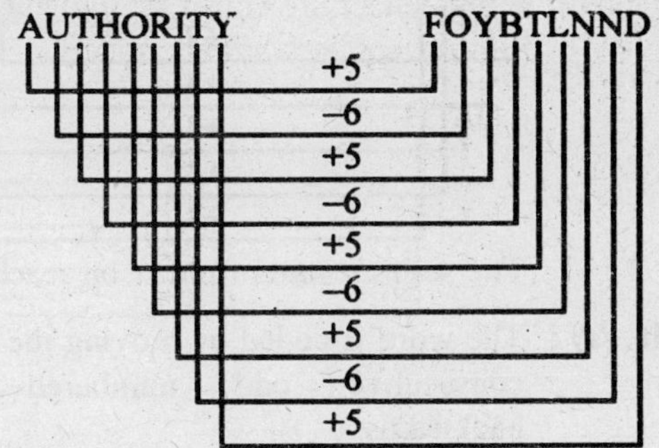

36. *(b)* : The letters of the given groups are coded by numbers and the word CAGE is formed by letters from the given words. So, to find the answer, select the respective numbers.

A B C D   E F G H → letters
2 4 6 8   1 3 5 7 → codes
So, C A G E → letters
6 2 5 1 → answer codes

37. *(a)* : The numbers represent letters and to find the answer, select the respective letters.

3 4 1 7 8 2 0 5 9 6 → codes
M O N K E Y R A G S → letters
So,
7 5 1 9 5 0 4 4 → codes
K A N G A R O O → answer letters

38. *(c)* : The numbers represent letters and to find the answer, select the respective letters.

1 3 5 7   2 4 6 8 → codes
H A R D   S O F T → letters
So, 2 1 4 4 8 → codes
S H O O T → answer letters

39. *(b)* : The word is coded by moving the first letter eight steps forward, and reducing the difference by one.

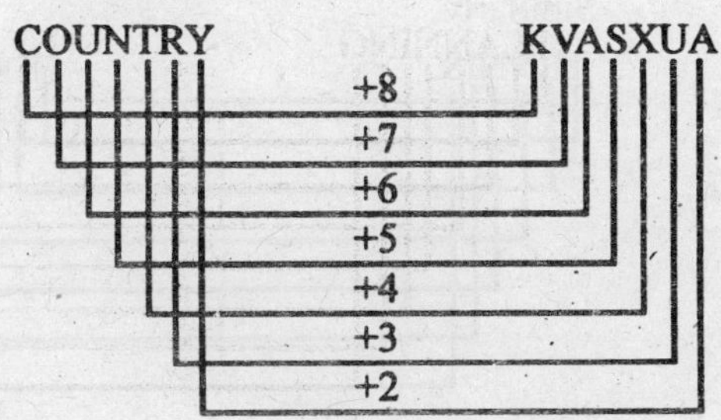

(The series restarts from A on reaching Z)
Similarly,

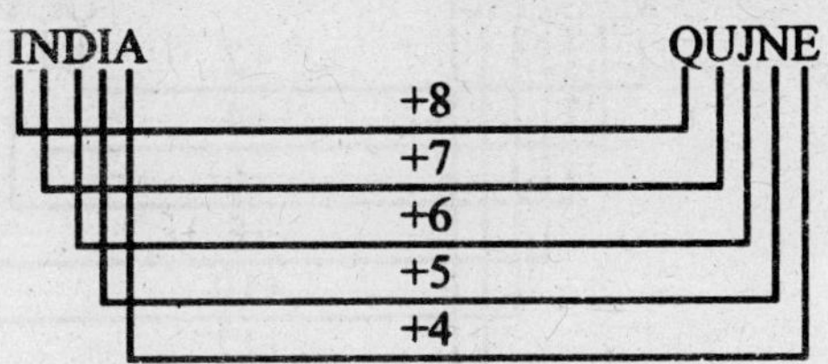

40. *(c)* : The letters of the words are coded by substituted letters. To find the answer code, select the respective substituted letters.

GASP BROW → letters
LNPQ XABF → substituted letter codes
So,
SPARROW → letters
PQNAABF → substituted letter answer codes

41. *(b)* : The letters of the word are coded by substituted letters. To find the answer code, select the respective substituted letters.

CORRESPONDENCE → letters
NUTTRAXUPQRPNR → substituted letter codes
So,
S C O P E—letters
A N U X R—substituted letter answer codes

42. *(d)* : The word is coded by moving the letters forward by consecutive even numbered steps.

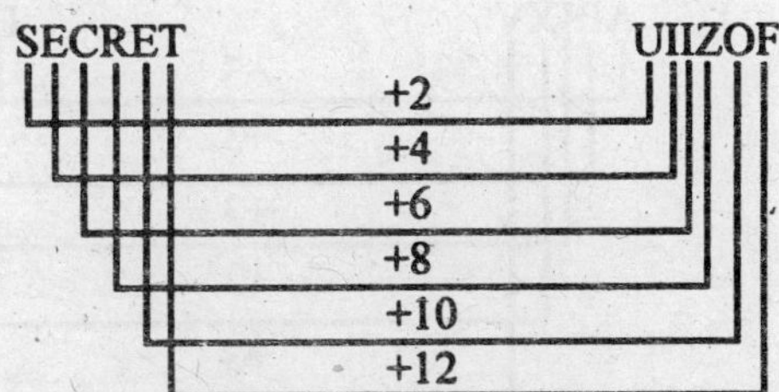

Similarly,

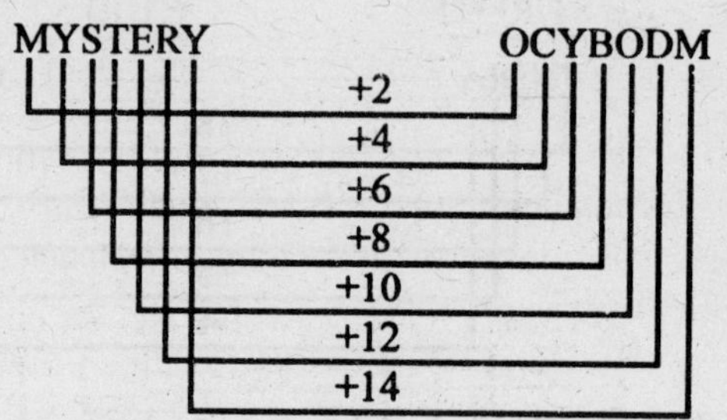

(The series restarts from A on reaching Z)

43. *(a)* : The letters are coded by numbers and to find the answer code, select the respective numbers.

L O C A T E S P A R K → letters
9 8 1 2 6 5 4 7 2 3 0 → codes

So,

C A S K E T → letters
1 2 4 0 5 6 → answer codes

44. *(b)* : The letters of the word are coded by their represented letters in reverse series.

H A L T → letters in natural series
S Z O G → letters in reverse series
8th 1st 12th 20th → position of letters

So,

S T O P → letters in natural series
H G L K → letters in reverse series
19th 20th 15th 16th → position of letters

45. *(c)* : The word is obtained by decoding the letters. The coded letters are moved three steps forward.

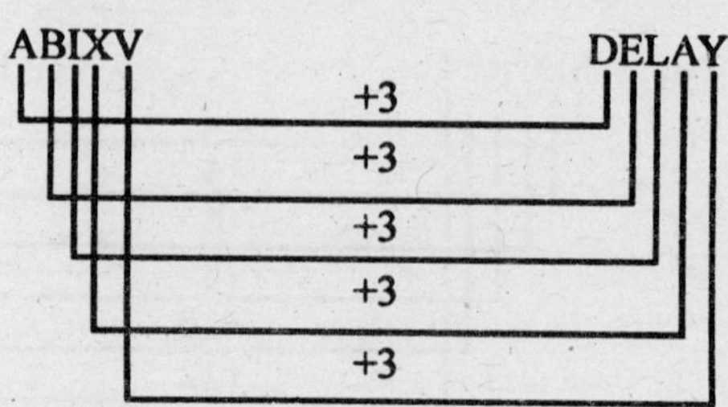

Similarly,

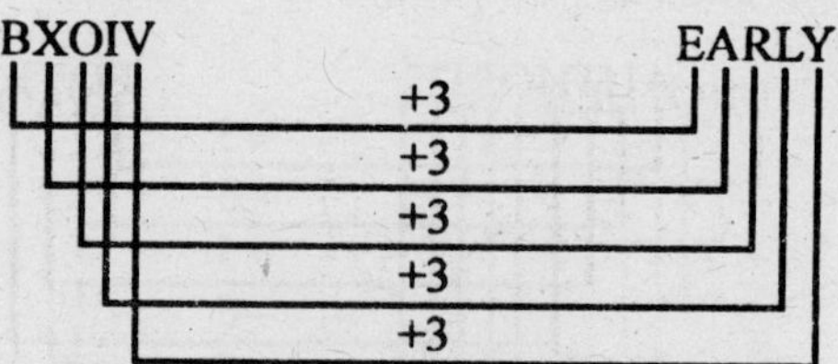

(The series restarts from A on reaching Z)

46. *(d)* : The word is coded by moving the letters, consecutive odd numbered steps backwards.

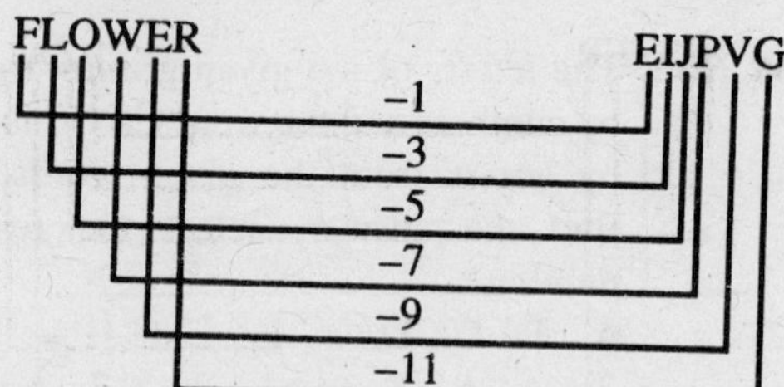

Similarly,

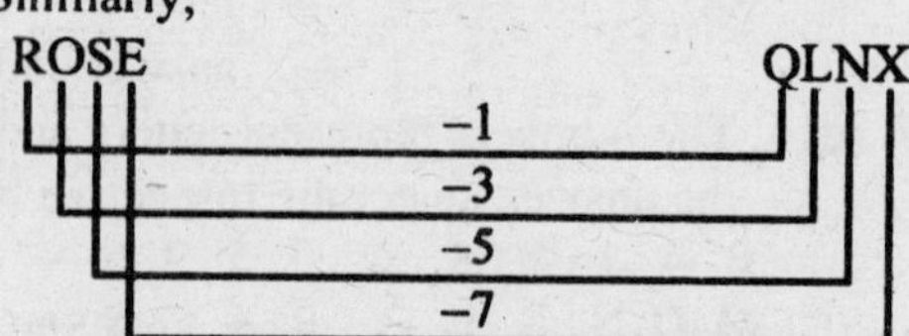

(The series restarts from Z on reaching A)

47. *(d)* : The word is coded by moving the letters one step forward and one step backward alternately.

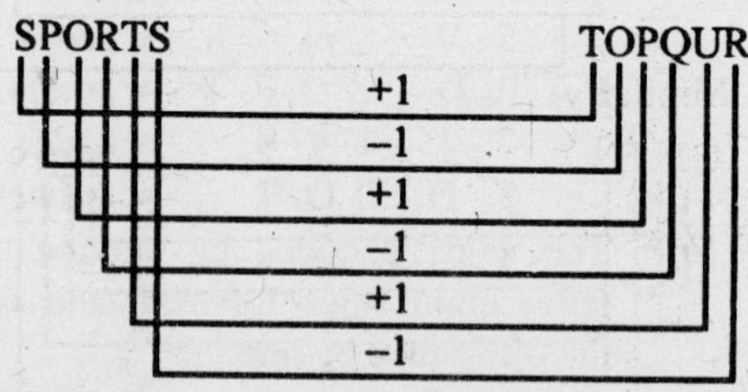

Similarly,

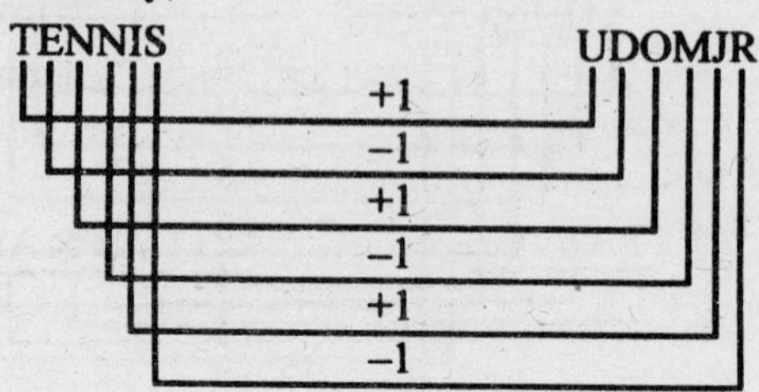

48. *(c)* : The word is coded by moving the letters seven steps forward.

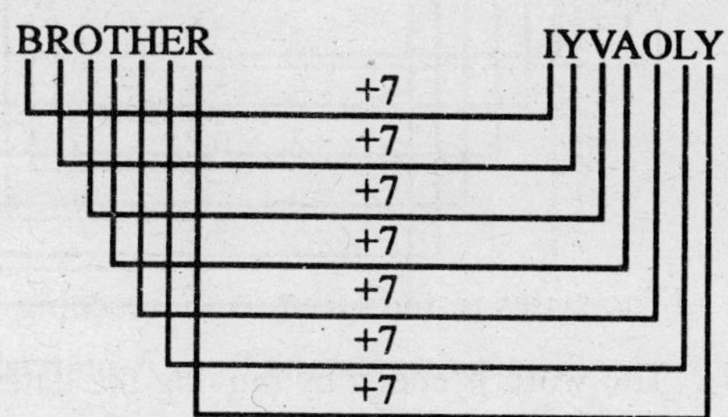

Similarly,

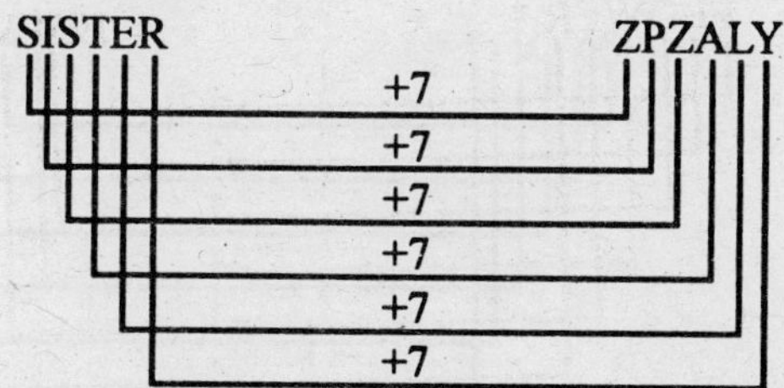

(The series restarts from A on reaching Z)

49. *(c)* : The coded letters are decoded to obtain the word. The letters are moved one step backward.

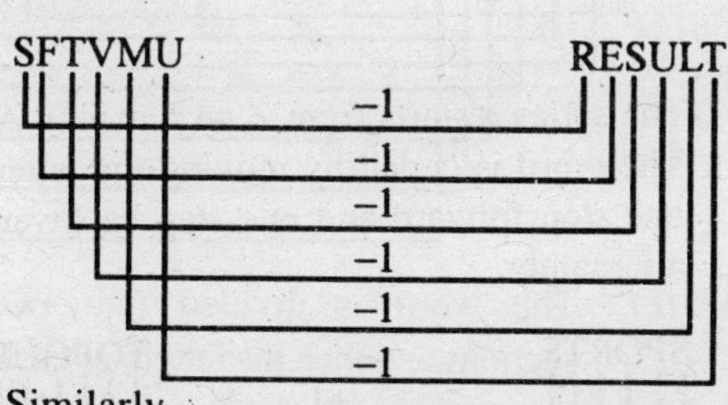

Similarly,

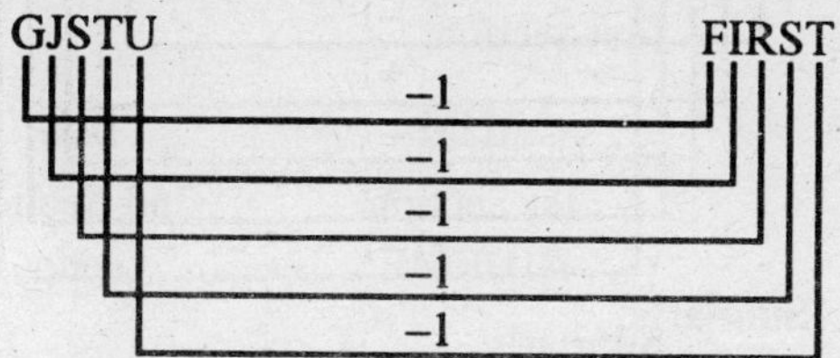

50. *(c)* : The word is divided into sections containing two letters each, and then the sections are written backwards.

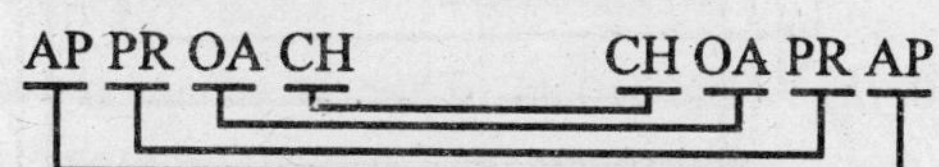

Similarly,

51. *(a)* : The word is divided into sections containing two letters each and the positions of the letters are interchanged.

Similarly,

52. *(b)* : The word is coded by moving the letters three and two steps forward alternately.

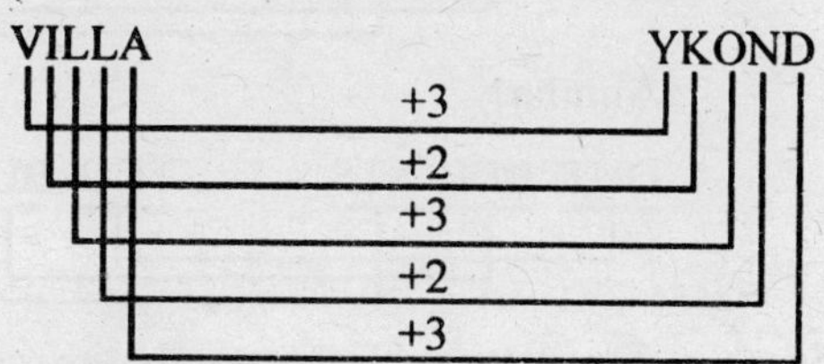

Similarly,

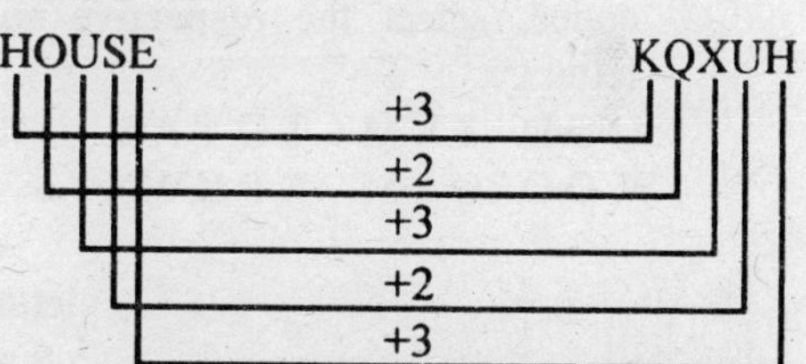

53. *(b)* : The word is divided into three equal sections, and the letters in each section are written backwards.

Similarly,

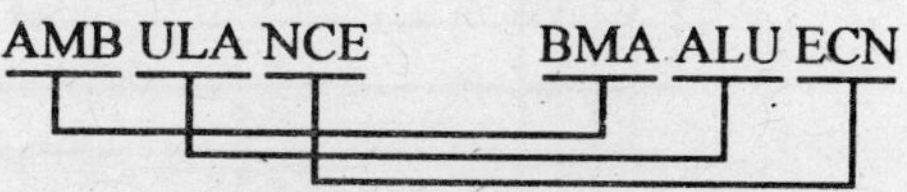

54. *(a)* : Only the letters at the odd positions are moved two steps forward.

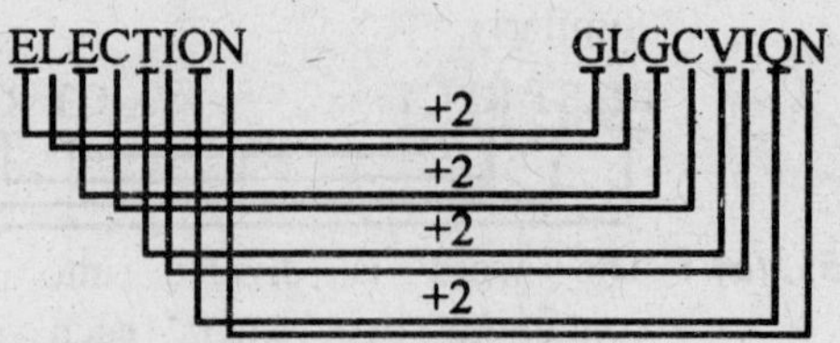

Similarly,

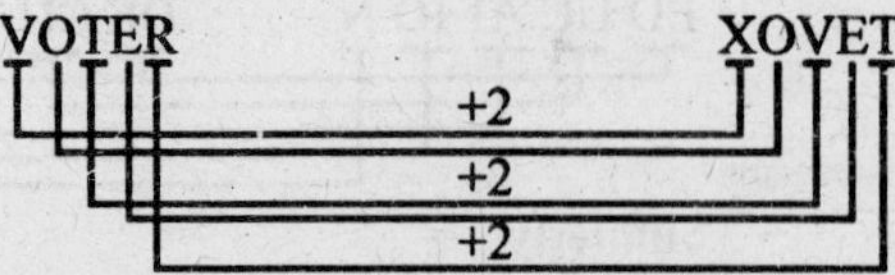

55. (c) : The word is divided into three equal sections, and the letters of first and third sections are written backwards.

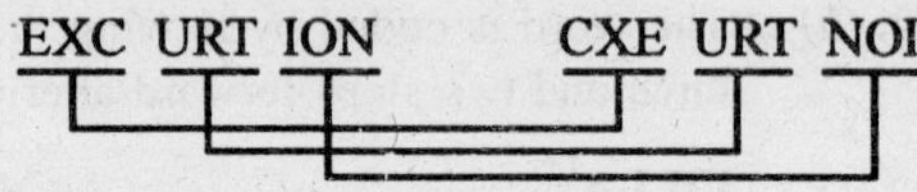

Similarly,

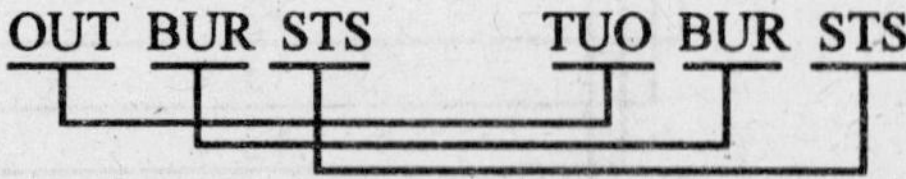

56. (c) : The letters of the words are coded by substituted letters. To find the answer codes, select the respective substituted letters.

A DD SUM TOTAL → letters
W OO QJM KPKWX → substituted letters codes

So,

T O A D S → letters
K P W O Q → substituted answer letter codes

57. (d) : The letters of the word are moved five steps forward and three steps backward alternately.

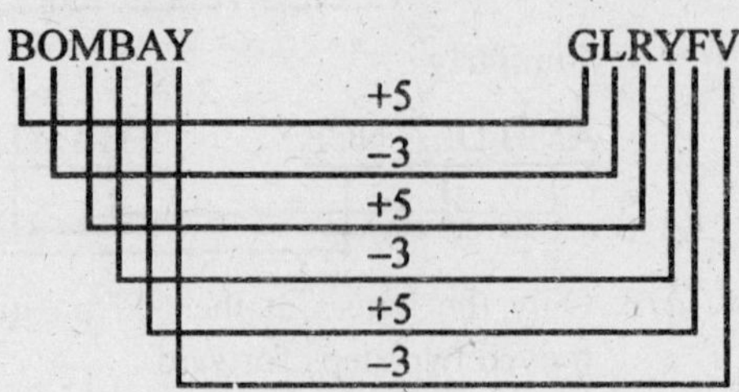

Similarly,

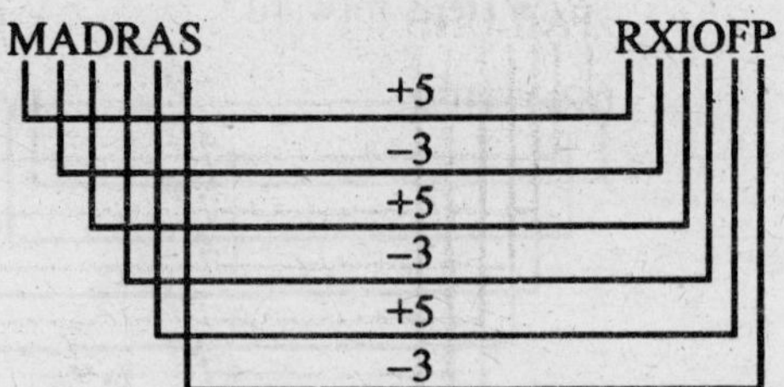

(The series restarts from A on reaching Z)

58. (b) : The code is decoded to obtain the word. The letters are moved one step backward.

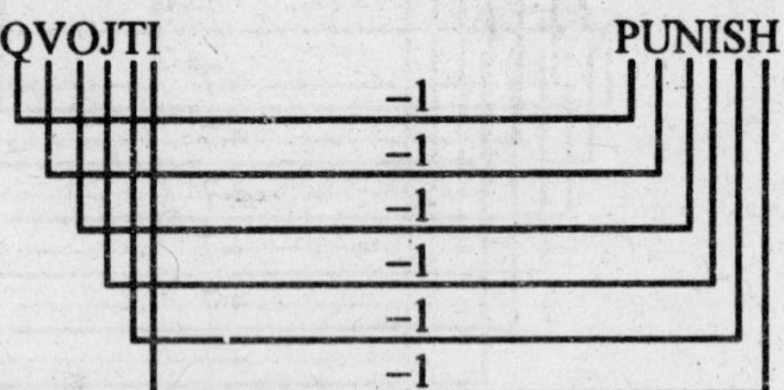

Similarly,

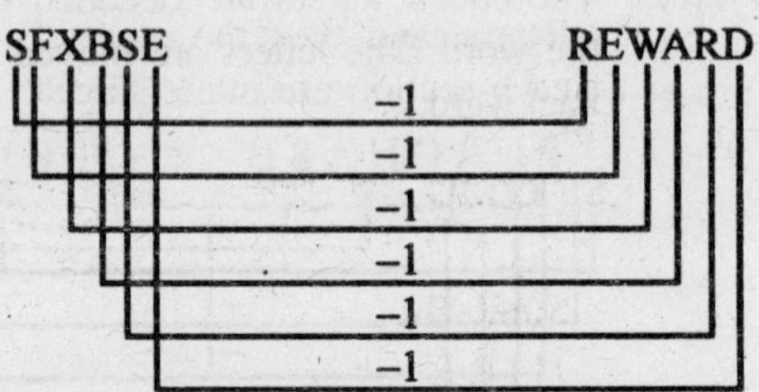

59. (c) : The word is divided into two equal sections and then the letters of each section are written alternately starting from the first section.

<u>ADM</u>		<u>IRE</u>
1st Section		2nd Section
AIDRME	→	code

Similarly,

<u>ADO</u>		<u>RES</u>
1st Section		2nd Section
ARDEOS	→	answer code

60. (b) : The letters of the word are moved nine and seven steps forward alternately.

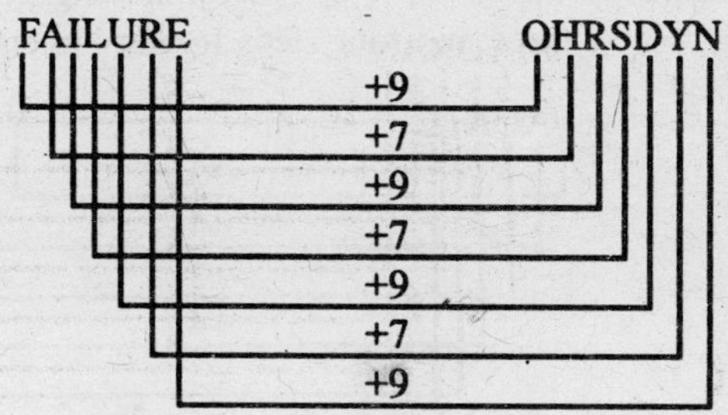

Similarly,

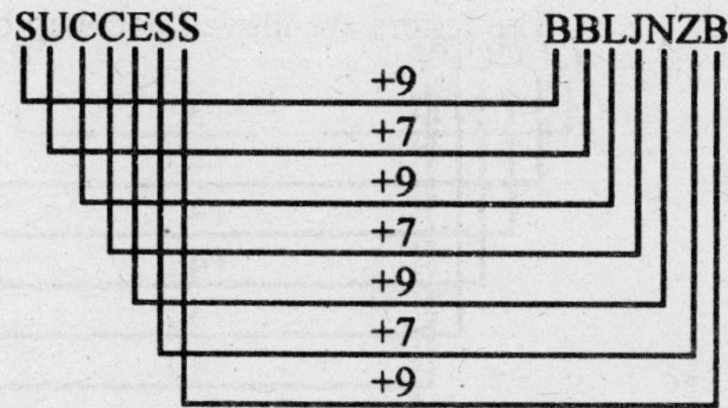

(The series restarts from A on reaching Z)

61. ***(d)*** **:** The word is divided into sections of two letters, and then the places of letters in each section are interchanged.

Similarly,

HIRE IHER

62. ***(a)*** **:** The letters of the coded word are decoded by the represented letters in the reverse series.

U	Z	W	V	→ (letters in natural series)
F	A	D	E	→ (letters in
↓	↓	↓	↓	reverse series)
21st	26th	23rd	22nd	→ (position of letters)

Similarly,

I	F	G	H	→ (letters in natural series)
R	U	S	T	→ (letters in
↓	↓	↓	↓	reverse series)
9th	6th	7th	8th	→ (position of letters)

63. ***(c)*** **:** The letters of the word are moved four steps forward.

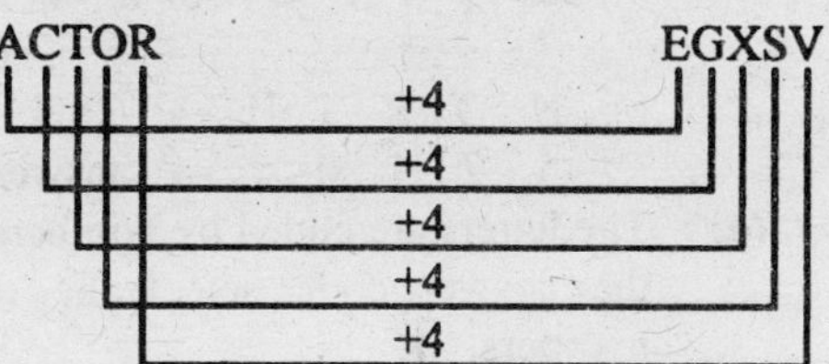

Similarly

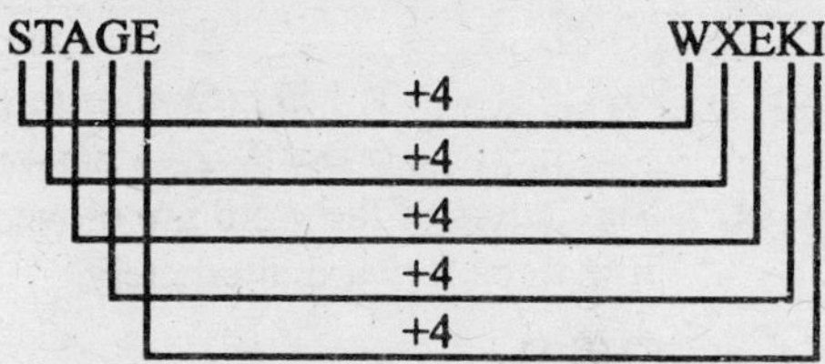

64. ***(b)*** **:** The letters of the word are moved five steps forward and backward alternately.

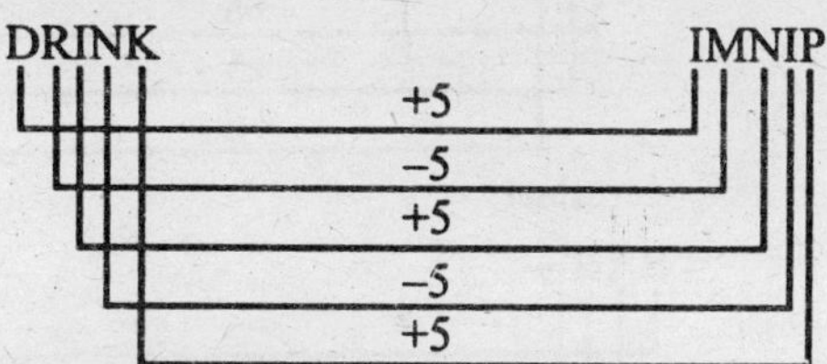

Similarly,

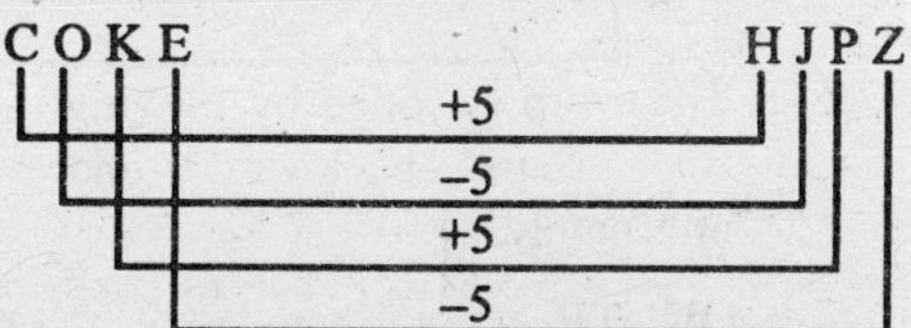

(The series restarts from Z on reaching A)

65. ***(d)*** **:** The letters of the word are coded by represented letters. To find the answer code, select the coded represented letters.

HORSE CAT → letters
BUNGY HOW → substituted letter codes

So,

CHEST → letters
HBYGW → substituted answer letter codes

66. ***(d)*** **:** The letters are coded by respective numbers. To find the answer code, select the respective numbers.

M O T H E R L A N D → letters
9 2 0 6 3 1 4 7 5 8 → number codes

So, N O R T H → letters
5 2 1 0 6 → answer codes

67. (a) : The letters are coded by numbers. To find the answer code select the respective numbers.

B A D G I V E F O R → letters
5 1 4 3 0 6 8 7 2 9 → number codes

So, V I D E O → letters
6 0 4 8 2 → answer codes

68. (a) : The letters of the word are moved six and five steps forward alternately.

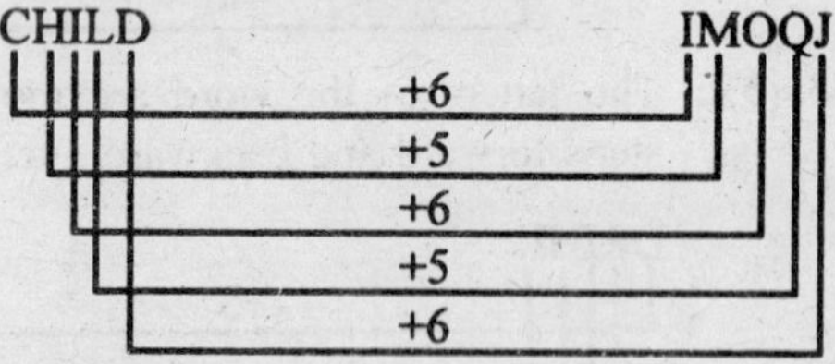

Similarly,

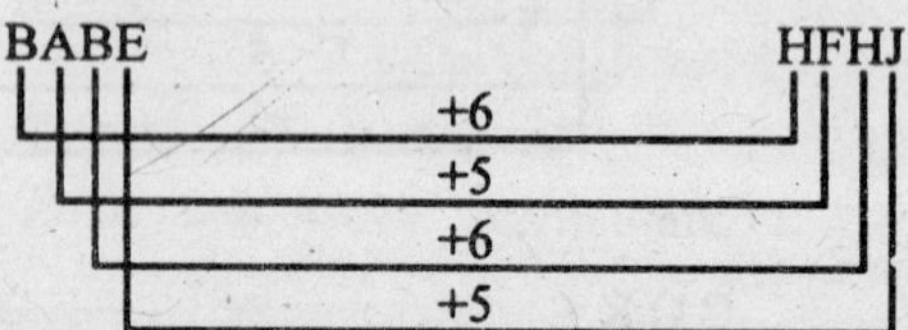

69. (b) : The word is coded by moving the letters two steps backward and forward alternately.

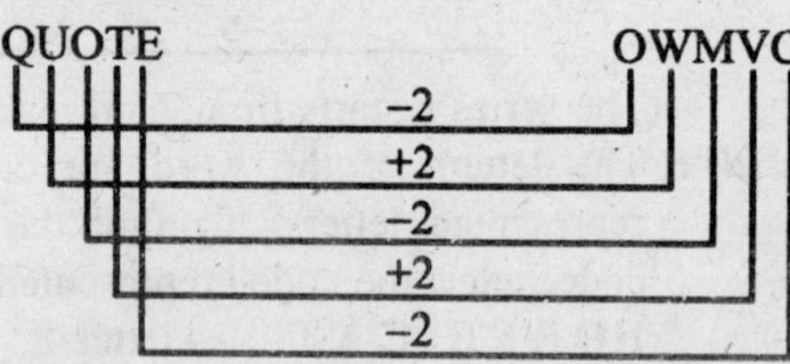

Similarly,

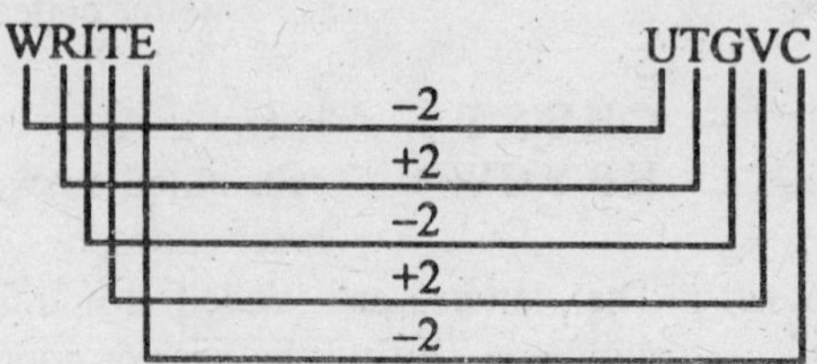

70. (d) : The word is coded by moving the letters three and four steps forward alternately.

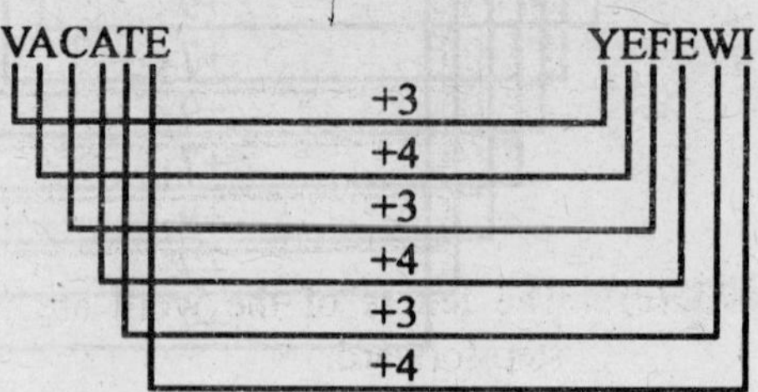

Similarly,

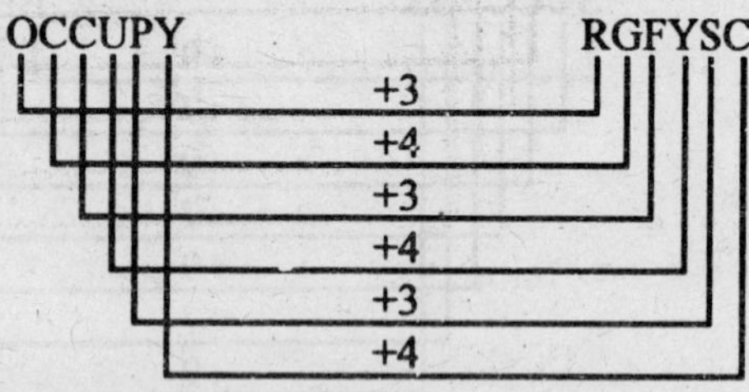

(The series restarts from A on reaching Z)

71. (a) : The word is coded by moving the letters four steps forward.

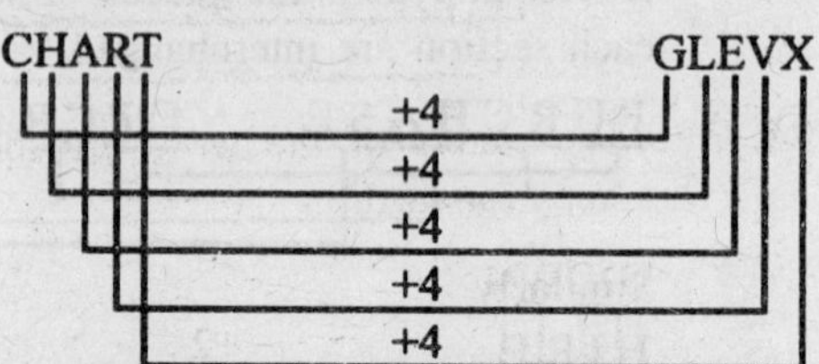

Similarly,

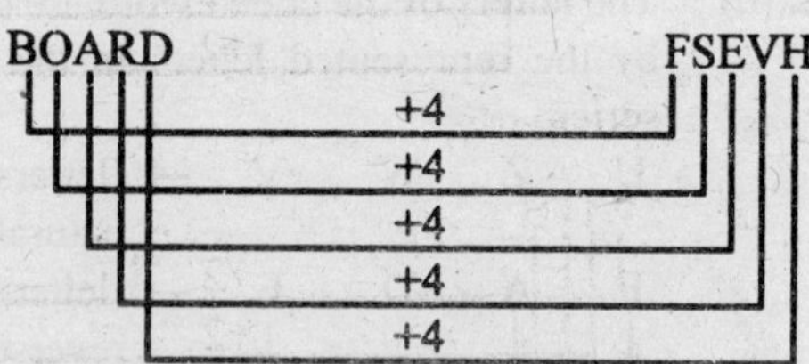

72. (b) : The word is coded by moving the letters one step forward and backward alternately.

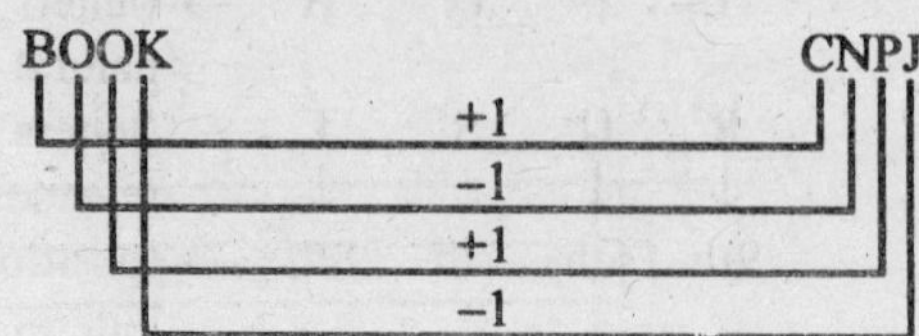

Similarly,

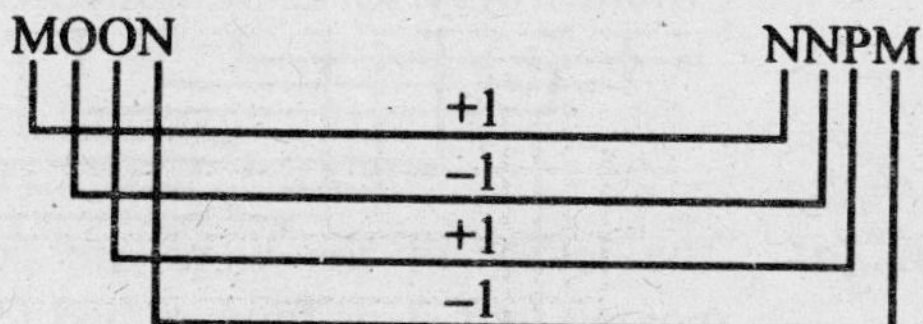

73. ***(c)*** **:** The letters of the word are moved one step forward.

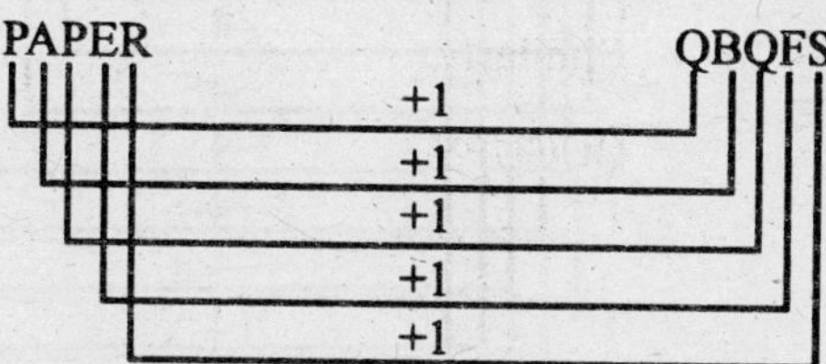

Similarly,

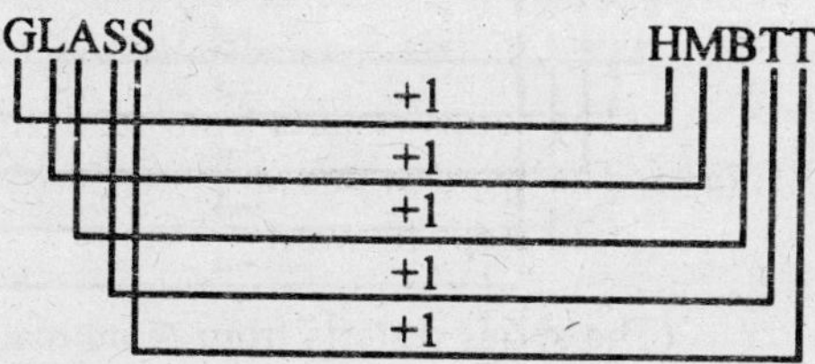

74. ***(c)*** **:** The letters of the word are moved two steps forward.

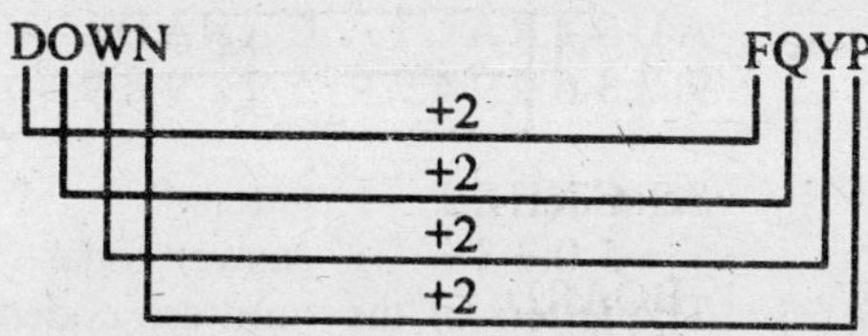

Similarly,

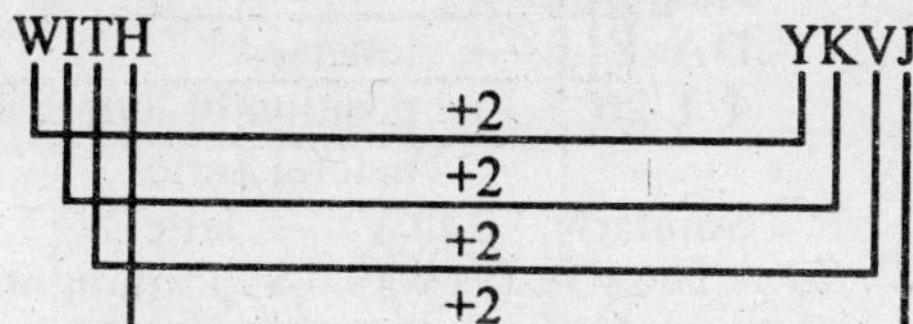

75. ***(b)*** **:** The letters of the word are moved two steps forward.

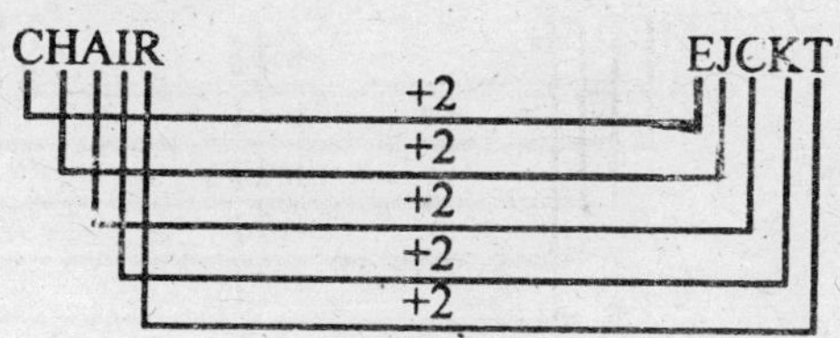

Similarly,

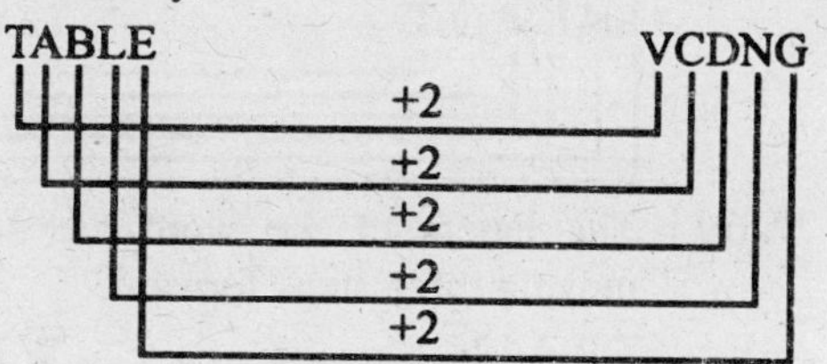

76. ***(c)*** **:** The letters of the word are moved forward by increasing steps starting from two.

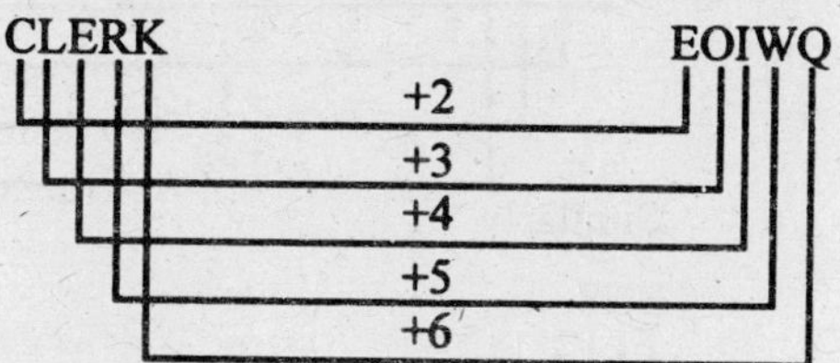

Similarly,

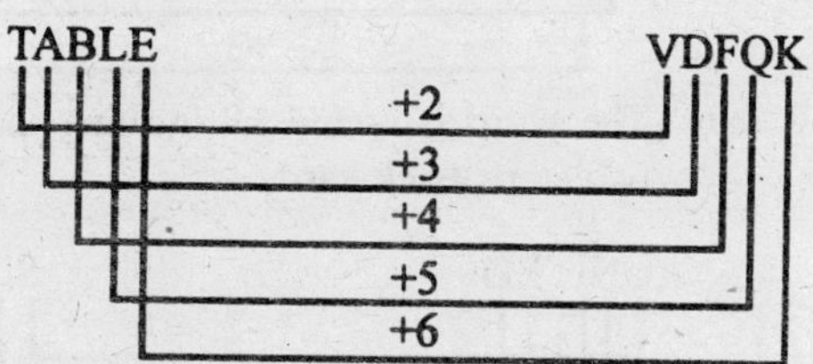

77. ***(c)*** **:** The letters of the word are moved four steps forward.

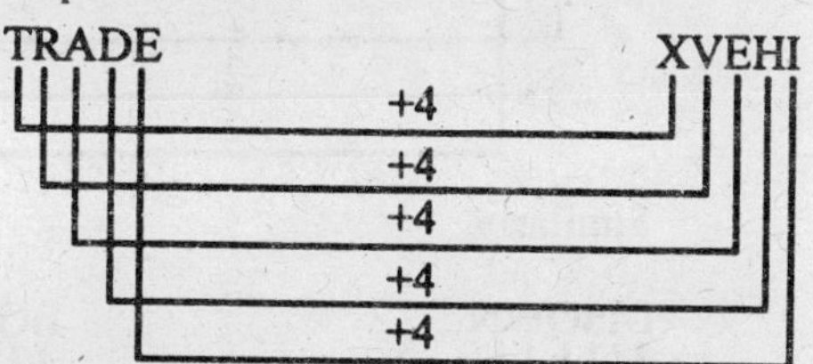

Similarly,

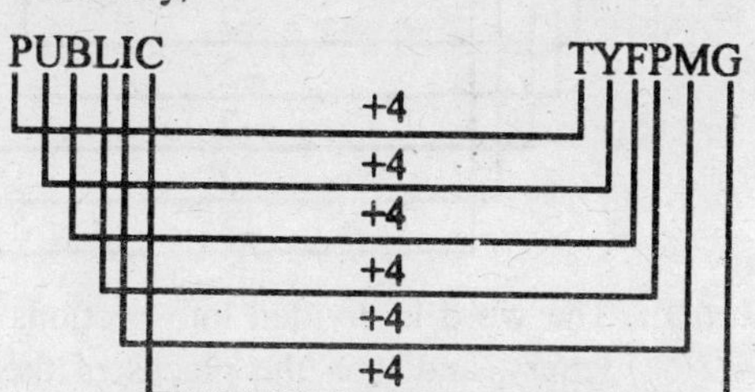

78. ***(d)*** **:** The letters of the word are written backward.

Similarly,

79. (c) : The letters of the word are coded by moving three steps forward.

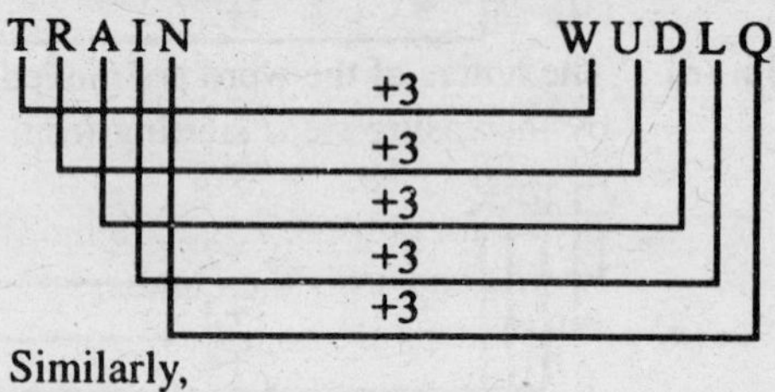

Similarly,

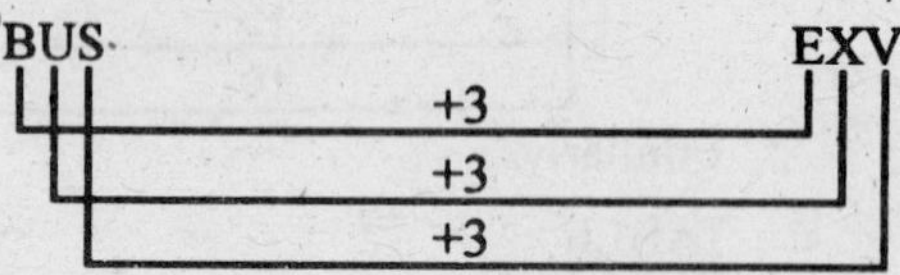

80. (a) : The word is coded by moving the letters two steps backward.

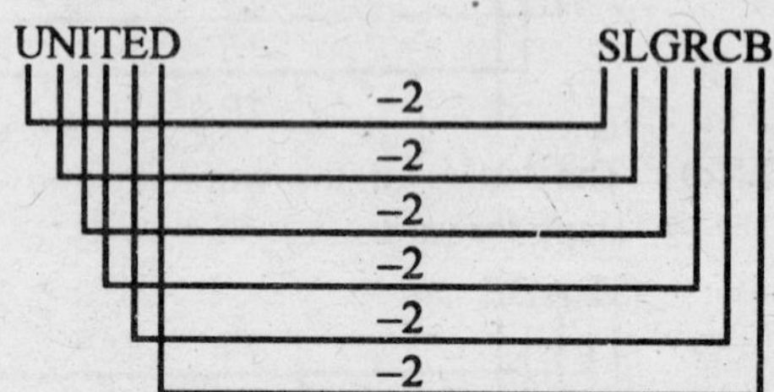

Similarly,

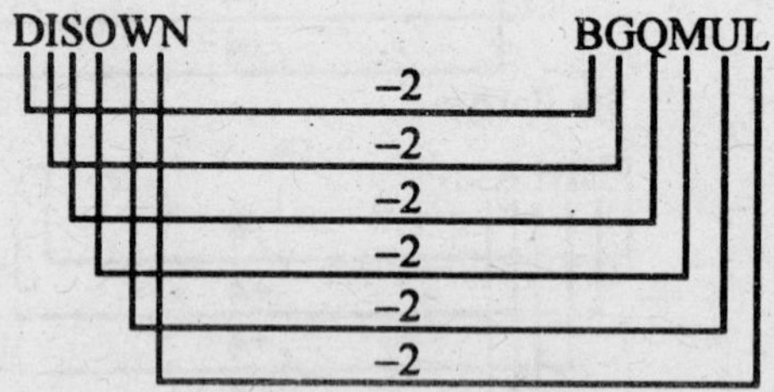

81. (d) : The word is divided into sections of two letters, and then the places of the letters of the odd numbered sections are interchanged.

Similarly,

82. (a) : The letters of the word are coded by moving four steps forward and four steps backward alternately.

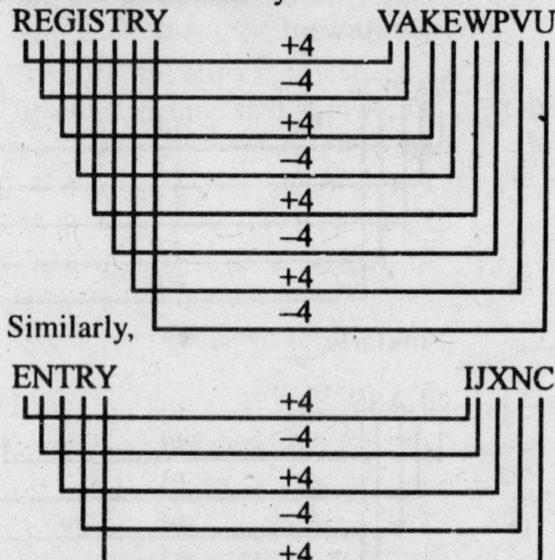

(The series restarts from A on reaching Z)

83. (d) : The letters are coded by numbers. To find the answer code, select the respective numbers.

A U S T R A L I A C A N A D A →letters
9 7 3 6 0 9 4 2 9 5 9 1 9 8 9 →number codes

So, C R U S T → letters
5 0 7 3 6 → answer codes

84. (c) : The letters of the word are coded by the numbers representing their position in the natural series.

D A Z E → letters
4 1 26 5 → position of letters in natural series

Similarly, B O Y → letters
2 15 25 → position of letters in natural series

85. (a) : The word is coded by moving the letters eleven steps forward.

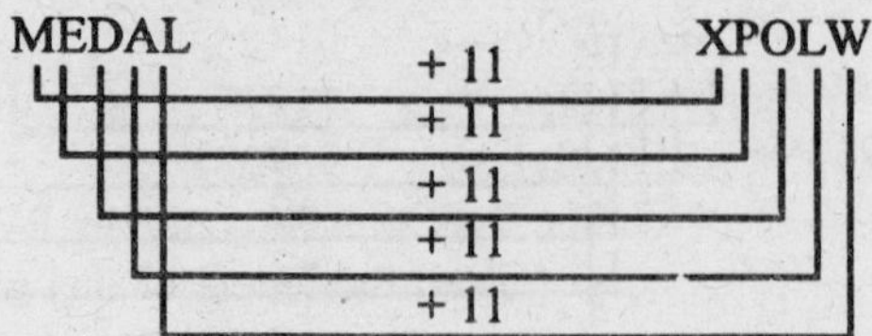

Similarly,

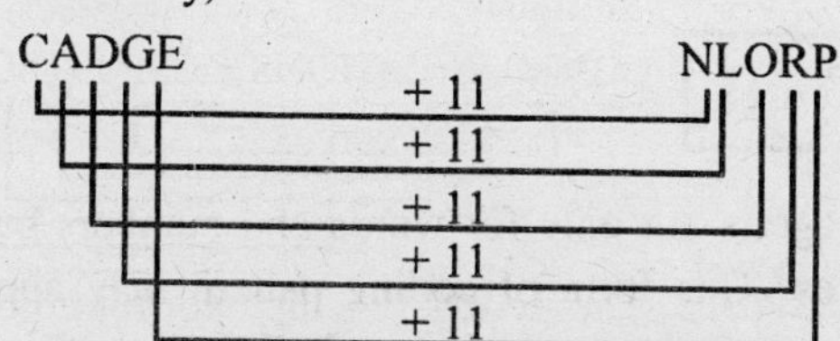

86. *(c)* : The words which have letter D in them are:
GRADE & DRAIN → letters
7 2 3 0 8   0 2 3 4 5 → codes
It is clear that code for 'D' is '0'.

87. *(b)* : The words that contain letter 'R' in them are :

F I R S T → 3 6 5 0 9
M O R E → 4 8 3 7
M E R I T → 8 3 5 7 9

Observation reveals that letter 'R' is common in the three words and so is the number '3'.

88. *(c)* : The manner of coding is :
TODAY WROTE DATE DIRTH
4 5 7 3 8 1 0 5 4 2 7 3 4 2 7 9 0 4 6
The number '5' is common in words TODAY and WROTE, and so is the letter 'O'. Letter 'T' cannot be the answer because it is common in all the four words and so is its number code '4'.

89. *(a)* : The words are coded in the following manner :

JOKER → 29750
TRUMP → 45813
PROJECT → 1572064

Letter 'C' is present in one word only, *i.e.*, PROJECT, and so is the code 6. All other number codes of this word are repeated in codes for JOKER and TRUMP.

90. *(b)* : The letter 'A' is present in three words and so is the number '1' in all the three words.
FACE HAD BADGE
6 135 8 1 4 2 1 4 7 5

91. *(d)* : The words are coded as :

ACTION → 014853
FORCE → 25916
REGAIN → 967083

Number 7 is present only in REGAIN. Except 'G' all the letters of this word are repeated in other two words. So '7' is the code for 'G'.

92. *(b)* : The words are coded as :
WORK ROUND KIND BRING BROOD
0918 19354 8654 71652 71994
It is clear that letter 'G' is represented by '2'.

93. *(c)* : The words are coded as :

BEAR → 9218
DRUM → 0863
PRY → 485
DOOR → 7998

Code for R is 8. R is common in all the words and so is the number '8'.

94. *(a)* : The letters are coded as :

FRANK → 93210
AFTER → 29463
MUFFET → 879964
FERRY → 96335
REEF → 3669

Code for F is 9. 'F' is common in all the words and so is the number '9'.

95. *(b)* : The words are coded as :
SAY ASK YES DYE EYE
069 608 930 493 393
It is clear that code for 'Y' is 9.

96. *(c)* : The words are coded as :
STABILITY RESTICATE
3 2 1 9 5 6 5 2 7 4 0 3 2 5 8 1 2 0
It is clear that code of 'I' is 5.

97. *(b)* : The word is coded as :
E X A M I N A T I O N
8 3 6 9 0 5 6 7 0 4 5
Code for N is 5 and for A is 6.

98. *(a)* : The words are coded as :
BEAUTY DEVIL ABIDE
8 3 5 2 4 7 0 3 9 1 6 5 8 1 0 3
It is clear that 3 is the code for E.

99. *(b)* : The words are coded as :

BARK → 0375
DIRT → 4972
WAGE → 4086
RISK → 7518

'R' is common in three words and so is the number '7'.

100. *(a)* : The words with the letter G are :
B A D G E & G R A D E
9 3 2 7 1   7 4 3 2 1
It is clear that code for G is 7.

PART - II

There is variety in ways of coding. Coding language is not only for words and numbers but also for hiding a group of words, statements or even sentences. This form of coding pattern may appear to be confusing but after solving only a few questions it is very easy to understand. Questions based on this coding pattern require no moving of steps or straining efforts of calculations, but only quick tallying or comparing ability. The codes can be letters or numbers.

SOLVED EXAMPLES

1. In a certain code 'ra mei ket' means 'he is rich'; 'rui pha jeu' means 'run for money'; and 'pha rui ket' means 'money for rich'. Which of the following is the code for 'rich'?

(*a*) ra (*b*) pha (*c*) ket (*d*) jeu

Ans. ***(c)*** **:** The given information is :

Code	*Sentence*
1. ra mei *ket*	he is *rich*
2. rui pha jeu	run for money
3. pha rui *ket*	money for *rich*

After comparing codes and sentences 1 and 3, it is clear that word 'rich' is common and so is the code 'ket'.

2. In a certain code 'ni ra ge' stands for 'who are you'; 'boi wo dur' stands for 'going far away'; and 'wo ge chi' stands for 'you went away'. Which of the following is the code for 'went'?

(*a*) ra (*b*) chi (*c*) wo (*d*) boi

Ans. ***(b)*** **:** The given information is :

Code	*Sentence*
1. ni ra *ge*	who are *you*
2. boi *wo* dur	going far *away*
3. *wo ge* **chi**	*you* **went** *away*

The word 'went' is in third sentence only. The word 'you' is common in first and third sentence and so is the code 'ge'. The word 'away' is common in second and third sentence and so is the code 'wo'. The only code remaining is 'chi' which stands for 'went'.

3. In a certain code 923 means 'beautiful and ugly', 249 means 'ugly and sensible', and 281 means 'bold and braven'. Which of the following is the code for 'and' ?

(*a*) 9 (*b*) 4 (*c*) 8 (*d*) 2

Ans. ***(d)*** **:** The given information is :

Code	*Sentence*
1. 9 2 3	beautiful *and* ugly
2. 2 4 9	ugly *and* sensible
3. 2 8 1	bold *and* braven.

In all the given codes and sentences the word 'and' is common and so is the code '2'.

EXERCISE

Directions : *In the following questions study the coded patterns and then select the right option from the given alternatives.*

1. In a certain language, (a) 'go ju mi' stands for 'plenty of money'; (b) pao ju go nei vu' for 'money creates lots of problems'; (c) 'kol vu nei' for 'problems create tension'; and (d) 'sol tun ju haw' for 'still money is needed'. Which of the following words stand for 'money'?

(*a*) nei (*b*) ju
(*c*) haw (*d*) go

2. In a certain language, (a) 'FOR' stands for 'old is gold'; (b) 'ROT' stands for 'gold is pure'; (c) 'ROM' stands for 'gold is costly'. How will 'pure old gold is costly' be written?

(*a*) TFROM (*b*) FOTRM
(*c*) FTORM (*d*) TOMRF

3. In a certain code '415' means 'milk is hot'; '18' means 'hot soup'; and '895' means 'soup is tasty'. What number will indicate the word 'tasty'?

(*a*) 9 (*b*) 8
(*c*) 5 (*d*) 4

4. In a certain code '643' means 'she is beautiful', '593' means 'he is handsome', and '567' means 'handsome meets beautiful'. What number will indicate the word 'meets'?

(*a*) 5 (*b*) 3
(*c*) 7 (*d*) 6

5. In a certain code language, (a) 'dugo hui mul zo' stands for 'work is very hard'; (b) 'hui dugo ba ki' for 'Bingo is very smart'; (c) 'nano mul dugo' for 'cake is hard', and (d) 'mul ki qu' for 'smart and hard'. Which of the following words stand for 'Bingo'?

(*a*) jalu (*b*) dugo
(*c*) ki (*d*) ba

6. In a certain code language, (a) 'pic vic nic' stands for 'winter is cold'; (b) 'to nic re' for 'summer is hot'; (c) 're pic boo' for 'winter and summer' and (d) 'vic tho pa' for 'nights are cold'. Which of the following word is the code for 'summer'?

(*a*) nic (*b*) boo
(*c*) to (*d*) re

7. In a certain language, (a) 'mx das sci' means 'good little frock'; (b) 'jm coz sci' means 'girl behaves good'; (c) 'ngv drs coz' means 'girl makes mischief'; and (d) 'das gp coz' means 'little girl fell'. What is the code for 'frock' in this language?

(*a*) mx (*b*) das
(*c*) sci (*d*) gp

8. In a certain language 'mu mit es' means 'who is she' and 'elb mu es' means 'where is she'. What is the code for 'where' in this language?

(*a*) es (*b*) elb
(*c*) mu (*d*) mit

9. In a certain code language '069' means 'grapes are sweet', '476' means 'very sweet fruit' and '509' means 'grapes are ripe'. Which of the following digits means 'ripe' in that language?

(*a*) 0 (*b*) 5
(*c*) 9 (*d*) 7

10. In a certain code language 'roi ja kyo twa' means 'Moody is writing letters', 'pok ju ja twa' means 'Woody is writing cards', 'trn kyo pos un' means 'they are writing letters', and 'koi rus pok' means 'gifts and cards'. What is the code word for 'Moody'?

(*a*) ja (*b*) twa
(*c*) roi (*d*) kyo

11. In a certain code language 'wre asi amoh kedo' means 'Polo is drinking tea', 'wre epu uki' means 'Polo buys books', and 'buen eld kedo' means 'Libbo drinks tea'. Which of the following code words mean 'Polo' and 'tea' in the above language?

(*a*) kedo and wre (*b*) asi and buen
(*c*) wre and kedo (*d*) amoh and wre

12. In a certain code, (i) 'juka lal mit sut' stands for 'Hello, how are you?'; (ii) 'mudi sut em nif' for 'Where are they going?'; (iii) 'hu zul met sut' for 'What are their names?'; and (iv) 'lal sut zul pe' for 'Are you going

too?'. Which of the following words in the above code language stand for 'are you'?
(*a*) sut mit (*b*) mudi sut
(*c*) juka nif (*d*) sut lal

13. In a certain code 'gri chri' means 'brand new', 'gyp twoh' means 'very old', 'gri bur twoh' means 'old and new' and 'chri deh gyp' means 'old brand car'. Which of the following codes means 'new car'?
(*a*) chri gri (*b*) gri deh
(*c*) deh gyp (*d*) twoh deh

14. If 'luma papa jano' stands for 'he speaks softly', 'papa lo hedi lami' for 'wind blows softly downhill'; and 'lo puki luma jano lami sod' for 'he sings like wind blows whisper; then what word will be written for 'downhill'?
(*a*) papa (*b*) lami
(*c*) hedi (*d*) lo

15. In a certain language, (a) 'sun shines brightly' is written as 'ba lo sul'; (b) 'houses are brightly lit' as 'kadó udo ari ba'; and (c) 'light comes from sun' as 'dapi kup lo nro'. What words will be written for 'sun' and 'brightly'?
(*a*) lo, ba (*b*) ba, lo
(*c*) snl, lo (*d*) ba, sul

16. In a certain code language, (1) 'lo ni hie pun' stands for 'he is drinking coke'; (2) 'hol ful gui pun' stands for 'she is eating food'; and (3) 'ne ful ni lo' stands for 'drinking coke and food'. Which of the following words is the code for 'he'?
(*a*) hie (*b*) lo
(*c*) pun (*d*) ni

17. In a certain code language,
1. Gor Paku Means 'Best Gift'
2. Mull Gor Sot Means 'Gift of Love'
3. Sot Hed Paku Means 'Best of Luck' and
4. Hed Sot Paku Means 'Love is Best'

Which of the following codes stand for the word 'Love'?
(*a*) Paku (*b*) Hed
(*c*) Sot (*d*) Mull

18. In a certain code language, 'pe sa de mi' means 'yes well no mean' and 'pa mi sa de' means 'sell mean well no'. What would 'yes' mean in that language?
(*a*) de (*b*) pe
(*c*) mi (*d*) sa

19. In a certain code 'hua pih uf pu' means 'he is very intelligent'; 'pih hua kup kit' means 'she is very fair'; 'luck uf hua' means 'Jai is intelligent'; and 'uf kit pod' means 'fair and intelligent'.
Which of the following codes stand for 'Jai'?
(*a*) kit (*b*) hua
(*c*) luck (*d*) pih

20. In a certain code language 'jo mi rei ma' stands for 'rest work no play'; 'rei kol puihi mesi' for 'less ground play tour'; and 'puihi ma jo mati' for 'rest group ground work'.
Which of the following codes stand for word 'no'?
(*a*) mi (*b*) mesi
(*c*) rei (*d*) jo

21. In a certain code '7 8 6' means 'bring me apple', '9 5 8' means 'peel green apple' and '6 4 5' means 'bring green fruit'. Which of the following is the code for 'me'?
(*a*) 8
(*b*) 6
(*c*) 7
(*d*) Cannot be determined

22. If 'ish lto inm' stands for 'neat and tidy'; 'qpr inm sen' stands for 'small but neat'; 'hsm sen rso' stands for 'good but erratic'; what would 'but' stand for?
(*a*) inm (*b*) sen
(*c*) qpr (*d*) hsm

23. If 'nso ptr kli chn' stands for 'Sharma gets marriage gift': 'ptr lnm wop chn' stands for 'wife gives marriage gift': 'tti wop nhi' stands for 'he gives nothing'; what would 'gives' stand for?
(*a*) wop (*b*) ptr
(*c*) nhi (*d*) chn

24. In a certain code language, 'col tip mot' means 'singing is appreciable', 'mot baj min' means 'dancing is good' and 'tip nop baj' means 'singing and dancing'. Which of the following means 'Good' in that code language?
(*a*) mot (*b*) min

(*c*) baj
(*d*) Cannot be determined

25. In a certain code '7 8 6' means 'study very hard', '9 5 8' means 'hard work pays' and '6 4 5' means 'study and work', which of the following is the code for 'very'?
(*a*) 8
(*b*) 6
(*c*) 7
(*d*) Cannot be determined

26. In a certain code language '1 2 3' means 'hot filter coffee', '3 5 6' means 'very hot day' and '5 8 9' means 'day and night'. Which digit in that language means 'very'?
(*a*) 8 (*b*) 6
(*c*) 9 (*d*) 5

27. In a certain code, '3 5 7' means 'get me toy', '8 4 3' means 'bring good toy' and '7 4 6' means 'bring me water'. Which of the following digits represents 'good' in that code?
(*a*) 7 (*b*) 6
(*c*) Data inadequate
(*d*) None of these

28. In a certain code 721 means 'good college life'. 526 means 'you are good' and 257 means 'life are good', which digit stands for 'you' as the code?
(*a*) 6 (*b*) 5
(*c*) 7 (*d*) None of these

29. In a certain code language 'dom pul ta' means 'bring hot food', 'pul tir sop' means 'food is good' and 'tak da sop' means 'good bright boy'. Which of the following does mean 'hot' in that language?
(*a*) dom
(*b*) pul
(*c*) ta
(*d*) Cannot be determined

30. In a certain code '3 7' means 'which class' and '5 8 3' means 'caste and class'. What is the code for 'caste'?
(*a*) 3 (*b*) 7
(*c*) Either 5 or 3 (*d*) Either 5 or 8

31. In a code language 'mu kay cit' means 'very lucky person' and 'dis hu mu' means 'fortunate and lucky'. Which is the word in that language for 'lucky?'
(*a*) mu (*b*) kay
(*c*) cit (*d*) dis

Directions : (Qs. 32-33) : *In a code language, (A) 'pit dar na' means 'you are good'; (B) 'dar tok pa' means 'good and bad'; (C) 'tim na tok' means 'they are bad'.*

32. In that language, which word stands for 'they'?
(*a*) na (*b*) tok
(*c*) tim (*d*) None of these

33. To find the answer to the above question, which of the following statements can be dispensed with?
(*a*) Only A (*b*) Only B
(*c*) A or B (*d*) None of these

Directions : (Qs. 34-35) : *In a certain code language :*

(A) 'tom na rod' means 'give me sweet'.
(B) 'jo ta rod' means 'you and me'.
(C) 'pot ta noc' means 'you are good'.
(D) 'jo mit noc' means 'good and bad'.

34. Which of the following represents 'bad' in that language?
(*a*) mit (*b*) noc
(*c*) jo (*d*) None of these

35. To arrive at the answer to the above question which of the following can be dispensed with?
(*a*) All are necessary
(*b*) A or B only
(*c*) A or C only
(*d*) None of these

Directions : (Qs. 36-37) : *In a certain code language :*

(A) 'pit na som' means 'bring me water'.
(B) 'na jo tod' means 'water is life'.
(C) 'tub od pit' means 'give me toy'.
(D) 'jo lin kot' means 'life and death'.

36. Which of the following represents 'is' in that language?
(*a*) jo (*b*) na
(*c*) tod (*d*) lin

37. To find out the answer to the above question, which of the following statements can be dispensed with?
(*a*) A only (*b*) C only

(*c*) D only (*d*) B or C only

Directions : (Qs. 38 to 40) : ***In a certain code language :***

(A) '1 3 4' means 'you are well'

(B) '7 5 8' means 'they go home'

(C) '8 3 9' means 'we are home'.

38. Which of the following represents 'they' in that code language?

(*a*) 5 (*b*) 7

(*c*) 3 (*d*) Data inadequate

39. Which of the statements can be dispensed with while answering the above question?

(*a*) A only (*b*) B only

(*c*) A or C only (*d*) B and C only

40. Which of the following represents 'are' in that code language?

(*a*) 1 (*b*) 3

(*c*) 4 (*d*) 7

EXPLANATORY ANSWERS

1. (*b*) :

Code	*Sentence*
1. go *ju* mi	plenty of *money*
2. pao *ju* go nei vu	*money* creates lots of problems
3. kol vu nei	problems create tension
4. sol tun *ju* haw	still *money* is needed

In 1st, 2nd and 4th codes and their sentences the word 'ju' is repeated and so is 'money'.

2. (*a*) :

Code	*Sentence*
1. FOR	old is gold
2. ROT	gold is pure
3. ROM	gold is costly

Therefore,

F stands for old

O stands for is

R stands for gold

T stands for pure

M stands for costly

So, 'pure old gold is costly' will be written as 'TFROM'.

3. (*a*) :

Code	*Sentence*
1. 415	milk is hot
2. 18	hot soup
3. 895	soup is *tasty*

From 3rd code and its sentence neither number '9' is repeated nor the word 'tasty'.

4. (*c*) :

Code	*Sentence*
1. 643	she is beautiful
2. 593	he is handsome
3. 567	handsome *meets* beautiful

From 3rd code and its sentence, neither number '7' nor the word 'meets' is repeated.

5. (*d*) :

Code	*Sentence*
1. *dugo hui* mul zo	work *is very* hard
2. *hui dugo* **ba** *ki*	**Bingo** *is very smart*
3. nano mul *dugo*	cake is *hard*
4. mul *ki* qu	*smart* and hard

From 2nd code and its sentence, neither 'ba' nor 'Bingo' is repeated.

(Words repeated are in italics)

6. (*d*) :

Code	*Sentence*
1. pic vic nic	winter is cold
2. to nic *re*	*summer* is hot
3. *re* pic boo	winter and *summer*
4. vic tho pa	nights are cold

The word 'summer' is common in 2nd and 3rd sentences and so is the code 're'.

7. (*a*) :

Code	*Sentence*
1. **mx** *das sci*	*good little* **frock**
2. jm coz *sci*	girl behaves *good*
3. ngv drs coz	girl makes mischief
4. *das* gp coz	*little* girl fell

Word 'frock' is only in the 1st sentence. The code word 'das' is repeated in 4th sentence and 'sci' in 2nd sentence. So, 'mx' is the code for 'frock'.

8. (*b*) :

Code	*Sentence*
1. *mu* mit *es*	who *is she*
2. **elb** *mu* es	**where** *is she*

The code words 'mu' and 'es' are repeated in Ist sentence. The only code left is 'elb' which means 'where'.

9. (*b*) : *Code* *Sentence*
1. *069* *grapes are* sweet
2. 476 very sweet fruit
3. 509 *grapes are* **ripe**

The code numbers '0' and '9' are repeated in 1st and 3rd sentences. The only code remaining is '5' which stands for 'ripe'.

10. (*c*) : *Code* *Sentence*
1. **roi** *ja kyo twa* **Moody** *is writing letters*
2. pok ju *ja twa* Woody *is writing* cards
3. trn *kyo* pos un they are writing *letters*
4. koi rus pok gifts and cards

'Moody' is in 1st sentence only. The code words 'ja' and 'twa' are repeated in 2nd sentence and 'kyo' in 3rd sentence. Only code word 'roi' remains which stands for 'Moody'.

11. (*c*) : *Code* *Sentence*
1. *wre* asi amoh **kedo** *Polo* is drinking **tea**.
2. *wre* epu uki *Polo* buys books
3. buen eld **kedo** Libbo drinks **tea**

The word 'Polo' is common in 1st and 2nd sentence and so is the code 'wre'. The word 'tea' is common in 1st and 3rd sentences and so is the code 'kedo'.

12. (*d*) : *Code* *Sentence*
1. juka *lal* mit **sut** hello, how **are** *you*?
2. mudi **sut** em nif where **are** they going?
3. hu zul met **sut** what **are** their names?
4. *lal* **sut** zul pe **are** *you* going too?

The word 'are' is present in all the four sentences and so is the code 'sut. The word 'you' is common in 1st and 4th sentences and so is the code 'lal'.

13. (*b*): *Code* *Sentence*
1. **gri** chri brand **new**
2. gyp twoh very old
3. **gri** bur twoh old and **new**
4. chri *deh* gyp old brand *car*

The word 'new' is present in 1st and 3rd sentences and so is the code 'gri. The word 'car' is only in the 4th sentence and code 'deh' is not repeated in any other sentence.

14. (*c*) : *Code* *Sentence*
1. luma *papa* jano → he speaks *softly*
2. *papa lo* **hedi** *lami*→ *wind blows softly* **downhill**
3. *lo* puki luma jano→ he sings like *lami* sod *wind blows* whisper

Code 'papa' is repeated in 1st and 2nd sentence but the word 'downhill' is not. Of the other coded words in 2nd sentence 'lo' and 'lami' are repeated in 3rd sentence, but again the word 'downhill' is not. The only code remaining is 'hedi' which should mean 'downhill'.

15. (*a*) : *Sentence* *Code*
1. *sun* shines **brightly** → **ba** *lo* sul
2. houses are **brightly** lit → kado udo ari **ba**
3. light comes from *sun* → dapi kup *lo* nro. In 1st and 3rd sentences, the word 'sun' is repeated and so is the code 'lo'. Similarly, in 1st and 2nd sentences the word 'brightly' is repeated and so is the code 'ba'.

16. (*a*) : *Code* *Sentence*
1. *lo ni* **hie** *pun* → **he** *is drinking coke*
2. hol ful gui *pun* → she *is* eating food
3. ne ful *ni lo* → *drinking coke* and food

In the 1st and 2nd sentences, the code 'pun' for 'is' is repeated but the word 'he' is not. In the 1st and 3rd sentences, the codes 'ni' and 'lo' are repeated. So, the code 'hie' stands for 'he'.

17. (*c*) : *Code* *Sentence*
1. Gor Paku → Best Gift
2. Mull Gor *Sot* → Gift of *Love*
3. Sot Hed Paku → Best of Luck
4. Hed *Sot* Paku → *Love* is Best

Only in sentences 2nd and 4th, the word 'Love' is repeated and the only code repeated is 'Sot'.

18. (*b*) : *Code* *Sentence*
1. **pe** *sa de mi* → **yes** *well no mean*
2. pa *mi sa de* → sell *mean well no*

In both the sentences, "well no mean" is repeated and so the coded words 'sa de mi' So, only 'pe' stands for 'yes'.

19. ***(c)*** **:** *Code* *Sentence*

1. *hua* pih uf pu → he *is* very intelligent
2. pih *hua* kup kit → she *is* very fair
3. **luck** *uf hua* → **Jai** *is intelligent*
4. *uf* kit pod → fair and *intelligent*

The word 'Jai' is in 3rd sentence. Of the three codes, 'hua' is repeated in 1st and 2nd sentences and 'uf' is repeated in 3rd and 4th sentences. So, code 'luck' stands for 'Jai'.

20. ***(a)*** **:** *Code* *Sentence*

1. *jo* **mi** *rei ma* → *rest work* **no** *play*
2. *rei* kol puihi mesi→ less ground *play* tour
3. puihi *ma jo* mati→ *rest* group ground *work*

The word 'no' is only in 1st sentence. Of the other codes 'rei' is repeated in 2nd sentence and 'jo' and 'ma' are repeated in 3rd sentence. So, 'mi' code stands for word 'no'.

21. ***(c)*** **:** *Code* *Sentence*

1. *7***8***6* *bring* **me** *apple*
2. 95*8* peel green *apple*
3. *6*45 *bring* green fruit

The word 'me' is in 1st sentence only. The word 'bring' is common in 1st and 3rd sentences and so is the code 6. The word 'apple' is common in 1st and 2nd sentences and so is the code 8. Only word remaining is 'me' and its code is 7.

22. ***(b)*** **:** *Code* *Sentence*

1. ish lto inm neat and tidy
2. qpr inm *sen* small *but* neat
3. hsm *sen* rso good *but* erratic

In 2nd and 3rd sentences word 'but' is repeated and so is the code 'sen'.

23. ***(a)*** **:** *Code* *Sentence*

1. nso ptr kli chn Sharma gets marriage gift
2. ptr lnm *wop* chn wife *gives* marriage gift
3. tti *wop* nhi he *gives* nothing

In 2nd and 3rd sentences word 'gives' is repeated and so is the code 'wop'.

24. ***(b)*** **:** *Code* *Sentence*

1. col tip *mot* singing *is* appreciable
2. *mot baj* **min** *dancing is* **good**
3. tip nop *baj* singing and *dancing*

The word 'good' is in 2nd sentence only. The word 'dancing' is common in 2nd and 3rd sentences and so is the code 'baj'. The word 'is' common in 1st and 2nd sentences and so is the code 'mot'. The only code remaining is 'min' which stands for 'good'.

25. ***(c)*** **:** *Code* *Sentence*

1. *786* *study* **very** *hard*
2. 958 *hard* work pays
3. *645* *study* and work

The word 'very' is in 1st sentence only. The word 'study' is common in 1st and 3rd sentences and so is the code '6'. The word 'hard' is common in 1st and 2nd sentences and so is the code '8'. The only code remaining is '7' which stands for 'very'.

26. ***(b)*** **:** *Code* *Sentence*

1. 123 *hot* filter coffee
2. *356* **very** *hot day*
3. *589* *day* and night

The word 'very' is in 2nd sentence only. The word 'hot' is common in 1st and 2nd sentences and so is the code '3'. The word 'day' is common in 2nd and 3rd sentences and so is the code '5'. The only code remaining is '6' which stands for 'very'.

27. ***(d)*** **:** *Code* *Sentence*

1. *357* get me *toy*
2. **8***43* *bring* **good** *toy*
3. *746* *bring* me water

The word 'good' is in 2nd sentence only. The word 'bring' is common in 2nd and 3rd sentences and so is the code '4'. The word 'toy' is common in 1st and 2nd sentences and so is the code '3'. The only code remaining is '8' which stands for 'good'.

28. *(a)* :

	Code	*Sentence*
1.	721	good college life
2.	*52*6	**you** *are good*
3.	*257*	life *are good*

The word 'you' is in 2nd sentence only. The words 'are good' are common in 2nd and 3rd sentences and so are the codes '2' and '5'. The only code remaining is '6' which stands for 'you'.

29. *(d)* :

	Code	*Sentence*
1.	dom *pul* ta	bring **hot** *food*
2.	*pul* tir sop	*food* is good
3.	tak da sop	good bright boy

From 1st and 2nd codes and sentences it is clear that code for 'food' is 'pul'. Neither the words 'bring' and 'hot' are repeated nor the codes 'dom' and 'ta'. So, the codes for the words cannot be detected.

30. *(d)* :

	Code	*Sentence*
1.	*3*7	which *class*
2.	58*3*	caste and *class*

In both the codes and sentences code '3' stands for 'class'. So the code for 'caste' can be either '5' or '8'. The same applies for word 'and'. More information is needed.

31. *(a)* :

	Code	*Sentence*
1.	*mu* kay cit	very *lucky* person
2.	dis hu *mu*	fortunate and *lucky*

In both the codes and sentences word 'lucky' is common and so is the code 'mu'.

32. *(c)* :

	Code	*Sentence*
A.	pit dar *na*	you *are* good
B.	dar *tok* pa	good and *bad*
C.	**tim** *na tok*	**they** *are bad*

The word 'they' is in sentence B only. The word 'are' is repeated in sentence A and so is the code 'na'. The word 'bad' is repeated in sentence B and so is the code 'tok'. The only code remaining is 'tim' which stands for 'they'.

33. *(d)* : The answer to the above question was arrived at only after comparing all the three codes and sentences.

34. *(a)* :

	Code	*Sentence*
A.	tom na rod	give me sweet
B.	*jo* ta rod	you *and* me
C.	pot ta *noc*	you are *good*
D.	*jo* **mit** *noc*	*good* and **bad**

The word 'bad' is in sentence 'D' only. The word 'good' is repeated in sentence 'C' and so is the code 'noc'. The word 'and' is repeated in sentence 'B' and so is the code 'jo'. The only code remaining is 'mit' which stands for 'bad'.

35. *(d)* : The answer to the above question was arrived at by comparing codes and sentences B, C and D. Only sentence 'A' could be dispensed with.

36. *(c)* :

	Code	*Sentence*
A.	pit *na* som	bring me *water*
B.	*na jo* **tod**	*water* **is** *life*
C.	tub od pit	give me toy
D.	*jo* lin kot	*life* and death

The word 'is' is in Sentence 'B' only. The word 'water' is repeated in Sentence 'A' and so is the code 'na'. The word 'life' is repeated in sentence 'D' and so is the code 'jo'. The only code remaining is 'tod' which stands for 'is'.

37. *(b)* : The answer to the above question was arrived at by comparing codes and sentences A, B and D. Only sentence 'C' could be dispensed with.

38. *(d)* :

	Code	*Sentence*
A.	1*3*4	you *are* well
B.	75*8*	they go *home*
C.	*8*3*9*	we *are home*

In codes and sentences B and C the word 'home' is repeated and so is the code '8'. The code for word 'they' can be either '7' or '5'. The same applies for 'go'. More information is needed.

39. *(a)* : Sentence 'A' has nothing in common with sentence 'B'.

40. *(b)* : In codes and sentences A and C the word 'are' is repeated and so is the code '3'.

PART - III

In yet another manner of coding particular words are assigned code names which are further coded. The questions on this pattern may appear meaningless but the codes must not be confused with the basic properties of reality.

SOLVED EXAMPLES

1. If 'banana' is called 'jelly', 'jelly' is called 'green', 'green' is called 'apple', 'apple' is called 'mango', what is the colour of leaf?

(*a*) green (*b*) mango (*c*) apple (*d*) banana (*e*) jelly

Ans. *(c)* : Leaf is green in colour and according to the codes in the question 'green' is called 'apple'.

2. If 'grey' is called 'brown', 'white' is called 'pink', 'red' is called 'grey', 'black' is called 'red', and 'brown' is called 'white', what is the colour of 'coal'?

(*a*) brown (*b*) white (*c*) black (*d*) pink (*e*) red

Ans. *(e)* : Coal is black in colour and according to the codes in the question 'black' is called 'red'.

3. If 'element' is called 'animal', 'atom' is called 'bird', 'bird' is called 'element', 'animal' is called 'android', 'android' is called 'robot', 'robot' is called 'ion', what is a lion?

(*a*) element (*b*) android (*c*) animal (*d*) bird (*e*) robot

Ans. *(b)* : Lion is an animal and according to the codes in question 'animal' is called 'android'.

EXERCISE

Directions : *Read the given coded information and choose the correct answer from the given options.*

1. If 'water' is called 'blue', 'blue' is called 'red', 'red' is called 'white', 'white' is called 'sky', 'sky' is called 'rain', 'rain' is called 'green', 'green' is called 'air' and 'air' is called 'table', which of the following is the colour of milk?

(*a*) white (*b*) rain
(*c*) sky (*d*) green
(*e*) air

2. If 'light' is called 'dark', 'dark' is called 'green', 'green' is called 'blue', 'blue' is called 'red', 'red' is called 'white' and 'white' is called 'yellow', what is the colour of blood?

(*a*) red (*b*) dark
(*c*) white (*d*) yellow
(*e*) None of these

3. If 'sky' is called 'sea', 'sea' is called 'water', 'water' is called 'air', 'air' is called 'cloud' and 'cloud' is called 'river', then what do we drink when thirsty?

(*a*) sky (*b*) air
(*c*) water (*d*) sea
(*e*) cloud

4. If 'yellow' means 'red', 'white' means 'green', 'red' means 'orange', 'blue' means 'white' and 'green' means 'blue', then the colour of sky is :

(*a*) white (*b*) green
(*c*) blue (*d*) yellow
(*e*) red

5. If 'land' is called 'sky', 'sky' is called 'air', 'air' is called 'water', 'water' is called 'sand' and 'sand' is called 'solid', where do fishes swim?

(*a*) air (*b*) sky
(*c*) water (*d*) solid
(*e*) sand

6. If 'house' is called 'hut', 'hut' is called 'canal', 'canal' is called 'school', 'school' is

called 'lawn', 'lawn' is called 'jug' and 'jug' is called 'cable', where do students study?
(*a*) lawn (*b*) jug
(*c*) hut (*d*) school
(*e*) canal

7. If 'cat' is called 'horse', 'horse' is called 'mouse', 'dog' is called 'rabbit', 'rabbit' is called 'cat', 'mouse' is called 'dog' and 'lion' is called 'ant', which is the animal that barks?
(*a*) dog (*b*) cat
(*c*) lion (*d*) rabbit
(*e*) horse

8. If 'light' is called 'morning', 'morning' is called 'dark', 'dark' is called 'night', 'night' is called 'sunshine' and 'sunshine' is called 'dusk', when do we sleep?
(*a*) morning (*b*) night
(*c*) dusk (*d*) dark
(*e*) sunshine

9. If 'ground' is called 'lake', 'lake' is called 'stone', 'stone' is called 'heavy', 'heavy' is called 'stadium', 'stadium' is called 'ocean', 'ocean' is called 'rain' and 'rain' is called 'fire', where are the testmatches held?
(*a*) heavy (*b*) ocean
(*c*) stone (*d*) ground
(*e*) stadium

10. If 'birds' are called 'kings', 'kings' are called 'flowers', 'flowers' are called 'cubes', 'cubes' are called 'tables', 'tables' are called 'humans' and 'humans' are called 'birds', what are roses?
(*a*) tables (*b*) flowers
(*c*) cubes (*d*) human
(*e*) birds

11. If 'water' is called 'stone', 'stone' is called 'oil', 'oil' is called 'air', 'air' is called 'wood', 'wood' is called 'gas' and 'gas' is called 'liquid', what is furniture made of?
(*a*) gas (*b*) air
(*c*) oil (*d*) liquid
(*e*) wood

12. If 'cages' are called 'rockets', 'rockets' are called 'traps', 'traps' are called 'planets', 'planets' are called 'aeroplanes', 'aeroplanes' are called 'cycles' and 'cycles' are called 'cars', what is Earth?
(*a*) cycles (*b*) rockets
(*c*) planet (*d*) aeroplanes
(*e*) traps

13. If 'red' is called 'air', 'air' is called 'black', 'black' is called 'sky', 'sky' is called 'blue', 'blue' is called 'wind' and 'wind' is called 'white', where to birds fly?
(*a*) air (*b*) sky
(*c*) blue (*d*) wind
(*e*) black

14. If 'dark' is called 'clear', 'clear' is called 'wind', 'wind' is called 'light', 'light' is called 'dull', 'dull', is called 'brown', 'brown' is called 'heavy', and 'heavy' is called 'bright', what is the colour of sand?
(*a*) dull (*b*) bright
(*c*) light (*d*) heavy
(*e*) clear

15. If 'orange' is called 'ashen', 'ashen' is called, 'red', 'red' is called 'blue', 'blue' is called 'brown', 'brown' is called 'black', 'black' is called 'white' and 'white' is called 'pale', what is the colour of a tree trunk?
(*a*) black (*b*) brown
(*c*) blue (*d*) white
(*e*) red

16. If 'green' is called 'pink', 'pink' is called 'blue', 'blue' is called 'purple', 'purple' is called 'white', 'white' is called 'orange' and 'orange' is called 'peach', what is the colour of snow?
(*a*) peach (*b*) orange
(*c*) purple (*d*) blue
(*e*) white

17. If 'engineers' are 'carpenters', 'carpenters' are 'painters', 'painters' are 'cobblers', 'cobblers' are 'doctors', 'doctors' are 'authors', 'authors' are 'jewellers' and 'jewellers' are 'robbers', who cures the sick people?
(*a*) jewellers (*b*) painters
(*c*) cobblers (*d*) doctors
(*e*) authors

18. If 'copper' is called 'gold', 'lead' is called 'silver', 'iron' is called 'lead', 'gold' is called 'tin' and 'silver' is called 'steel', what is in

a pencil?
(*a*) lead (*b*) gold
(*c*) tin (*d*) silver
(*e*) iron

19. If 'colour' is called 'blue', 'blue' is called 'light', 'light' is called 'showy', 'showy' is called 'dark' and 'dark' is called 'colour', what is the colour of ink?
(*a*) blue (*b*) showy
(*c*) dark (*d*) colour
(*e*) light

20. If 'violet' is called 'yellow', 'yellow' is called 'blue', 'blue' is called 'red', 'red' is called 'fawn', 'fawn' is called 'green' what is the colour of brick?
(*a*) blue (*b*) green
(*c*) yellow (*d*) fawn
(*e*) red

21. If 'cars' are called 'flowers', 'flowers' are called 'cakes', 'cakes' are called 'fruits', 'fruits' are called 'birds', 'birds' are called 'ants' and 'ants' are called 'pigs', what is a crow?
(*a*) pig (*b*) ant
(*c*) bird (*d*) fruit
(*e*) cake

22. If 'yellow', is called 'pale', 'pale' is called 'blue', 'blue' is called 'orange', 'orange' is called 'dull', 'dull' is called 'green' and green' is called 'yellow', what is the colour of grass in a lawn?
(*a*) pale (*b*) yellow
(*c*) blue (*d*) green
(*e*) orange

23. If 'light' is called 'colour', 'colour' is called 'red', 'power' is called 'light', 'red' is called 'dust' and 'dust' is called 'waste', what do we get from Sun?
(*a*) colour (*b*) light
(*c*) red (*d*) power
(*e*) dust

24. If 'mud' is called 'water', 'water' is called 'heat', 'heat' is called 'gas', 'gas' is called 'air', 'air' is called 'fire', where do fishes swim?
(*a*) water (*b*) air
(*c*) heat (*d*) fire
(*e*) gas

25. If 'black' is called 'pink', 'pink' is called 'blue', 'blue' is called 'brown', 'brown' is called 'orange', 'orange' is called 'violet', violet' is called 'red' and 'red' is called 'black', what is the colour of blood?
(*a*) black (*b*) brown
(*c*) pink (*d*) orange
(*e*) red

EXPLANATORY ANSWERS

1. (*c*) : Colour of milk is 'white' and 'white' is called 'sky'.

2. (*c*) : Colour of blood is 'red' and 'red' is called 'white'.

3. (*b*) : We drink 'water' when we are thirsty and 'water' is called 'air'.

4. (*a*) : Colour of sky is 'blue' and 'blue' means 'white'.

5. (*e*) : Fishes swim in 'water' and 'water' is called 'sand'.

6. (*a*) : Students study in 'school' and 'school' is called 'lawn'.

7. (*d*) : Animal that barks is 'dog' and 'dog' is called 'rabbit'.

8. (*e*) : We sleep during the 'night' and 'night' is called 'sunshine'.

9. (*b*) : Test-matches are held in 'stadium' and 'stadium' is called 'ocean'.

10. (*c*) : Roses are 'flowers' and 'flowers' are called 'cubes'.

11. (*a*) : Furniture is made of 'wood' and 'wood is called 'gas'.

12. (*d*) : Earth is a 'planet' and 'planets' are called 'aeroplanes'.

13. (*c*) : Birds fly in the 'sky' and 'sky' is called 'blue'.

14. (*d*) : Colour of sand is 'brown' and 'brown' is called 'heavy'.

15. (*a*) : Colour of tree trunk is 'brown' and 'brown' is called 'black'.

16. ***(b)*** **:** Colour of snow is 'white' and 'white' is called 'orange'.

17. ***(e)*** **:** Sick people are cured by a 'doctor' and 'doctors' are called 'authors'.

18. ***(d)*** **:** Pencil has 'lead' in it and 'lead' is called 'silver'.

19. ***(e)*** **:** Colour of ink is 'blue' and 'blue' is called 'light'.

20. ***(d)*** **:** Colour of brick is 'red' and 'red' is called 'fawn'.

21. ***(b)*** **:** Crow is a 'bird' and 'birds' are called 'ants'.

22. ***(b)*** **:** The colour of grass in a lawn is 'green' and 'green' is called 'yellow'.

23. ***(a)*** **:** We get 'light' from sun and 'light' is called 'colour'.

24. ***(c)*** **:** Fishes swim in 'water' and 'water' is called 'heat'.

25. ***(a)*** **:** Colour of blood is 'red' and 'red' is called 'black'.

PART - IV

Coding-Decoding can be really easy and simplified if one has to tally the given codes. In this type of coding, the Digits and its coded Letters or *vice versa* are already given. One has to find out the answers to the given questions just by tallying the given codes.

SOLVED EXAMPLES

1. *Digits* : 3 7 2 0 1 9 8 5 4
Letters : A X M W Z B L N D
Which of the following options has the correct coded form of the given number 90342?
(*a*) BMADX (*b*) BWADX (*c*) BWADM (*d*) BMADW
Ans. (*c*)

2. *Letters* : J N I Q V R F A D S
Digits : 4 7 2 5 9 1 8 6 3 0
Which of the following options has the correct coded form of the given letter FRNIS?
(*a*) 81720 (*b*) 81270 (*c*) 61750 (*d*) 18720
Ans. (*a*)

EXERCISE

Directions (Qs. 1 to 5) : *The following questions are based on the code pattern given below :*

Digits : 2 6 4 1 0 8 3 7 5 9
Letters : M E N H V F I W L X

Which of the given options has the correct coded form of the given numbers?

1. 435216
(*a*) HILMNE (*b*) NILMHE
(*c*) VFLMNE (*d*) NILHME

2. 897615
(*a*) FXWEHL (*b*) VXLENH
(*c*) FXLWHE (*d*) VXELHI

3. 146738
(*a*) HNEIWF (*b*) HNWEIF
(*c*) HENWIF (*d*) HNEWIF

4. 092863
(*a*) VXMFEI (*b*) VXMIFE
(*c*) VXMIEF (*d*) VXFMEI

5. 702439
(*a*) LVMIEX (*b*) INEMHV
(*c*) WVMNIX (*d*) VWNMEX

Directions (Qs. 6 to 10) : *The following questions are based on the following code pattern :*

Digits : 7 0 5 9 2 4 8 3 1 6
Letters : J R S D Q C A K G O

Which of the given options has the correct coded form of the given numbers?

6. 251460
(*a*) QSGCOR (*b*) CRGCOS
(*c*) QSCGOJ (*d*) CSGROS

7. 357698
(*a*) GSRODA (*b*) KSJOSA
(*c*) GSORSA (*d*) KSJODA

8. 735021
(*a*) JASRDG (*b*) JKDRQG
(*c*) JKSRQG (*d*) JKSQRG

9. 850394
(*a*) ASRKDC (*b*) ASRDKC
(*c*) CARKDQ (*d*) AKRDSQ

10. 176203
(*a*) GJODQR (*b*) GJOQRK
(*c*) KJOQAR (*d*) KOQRJA

Directions (Qs. 11 to 15) : *The following questions are based on the code pattern given below.*

Digits : 4 7 3 9 1 6 5 0 8 2
Letters : T N J Z B R V S W D

Which of the given options has the correct coded form of the given numbers?

11. 627958
(*a*) VBZJWT (*b*) RDNZVW
(*c*) BRZNTW (*d*) ZVSJTN

12. 104329
(*a*) ZSTNZB (*b*) RBNSJD
(*c*) BSTJDZ (*d*) WRDSJN

13. 258306
(*a*) VDJWRS (*b*) BRJNTS
(*c*) DVWJSR (*d*) SWVRJT

14. 921473
(*a*) ZDBTNJ (*b*) JRVTNB
(*c*) RNTJWD (*d*) SDBTNJ

15. 058934
(*a*) VRSBZN (*b*) SVWZJT
(*c*) WSDJNT (*d*) RBVBJT

Directions (Qs. 16 to 20) : *Based on the code pattern given below answer the following questions.*

Numbers :	5	9	2	0	6	3	8	1	4	7
Alphabet :	C	X	O	A	Q	V	J	S	G	B

16. 862309
(*a*) SVAQOX (*b*) JQOVAX
(*c*) GVQVAO (*d*) VQAVXC

17. 241753
(*a*) OGSBCV (*b*) OGBSCV
(*c*) OGSCBV (*d*) OGSBQV

18. 045296
(*a*) OGCAXQ (*b*) JAXCSG
(*c*) AGCOXQ (*d*) QACOJV

19. 321987
(*a*) JAGOJB (*b*) QXSCJB
(*c*) VOSXJB (*d*) VOCXJG

20. 695430
(*a*) QXCSJA (*b*) QXCJVA
(*c*) QXCSVA (*d*) QXCGVA

Directions (Qs. 21 to 25) : *The following questions are based on the code pattern given below :*

Digits :	5	6	9	0	3	4	8	7	2	1
Letters :	J	L	P	Q	S	T	N	I	K	R

Which of the given options has the correct coded form of the given numbers?

21. 368204
(*a*) SPNKQT (*b*) SLNKQT
(*c*) SLNIQT (*d*) SLNKPT

22. 964815
(*a*) PLNTRJ (*b*) QSTNRJ
(*c*) PLTNRJ (*d*) QLTNRJ

23. 69087
(*a*) LPQNI (*b*) LPQIK
(*c*) JLPNI (*d*) QSTJN

24. 71035
(*a*) NSTJL (*b*) IRQSJ
(*c*) QSJLP (*d*) KRPQJ

25. 54792
(*a*) ITPJK (*b*) PTIKJ
(*c*) KPITJ (*d*) JTIPK

Directions (Qs. 26 to 30) : *The following questions are based on the code pattern given below :*

Letters :	X	S	M	A	P	E	D	L	W	T
Digits :	1	6	9	8	3	5	0	2	4	7

Which of the given options has the correct coded form of the given letters?

26. WDSTP
(*a*) 40638 (*b*) 40975
(*c*) 40948 (*d*) 40673

27. AMLXE
(*a*) 89213 (*b*) 89210
(*c*) 89215 (*d*) 89015

28. XTDMSW
(*a*) 170946 (*b*) 179064
(*c*) 170964 (*d*) 176904

29. MLADPS
(*a*) 928036 (*b*) 928536
(*c*) 698036 (*d*) 960836

30. EXWTM
(*a*) 51497 (*b*) 51479
(*c*) 54179 (*d*) 51749

Directions (Qs. 31 to 35) : *The following questions are based on the code pattern given below :*

Letters :	B	Y	E	V	R	C	X	I	G	W
Numbers :	7	5	6	0	4	3	9	8	1	2

Which of the following options is the correct coded form of the given letters?

31. RYWBCV
(*a*) 452780 (*b*) 452790
(*c*) 452730 (*d*) 327590

32. WEXIYC
(*a*) 209853 (*b*) 269853
(*c*) 268953 (*d*) 296853

33. YXGIEB
(*a*) 591867 (*b*) 594167
(*c*) 521867 (*d*) 539628

34. EXBRGV
(*a*) 697041 (*b*) 235971
(*c*) 237951 (*d*) 697410

35. CRWBGV
(*a*) 342610 (*b*) 342710
(*c*) 254610 (*d*) 245610

Directions (Qs. 36 to 40) : *Based on the given coded pattern answer the following questions :*

Letters :	N	L	K	V	S	R	B	Y	M	J
Numbers :	2	1	6	3	5	0	8	9	7	4

36. RLYJNK
(*a*) 091426 (*b*) 019246
(*c*) 019423 (*d*) 019426

37. NVLYMB
(*a*) 231987 (*b*) 235078
(*c*) 231978 (*d*) 239610

38. SRBNJY
(*a*) 508249 (*b*) 594208
(*c*) 631970 (*d*) 642170

39. SVLMBR
(*a*) 531980 (*b*) 531780
(*c*) 531805 (*d*) 561780

40. KRMSJN
(*a*) 608542 (*b*) 689542
(*c*) 607542 (*d*) 607524

Directions (Qs. 41 to 45) : *Based on the given coded pattern answer the following questions :*

Letters :	S	D	Q	P	N	C	Y	M	O	E
Numbers :	7	5	2	8	0	3	6	1	9	4

41. COEDPQ
(*a*) 394082 (*b*) 394582
(*c*) 394508 (*d*) 394502

42. MODYSP
(*a*) 195378 (*b*) 195678
(*c*) 195078 (*d*) 195638

43. OQNCMD
(*a*) 920615 (*b*) 920365
(*c*) 920312 (*d*) 920315

44. PSNEYO
(*a*) 870469 (*b*) 874609
(*c*) 876409 (*d*) 879046

45. DMSCNQ
(*a*) 517392 (*b*) 517382
(*c*) 517302 (*d*) 517362

Directions (Qs. 46 to 50) : *The following questions are based on the code pattern given below :*

Letters :	T	R	A	H	U	X	C	I	B	L
Numbers :	3	0	1	7	4	9	6	8	2	5

Which of the following options is the correct coded form of the given letters?

46. RACIXT
(*a*) 016823 (*b*) 016873
(*c*) 016843 (*d*) 016893

47. BUHLAI
(*a*) 247018 (*b*) 247508
(*c*) 247538 (*d*) 247518

48. LBIHAR
(*a*) 528471 (*b*) 528710
(*c*) 528947 (*d*) 528103

49. UBAXTC
(*a*) 421736 (*b*) 421956
(*c*) 421936 (*d*) 421906

50. HULBRT
(*a*) 745203 (*b*) 723045
(*c*) 752340 (*d*) 732145

ANSWERS

1	2	3	4	5	6	7	8	9	10
(*b*)	(*a*)	(*d*)	(*a*)	(*c*)	(*a*)	(*d*)	(*c*)	(*a*)	(*b*)
11	**12**	**13**	**14**	**15**	**16**	**17**	**18**	**19**	**20**
(*b*)	(*c*)	(*c*)	(*a*)	(*b*)	(*b*)	(*a*)	(*c*)	(*c*)	(*d*)
21	**22**	**23**	**24**	**25**	**26**	**27**	**28**	**29**	**30**
(*b*)	(*c*)	(*a*)	(*b*)	(*d*)	(*d*)	(*c*)	(*c*)	(*a*)	(*b*)
31	**32**	**33**	**34**	**35**	**36**	**37**	**38**	**39**	**40**
(*c*)	(*b*)	(*a*)	(*d*)	(*b*)	(*d*)	(*c*)	(*a*)	(*b*)	(*c*)
41	**42**	**43**	**44**	**45**	**46**	**47**	**48**	**49**	**50**
(*b*)	(*b*)	(*d*)	(*a*)	(*c*)	(*d*)	(*d*)	(*b*)	(*c*)	(*a*)

PART - V

In this type of coding, the capital letters A to Z are coded by using the small letters a to z. With the help of the coding pattern, one has to find the right code from the columns which has equivalent to the group of capital letters.

SOLVED EXAMPLES

Below are given letters A to Z and under each capital letter a small letters is written which is to be used as its code.

A	B	C	D	E	F	G	H	I	J	K	L	M
g	l	x	b	k	q	z	n	u	d	s	p	i
N	O	P	Q	R	S	T	U	V	W	X	Y	Z
r	t	f	y	v	h	w	a	j	o	e	c	m

In each of the following Questions (1-5), a group of six capital letters is given and its code equivalent is given in one of the columns (a), (b), (c) or (d). The correct answer is the column in which the group of code equivalent letters is found.

(a)	(b)	(c)	(d)
puinex	rmvjkl	undcfv	jqlmbh
dwyflo	qrodte	frhpni	rmvkpl
rmyxtu	jfnhdp	zglqde	cxrnuw
fdcwae	cubkfj	onrdlt	fcdaen
cxraen	zykpos	jpqmls	ofvcjy

1. NZRVEB

   Ans. ***(b)*** **:** The code equivalent 'rmvjkl' is in column (b).

2. PJYTUX

   Ans. ***(a)*** **:** The code equivalent 'fdcwae' is in column (a).

3. YCNHIT

   Ans. ***(d)*** **:** The code equivalent 'cxrnuw' is in column (d).

4. VFBZDS

   Ans. ***(d)*** **:** The code equivalent 'jqlmbh' is in column (d).

5. WHNJBO

   Ans. ***(c)*** **:** The code equivalent 'onrdlt' is in column (c).

EXERCISE

Directions (Qs. 1 to 10) : *Below are given letters A to Z. Under each capital letter a small letter is written which is to be used as a code for the capital letter.*

A	B	C	D	E	F	G	H	I
p	t	x	q	v	y	r	z	e
J	K	L	M	N	O	P	Q	R
n	a	s	g	c	j	l	u	m

S	T	U	V	W	X	Y	Z
o	w	k	d	i	b	h	f

In each of the following questions, a group of six capital letters is given and its code equivalent is given in one of the columns (a), (b), (c) or (d). The correct answer is the column in which the group of code equivalent letters is found

(a)	(b)	(c)	(d)
muvgto	zcuysm	wlhxct	ribgpq
xfwlmd	rsqwui	zcyums	mvquot
gwdnje	qvlmzi	xfdwlm	dgjtlq
muqvot	dgtjql	rigbqp	rqswui
qwjvrx	muvqto	rsqiwu	wlhzbt
wlhcxf	gwndej	qwjrvx	zcsmuy

1. DTOEGC
2. CZVTPR
3. MTVJOI
4. DEPRHW
5. TPYCNB
6. GWXMAD
7. GLDWTQ
8. RQEMBS
9. HNQFLR
10. VMOBPD

Directions (Qs. 11 to 20) : *Below are given letters A to Z. Under each capital letter is its code equivalent in small letters.*

A	B	C	D	E	F	G	H	I	J	K	L	M
g	m	x	k	z	r	a	l	p	v	u	c	o

N	O	P	Q	R	S	T	U	V	W	X	Y	Z
t	j	b	w	e	q	h	z	d	i	s	n	f

In each of the following questions a group of capital letters is given and its code equivalent is given in one of the columns (a), (b), (c) or (d). The correct answer is the column in which the group of code equivalent letters is found.

(a)	(b)	(c)	(d)
womghz	nuarlk	trbhzy	xepush
defats	fnrsan	jgobka	deiots
moplqt	xelvsh	baifzu	womjhz
nurapk	deiats	mkisny	atzefh
ztmrqw	wonglq	cqjuwt	duwpfj
atzwots	lqxcob	onqglz	nurlpk

11. BDWXZY
12. OAMPDG
13. CRHJXT
14. UNBFSQ
15. GNURZT
16. HSCLMP
17. VRWMNX
18. YKFGID
19. QMBATE
20. LSOKQN

ANSWERS

1	2	3	4	5	6	7	8	9	10
(a)	*(c)*	*(a)*	*(b)*	*(c)*	*(d)*	*(c)*	*(a)*	*(b)*	*(d)*
11	**12**	**13**	**14**	**15**	**16**	**17**	**18**	**19**	**20**
(c)	*(c)*	*(b)*	*(a)*	*(d)*	*(b)*	*(d)*	*(a)*	*(a)*	*(c)*

PART - VI

Column coding is a very complex form of coding. It needs a lot of attention and swift eye movement to decode the code for each letter of the given words. Proper words in capital letters are given in one column and the codes in small letters are given in another column. Based on the information given in both columns the candidate has to arrive at the correct answer option.

SOLVED EXAMPLES

Directions (Qs. 1 to 5) : *Below in Column I are given some words and in Column II are given their equivalent small letter codes. The letters in Column II are jumbled up. Decode the language and select the correct code for the words given in each question.*

Column I	*Column II*
1. SUCRE	A. kifpo
2. CURING	B. lcbfop
3. LATELY	C. gkhugv
4. TRACED	D. kofhru
5. PRIDE	E. tokcr
6. GRAVY	F. whlov
7. BUILT	G. cgpum

1. CREDIT

(*a*) idkrsp (*b*) holitb (*c*) fokrcu (*d*) uhvpci

2. PLUNGE

(*a*) ugtmlo (*b*) tgpblk (*c*) iupmob (*d*) wvfbit

3. YEARN

(*a*) tshdg (*b*) vkhob (*c*) wpcmk (*d*) folgt

4. BRAVE

(*a*) mbgfp (*b*) hvotw (*c*) poilb (*d*) mohwk

5. SPRING

(*a*) itocbl (*b*) hibmkl (*c*) ortvwc (*d*) kcgmpr

EXPLANATORY ANSWERS

The decoding steps will be :

(*i*) In LATELY the repeated letter is 'L' and so is the code 'g'.

(*ii*) In SUCRE and GRAVY the common letter is 'R' and so is the code 'o'.

(*iii*) In GRAVY and CURING the common letters are 'R' and 'G' and the common codes 'o' and 'l' with reference to (*ii*) code for 'G' is 'l'.

(*iv*) In GRAVY and TRACED the common letters are 'R' and 'A' and the common codes 'o' and 'h'. With reference to (*ii*) code for 'A' is 'h'.

(*v*) In GRAVY and LATELY the common letters are 'A' and 'Y' and the common codes 'h' and 'v'. With reference to (*iv*) code for 'Y' is 'v'.

(*vi*) The only letter remaining in GRAVY is 'V' and so is the code 'w'

(*vii*) In TRACED and BUILT the common letters is 'T' and so is the code 'u' *(viii)* In BUILT and SUCRE the common letter is 'U' and so is the code 'p'.

(ix) In BUILT and CURING the common letters are 'U' and 'I' and the common codes 'p' and 'c'. With reference to *(viii)* code for 'I' is 'c'.

(x) The only letter remaining in BUILT is 'B' and so is the code 'm'.

(xi) In TRACED and LATELY the common letters are 'A' and 'E' and the common codes 'h' and 'k'. With reference to *(iv)* code for 'E' is 'k'.

(xii) In TRACED and PRIDE the common letters are 'R', 'E' and 'D' and the common codes 'o', 'k' and 'r'. With reference to *(ii)* and *(xi)* code for 'D' is 'r'.

(xiii) The only letter remaining in TRACED is 'C' and so is the code 'f'.

(xiv) The only letter remaining in SUCRE is 'S' and so is the code 'i'.

(xv) The only letter remaining in CURING is 'N' and so is the code 'b'

(xvi) The only letter remaining in PRIDE is 'P' and so is the code 't'.

Based on above decoding steps the capital letters and their equivalent small letter codes will be :

Letters :	L	R	G	A	Y	V	T	U	I	B	E	D	C	S	N	P
Codes :	g	o	l	h	v	w	u	p	c	m	k	r	f	i	b	t

1. *(c)* **2.** *(b)* **3.** *(b)* **4.** *(d)* **5.** *(a)*

EXERCISE

Directions (Qs. 1-5) : *Below in Column I are given some words and in column II are given their equivalent small letter codes. The letters in column II are jumbled up. Moreover, the codes in Column II do not appear in the same order as in column I. Decode the language and select the correct code for the words given in each question.*

Column I	*Column II*
1. BIRD	A. wgo
2. SPORT	B. tnugn
3. SAD	C. euk
4. IF	D. wknxy
5. CARRY	E. cnoe
6. PACE	F. pc
7. BOY	G. thyg

1. POISE
   (*a*) exkuoc (*b*) ghyoet
   (*c*) ykcwh (*d*) hnxcgy
2. STRAY
   (*a*) nkxhp (*b*) noxgc
   (*c*) eykgw (*d*) wxngu
3. CREDIT
   (*a*) ckgwxn (*b*) oughpt
   (*c*) tnhocx (*d*) pewnoc
4. DIFFER
   (*a*) ocpphn (*b*) uhnncg
   (*c*) ytokon (*d*) uxnkyg
5. ORBIT
   (*a*) ywthk (*b*) knecx
   (*c*) ouxkn (*d*) etnguy

EXPLANATORY ANSWERS

(i) The only two letter word is IF and so, its code is pc.

(ii) The five letter words are SPORT and CARRY and their codes tnvgn and wknxy. The word CARRY has one letter 'R' repeated and the code tnugn has 'n'. So, the code for CARRY is tnugn and code for SPORT is wknxy.

(iii) The four letter words are BIRD and PACE and their codes cnoe and thyg. According to *(ii)* code for 'R' is 'n' and BIRD which has 'R' in it has the code cnoe. So, the code for PACE is thyg.

(iv) The three letter words are SAD and BOY and their codes wgo and euk. SAD and PACE (in *iii*) have 'A' common and the code which has 'g' in it is the code for SAD. So, code

for SAD is wgo and code for BOY is euk. Now, when the words and codes are set in order they will be :

IF	pc
SPORT	wknxy
CARRY	tnugn
BIRD	cnoe
PACE	thyg
SAD	wgo
BOY	euk

The decoding steps will be :

(i) In word CARRY there are two 'R's and in the code there are two 'n's. So, code for 'R' is 'n'.

(ii) In SPORT and SAD the common letter is 'S' and so is the code 'w'.

(iii) In SPORT and PACE the common letter is 'P' and so is the code 'y'.

(iv) In SPORT and BOY the common letter is 'O' and so is the code 'k'.

(v) The only letter remaining in SPORT is 'T' and its code 'x'.

(vi) In CARRY and SAD the common letter is 'A' and so is the code 'g'.

(vii) In CARRY and BOY the common letter is 'Y' and so is the code 'u'.

(viii) The only letter remaining in SAD is 'D' and its code 'o'.

(ix) The only letter remaining in 'BOY' is 'B' and its code 'e'.

(x) In CARRY and PACE the commo letters are 'C' and ' and the common codes 't' and 'g'. With refere e to *(vi)* code for 'C' is 't'.

(xi) The letter remaining in BIRD is 'I' and its code 'c',

(xii) The letter remaining in PACE is 'E' and its code 'h'.

(xiii) The letter remaining in IF is 'F' and its code 'p'.

Based on above decoding steps the capital letters and their equivalent small letter codes will be :

Letters :	R	S	P	O	T	A	Y	D	B	C	I	E	F
Codes :	n	w	y	k	x	g	u	o	e	t	c	h	p

1. *(c)* **2.** *(d)* **3.** *(c)* **4.** *(a)* **5.** *(b)*

STATEMENT ANALYSIS

In these type of questions, a few statements are given. Certain facts are broken up and mentioned in these statements. What is required is to analyse the statements, arrange and sort out the given facts and then answer the questions related to the given statements.

SOLVED EXAMPLES

1. Icecream is as cold as snow. Ice is not as cold as hail. Flakes are not as cold as ice but colder than icecream. What is the coldest?

(*a*) Hail (*b*) Icecream (*c*) Flakes (*d*) Ice (*e*) Snow

Ans. ***(a)*** : The order showing an increase in coldness, is Icecream/Snow, Flakes, Ice, Hail.

2. *Read the following statements and answer the questions a and b.*

Five men Heavy, Fat, Thin, Short and Tall are running one behind the other. Of the Heavy and the Tall man one is an Artist and the other is Talkative. Thin man who is a Genius is in the centre. Short man is not Dark and the one who is Fair is ahead of Thin man. The Heavy man, who is not an Artist, is in front of the Fat man.

a. Who is Fair?

(*a*) Tall man (*b*) Fat man (*c*) Short man (*d*) Heavy man (*e*) Thin man

Ans. ***(b)***

b. What is the Tall Man?

(*a*) Genius (*b*) Talkative (*c*) Artist (*d*) Dark (*e*) Fair

Ans. ***(c)***

The chart of the characteristics of five men is :

Heavy man is Talkative.
Fat man is Fair.
Thin man is Genious.
Short man is not Dark.
Tall man is the artist.

EXERCISE

1. Among five friends, A is heavier than B; C is lighter than D; B is lighter than D but heavier than E. Who among them is the heaviest?

(*a*) B (*b*) C
(*c*) A (*d*) D
(*e*) Can't say

2. Pune is bigger than Jhansi, Sitapur is bigger than Chittor. Raigarh is not as big as Jhansi, but is bigger than Sitapur. Chittor is not as big as Sitapur. Which is the smallest?

(*a*) Jhansi (*b*) Pune
(*c*) Chittor (*d*) Sitapur
(*e*) None of these

3. Ajay works more than Ram. Alok works as much as Raju. Pankaj works less than Alok. Ram works more than Alok. Who works the most of all?

(*a*) Ajay (*b*) Ram
(*c*) Alok (*d*) Raju
(*e*) Pankaj

4. Vipul is taller than Hans. Hans is taller than Anand. Alok is taller than Ashok. Ashok is taller than Hans. Who among them is the tallest?

(*a*) Vipul
(*b*) Alok
(*c*) Ashok
(*d*) Cannot be determined
(*e*) None of these

5. Pramod is taller than Gopal. Gopal is shorter than Madhu. To find out who among them is the tallest, which of the following further informations is necessary?

(*a*) Madhu is taller than Gopal.
(*b*) Madhu is shorter than Pramod's brother
(*c*) Pramod is taller than Madhu.
(*d*) Pramod is taller than Madhu's brother.
(*e*) No further information is necessary.

6. Among five friends P, Q, R, S and T, who is the youngest? To arrive at the answer which of the following information given in the statements (A) and (B) is sufficient?

(A) R is younger than P and T.
(B) S is younger than Q.

(*a*) Only A alone is sufficient
(*b*) Either A or B is sufficient
(*c*) Both A and B together are needed
(*d*) Only B alone is sufficient
(*e*) Both A and B together are not sufficient

7. Sushma is richer than Rashmi whereas Anand is richer than Priya. Arun is as rich as Rashmi. Shoba is richer than Sushma. Which of the following statements is correct according to the above propositions?

(*a*) Rashmi is poorer than Priya.
(*b*) Priya is richer than Arun
(*c*) Arun is poorer than Sushma.
(*d*) Anand is richer than Rashmi
(*e*) None of these

8. A is elder to B while C and D are elder to E who lies between A and B. If C be elder to B, which one of the following statements is necessarily true?

(*a*) E is elder to B
(*b*) A is elder to C
(*c*) C is elder to D
(*d*) D is elder to C
(*e*) None of these

9. Vikram is taller than Rajan but shorter than Annie. Jamal is taller than Annie. Sita is taller than Vikram. Rajan is shorter than Sita. Who is the shortest of all in the group?

(*a*) Sita
(*b*) Rajan
(*c*) Vikram
(*d*) Cannot be determined
(*e*) None of these

10. Suresh is as much older than Kamal as he is younger than Prabodh. Navin is as old as Kamal. Which of the following statements is wrong?

(*a*) Suresh is older than Navin
(*b*) Kamal is younger than Suresh
(*c*) Prabodh is not the oldest
(*d*) Navin is younger than Prabodh
(*e*) Kamal is younger than Prabodh

11. Ashok is heavier than Gopal. Mahesh is lighter than Jayesh. Prashant is heavier than Jayesh but lighter than Gopal. Who among them is the heaviest?

(*a*) Gopal (*b*) Jayesh
(*c*) Prashant (*d*) Ashok
(*e*) Mahesh

12. Subodh's marks in English are as much more than Gopal's marks in History as less than Pramod's marks in English. To find out Subodh's marks in English, which of the following informations given in the statements (A) and (B) is/ are sufficient?

(A) Gopal's marks in History.
(B) Pramod's marks in History.

(*a*) Both A and B together are needed
(*b*) Only B is sufficient
(*c*) Either A or B is sufficient
(*d*) Both A and B together are not sufficient
(*e*) Only A is sufficient

13. Pramod is older than Jayesh and Sudhir. Vikas is younger than Anil. To find out who among them is the oldest, which of the following further information will be required, if any?

(*a*) Sudhir is older than Jayesh
(*b*) Anil is older than Jayesh
(*c*) Vikas is older than Pramod
(*d*) Vikas is younger than Pramod
(*e*) No further information is required

14. Ashok is younger than Prabir and Gopal.

Sohan is younger than Prabir but older than Gopal. Which of the following statements is definitely true?

(*a*) Ashok is older than Sohan
(*b*) Sohan is the oldest among them
(*c*) Gopal is younger than Ashok
(*d*) Gopal is older than Prabir
(*e*) Gopal is next to the youngest among them

15. Among five boys, Vasant is taller than Manohar, but not as tall as Raju. Jayant is taller than Datta, but shorter than Manohar. Who is the tallest in their group?

(*a*) Raju
(*b*) Manohar
(*c*) Vasant
(*d*) Cannot be determined
(*e*) None of these

16. A and D study in the same class. K and L study in the same class. In which class does D study? To answer the above question, which of the following informations given in the statements A and B is/are necessary?

(A) D studies one standard below L.
(B) A's elder brother studies with K.

(*a*) Both A and B together are not sufficient
(*b*) Both A and B together are needed
(*c*) Only A is sufficient
(*d*) Only B is sufficient
(*e*) Either A or B is sufficient

Directions (Qs. 17-18) : *(A) Gopal is shorter than Ashok but taller than Kuhav; (B) Navin is shorter than Kuhav; (C) Jayesh is taller than Navin; (D) Ashok is taller than Jayesh.*

17. Who among them is the tallest?

(*a*) Gopal (*b*) Ashok
(*c*) Jayesh (*d*) Navin
(*e*) Kuhav

18. Which of the following informations is not necessary to answer the above question?

(*a*) A (*b*) B
(*c*) C (*d*) D
(*e*) All are necessary

Directions (Qs. 19-20) : *Five men A, B, C, D and E read a newspaper. The one who reads first gives it to C. The one who reads last had taken from A. E was not the first or last to read. There were two readers between B and A.*

19. B passed the newspaper to whom?

(*a*) E
(*b*) B
(*c*) A
(*d*) Cannot be determined
(*e*) None of these

20. Who read the newspaper last?

(*a*) E (*b*) B
(*c*) D
(*d*) Cannot be determined
(*e*) None of these

Directions (Qs. 21 to 23) : *Ram, Sohan and Mohan play football, hockey and cricket. Ram, Ramesh and Mohan play hockey, cricket and basketball. Ram, Sohan, Rahim and Mohan play football and cricket. Now answer the following questions based on the above statements :*

21. Which game is played by all the boys?

(*a*) Football (*b*) Hockey
(*c*) Cricket (*d*) Basketball
(*e*) None of these

22. Which two boys play all the games?

(*a*) Ram, Sohan (*b*) Ram, Ramesh
(*c*) Sohan, Mohan (*d*) Ram, Mohan
(*e*) Ram, Rahim

23. Who does not play football?

(*a*) Ramesh (*b*) Sohan
(*c*) Rahim (*d*) Mohan
(*e*) Ram

Directions (Qs. 24-26) : *Read the following directions and answer the questions given below :*

There are four friends Ravi, Hari, Manu and Jatin. One of them lives at Kanpur and his hobbies are reading and writing. Hari and Jatin live at Lucknow. Hari's hobby is stamp collection. Common Hobby of two friends staying at Lucknow is coin collection. Ravi lives at Allahabad. One boy staying at Lucknow also loves to hear music. The boy staying at Allahabad loves to travel and read comics. If all the boys have two hobbies each answer the following questions :

24. Who lives at Kanpur?

(*a*) Jatin (*b*) Manu
(*c*) Ravi (*d*) Hari

(*e*) None of the above

25. Coin collection and listening to music are the hobbies of :

(*a*) Manu (*b*) Ravi
(*c*) Hari (*d*) Jatin
(*e*) None of the above

26. Which of the following is not the hobby of Ravi?

(*a*) Reading comics
(*b*) Reading
(*c*) Travelling
(*d*) Cannot be said
(*e*) None of the above

Directions (Qs. 27 to 29) : *Read the following directions and answer the questions given below :*

There are five persons in a group. Out of these two are men. Only three persons know swimming, of which one is a man. There is a couple, of which the husband knows swimming. A is the younger sister of D and B is the husband of E. C is a swimming champion.

27. Who is the other man in the group?

(*a*) C (*b*) B
(*c*) A (*d*) D
(*e*) Can't say

28. The two women who know how to swim are :

(*a*) A and C (*b*) C and D
(*c*) D and E (*d*) A and E
(*e*) Data inadequate

29. The two persons who do not know how to swim are :

(*a*) B and D (*b*) D and E
(*c*) A and E (*d*) A and D
(*e*) None of the above

Directions (Qs. 30 to 33) : *Read the following directions and answer the questions given below :*

There are five books, out of which two books are on gardening, two on cookery and one on photography. Three of the books are in red cover and two in blue. There is a red cover on the photography book but not on the cookery book. There is no blue cover on the gardening books. B is a book on cookery, D on photography and E on gardening. C and D are not the books on gardening.

30. Which of the following books is in red cover and deals with gardening?

(*a*) E (*b*) C
(*c*) B (*d*) D
(*e*) None of the above

31. Which of the following books are in red cover and neither deals with cookery nor photography?

(*a*) B and C (*b*) A and E
(*c*) D and E (*d*) D and C
(*e*) None of the above

32. Which of the following are not the books on gardening?

(*a*) A and D (*b*) E and C
(*c*) B and D (*d*) E and D
(*e*) None of the above

33. Blue cover is not on the book dealing with the subject :

(*a*) Cookery (*b*) Gardening
(*c*) Photography (*d*) Both (b) and (c)
(*e*) None of the above

Directions (Qs. 34 to 38) : *Read the following statements and answer the questions given below :*

Raghu and Gyan are good at cricket and hockey. Sohan and Gyan are good at hockey and chess. Raghu and Govind are good at swimming and cricket.

34. Who is good at cricket, hockey and chess?

(*a*) Raghu (*b*) Gyan
(*c*) Sohan (*d*) Govind
(*e*) None of the above

35. Who is good at cricket and swimming ?

(*a*) Gyan (*b*) Govind
(*c*) Sohan (*d*) All of them
(*e*) Cannot be determined

36. Who is good at hockey, chess and swimming?

(*a*) Raghu (*b*) Govind
(*c*) Sohan (*d*) All the three
(*e*) None of the above

37. Who is good at swimming, hockey and cricket?

(*a*) Raghu (*b*) Sohan
(*c*) Govind (*d*) Gyan
(*e*) None of the above

38. Who is good at hockey but not so in swimming?

(*a*) Govind (*b*) Raghu
(*c*) Sohan (*d*) No one
(*e*) All the three

Directions (Qs. 39 to 41) : *Read the following statements and answer the questions given below :*

Rajat, Sushil and Nagesh play football, hockey and cricket. Rajat, Ramu and Nagesh play hockey, cricket and basketball. Rajat, Sushil, Mayank and Nagesh play football and cricket.

39. Which game is played by all the boys?
(*a*) Hockey (*b*) Basketball
(*c*) Football (*d*) Cricket
(*e*) None of the above

40. Who does not play football?
(*a*) Rajat (*b*) Nagesh
(*c*) Sushil (*d*) Ramu
(*e*) None of the above

41. Which of the following two boys play all the games?
(*a*) Nagesh, Rajat (*b*) Mayank, Ramu
(*c*) Ramu, Nagesh (*d*) Sushil, Mayank
(*e*) None of the above

Directions (Qs. 42 to 46) : *Read the following statements and answer the questions given below :*

There are four girls–Eena, Mira, Meena and Moe. One of them lives at Chennai and her hobbies are clay modelling and reading. Mira lives at Mumbai. Eena also lives at Mumbai and her hobby is dancing. Both girls staying at Mumbai are fond of gardening. Moe lives at Delhi and her hobbies are painting and photography. One girl staying at Mumbai enjoys travelling. If all the girl have two hobbies each, answer the following questions :

42. Who enjoys travelling?
(*a*) Eena (*b*) Mira
(*c*) Meena (*d*) Moe
(*e*) None of the above

43. Who is the girl with the hobbies dancing and gardening?
(*a*) Eena (*b*) Moe
(*c*) Mira (*d*) Meena
(*e*) None of the above

44. Who is staying at Chennai?
(*a*) Meena (*b*) Eena
(*c*) Both (*d*) None of the above
(*e*) Cannot be determined

45. Who among the following is fond of gardening?
(*a*) Meena (*b*) Mira
(*c*) Both (*d*) None of the above
(*e*) Cannot be determined

46. What are Meena's hobbies?
(*a*) Reading, dancing
(*b*) Gardening, painting
(*c*) Travelling, dancing
(*d*) Clay modelling, reading
(*e*) None of the above

Directions (Qs. 47 to 50) : The following information is given about four persons P, Q, R and S who are mother, father, grandfather and grand-mother of U.

(*i*) P took birth before S.
(*ii*) R died before P.
(*iii*) Q died after P, R and S.

47. If Q took birth after the death of P, then which of the following statements can be correct?
(*a*) S was the guardian of P
(*b*) P was the guardian of R
(*c*) Q was the guardian of R
(*d*) Q is the life partner of P
(*e*) R is the grandson of Q

48. If S died before P and P died before the birth of Q, then which of the following statements is correct?
(*a*) R was not alive during P's life span
(*b*) S was not alive during Q's life span
(*c*) R was not alive during S's life span
(*d*) S neither took birth nor died during R's life span
(*e*) R was born and dead during P's life span

49. If Q took birth before P, then which of the following statements should be correct one?
(*i*) Q's life span was more than P's.
(*ii*) Q's life span was more than S's.
(*iii*) Q's life span was more than R's.
(*a*) Only (*i*) is correct
(*b*) Only (*ii*) is correct
(*c*) Only (*i*) and (*ii*) are correct
(*d*) Only (*ii*) and (*iii*) are correct
(*e*) All are correct

50. Which of the following statements should be correct one?
(*a*) S was born before the birth of Q
(*b*) R was born before the death of S
(*c*) R was born before the birth of Q, S and P

(*d*) Q was born after birth of P, R and S
(*e*) R was born before the death of P

Directions (Qs. 51 to 55) : Four youngmen, Raj, Prem, Ved and Ashok are friendly with four girls Sushma, Kusum, Vimla and Poonam. Sushma and Vimla are friends. Ved's girlfriend does not like Sushma and Vimla. Kusum does not care for Ved. Prem's girlfriend is friendly with Sushma. Sushma does not like Raj.

51. Who does not like Sushma and Vimla?
(*a*) Raj (*b*) Ashok
(*c*) Ved (*d*) Poonam
(*e*) Data inadequate

52. Who does not like Ved?
(*a*) Sushma (*b*) Poonam
(*c*) Kusum (*d*) Vimla
(*e*) Data inadequate

53. Who is Poonam's boy friend?
(*a*) Raj (*b*) Ashok
(*c*) Prem (*d*) Ved
(*e*) Data inadequate

54. With whom is Sushma friendly?
(*a*) Kusum (*b*) Ashok
(*c*) Raj (*d*) Prem
(*e*) Data inadequate

55. Who is Raj's girl friend?
(*a*) Poonam (*b*) Vimla
(*c*) Sushma (*d*) Kusum
(*e*) Data inadequate

Directions (Qs. 56 to 60) : *Read the following information and asnwer the questions given below :*

(*i*) P, Q, R, S, T and U are six members in a family in which there are two married couples.
(*ii*) T a teacher is married to the doctor who is mother of R and U.
(*iii*) Q the lawyer is married to P.
(*iv*) P has one son and one grandson.
(*v*) Of the two married ladies one is a housewife.
(*vi*) There is also one student and one male engineer in the family.

56. Who among the following is the housewife?
(*a*) Q (*b*) P
(*c*) S (*d*) T
(*e*) None of these

57. Which of the following represents the group of females in the family?
(*a*) QTR (*b*) PSR
(*c*) PSU (*d*) Data inadequate
(*e*) None of these

58. Which of the following is true about the granddaughter in the family?
(*a*) She is a student
(*b*) She is an engineer
(*c*) She is a lawyer
(*d*) Data Inadequate
(*e*) None of these

59. How R is related to U?
(*a*) Brother
(*b*) Sister
(*c*) Brother or Sister
(*d*) Data inadequate
(*e*) None of these

60. How is P related to R?
(*a*) Grandfather (*b*) Mother
(*c*) Sister (*d*) Grandmother
(*e*) None of these

Directions (Qs. 61 to 65) : *Read the following information carefully to answer the questions given below it.*

(*i*) A, B, C, D, E and F are six students in a class.
(*ii*) B and C are shorter than F but heavier than A.
(*iii*) D is heavier than B and taller than C.
(*iv*) E is shorter than D but taller than F.
(*v*) F is heavier than D.
(*vi*) A is shorter than E but taller than F.

61. Who is third from the top when they are arranged in descending order of their height?
(*a*) A (*b*) E
(*c*) B (*d*) C
(*e*) None of these

62. Who among them is the tallest?
(*a*) B (*b*) A
(*c*) D (*d*) E
(*e*) None of these

63. Who among them is the lightest?
(*a*) B (*b*) C
(*c*) B or C (*d*) A
(*e*) Data inadequate

64. Which of the following groups of friends is

shorter than A?
(*a*) D, B, C only (*b*) E, B, C only
(*c*) B, C only (*d*) F, B, C only
(*e*) None of these

65. Which of the following statements is true for F as regards height and weight?
(*a*) He is heavier than B and C but shorter than D
(*b*) He is lighter than B and C but taller than D
(*c*) He is heavier than B and taller than E
(*d*) He is lighter than E and also shorter than E
(*e*) He is lighter than E and taller than E.

Directions (Qs. 66 to 70) : *Study the following information to answer the given questions :*

(*i*) There are eight faculty members A, B, C, D, E, F, G and H in the institute, each teaching different subject.
(*ii*) There are three lady members and of the eight, four are holding Ph. D. Degree
(*iii*) E teaches Psychology and is Ph.D. A teaches Chemistry.
(*iv*) The one who teaches Economics is not Ph.D. No lady member teaches either Commerce or Law. Law faculty does not award Ph.D.
(*v*) D and G do not teach either Commerce or Physics.
(*vi*) H and C are lady members and are not Ph.D. F who is Ph.D. teaches Zoology.
(*vii*) B and G are Ph.Ds and G is a lady member.

66. Which of the following lady members is/are Ph.D.?
(*a*) G (*b*) C and D
(*c*) G and H (*d*) Can't be determined
(*e*) None of these

67. Which of the following combinations is NOT correct?
(*a*) Chemistry - Male - Not Ph.D.
(*b*) Zoology - Male - Ph.D.
(*c*) Physics - Lady - Ph.D.
(*d*) Economics - Lady - Not-Ph.D.
(*e*) Commerce - Male - Ph.D.

68. Who teaches Physics?
(*a*) C (*b*) H
(*c*) Either H or C (*d*) Either C or G
(*e*) None of these

69. Which of the following statements is true?
(*a*) Three male members are Ph.D.
(*b*) Two lady members are Ph.D.
(*c*) The person who teaches Economics is Ph.D.
(*d*) The person who teaches Zoology is not Ph.D.
(*e*) None of these

70. What is the subject taught by G?
(*a*) Zoology
(*b*) Either Physics or Economics
(*c*) Either Physics or Zoology
(*d*) Cannot be determined
(*e*) None of these

Directions (Qs. 71 to 75) : *Read the following information carefully and answer the questions given below it.*

(*i*) A, B, C, D, E and F are six members of a family.
(*ii*) There are two married couples among them.
(*iii*) C is the mother of A and F.
(*iv*) E is the father of D.
(*v*) A is the grandson of B.
(*vi*) The total number of female members in the family is three.

71. Who is the wife of E?
(*a*) B (*b*) C
(*c*) F (*d*) Data inadequate
(*e*) None of these

72. Which of the following pairs is one of the married couples?
(*a*) EF (*b*) BD
(*c*) EB (*d*) AF
(*e*) None of these

73. Which of the following is a group of female members?
(*a*) BDE (*b*) AFB
(*c*) DCF (*d*) BCF
(*e*) None of these

74. How is F related to A?
(*a*) Brother (*b*) Daughter
(*c*) Son (*d*) Mother
(*e*) None of these

75. How is B related to F?
(*a*) Sister (*b*) Grandmother

(*c*) Wife (*d*) Data inadequate
(*e*) None of these

Directions (Qs. 76 to 80) : *Read the following information carefully and answer the questions given below it.*

(*i*) P, Q, R, S, T and U are travelling in a bus.
(*ii*) There are two reporters, two technicians, one photographer and one writer in the group.
(*iii*) The photographer P is married to S who is a reporter.
(*iv*) The writer is married to Q who is of the same profession as that of U.
(*v*) P, R, Q, S are two married couples and nobody in the group has same profession.
(*vi*) U is brother of R.

76. How is R related to U?
(*a*) Brother (*b*) Sister
(*c*) Mother (*d*) Uncle
(*e*) Can't be definitely said

77. Which of the following is a pair of husband?
(*a*) PR (*b*) QS
(*c*) PQ (*d*) QR
(*e*) Can't be determined

78. Which of the following is a pair of reporters?
(*a*) ST (*b*) PQ
(*c*) RT (*d*) SU
(*e*) Can't be definitely said

79. Which of the following is a pair of technicians?
(*a*) PT (*b*) QU
(*c*) SU (*d*) RS
(*e*) PR

80. Which of the following pairs is a couple?
(*a*) QS (*b*) PT
(*c*) QR (*d*) PQ
(*e*) ST

Directions (Qs. 81 to 85) : *Read the following information to answer the given questions :*

Six lectures A, B, C, D, E and F are to be organised only once on each day from Monday to Sunday in accordance with the following ......

(*i*) C should not be organised on Friday.
(*ii*) A should be organised immediately after D.
(*iii*) There should be a gap of two days between B and F.
(*iv*) On one day there will be no lecture (Saturday is NOT that day), just before that day F will be organised.
(*v*) E should be organised on Wednesday and should not be followed by F.

81. Which of the information is NOT required in finding the complete sequence of organisation of lectures?
(*a*) (*i*) only (*b*) (*ii*) only
(*c*) (*v*) only (*d*) (*i*) and (*ii*) only
(*e*) All are required

82. Which of the following is the last lecture in the series?
(*a*) A (*b*) C
(*c*) B (*d*) Can't be determined
(*e*) None of these

83. How many lectures are organised between F and D?
(*a*) None (*b*) One
(*c*) Two (*d*) Three
(*e*) None of these

84. On which day will the lecture D be organised?
(*a*) Friday (*b*) Saturday
(*c*) Sunday (*d*) Thursday
(*e*) None of these

85. On which day, there is no lecture?
(*a*) Sunday (*b*) Friday
(*c*) Monday (*d*) Can't be determined
(*e*) None of these

Directions (Qs. 86 to 90) : *Read the following information carefully and then answer the questions given under it.*

Ramesh, Kamal, Ahmed and John are students of a school. Three of them stay far from the school and one near it. Two study in Class IV, one in Class V and one in Class VI. They study Hindi, Mathematics, Social Science and Science. One is good at all the four subjects while another is weak in all of these. Ramesh stays far from the school and is good at Mathematics only while Kamal is weak in Mathematics only and stays close to the school. Neither of these two nor Ahmed studies in Class VI. One who is good at all the subjects studies in Class V.

86. Name the boy who is good at all the subjects.
(*a*) Ramesh (*b*) Kamal
(*c*) Ahmed (*d*) John
(*e*) None of these

87. Other than Ramesh and the boy good at all the subjects, who else stays far from the school?
(*a*) Ramesh (*b*) Kamal
(*c*) Ahmed (*d*) John
(*e*) Can't be definitely said

88. Which two boys are good at Hindi?
(*a*) Ramesh and Kamal
(*b*) Kamal and Ahmed
(*c*) Ahmed and John
(*d*) John and Ramesh
(*e*) Can't say

89. Which two boys are good at Mathematics?
(*a*) Ramesh and Ahmed
(*b*) Kamal and Ahmed
(*c*) John and Ahmed
(*d*) Ramesh and John
(*e*) Data inadequate

90. Name the boy who is weak in all the subjects.
(*a*) Ramesh (*b*) Kamal
(*c*) Ahmed (*d*) John
(*e*) All the above

Directions (Qs. 91 to 95) : *Study the following information carefully and answer the questions given below it.*

(i) A, B, C, D, E and F are six members in a family in which there are two married couples.
(ii) D is brother of F. Both D and F are lighter than B.
(iii) B is mother of D and lighter than E.
(iv) C, a lady, is neither heaviest nor the lightest in the family.
(v) E is lighter than C.
(vi) The grandfather in the family is the heaviest.

91. How is E related to F?
(*a*) Grandmother (*b*) Brother
(*c*) Father (*d*) Data inadequate
(*e*) None of these

92. How is C related to D?
(*a*) Sister (*b*) Grandmother
(*c*) Mother (*d*) Cousin
(*e*) None of these

93. How many male members are there in the family?
(*a*) Data inadequate
(*b*) 2
(*c*) 4
(*d*) 3
(*e*) None of these

94. Which of the following is a pair of married couples?
(*a*) AD (*b*) BC
(*c*) AB (*d*) BE
(*e*) None of these

95. Who among the following will be in the second place if all the members in the family are arranged in the descending order of their weight?
(*a*) D (*b*) A
(*c*) C (*d*) Data inadequate
(*e*) None of these

Directions (Qs. 96 to 100) : *Read the following information carefully and answer the questions based on that information :*

(i) A, B, C, D and E are five friends.
(ii) B is elder to E, but not as tall as C.
(iii) C is younger to A, and is taller to D and E.
(iv) A is taller to D, but younger to E.
(v) D is elder to A but is shortest in the group.

96. If F, another friend is taller than C, how many of them will be between F and E according to their height?
(*a*) None (*b*) One
(*c*) Two (*d*) Three
(*e*) None of these

97. If selection is to be made among them who would be relatively older and also taller, who among them should be chosen?
(*a*) A (*b*) E
(*c*) D (*d*) C
(*e*) None of these

98. Who among the following is the eldest?
(*a*) C (*b*) B
(*c*) D (*d*) A
(*e*) None of these

99. Which of the following pairs of students is elder to D?
(*a*) BA (*b*) BC
(*c*) EA (*d*) BE
(*e*) None of these

100. Which of the following statements is correct about B?
(i) B is not the tallest.

(ii) B is shorter to E.

(iii) When they are asked to stand in ascending order with respect to their heights, B is in the middle.

(*a*) Only (i) is correct
(*b*) All are correct
(*c*) All are incorrect
(*d*) Only (i) and (ii) are correct
(*e*) None of these

Directions (Qs. 101 to 105) : *Study the following information carefully and answer the questions given below it :*

(i) A, B, C, D, E, F and G are seven members of a family.

(ii) Six of them have a different profession of Accountant, Lawyer, Teacher, Manager, Doctor, Engineer and one is a Student.

(iii) There are two married couples in the family.

(iv) A and F are Accountant and Doctor respectively.

(v) D is the father of B and the grandfather of G and is an Engineer.

(vi) No lady is either an Engineer or a lawyer.

(vii) G, who is a student, is the grandson of E.

101. How many male members are there in the family?
(*a*) 4 (*b*) 5
(*c*) 3 (*d*) Data inadequate
(*e*) None of these

102. Which of the following is one of the married couples?
(*a*) BC (*b*) BD
(*c*) BF (*d*) AC
(*e*) None of these

103. How is F related to G?
(*a*) Brother (*b*) Sister
(*c*) Uncle (*d*) Data inadequate
(*e*) None of these

104. How is C related to G?
(*a*) Mother (*b*) Aunt
(*c*) Sister (*d*) Data inadequate
(*e*) None of these

105. What is E's profession?
(*a*) Teacher
(*b*) Manager
(*c*) Teacher or Manager
(*d*) Doctor
(*e*) None of these

Directions (Qs. 106 to 110) : *Read the following information carefully and based on that information, answer the following questions :*

(i) P, Q, R, S, T and U are members of a club. Each one of them has a different occupation such as Lawyer, Engineer, Architect, Doctor, Teacher and Housewife.

(ii) There are two ladies in the group.

(iii) R is a Housewife and is married to T.

(iv) Doctor is married to P who is a Lady Teacher.

(v) Q is a lawyer and U is unmarried.

106. Who is Doctor in the group?
(*a*) S (*b*) U
(*c*) T (*d*) Data inadequate
(*e*) None of these

107. How is P related to Q?
(*a*) Brother (*b*) Nephew
(*c*) Father (*d*) Data inadequate
(*e*) None of these

108. What is the occupation of T?
(*a*) Engineer
(*b*) Architect
(*c*) Engineer or Architect
(*d*) Data inadequate
(*e*) None of these

109. Which of the following pairs represents the two husbands?
(*a*) T, R (*b*) P, S
(*c*) T, U (*d*) Q, T
(*e*) None of these

110. Which of the following is the married pair?
(*a*) QT (*b*) PT
(*c*) PS (*d*) QR
(*e*) None of these

Directions (Qs. 111 to 115) : *There are five men A, B, C, D and E and six women, P, Q, R, S, T, and U. A, B and R are advocates, C, D, P, Q and S are doctors and the rest are teachers. Some teams are to be selected from amongst these eleven persons subject to the following conditions :*

A, P and U have to be together
B cannot go with D or R
E and Q have to be together
C and T have to be together
D and P cannot go together

C cannot go with Q.

111. If the team is to consist of one advocate, two doctors, three teachers and C may not go with T, the members of the team are :
(*a*) AEPQSU (*b*) AEPQTU
(*c*) BEQSTU (*d*) EQRSTU
(*e*) None of these

112. If the team is to consist of two advocates, two doctors, two teachers and not more than three ladies, the members of the team are :
(*a*) ACPRTU (*b*) BCEQRT
(*c*) AEPQRT (*d*) ABCPTU
(*e*) None of these

113. If the team is to consist of one male advocate, one male doctor, one lady doctor and two teachers, the members of the team are :
(*a*) ACPTU (*b*) BCEQT
(*c*) ADEPT (*d*) ADEPU
(*e*) None of these

114. If the team is to consist of two male advocates, two lady doctors and one teacher, the members of the team are :
(*a*) BEQRS (*b*) ABPQU
(*c*) ABPUS (*d*) APRSU
(*e*) None of these

115. If the team is to consist of one advocate, three doctors and one male teacher, the members of the team are :
(*a*) ADPSU (*b*) DEQRS
(*c*) CDRST (*d*) DEQRT
(*e*) None of these

Directions (Qs. 116 to 120) : *Read the following information to answer the given questions :*

Six lectures A, B, C, D, E and F are to be organised in a span of seven days - from Sunday to Saturday, only one lecture on each day in accordance with the following :

(*i*) A should not be organised on Thursday.
(*ii*) C should be organised immediately after F.
(*iii*) There should be a gap of two days between E and D.
(*iv*) One day there will be no lecture (Friday is NOT that day), just before that day D will be organised.
(*v*) B should be organised on Tuesday and should not be followed by D.

116. Which day will the lecture F be organised?
(*a*) Friday (*b*) Saturday
(*c*) Sunday (*d*) Thursday
(*e*) None of these

117. On which day is there no lecture?
(*a*) Sunday (*b*) Friday
(*c*) Monday (*d*) Can't be determined
(*e*) None of these

118. How many lectures are organised between C and D?
(*a*) None (*b*) One
(*c*) Two (*d*) Three
(*e*) None of these

119. Which of the informations is NOT required in finding the complete sequence of organisation of lectures?
(*a*) (*i*) only (*b*) (*ii*) only
(*c*) (*v*) only (*d*) (*i*) and (*ii*) only
(*e*) All are required

120. Which of the following is the last lecture in the series?
(*a*) A (*b*) C
(*c*) B (*d*) Can't be determined
(*e*) None of these

Directions (Qs. 121 to 125) : *Read the following information to answer the questions given below :*

(*i*) Five friends A, B, C, D and E wore shirts of green, yellow, pink, red and blue colours and shorts of black, white, grey, blue and green colours.
(*ii*) Nobody wore shirt and short of same colour.
(*iii*) D wore blue shirt and C wore green short.
(*iv*) The one who wore green shirt, wore black short and the one who wore blue short, wore red shirt.
(*v*) A wore white short and pink shirt.
(*vi*) E did not wear red shirt.

121. What was the colour combination of D's shirt and short?
(*a*) Green and black
(*b*) Red and blue
(*c*) Blue and grey
(*d*) Blue and white
(*e*) None of these

122. Who wore black short?
(*a*) C (*b*) E

(*c*) B (*d*) D
(*e*) A

123. Who wore white short?
(*a*) E (*b*) Data inadequate
(*c*) B (*d*) A
(*e*) None of these

124. Which colour shirt did C wear?
(*a*) Yellow (*b*) Blue
(*c*) Green (*d*) Pink
(*e*) Data inadequate

125. Which colour short did B wear?
(*a*) Grey (*b*) Blue
(*c*) White (*d*) Black
(*e*) Green

Directions (Qs. 126 to 130) :

(*i*) P, Q, R, S, T and U are six members of a group of which three are males and three are females.

(*ii*) There are two engineers, two lawyers, one teacher and one doctor in the group.

(*iii*) Q, T, P and R are two married couples and no person in this group has the same profession.

(*iv*) T, a teacher with blue dress married a male lawyer with brown dress.

(*v*) Colour of the dresses of both the husbands and that of both the wives is the same.

(*vi*) Two persons have blue dress, two have brown and the remaining one each has black and green.

(*vii*) P is a male engineer and whose sister S is also an engineer.

(*viii*) Q is a doctor.

126. Which of the following is a group of female members ?
(*a*) QSU (*b*) QSR
(*c*) QST (*d*) QTU
(*e*) None of these

127. Who is the wife of P?
(*a*) R (*b*) T
(*c*) S (*d*) Q
(*e*) None of these

128. What is the colour of U's dress?
(*a*) Black
(*b*) Green
(*c*) Black or Green
(*d*) Data inadequate
(*e*) None of these

129. Which of the following is a pair of married ladies?
(*a*) QT (*b*) PR
(*c*) TS (*d*) Data inadequate
(*e*) None of these

130. What is the profession of R?
(*a*) Teacher (*b*) Lawyer
(*c*) Engineer (*d*) Doctor
(*e*) Cannot be determined

Directions (Qs. 131 to 135) : *At an Electronic Data Processing Unit, five out of the eight program sets P, Q, R, S, T, U, V and W are to be operated daily. On any one day, except for the first day of a month, only three of the program sets must be the ones that were operated on the previous day. The program operating must also satisfy the following conditions :*

(*i*) If program 'P' is to be operated on a day, 'V' cannot be operated on that day.

(*ii*) If 'Q' is to be operated on a day, 'T' must be one of the programs to be operated after 'Q'.

(*iii*) If 'R' is to be operated on a day, 'V' must be one of the programs to be operated after 'R'.

(*iv*) The last program to be operated on any day must be either 'S' or 'U'.

131. If the program sets 'R' and 'W' are to be operated on the first day, which of the following could be the other programs on that day?
(*a*) P, T, U (*b*) Q, S, V
(*c*) Q, T, V (*d*) T, S, U
(*e*) None of these

132. Which of the following is TRUE of any day's valid program set operation?
(*a*) 'P' cannot be operated at third place
(*b*) 'Q' cannot be operated at third place
(*c*) 'T' cannot be operated at third place
(*d*) 'R' cannot be operated at fourth place
(*e*) 'U' cannot be operated at fourth place

133. If the program sets operated on a day, P, Q, W, T, U, each of the following could be the next day's program set EXCEPT
(*a*) Q, R, V, T, U (*b*) Q, T, V, W, S
(*c*) W, T, U, V, S (*d*) W, R, V, T, U
(*e*) W, T, S, P, U

134. If 'R' is operated at third place in a sequence, which of the following CANNOT be the second program in that sequence?
(*a*) Q (*b*) S
(*c*) T (*d*) U
(*e*) W

135. Which of the following could be the set of programs to be operated on the first day of a month?
(*a*) P, R, V, S, U (*b*) Q, S, R, V, U
(*c*) T, U, R, V, S (*d*) U, Q, S, T, W
(*e*) V, Q, R, T, S

EXPLANATORY ANSWERS

1. (*e*) : The five friends in descending order of weight are : A/D, B/C, E or A/D, B, C/E. Either A or D is the heaviest.

2. (*c*) : The order of cities in descending order of size is : Pune, Jhansi, Raigarh, Sitapur, Chittor.

3. (*a*) : On the basis of doing work, the descending order will be : Ajay, Ram, Alok/Raju, Pankaj.

4. (*d*) : On the basis of height, the descending order will be Vipul/Alok, Ashok, Hans, Anand. Either Vipul or Alok is the tallest.

5. (*c*) : According to the information both Pramod and Madhu are taller than Gopal. Option (c) decides who is the tallest.

6. (*e*) : Statements are not inter-related.

7. (*c*) : On the basis of wealth, the descending order will be :
1. Shobha, Sushma, Rashmi/Arun
2. Anand, *and* Priya
(The two statements are not inter-related.)

8. (*a*) : The order in descending seniority will be : A/C/D, E, B.

9. (*b*) : On the basis of height the descending order will be :
Jamal/Sita, Annie, Vikram, Rajan.
or
Jamal, Sita/Annie, Vikram, Rajan.

10. (*c*) : On the basis of age the descending order will be : Prabodh, Suresh, Kamal/Navin.

11. (*d*) : On the basis of weight, the descending order will be : Ashok, Gopal, Prashant, Jayesh, Mahesh.

12. (*d*) : Comparison in marks do no clarify Subodh's marks in a subject.

13. (*c*) : On the basis of age the descending order will be :
1. Pramod, Jayesh/ Sudhir
and
2. Anil, Vikas
Option (c) connects these two statements.

14. (*e*) : On the basis of age the descending order will be : Prabir, Sohan, Gopal, Ashok.

15. (*a*) : The boys in descending order of height will be: Raju, Vasant, Manohar, Jayant, Datta.

16. (*a*) : There is no useful information in either of the two statements.

17. (*b*) : On the basis of height the descending order will be :
Ashok, Gopal/Jayesh, Kuhav, Navin
or
Ashok, Gopal, Kuhav/Jayesh, Navin.

18. (*c*)

19. (*e*) : The men read the newspaper in this order : B, C, E, A, D, and B passed the newspaper to C.

20. (*c*) : See answer 19 explanation.

Chart for Answers 21 to 23

Boy	*Games Played*
Ram	Football, Hocky, Cricket, Basketball
Sohan	Football, Hockey, Cricket
Mohan	Football, Hockey, Cricket, Basketball
Ramesh	Hockey, Cricket, Basketball
Rahim	Football, Cricket.

21. (*c*) 22. (*d*) 23. (*a*)

Chart for Answers 24 to 26

Name	*Staying at*	*Hobbies*
Ravi	Allahabad	Travelling, Reading comics
Hari	Lucknow	Stamp & Coin collection
Manu	Kanpur	Reading, Writing
Jatin	Lucknow	Music, Coin collection

24. *(b)* **25.** *(d)* **26.** *(b)*

For Answers 27 to 29 the information chart will be :

A. Woman ((younger sister of D); knows swimming.
B. Man (husband of E); knows swimming
C. Woman; Swimming champion
D. Man (brother of A)
E. Woman (wife of B)

From the couple B & E, B (husband) knows swimming. C is a swimming champion. Three persons know how to swim of which only B is a man. So, the two women who know how to swim are C and A (the younger sister of D). There are two men in the group of five. One is B and the other will be D.

27. *(d)* **28.** *(a)* **29.** *(b)*

For Answers 30 to 33 the information chart will be :

Books	*Cover colour*	*Subject*
A	Red	Gardening
B	Blue	Cookery
C	Blue	Cookery
D	Red	Photography
E	Red	Gardening

30. *(a)* **31.** *(b)* **32.** *(c)* **33.** *(d)*

Chart for Answers 34 to 38

Raghu—	Cricket,	Hockey,	×	Swimming
Gyan —	Cricket,	Hockey,	Chess,	×
Sohan —	×	Hockey,	Chess,	×
Govind—	Cricket,	×	×	Swimming

34. *(b)* **35.** *(b)* **36.** *(e)* **37.** *(a)* **38.** *(c)*

Chart for Answers 39 to 41

Boy	*Games Played*
Rajat	— Football, Hockey, Cricket, Basketball
Sushil	— Football, Hockey, Cricket, Basketball
Nagesh	— Football, Hockey, Cricket, Basketball
Ramu	— Hockey, Cricket, Basketball
Mayank	— Football, Cricket

39. *(d)* **40.** *(d)* **41.** *(a)*

Chart for Answers 42 to 46

Girls	*Live at*	*Hobbies*
Eena	— Mumbai	Dancing, Gardening
Mira	— Mumbai	Travelling, Gardening
Meena	— Chennai	Clay Modelling, Reading
Moe	— Delhi	Painting, Photography

42. *(b)* **43.** *(a)* **44.** *(a)* **45.** *(b)* **46.** *(d)*

47. *(a)* **:** If Q took birth after the death of P and given that P took birth before S, then S was the guardian of P.

48. *(b)* **:** If S died before P and P died before the birth of Q, then S was not alive during the life span of Q.

49. *(c)* **:** If Q took birth before P, who took birth before S, and given that Q died after P, R and S, then Q's life span was more than both P and S.

50. *(e)* **:** Compare given statements *(i)* and *(ii)*

Chart for Answers 51 to 55

Boys →	*Friendly With*	← *Girls*
Raj		Kusum
Prem		→ Vimla
Ved	Friends	Poonam
Ashok		→ Sushma

51. *(d)* **:** 'Ved's girlfriend does not like Vimla and Sushma'.

52. *(c)* **:** 'Kusum does not care for Ved'.

53. *(d)* **54.** *(b)* **55.** *(d)*

Chart for Answers 56 to 60

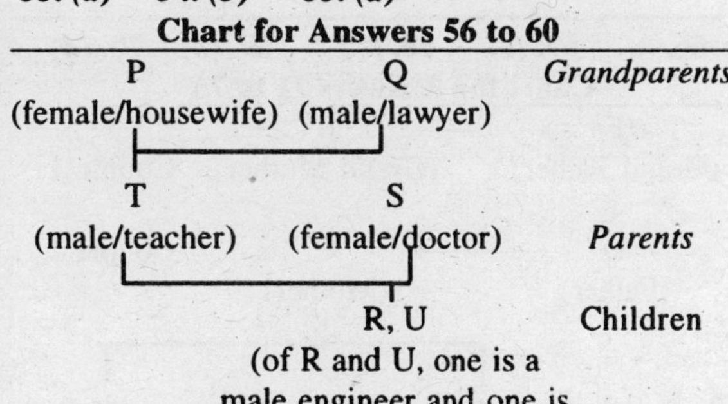

56. *(b)* **:** One married lady S who is mother of R and U is a doctor. Q the lawyer is married to P. Of the two married ladies one is a housewife. As Q is a lawyer the other married lady who is a housewife should be P.

57. (d) : Sex of R and U is not given.

58. (a) : P has one son T and one grandson either R or U one of whom is as engineer. So, the grand daughter is a student.

59. (c) : Sex of R and U is not given, but as both are children of S and one is a male engineer, the relationship between the two is of brother and sister.

60. (d)

Information summary for Answers 61 to 65

The students in the order

(i) tallest to shortest one :

D, E, A, F, B/C

(ii) heaviest to lightest are

F, D, B/C, A

61. (a) **62. (c)**

63. (e) : Weight of E is not given.

64. (d) **65. (a)**

Chart for Answers 66 to 70

Faculty member	*Sex*	*Subject taught*	*Ph.D/ Not-Ph.D.*
A	Male	Chemistry	Not Ph.D.
B	Male	Commerce	Ph.D.
C	Lady	Physics or Economics	Not Ph.D.
D	Male	Law	Not. Ph.D.
E	Male	Psychology	Ph.D.
F	Male	Zoology	Ph.D.
G	Lady	X	Ph.D.
H	Lady	Physics or Economics	Not Ph.D.

66. (a) **67. (c)** **68. (c)** **69. (a)** **70. (d)**

Chart for Answers 71 to 75

E ←——→ B
(Grand Father) (Grand Mother) Couple 1.
↓
D ←——→ C Couple 2.
(Father) (Mother)
↓
A (Sister) F
(Son) ←—— (Daughter)

71. (a) **72. (c)** **73. (d)** **74. (e)** **75. (b)**

Information summary for Answers 76 to 80

P and S — Couple 1.
Q and R — Couple 2.

P — Photographer
Q — Technician
R — Writer
S — Reporter
T — Reporter
U — Technician

Note : The sex of P, Q, R, S, T or U is not given.

76. (e) : U is the brother of R, but sex of R is not given.

77. (e) **78. (a)** **79. (b)** **80. (c)**

Information summary for Answers 81 to 85

Day		*Lecture*
Monday	—	No lecture
Tuesday	—	C
Wednesday	—	E
Thursday	—	B
Friday	—	D
Saturday	—	A
Sunday	—	F

81. (e) **82. (e)** **83. (b)** **84. (a)** **85. (c)**

Chart for Answers 86 to 90

Name	*Location*	*Performance*	*Class*
Ramesh	Far from the school	Good at Maths only	IV
Kamal	Close to the school	Weak in Maths only	IV
Ahmed	Far from the school	Good at all the subjects	V
John	Far from the school	Weak in all the subjects	VI

86. (c) **87. (d)** **88. (b)** **89. (a)** **90. (d)**

Information summary for Answers 91 to 95

A is the grandfather.
B is the mother of D and F, D is the brother of F.
C is a lady.
In descending order of weight the family members are — A, C, E, B, D/F.

91. (d) : There are no relationship details about E.

92. (e) : There are no relationship details between C and D.

93. (a) : Sex of all the family members is not given.

94. (e) : There are no details that can detect a couple in the family.

95. *(c)*

Information summary for Answers 96 to 100

1. From eldest to the youngest the order of friends is :
   B/D, E, A, C *or* B, D/E, A,C
2. From tallest to the shortest the confirmed order of friends is : F, C, E, D.
   A can be in-between, F, C *or* C, E or E, D
   B can be in-between, C, E, *or* E, D

96. *(e)* : C is definitely in-between F and E but nothing is certain about A and B.

97. *(e)*

98. *(e)* : Either B or D is the eldest

99. *(e)* **100.** *(a)*

Information summary for Answers 101 to 105

Members	*Profession*	*Sex*
A	— Accountant	— Not known
B	— Lawyer	— Male
C	— Teacher or Manager	— Not known
D	— Engineer	— Male
E	— Teacher or Manager	— Female
F	— Doctor	— Not known
G	— Student	— Male

1. D is grandfather of G
   G is grandson of E
   So, E must be the grandmother of G
2. D is the father of B and the grandfather of G, so B is the father of G
3. No lady is a lawyer, so B is the lawyer
4. So, C or A or F is the wife of B (E is the wife of D)

101. *(d)* **102.** *(e)* **103.** *(d)* **104.** *(d)* **105.** *(c)*

Chart for Answers 106 to 110

Members	*Occupation*	*Sex*
P	Teacher	F
Q	Lawyer	M
R	Housewife	F
S	Doctor	M
T	Engineer or Architect	M
U	Engineer or Architect	Unmarried Male

P and S — Couple 1.
R and T — Couple 2.

106. *(a)* **107.** *(d)* **108.** *(c)* **109.** *(e)* **110.** *(c)*

Information Summary for Answers 111 to 115

Men	*Women*
A - Advocate	P - Doctor
B - Advocate	Q - Doctor
C - Doctor	R - Advocate
D - Doctor	S - Doctor
E - Teacher	T - Teacher, U - Teacher

Those who must be together in a team : (1) A, P, U (2) E, Q (3) C, T

Those who cannot go together in a team : (i) B, D (2) B, R (3) D, P (4) C, Q

111. *(b)* **112.** *(d)* **113.** *(a)* **114.** *(c)* **115.** *(b)*

Information summary for Answers 116 to 120

Day		*Lecture*
Sunday	→	D
Monday	→	No Lecture
Tuesday	→	B
Wednesday	→	E
Thursday	→	F
Friday	→	C
Saturday	→	A

116. *(d)* **117.** *(c)* **118.** *(d)* **119.** *(e)* **120.** *(a)*

Chart for Answers 121 to 125

Friend	*Shirt*	*Short*
A	Pink	White
B	Red	Blue
C	Yellow	Green
D	Blue	Grey
E	Green	Black

121. *(c)* **122.** *(b)* **123.** *(d)* **124.** *(a)* **125.** *(b)*

Chart for Answers 126 to 130

Member	*Profession*	*Dress*	*Sex*
P	Engineer	Brown	M
Q	Doctor	Blue	F
R	Lawyer	Brown	M
S	Engineer	Black or Green	F
T	Teacher	Blue	F
U	Lawyer	Black or Green	M

P and Q — Couple 1.
R and T — Couple 2.

126. *(c)* **127.** *(d)* **128.** *(c)* **129.** *(a)* **130.** *(b)*

131. *(e)* : Other programmes are : R, T, W, V, S

132. *(e)* : U can be the last programme on any day.

133. *(e)* : Four of the program sets cannot be operated the next day out of those operated on the first day.

134. *(a)* **135.** *(c)*

PLACE ARRANGEMENT

Place arrangement generally refers to the positioning of persons or objects in a manner indicated by set of information given. One has to understand the order of placement and then attempt questions following the given information.

SOLVED EXAMPLES

1. Five boys are climbing the stairs. David is in the centre. Kartik is in the last. Anmol is ahead of Nitin who is behind Anmol as well as Danny. Who is ahead of all?
   (*a*) Danny (*b*) Anmol
   (*c*) Either Danny or Anmol (*d*) Cannot be determined
   (*e*) None of the two

   Ans. (*c*) : The order in which the boys are climbing is :

Danny		Anmol
Anmol		Danny
David	or	David
Nitin		Nitin
Kartik		Kartik

   So, there is every possibility that either Danny or Anmol is ahead of all.

2. Five persons are walking in a line one behind the other. Of the first and the last persons in the line, one is intelligent and the other a fool. One strong man is behind the short man. The weak man is in front of the fool. Short man is in-between the intelligent man and the strong man. Who is the man in the centre?
   (*a*) Short man (*b*) Strong man
   (*c*) Weak man (*d*) Intelligent man
   (*e*) Cannot be said

   Ans. (*b*) : The order in which the five men are walking is :
   Fool, Weak man, Strong man, Short man, Intelligent man

EXERCISE

Directions : *In the following questions, under-stand the arrangement pattern and then select the right answer from the given options :*

1. Five boys are sitting in a row. Raghu is not adjacent to Shyam or Amit. Ajay is not adjacent to Shyam. Raghu is adjacent to Mayank. If Mayank is at the middle in the row, then Ajay is adjacent to whom out of the following?
   (*a*) Amit (*b*) Raghu
   (*c*) Mayank (*d*) Shyam
   (*e*) Data Inadequate
2. Mini is to the right of Rajni but to the left of Ananta. Saya is to the right of Mini but to the left of Jaya. Who is on the extreme left if all the girls are facing North?
   (*a*) Jaya (*b*) Mini
   (*c*) Rajni (*d*) Saya
   (*e*) Ananta
3. Kittu is in-between Mohan and Sohan. Raju is to the left of Sohan and Shyam is to the right of Mohan. If all of the friends are sitting

facing South, then who is on their extreme right?
(*a*) Mohan (*b*) Sohan
(*c*) Kittu (*d*) Shyam
(*e*) Data Inadequate

4. A, B, C, D and E are running one behind the other. C is not near E and A is not near D. B is next to A and E is not near D. Who is in the middle?
(*a*) B (*b*) E
(*c*) A (*d*) Cannot be said
(*e*) None of these

5. O, P, Q, R, S and T are standing on a bench according to their height. P is taller than O but shorter than S. Only S is taller than T. R is shorter than P but taller than Q. Who is the shortest?
(*a*) O (*b*) Q
(*c*) P (*d*) Cannot be said
(*e*) None of these

6. Five personalities are living in a multistoried building. Mr. Effortless lives in a flat above Mr. Active, Mr. Charge lives in a flat below Mr. Diligent, Mr. Active lives in a flat above Mr. Diligent and Mr. Behaved lives in a flat below Mr. Charge. Who lives in the topmost flat?
(*a*) Mr. Charge (*b*) Mr. Diligent
(*c*) Mr. Effortless (*d*) Mr. Behaved
(*e*) Cannot be said

7. Six friends are sitting in a circle and playing cards. Kenny is to the left of Danny. Michael is in-between Bob and John. Roger is in between Kenny and Bob. Who is sitting to the right of Michael?
(*a*) Danny (*b*) John
(*c*) Kenny (*d*) Bob
(*e*) Cannot be said

8. From the above question, if the places of Danny and Bob are interchanged and so also of Kenny and Roger, then who will be sitting to the left of Bob?
(*a*) Roger (*b*) John
(*c*) Kenny (*d*) Michael
(*e*) Data inadequate

9. Four girls A, B, C and D are sitting in a circle. B and C are facing each other. Which of the following is definitely true?
(*a*) A is to the left of C
(*b*) D is to the left of C
(*c*) A and D are facing each other
(*d*) A is not between B and C
(*e*) None of these

10. Brajesh, Jayesh, Amar and Praveer are playing a game of cards. Amar is to the right of Jayesh who is to the right of Brajesh. Who is to the right of Amar?
(*a*) Brajesh
(*b*) Praveer
(*c*) Brajesh or Praveer
(*d*) Jayesh
(*e*) None of these

11. Four girls are sitting on a bench to be photographed. Seema is to the left of Rani. Mary is to the right of Rani. Rita is between Rani and Mary. Who would be second from the left in the photography?
(*a*) Rani (*b*) Seema
(*c*) Mary (*d*) Rita
(*e*) None of these

12. In a pile of 10 books there are 3 of History, 3 of Hindi, 2 of Maths, and 2 of English. Taking from above there is an English book between a History and Maths book, a History book between a Maths and an English book, a Hindi book between an English and a Maths book, a Maths book between two Hindi books, and two Hindi books between a Maths and a History book. Book of which subject is at the sixth position from the top?
(*a*) English (*b*) Hindi
(*c*) History (*d*) Maths
(*e*) Data Inadequate

13. Five persons A, B, C, D and E are sitting in a row facing you such that D is on the left of C and B is on the right of E. A is on the right of C and B is on the left of D. If E occupies a corner position, then who is sitting in the centre?
(*a*) A (*b*) B
(*c*) C (*d*) D
(*e*) Data Inadequate

14. Of the five members of a panel sitting in a row, R is on the left of P but right of T, and

Q is on the left of S but right of P. Who is sitting in the middle?

(*a*) P (*b*) Q
(*c*) R (*d*) S
(*e*) T

15. Six friends A, B, C, D, E and F are standing in a circle. B is between F and C; A is between E and D; F is to the left of D. Who is between A and F?

(*a*) C (*b*) B
(*c*) D (*d*) E
(*e*) Cannot be determined

Directions (Qs. 16 to 18) : *Read the following statements and answer the questions given below :*

A, B, C, D and E are standing in a row. On one end of the row is D and on the other is C. B is to the right of E. A is to the left of C. E is in-between D and B.

16. Who is in the centre of the row?

(*a*) E (*b*) D
(*c*) B (*d*) A
(*e*) C

17. A is standing between :

(*a*) B & D (*b*) E & B
(*c*) C & E (*d*) B & C
(*e*) Cannot be said

18. Who is to the right of B?

(*a*) C (*b*) E
(*c*) A (*d*) D
(*e*) Cannot be said

Directions (Qs. 19-20) : *Read the following statements and answer the questions given below :*

Six persons are sitting around the camp-fire. Vidur is to the left of Sonu. Adil is between Roy and Shyam. Negi is at the second place to the left of Adil.

19. Who is at the second place to the right of Vidur?

(*a*) Roy (*b*) Negi
(*c*) Shyam (*d*) None of the above
(*e*) Date Inadequate

20. Who is to the left of Roy?

(*a*) Sonu (*b*) Adil
(*c*) Negi (*d*) Cannot be said
(*e*) Data Inadequate

Directions (Qs. 21-22) : *Read the following statements and answer the questions given below :*

Five shirts are placed on a shelf in a heap. Red shirt is above the Blue shirt and Green shirt is below the Orange shirt. Blue shirt is above the Orange shirt and White is below the Green shirt.

21. The colour of the shirt between Red and Orange shirts is :

(*a*) White (*b*) Green
(*c*) Blue (*d*) Data is insufficient
(*e*) None of these

22. Which colour shirt is at the bottom?

(*a*) Red (*b*) White
(*c*) Orange (*d*) Cannot be said
(*e*) None of these

Directions (Qs. 23 to 27) : *Read the following statements and answer the questions given below :*

Nine family members are sitting in a theatre in one row. They are J, K, L, M, N, O, P, Q and R. L is at the right of M and at third place at the right of N. K is at one end of the row. Q is immediately next to O and P. O is at third place at the left of K. J is right next to the left of O.

23. Which of the following statement is true?

(*a*) There is one person between L and O
(*b*) R and P are neighbours
(*c*) M is at one extreme end
(*d*) N is at two seats away from J.
(*e*) None of the above

24. The family members sitting on the right of O are :

(*a*) RML (*b*) JQP
(*c*) QPK (*d*) KPR
(*e*) Cannot be determined

25. Who is sitting in the centre of the row?

(*a*) L (*b*) J
(*c*) O (*d*) Q
(*e*) None of the above

26. Who are sitting next to L?

(*a*) A and O (*b*) M and J
(*c*) M and O (*d*) P and J
(*e*) Data Inadequate

27. Who is at the other end of the row?

(*a*) R (*b*) J
(*c*) P (*d*) N
(*e*) Q

Directions (Qs. 28 to 30) : (A) There are five friends; (B) They are standing in a row facing south;

(C) Jayesh is to the immediate right of Alok; (D) Pramod is between Babir and Subodh; (E) Subodh is between Jayesh and Pramod.

28. Who is at the extreme left end?
(*a*) Alok (*b*) Babir
(*c*) Subodh (*d*) Data inadequate
(*e*) None of these

29. Who is in the middle?
(*a*) Babir (*b*) Pramod
(*c*) Subodh (*d*) Jayesh
(*e*) Alok

30. To find answers to the above two questions, which of the given statements can be dispensed with?
(*a*) None (*b*) A only
(*c*) B only (*d*) C only
(*e*) D only

Directions (Qs. 31 to 33) : *Read the following information and answer the questions given below :*

(*i*) A, B, C, D and E reside in a five-storey building.
(*ii*) B and E do not reside on the ground floor.
(*iii*) D resides one storey above A and one storey below C.
(*iv*) E does not reside on the top floor.

31. On which floor does D reside?
(*a*) Second (*b*) Fourth
(*c*) Fifth (*d*) First
(*e*) Data inadequate

32. How many of them do reside above C?
(*a*) 3 (*b*) 2
(*c*) 4 (*d*) 1
(*e*) Data inadequate

33. To find out the answers to the above two questions, which of the four given statements can be dispensed with ?
(*a*) Only (*iv*) (*b*) Only (*ii*) and (*iii*)
(*c*) None (*d*) Only (*i*)
(*e*) Only (*ii*) and (*iv*)

Directions (Qs. 34 to 36) : *Read the following information and answer the questions given below :*

(A) Six friends are playing a card game facing at the centre.
(B) Subodh is to the right of Prabodh.
(C) There is one person between Uma and Sudha.
(D) Prabir is between Subodh and Uma and second to the left of Aloke.

34. Who is to the right of Sudha?
(*a*) Prabodh (*b*) Uma
(*c*) Aloke (*d*) Prabir
(*e*) Data inadequate

35. If Aloke and Subodh interchange their positions, who will be second to the right of Prabir?
(*a*) Prabodh (*b*) Subodh
(*c*) Uma (*d*) Sudha
(*e*) None of these

36. To answer the above two questions, which of the following statements can be dispensed with?
(*a*) C only (*b*) D only
(*c*) C or D only (*d*) None
(*e*) B only

Directions (Qs. 37 to 39) : *Read the following information carefully and answer the questions given below it :*

(*i*) There are seven books one each on Psychology, Hindi, English, Sociology, Economics, Education and Accountancy, lying on a table one above the other.
(*ii*) Sociology is on the top of all the books.
(*iii*) Accountancy is immediately below Education which is immediately below Sociology.
(*iv*) Economics is immediately above Psychology but not in the middle.
(*v*) Hindi is immediately below Psychology.

37. Which three books are between Accountancy and Hindi?
(*a*) Economics, Psychology and Hindi.
(*b*) Economics, Psychology and Education
(*c*) English, Economics and Psychology
(*d*) Cannot be determined
(*e*) None of these

38. Economics is between which of the following books?
(*a*) Accountancy and Education
(*b*) Psychology and Hindi
(*c*) English and Psychology
(*d*) Cannot be determined
(*e*) None of these

39. If Sociology and English, Accountancy and Hindi & Education and Psychology

interchange their positions, which book will be between Psychology and Sociology?
(*a*) Hindi (*b*) Accountancy
(*c*) Psychology (*d*) Economics
(*e*) None of these

Directions (Qs. 40 to 44) : *Read the following information carefully and answer the questions given below :*

(*i*) Six flats on a floor in two rows facing North and South are allotted to P, Q, R, S, T and U.
(*ii*) Q gets a North facing flat and is not next to S.
(*iii*) S and U get diagonally opposite flats.
(*iv*) R, next to U, gets a South facing flat and T gets a North facing flat.

40. Which of the following combinations get South facing flats?
(*a*) URP (*b*) UPT
(*c*) QTS (*d*) Data inadequate
(*e*) None of these

41. The flats of which of the other pairs than SU, is diagonally opposite to each other?
(*a*) PT (*b*) QP
(*c*) QR (*d*) TS
(*e*) None of these

42. Whose flat is between Q and S?
(*a*) T (*b*) U
(*c*) R (*d*) P
(*e*) Data inadequate

43. If the flats of T and P are interchanged, whose flat will be next to that of U?
(*a*) Q (*b*) T
(*c*) P (*d*) R
(*e*) None of these

44. To arrive at the answers to the above questions, which of the following statements can be dispensed with?
(*a*) None (*b*) (i) only
(*c*) (ii) only (*d*) (iii) only
(*e*) None of these

Directions (Qs. 45 to 49) : *Study the following information carefully and answer the questions given below it :*

(*i*) Eleven students A, B, C, D, E, F, G, H, I, J and K are sitting in the first row of the class facing the teacher.
(*ii*) D who is to the immediate left of F is second to the right of C.
(*iii*) A is second to the right of E, who is at one of the ends.
(*iv*) J is the immediate neighbour of A and B and third to the left of G.
(*v*) H is to the immediate left of D and third to the right of I.

45. In the above sitting arrangement which of the following statements is superfluous?
(*a*) (*i*) (*b*) (*ii*)
(*c*) (*iii*) (*d*) (*iv*)
(*e*) None is superfluous

46. Which of the following groups of friends is sitting to the right of G?
(*a*) IBJA (*b*) ICHDF
(*c*) CHDF (*d*) CHDE
(*e*) None of these

47. Who is sitting in the middle of the row?
(*a*) C (*b*) I
(*c*) B (*d*) G
(*e*) None of these

48. Which of the following statements is TRUE in the context of the above sitting arrangements?
(*a*) There are three students sitting between D and G
(*b*) G and C are neighbours sitting to the immediate right of H.
(*c*) B is sitting between J and I
(*d*) K is between A and J
(*e*) None of these

49. If E and D, C and B, A and H and K and F interchange their positions, which of the following pairs of students is sitting at the ends?
(*a*) D and E (*b*) E and F
(*c*) D and K (*d*) K and F
(*e*) None of these

Directions (Qs. 50 to 54) : *Some friends are sitting on a bench. Sunil is sitting next to Sunita and Sanjoy is next to Bindu. Bindu is not sitting with Sumit. Sumit is on the left end of the bench and Sanjoy is on second position from right hand side. Sunil is on the right side of Sunita and to the right side of Sumit. Sunil and Sanjoy are sitting together.*

Based on the above sitting arrangements select the correct alternatives out of the five given in the following questions.

50. Sanjoy is sitting in-between :
(*a*) Bindu and Sunita
(*b*) Sunil and Sumit
(*c*) Sunita and Bindu
(*d*) Sunil and Bindu
(*e*) Sumit and Bindu

51. Bindu is sitting on the :
(*a*) Extreme right side
(*b*) Extreme left side
(*c*) Second from left side
(*d*) Third from left
(*e*) In the centre

52. Sumit is sitting on the :
(*a*) Second place from right
(*b*) Second place from left
(*c*) Extreme left
(*d*) Extreme right
(*e*) In the middle of all

53. Sunil is sitting between :
(*a*) Sunita and Sanjoy
(*b*) Sunita and Bindu
(*c*) Sanjoy and Sumit
(*d*) Bindu and Sanjoy
(*e*) Sumit and Bindu

54. Who is sitting in the centre?
(*a*) Sunil (*b*) Sanjoy
(*c*) Sunita (*d*) Bindu
(*e*) Sumit

Directions (Qs. 55 to 60) : *Read the following information and answer the questions given below :*
(i) A, B, C, D, E, F, and G are sitting on a wall and all of them are facing east.
(ii) C is on the immediate right of D.
(iii) B is at an extreme end and has E as his neighbour.
(iv) G is between E and F.
(v) D is sitting third from the south end.

55. Which of the conditions (i) to (v) given above is not required to find out the place in which A is sitting?
(*a*) *(i)*
(*b*) *(ii)*
(*c*) *(iii)*
(*d*) All statements are required
(*e*) None of these

56. Which of the following pairs of people are sitting at the extreme ends?
(*a*) AE (*b*) AB
(*c*) FB (*d*) CB
(*e*) Cannot be determined

57. Immediately between which of the following pairs of people is D sitting?
(*a*) CE (*b*) AC
(*c*) CF (*d*) AF
(*e*) None of these

58. Name the person who should change places with C such that he gets the third place from the north end?
(*a*) G (*b*) F
(*c*) E (*d*) Can't be determined
(*e*) None of these

59. Who is sitting to the right of E?
(*a*) F (*b*) D
(*c*) C (*d*) A
(*e*) None of these

60. Which of the following pairs of people are sitting next to F?
(*a*) EG (*b*) DC
(*c*) ED (*d*) GD
(*e*) None of these

EXPLANATORY ANSWERS

1. (*b*) : The order of sitting is :
Amit, Shyam, Mayank, Ajay, Raghu
or
Ajay, Raghu, Mayank, Amit, Shyam

2. (*c*) : The order in which the girls are positioned is :
Rajni, Mini, Ananta, Saya, Jaya
or
Saya, Jaya, Ananta
or
Saya, Ananta, Jaya

3. (*d*) : The order of sitting while facing South is: Shyam, Mohan, Kittu, Sohan, Raju.

4. (*a*) : The positions while running behind the other is :

E E
A A
B *or* B
C D
D C

5. *(d)* : In descending order of height, the standing positions are :

S S
T T
P *or* P
R R
O Q
Q O

Either O or Q is the shortest. The information given is not enough to clarify the answer.

6. *(c)* : The personalities living in flats in multi-storied building are in order given below :

Mr. Effortless
Mr. Active
Mr. Diligent
Mr. Charge
Mr. Behaved

7. *(d)* : The order in which the friends are sitting is :

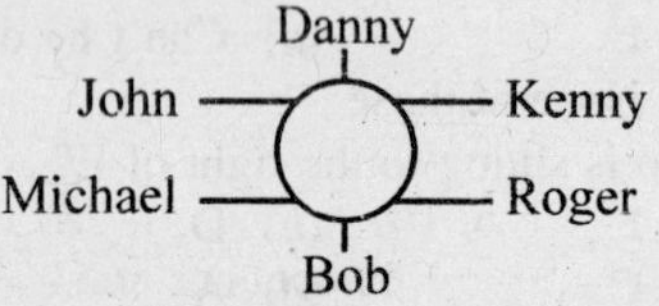

8. *(a)* : The order of sitting in new positions will be :

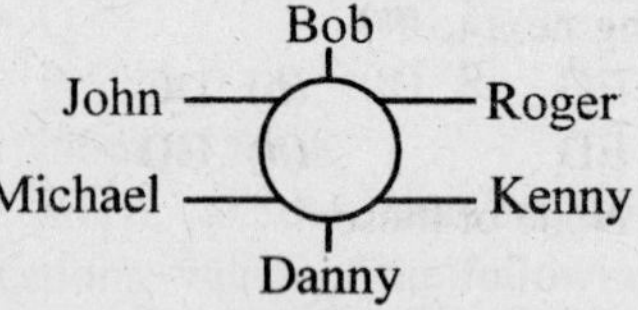

9. *(c)* : The sitting positions are :

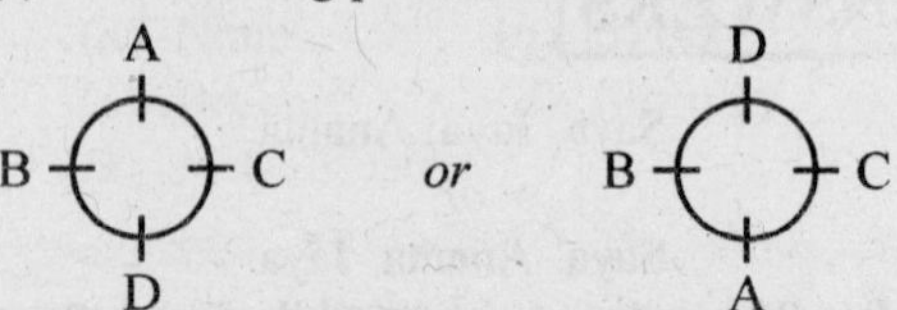

10. *(b)* : The order from left to right is :
Brijesh, Jayesh, Amar, Praveer

11. *(d)* : Sitting order as seen for the photograph is :
Mary, Rita, Rani, Seema
1st left for the photography is Mary and then 2nd is Rita.

12. *(b)* : The pile of books is in the order :

1st — History
English
Maths
History
English
6th — Hindi
Maths
Hindi
Hind
10th — History

13. *(d)* : Sitting order while facing us is :
A, C, D, B, E

14. *(a)* : Members of the panel are sitting in the order —
T, R, P, Q, S

15. *(c)* : The pattern of standing is :

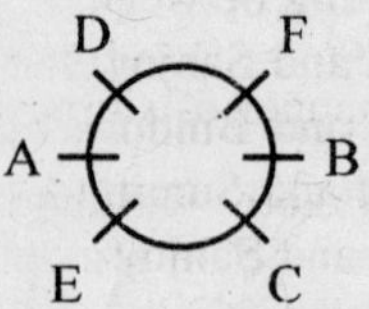

16. *(c)* : For questions 16 to 18 the order in which the five persons are standing is :
D, E, B, A, C.

17. *(d)* **18. *(c)***

19. *(b)* : For questions 19 and 20, the order of sitting around the camp fire is :

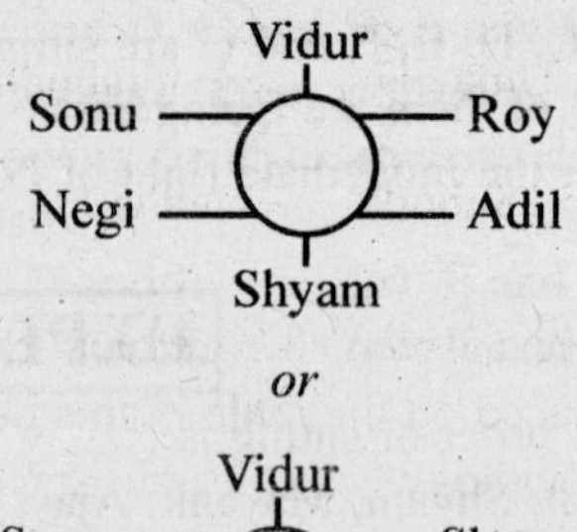

or

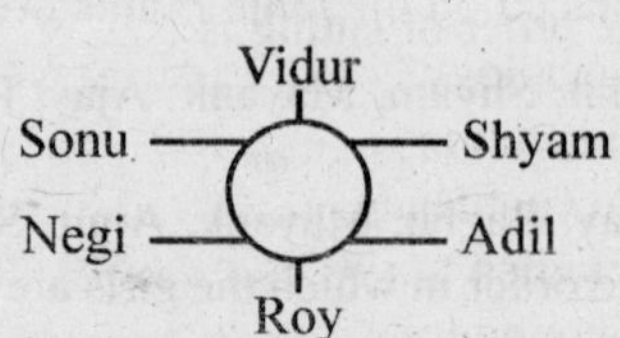

20. *(d)* : Person to the left of Roy can be Adil or Negi. So, the answer cannot be decided.

21. ***(c)*** **:** For questions 21 and 22, the placement of shirts on the shelf is :

Red
Blue
Orange
Green
White

22. ***(b)***

23. ***(a)*** **:** Order of sitting for questions 23 to 27 is : N, R, M, L, J, O, Q, P, K.

24. ***(c)*** **25.** ***(b)*** **26.** ***(b)*** **27.** ***(d)***

28. ***(a)*** **:** For questions 28 to 30 five friends are standing in this order :

Alok, Jayesh, Subodh, Pramod, Babir

29. ***(c)*** **30.** ***(b)***

31. ***(d)*** **:** For answers 31 to 33 the manner of residing in a five-storey building is :

B
E
C
D
Ground floor - A

32. ***(b)*** **33.** ***(c)***

34. ***(a)*** **:** The manner of sitting is :

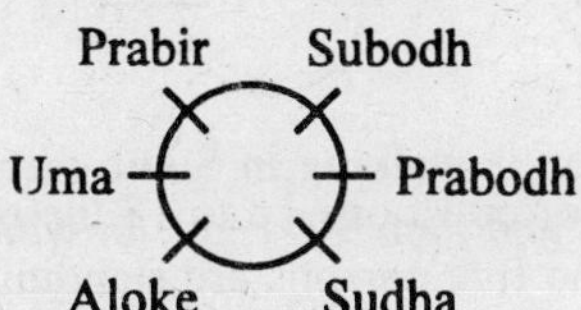

35. ***(b)*** **:** After interchanging positions the order will be :

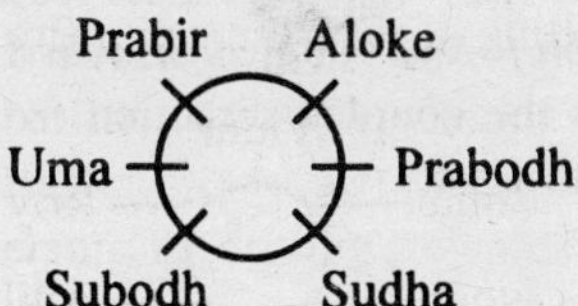

36. ***(a)***

37. ***(c)*** **:** For answers 37 and 38 the books are placed on the table in this order :

Sociology
Education
Accountancy
English
Economics
Psychology
Hindi

38. ***(c)***

39. ***(a)*** **:** After interchanging the positions of the books the new positions will be :

English
Psychology
Hindi
Sociology
Economics
Education
Accountancy

40. ***(a)*** **:** For answerws 40-44 the positions of flats occupied are :

(Q) (T) (S) ↑N
(U) (R) (P) ↓S

41. ***(b)*** **42.** ***(a)***

43. ***(d)*** **:** The new positions will be :

(Q) (P) (S) ↑N
(U) (R) (T) ↓S

44. ***(a)***

45. ***(e)*** **:** For answers 45 to 48 the sitting arrangement of the students is :

E, K, A, J, B, I, G, C, H, D, F

46. ***(c)*** **47.** ***(b)*** **48.** ***(c)***

49. ***(c)*** **:** The new sitting arrangement will be :

D, F, H, J, C, I, G, B, A, E, K

50. ***(d)*** **:** For answers 50 to 54 the order of sitting is :

Sumit, Sunita, Sunil, Sanjoy, Bindu

51. ***(a)*** **52.** ***(c)*** **53.** ***(a)*** **54.** ***(a)***

55. ***(d)*** **:** For answers 55 to 60 the sitting arrangement as facing East is :

7th → B
E
G
F
D
C
1st → A

56. ***(b)*** **57.** ***(c)*** **58.** ***(a)*** **59.** ***(e)*** **60.** ***(d)***

DIRECTION SENSE

In these type of tests, the directions in questions needs to be perceived. Such questions are based on the direction chart.

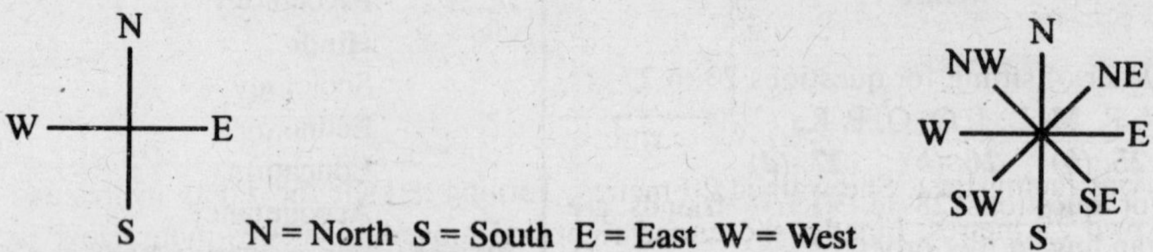

The sense of the different directions are guided by the left and right turns or angular turns.

SOLVED EXAMPLES

1. A person is walking in the North direction. He turns right two times and continues to walk. In which direction is he walking now ?

(*a*) North (*b*) South (*c*) East (*d*) West

Ans. (*b*) :

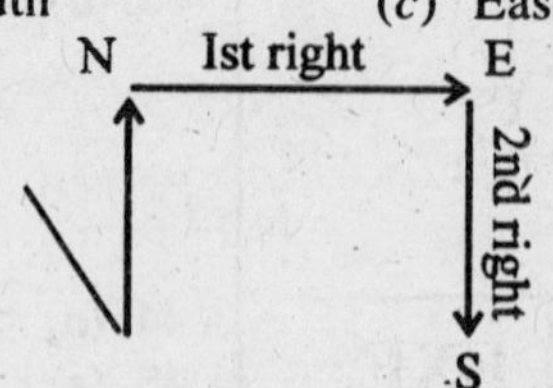

By following the direction chart it is clear that the person is walking in South direction.

2. A person is walking in the East direction. He turns 45° left and then 90° right. In which direction is he now ?

(*a*) North (*b*) North-West (*c*) North-East (*d*) West

Ans. (*c*) :

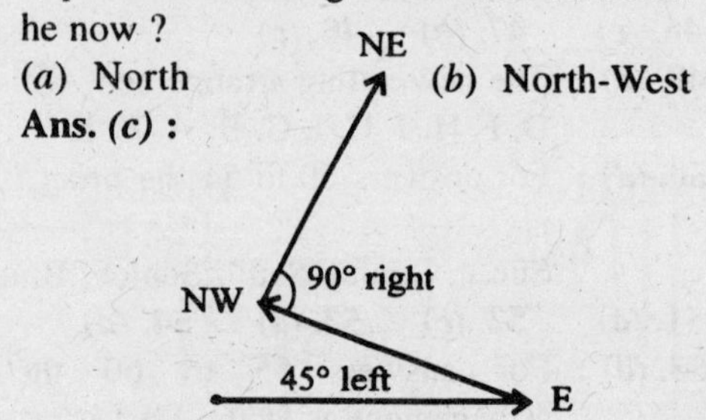

The 45° turn escapes from the straight direction to the coupled direction. 90° turn also follows the coupled direction from North-West to North-East.

The directions to be followed for changing one direction to another can also be routed by making proper use of the direction sense. The distances can also be measured easily.

3. Maya is travelling towards South. Which of the following directions should she take in order to travel towards North ?

(*a*) right, left, right, right (*b*) left, right, right

(*c*) right, right, left (*d*) left, left, left, left

Ans. (*a*) : Maya's first right turn is towards West, second turn to the left turns her to South again.

The third turn to the right takes her to the West once again, but by taking the final right turn, she is going towards North.

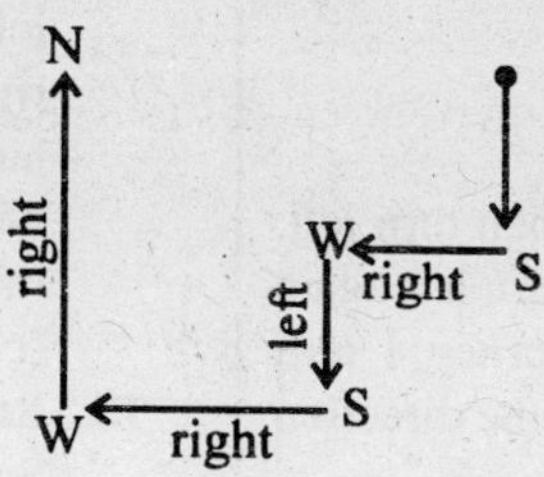

4. Shobha was facing East. She walked 20 metres. Turning left she moved 15 metres and then turning right moved 25 metres. Finally, she turned right and moved 15 metres more. How far is she from her starting point?

(*a*) 25 metres (*b*) 35 metres (*c*) 50 metres (*d*) 45 metres

Ans. (*d*) :

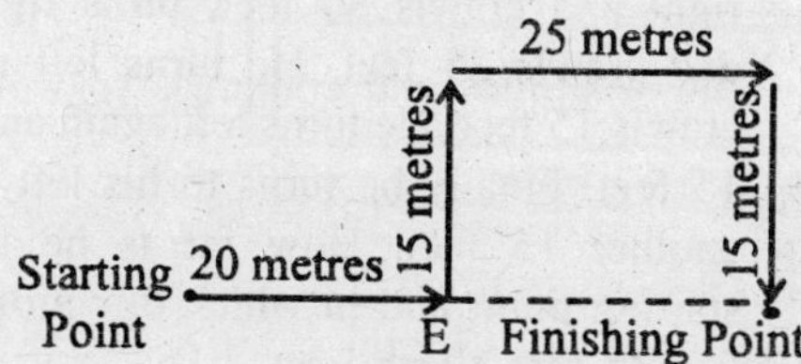

Shobha turns left after walking 20 metres towards East. Now she walks 15 metres towards North. She turns right towards East again and walks 25 metres further. Finally turning right towards South, she walks 15 metres. The distance moved towards North and towards South is same, *i.e.,* 15 metres. So, Shobha is 20 + 25 metres = 45 metres away from her starting point.

EXERCISE

Directions : *In the following questions, select the right answer from the given options to depict the correct direction/distance.*

1. Kittu walks towards East and then towards South. After walking some distance he turns towards West and then turns to his left. In which direction is he walking now?

(*a*) North (*b*) South
(*c*) East (*d*) West

2. A person is driving towards West. What sequence of directions should he follow so that he is driving towards South?

(*a*) left, right, right
(*b*) right, right, left
(*c*) left, left, left
(*d*) right, right, right

3. Richa drives 8 km to the South, turns left and drives 5 km. Again, she turns left and drives 8 km. How far is she from her starting point?

(*a*) 3 km (*b*) 5 km
(*c*) 8 km (*d*) 13 km

4. Dingi runs 40 km towards North then turns right and runs 50 km. He turns right and runs 30 km, and once again turns right and runs 50 km. How far is he from his starting point?

(*a*) 90 km (*b*) 50 km
(*c*) 10 km (*d*) 5 km

5. Debu walks towards East then towards North and turning 45° right walks for a while and lastly turns towards left. In which direction is he walking now?

(*a*) North (*b*) East
(*c*) South-East (*d*) North-West

6. If North is called North-West, North-West is called West, West is called South-West and so on. What will South-East be called?

(*a*) East (*b*) West
(*c*) North-East (*d*) South-East

7. I went 15 m to the North, then I turned West and covered 10 m, then I turned South and

covered 5 m, and then turned East and covered 10 m. In which direction am I from the starting point?
(*a*) East (*b*) West
(*c*) North (*d*) South

8. I travel in North direction and then turn left. After travelling for some time I turn left again and then right. Later in the journey I turn left and left once again. What is the direction I am facing?
(*a*) North (*b*) South
(*c*) East (*d*) West

9. Raj is walking towards West. He takes three turns while walking, all at an angle of 45° towards right, right and left. What direction is he facing now?
(*a*) North-East (*b*) South-East
(*c*) East (*d*) West

10. Jatin leaves his house and walks 12 km towards North. He turns right and walks another 12 km. He turns right again, walks 12 km more and turns left to walk 5 km. How far is he from his home and in which direction?
(*a*) 7 km East (*b*) 10 km East
(*c*) 17 km East (*d*) 24 km East

11. A lady runs 12 km towards North, then 6 km towards South and then 8 km East. How far is she from her starting point and in which direction?
(*a*) 5 km North-East
(*b*) 5 km East
(*c*) 10 km North-East
(*d*) 10 km West.

12. Diva journeys 10 km to East then 10 km to South-West. He turns again and journeys 10 km to North-West. Which direction is he in from the starting point?
(*a*) South (*b*) North
(*c*) West (*d*) East

13. Manu goes 40 km North, turns right and goes 80 km, turns right again and goes 30 km. In the end he turns right again and goes 80 km. How far is he from his starting point if he goes straight ahead another 50 km and turns left to go his last 10 km?
(*a*) 10 km (*b*) 30 km
(*c*) 40 km (*d*) 50 km

14. I walked 18 km towards North, then turned left and having walked another 4 km, I turned right and walked for 12 km more. How far have I walked from the starting point and in which direction?
(*a*) 8 km North (*b*) 10 km West
(*c*) 16 km South (*d*) 34 km North

15. Ravi drives 12 km towards West. He turns South and drives 3 km. He again turns East and drives 8 km. How far is he from his starting point?
(*a*) 3 km (*b*) 5 km
(*c*) 7 km (*d*) 11 km

16. A child crawls 20 feet towards North, turns right and crawls 30 feet, turns right again and crawls 35 feet. He turns left now and crawls 15 feet. He turns left again and crawls 15 feet. Finally he turns to his left to crawl another 15 feet. How far is he from his starting point and in which direction?
(*a*) 45 feet North-East
(*b*) 30 feet East
(*c*) 30 feet West
(*d*) 15 feet West

17. A man travels 100 km towards South. From there he turns right and travels 100 km and again turns right to travel 50 km. Which direction is he in from his starting point?
(*a*) North (*b*) North-East
(*c*) East (*d*) South-West

18. A train runs 120 km in West direction, 30 km in South direction and then 80 km in east direction before reaching the station. In which direction is the station from the train's starting point?
(*a*) South-West (*b*) North-West
(*c*) South-East (*d*) South

19. Facing the West direction, Priya jogs for 20 m, turns left and goes further 40 m. She turns left again and jogs for 20 m. Then she turns right to go 20 m to reach the park. How far is the park from her starting point and in which direction?
(*a*) 20 m South (*b*) 40 m West
(*c*) 60 m South (*d*) 100 m East

20. If all the directions are rotated, *i.e.*, if North

is changed to West and East to North and so on, then what will come in place of North-West?

(*a*) South-West (*b*) North-East
(*c*) East-North (*d*) East-West

21. Raj's car is facing towards West. He turns left and drives 10 km and turns left again and drives 10 km. Then he turns right and drives 40 km. He turns right again and drives 30 km. Lastly, he turns right and drives 50 km. How far is Raj from the starting point?

(*a*) 10 km (*b*) 20 km
(*c*) 40 km (*d*) 60 km

22. A and B start together from one point. They walk 10 km towards North. A turns left and covers 5 km whereas B turns right and covers 3 km. A turns left again and covers 15 km whereas B turns right and covers his 15 km. How far is A from B?

(*a*) 18 km (*b*) 10 km
(*c*) 5 km (*d*) 8 km

23. Tarun is walking towards East. What direction he should not follow if he should walk towards North?

(*a*) right, right, left, right, right
(*b*) right, right, left, left, left
(*c*) right, right, right
(*d*) right, left, right, left

24. Sony and Moni start walking from a point. Sony walks in West direction and Moni in South direction. After covering 20 km, Sony turns left and walks 15 km. Moni walks 10 km, turns left and walks 5 km. Sony, then turns left again and walks 25 km, whereas Moni turns right and walks 5 km. How far are Sony and Moni from each other?

(*a*) 5 km
(*b*) They are back at the starting point
(*c*) They are at same place at the finishing point
(*d*) Data is insufficient

25. Sita's house faces South direction. She runs ahead 10 m, turns left and runs 5 m. Then she turns left again and runs 15 m and then again turns left and runs 10 m. Finally she turns right and runs 5 m to reach her friend's house. What direction is Sita's friend's house facing?

(*a*) North (*b*) South
(*c*) West (*d*) East

26. If a person is walking towards North, what direction should he follow so that he is walking towards West?

(*a*) right, right, left
(*b*) left, left, right
(*c*) left, right, right
(*d*) left, left, left

27. If all the directions are changed in the manner that North becomes South and vice versa, then North-West will be :

(*a*) South-East (*b*) North-East
(*c*) South-West (*d*) None of the above

28. I was walking in South-East direction. After a while I turned 90° to the right and walked ahead. Later I turned 45° to the right. In which direction am I walking now?

(*a*) North (*b*) North-East
(*c*) South-West (*d*) East

29. Maria crawls 10 ft, turns right and crawls another 10 ft, then turns left two times and crawls 15 ft each time. If she started crawling in the western direction, towards which direction is she crawling now?

(*a*) East (*b*) South
(*c*) North (*d*) West

30. Two friends Jack and Bunny start a race, and together they run for 50 mts. Jack turns right and runs 60 mts while Bunny turns left and runs 40 mts. Then Jack turns left and runs 50 mts while Bunny turns right and runs 50 mts. How far are the two friends now from each other?

(*a*) 60 mts (*b*) 100 mts
(*c*) 20 mts (*d*) 150 mts

31. A policeman left his police post and proceeded south 4 km, after hearing a loud sound from point A. On reaching the place he heard another sound and proceeded 4 km to his left to the point B, only to find that the sound was coming from left of B. From B he proceeded left to reach that place 4 km away. In which direction he has to go to reach his police post?

(*a*) North (*b*) South

(*c*) East (*d*) West

32. Rahim started from point X and walked straight five km West, then turned left and walked straight two km and again turned left and walked straight seven km. In which direction is he from point X?
(*a*) North-East
(*b*) South-West
(*c*) South-East
(*d*) North-West

33. Ravi trávelled four km straight towards south. He turned left and travelled six km straight, then turned right and travelled four km straight. How far is he from the starting point?
(*a*) 8 km (*b*) 10 km
(*c*) 12 km (*d*) 18 km

34. One day John left home and cycled 10 km Southwards, turned right and cycled 5 km and turned right and cycled 10 km and turned left and cycled 10 km How many kms will he have to cycle to reach his home straight?
(*a*) 10 km (*b*) 15 km
(*c*) 20 km (*d*) 25 km

35. Sub-Inspector Jatin travelled from his Police-post straight for 400 metres. He then turned left and travelled 500 metres straight after which he turned left again and travelled for 400 metres straight. He then turned right and walked for another 600 metres straight. How far is he from the Police-post?
(*a*) 1.0 km (*b*) 1.1 km
(*c*) 1.4 km (*d*) 1.8 km

36. Starting from a point, Raju walked 12 metres towards North, he turned right and walked 10 metres, he again turned right and walked 12 metres, then he turned left and walked 5 metres. How far is he now and in which direction from the starting point?
(*a*) 27 metres towards East
(*b*) 5 metres towards East
(*c*) 10 metres towards West
(*d*) 15 metres towards East

37. Samir started from his Police Station on inspection duty. After travelling straight for a distance of four (4) km, he turned left for the market and travelled straight for 600 metres. He now turned left again and travelled straight for another 200 metres, and turned left and travelled straight for 600 metres. How far is Samir from the Police Station?
(*a*) 3.4 km (*b*) 3.8 km
(*c*) 4.4 km (*d*) 4.8 km

38. Suman is 40 metres South-West of Ashok, Prakash is 40 metres South-East of Ashok. Prakash is in which direction of Suman?
(*a*) South (*b*) West
(*c*) East (*d*) North-East

39. I go 10 m to the East, then I turn left and go 5 m, I turn left again and go 10 m and then again I turn left and go 10 m. In which direction am I from the starting point?
(*a*) East (*b*) West
(*c*) North (*d*) South

40. Mohan started from point 'A' and proceeded 7 km straight towards East, then he turned left and proceeded straight for a distance of 10 km. He then turned left again and proceeded straight for a distance of 6 km, and then turned left again and proceeded straight for another 10 km. In which direction is Mohan from his starting point?
(*a*) East (*b*) West
(*c*) North (*d*) South

41. Arun started walking from a point 'P' towards North and walked 30 metres. He then turned left and walked 40 metres and reached 'Q'. At what minimum straight line distance is the point 'Q' from 'P' and in which direction?
(*a*) 50 metres North-East
(*b*) 60 metres North-West
(*c*) 50 metres North-West
(*d*) 80 metres North-West

42. A Station Director starts from the Radio Station and drives 15 km towards West, turns left and covers another 10 km and again turns right and covers 18 km. To which direction she is now driving?
(*a*) South (*b*) South-West
(*c*) West (*d*) North-East

43. A policeman goes straight seven (7) kilometres eastwards, then turns right and goes straight three (3) kilometres and turns right again and goes straight ten (10) kilometres. In which direction is he from the starting point?

(*a*) South-West
(*b*) North-West
(*c*) North-East
(*d*) South-East

44. In an open ground, Maithili starts walking towards east and stops after 35 metres and turns right and walks another 15 metres and again turns right and walks 15 metres and then stops. What is the minimum distance she has to walk to reach the starting point?

(*a*) 25 metres
(*b*) 20 metres
(*c*) 30 metres
(*d*) 35 metres

45. Vijayan started walking towards South. After walking 15 metres he turned to the left and walked 15 metres. He again turned to his left and walked 15 metres. How far is he from his original position and in which direction?

(*a*) 15 metres, North
(*b*) 15 metres, East
(*c*) 30 metres, South
(*d*) 15 metres, West

Directions (Qs. 46 to 50) : *P, Q, R and S are standing on four corners of a square piece of plot as shown in the given figure. They start moving, and the movements are explained in each of the questions. Read the question and select the right alternative.*

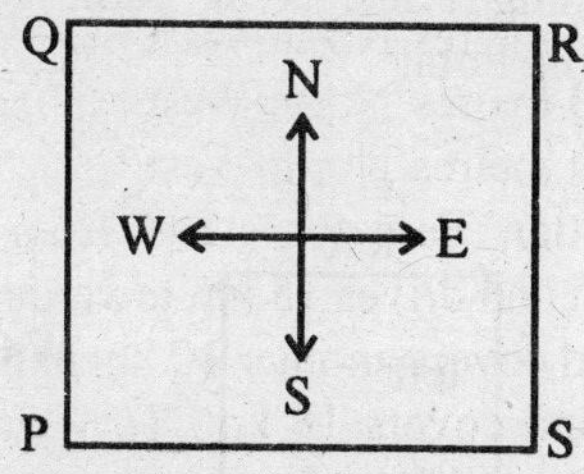

46. P, Q, R and S walk diagonally to opposite corners and from there Q and R walk one and a half sides anti-clockwise while P and S walk one side clockwise along the sides. Where is S now?

(*a*) At the North-West corner
(*b*) At the North-East
(*c*) At the South-West corner
(*d*) None of these

47. Q travelled straight to R, a distance of 10 km. He turned right and walked 7 km. towards S, again he turned right and walked 8 km, and then finally turned right and walked 7 km. How far is he from his original position?

(*a*) 7 km (*b*) 8 km
(*c*) 2 km (*d*) 3 km

48. From the original position, S starts crossing the field diagonally. After walking half the distance he turns right; walks some distance and turns left. Which direction is S facing now?

(*a*) South-East
(*b*) North-West
(*c*) South-West
(*d*) North

49. P and S walk one and a half length of the side clockwise and anti-clockwise respectively. Which one of the following statements is true?

(*a*) P is at midpoint between Q and R and S at the corner originally occupied by P
(*b*) P and S are both at the midpoint between R and S
(*c*) P and S are both at the midpoint between Q and R
(*d*) S is at midpoint between Q and R and P is at the midpoint between original side of R and S

50. P, Q, R, and S walk one and a half sides clockwise. Who is on the left of Q if he is facing West?

(*a*) P (*b*) R
(*c*) S (*d*) No one

EXPLANATORY ANSWERS

1. (*b*) :

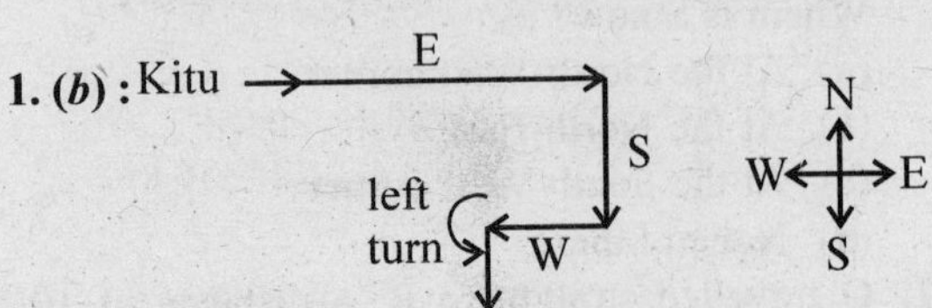

2. (*d*) :

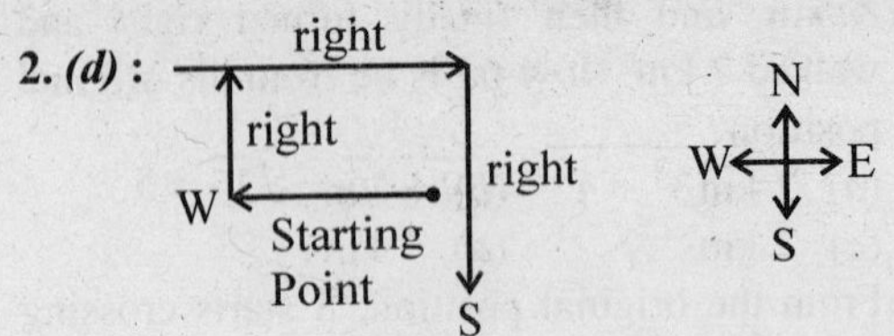

3. (*b*) :

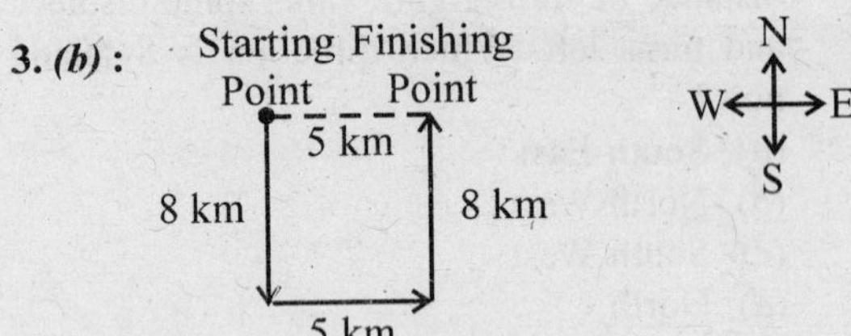

4. (*c*) :

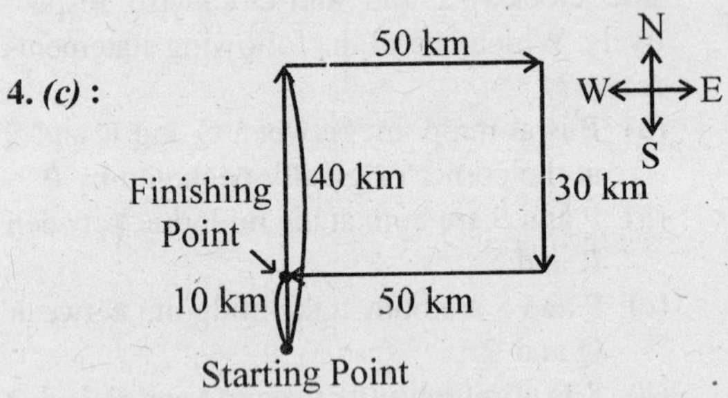

5. (*d*) :

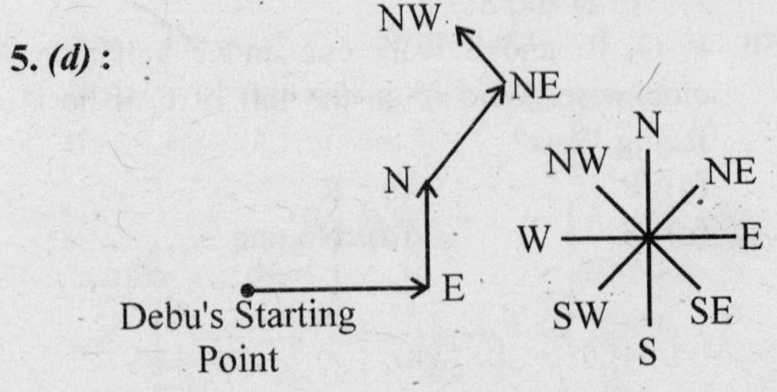

6. (*a*) :

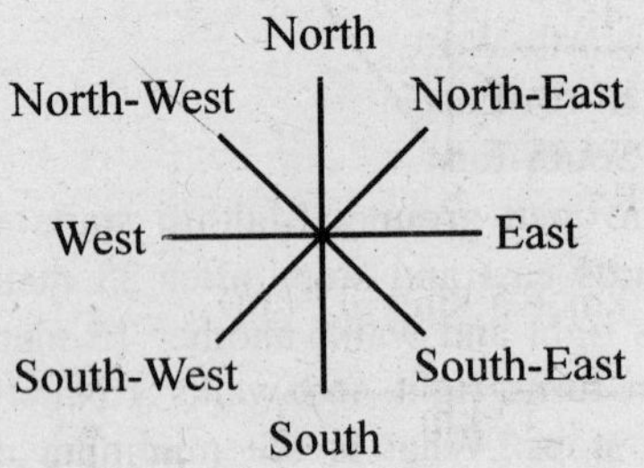

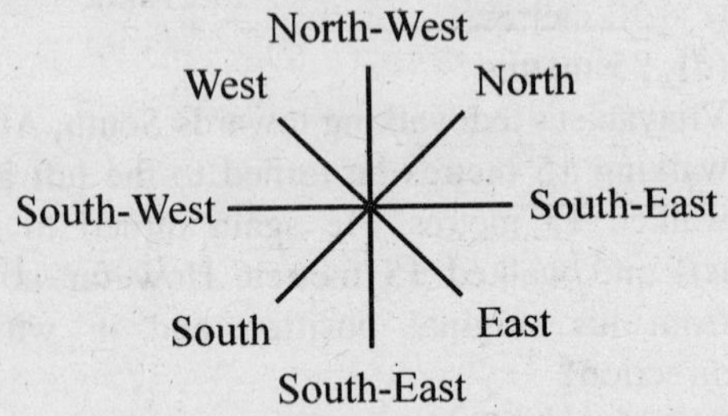

7. (*c*) :

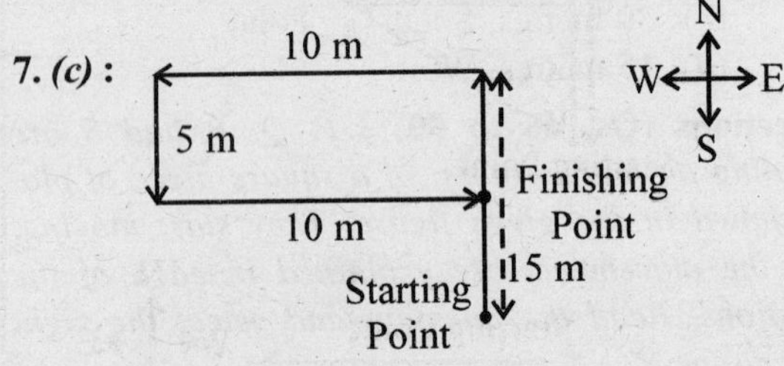

Finishing Point is at 10m North from Starting Point

8. (*c*) :

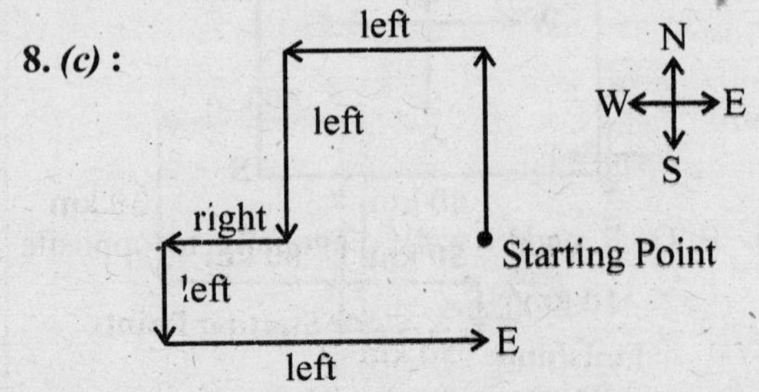

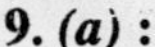

9. (a) :

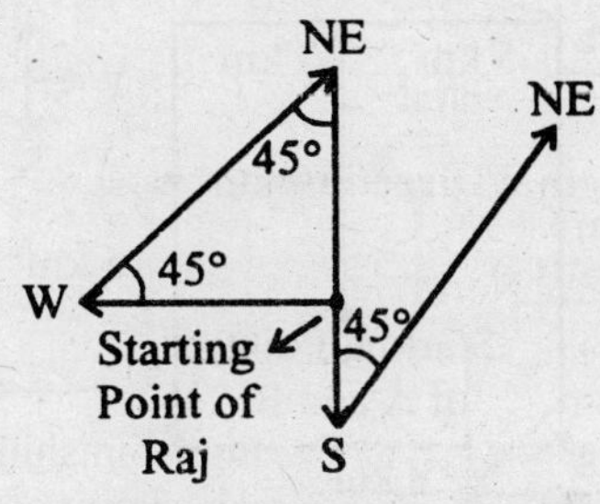

10. (c) : (12 km + 5 km = 17 km)

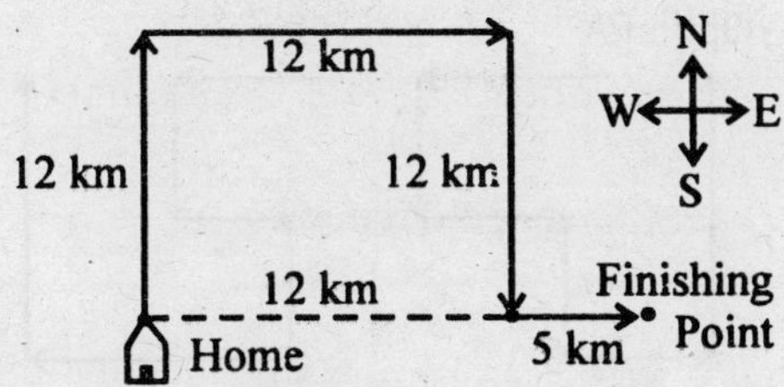

11. (c) : $ab = \sqrt{ac^2 + bc^2}$

$? = \sqrt{8^2 + 6^2} = \sqrt{64 + 36} = \sqrt{100} = 10$

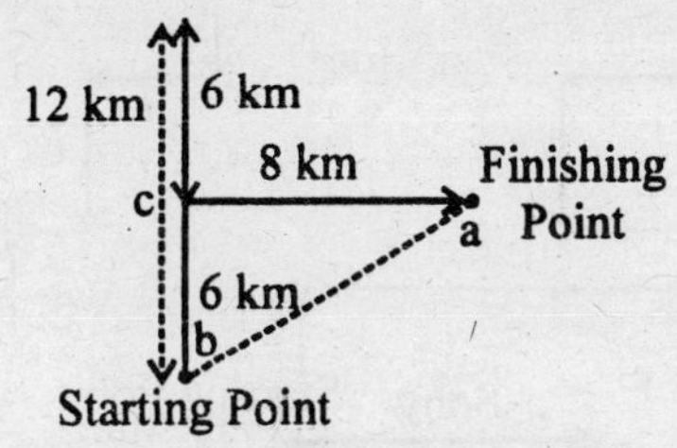

12. (c) :

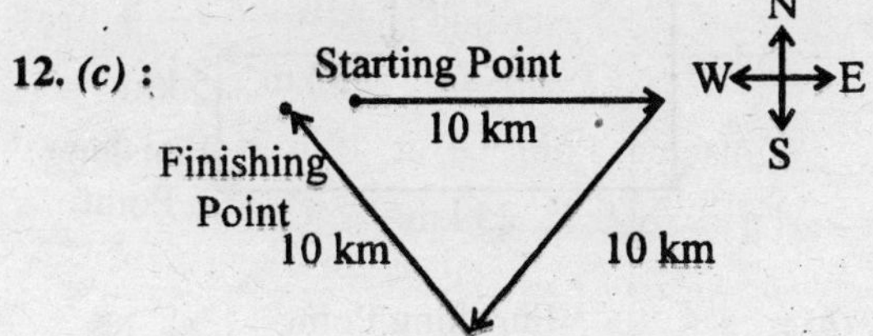

13. (d) :

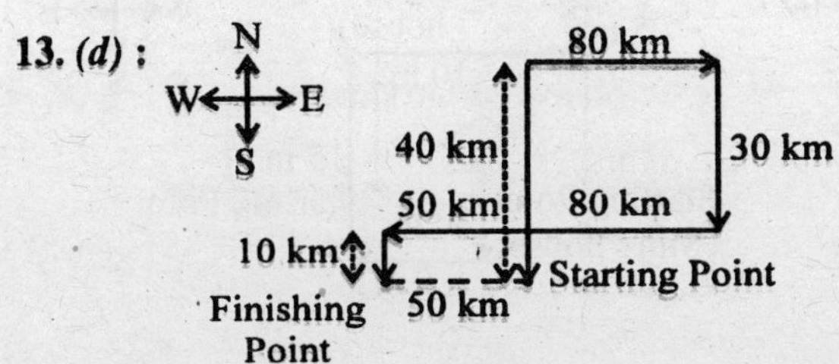

14. (d) : Finishing Point

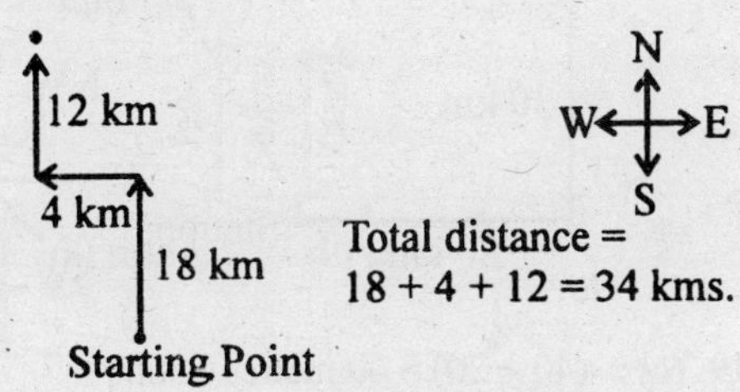

15. (b) : $ab = \sqrt{bc^2 + ca^2}$

$? = \sqrt{3^2 + 4^2} = \sqrt{9 + 16} = \sqrt{25} = 5$

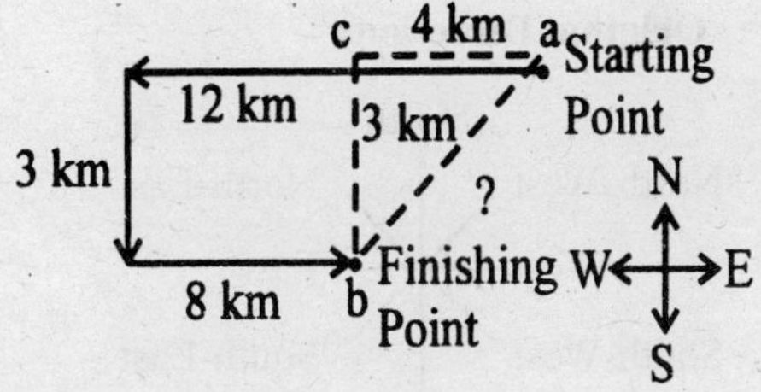

16. (b) :

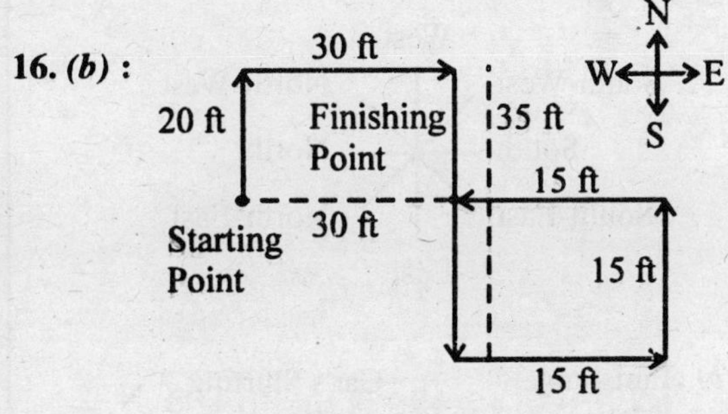

17. (d) :

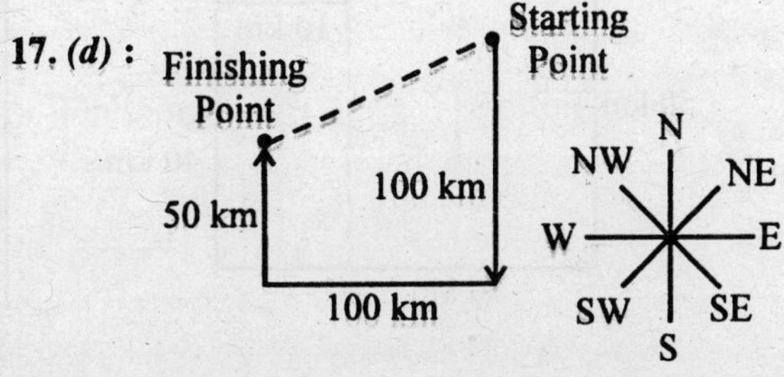

18. ***(a)*** **:**

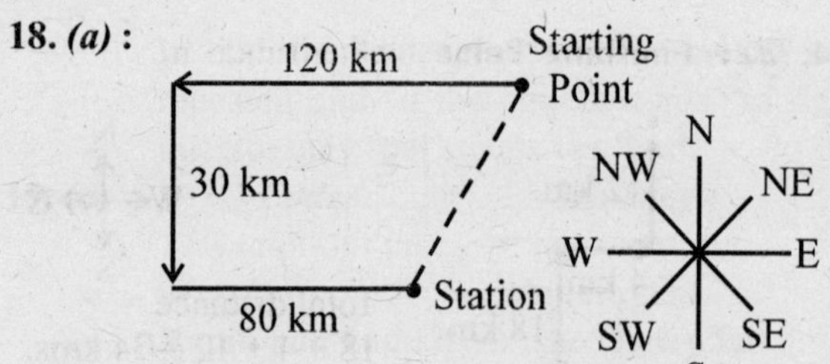

19. ***(c)*** **:** (40 + 20) = 60 metres South

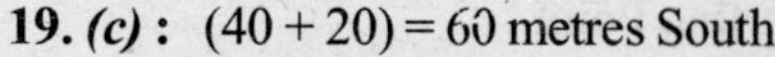

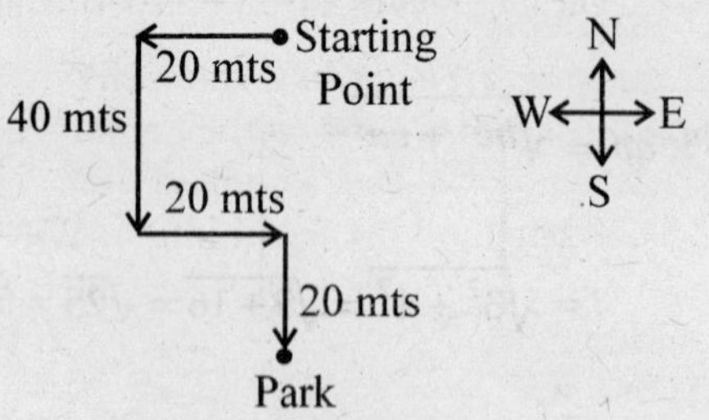

20. ***(a)*** **: Original Directions**

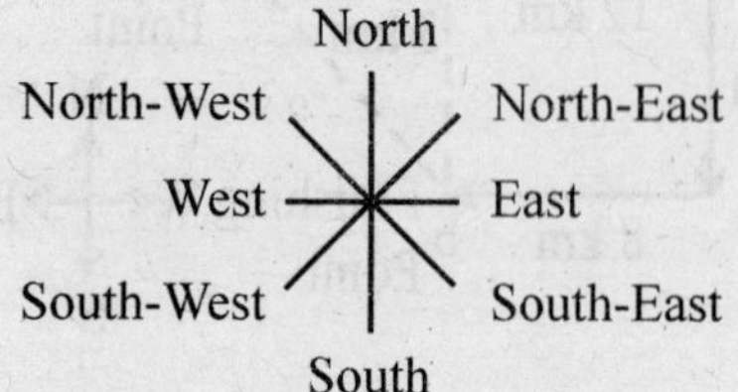

Changed Directions

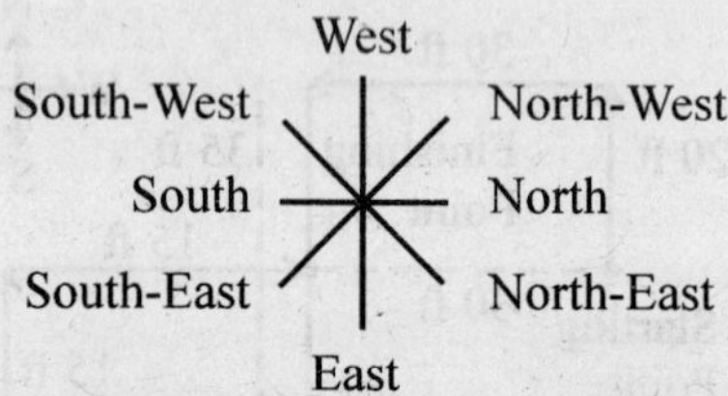

21. ***(b)*** **:**

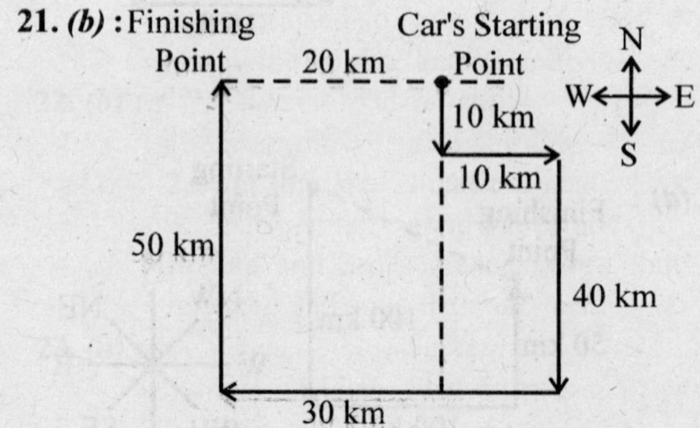

22. ***(d)*** **:**

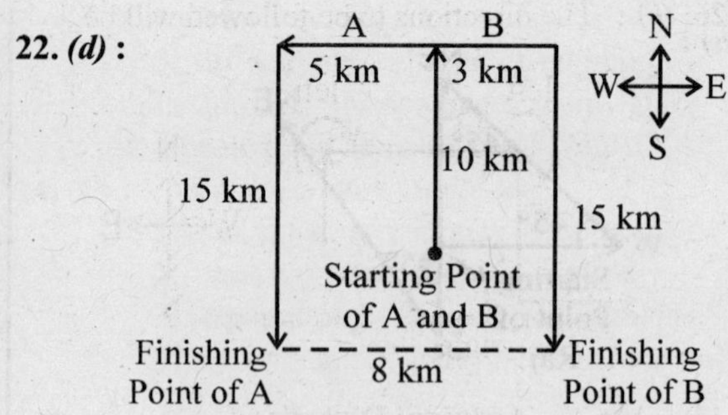

23. ***(d)*** **:**

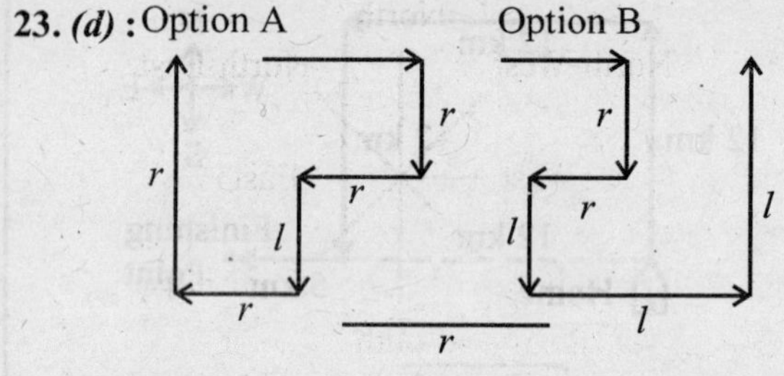

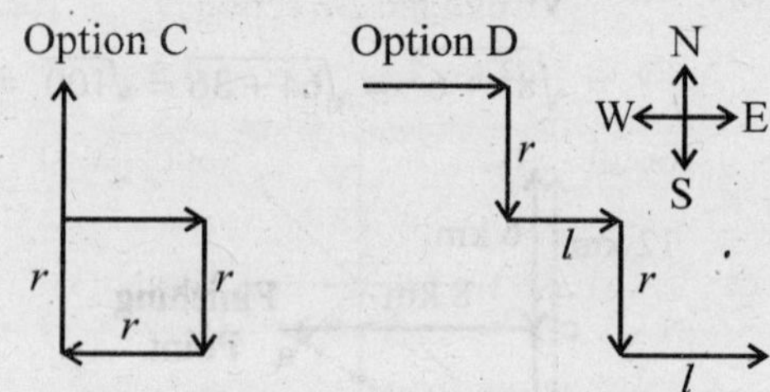

24. ***(c)*** **:**

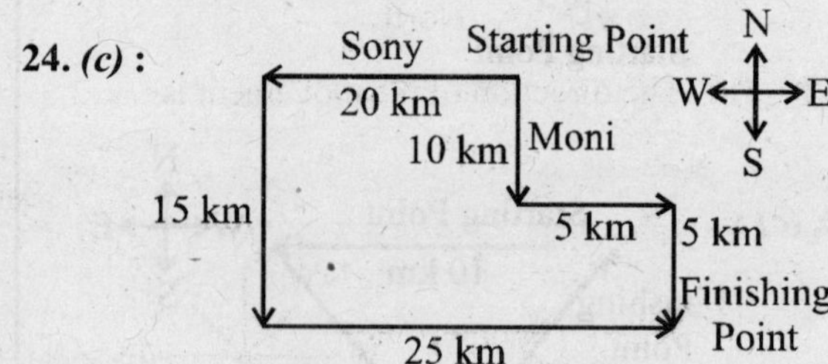

25. ***(b)*** **:**

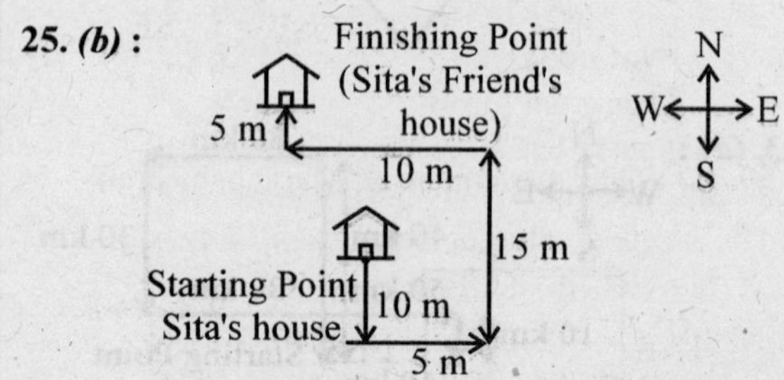

26. ***(b)*** **:** The directions to be followed will be :

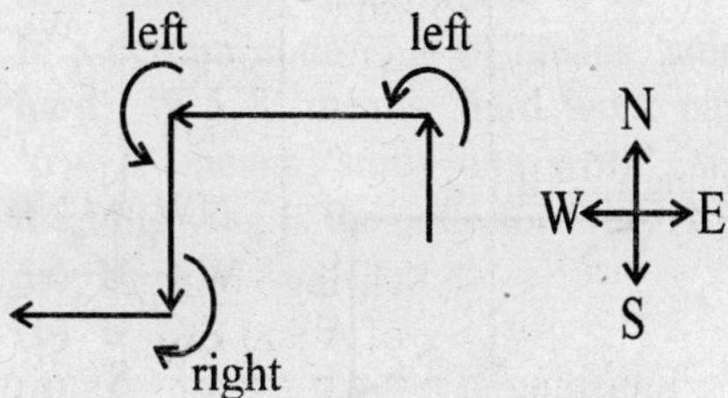

27. ***(a)*** **:** **Original Directions**

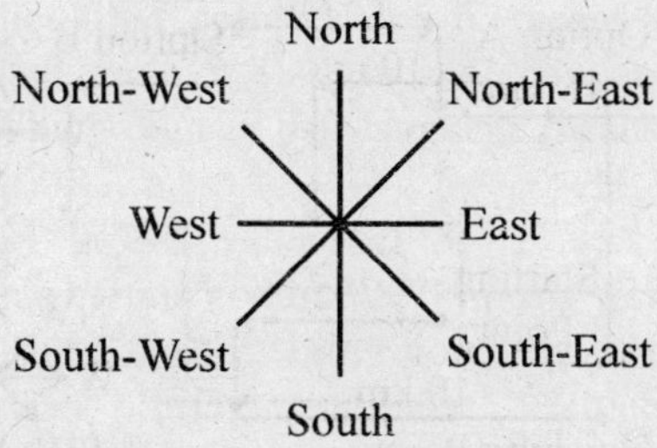

Changed Directions

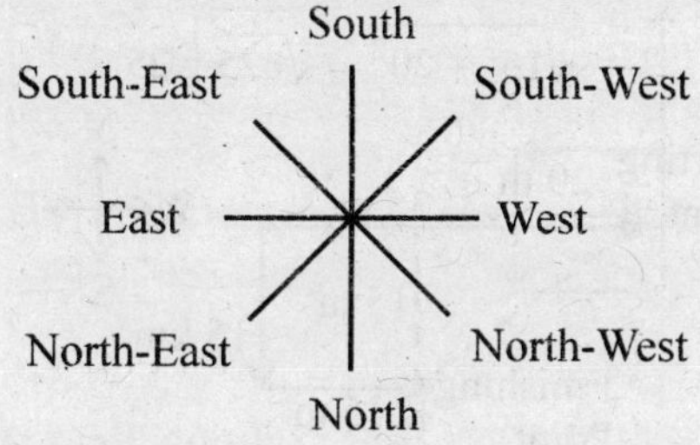

28. ***(a)*** **:** The direction of the movement is :

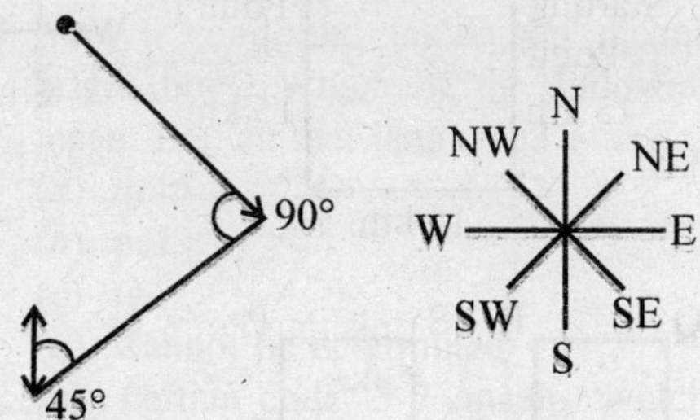

29. ***(b)*** **:** The movements of Maria baby are :

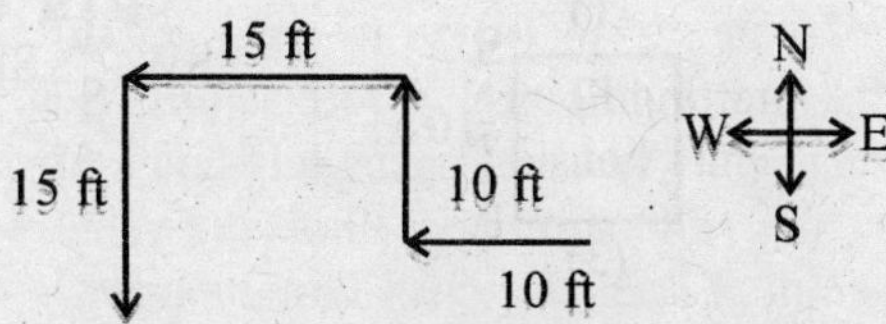

30. ***(b)*** **:** The track of both the friends is :

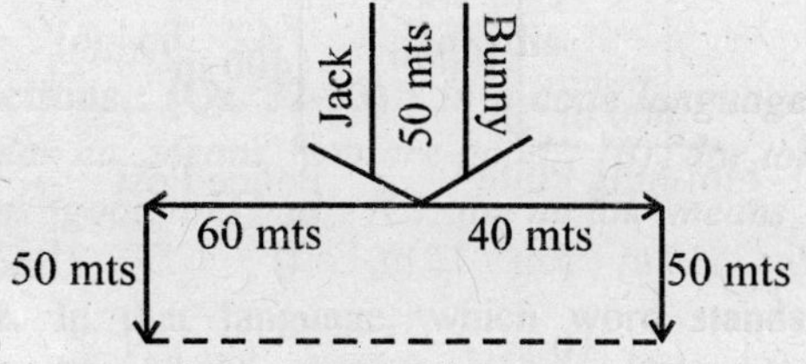

The two friends are 60 + 40 = 100 mts apart

31. ***(d)*** **:**

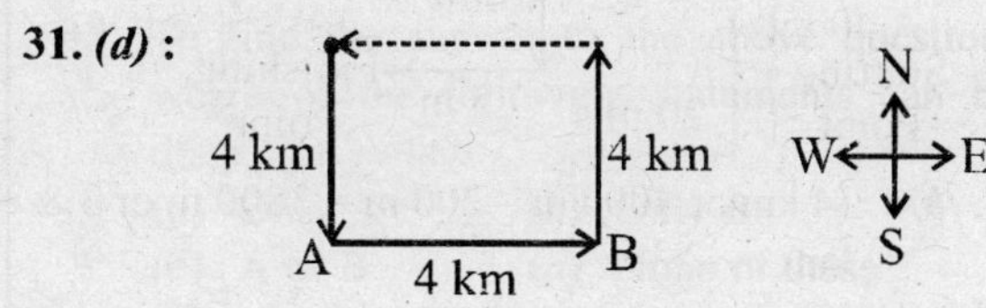

32. ***(c)*** **:**

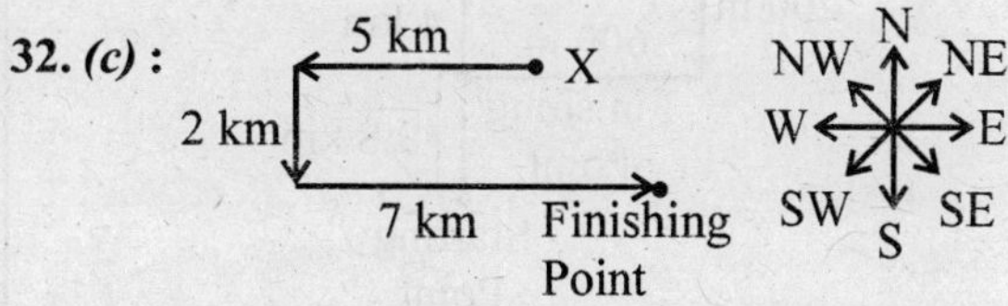

33. ***(b)*** **:**

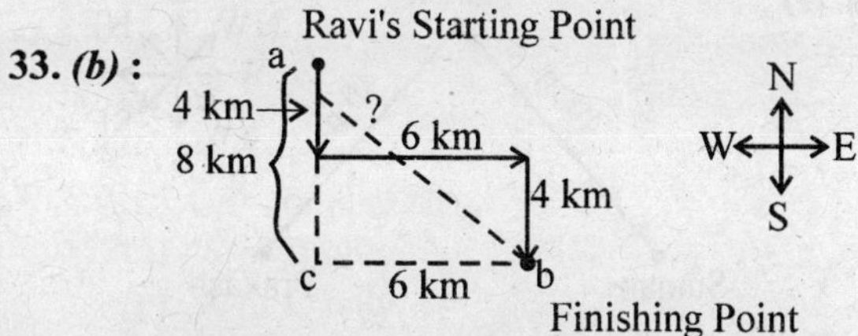

$$ab = \sqrt{bc^2 + ca^2}$$

$$? = \sqrt{6^2 + 8^2} = \sqrt{36 + 64} = \sqrt{100} = 10 \text{ km}$$

34. ***(b)*** **:** (10 km + 5 km = 15 km)

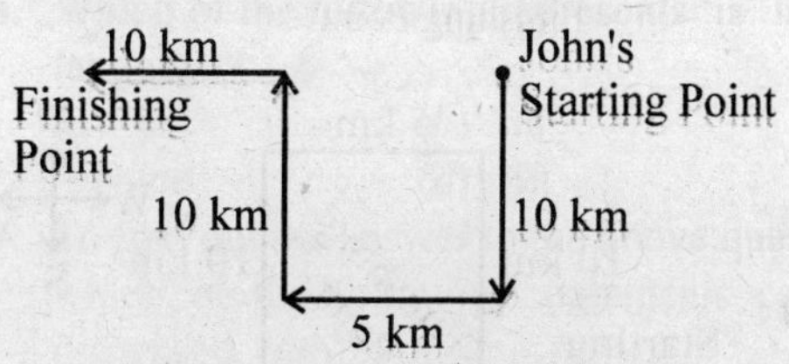

35. ***(b)*** **:** (600 m + 500 m = 1100 m or 1.1 km)

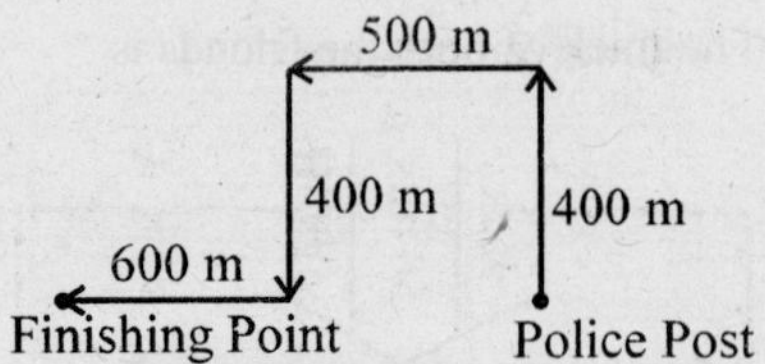

36. (d) : (10 m + 5 m = 15 m, East)

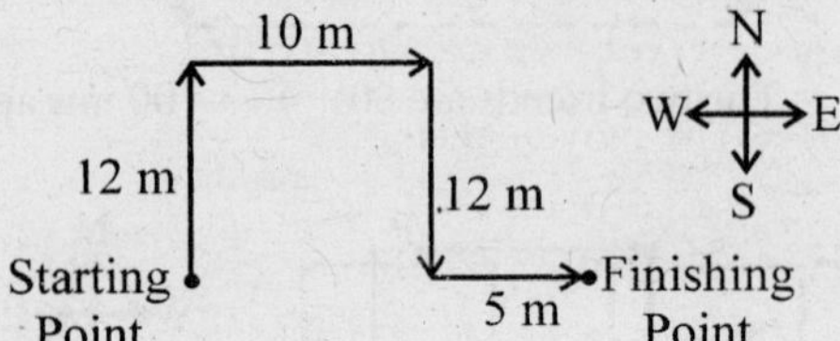

37. (b) : (4 km or 4000 m – 200 m = 3800 m or 3.8 km)

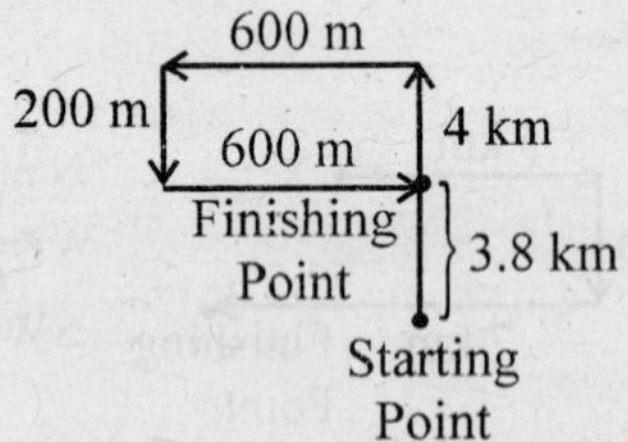

38. (c) :

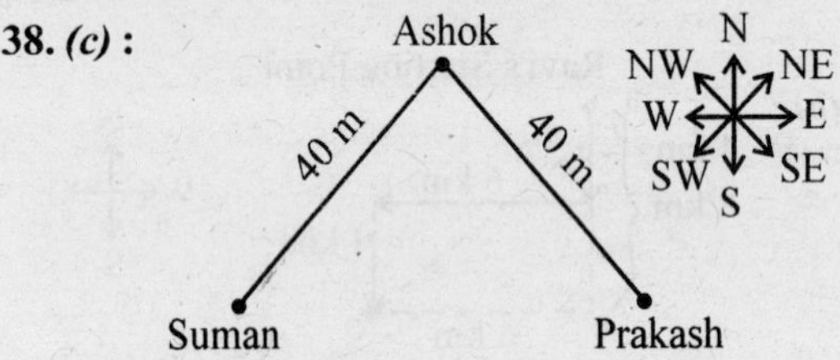

39. (d) :

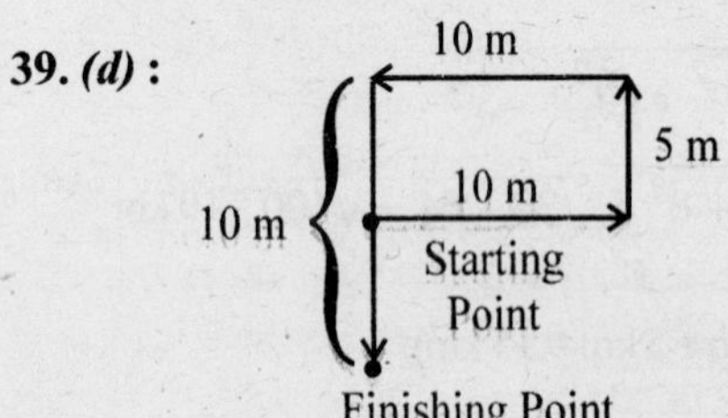

40. (a) :

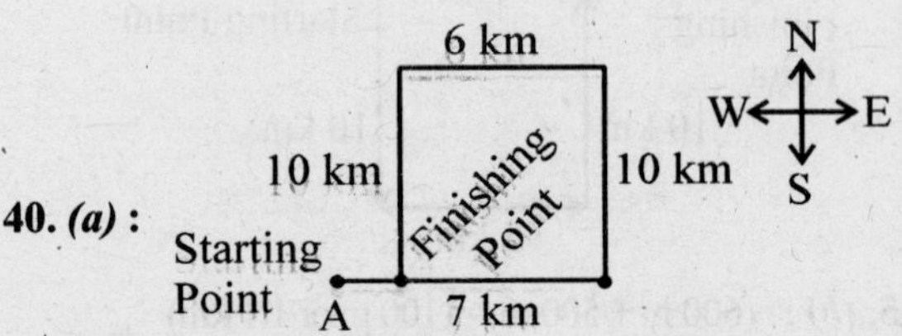

41. (c) : $ab = \sqrt{bc^2 + ca^2}$

$$? = \sqrt{30^2 + 40^2} = \sqrt{2500} = 50$$

Finishing Point 'Q' a — 40 m — c — 30 m — b Starting Point 'P' ?

42. (c) :

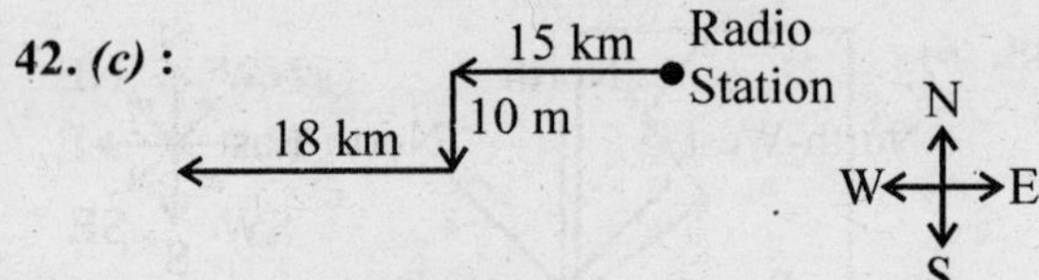

43. (a) :

Starting Point — 7 km — 3 km — 10 km — Finishing Point

44. (a) : $ab^2 = \sqrt{bc^2 + ca^2}$

$$? = \sqrt{15^2 + 20^2} = \sqrt{625} = 25$$

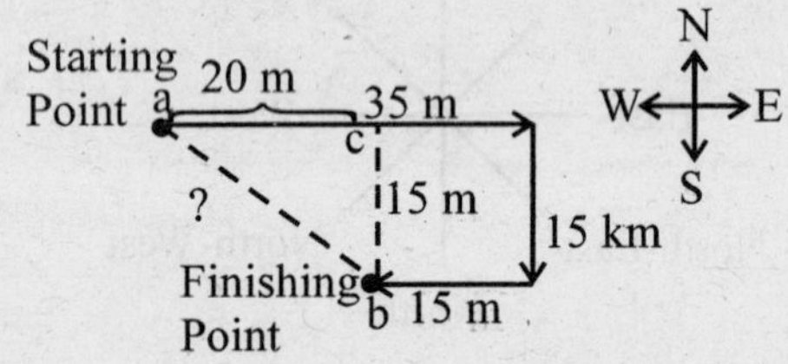

45. (b) :

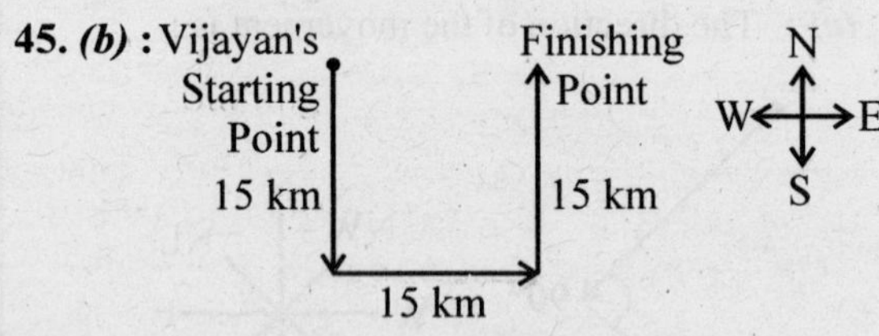

46. (b) :

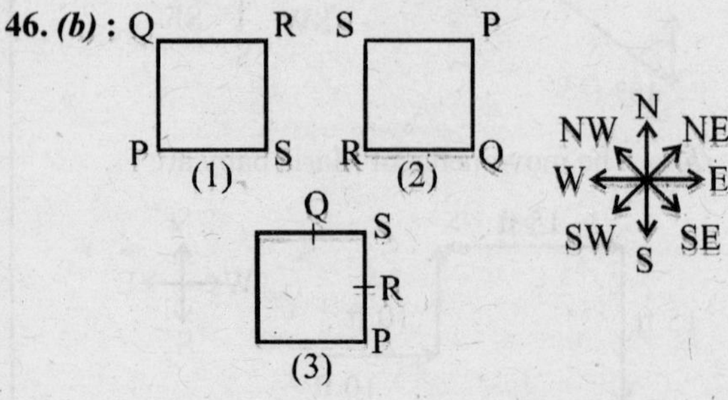

47. *(c)* **:** (10 km – 8 km = 2 km)

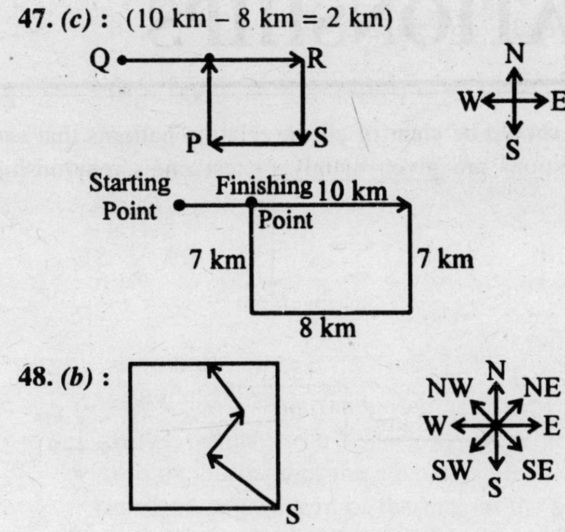

48. *(b)* **:**

49. *(c)* **:** The movements are :

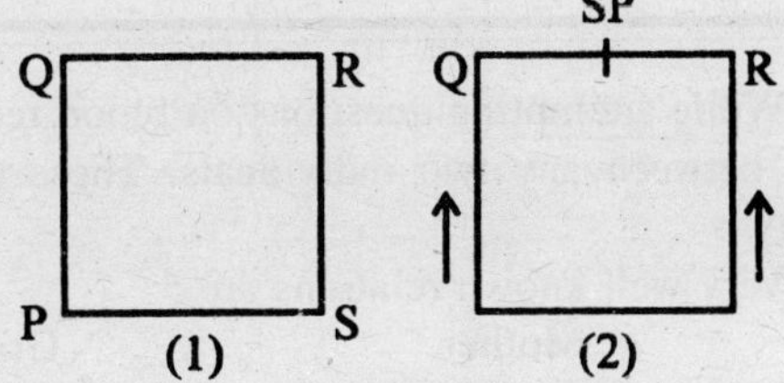

50. *(b)* **:** The movements are :

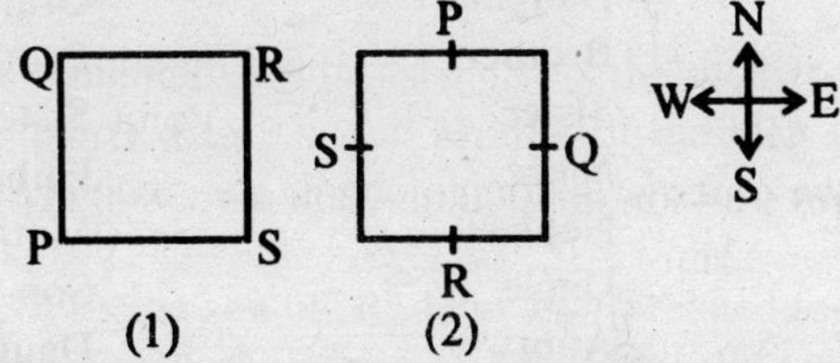

BLOOD RELATIONSHIPS

While attempting questions on blood relations, one should be clear of all the relation patterns that can exist between any two individuals. These type of questions are given mainly to test one's relationship ability.

Very well known relations are :

Mother	Grandmother
Father	Grandfather
Son	Grandson
Daughter	Granddaughter
Brother	Brother-in-law
Sister	Sister-in-law
Niece	Father-in-law
Nephew	Mother-in-law
Uncle	Son-in-law
Aunt	Daughter-in-law
Husband	Cousin
Wife	

The patterns of some relationships which help in solving questions in these tests are :

Father's *or* Mother's Father	—	Grandfather (Paternal *or* Maternal)
Father's *or* Mother's Mother	—	Grandmother (Paternal *or* Maternal
Father's *or* Mother's Son	—	Brother
Father's *or* Mother's Daughter	—	Sister
Father's Brother	—	Paternal Uncle
Father's Sister	—	Paternal Aunt
Mother's Brother	—	Maternal Uncle
Mother's Sister	—	Maternal Aunt
Uncle *or* Aunt's Son *or* Daughter	—	Cousin
Son's Wife	—	Daughter-in-law
Daughter's Husband	—	Son-in-law
Husband's *or* Wife's Brother	—	Brother-in-law
Husband's *or* Wife's Sister	—	Sister-in-law
Brother's Wife	—	Sister-in-law
Sister's Husband	—	Brother-in-law
Brother's Son	—	Nephew
Brother's Daughter	—	Niece

SOLVED EXAMPLES

1. Pointing to a photograph, a woman said, "This man's son's sister is my mother-in-law". How is the woman's husband related to the man in the photograph?

(*a*) Son (*b*) Grandson (*c*) Nephew (*d*) Son-in-law

(*e*) None of these

Ans. (*b*) : The relationship chart based on the given problem can be worked out as given below :

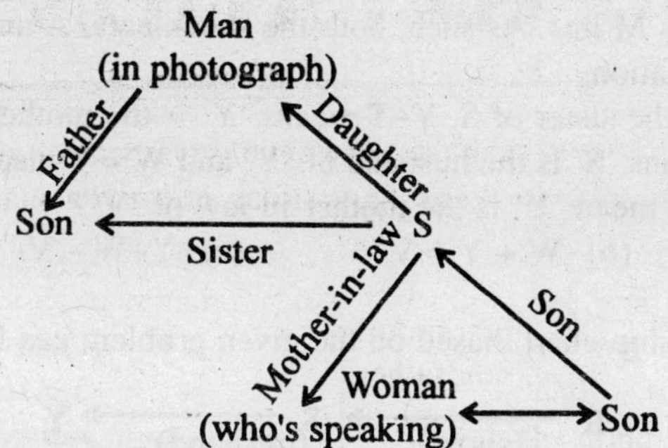

Man's son's sister (supposed as 'S'), will be man's daughter. If this sister 'S' is the mother-in-law of the woman, who's speaking, then the woman is married to S's son. Mother of the man who is also the husband of the woman is S and S is the daughter of man in photograph. Therefore woman's husband is grandson of the man in the photograph.

2. 'X' is the wife of 'Y' and 'Y' is the brother of 'Z'. 'Z' is the son of 'P'. How is 'P' related to 'X'?
(*a*) Sister (*b*) Aunt (*c*) Brother (*d*) Father-in-law
(*e*) None of these

Ans. (*d*) : The relationship chart, based on the given problem can be worked out as given below :

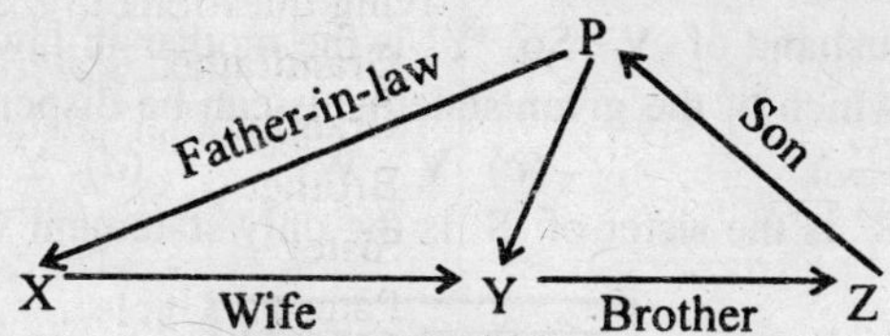

'Y' is the brother of 'Z' who is son of 'P'. So 'Z' is also the son of 'P'. When 'P' is the father of 'Y' and 'X' is the wife of 'Y', then 'P' is the father-in-law of 'X'.

3. How many daughters does M have? To answer the above question, which of the following informations given in the statements (A) and (B) is/are sufficient?
(A) B is sister of R.
(B) K, who is married to M, is mother of B and D.
(*a*) Both A and B together are needed
(*b*) Both A and B together are not sufficient
(*c*) Either A or B is sufficient
(*d*) Only B is sufficient
(*e*) Only A is sufficient

Ans. (*b*) : The relationship chart that is drawn on the basis of information in both the statements is given below :

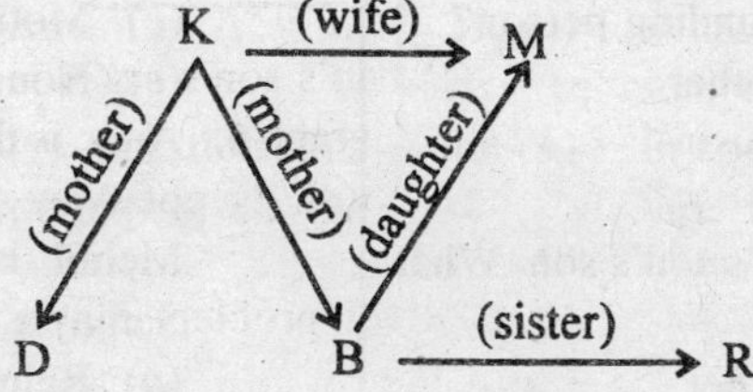

Only the Sex of B is depicted. Sex of D and R is not given. So, it is not possible to conclude the number of daughters M has. As such, both the statements, A and B together are not sufficient to get the right information.

4. *(a)* : If R × S means 'R' is the sister of S, Y÷T means 'Y' is the mother of 'T', V + W means 'V' is the wife of 'W', S – Y means 'S' is the husband of 'Y' and W = T means W is the brother of 'T', which of the following would mean 'Y' is the mother-in-law of 'V'?

(*a*) V – Y+W (*b*) W + Y = V (*c*) Y÷W – V (*d*) W = Y + V
(*e*) None of these

Ans. *(c)* : The relationship chart, based on the given problem can be worked out as given below :

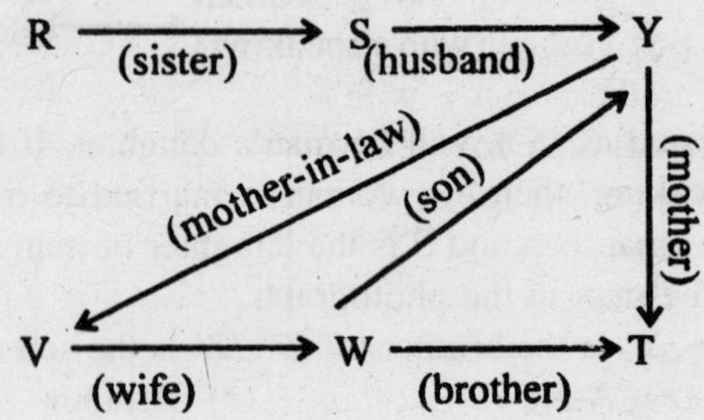

'Y' is the mother of 'T' and 'W' is the brother of 'T'. So, 'W' is the son of 'Y',
Y ÷ W means 'Y' is the mother of 'W' and
W – V means 'W' is the husband of 'V'. So, 'Y' is the mother-in-law of 'V'.

(*b*) : In the above question which of the given statements can be dispensed with to arrive at the answer?

(*a*) R × S (*b*) S – Y (*c*) V + W (*d*) Y ÷ T (*e*) All are required

Ans. *(a)* : R × S, *i.e.*, 'R' is the sister of 'S' is the only statement which can be dispensed with.

EXERCISE

Directions : *In each of the following questions keenly study the relationship mentioned between the persons, and then from the given options select the right relationship as the answer.*

1. 'A' is the father of 'B' and 'C'. 'B' is the son of 'A' but 'C' is not the son of 'A'. What is 'C's' relation with 'A'?
(*a*) Daughter (*b*) Son
(*c*) Niece (*d*) Nephew
(*e*) None of these

2. A lady said, "The person standing there is my grandfather's only son's daughter". How is the lady related to the standing person?
(*a*) Sister (*b*) Mother
(*c*) Aunt (*d*) Cousin
(*e*) None of these

3. Ravi is the brother of Amit's son's son. What is Amit's relation to Ravi?
(*a*) Cousin (*b*) Father
(*c*) Grandfather (*d*) Son
(*e*) None of these

4. Mayank said, "My mother is the sister of Rajat's brother." What is Rajat's relation with Mayank?
(*a*) Cousin (*b*) Maternal uncle
(*c*) Uncle (*d*) Brother-in-law
(*e*) None of these

5. Introducing Lily, Raghav said, "Her father is my mother's only son". How is Lily related to Raghav?
(*a*) Aunt (*b*) Daughter
(*c*) Mother (*d*) Sister
(*e*) None of these

6. Ajay is the brother of Vijay. Mili is the Sister of Ajay. Sanjay is the brother of Rahul and Mehul is the daughter of Vijay. Who is Sanjay's Uncle?
(*a*) Rahul (*b*) Ajay

(*c*) Mehul (*d*) Data inadequate
(*e*) None of these

7. Adity is Bhavi's brother, Bharat is Jayant's father. Ella is Bhavi's mother. Aditya and Jayant are brothers. What is Ella's relationship with Bharat?
(*a*) Sister (*b*) Mother
(*c*) Daughter (*d*) Wife
(*e*) None of these

8. A man introduced the boy coming with him as "He is son of the father of my wife's daughter". What relation did the boy bear to the man?
(*a*) Son-in-law (*b*) Son
(*c*) Brother (*d*) Father
(*e*) None of these

9. A and B are two brothers. C is sister of B. D is sister of E. E is son of A. Who is D's uncle?
(*a*) D (*b*) E
(*c*) B (*d*) C
(*e*) None of these

10. Varun said pointing towards Arun, "He is my sister's only brother's son". How is Arun related to Varun?
(*a*) Son (*b*) Brother
(*c*) Nephew (*d*) Data insufficient
(*e*) None of these

11. Pointing to a man, a lady said, "His brother's father is my grandfather's only son." How is the lady related to the man?
(*a*) Mother (*b*) Sister
(*c*) Daughter (*d*) Aunt
(*e*) None of these

12. Vidya is the wife of Gopi and Gopi is the brother of Akhil. Akhil is the uncle of Vijay. What is Vijay's relation with Vidya?
(*a*) Son (*b*) Nephew
(*c*) Brother-in-law (*d*) Brother
(*e*) None of these

13. If Amit's father is Billoo's father's only son and Billoo has neither a brother nor a daughter, what is the relationship between Amit and Billoo?
(*a*) Uncle - Nephew
(*b*) Father- Daughter
(*c*) Father - Son
(*d*) Cousins (*e*) None of these

14. A is the sister of B. B is the son of C, and E is the daughter of D, and sister of A. What is D to C?
(*a*) Brother (*b*) Husband
(*c*) Wife (*d*) Data is inadequate
(*e*) None of these

15. A Man said to a lady, "Fagu's mother is the only daughter of your father". How is the lady related to Fagu?
(*a*) Daughter (*b*) Sister
(*c*) Wife (*d*) Mother
(*e*) None of these

16. Pointing to a man, a woman said, "He is the only son of my mother's mother". How is the woman related to the man?
(*a*) Aunt (*b*) Daughter
(*c*) Niece (*d*) Sister
(*e*) None of these

17. If B's mother was A's mother's daughter, how was A related to B?
(*a*) Uncle (*b*) Aunt
(*c*) Sister (*d*) Data is insufficient
(*e*) None of these

18. Pointing to a woman in the photograph a man said, "She is the daughter of my grandmother's only son. How is the woman related to the man?
(*a*) Mother (*b*) Daughter
(*c*) Sister-in-law (*d*) Sister
(*e*) None of these

19. A man and a woman are sitting in a room. Man's mother-in-law and woman's mother-in-law are mother and daughter respectively. Man is the .... of the woman.
(*a*) Father (*b*) Father-in-law
(*c*) Uncle (*d*) Grandfather-in-law
(*e*) None of these

20. Pointing to Suman, Amit said, "He is my sister's only brother's son". How is Suman related to Amit?
(*a*) Grandson
(*b*) Son
(*c*) Nephew
(*d*) Cannot be determined
(*e*) None of these

21. Pointing to someone, I said, "She is my

father's sister and she is the only daughter". How many children did my paternal grand-parents have in all?
(*a*) Two sons
(*b*) One daughter
(*c*) One son and one daughter
(*d*) Cannot be determined
(*e*) None of these

22. Pointing to a photograph, a woman said, "She is the only daughter of my mother's father." How is the woman related to the person in the photograph?
(*a*) Mother
(*b*) Grandmother
(*c*) Daughter
(*d*) Cannot be determined
(*e*) None of these

23. Sandip's mother is the only daughter of Rekha's father. How is Rekha's husband related to Sandip?
(*a*) Uncle (*b*) Brother
(*c*) Grandfather (*d*) Data inadequate
(*e*) Father

24. If P is the husband of Q and R is the mother of S and Q, what is R to P?
(*a*) Mother (*b*) Sister
(*c*) Aunt (*d*) Mother-in-law
(*e*) Cannot be determined

25. Ram is the brother of Shyam and Mahesh is the father of Ram. Jagat is the brother of Priya and Priya is daughter of Shyam. Who is the uncle of Jagat ?
(*a*) Shyam (*b*) Mahesh
(*c*) Ram (*d*) Data insufficient
(*e*) None of these

26. Pointing to a photograph, a woman says, "This man's son's sister is my mother-in-law". How is the woman's husband related to the man in the photograph ?
(*a*) Son-in-law (*b*) Son
(*c*) Grandson (*d*) Nephew
(*e*) None of these

27. Pointing towards a person in a photograph, Aruna said, "He is the only son of the father of my sister's brother". How is that person related to Aruna?
(*a*) Mother (*b*) Maternal Uncle
(*c*) Father (*d*) Cousin
(*e*) None of these

28. If Vijay says "Viju's mother is the only daughter of my mother", how is Vijay related to Viju ?
(*a*) Brother
(*b*) Grandfather
(*c*) Father
(*d*) Cannot be determined
(*e*) None of these

29. Pointing to a photograph a lady tells Mohan, "I am the only daughter of this lady and her son is your maternal uncle." How is the speaker related to Mohan's father ?
(*a*) Wife
(*b*) Sister-in-law
(*c*) Either of the two
(*d*) Neither of the two
(*e*) Cannot be determined

30. Q's mother is sister of P and daughter of M. S is daughter of P and sister of T. How is M related to T ?
(*a*) Father
(*b*) Grandfather
(*c*) Grandmother
(*d*) Grandfather or Grandmother
(*e*) None of these

31. A is the mother of B'. B's father C has three children. Based on this information, state which of the following statements is definitely true ?
(*a*) C has three daughters
(*b*) C has three sons
(*c*) B is a male child
(*d*) B has two sisters
(*e*) None of these

32. Daya has a brother Anil. Daya is a son of Chandra. Bimal is Chandra's father. In terms of relationship, what is Anil of Bimal ?
(*a*) Grandfather (*b*) Brother
(*c*) Grandson (*d*) Son
(*e*) Uncle

33. 'A' is the brother of 'B', 'C' is the sister of 'B'. How is 'B' related to 'A'?
(*a*) Cousin
(*b*) Sister
(*c*) Brother

(*d*) Cannot be determined
(*e*) None of these

34. Pointing to Snehal, Mahesh said, "Her mother's only daughter is my daughter". How is Mahesh related to Snehal?
(*a*) Brother (*b*) Uncle
(*c*) Son (*d*) Father
(*e*) None of these

35. Is 'C' mother of 'D'? To find out the answer which of the following informations given in the statements 'A' and 'B' is/are sufficient?
(A) B has two children of which D is one.
(B) D's sister is daughter of C.
(*a*) Both A and B together are needed
(*b*) Both A and B together are not sufficient
(*c*) Only A is sufficient
(*d*) Only B is sufficient
(*e*) Either A or B is sufficient

36. A is B's brother. A is C's brother. To find out how B is related to C, which of the following is the minimum further information necessary, is any?
I. C's sex II. B's sex
(*a*) Only I is necessary
(*b*) Only II is necessary
(*c*) Either I or II is necessary
(*d*) Both I and II are needed
(*e*) Neither I nor II is necessary

37. Is D brother of F? To find out the answer which of the following informations given in the statements A and B is/are sufficient?
(A) B has two sons of which F is one.
(B) D's mother is married to B.
(a) Both A and B together are needed
(*b*) Both A and B together are not sufficient
(*c*) Only A is sufficient
(*d*) Only B is sufficient
(*e*) Either A or B is sufficient

38. Neera is daughter of Mahender. Mala, Achla's sister has a son Mohan and daughter Sushila. Kamla is maternal aunt of Sushila and mother of Krishna. Mohan is cousin of Krishna. Krishna is brother of Neera. How is Achla related to Mahender?
(*a*) Cousin (*b*) Sister-in-law
(*c*) Niece (*d*) Daughter
(*e*) Sister

39. B is maternal uncle of A. C is maternal grandfather of B. D is grandson of C. How is D related to A?
(*a*) Maternal uncle
(*b*) Cousin brother
(*c*) Nephew
(*d*) Maternal grandfather
(*e*) None of these

40. Introducing a man, a woman said, "His wife is the only daughter of my father". How is the man related to the woman?
(*a*) Husband (*b*) Father
(*c*) Father-in-law (*d*) Brother
(*e*) None of these

41. B's mother is the only daughter of A's mother. How is A related to B?
(*a*) Niece (*b*) Brother
(*c*) Father (*d*) Uncle
(*e*) Cannot be determined

42. Introducing a man to her husband, a woman said, "His brother's father is the only son of my grandfather." How is the woman related to the man?
(*a*) Aunt (*b*) Mother
(*c*) Daughter (*d*) Mother-in-law
(*e*) Sister

43. A said to B that B's mother was the mother-in-law of A's mother. How is A's mother related to B's mother?
(*a*) Mother (*b*) Daughter-in-law
(*c*) Daughter (*d*) Cousin
(*e*) Aunt

44. If A is the mother of B and C, and D is the husband of C, then what is A to D?
(*a*) Aunt (*b*) Mother-in-law
(*c*) Sister-in-law (*d*) Sister
(*e*) Daughter-in-law

45. Introducing a man, a woman said, "His mother is the only daughter of my father." How is the man related to the woman?
(*a*) Father (*b*) Uncle
(*c*) Husband (*d*) Brother
(*e*) Son

46. If Maya is the only daughter of Richa's grandmother's brother, how is Maya's daughter related to Richa?
(*a*) Niece (*b*) Cousin
(*c*) Aunt (*d*) Mother

(*e*) None of these

47. Pointing to a woman, a man said, "Her husband's mother is the wife of my father's only son". How is the man related to the woman?

(*a*) Son (*b*) Brother-in-law
(*c*) Uncle (*d*) Father-in-law
(*e*) Grandfather

48. Bela is the mother of Chinu and Miki. If Kavind is the husband of Miki, what is Bela to Kavind?

(*a*) Daughter (*b*) Sister
(*c*) Mother (*d*) Mother-in-law
(*e*) None of these

49. Pointing to a woman, a man says, "Her mother is the only daughter of my mother-in-law". How is the woman related to the man?

(*a*) Sister (*b*) Daughter
(*c*) Aunt (*d*) Data is insufficient
(*e*) None of these

50. Introducing a lady, a man said that her mother's husband's sister is his mother. What is the man's relationship with the lady?

(*a*) Cousin (*b*) Nephew
(*c*) Father (*d*) Data insufficient
(*e*) None of these

51. A lady said to a man, "The daughter of your only sister is the sister of my husband." What is the man's sister to the lady?

(*a*) Mother (*b*) Sister-in-law
(*c*) Sister (*d*) Mother-in-law
(*e*) None of these

52. Bilie's mother is Chaya's mother's daughter. How is Bilie related to Chaya?

(*a*) Sister
(*b*) Niece
(*c*) Maternal Aunt
(*d*) Mother
(*e*) None of these

53. 'D' is the son of 'J' who is son of 'F'. 'P' is the daughter of 'R'. If 'N' is the sister of P and daughter of 'J', what is 'J's' relationship with 'R'?

(*a*) Brother (*b*) Father
(*c*) Husband (*d*) Uncle
(*e*) None of these

54. A woman said pointing to a photograph, "The man in picture is the brother of my mother-in-law's son". What relationship does the woman have with the man in the picture?

(*a*) Husband (*b*) Brother-in-law
(*c*) Son (*d*) Data is insufficient
(*e*) None of these

Directions (Qs. 55 to 57) : *Read the following statements and answer the questions given below :*

A is the father of C. But C is not his son.
E is the daughter of C. F is the spouse of A.
B is the brother of C. D is the son of B.
G is the spouse of B. H is the father of G.

55. Who is the son-in-law of H?

(*a*) C (*b*) A
(*c*) D (*d*) B
(*e*) None of these

56. Who is the grand-daughter of A ?

(*a*) H (*b*) D
(*c*) B (*d*) E
(*e*) None of these

57. Who is the common grandchild of both F and H?

(*a*) D (*b*) E
(*c*) C (*d*) B
(*e*) None of these

Directions (Qs. 58-59) : *Read the following statements and answer the questions :*

S and R are brothers. T is the daughter of S. U is the spouse of R and mother of Q. P is the daughter of V, who is the spouse of T.

58. Who is the grandfather of P?

(*a*) U (*b*) S
(*c*) R (*d*) V
(*e*) None of these

59. Who is the cousin of Q ?

(*a*) T (*b*) V
(*c*) R (*d*) P
(*e*) None of these

Directions (Qs. 60 to 64) : *Read the statements carefully and answer the following questions :*

P is the father of R, but R is not his son.
T is the daughter of R. U is the spouse of P.
Q is the brother of R. S is the son of Q.

V is the spouse of Q. W is the father of V.

60. Who is the Grandmother of S?
(*a*) W (*b*) P
(*c*) R (*d*) U
(*e*) None of these

61. Who is the son of U ?
(*a*) Q (*b*) R
(*c*) T (*d*) S
(*e*) Cannot be determined

62. Who is the father-in-law of Q?
(*a*) R (*b*) P
(*c*) T (*d*) W
(*e*) None of these

63. Who is the sister-in-law of R?
(*a*) S (*b*) V
(*c*) U (*d*) T
(*e*) Cannot be determined

64. Who is the cousin of T?
(*a*) R (*b*) Q
(*c*) W (*d*) S
(*e*) None of these

Directions (Qs. 65 to 69) : *Read the following statements and answer the questions given below :*

Radha and Minnilal have two children Simmi and Divya, Divya is married to Anuj who is the son of Madhu and Jabbar. Resham is daughter of Anuj. Kiran who is Anuj's sister is married to Subodh and has two sons Tarun and Aman. Tarun is grandson of Madhu and Jabbar.

65. What is the relationship between Aman and Resham?
(*a*) Uncle - Niece
(*b*) Father - Daughter
(*c*) Husband - Wife
(*d*) Cousins
(*e*) None of these

66. How is Subodh related to Jabbar?
(*a*) Son-in-law (*b*) Son
(*c*) Brother (*d*) Father-in-law
(*e*) None of these

67. How is Resham related to Kiran?
(*a*) Niece (*b*) Daughter
(*c*) Mother (*d*) Aunt
(*e*) None of these

68. How is Kiran related to Divya?
(*a*) Aunt (*b*) Grandmother
(*c*) Sister-in-law (*d*) Sister
(*e*) None of these

69. Which of the following statements is definitely true?
(*a*) Aman is the son of Simmi
(*b*) Madhu is the mother-in-law of Subodh
(*c*) Resham is the cousin of Kiran
(*d*) All the three are true
(*e*) None of these

Directions (Qs. 70 to 75) : *Read the following statements and answer the questions given below :*

Raju has two sons 'X' and 'Y' and a daughter 'Z'. Biju has two sons 'A' and 'B' and daughter 'C'. 'A' and 'Z' are married and have two sons 'J' and 'K'. Laloo has a son 'P' and a daughter 'Q'. 'Q' is married to 'Y' and they have two daughters 'F' and 'G' and a son 'H'.

70. How is Raju related to 'Q'?
(*a*) Uncle (*b*) Father-in-law
(*c*) Brother (*d*) Son
(*e*) None of these

71. How is 'Z' related to Biju?
(*a*) Daughter (*b*) Sister
(*c*) Sister-in-law (*d*) Daughter-in-law
(*e*) None of these

72. How is 'Y' related to 'P'?
(*a*) Son
(*b*) Uncle
(*c*) Brother-in-law
(*d*) Brother
(*e*) None of these

73. How is 'G' related to Laloo?
(*a*) Granddaughter
(*b*) Aunt
(*c*) Daughter
(*d*) Mother
(*e*) None of these

74. How is 'J' related to 'C'?
(*a*) Nephew (*b*) Brother
(*c*) Uncle (*d*) Grandfather
(*e*) None of these

75. How is 'F' related to 'K'?
(*a*) Father (*b*) Cousin
(*c*) Husband (*d*) Uncle
(*e*) None of these

76. If M + N means 'M' is the brother of 'N',

M – N means 'M' is the sister of 'N',
M × N means 'M' is the mother of 'N' and
M ÷ N means 'M' is the father of 'N'. Which of the following would mean 'E' is the paternal Aunt of 'F'?

(*a*) E – G ÷ F (*b*) E + G × F
(*c*) E × F – G (*d*) F × G + E
(*e*) None of these

77. If S – T means 'S' is the wife of 'T', S + T means 'S' is the daughter of 'T' and S ÷ T means 'S' is the son of 'T'. What will M + J ÷ K mean?
(*a*) 'K' is the father of 'M'
(*b*) 'M' is the grand-daughter of K
(*c*) 'J' is wife of 'K'
(*d*) 'K' and 'M' are brothers
(*e*) None of these

78. If A × B means 'A' is the brother of 'B', and A + B means 'A' is the father of 'B', which of the following means 'M' is the nephew of N'?
(*a*) N × K + M (*b*) N + M × K
(*c*) M × K + N (*d*) Data inadequate
(*e*) None of these

79. A × B means 'A' is the mother of 'B',
A ÷ B means 'A' is the son of 'B'
A – B means 'A' is the sister of 'B'
Which of the following would mean 'Q' is the maternal uncle of 'P'?
(*a*) P ÷ R – Q (*b*) Q ÷ R – P
(*c*) Q × R + P (*d*) P × R – Q
(*e*) None of these

80. If A + B means 'A' is the brother of 'B', A × B means 'A' is the mother of 'B', A ÷ B means 'A' is the sister of 'B', which of the following would mean 'P' is the uncle of 'S'?
(*a*) P ÷ S × R (*b*) Q ÷ S × P
(*c*) P + R × S (*d*) Data inadequate
(*e*) None of these

81. If A ÷ B means 'A' is the father of 'B', A × B means 'A' is the mother of 'B', A + B means 'A' is the sister of 'B' and A – B means 'A' is the grandfather of 'B', which of the following would mean 'M' is the grandson of 'N'?
(*a*) M – O + N (*b*) N × O ÷ M
(*c*) M + N × O (*d*) Data inadequate
(*e*) None of these

Directions (Qs. 82-83) : *Read the following information to answer the given questions :*

(A) 'P + Q' means 'P is the brother of Q'
(B) 'P × Q' means 'P is the father of Q'
(C) 'P ÷ Q' means 'P is the mother of Q'

82. Which of the following would mean 'R' is the son of 'M'?
(*a*) M + R × S (*b*) M × S ÷ R
(*c*) M ÷ R × S (*d*) M × S × R
(*e*) None of these

83. To arrive at the answer to the above question, which of the statements can be dispensed with?
(*a*) Only A (*b*) B or C
(*c*) A or B (*d*) Only B
(*e*) None

Directions (Qs. 84-85) : *Read the following information and answer the questions given below :*

(A) P + Q means 'P' is the mother of 'Q'.
(B) P ÷ Q means 'P' is the father of 'Q'.
(C) P – Q means 'P' is the sister of 'Q'.

84. Which of the following represents 'M' is the daughter of 'R'?
(*a*) R + M + N (*b*) R + N ÷ M
(*c*) R – M ÷ N (*d*) Data inadequate
(*e*) None of these

85. To find the answer to the above question, which of the statements can be dispensed with?
(*a*) Only A (*b*) B or C
(*c*) A or B (*d*) Only C
(*e*) None of these

Directions (Qs. 86-87) : *Read the following information to answer the question given below :*

(A) 'P + Q' means 'P' is the brother of 'Q'.
(B) 'P × Q' means 'P' is the father of 'Q'.
(C) 'P – Q' means 'P' is the sister of 'Q'.

86. Which of the following represents 'S' is the niece of 'T'?
(*a*) T × S + M – K (*b*) T + M × S – K
(*c*) K – S × M + T (*d*) T × M + S – K
(*e*) None of these

87. To find out the answer to the above question which of the statements can be dispensed with?
(*a*) A only (*b*) B only

(*c*) C only (*d*) B or C only

(*e*) All are necessary

Directions (Qs. 88 to 90) : *Read the following information to answer questions given below :*

(A) A × B means 'A' is the brother of 'B'

(B) A + B means 'A' is the mother of 'B'

(C) A ÷ B means 'A' is the son of 'B'

(D) A – B means 'A' is the husband of 'B'

88. Which of the following would mean 'M' is the father of 'N'?

(*a*) M ÷ N + O (*b*) M × O – N

(*c*) M + O ÷ N (*d*) M – O + N

(*e*) None of these

89. Which of the following is definitely true if 'N' is the son of 'M'?

(*a*) M + N × O (*b*) M + N – O

(*c*) N ÷ M (*d*) All the three are true

(*e*) None of the three are true

90. Which of the following would mean 'M' is the Aunt of 'N'?

(*a*) M + N – O (*b*) M × O ÷ N

(*c*) N + O × M (*d*) N ÷ M + O

(*e*) None of these

EXPLANATORY ANSWERS

1. (*a*) :

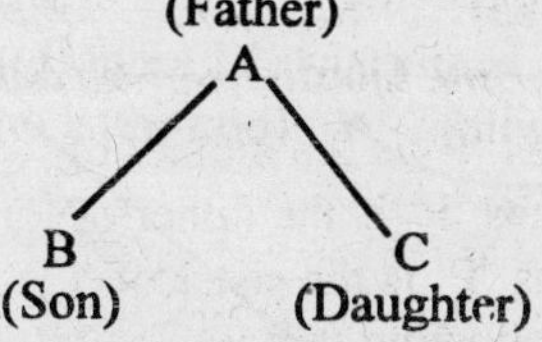

'C' is not the son of 'A', but 'A' is the father of 'C'. So, 'C' is the daughter of 'A'.

2. (*a*) :

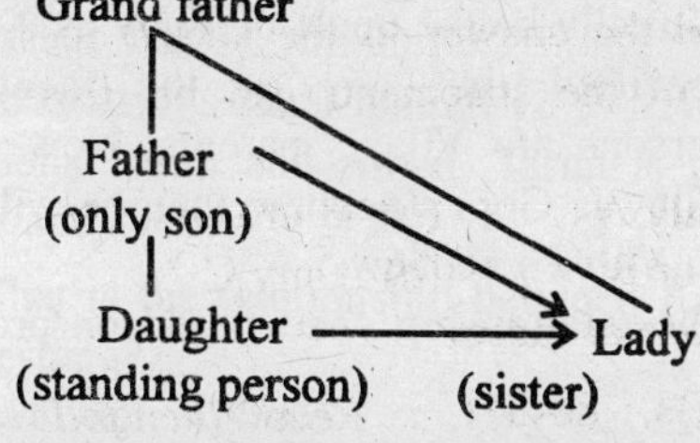

Lady's grandfather's son is lady's father and father's daughter will only be lady's sister.

3. (*c*) :

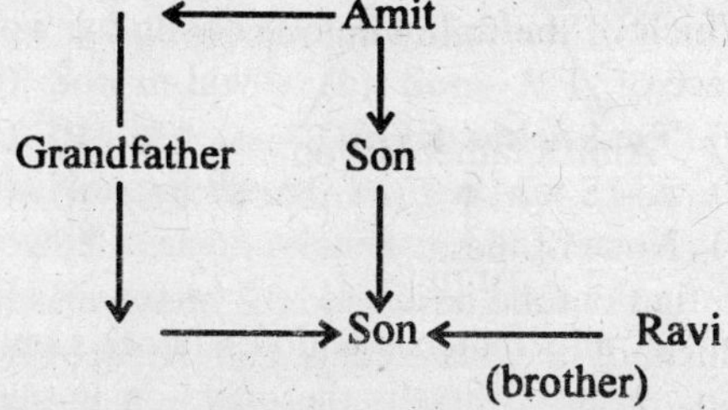

Amit's son's son is Amit's grandson. Ravi is the brother of Amit's son's son. So, Amit is also the grandfather of Ravi.

4. (*b*) : Mother —(sister)→ Rajat's brother ←(brother)— Rajat

Mayank (child of Mother); Rajat —Maternal Uncle→ Mayank

Mayank's mother is the sister of Rajat's brother. So Rajat is also the brother of Mayank's mother. Relation of the brother with his sister's child is maternal. So Rajat is Mayank's maternal uncle.

5. (*b*) : The relation is : Mother

↑ (Son)

Raghav

↓ (Father)

Lily (Daughter)

'My mother's only son' means Raghav himself. 'Her father' means Lily's father; *i.e.* Raghav and so, Lily is Raghav's daughter.

6. (*d*) : 1. Mili —(sister)→ Ajay —(brother)→ Vijay ↓ Mehul (daughter)

2. Sanjay —(brother)→ Rahul

There are two sets of relationship. Information given is incomplete and no relation can be established between the two sets.

7. (*d*) : The relationship chart based on problem is :

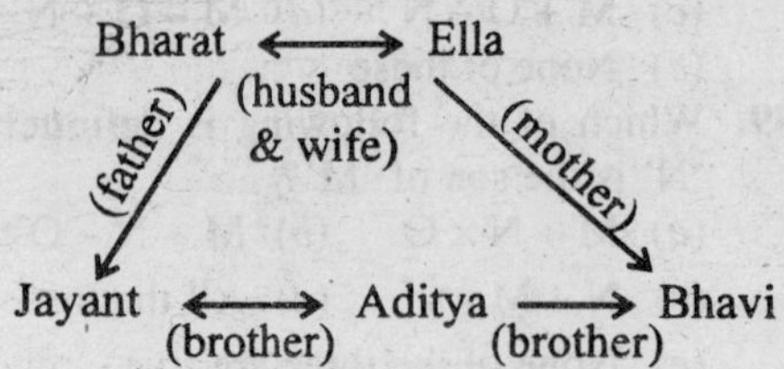

Jayant and Aditya are brothers. If Aditya is Bhavi's brother, then Jayant is also Bhavi's brother. If Bharat is Jayant's father, then he is also the father of Aditya and Bhavi. If Ella is Bhavi's mother, then she is also the mother of Aditya and Jayant. This means Bharat and Ella are husband and wife and the parents of three.

8. (*b*) : The relationship chart based on problem is :

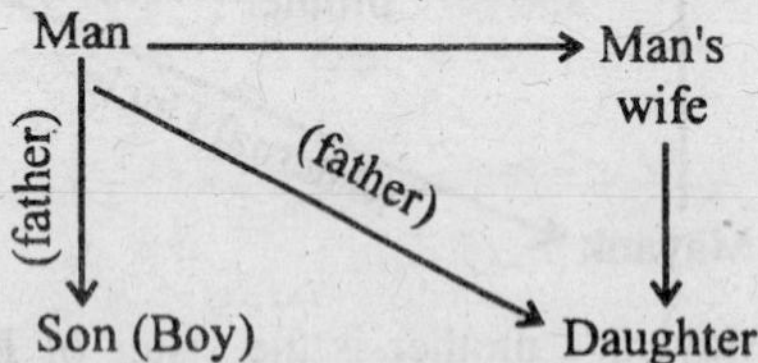

'Father of the man's wife's daughter' is the man himself and the boy in question is the man's son.

9. (*c*) : The relationship chart based on the problem is :

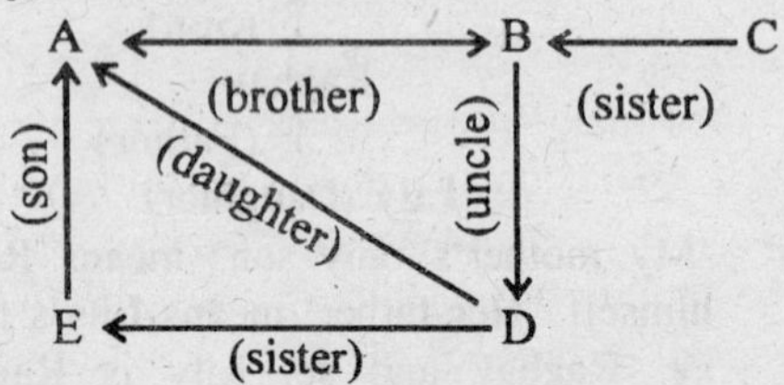

When D is sister of E, who is son of A then D is daughter of A. Brother of A is B and so, B is D's uncle.

10. (*a*) :

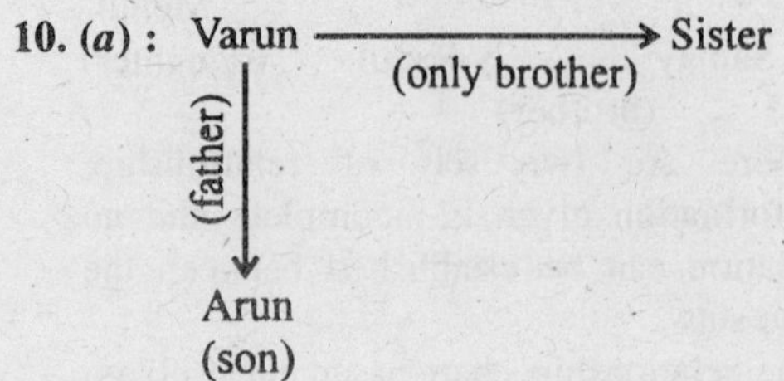

Varun's sister's only brother is Varun himself and Arun is his son.

11. (*b*) :

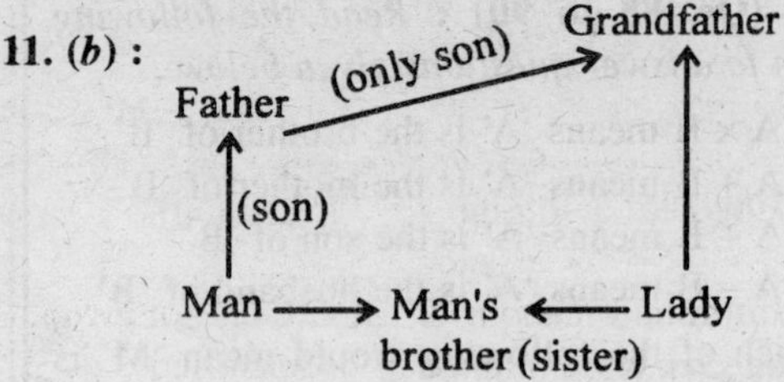

Man's brother's father is also the lady's father as he is the only son of lady's grandfather. So, the lady is man's sister.

12. (*b*) : The relationship chart based on problem is :

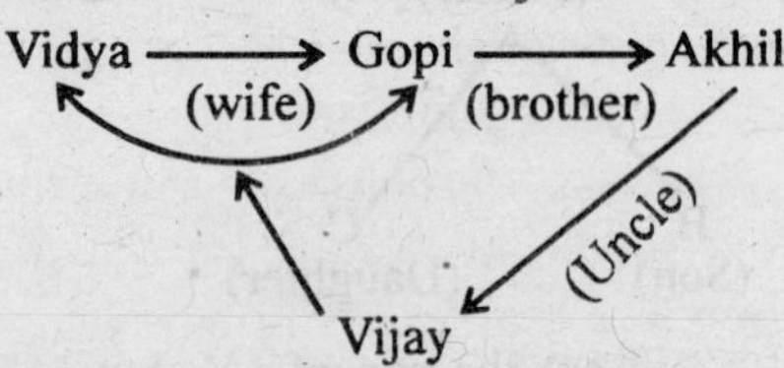

Vidya is wife of Gopi who is brother of Akhil. So, Vidya is sister-in-law of Akhil. If Akhil is uncle of Vijay then Gopi will naturally be the uncle of Vijay as it is not specified that any of the mentioned persons are Vijay's parents. Now, when Vijay is Gopi's nephew then he will also be Vidya's nephew.

13. (*c*) : The relationship chart based on problem is :

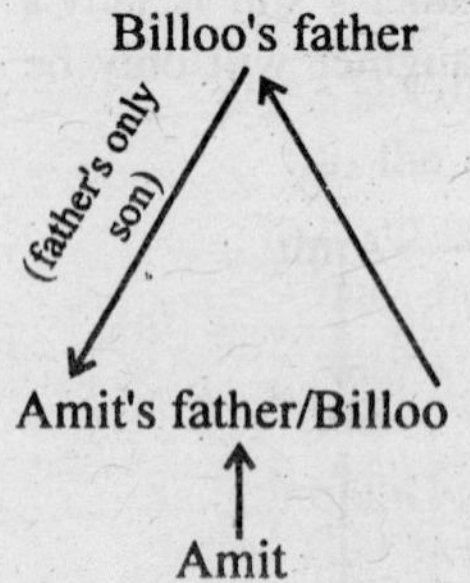

Amit's father is Billoo's father's only son means Billoo is the only son in question also, he is the father of Amit. It must be noted that Billoo has no brother which means he is single and also, when he has no daughter, Amit is his only son.

14. (*d*) :

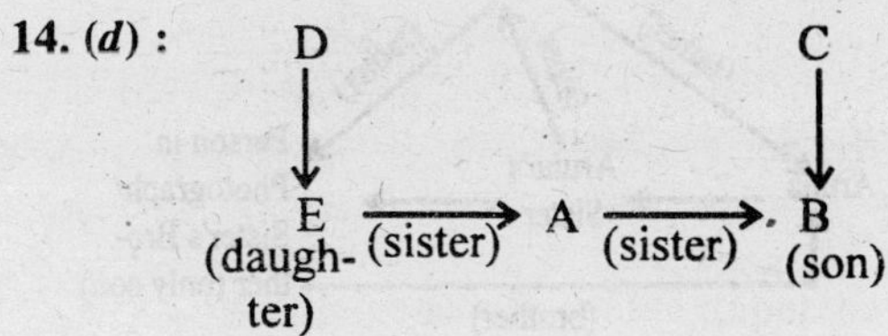

Information about 'D' and 'C' is not given as such no relation can be specified.

15. (*d*) :

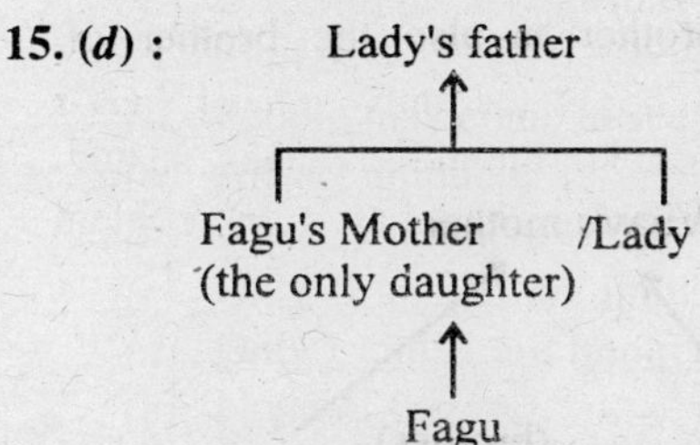

The only daughter of Lady's father is Fagu's mother.

16. (*c*) :

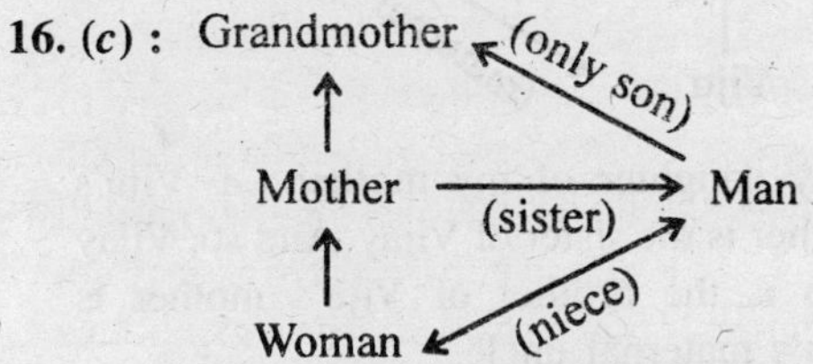

The man is the brother of the woman's mother. So, the woman is man's niece.

17. (*e*) :

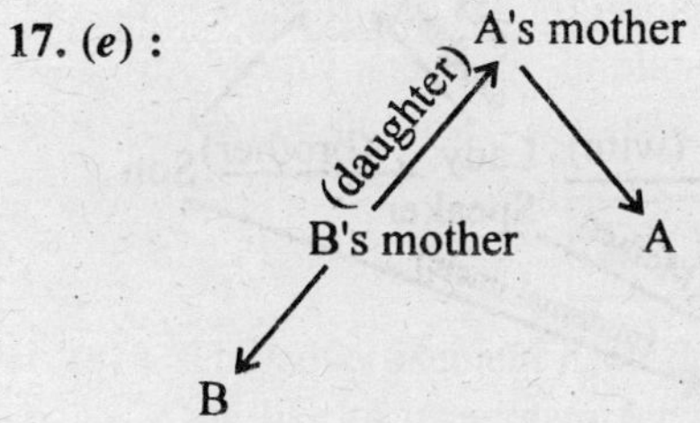

Sex of 'A' is not known. Either option A or B is correct.

18. (*d*) :

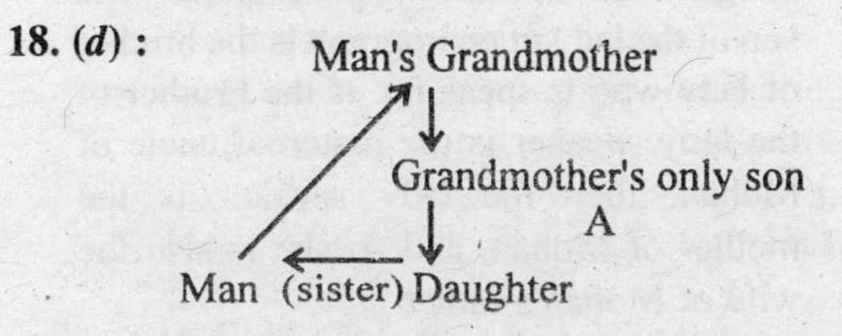

'My grandmother's only son' is the father of the man, and 'daughter of my grandmother's only son' is the sister of the man.

19. (*b*) :

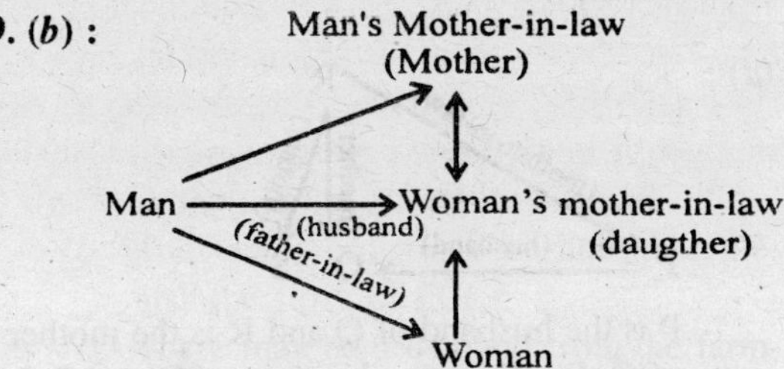

Woman's mother-in-law is the daughter of Man's mother-in-law. So, the man is the husband of woman's mother-in-law and the father-in-law of the woman.

20. (*b*) : Amit ⟷ Amit's Sister
(only brother)
↓
Son (Suman)

'My sister's only brother's is Amit himself and 'Sister's only brother's son' is the son of Amit *i.e.,* Suman is the son of Amit.

21. (*d*) :

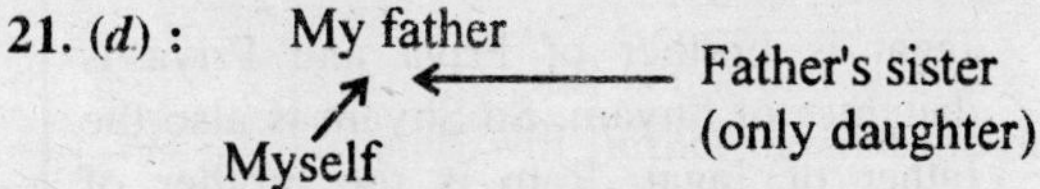

Nothing can be determined from this information.

22. (*c*) : Woman's mother's father
↕
Person in photograph
(woman's mother/only daughter)
↑ (daughter)
Woman

'Only daughter of my mother's father' is the person in the photograph and she is also the mother of the woman. So, the woman is the daughter of the person in the photograph.

23. (*e*) :

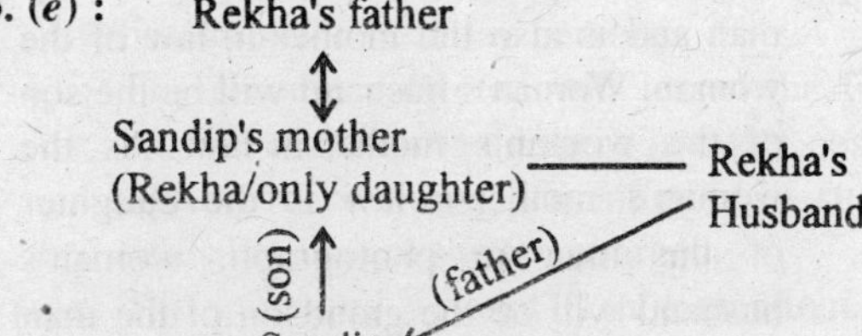

'Only daughter of Rekha's father's is

Rekha who is also Sandip's mother. And so, Rekha's husband is the father of Sandip.

24. (*d*) :

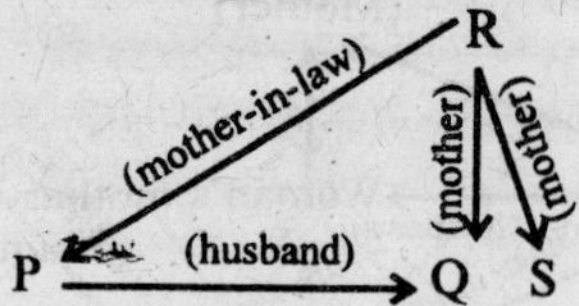

P is the husband of Q and R is the mother of Q. So, Q is the daughter of R and R is the mother-in-law of daughter's husband P.

25. (*c*) :

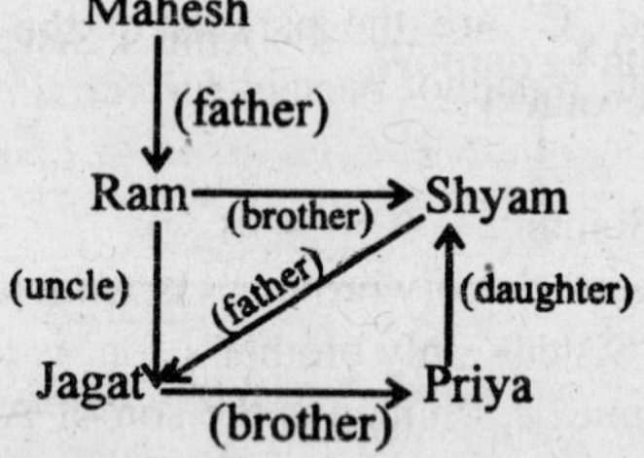

Jagat is brother of Priya and Priya is daughter of Shyam. So Shyam is also the father of Jagat. Ram is the brother of Shyam. So, Jagat's father's brother Ram is the uncle of Jagat.

26. (*c*) :

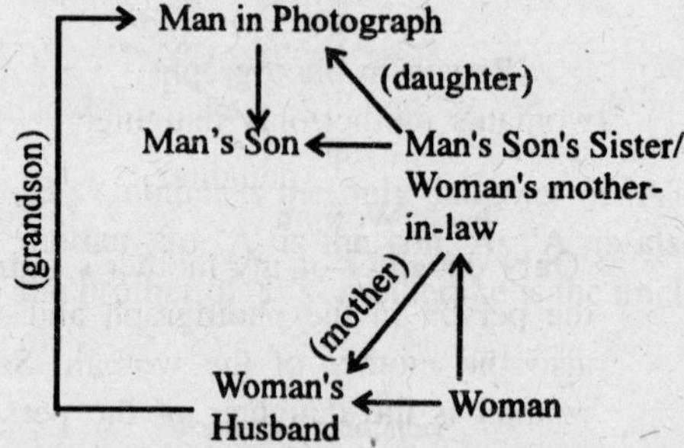

'Man's son's sister' is the daughter of the man and is also the mother-in-law of the woman. Woman's husband will be the son of the woman's mother-in-law. As the woman's mother-in-law is the daughter of the man in photograph, woman's husband will be the grandson of the man in photograph.

27. (*e*) :

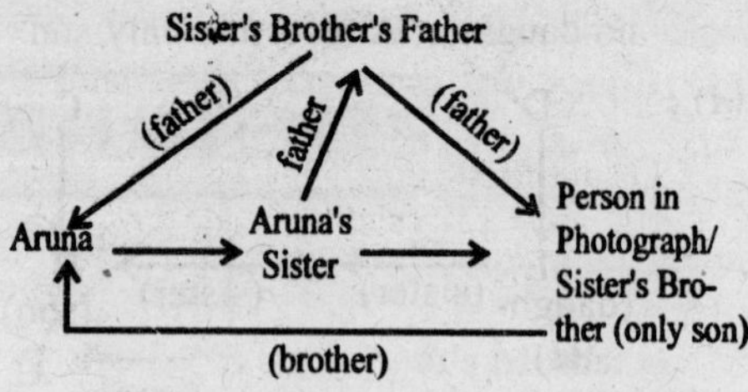

'The only son of the father of my sister's brother' is the brother himself. Aruna's sister's brother is also the brother of Aruna.

28. (*e*) :

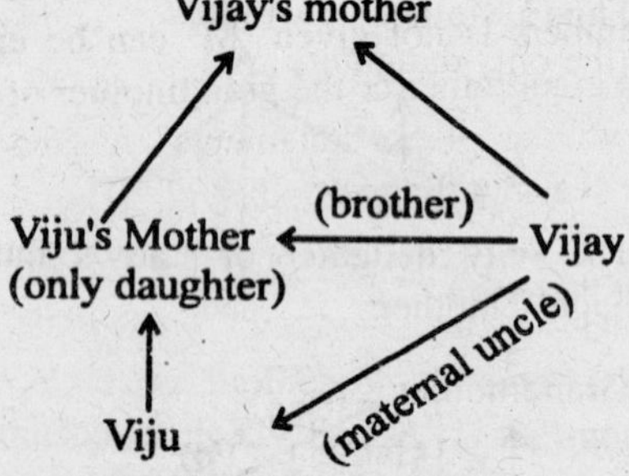

Only daughter of my mother *i.e.* Viju's mother is the sister of Vijay. And so, Vijay who is the brother of Viju's mother is Viju's maternal uncle.

29. (*a*) :

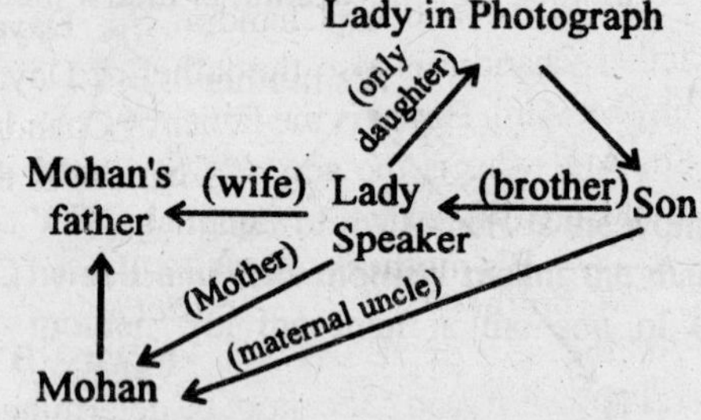

The lady who is speaking is the only daughter of the lady in photograph. The son of the lady in photograph is the brother of lady who is speaking. If the brother of the lady speaker is the maternal uncle of Mohan, then the lady speaker is the mother of Mohan, and so she is also the wife of Mohan's father.

30. (*d*) :

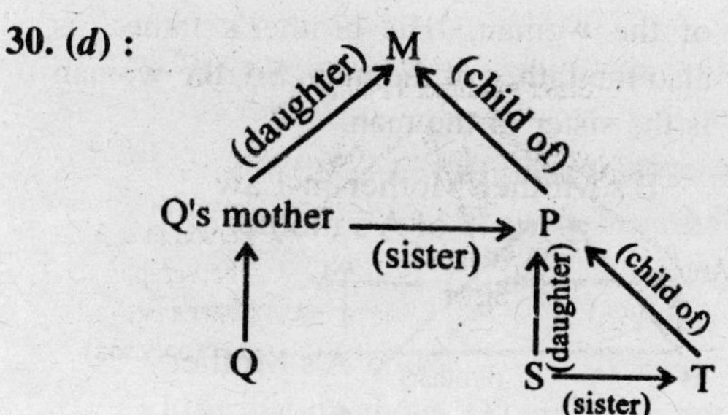

'Q's' mother is the sister of 'P' and daughter of 'M'. So, 'P' is also the child of 'M'. 'S' is the daughter of 'P' and sister of 'T'. So 'T' is also the child of 'P'; who is the child of 'M'. As the sex of the members is not given 'M' can be either the grandfather or the grandmother of 'T'.

31. (*e*) : From the given statements 'A' and 'C' are the mother and father of 'B' and two more children. None of the given options can be true.

32. (*c*) : Bimal (father) Chandra (son) (father) (grandson) Daya (brother) Anil

Daya is the son of Chandra. So, Daya's father Chandra is also the father of Daya's brother Anil. Bimal is the father of Chandra. So, Anil who is the son of Chandra is the grandson of Bimal.

33. (*d*) : A ⟶ B ⟵ C (brother) (sister)

As the sex of 'B' is not known, 'B's' relationship with 'A' cannot be determined.

34 (*d*) :

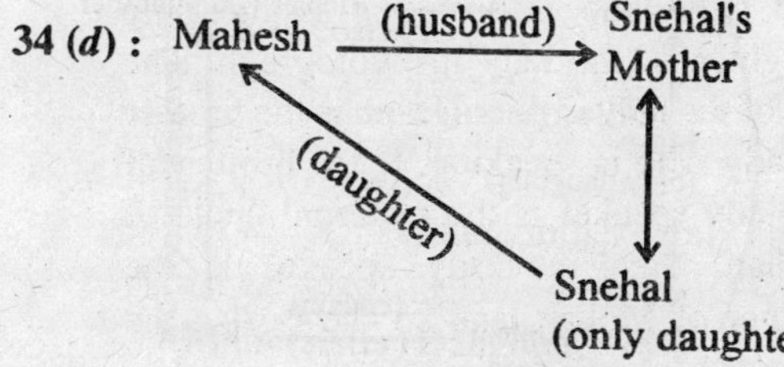

'Her (Snehal's) mother's only daughter' is Snehal herself. So Snehal is the daughter of Mahesh who in turn is her father.

35. (*b*) :

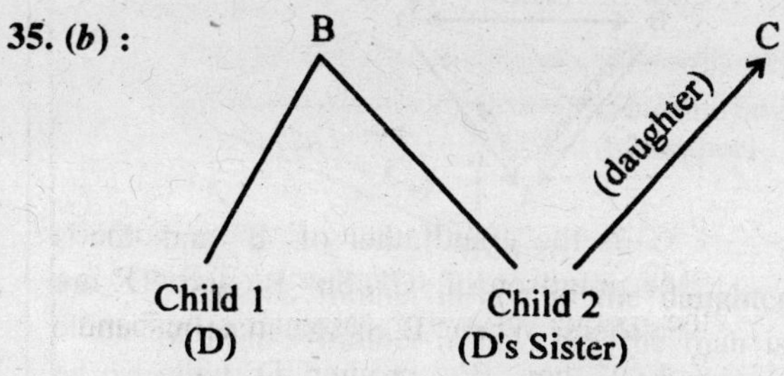

Though both the statements suggest that 'B' and 'C' are the parents of the two children; it cannot be said for certain that 'C' is the mother of 'D' as the sex of 'B' and 'C' is not given.

36. (*c*) : B ⟵ A ⟶ C (brother) (brother)

Either of the two information is necessary to find how 'B' is related to 'C'.

37. (*a*) :

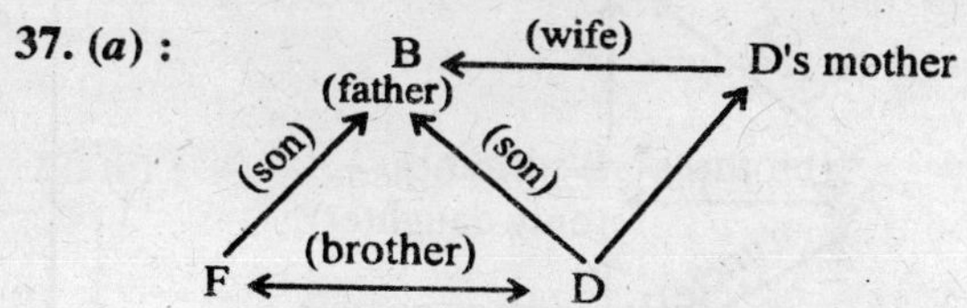

Both the statements are needed to know that 'D' is the brother of 'F'.

38. (*b*) :

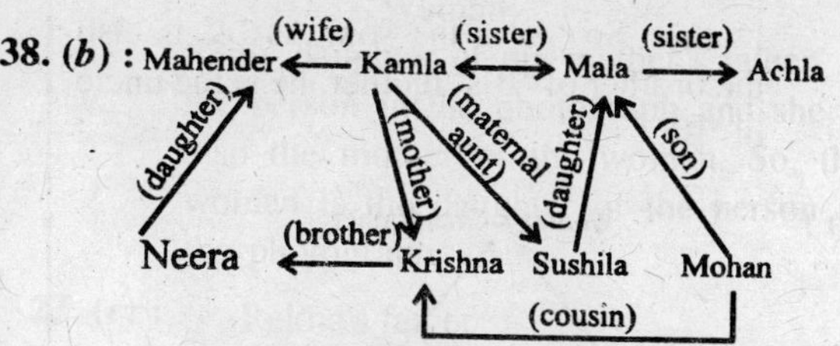

From the relationship chart, Kamla, Mala and Achla are sisters and also Kamla is maternal aunt of Mala's daughter Sushila. Kamla is the wife of Mahender. A wife's sister is a sister-in-law. So, Achla is the sister-in-law of Mahender.

39. (*a*) :

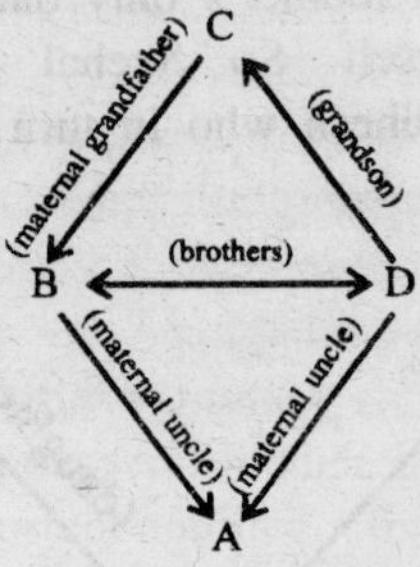

'C' is the grandfather of 'B' and 'D' is the grandson of 'C'. So 'B' and 'D' are brothers. When 'B' is the maternal uncle of 'A' then 'B's' brother 'D' will also be the maternal uncle of 'A'.

40. (*a*) :

Woman's Father

Man —(husband)→ Man's wife (only daughter)

'Only daughter of my father' is the woman herself and the man is her husband.

41. (*d*) :

A's Mother

A —(son)→ A's Mother; A —(brother)→ B's Mother (only daughter); A —(uncle)→ B

'B's' mother is the only daughter of 'A's' mother. So 'A' is the son. As 'A' is also the brother of 'B's' mother, he is the uncle of 'B'.

42. (*e*) :

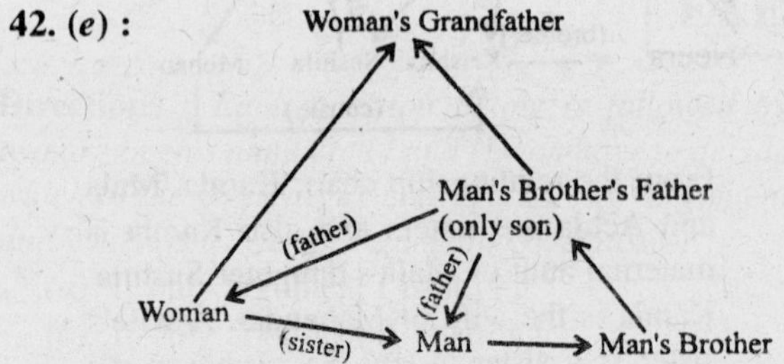

'Only son of my grandfather' is the father of the woman. 'His brother's father' is also the father of the man. So, the woman is the sister of the man.

43. (*b*) :

B's Mother/Mother-in-Law of A's mother

B → B's Mother; A's Mother —(daughter-in-law)→ B's Mother/Mother-in-Law of A's mother; A → A's Mother

'B's' mother is the mother-in-law of 'A's' mother. So, 'A's' mother is the daughter-in-law of 'B's' mother.

44. (*b*) :

A —(mother)→ B; A —(mother)→ C; A —(mother-in-law)→ D; D —(husband)→ C

'A' is the mother of 'C' and 'D' is the husband of 'C'. So, 'A' is the mother-in-law of 'C's' husband 'D'.

45. (*e*) :

Woman's Father

(Woman/only daughter) Man's Mother

Man —(son)→ Man's Mother

'Only daughter of my father' is the woman herself and 'His mother' means the man's mother. So, the man is the son of the woman.

46. (*b*) :

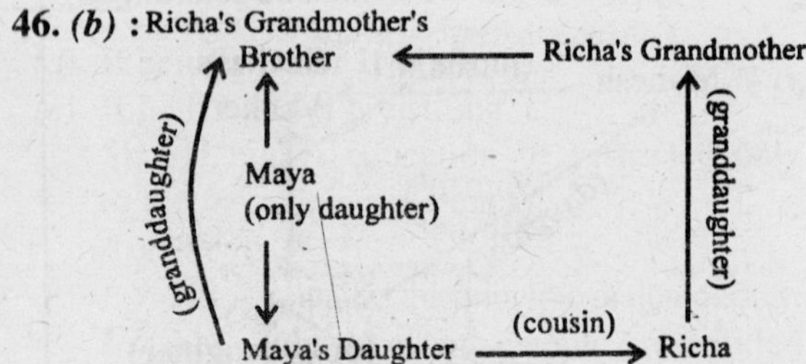

Both Maya's Daughter and Richa are

granddaughters of a brother and a sister respectively. So Maya's daughter is the cousin of Richa.

47. (*d*) :

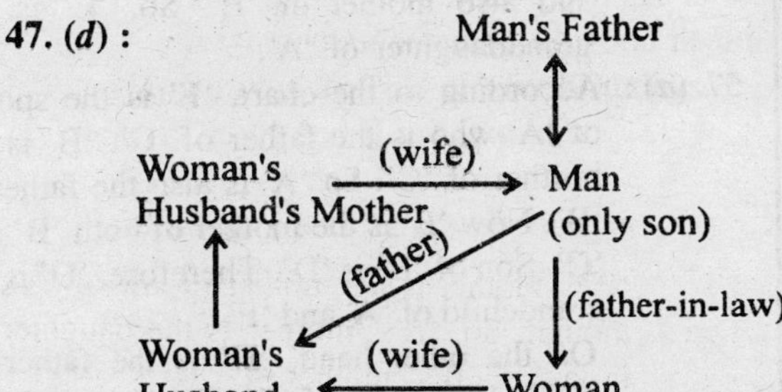

'My father's only son' is the man himself. 'Her husband's mother' is the wife of the man and so the man is the father of the woman's husband. As the woman is the wife of man's son, the man is the father-in-law of the woman.

48. (*d*) : The relationship chart based on the problem is :

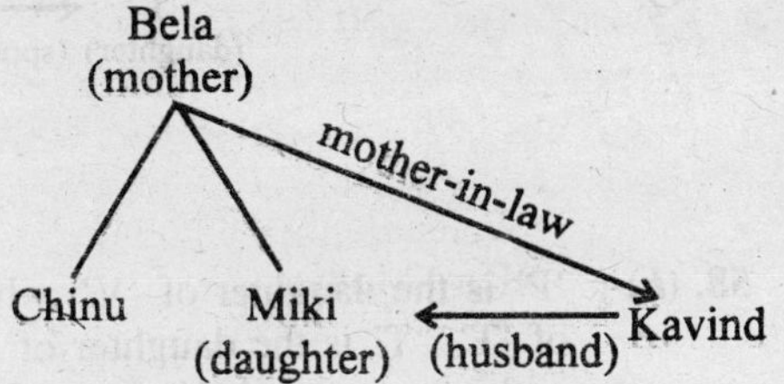

Bela is mother of Miki. Kavind is Miki's husband. So, Bela is Kavind's mother-in-law as wife's mother is the husband's mother-in-law.

49. (*b*) : The relationship chart based on the given statements is :

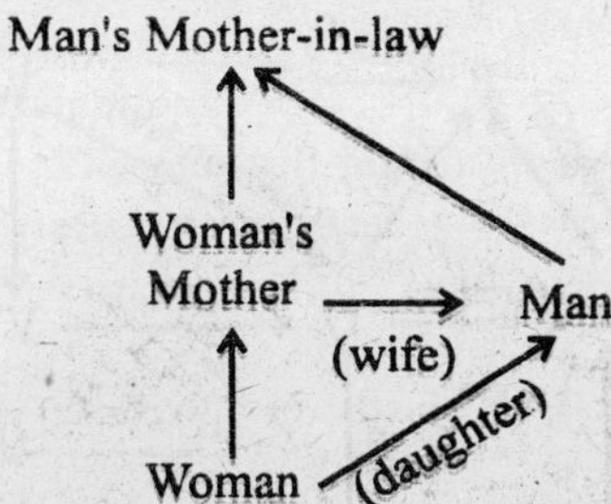

The woman, who is pointed out is the man's daughter and the man's mother-in-law's only daughter is man's wife.

50. (*a*) : The relationship chart based on problem is :

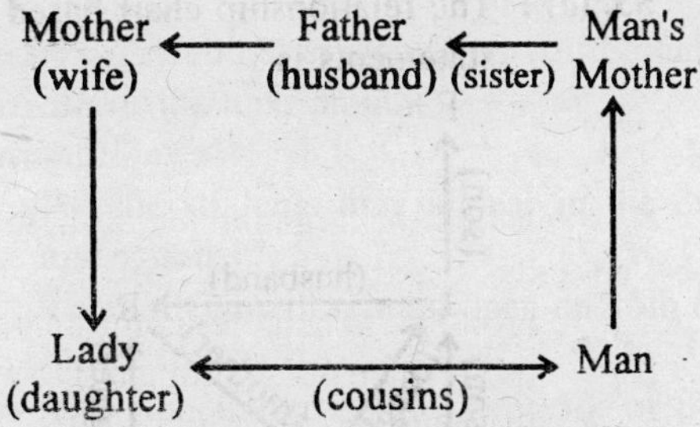

As the children of brother and sister are cousins, so are the man and the lady. Lady is the daughter of brother of man's mother and man is the son of brother's sister.

51. (*d*) : The relationship chart based on problem is :

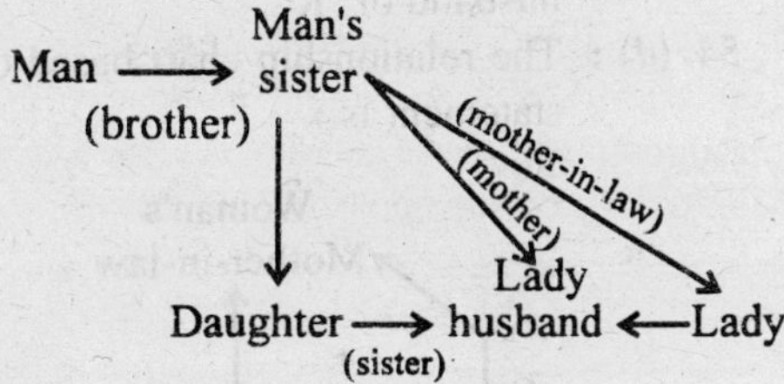

Man's sister's daughter is the sister of lady's husband. This means that man's sister is the mother of lady's husband, and further the mother-in-law of the lady. So, the man's sister is the lady's mother-in-law.

52. (*b*) : The relationship chart based on the given statements is :

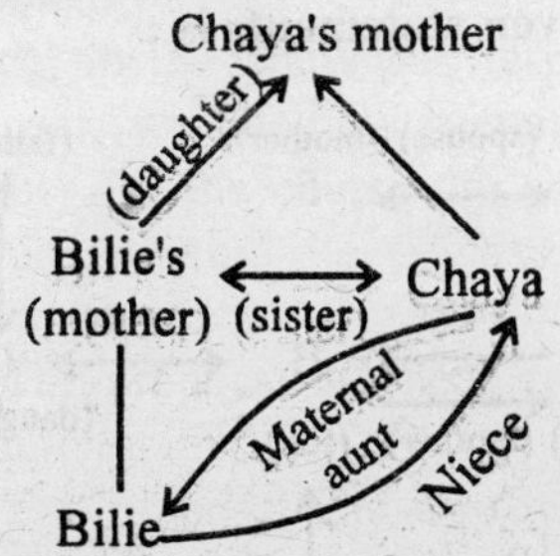

Bilie's mother is Chaya's mother's daughter. So, Bilie and Chaya are sisters. Sister's child is either a niece (girl) or a nephew (boy). Here, the optional name given is feminine. So, Bilie is the niece of Chaya.

53. (*c*) : The relationship chart based on the given statements is :

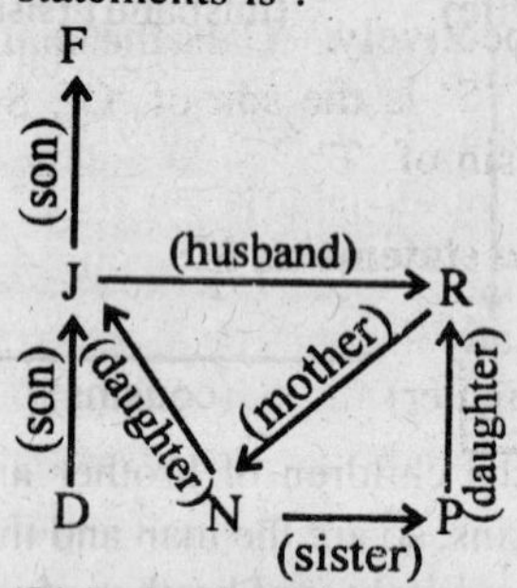

'P' is the daughter of 'R'. 'N' is the sister of 'P' and daughter of 'J'. So, 'R' is also the mother of 'N'. When 'J' is the father and 'R' is the mother, then 'J' is the husband of 'R'.

54. (*d*) : The relationship chart based on the given statement is :

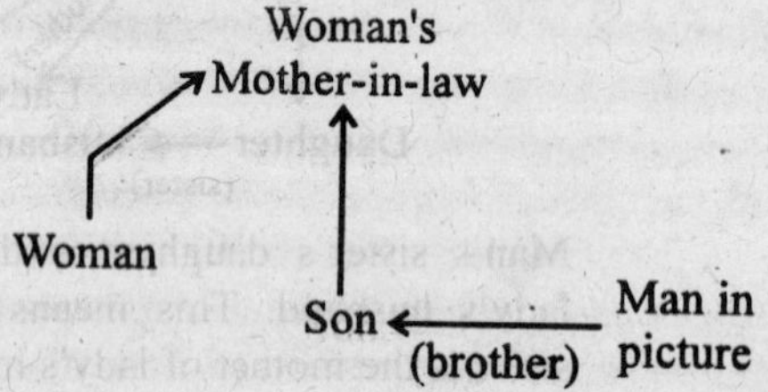

The man in photograph can be woman's husband or brother-in-law, if the mother-in-law's son is her husband. As such a definite relationship cannot be worked out.

For answers 55 to 57 the relationship chart based on given statements is :

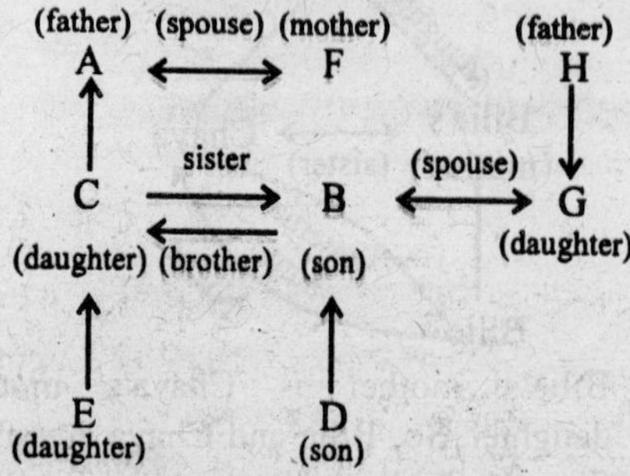

55. (*d*) : 'H' is the father of 'G' and 'G' is the wife of 'B'. So, 'B' is the son-in-law of 'H'.

56. (*d*) : 'E' is the daughter of 'C'. 'C' is not a son of 'A' means 'C' is the daughter of 'A' and also mother of 'E'. So, 'E' is the granddaughter of 'A'.

57. (*a*) : According to the chart, 'F' is the spouse of 'A' who is the father of 'C'. 'B' is the brother of 'C'. So 'A' is also the father of 'B'. Now 'F' is the mother of both 'B' and 'C'. Son of 'B' is 'D'. Therefore, 'D' is the grandchild of 'A' and 'F'.

On the other hand, 'H' is the father of 'G', who is wife of 'B'. 'D' is son of 'B', so also of 'G'. Therefore, 'D' is the grandchild of 'H'. It can be concluded that the common grandchild of 'F' and 'H' is 'D'.

For answers 58 and 59, the relationship chart based on given statements is :

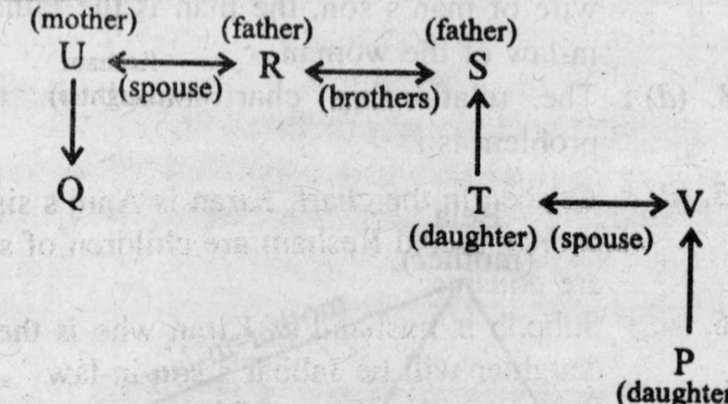

58. (*b*) : 'P' is the daughter of 'V', who is spouse of 'T'. 'T' is the daughter of 'S'. So, 'T' is the mother and 'V' is the father of 'P'. Therefore, 'S' is the grandfather of 'P'.

59. (*a*) : 'R' and 'S' are brothers. 'Q' is the child of 'R' and 'T' is the child of 'S'. So, cousin of 'Q' is 'T'.

For answers 60 to 64 the relationship chart based on given statements is :

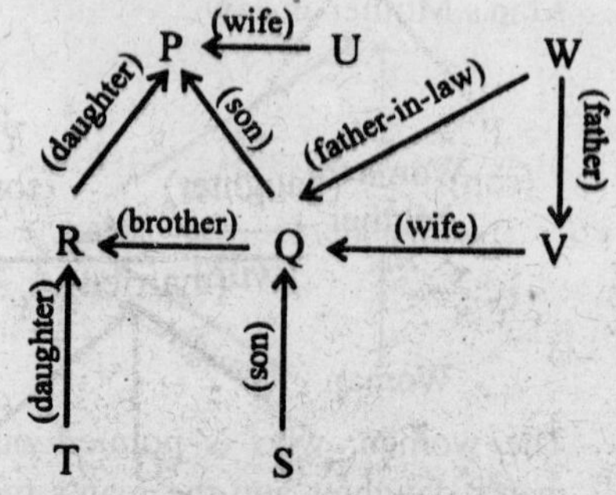

60. (*d*) : 'P' is the father of 'R' and 'Q' is the

brother of 'R'. So, 'Q' is the son of 'P'. 'U' is the wife of 'P' and so the mother 'Q'. 'S' is the son of 'Q' and 'Q's' mother 'U' is the grandmother of 'S'.

61. (*a*) : 'P' is the father of 'R' and 'Q' is the brother of 'R' so 'Q' is the son of 'P'. 'U' is the wife of 'P', so 'Q' is the son of 'U'.

62. (*d*) : 'W' is the father of 'V' and 'V' is the wife of 'Q', so W is the father-in-law of 'Q'.

63. (*b*) : 'Q' is the brother of 'R' and 'V' is the wife of 'Q'. So 'V' is the sister-in-law of 'R'.

64. (*d*) : 'R' and 'Q' are sister and brother respectively. 'T' is the daughter of 'R' and 'S' is the son of 'Q'. So, 'S' is the cousin of 'T'.

For answers 65 to 69 the relationship chart based on the given statements is :

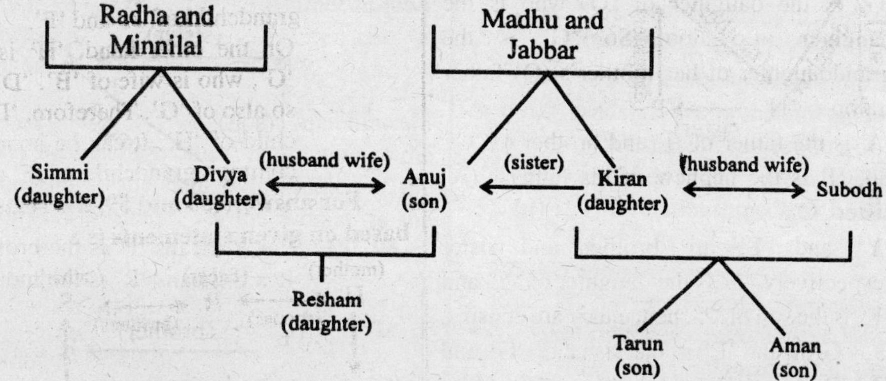

65. (*d*) : As seen in the chart, Kiran is Anuj's sister. Aman is Kiran's son and Resham is Anuj's daughter. So Aman and Resham are children of sister (Kiran) and brother (Anuj) respectively, hence, they are cousins.

66. (*a*) : Subodh is husband of Kiran who is the daughter of Madhu and Jabbar. So husband of Jabbar's daughter will be Jabbar's son-in-law.

67. (*a*) : Resham is daughter of Divya and Anuj. Kiran is sister of Anuj and aunt of Resham. So, Resham is the niece of Kiran.

68. (*c*) : Divya is wife of Anuj and Kiran is sister of Anuj. Brother's wife is a sister-in-law and so is the relation of Kiran with Divya.

69. (*b*) : Kiran is the daughter of Madhu and wife of Subodh. So, Madhu is the mother-in-law of her daughter Kiran's husband Subodh.

For answers 70 to 75 the relationship chart based on the information given is :

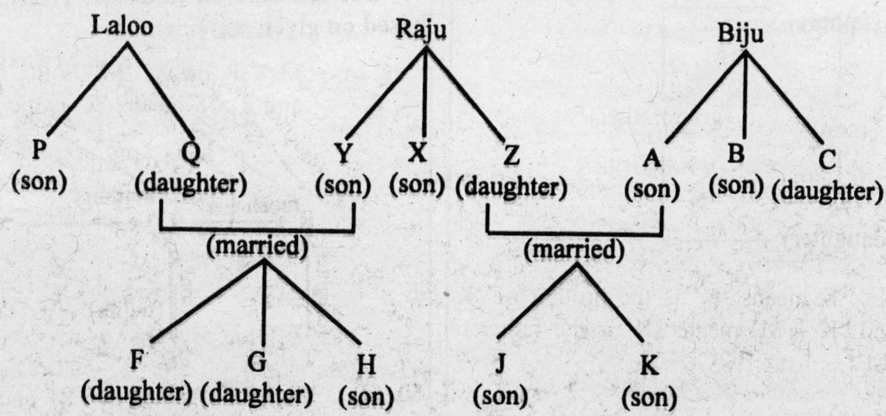

70. (*b*) : As seen in the chart 'Y' is the son of Raju and the husband of 'Q'. So Raju is the father-in-law of his son's 'Y' wife 'Q'.

71. (*d*) : 'A' is the son of Biju and husband of 'Z'. So, 'Z' is the daughter-in-law of her husband's (A) father Biju.

72. (*c*) : 'Q' is the wife of 'Y' and sister of 'P'. So 'Y' is the brother-in-law of his wife's (Q) brother 'P'.

73. (*a*) : 'G' is the daughter of 'Q' who is the daughter of Laloo. So 'G' is the granddaughter of her mother's (Q) father Laloo.

74. (*a*) : 'A' is the father of 'J' and brother of 'C'. So, 'J' is the nephew of his father's (A) sister 'C'.

75. (*b*) : 'Y' and 'Z' are brother and sister respectively. 'F' is the daughter of 'Y' and 'K' is the son of 'Z', hence they are cousins.

76. (*a*) : E – G means 'E' is the sister of 'G' and G ÷ F means 'G' is the father of F.

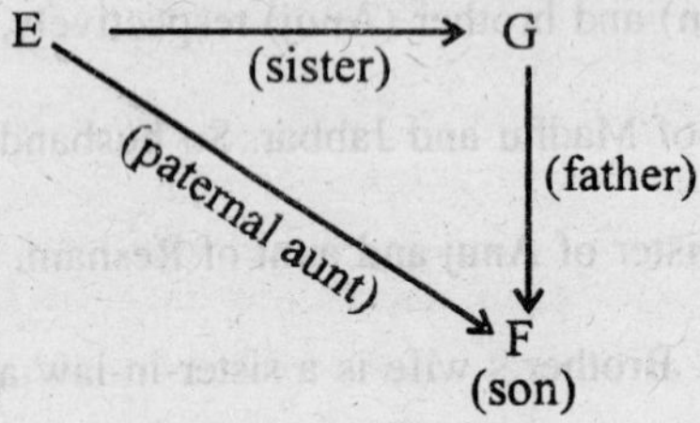

77. (*b*) : M + J means 'M' is the daughter of 'J'. J ÷ K means 'J' is the son of 'K'

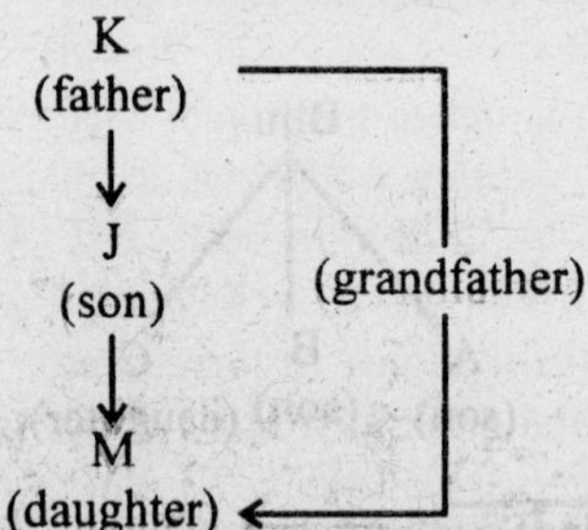

78. (*a*) : N × K means 'N' is the brother of 'K' and 'K + M' means 'K' is the father of 'M'.

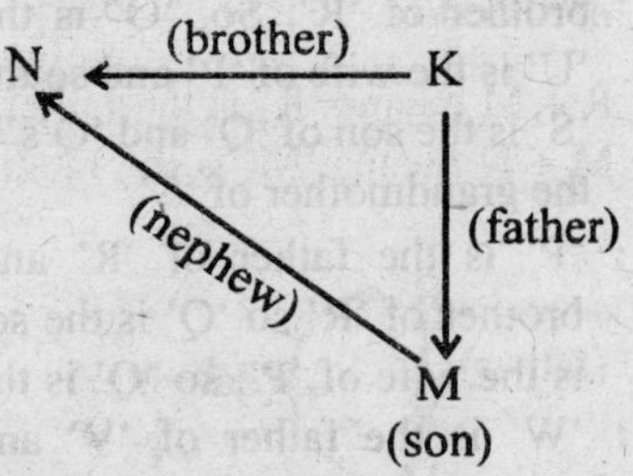

79. (*a*) : P ÷ R means 'P' is the son of 'R' and R – Q means 'R' is the sister of 'Q'.

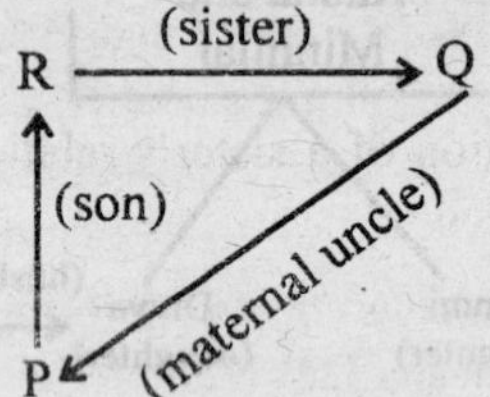

80. (*c*) : P + R means 'P' is the brother of 'R' and R × S means 'R' is the mother of 'S'.

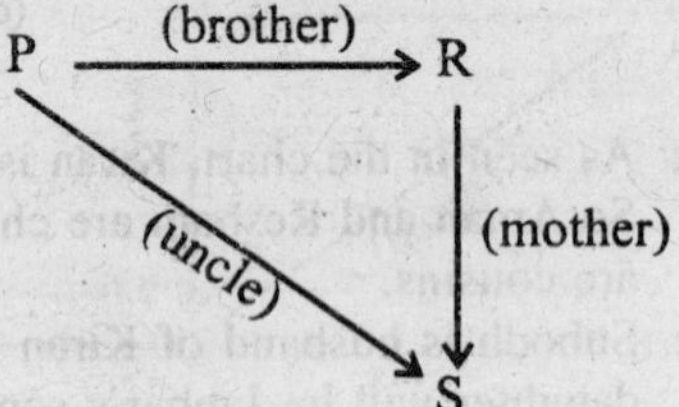

81. (*e*) : N × O means 'N' is the father of 'O' and O × M means 'O' is the father of M.

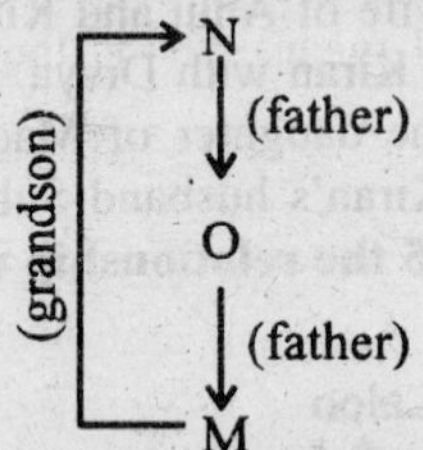

82. (*c*) : M ÷ R means 'M' is the mother of 'R' and R × S means 'R' is the father of 'S'.

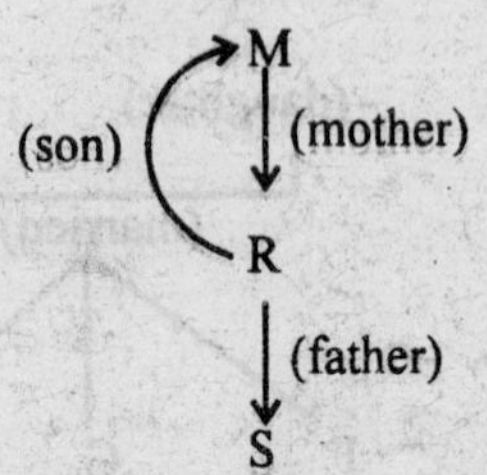

83. (*a*) : Information of a brother's relationship was not needed.

84. (*a*) : R ÷ M means 'R' is the father of 'M' and M + N means 'M' is the mother of 'N'.

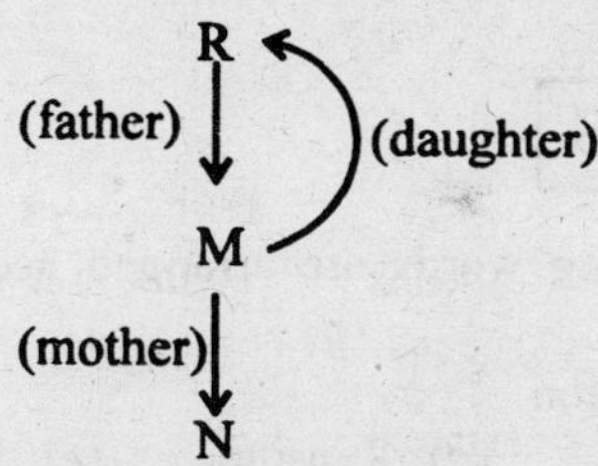

85. (*d*) : Information of a sister's relationship was not needed.

86. (*b*) : T + M means 'T' is the brother of 'M', M × S means 'M' is the father of 'S' and S – K means 'S' is the sister of 'K'.

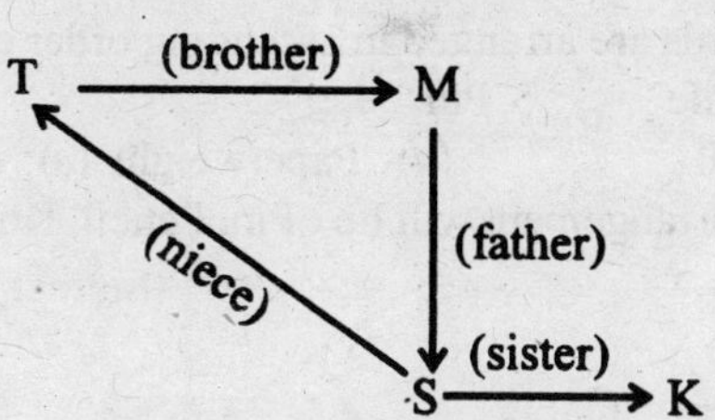

87. (*e*)

88. (*d*) : M – O means 'M' is the husband of 'O' and O + N means 'O' is the mother of 'N'.

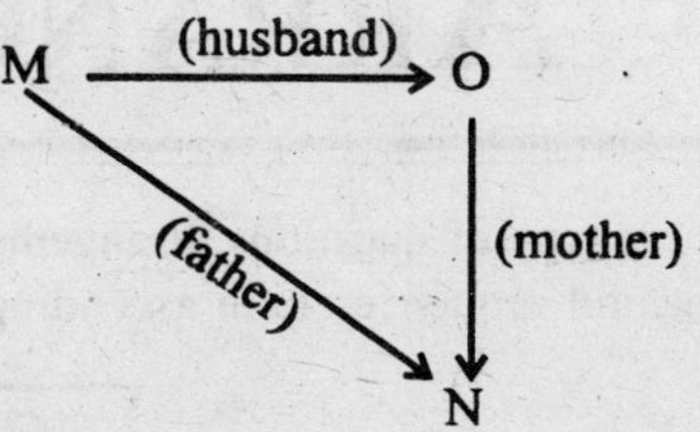

89. (*d*) : (A) M + N means 'M' is the mother of 'N' and N × O means 'N' is the brother of 'O'.

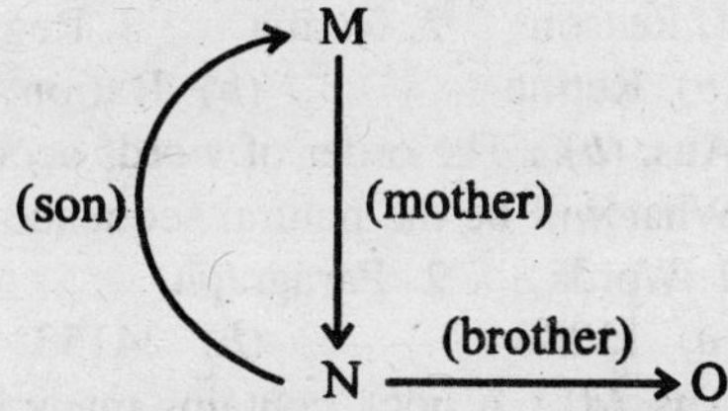

(B) M + N means 'M' is the mother of 'N' and N – O means 'N' is the husband of 'O'.

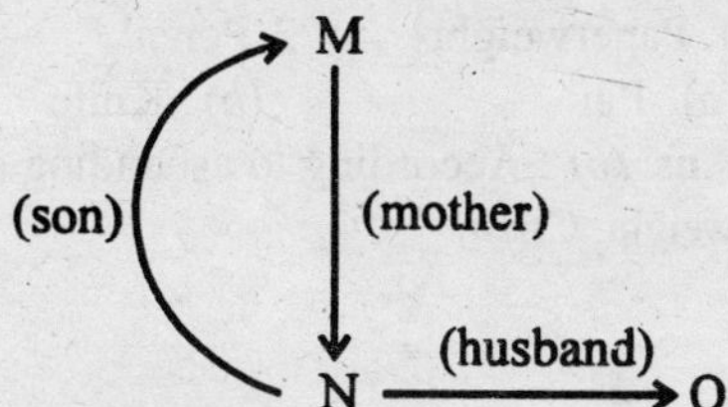

(C) N ÷ M means 'N' is the son of 'M'

90. (*e*) : The answer cannot be determined. Information about a sister's relationship is required to work out the relationship between 'M' and 'N'.

ARRANGING IN ORDER

In these type of questions arrangement of given options is done on the basis of dictionary, size, rank, weight, natural sequence etc in ascending or descending order.

SOLVED EXAMPLES

1. Which word will come in the second place if the following words are arranged according to dictionary?
1. Reason 2. Retina 3. Regard 4. Ransom 5. Ration
(*a*) Retina (*b*) Ration (*c*) Regard (*d*) Ransom (*e*) Reason

Ans. *(b)* : The order of words according to dictionary is Ransom, Ration, Reason, Regard, Retina.

2. What will be the natural sequence of the given words in descending manner?
1. Words 2. Paragraph 3. Book 4. Lesson 5. Sentence
(*a*) 15243 (*b*) 24153 (*c*) 32451 (*d*) 34251 (*e*) 54213

Ans. *(d)* : A book contains many lessons, a lesson contains many paragraphs, a paragraph contains many sentences and a sentence contains many words.
(**Note** : Option *(a)* is in ascending manner.)

3. What word will come in the middle if the following words are arranged in ascending order of weight?
1. Paperweight 2. Pencil 3. Chair 4. Knife 5. Pin
(*a*) Pin (*b*) Knife (*c*) Pencil (*d*) Paperweight (*e*) Chair

Ans. *(b)* : According to ascending order of weight the arrangement will be - Pin, Pencil, Knife, Paperweight, Chair.

EXERCISE

1. Which of the following words would appear in the middle if they are arranged as in the dictionary order?
(*a*) Delude (*b*) Delirium
(*c*) Defer (*d*) Demean
(*e*) Delete

2. Which one would be a meaningful order of the following?
1. Key 2. Door
3. Lock 4. Room
5. Switch on
(*a*) 5 1 2 4 3 (*b*) 4 2 1 5 3
(*c*) 1 3 2 4 5 (*d*) 1 2 3 5 4

3. If the following words are rearranged in the alphabetical order as in a dictionary, which will be the third word?
(*a*) Amphibian (*b*) Amorphous
(*c*) Ambiguous
(*d*) Amphidextrous
(*e*) Ambivalent

4. Which one would be a meaningful order of the following?
1. Consultation 2. Illness
3. Doctor 4. Treatment
5. Recovery
(*a*) 4 3 1 2 5 (*b*) 2 3 4 1 5
(*c*) 5 1 4 3 2 (*d*) 2 3 1 4 5
(*e*) 4 1 5 3 2

5. In a telephone directory, which of the following names will appear in the middle?
(*a*) Randhir (*b*) Randesh
(*c*) Rama (*d*) Ramesh
(*e*) Renmurthi

6. What would be a meaningful order of the

following?
1. Andhra Pradesh
2. Universe
3. Tirupathi
4. World
5. India

(*a*) 1 5 3 2 4 (*b*) 4 1 5 3 2
(*c*) 5 4 2 1 3 (*d*) 2 1 3 5 4
(*e*) 3 1 5 4 2

7. Which one would be a meaningful order of the following?
1. Mother 2. Child
3. Milk 4. Cry
5. Smile

(*a*) 3 2 1 5 4 (*b*) 2 4 1 3 5
(*c*) 1 5 2 4 3 (*d*) 2 4 3 1 5
(*e*) 3 4 1 2 5

8. Which would be the proper order of the following?
1. Rainbow 2. Rain
3. Sun 4. Happy
5. Child

(*a*) 4 2 3 5 1 (*b*) 4 5 1 2 3
(*c*) 2 1 4 3 5 (*d*) 2 3 1 5 4
(*e*) 4 3 1 2 5

9. Which one will be a meaningful order of the following :
1. Birth 2. Death
3. Funeral 4. Marriage
5. Education

(*a*) 1 3 4 5 1 (*b*) 4 5 3 1 2
(*c*) 1 5 4 2 3 (*d*) 2 3 4 5 1
(*e*) 3 1 4 2 5

10. In a telephone directory which of the following names will appear in the middle?

(*a*) Sajewet (*b*) Sajewat
(*c*) Segvan (*d*) Salwar
(*e*) Sajevar

11. Which would be the proper order of the following? (in ascending order)
1. Trillion 2. Thousand
3. Billion 4. Hundred
5. Million

(*a*) 4 2 5 3 1 (*b*) 1 5 3 2 4
(*c*) 4 2 3 5 1 (*d*) 1 2 3 4 5
(*e*) 4 2 5 1 3

12. What would be the meaningful order of the following?
1. Table 2. Tree
3. Wood 4. Seed
5. Plant

(*a*) 1 3 2 4 5 (*b*) 4 5 3 2 1
(*c*) 4 5 2 3 1 (*d*) 1 2 3 4 5
(*e*) 1 4 2 5 3

13. Which one would be a meaningful order of the following?
1. Snake 2. Grass
3. Eagle 4. Frog
5. Insect

(*a*) 3 2 1 4 5 (*b*) 5 2 1 4 3
(*c*) 2 5 4 1 3 (*d*) 2 4 5 3 1
(*e*) 2 4 5 1 3

14. Which one would be a meaningful order of the following?
1. Windows 2. Walls
3. Floor 4. Foundation
5. Roof 6. Room

(*a*) 4 2 1 5 3 6 (*b*) 4 3 5 6 2 1
(*c*) 4 5 3 2 1 6 (*d*) 4 1 5 6 2 3
(*e*) 4 1 5 3 6 2

15. Which would be a meaningful order of the following?
1. Index 2. Contents
3. Title 4. Chapters
5. Introduction

(*a*) 2 3 4 5 1 (*b*) 3 2 5 4 1
(*c*) 5 1 4 2 3 (*d*) 3 2 5 1 4
(*e*) 5 4 2 1 3

16. If the following words are arranged in their natural sequence in descending order, which word will occur in the second place?
1. Book 2. Paragraph
3. Library 4. Alphabet
5. Page

(*a*) Page (*b*) Paragraph
(*c*) Book (*d*) Library
(*e*) Alphabet

17. What would be the proper order of the following :
1. Decameter 2. Meter
3. Kilometer 4. Centimeter
5. Milimeter

(*a*) 1 4 3 2 5 (*b*) 5 4 1 2 3
(*c*) 5 4 3 2 1 (*d*) 5 4 2 1 3

(e) 1 3 4 5 2

18. If the following words are arranged in natural order then what will come in the second place?

1. Producer 2. Raw material
3. Seller 4. Consumer
5. Distributor

(a) Producer (b) Seller
(c) Consumer (d) Distributor
(e) Raw Material

19. If the words are arranged in ascending order which word will occur in the fourth place?

1. Youth 2. Infant
3. Adult 4. Childhood
5. Teenager

(a) Teenager (b) Childhood
(c) Adult (d) Youth
(e) Infant

20. If the following words are arranged according to dictionary, what will be the correct order?

1. Martial 2. Marital
3. Matrimony 4. Material
5. Matriarch

(a) 2 1 4 5 3 (b) 2 4 5 1 3
(c) 3 4 1 5 2 (d) 2 1 5 3 4
(e) 3 1 5 2 4

21. What would be the proper order of the following words in descending order?

1. Gram 2. Decigram
3. Hectogram 4. Kilogram
5. Centigram

(a) 4 3 1 2 5 (b) 4 2 3 1 5
(c) 5 2 1 4 3 (d) 4 3 2 1 5
(e) 5 4 1 3 2

22. What will be the middle word in natural order of the words given?

1. Medication 2. Patient
3. Diagnosis 4. Recuperation
5. Doctor

(a) Doctor (b) Patient
(c) Medication (d) Recuperation
(e) Diagnosis

23. Which would be the proper order of the following?

1. Country 2. Furniture
3. Forest 4. Wood
5. Trees

(a) 4 3 2 1 5 (b) 2 4 1 5 3
(c) 1 3 5 4 2 (d) 1 2 3 4 5
(e) 2 1 5 4 3

24. If the following words are arranged in natural order, what will come in the last place in ascending order?

1. Captain 2. Brigadier
3. Major 4. Lieutenant-General
5. Lieutenant

(a) Lientenant-General
(b) Brigadier
(c) Captain
(d) Major
(e) Lieutenant

25. What will be the natural order of the following words according to speed?

1. Jet 2. Bus
3. Cycle 4. Aeroplane
5. Train

(a) 3 5 2 4 1 (b) 3 2 5 1 4
(c) 3 2 5 4 1 (d) 3 2 1 4 5
(e) 3 1 4 2 5

26. If these words are arranged according to dictionary then what word will come in the third place?

1. Originality 2. Originally
3. Originator 4. Original
5. Originate

(a) Originality (b) Originator
(c) Originate (d) Originally
(e) Original

27. Which word will come in the third place in the natural sequence of the following words in descending order?

1. Town 2. Country
3. Family 4. Neighbourhood
5. State

(a) Town (b) Country
(c) State (d) Neighbourhood
(e) Family

28. What will be the natural order of the following words?

1. Digest 2. Cut
3. Chew 4. Purchase
5. Cook

(a) 4 5 2 3 1 (b) 4 2 5 1 3

(*c*) 4 5 3 1 2 (*d*) 4 2 5 3 1
(*e*) 4 2 1 5 3

29. If the following words are arranged according to dictionary what will come in the last?

1. Institutist 2. Institutional
3. Institute 4. Institutor
5. Institutionalism

(*a*) Institutist
(*b*) Institutor
(*c*) Institutionalism
(*d*) Institutional
(*e*) Institute

30. What will be the natural order of the following?

1. Independence Day
2. Christmas
3. Diwali
4. Holi
5. Republic Day

(*a*) 5 4 1 3 2 (*b*) 5 1 4 3 2
(*c*) 4 1 5 3 2 (*d*) 2 3 4 1 5
(*e*) 4 3 1 5 2

31. What will be the natural order of the following words according to weight?

1. Drum 2. Pin
3. Paper weight 4. Pebble
5. Coffee cup

(*a*) 4 2 3 5 1 (*b*) 2 4 5 3 1
(*c*) 4 2 5 1 3 (*d*) 2 4 3 5 1
(*e*) 4 2 5 3 1

32. What word will come in the third place if these words are arranged in descending order?

1. Judge 2. Listen
3. Act 4. Analyse
5. Observe

(*a*) Listen (*b*) Observe
(*c*) Act (*d*) Judge
(*e*) Analyse

33. If the following words are arranged in ascending order what word will be in the fourth place?

1. Air commodore
2. Wing Commander
3. Pilot Officer
4. Squadron Leader
5. Air Marshal

(*a*) Air Marshal
(*b*) Air Commodore
(*c*) Wing Commander
(*d*) Pilot Officer
(*e*) Squadron leader

34. If the following words are arranged in natural sequence in descending order, what will come in the second place from the last?

1. Teacher 2. Lecturer
3. Dean 4. Tutor
5. Reader

(*a*) Dean (*b*) Lecturer
(*c*) Tutor (*d*) Reader
(*e*) Teacher

35. If the words are arranged according to dictionary, what will come in the second place from the last?

1. Spastically 2. Spasmatic
3. Spasticity 4. Spastic
5. Spasmodical

(*a*) Spastic (*b*) Spasmodical
(*c*) Spastically (*d*) Spasmatic
(*e*) Spasticity

36. What will be the natural order of the following words according to size?

1. Dog 2. Horse
3. Ant 4. Giraffe
5. Mouse

(*a*) 3 5 1 2 4 (*b*) 3 1 5 2 4
(*c*) 3 5 1 4 2 (*d*) 3 5 2 1 4
(*e*) 3 5 2 4 1

37. What will be the natural order of the following in descending order?

1. Hut 2. Skyscraper
3. Palace 4. Room
5. House

(*a*) 2 3 1 5 4 (*b*) 4 1 5 3 2
(*c*) 2 3 5 1 4 (*d*) 3 2 5 4 1
(*e*) 2 3 5 4 1

38. Which would be the proper order of the following?

1. Euphoria 2. Happiness
3. Ambivalence 4. Ecstasy
5. Pleasure

(*a*) 3 4 1 2 5 (*b*) 3 2 5 4 1
(*c*) 5 4 1 3 2 (*d*) 3 5 2 1 4
(*e*) 1 4 3 2 5

39. What will be the proper order of the words

according to dictionary?
1. Rural 2. Rugby
3. Rugged 4. Rummage
5. Ruffle
(*a*) 5 3 2 4 1 (*b*) 5 2 3 1 4
(*c*) 5 2 4 3 1 (*d*) 5 2 3 4 1
(*e*) 5 2 1 3 4

40. Which name will come in the middle if these names are arranged in a telephone directory?
1. Priyanka 2. Priyana
3. Priti 4. Pratima
5. Protima
(*a*) Priti (*b*) Pratima
(*c*) Protima (*d*) Priyana
(*e*) Priyanka

41. Arrange the following in a meaningful sequence :
1. Senescence 2. Infancy
3. Puberty 4. Going adulthood
5. Babyhood
(*a*) 5 3 2 4 1 (*b*) 1 3 4 2 5
(*c*) 2 3 4 5 1 (*d*) 2 5 3 4 1
(*e*) 5 4 2 1 3

42. Arrange the following words in the sequence in which they occur in dictionary :
Liver Long Late Load Luminous Letter
1 2 3 4 5 6
(*a*) 3 6 1 4 2 5 (*b*) 3 6 1 2 4 5
(*c*) 3 1 6 2 4 5 (*d*) 3 1 6 2 5 4
(*e*) 3 4 1 6 2 5

43. Which number-sequence of the following represents a correct sequence from small to big?
1. Bungalow 2. Flat
3. Cottage 4. House
5. Palace 6. Mansion
(*a*) 3 2 1 4 6 5 (*b*) 3 2 4 1 6 5
(*c*) 3 2 4 1 5 6 (*d*) 5 6 4 1 2 3
(*e*) 5 4 6 2 1 3

44. Arrange the following words in a meaningful order :
1. Gold 2. Iron
3. Sand 4. Platinum
5. Diamond
(*a*) 3 2 1 5 4 (*b*) 2 4 3 5 1
(*c*) 5 4 3 2 1 (*d*) 4 5 1 3 2
(*e*) 4 2 3 1 5

45. Arrange the following words in a meaningful order :
1. Site 2. Plan
3. Rent 4. Money
5. Building
(*a*) 2 3 5 1 4 (*b*) 4 1 2 5 3
(*c*) 1 2 3 5 4 (*d*) 3 4 2 5 1
(*e*) 3 1 4 2 5

46. Which one would be a meaningful order of the following?
1. Probation 2. Interview
3. Selection 4. Appointment
5. Advertisement 6. Application
(*a*) 5 6 4 2 3 1 (*b*) 5 6 3 2 4 1
(*c*) 5 6 2 3 4 1 (*d*) 6 5 4 2 3 1
(*e*) 6 5 2 1 3 4

47. What would be a meaningful order of the following?
1. Caste
2. Family
3. Newly-married couple
4. Clan
5. Species
(*a*) 3 4 5 1 2 (*b*) 5 2 1 4 3
(*c*) 2 3 1 4 5 (*d*) 4 5 3 2 1
(*e*) 4 3 2 1 5

48. Which one would be a meaningful order of the following?
1. College 2. Child
3. Salary 4. School
5. Employment
(*a*) 1 2 4 3 5 (*b*) 4 1 3 5 2
(*c*) 2 4 1 5 3 (*d*) 5 3 2 1 4
(*e*) 3 4 1 2 5

49. What will be the dictionary order of these words?
Bungling, Burgling, Bubble, Bundle, Bushy, Bully
1 2 3 4 5 6
(*a*) 2 4 5 6 1 3 (*b*) 5 6 1 4 3 2
(*c*) 1 4 6 5 2 3 (*d*) 6 1 2 3 5 2
(*e*) 3 6 4 1 2 5

50. Which word would be in the second place if the following are arranged in a natural sequence?
1. Noon 2. Night
3. Evening 4. Dusk
5. Dawn
(*a*) Night (*b*) Noon
(*c*) Dusk (*d*) Dawn
(*e*) Evening

EXPLANATORY ANSWERS

1. (*b*) : The dictionary order of word is — Defer, Delete, **Delirium,** Delude, Demean

2. (*c*) : With the Key you open a Lock, then open the Door to enter the Room and Switch on the light.

3. (*b*) : The dictionary order of the words is — Ambiguous, Ambivalent, **Amorphous,** Amphibian, Amphidextrous.

4. (*d*) : An Ill person goes to a Doctor for Consultation who prescribes Treatment for Recovery.

5. (*b*) : In telephone directory the order of names is — Ramesh, Rana, Randesh, Randhir, Renmurthi.

6. (*e*) : Tirupathi is in Andhra Pradesh which is a state in India and India is a part of the World which is in Universe.

7. (*b*) : When a Child Cries the Mother gives him Milk and then he Smiles.

8. (*d*) : When it rains in the Sun a Rainbow is formed and the Child is Happy to see it.

9. (*c*) : After the Birth of a child, his Education is important. When he is grown up he is Married. When he is old he Dies and is taken for the Funeral.

10. (*a*) : In telephone directory the order of names is—Sajevar, Sajewat, **Sajewet**, Salwar, Segvan.

11. (*a*) : The words are arranged in order of increasing amount.

12. (*c*) : From a Seed a Plant is grown into a Tree whose Wood is used to make a Table.

13. (*c*) : In the Grass there are many Insects. Frog who eats them is a prey of Snake who in turn is the prey of an Eagle.

14. (*a*) : The order of words depict the right order of constructing a building/room.

15. (*b*) : A Title comprises Contents of Introduction for Chapter Index.

16. (*c*) : The words in descending order of natural sequence are—Library, **Book,** Page, Paragraph, Alphabet. Library is a collection of Books, a Book is a collection of many Pages, in a Page there are many Paragraphs which contain a lot of Alphabet.

17. (*d*) : The proper order of measurement in increasing order is—Milimeter, Centimeter, Meter, Decameter, Kilometer.

18. (*a*) : The natural order of words is—Raw material, **Producer,** Distributor, Seller, Consumer. Raw material is used by the Producer to make a product which its Distributor gives to the Seller from whom the Consumer can purchase it.

19. (*d*) : The words in ascending order depict the natural growth of a human being — Infant, Childhood, Teenager, **Youth,** Adult.

20. (*a*) : The dictionary order of words is — Marital, Martial, Material, Matriarch, Matrimony.

21. (*a*) : The arrangement of weights in descending order is — Kilogram, Hectogram, Gram, Decigram, Centigram.

22. (*e*) : The words in natural order are — Patient, Doctor, **Diagnosis,** Medication, Recuperation. A Patient goes to the Doctor who gives the Diagnosis and Prescribes the Medication for Recuperation.

23. (*c*) : The proper order of the words is—Country, Forest, Trees, Wood, Furniture. In a Country there are Forests comprising Trees the Wood of which are used to make Furniture.

24. (*a*) : The arrangement of ranks in ascending order is—Lieutenant, Captain, Major, Brigadier, **Lieutenant-General.**

25. (*c*) : The natural order of modes of transport according to increasing speed is — Cycle, Bus, Train, Aeroplane, Jet.

26. (*d*) : The dictionary order of words is — Original, Originality, **Originally,** Originate, Originator.

27. (*a*) : The words in natural sequence of descending order are — Country, State, **Town,** Neighbourhood, Family.
In a country there are many States which comprises of many Towns wherein in the

Neighbourhood live Families.

28. (*d*) : The natural order of the words is — Purchase, Cut, Cook, Chew, Digest. After Purchasing vegetables we Cut them, then Cook them and while eating Chew them and Digest them in our stomach.

29. (*b*) : The dictionary order of words is — Institute, Institutional, Institutionalism, Institutist, **Institutor**.

30. (*a*) : The natural order of National/Gazetted Holidays in Calendar is — Republic Day (January), Holi (March), Independence Day (August), Diwali (October/November), Christmas (December).

31. (*b*) : The arrangement of words according to weight in ascending order is — Pin, Pebble, Coffee Cup, Paper Weight, Drum.

32. (*e*) : The arrangement of words in descending order is — Act, Judge, **Analyse,** Observe, Listen *Or* Act, Judge, **Analyse,** Listen, Observe.

33. (*b*) : The arrangement of ranks in ascending order is — Pilot Officer, Squadron Leader, Wing Commander, **Air Commodore,** Air Marshal.

34. (*e*) : The arrangement of educational posts in descending order is — Dean, Reader, Lecturer, **Teacher,** Tutor.

35. (*c*) : The dictionary order of words is — Spasmatic, Spasmodical, Spastic, **Spastically,** Spasticity.

36. (*a*) : The natural order of living beings according to increasing size is — Ant, Mouse, Dog, Horse, Giraffe.

37. (*c*) : The words in descending order are — Sky-scraper, Palace, House, Hut, Room.

38. (*d*) : The order of expressions of feeling of joy is — Ambivalence, Happiness, Pleasure, Euphoria, Ecstacy.

39. (*d*) : The dictionary order of words is — Ruffle, Rugby, Rugged, Rummage, Rural.

40. (*d*) : Order of names in telephone directory is Pratima, Priti, **Priyana**, Priyanka, Protima.

41. (*d*) : The meaningful sequence of the words is—Infancy, Babyhood, Puberty, Going Adulthood, Senescence.

42. (*a*) : The dictionary order of words is — Late, Letter, Liver, Load, Long, Luminous.

43. (*b*) : The sequence of letters from small to big is — Cottage, Flat, House, Bungalow, Mansion, Palace.

44. (*a*) : The meaningful order of words is — Sand, Iron, Gold, Diamond, Platinum. (The order is based on the dearness.)

45. (*b*) : The meaningful order of words is — Money, Site, Plan, Building, Rent — based on proper planning.

46. (*c*) : The meaningful order of the words is — Advertisement, Application, Interview, Selection, Appointment, Probation.

47. (*b*) : The meaningful order of words is — Species, Family, Caste, Clan, Newly-married Couple.

48. (*c*) : The meaningful order of words is — Child, School, College, Employment, Salary.

49. (*e*) : The dictionary order of words is—Bubble, Bully, Bundle, Bungling, Burgling, Bushy.

50. (*e*) : The natural order of words is— Dawn, Noon, Evening, Dusk, Night.

CALENDAR, CLOCK, TIME, DISTANCE

These are mathematical problem based on calculations of time by a clock or calendar and computations of speed or distances.

SOLVED EXAMPLES

1. If day-after-tomorrow is Sunday, what was day-before-yesterday?

(*a*) Wednesday (*b*) Thursday (*c*) Friday (*d*) Saturday
(*e*) None of the above

Ans. (*a*) :

Day-after-tomorrow	—	Sunday
Tomorrow	—	Saturday
Today	—	Friday
Yesterday	—	Thursday
Day-before-yesterday	—	Wednesday

2. If the next day after 3rd Monday in a month is 16th, what will be the date on day before 5th Monday?

(*a*) 27 (*b*) 28 (*c*) 29 (*d*) 30
(*e*) None of these

Ans. (*b*) : Next day after 3rd Monday is 16th
So Monday is 15th
4th Monday is 22nd.... (15 + 7)
5th Monday is 29th .... (15 + 14) or (22 + 7)
So, date on day before 5th Monday is 28th

3. How many times in 12 hours the hands of a clock will be at right angles?

(*a*) 12 (*b*) 16 (*c*) 18 (*d*) 24
(*e*) 36

Ans. (*d*) : In every hour the hands are at right angles twice.

4. If a train runs at a speed of 92.7 km/hr, then the distance covered in metres in 20 minutes will be :

(*a*) 3009 (*b*) 308.9 (*c*) 309 (*d*) 3090
(*e*) 30900

Ans. (*e*) : Speed of the train is 92.7 km/hr *i.e.*
92700 metres in 60 minutes
In 20 minutes the distance covered will be :

$$\frac{92700}{60} \times 20 = 30900 \text{ metres}$$

5. Prabhat remembers that his mother's birthday is after seventeenth April but before twenty-first April, whereas his sister Urmila remembers that their mother's birthday is after nineteenth but before twenty-fourth April. Which of the following days in April is definitely their mother's birthday?

(*a*) Nineteenth (*b*) Twenty-first (*c*) Twenty-second (*d*) Twentieth

(e) None of these

Ans. *(d)* : Mother's birthday in the month of April :

According to Prabhat: is from 17th —— 21st

According to Urmila: is from 19th —— 24th

It is clear that the mother's birthday is between 19th and 21st April and so the definite date is 20th April.

EXERCISE

1. If the day before yesterday was Thursday, when will Sunday be?
(a) Tomorrow (b) Day after tomorrow
(c) Today (d) Two days after today
(e) None of these

2. There are twenty people working in an office. The first group of five works between 8:00 A.M. and 2:00 PM. The second group of ten works between 10:00 AM to 4:00 PM. And the third group of five works between 12 noon to 6:00 PM. There are three computers in the office which all the employees frequently use. During which of the following hours the computers are likely to be used most?
(a) 1:00 PM - 3:00 PM
(b) 12 noon - 2:00 PM
(c) 2:00 PM - 4:00 PM
(d) 10:00 AM - 12 noon
(e) None of these

3. If the seventh day of a month is three (3) days earlier than Friday, what day will it be on the nineteenth day of the month?
(a) Sunday (b) Monday
(c) Wednesday (d) Friday
(e) Tuesday

4. Radha remembers that her father's birthday is after 16th but before 21st of March, while her brother Mangesh remembers that his father's birthday is before 22nd but after 19th of March. On which date is the birthday of their father?
(a) 19th
(b) 20th
(c) 21st
(d) Cannot be determined
(e) None of these

5. A man is three (3) years older than his wife and four (4) times as old as his son. If the son attains an age of fifteen (15) years after three (3) years, what is the present age of the mother?
(a) 60 years (b) 51 years
(c) 48 years (d) 45 years
(e) 65 years

6. A clock is so placed that at 12 noon its minute hand points towards north-east. In which direction does its hour hand point at 1.30 P.M.?
(a) East (b) West
(c) North (d) South
(e) None of these

7. If in the above question clock is turned through an angle of 135° in an anticlockwise direction, in which direction will its minute hand point at 8.45 P.M.?
(a) East (b) West
(c) North (d) South
(e) None of these

8. A couple married in 1980 had two children, one in 1982 and the other in 1984. Their combined ages will equal the years of the marriage in?
(a) 1986 (b) 1985
(c) 1987 (d) 1988
(e) 1989

9. Manoj left home for the bus stop 15 minutes earlier than the usual time. It takes 10 minutes to reach the stop. He reached the stop at 8.40 a.m. What time does he usually leave home for the bus stop?
(a) 8.30 a.m. (b) 8.55 a.m.
(c) 8.45 p.m. (d) Data inadequate
(e) None of these

10. Mamuni went to the movies nine days ago.

She goes to the movies only on Thursday. What day of the week is today?

(*a*) Sunday (*b*) Tuesday
(*c*) Thursday (*d*) Saturday
(*e*) Friday

11. If Thursday was the day after the day before yesterday five days ago, what is the least number of days ago when Sunday was three days before the day after tomorrow?

(*a*) Two days ago (*b*) Three days ago
(*c*) Four days ago (*d*) Five days ago
(*e*) None of these

12. 1.12.91 is the first Sunday. Which is the fourth Tuesday of December 91?

(*a*) 31.12.91 (*b*) 24.12.91
(*c*) 17.12.91 (*d*) 26.12.91
(*e*) None of these

13. If the third day of a month is Monday, which of the following will be the fifth day from 21st of that month?

(*a*) Tuesday (*b*) Monday
(*c*) Wednesday (*d*) Thursday
(*e*) None of these

14. Keshav runs a factory in three shifts of eight hours each with 210 employees. In each shift minimum of 80 employees are required to run the factory effectively. No employee can be allowed to work for more than 16 hours a day. At least how many employees will be required to work for 16 hours every day?

(*a*) 30
(*b*) 60
(*c*) Data inadequate
(*d*) 20
(*e*) None of these

15. If 15 horses eat 15 bags of gram in 15 days, in how many days will one horse eat one bag of grain?

(*a*) 15 days (*b*) 1/15 days
(*c*) 1 day (*d*) 30 days
(*e*) 225 days

16. A century leap year is divisible by :

(*a*) 4 (*b*) 16
(*c*) 40 (*d*) 400
(*e*) None of these

17. If the fifth day of a month is Friday, which of the following will be the Seventh day from 10th of that month?

(*a*) Tuesday (*b*) Monday
(*c*) Wednesday (*d*) Thursday
(*e*) None of these

18. Day after tomorrow is my birthday. On the same day next week falls 'Holi'. Today is Monday. What will be the day after 'Holi'?

(*a*) Wednesday (*b*) Thursday
(*c*) Friday (*d*) Saturday
(*e*) None of these

19. A clock shows the time as 3 : 30 p.m. If the minute hand gains 2 minutes every hour, how many minutes will the clock gain by 4 a.m.?

(*a*) 23 Minutes (*b*) 24 Minutes
(*c*) 25 Minutes (*d*) 26 Minutes
(*e*) None of these

20. Two brothers were expected to return home on the same day. Rajat returned 3 days earlier but Rohit returned 4 days later. If Rajat returned on Thursday, what was the expected day when both the brothers were to return home and when did Rohit Return?

(*a*) Wednesday, Sunday
(*b*) Thursday, Monday
(*c*) Sunday, Thursday
(*d*) Monday, Friday
(*e*) None of these

21. A train started from station 'A' and proceeded towards station 'B' at a speed of 48 km/hr. Forty-five minutes later another train started from station 'B' and proceeded towards station 'A' at 50 km/hr. If the distance between the two stations is 232 km, at what distance from station 'A' will the trains meet?

(*a*) 132 km (*b*) 144 km
(*c*) 108 km (*d*) 160 km
(*e*) None of these

22. A, B and C are pipes attached to a cistern. A and B can fill it in 15 and 10 minutes respectively, while C can empty it in 20 minutes. If A, B and C be kept open successively for 1 minute each, find the last integral number of minutes required for the cistern to get filled.

(*a*) 20 (*b*) 23
(*c*) 25 (*d*) 26
(*e*) None of these

23. How many minutes does the minute hand gain in every one hour?
(*a*) 55 (*b*) 60
(*c*) 65 (*d*) No gain
(*e*) None of these

24. A 260 metres long train runs at a speed of 55 kmph. How much time will it take to cross a platform 290 metres long?
(*a*) 20 seconds (*b*) 36 seconds
(*c*) 18 seconds (*d*) 60 seconds
(*e*) None of these

25. Bunny's brother Sunny is 562 days older to him while his sister Jenny is 75 weeks older to Sunny. If Jenny was born on Tuesday, on which day was Bunny born?
(*a*) Monday (*b*) Tuesday
(*c*) Friday (*d*) Saturday
(*e*) Thursday

26. My uncle shall visit me after 64 days of my father's birthday. If my father's birthday falls on Tuesday, what shall be the day on my Uncle's visit?
(*a*) Wednesday (*b*) Sunday
(*c*) Tuesday (*d*) Monday
(*e*) Saturday

27. If 21st November falls five days before Wednesday then what will be the day on 25th December?
(*a*) Wednesday (*b*) Sunday
(*c*) Friday (*d*) Thursday
(*e*) Monday

28. How much time will 160 m long train travelling at a speed of 40 km/hr take to cross a man going in the same direction with a speed of 4 km/hr?
(*a*) 15 seconds (*b*) 40 seconds
(*c*) 24 seconds (*d*) 16 seconds
(*e*) None of these

29. If in a clock the numbers 1 to 12 are replaced with alphabet starting from F, then which of the following options shall indicate the time as 9'o clock?
(*a*) M - P (*b*) Q -N
(*c*) P - M (*d*) N - P
(*e*) N - Q

30. Arjun remembers that his mother's birthday is between fifteenth and twenty-first November. His sister remembers that their mother's birthday is between nineteenth and twenty-fifth November. If both of them remember correctly, on which day is their mother's birthday?
(*a*) Twentieth
(*b*) Twenty-first
(*c*) Twentieth or Twenty-first
(*d*) Twenty-second
(*e*) None of these

31. If 3rd December 1999 is Sunday, what day is 3rd January 2000?
(*a*) Tuesday (*b*) Wednesday
(*c*) Thursday (*d*) Friday
(*e*) Sunday

32. Prabir starts for office every morning at 9.15 a.m. and reaches there at 9.55 a.m. On Wednesday he started five minutes later than the time he started on Friday. Three days out of five days in the week he started late, out of which Friday was one of the days. On how many days he started in time?
(*a*) Two (*b*) Three
(*c*) Four (*d*) One
(*e*) None of these

33. In the question above, at what time did he start on Wednesday?
(*a*) 9.25 a.m.
(*b*) 9.15 a.m.
(*c*) Data inadequate
(*d*) 9.20 a.m.
(*e*) None of these

34. What is the birthdate of Nutan's mother? To answer this question, which of the following informations given in the statements A and B is/are sufficient?
(A) Nutan's father remembers that his wife's birthday is after 20th and before 23rd February.
(B) Nutan's brother remembers that their mother's birthday was after 21st but before 25th February.
(*a*) Only B is sufficient
(*b*) Only A is sufficient
(*c*) Both A and B together are not sufficient
(*d*) Both A and B together are needed
(*e*) Either A or B is sufficient

35. On which day in April was Gopal's birthday? To find out the answer which of the following informations given in the statements A and B is/are sufficient?

(A) Gopal was born exactly 28 years after his mother was born.

(B) His mother will be 55 years 4 months and 5 days on August 18 this year.

(*a*) Either A or B is sufficient
(*b*) Only B is sufficient
(*c*) Both A and B together are needed
(*d*) Both A and B together are not sufficient
(*e*) Only A is sufficient.

Directions (Qs. 36 to 38) : *Read the following information and answer the questions given below :*

(*I*) Kundanmal is available at home between 12 noon to 4 p.m. on Tuesday, Thursday and Sunday.

(*II*) His younger brother Nainamal is available at home on Monday, Thursday, Friday and Sunday between 10 a.m. to 2 p.m.

(*III*) The eldest brother Jethamal is available between 9 a.m. to 12 noon on Monday, Wednesday and Thursday and 2 p.m. to 4 p.m. on Friday, Saturday and Sunday.

36. On which day(s) of a week, the youngest and the eldest brothers are available at home at the same time?

(*a*) Only Monday
(*b*) Only Thursday
(*c*) Only Friday
(*d*) Both Monday and Thursday
(*e*) Both Sunday and Friday

37. At a time, on which day of a week all the three brothers are available at home?

(*a*) Sunday (*b*) Thursday
(*c*) None (*d*) Can't be determined
(*e*) None of these

38. For how many days only one brother is available at a particular time in a week?

(*a*) Four (*b*) Three
(*c*) Two (*d*) One
(*e*) None of these

Directions (Qs. 39 to 42) : *Read the following information and answer the questions given below :*

(*i*) A city bus company operates 7 buses M, N, O, P, Q, R and S each once for daily 4 hours sight-seeing tours.

(*ii*) From Monday to Friday first bus leaves at 8 a.m. sharp, subsequent bus leaves alternatively after a gap of 45 minutes, followed by 30 minutes, again 45 minutes and 35 minutes and so on.

(*iii*) On Saturday and Sunday, first bus leaves at 7.30 a.m. and others follows regularly after a gap of 1 hour.

(*iv*) Bus 'Q' leaves immediately after 'M' and is immediately followed by 'S'.

(*v*) Bus 'O' is not followed by any other bus.

(*vi*) Bus 'R' leaves immediately before 'M' but not immediately after 'P'.

39. At what time, bus 'M' leaves on Saturday?

(*a*) 10 a.m. (*b*) 9.45 a.m.
(*c*) 10.30 a.m. (*d*) Data inadequate
(*e*) None of these

40. On Sunday, when bus 'P' completes its tour, which of the following buses begins its tour?

(*a*) Q (*b*) S
(*c*) O (*d*) Data inadequate
(*e*) None of these

41. If the time gap after bus 'M' leaves on Saturday-Sunday is increased by 30 minutes for the subsequent trips, at what time, tour of bus 'O' will be completed?

(*a*) 3 p.m. (*b*) 2 p.m.
(*c*) 6 p.m. (*d*) 7 p.m.
(*e*) None of these

42. If the time gap between two buses is uniformly kept as 45 minutes from Monday to Friday, then the beginning of tour of bus 'O' will mark completion of tour of which of the following buses?

(*a*) N (*b*) R
(*c*) M (*d*) Data inadequate
(*e*) None of these

Directions (Qs. 43 to 45) : *Read the following information and answer the questions given below :*

(*i*) Eight doctors P, Q, R, S, T, U, V and W visit a charitable dispensary run by Shram-Mandir Trust every day except on a holiday, *i.e.* Monday.

(*ii*) Each doctor visits for 1 hour from Tuesday

to Sunday except Saturday. The timings are 9 a.m. to 1 p.m. and 2 p.m. to 6 p.m., 1 p.m. to 2 p.m. is lunch break.

(iii) On Saturday, it is open only in the morning, *i.e.,* 9 a.m. to 1 p.m. and each doctor visits for only half an hour.

(iv) No other doctor visits the dispensary before doctor 'Q' and after doctor 'U'.

(v) Doctor 'W' comes immediately after lunch break and is followed by 'R'.

(vi) 'S' comes in the same order as 'P' in the afternoon session.

43. At what time the visit of Doctor 'T' would be over on Saturday?

(*a*) 10 a.m.
(*b*) 11 a.m.
(*c*) Either 10 a.m. or 11 a.m.
(*d*) Data inadequate
(*e*) None of these

44. Doctor 'P' visits in-between which of the following pairs of doctors?

(*a*) R and W (*b*) S and T
(*c*) U and W (*d*) S and V
(*e*) None of these

45. If the lunch break and subsequent visiting hours are reduced by 15 minutes, at what time Doctor 'U' is expected to attend the dispensary?

(*a*) 3.15 p.m. (*b*) 4.15 p.m.
(*c*) 4.45 p.m. (*d*) 4 p.m.
(*e*) None of these

EXPLANATORY ANSWERS

1. (*a*) : Thursday —Day-before-yesterday
Friday —Yesterday
Saturday —Today
Sunday —Tomorrow

2. (*b*) : 1. 5 people work between 8 a.m. to 2 p.m.
2. 10 people work between 10 a.m. to 4 p.m.
3. 5 people work between 12 noon to 6 p.m.
So, computers are used most between 12 noon to 2 p.m.

3. (*a*) : 7th day is 3 days earlier than Friday so, 10th day is Friday, so also is 17th.
∴ 19th day will be 2nd day ahead of Friday, *i.e.,* Sunday.

4. (*b*) : Father's birthday

According to Radha: March 16th — March 21st
According to Mangesh: 19th March — 22nd March

∴ Their father's birthday is on 20th March.

5. (*d*) : Present age of son is 15-3 = 12 years. Age of the man is 4 times the age of son, *i.e.,* 12 × 4 = 48 years
Man is 3 years elder to his wife/son's mother.
So Age of the mother is 48 – 3 = 45 years

6. (*a*) :

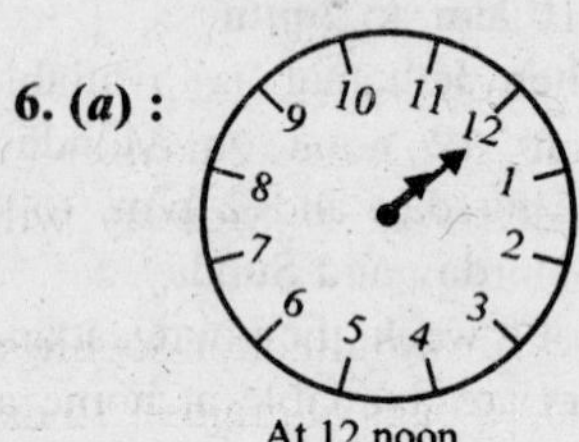

At 12 noon

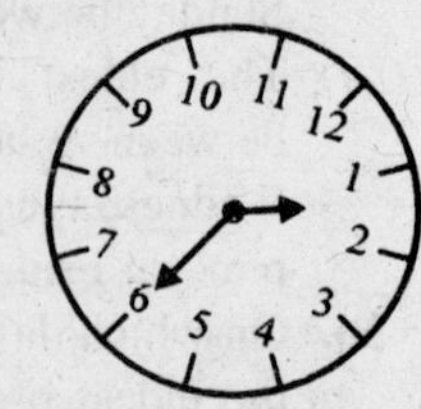

At 1.30 p.m. the hour hand will point towards East.

7. (*d*) :

After rotating the clock in earlier question, its minute hand will point towards South at 8:45 p.m.

8. (*a*) : 1982 — 2 years later — 1st child
1984 — 4 years later — 2nd child
Total age of children — 2 years.
1985 — 5 years later — Total age of children : 4 years.
1986 — 6 years later — Total age of children : 6 years.

9. (*e*) : Manoj reached the bus stop at 8.40 a.m. He left his home at 8:40 – 10 minutes = 8:30 a.m. He left 15 minutes earlier than usual, so his actual time of leaving home is 8:30 am + 15 minutes = 8:45 a.m.

10. (*d*) : Mamuni goes to the movies on Thursday, so nine days ago was Thursday.
∴ Two days ago was also Thursday. So, today is Saturday.

11. (*a*) : Day after the day-before-yesterday five days ago is the 6th day which is Thursday. And so, the 3rd day will be Sunday. Three days before the day-after-tomorrow is Yesterday which is the 1st day of the five days. So, two days ago was Sunday.

12. (*b*) : First Sunday is on 1st December
First Tuesday is on 3rd December
3 weeks later, Fourth Tuesday will be on 3 + (7 × 3) = 24th December.

13. (*c*) : 3rd day of the month is Monday
5th day from 21st is 26th
26 – 3 = 23 days
23 days later, 23/7 leaves 2 days.
So, two days ahead of Monday will be Wednesday.

14. (*e*) : 80 employees are required for double shift.

15. (*a*) : 15 horses eat 15 bags of grain in 15 days
15 horses eat 1 bag of grain in 1 day
1 horse eats 1 bag of grain in 15 days

16. (*d*) : A leap year is divisible by 4 and a century leap year is divisible by 400.

17. (*c*) : Seventh day from 10th is 17th.
5th day is Friday. Next Friday is on 12th
17 – 12 = 5, 5 days ahead of Friday will be Wednesday. So, 17th is Wednesday.

18. (*b*) : Today is Monday
Day-after-tomorrow is Wednesday
Next week 'Holi' is also on Wednesday
So, Day after Holi is Thursday.

19. (*c*) : Hours between 3:30 p.m. and 4 a.m. are — 12½ hours. Number of minutes gained will be 12½ × 2 = 25 minutes.

20. (*c*) : Rajat returned on Thursday. 3 days later was the day of expected return, *i.e.*, Sunday. Rohit returned 4 days after Sunday *i.e.* Thursday.

21. (*a*) : ←— d —→|←— $232 - d$ —→

i.e., $$\frac{d}{48} = \frac{232-d}{50} + \frac{3}{4}$$

$$\frac{d}{48} = \frac{464-2d+75}{100}$$

$$100\,d = (539-2d)\,48$$

$$100\,d = 25872 - 96\,d$$

$$196\,d = 25872$$

$$d = 25872 \div 196 = 132 \text{ km.}$$

22. (*c*) : In 3 minutes the cistern filled by A, B and C $= \frac{1}{15} + \frac{1}{10} - \frac{1}{20} = \frac{7}{60}$ th.
Time taken to fill the cistern completely
= 25 minutes

23. (*a*) : In every hour the minute hand moves 60 minutes whereas the hour hand moves 5 minutes.

24. (*b*) : Total length to be covered = 260 + 290 = 550 metres.
Time taken to cross the platform

$$= \frac{550}{55} \times \frac{3600}{1000} = 36 \text{ seconds}$$

25. (*e*) : Jaya is older to Sunny by 75 × 7 = 525 days.
Jaya is older to Bunny by 525 + 562 = 1087 days
1087 ÷ 7 gives 2 as remainder.
So, if Jaya was born on Tuesday, then Bunny was born 2 days later, *i.e.*, on Thursday.

26. (*a*) : My father's birthday is on Tuesday.
64 ÷ 7 gives 1 as remainder
So, 63rd day will be Tuesday and one day ahead is the day when uncle shall visit *i.e.*, on Wednesday.

27. (*d*) : 5 days before Wednesday is Friday.
So, 21st November is Friday
Number of days between 21st November and 25th December = 9 + 25 = 34 days
34 ÷ 7 gives 6 as remainder

∴ 28th day will be Friday and 6 days ahead will be Thursday.
So, 25th December will be Thursday.

28. (d) : Relative speed of the train will be 40 – 4 = 36 km/hr or 10 m/sec as both, the train and the man, are moving in same direction.
Time taken by the train to cross the man 160 ÷ 10 = 16 seconds.

29. (e) :

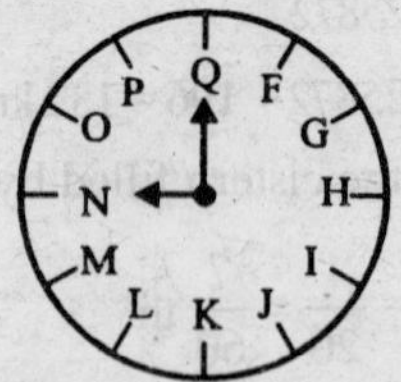

Note : Q – N will indicate the time as Quarter to twelve *i.e.* 11:45

30. (a) : Mother's birthday

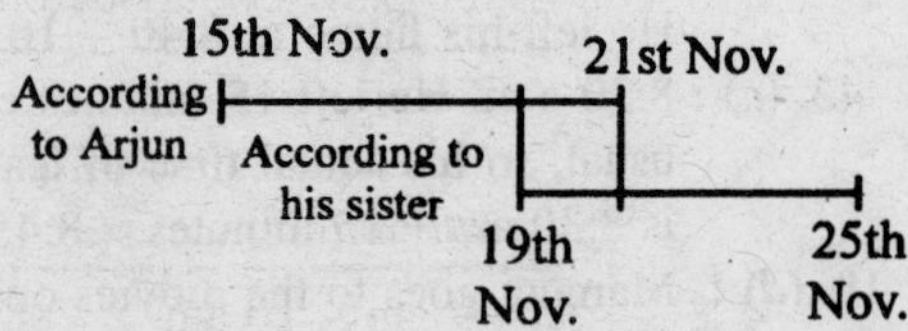

So, their mother's birthday is on 20th November.

31. (b) : 3rd December 1999 is Sunday. Number of days in-between 3rd December 1999 and 3rd January 2000 = 28 + 3 = 31 days
31 ÷ 7 gives 3 as remainder
So, 31st December 1999 will be Sunday and 3rd January 2000 will be 3 days ahead *i.e.* Wednesday.

32. (a) : Out of five days, he starts late on three days.

33. (c) : Time on Friday is not given.

34. (d) **35. (c)**

36. (d) : The availability of brothers in a week is :

	Jethamal	Kundanmal	Nainamal
Monday	9 a.m. - 12 noon	x	10 a.m. - 2 p.m.
Tuesday	x	12 noon - 4 p.m.	x
Wednesday	9 a.m. - 12 noon	x	x
Thursday	9 a.m. - 12 noon	12 noon - 4 p.m.	10 a.m. - 2 p.m.
Friday	2 p.m. - 4 p.m.	x	10 a.m. - 2 p.m.
Saturday	2 p.m. - 4 p.m.	x	x
Sunday	2 p.m. - 4 p.m.	12 noon - 4 p.m.	10 a.m. - 2 p.m.

37. (c) **38. (e)**

39. (c) :

Order in which the buses leave	*Leaving Time from Monday to Friday*	*Leaving Time on Saturday and Sunday*
P	8: a.m.	7:30 a.m.
N	8:45 a.m.	8:30 a.m.
R	9:15 a.m.	9:30 a.m.
M	10 a.m.	10:30 a.m.
Q	10:35 a.m.	11:30 a.m.
S	11:20 a.m.	12:30 p.m.
O	12 noon	1:30 p.m.

40. (a) : Bus P leaves at 7:30 a.m. and completes its four hours sight-seeing tour at 11:30 a.m. Bus Q begins its tour at 11:30 a.m.

41. (d) : Bus M leaves at 10:30 am. If time gap of 1 hr is increased by 30 minutes, bus Q will leave at 12 noon; bus S at 1:30 p.m. and bus O at 3 p.m. Bus O will complete its four hours tour at 7 p.m.

42. (*e*) : Bus N will leave at 8:45 a.m., R at 9:30 a.m., M at 10:15 a.m., Q at 11 a.m., S at 11:45 a.m, and O at 12:30 p.m. 4 hours before 12:30 p.m. is 8:30 a.m. No bus starts at 8:30 a.m.

43. (*c*) :

Timings on Monday to Friday and Sunday	*Timings on Saturday*	*The Order in which the Doctors visit*
9 am - 10 am	9 am - 9:30 am	Q
10 am - 11 am	9:30 am - 10 am	T or V
11 am - 12 noon	10 am - 10:30 am	S
12 noon - 1 pm	10:30 am - 11 am	T or V
(Lunch 1 pm - 2 pm)		
2 pm - 3 pm	11 am - 11:30 am	W
3 pm - 4 pm	11:30 am - 12 noon	R
4 pm - 5 pm	12 noon - 12:30 pm	P
5 pm - 6 pm	12:30 pm - 1 pm	U

44. (*e*)

45. (*d*) : The new lunch timings for the doctors will be :

Lunch	—	1 pm	-	1:45 pm
W	—	1:45 pm	-	2:30 pm
R	—	2:30 pm	-	3:15 pm
P	—	3:15 pm	-	4 pm
U	—	4 pm	-	4:45 pm

Doctor U will attend the dispensary at 4 pm.

ROWS AND RANKS

These type of problems need easy calculations to find out the number of objects in a row, lane or queue or to find a person's rank in a class of certain number of students; or to find the total number of students.

SOLVED EXAMPLES

1. In a row of trees, one tree is 8th from one end and 3rd from the other. How many trees are there in the row?

(*a*) 11 (*b*) 9 (*c*) 10 (*d*) 12 (*e*) None of these

Ans. (*c*) : The number of trees in the row are :

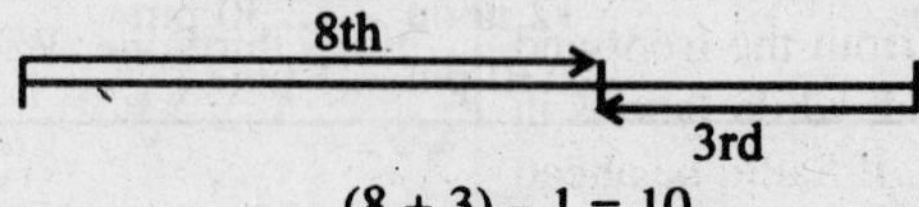

$(8 + 3) - 1 = 10$

2. If Janki is 12 ahead in rank of Pallavi who ranks 15th from last, then how many students are there in the class if Janki ranks 4th in order of merit?

(*a*) 23 (*b*) 27 (*c*) 31 (*d*) 33 (*e*) None of these

Ans. (*c*) : After calculations the answer will be :

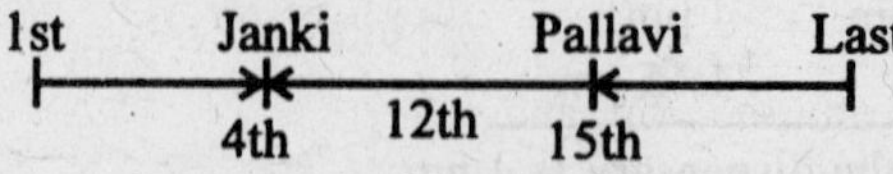

The total number of students are : $4 + 12 + 15 = 31$

EXERCISE

1. In a row of trees, one tree is fifth from either end of the row. How many trees are in the row?
(*a*) 11 (*b*) 8
(*c*) 10 (*d*) 9
(*e*) None of these

2. Jaya ranks 5th in a class of 53. What is her rank from the bottom in the class?
(*a*) 49th (*b*) 48th
(*c*) 47th (*d*) 50th
(*e*) None of these

3. Mohan ranks twenty-first in a class of sixty-five students. What will be his (Mohan's) rank if the lowest candidate is assigned rank 1?
(*a*) 44th (*b*) 45th
(*c*) 46th (*d*) Data inadequate
(*e*) None of these

4. If Rahul finds that he is 12th from the right in a line of boys and 4th from the left, how many boys should be added to the line such that there are 28 boys in the line?
(*a*) 12 (*b*) 14
(*c*) 20 (*d*) 13
(*e*) None of these

5. In a row of boys, Rajan is tenth from the right and Suraj is tenth from the left. When Rajan and Suraj interchange their positions, Suraj will be twenty-seventh from the left. Which of the following will be Rajan's position from the right?
(*a*) Tenth (*b*) Twenty-sixth
(*c*) Twenty-ninth (*d*) Twenty-fifth
(*e*) None of these

6. Mahesh and Suresh are ranked 11th and 12th respectively from the top in a class of 41

students. What will be their respective ranks from the bottom?
(*a*) 32nd and 33rd
(*b*) 29th and 30th
(*c*) 30th and 31st
(*d*) 31st and 30th
(*e*) None of these

7. Uma ranked 8th from the top and 37th from bottom in a class. How many students are there in the class?
(*a*) 47 (*b*) 46
(*c*) 45 (*d*) 48
(*e*) None of these

8. In a queue, Sadiq is 14th from the front and Joseph is 17th from the end, while Jane is in between Sadiq and Joseph. If Sadiq be ahead of Joseph and there be 48 persons in the queue, how many persons are there between Sadiq and Jane?
(*a*) 5 (*b*) 6
(*c*) 7 (*d*) 8
(*e*) None of these

9. Rohan ranked eleventh from the top and twenty-seventh from the bottom among the students who passed the annual examination in a class. If the number of students who failed in the examination was 12, how many students appeared for the examination?
(*a*) 48
(*b*) 49
(*c*) 50
(*d*) Cannot be determined
(*e*) None of these

10. Some boys are sitting in a row. P is sitting fourteenth from the left and Q is seventh from the right. If there are four boys between P and Q, how many boys are there in the row?
(*a*) 19 (*b*) 21
(*c*) 25 (*d*) 23
(*e*) None of these

11. There are five different houses, A to E, in a row. A is to the right of B and E is to the left of C and right of A, and B is to the right of D. Which of the houses is in the middle?
(*a*) B (*b*) A
(*c*) D (*d*) E
(*e*) None of these

12. Madhav ranks seventeenth in a class of thirtyone. What is his rank from the last?
(*a*) 13 (*b*) 14
(*c*) 15 (*d*) 16
(*e*) 17

13. Veena ranks 73rd from the top in a class of 182. What is her rank from the bottom if 22 students have failed the examination?
(*a*) 88 (*b*) 108
(*c*) 110 (*d*) 90
(*e*) 93

14. Rakesh ranked 9th from the top and 38th from the bottom in a class. How many students are there in the class?
(*a*) 47 (*b*) 45
(*c*) 46 (*d*) 48
(*e*) None of these

15. John ranks 19th in class and is 36th from the last. How many students are there in the class?
(*a*) 53 (*b*) 54
(*c*) 51 (*d*) 50
(*e*) None of these

EXPLANATORY ANSWERS

1. (*d*):

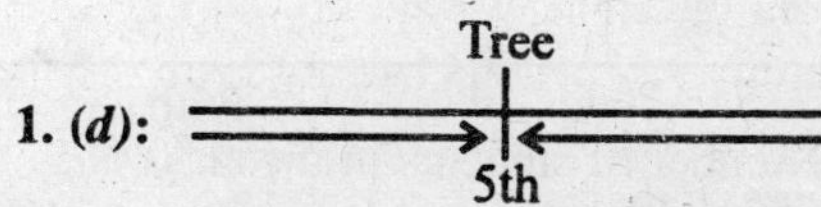

Total number of trees in the row are :
(5 + 5) – 1 = 9

2. (*a*):

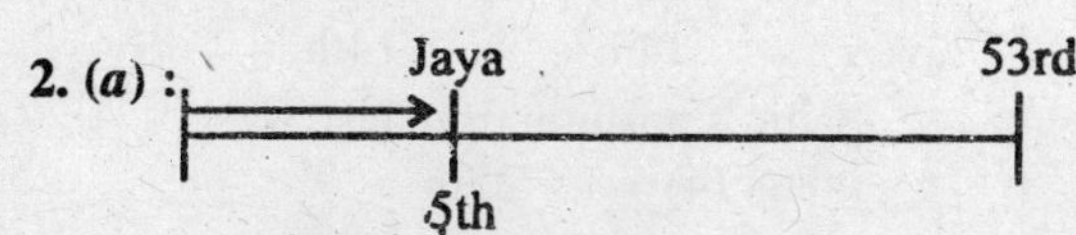

Jaya's rank from the bottom is :
(53 – 5) + 1 = 49th.

3. (*b*) : 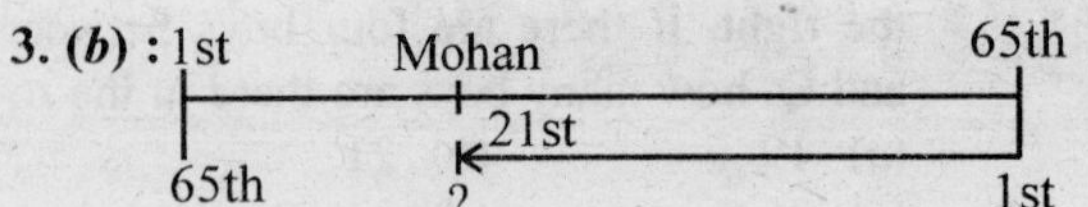

Note : Mohan's rank from the last or the question asked means the same.

Mohan's rank is (65 – 21) +1 = 45th

4. (*d*) : 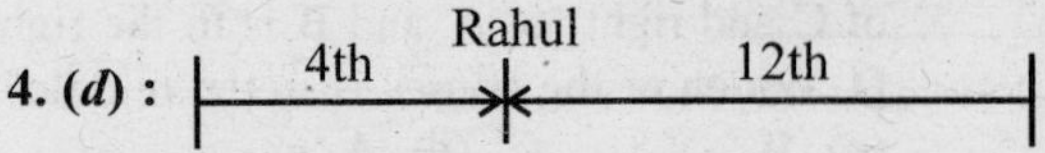

The number of boys in the line are :
(4 + 12) – 1 = 15
To make a line of 28 boys, (28 –15) *i.e.* 13 more boys are needed.

5. (*e*) : 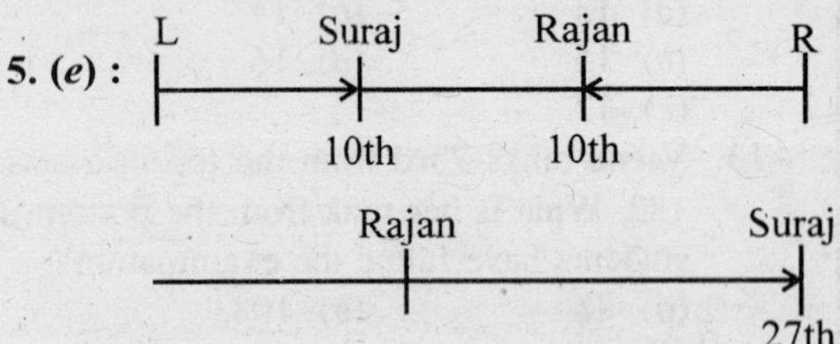

As the position of boys is equal from both ends, Rajan will also be 27th from the right after changing positions.

6. (*d*) : 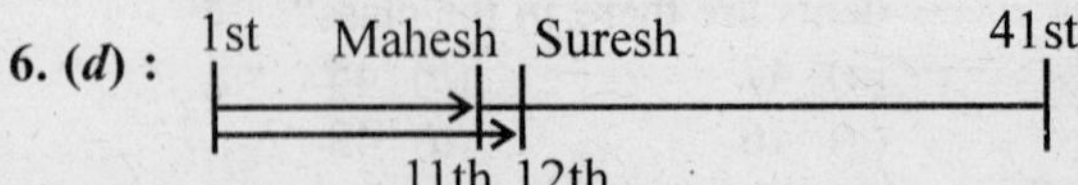

Mahesh's position from bottom is :
(41 – 11) + 1 = 31st
Suresh's position from bottom is :
(41 – 12) +1 = 30th

7. (*e*) : Uma — 8th → ← 37th

Total number of students in the class are :
(8 + 37) – 1 = 44

8. (*d*) : 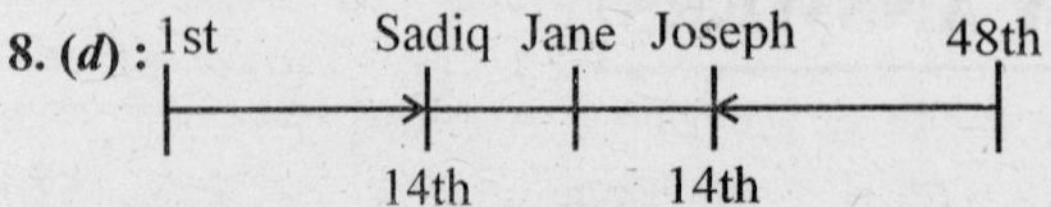

Sadiq's position from last is :
(48 – 14) + 1 = 35th
Number of persons between Sadiq and Joseph are (35 – 17) – 1 = 17
Jane is in-between Sadiq and Joseph *i.e.*, she's at 9th position from both the boys.
∴ there are 8 persons between Sadiq and Jane.

Note : (8 + 8) + 1 = 17

9. (*b*) : Rohan — 11th → ← 27th

Number of students who passed the examination (11+ 27) – 1 = 37
Those who failed = 12
Total number of students who appeared in the examination = 37 + 12 = 49.

10. (*c*) : P Q — 14th → 4 ← 7th

The number of boys in the row are :
(14 + 4 + 7) = 25

11. (*b*) : The houses in the row are :
D B A E C

12. (*c*) : 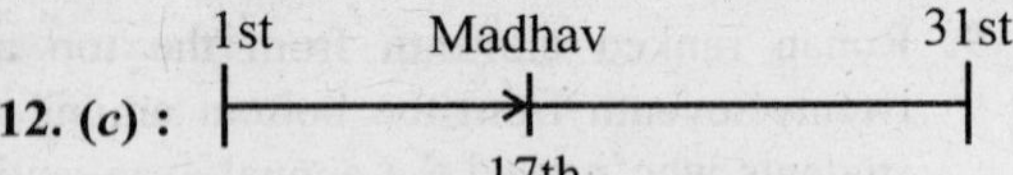

Madhav's rank from the last is :
(31 – 17) + 1 = 15th

13. (*a*) : 

Number of students who failed is 22.
Number of students who passed
= 182–22 = 160. So Veena's rank from the bottom will be : (160 – 73) + 1 = 88th

14. (*c*) : 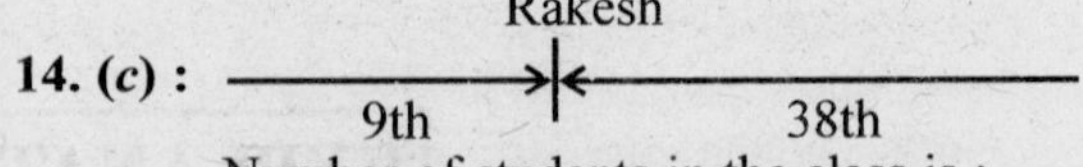

Number of students in the class is :
(9 + 38) – 1 = 46

15. (*b*) : John — 19th → ← 36th

Number of students in the class is :
(19 + 36) – 1 = 54

NUMBER PROBLEMS

Number problems consists of number sequences, problems with algebraic expressions, mathematical calculations and other compatiable problems.

SOLVED EXAMPLES

1. How many such 7s are there in the following number sequence which are immediately followed by 4 but not immediately preceded by 8?

5 4 7 8 9 7 4 3 8 7 5 7 4 8 7 4 1 2 7 4 5 7 9 4

(*a*) Two (*b*) Three (*c*) Four (*d*) Five (*e*) None of these

Ans. *(b)* : Number of 7s which are immediately followed by 4 but not immediately preceded by 8 are :

5 4 7 8 9 7 4 3 8 7 5 7 4 8 7 4 1 2 7 4 5 7 9 4

(underlined: "9 7 4" — 1; "5 7 4" — 2; "2 7 4" — 3)

2. A number is 9 times twice the other number. The sum of two numbers is 133. The two numbers are :

(*a*) 9, 124 (*b*) 11, 122 (*c*) 17, 166 (*d*) 7, 126 (*e*) 27, 136

Ans. *(d)* : If the smaller number is x, then

$$x + (2x \times 9) = 133$$
$$x + 18x = 133$$
$$19x = 133$$
$$x = 133 \div 19 = 7$$

If one number is 7, the other number is :

$$133 - 7 = 126$$

3. If all the numbers from 1 to 28 which are exactly divisible by 3 are arranged in descending order, which would come at the sixth place from the top?

(*a*) 12 (*b*) 21 (*c*) 15 (*d*) 18 (*e*) 24

Ans. *(a)* : The numbers divisible by 3 in descending order are : 27, 24, 21, 18, 15, 12, 9, 6, 3 and the number at the sixth place is 12.

EXERCISE

1. How many 6's are there in the following series of numbers which are preceded by 7 but not immediately followed by 9?

6 7 9 5 6 9 7 6 8 7 6 7 8 6 9 4 6 7 7 6 9 5 7 6 3

(*a*) One (*b*) Two
(*c*) Three (*d*) Four
(*e*) More than 4

2. In a chess tournament each of six players will play every other player exactly once. How many matches will be played during the tournament?

(*a*) 12 (*b*) 15
(*c*) 30 (*d*) 36
(*e*) 42

3. How many 4's are there in the following series which are preceded by 7, but are not preceded by 8?

3 4 5 7 4 3 7 4 8 5 4 3 7 4 9 8 4 7 2 7 4 1 3 6

(*a*) 1 (*b*) 2
(*c*) 3 (*d*) 4
(*e*) More than four

4. How many even numbers are there in the following series of numbers, each of which is immediately preceded by an odd number, but not immediately followed by an even number?

5 3 4 8 9 7 1 6 5 3 2 9 8 4 3 5

(*a*) Nil (*b*) 1

(*c*) 2 (*d*) 3
(*e*) None of these

5. If all the numbers from 1 to 51 which are exactly divisible by 3 are arranged in descending order, which of the following numbers will come at the seventh and tenth places from the top?
(*a*) 33 & 27 (*b*) 33 & 21
(*c*) 21 & 30 (*d*) 33 & 24
(*e*) 33 & 27

6. Nitin was counting down from 32. Shasank was counting upwards, the numbers starting from 1 and he was calling out only the odd numbers. Which common number will they call out at the same time if they were calling out at the same speed?
(*a*) 21 (*b*) 22
(*c*) 19
(*d*) They will not call out the same number
(*e*) None of these

7. In the following list of numerals, how many 3s are followed by 3, but NOT preceded by 3?
2 4 6 3 3 1 5 7 8 3 3 3 4 6 2 3 3 3 3 9 7 2 3
(*a*) 1 (*b*) 2
(*c*) 3 (*d*) 4
(*e*) None

8. If in a given number 5 8 9 4 3 2 7 6 1 4, we interchange the first and the second digits, the third and the fourth, the fifth and the sixth and so on, then counting from the right end, which digit will be sixth?
(*a*) 3 (*b*) 2
(*c*) 4 (*d*) 5
(*e*) None of these

9. Aparna cuts a cake into two halves and cuts one-half into smaller pieces of equal size. Each of the small pieces is twenty grams in weight. If she has seven pieces of the cake in all with her, how heavy was the original cake?
(*a*) 140 grams (*b*) 280 grams
(*c*) 240 grams (*d*) 120 grams
(*e*) None of these

10. In the following number sequence how many such even numbers are there which are exactly divisible by its immediate preceding number but not exactly divisible by its immediate following number?
3 8 4 1 5 7 2 8 3 4 8 9 3 9 4 2 1 5 8 2
(*a*) Two (*b*) Three
(*c*) Four (*d*) More than four
(*e*) One

11. How many 7s are there in the following series which are not immediately followed by 3 but immediately preceded by 8?
8 9 8 7 6 2 2 6 3 2 6 9 7 3 2 8 7 2 7 7 8 7 3 7 7 9 4
(*a*) Nil (*b*) One
(*c*) Two (*d*) Three
(*e*) More than three

12. How many 9's are there in the following sequence which are neither preceded by 6 nor immediately followed by 3?
9 3 8 6 9 9 5 9 3 7 8 9 9 9 3 9 6 3 9
(*a*) One (*b*) Two
(*c*) Three (*d*) Four
(*e*) None of these

13. If a number is five times as great as another number which is four less than forty, then the number is :
(*a*) 220 (*b*) 180
(*c*) 144 (*d*) 200
(*e*) 196

14. If 2/3rd of a number is 96, what will be the 3/4th of that number?
(*a*) 108 (*b*) 198
(*c*) 128 (*d*) 48
(*e*) 92

15. If such numbers which are divisible by 5, and also those which have 5 as one of the digits are eliminated from the numbers 1 to 60, how many numbers would remain?
(*a*) 53 (*b*) 47
(*c*) 40 (*d*) 45
(*e*) 50

16. How many 8's are there in the following number series which are exactly divisible by its immediately preceding and also exactly divisible by immediately succeeding numbers?
8 2 4 5 1 7 2 8 4 8 4 2 2 8 2 6 9 8 4 5 4 8 3 2 8 4 3 1 8 3
(*a*) 1 (*b*) 2
(*c*) 3 (*d*) 4

(*e*) None of these

17. Jagan was to either get one-seventh of a milk chocolate or one-fourteenth of a bigger fruit chocolate. Which chocolate would give him the larger piece if the fruit chocolate is three times as large as the milk chocolate?
(*a*) Milk chocolate
(*b*) Fruit chocolate
(*c*) The pieces will be of the same size
(*d*) Information inadequate
(*e*) None of these

18. How many such 3's are there in the following number sequence which are immediately preceded by an odd number and immediately followed by an even number?
5 3 8 9 4 3 7 2 3 8 1 3 8 4 2 3 5 7 3 4 2 3 6
(*a*) One (*b*) Two
(*c*) Three (*d*) Four
(*e*) More than four

19. Count each 7 which is not immediately preceded by 5 but is immediately followed by either 2 or 3. How many such 7's are there?
5 7 2 6 5 7 3 8 3 7 3 2 5 7 2 7 3 4 8 2 6 7 8
(*a*) 2 (*b*) 3
(*c*) 4 (*d*) 5
(*e*) Nil

20. A number is four less than two times the other number. If their difference is 21, what is the greater number?
(*a*) 50 (*b*) 46
(*c*) 31 (*d*) 21
(*e*) 15

21. Of the two digits number the total of the digits of the number is 6. If these digits are reversed there is an increasing difference of 18. What is the number?
(*a*) 12 (*b*) 24
(*c*) 42 (*d*) 36
(*e*) 33

22. Sony and Johnny caught 60 fishes. Sony caught four times as many as Johnny. How many fishes did Johnny catch?
(*a*) 12 (*b*) 16
(*c*) 34 (*d*) 38
(*e*) 42

23. 10 years ago Neha's mother was 4 times older than Neha. After 10 years Neha's mother will be twice Neha's age. How old is Neha now?
(*a*) 10 years (*b*) 15 years
(*c*) 17 years (*d*) 20 years
(*e*) 23 years

24. The sum of two consecutive numbers is 87. Which is the larger number?
(*a*) 42 (*b*) 43
(*c*) 44 (*d*) 45
(*e*) 46

25. How many numbers from 11 to 50 are there which are exactly divisible by 7 but not by 3?
(*a*) 2 (*b*) 4
(*c*) 5 (*d*) 6
(*e*) 7

26. How many 3's are there in the following sequence which are neither preceded by 6 nor immediately followed by 9?
9 3 6 6 3 9 5 9 3 7 8 9 7 6 3 9 6 3 9
(*a*) One (*b*) Two
(*c*) Three (*d*) Four
(*e*) None of these

27. How many 7's are there in the following series which are preceded by 6 which is not preceded by 8?
8 7 6 7 8 6 7 5 6 7 9 8 6 1 6 7 7 6 8 8 6 9 7 6 8 7
(*a*) 2 (*b*) 3
(*c*) 4 (*d*) Only 1
(*e*) Nil

28. If the odd numbers between 20 to 40 are arranged in a row, what will be the 6th number from the right?
(*a*) 27 (*b*) 31
(*c*) 33 (*d*) 25
(*e*) 29

29. How many numbers from 1 to 50 will be left out if the numbers which are exactly divisible by 7 and having 7 as one of the digits are removed?
(*a*) 43 (*b*) 30
(*c*) 42 (*d*) 39
(*e*) 37

30. How many numbers are there between 1 to 100 which are divisible by 9 and the sum of whose digits is 9?
(*a*) 13 (*b*) 11

(c) 7 (d) 9
(e) 10

31. How many numbers are there between 20 and 60 which are divisible by 3 and the total of two digits is 9?
(a) 4 (b) 3
(c) 2 (d) 1
(e) More than 4

32. The sum of odd numbers between 20 and 30 is :
(a) 105 (b) 120
(c) 125 (d) 140
(e) 145

33. If such numbers which are divisible by 7 and also those which have 7 as one of the digits are eliminated from the numbers 5 to 50, how many numbers would remain?
(a) 34 (b) 35
(c) 36 (d) 37
(e) 39

34. My age is two years more than twice that of Ram. If I am 34 years old, how old is Ram?
(a) 20 (b) 18
(c) 16 (d) 14
(e) 12

Directions (Qs. 35 to 37) : *Study the following number sequence and answer the questions given below it :*

5 1 4 7 3 9 8 5 7 2 6 3 1
5 8 6 3 8 5 2 2 4 3 4 9 6

35. How many odd numbers are there in the sequence which are immediately preceded and also immediately followed by an even number?
(a) 1 (b) 2
(c) 3 (d) 4
(e) More than 4

36. How many odd numbers are there in the sequence which are immediately followed by an odd number?
(a) 1 (b) 2
(c) 3 (d) 4
(e) More than 4

37. How many even numbers are there in the sequence which are immediately preceded by an odd number but immediately followed by an even number?
(a) 1 (b) 2
(c) 3 (d) 4
(e) More than 4

38. How many numbers amongst the numbers 7 to 41 are there which are exactly divisible by 9 but not by 3?
(a) Nil (b) 1
(c) 2 (d) 3
(e) More than 3

39. In the series given below, how many even numbers are immediately preceded by 6 as well as immediately followed by 3?
6 6 5 6 8 3 9 4 3 6 7 3 6 4 3 2 8 6 4 6 8 2 6 6 3
(a) 1 (b) 2
(c) 3 (d) 4
(e) More than 4

40. The sum of odd numbers between 0 and 10 is :
(a) 15 (b) 20
(c) 25 (d) 30
(e) 35

41. In a certain match all the teams were to play with each other. If there are 10 teams, how many matches will have to be played?
(a) 30 (b) 45
(c) 60 (d) 90
(e) None of the above

42. How many repeat sequence of three consecutive numbers are there in the given sequence?
6 9 6 2 4 2 9 6 2 9 2 6 9 4 9 6 2 6 9 2 4
(a) 3 (b) 2
(c) 1 (d) 4
(e) None of these

43. How many numbers are immediately preceded and immediately followed by different numbers?
7 7 7 5 7 5 7 5 7 7 7 7 5 7 5 7 5 7 7 7 7 7 5 7 5
(a) 2 (b) 3
(c) 4 (d) 5
(e) 1

44. How many 8's are there in the given sequence which are not immediately preceded by 09 and not immediately followed by 90?
9 0 8 0 9 0 9 8 9 0 8 9 0 8 0 9 8 9 0 9 8 0 9 8
9 0 8 9 0
(a) 1 (b) 2

(*c*) 3 (*d*) More than 3
(*e*) None of these

45. Which pair of numbers has least and maximum frequency in the given sequence?
8 7 5 6 4 5 8 3 8 6 7 2 3 5 8 3 5 7 6 4 7 6 5
(*a*) 4 and 5 (*b*) 2 and 6
(*c*) 3 and 8 (*d*) 2 and 5
(*e*) None of these

46. Number of Prime numbers between 30 and 50 is :
(*a*) 4 (*b*) 5
(*c*) 6 (*d*) 7
(*e*) 9

47. Which is the middle even number between 9 and 23?
(*a*) 14 (*b*) 16
(*c*) 18 (*d*) 20
(*e*) 22

48. A number which is divided by 9 gives 15 as quotient and 3 as remainder. Find that number.
(*a*) 205 (*b*) 108
(*c*) 138 (*d*) 132
(*e*) None of these

49. A number is four less than six times the other number. If the sum of both the numbers is 38, what are the numbers?
(*a*) 6, 32 (*b*) 7, 31
(*c*) 5, 33 (*d*) 4, 34
(*e*) None of these

50. The sum of two numbers is 99. If the two digits of a number are interchanged, the difference between the two numbers is 9. What is the larger number?
(*a*) 54 (*b*) 63
(*c*) 72 (*d*) 78
(*e*) 85

51. A student got twice as many sums wrong as he got right. If he attempted 48 sums in all, how many did he solve correctly?
(*a*) 9 (*b*) 12
(*c*) 18 (*d*) 24
(*e*) 16

52. The average age of 5 persons is 40 years while the average age of some other 10 persons is 25 years. The average age of all the 15 persons is :
(*a*) 27 years (*b*) 32 years
(*c*) 37 years (*d*) 30 years
(*e*) 35 years

53. A, B, C, D and E play a game of cards. A says to B, "If you give me three cards, you will have as many as E has and if I give you three cards, you will have as many as D has." A and B together have 10 cards more than what D and E together have. If B has two cards more than what C has and the total number of cards be 133, how many cards does B have?
(*a*) 35 (*b*) 25
(*c*) 23 (*d*) 22

54. When I was born, my mother was 23 years of age. After 6 years, when my sister was born, my father was 34 years of age. What is the difference between the ages of my parents?
(*a*) 5 years (*b*) 6 years
(*c*) 11 years (*d*) 17 years
(*e*) None of these

55. A father tells his son, "I was of your present age when you were born." If the father is 36 now, how old was the boy 5 years back?
(*a*) 15 years (*b*) 13 years
(*c*) 17 years (*d*) 20 years

EXPLANATORY ANSWERS

1. (*c*) : $6\,7\,9\,5\,6\,9\,\underset{1}{\underline{7\,6\,8}}\,\underset{2}{\underline{7\,6\,7}}\,8\,6\,9\,4\,6\,7\,7\,6\,9\,5\,\underset{3}{\underline{7\,6\,3}}$

2. (*b*) : When all the players have to play with each other then the method of calculating the number of matches to be played is $\frac{n(n-1)}{2}$ where '*n*' is the number of players playing the match. So, the number of matches played will be :
$(6 \times 5) \div 2 = 30 \div 2 = 15$

3. (*d*) : $3\,4\,5\,\underset{1}{\underline{7\,4}}\,3\,\underset{2}{\underline{7\,4}}\,8\,5\,4\,3\,\underset{3}{\underline{7\,4}}\,9\,8\,4\,7\,2\,\underset{4}{\underline{7\,4}}\,1\,3\,6$

4. (*c*) : $5\,3\,4\,8\,9\,7\,\underset{1}{\underline{1\,6\,5}}\,\underset{2}{\underline{3\,2\,9}}\,8\,4\,3\,5$

5. (*d*) : The numbers divisible by 3 in descending order are :

51, 48, 45, 42, 39, 36, $\underset{7th}{\underline{33}}$, 30, 27, $\underset{10th}{\underline{24}}$, 21, 18, 15, 12, 9, 6, 3.

6. (*d*) : When Nitin is on count 22, Shasank is on 21 and when Nitin is on count 21, Shasank is on 23.

7. (*c*) : 2 4 6 3 3 1 5 7 8 3 3 3 4 6 2 3 3 3 3 9 7 2 3 (1, 2, 3 marked)

8. (*b*) : The new number after interchanging the digits is :
8 5 4 9 2 3 6 7 4 1
6th

9. (*c*) : There is one bigger piece and six smaller pieces. One small piece weighs 20 gm. Total weight of six smaller speices is 120 gm.
∴ Weight of the bigger piece = 120 gm
∴ Weight of the original cake = 240 gm

10. (*a*) : 3 8 4 1 5 7 2 8 3 4 8 9 3 9 4 2 1 5 8 2 (1, 2 marked)

11. (*c*) : 898762263269732872778737794 (1, 2 marked)

12. (*d*) : 9 3 8 6 9 9 5 9 3 7 8 9 9 9 3 9 6 3 9 (1, 2, 3, 4 marked)

13. (*b*) : Number four less than forty is 40 – 4 = 36
Five times the number is = 36 × 5 =180

14. (*a*) : If the number is x, then

$$\frac{2}{3}x = 96$$

$$x = \frac{96 \times 3}{2} = 144$$

$\frac{3}{4}$ th of the number is $144 \times \frac{3}{4} = 108$

15. (*c*) : The eliminated twenty numbers are : 5, 10, 15, 20, 25, 30, 35, 40, 45 and 50 to 60. The remaining numbers are 60 – 20 = 40.

16. (*d*) : 8 2 4 5 1 7 2 8 4 8 4 2 2 8 2 6 9 8 4 5 4 8 3 2 8 4 3 1 8 3 (1, 2, 3, 4 marked)

17. (*b*) : If fruit chocolate (F) is equal to three times as milk chocolate (M) then —

$$F = 3M$$

or $$\frac{F}{M} = 3$$

$$\therefore \frac{1/14\ F}{1/7\ M} = \frac{3/14}{1/7}$$

When 3/14 > 1/7, then F (Fruit chocolate) will give him the larger piece.

18. (*c*) : 5 3 8 9 4 3 7 2 3 8 1 3 8 4 2 3 5 7 3 4 2 3 6 (1, 2, 3 marked)

19. (*a*) : 5 7 2 6 5 7 3 8 3 7 3 2 5 7 2 7 3 4 8 2 6 7 8 (1, 2 marked)

20. (*b*) : If smaller number is x, then

$$(2x – 4) – x = 21$$
$$2x – x = 21 + 4$$
$$x = 25$$

The greater number is

$$(25 \times 2) – 4 = 46$$

21. (*b*) : If the digit at the unit is x and at the tens is y, then

$$(10x + y) – (10y – x) = 18$$
$$9(x – y) = 18$$

i.e. $x – y = 2$
What is given is $x + y = 6$
What is obtained is $x – y = 2$
$2x = 8$

Now $x = 8/2$ *i.e.,* $x = 4$
Then $y = 6 – 4 = 2$
So, the number is 24.

22. (*a*) : Out of 5 fishes Sony caught 4 and Johnny 1. Out of 60 Sony caught $\frac{60}{5} \times 4 = 48$ fishes and Johnny caught $\frac{60}{5} \times 1 = 12$ fishes

23. (*d*) : If Neha's age be x, ten years ago her age was $x – 10$ and her mother's age $4(x – 10)$. After ten years Neha's age will be $x + 10$ and her mother's age $4(x – 10) + 20$ or $2(x + 10)$

$$\therefore 4(x – 10) + 20 = 2(x + 10)$$
$$4x – 40 + 20 = 2x + 20$$
$$4x – 2x = 20 + 20$$
$$2x = 40$$
$$x = \frac{40}{2} = 20 \text{ years}$$

24. (*c*) : If the smaller number is x, then

$$x + (x + 1) = 87$$
$$2x + 1 = 87$$
$$2x = 86$$
$$x = 86/2 = 43$$

The larger number is $x + 1$ or $43 + 1$ *i.e.,* 44.

25. (*b*) : The numbers divisible by 7 but not by 3 are :
14, 28, 35, 49

26. (*b*) : 9 3 6 6 3 9 5 9 3 7 8 9 7 6 3 9 6 3 9
(1, 2)

27. (*b*) : 8767867567986167768869 7687
(1, 2, 3)

28. (*e*) : 21, 23, 25, 27, 29, 31, 33, 35, 37, 39
↑ 6th

29. (*d*) : The eleven numbers removed are—7, 14, 17, 21, 27, 28, 35, 37, 42, 47, 49. The remaining numbers are 50 – 11 = 39

30. (*e*) : The numbers divisible by 9 and having sum of digits as 9 are— 9, 18, 27, 36, 45, 54, 63, 72, 81, 90

31. (*a*) : The numbers divisible by 3 and having 9 as the total of their digits are :
27, 36, 45, 54

32. (*c*) : 21 + 23 + 25 + 27 + 29 = 125

33. (*b*) : The eleven numbers eliminated are —
7, 14, 17, 21, 27, 28, 35, 37, 42, 47, 49
The remaining numbers are 46 – 11 = 35

34. (*c*) : If the age of Ram is x, then
$$2x + 2 = 34$$
$$2x = 32$$
$$x = 32/2 = 16 \text{ years.}$$

35. (*d*) : 51473985726315863852243496
(1 2 3 4)

36. (*e*) : 51473985726315863852243496
(1 2 3 4 5 6 7)

37. (*c*) : 51473985726315863852243496
(1 2 3)

38. (*a*) : Number divisible by 9 is also divisible by 3.

39. (*c*) : 665683943673643286468 2663
(1 2 3)

40. (*c*) : 1 + 3 + 5 + 7 + 9 = 25

41. (*b*) : The number of matches played will be —
(10 × 9) ÷ 2 = 90 ÷ 2 = 45

42. (*a*) : 6 9 6 2 4 2 9 6 2 9 2 6 9 4 9 6 2 6 9 2 4
(1 2 3)

43. (*d*) : 7 7 7 5 7 5 7 5 7 7 7 7 5 7 5 7 5 7 7 7 7 7 5 7 5
(1 2 3 4 5)

44. (*b*) : 9080909890890809890980989 0890
(1 2)

45. (*d*) : 2 appears only once and 5 appears five times
8 7 5 6 4 5 8 3 8 6 7 2 3 5 8 3 5 7 6 4 7 6 5
(1 2 1 3 4 5)

46. (*b*) : The prime numbers are—31, 37, 41, 43, 47

47. (*b*) : The even numbers between 9 and 23 are : 10, 12, 14, 16, 18, 20, 22 and the middle even number is 16.

48. (*c*) : The method for calculating the number will be :
(Divisor × Quotient) + Remainder = Number
∴ (9 × 15) + 3 = 135 + 3 = 138

49. (*a*) : If one number is x, then
$$x + (6x - 4) = 38$$
$$7x = 38 + 4$$
$$\therefore \quad x = 42/7 = 6$$
The other number is (6 × 6) – 4 = 36 – 4 = 32.

50. (*a*) : If one number is x and the other number is y, then
$$x + y = 99$$
$$x - y = 9$$
$$2x = 108$$
$$x = 108/2 = 54$$
$$y = 99 - 54 = 45$$
The two numbers are 45 and 54 of which the later is the larger number.

51. (*e*) : If the number of wrong sums be 'x' and the number of right sums be 'y' then
$$x = 2y$$
or $$-x + 2y = 0$$
Also, $$x + y = 48$$
$$3y = 48$$
$$\therefore \quad y = 16 \text{ sums}$$

52. (*d*) : Total of the ages of 5 persons is
5 × 40 = 200
Total of the ages of 10 persons is
10 × 25 = 250
Total of the ages of above 15 persons is

450 and their average age is 450/15 = 30 years

53. (*b*) : As per given information :

(1) B – 3 = E

(2) B + 3 = D

(3) A + B = D + E + 10

(4) B + 2 = C

(5) Total number of cards

i.e. A+B+C+D+E = 133

(6) According to (1) and (2) : B – 3 = E

B + 3 = D

2 B = D + E

(7) According to (3) and (6) A + B = D + E + 10

or A + B = 2 B + 10

i.e. A = B + 10

Now, Substituting (4), (6) and (7) in (5) we get the expression :

(B+10) + B + (B – 2) + 2B = 133

So, 5 B + 8 = 133

5 B = 133 – 8

B = 125/5 = 25

∴ B has 25 cards

54. (*a*) : Mother's age when I was born = 23 years

Father's age when sister was born = 34 years

Father's age when I was born = 34 – 6 = 28 years

Difference between the ages of my parents = 28 – 23 = 5 years

55. (*b*) : If boy's present age is 'x' then father's age when the boy was born is also 'x'.

So, $x + x = 36$

$2x = 36$

$x = 36/2 = 18$

5 year's back the boy was 18 – 5 = 13 years old.

COMMON PROPERTY

In this type of test the questions contain either numbers or words or letters which have a common property. From the given set of options the candidate has to select the one which bears the same property.

SOLVED EXAMPLES

1. Which set of numbers is like the given set?
(48, 24, 12)
(*a*) (46, 22, 11) (*b*) (44, 22, 10) (*c*) (42, 20, 10) (*d*) (40, 20, 10)
Ans. (*d*) : Half of 1st number is the next number.
$48 \div 2 = 24; 24 \div 2 = 12$
Similarly
$40 \div 2 = 20; 20 \div 2 = 10$

2. Which of the following is equivalent of Canada, Chile and Germany?
(*a*) Ottawa (*b*) Chicago (*c*) Paris (*d*) Singapore
Ans. (*d*) : Canada, Chile and Germany are countries and so is Singapore.

3. Which set of letter is like the given set?
HS, NC, TO
(*a*) WY (*b*) LU (*c*) ZA (*d*) CK
Ans. (*b*) : Of the two letters, the first is made up of straight lines and the second by curved line.

4. What is common among Saraswati, Ganga and Cauvery?
(*a*) Dams (*b*) Towns (*c*) Rivers (*d*) Movies
Ans. (*c*) : All three are rivers.

EXERCISE

1. Out of the given alternatives, choose the one that belongs to the given number group.
Given number group : (49, 25, 9)
(*a*) (39, 26, 13) (*b*) (36, 16, 4)
(*c*) (64, 27, 8) (*d*) (36, 25, 16

2. Which one number is like the given number set : (363, 489, 579)?
(*a*) 281 (*b*) 382
(*c*) 471 (*d*) 562

3. To which class do kerosene, petrol and diesel belong?
(*a*) Coal (*b*) Fuel
(*c*) Firewood (*d*) Engine

4. To which class do Mercury, Venus and Saturn belong?
(*a*) Planet (*b*) Jupiter
(*c*) Earth (*d*) Mars

5. Which set of numbers has the same property as the following numbers?
21, 38, 55
(*a*) 47, 64, 80 (*b*) 19, 36, 55
(*c*) 23, 40, 57 (*d*) 35, 62, 79

6. Which one is like tender, soft and fragile?
(*a*) Surplus (*b*) Sensitive
(*c*) Catchy (*d*) Honest

7. Which one is like school, college and institute?
(*a*) House (*b*) University
(*c*) Planetarium (*d*) Stadium

8. Which set of numbers is like the given number set : 1050, 210, 42?
(*a*) 75, 15, 3 (*b*) 60, 12, 2
(*c*) 125, 25, 6 (*d*) 95, 19, 3

9. Which set of letters is like the given letter

set : B, F, J ?
(*a*) M, Q, U (*b*) S, W, Z
(*c*) R, U, Y (*d*) D, G, K

10. Which set of numbers is like the given number set : 7, 77, 847?
(*a*) 9, 99, 989 (*b*) 1, 11, 131
(*c*) 6, 66, 726 (*d*) 8, 8, 948

11. Which one is like mother, sister and niece?
(*a*) Nephew (*b*) Guardian
(*c*) Father (*d*) Aunt

12. Which of the following has the same property as DFH, RTV, JLN, VXZ?
(*a*) ACD (*b*) NPQ
(*c*) CFI (*d*) OQS

13. Which of the following has the same property as RnTz, FnjK, BTbs, tfNL?
(*a*) FGhI (*b*) rRQd
(*c*) NOqB (*d*) GgTJ

14. What is common among eagle, bat and owl?
(*a*) Country Emblems
(*b*) Birds
(*c*) Pets
(*d*) None of these

15. Which one is like pear, plum and mango?
(*a*) Tree (*b*) Lady finger
(*c*) Guava (*d*) Cabbage

16. Which one is like car, aeroplane and truck?
(*a*) Bus (*b*) Ox-cart
(*c*) Roadways (*d*) All the above

17. Which set of numbers is like the given set : 53, 40, 27?
(*a*) 58, 27, 18 (*b*) 77, 63, 50
(*c*) 93, 80, 67 (*d*) 39, 26, 13

18. Which of the following words have same characteristics as Cap, Hat and Turban?
(*a*) Hair (*b*) Helmet
(*c*) Safety (*d*) Umbrella

19. Which set of letters is like the given set : WVU, EDC, LKJ?
(*a*) GHF (*b*) BAZ
(*c*) PON (*d*) WUT

20. Which number has the same property as the given numbers : 637, 399, 784?
(*a*) 161 (*b*) 535
(*c*) 493 (*d*) 257

EXPLANATORY ANSWERS

1. (*b*) : The numbers are squares of alternate numbers. $7^2 = 49$, $5^2 = 25$, $3^2 = 9$. Similarly, $6^2 = 36$, $4^2 = 16$, $2^2 = 4$.

2. (*c*) : The numbers are divisible by 3.

3. (*b*) : All three are fuel.

4. (*a*) : All three are planets.

5. (*c*) : The difference between the numbers is 17, *i.e.*, 21 + 17 = 38; 38 + 17 = 55. Similarly, 23 + 17 = 40; 40 + 17 = 57.

6. (*b*) : All three indicate delicacy, so does the word sensitive.

7. (*b*) : All three are places of education, so is University.

8. (*a*) : The number divided by 5 is the next number, *i.e.*, 1050 ÷ 5 = 210; 210 ÷ 5 = 42. Similarly 75 ÷ 5 = 15; 15 ÷ 5 = 3.

9. (*a*) : The difference between two adjacent letters in the question is increased as + 4, *i.e.*,
B F J; Similarly M Q U
+4 +4 +4 +4

10. (*c*) : The numbers are multiples of 11, *i.e.*, 7 × 11 = 77; 77 × 11 = 847. Similarly 6 × 11 = 66; 66 × 11 = 726.

11. (*d*) : All three are female genders and so is Aunt.

12. (*d*) : The letters are alternate. They skip one letter in-between.

13. (*b*) : Two letters are capital, two are small.

14. (*b*) : All three are birds.

15. (*c*) : All three are fruits and so is Guava.

16. (*a*) : All three run on petrol and so does the bus.

17. (*d*) : The difference between the numbers is 13 *i.e.* 53 – 13 = 40; 40 – 13 = 27. Similarly 39 – 13 = 26; 26 – 13 = 13.

18. (*b*) : All three are worn on the head and so is helmet.

19. (*c*) : The letters are in reverse consecutive order.

20. (*a*) : The numbers are divisible by 7.

PERMUTATIONS AND COMBINATIONS

In these type of questions the only factor essential is alertness. In every question a word is given. By using the letters of this given word the options are formed. The candidates are required to find from the given options the word *(i)* which cannot be formed by using the letters of the given word or *(ii)* which can be formed by using the letters of the given word.

SOLVED EXAMPLES

1. Find out the one word among the options which cannot be formed by using the letters of the word given.
MATURITY
(a) MART *(b)* TRAY *(c)* TRUE *(d)* TRAM
Ans. Option '*c*' has the word formed also by using the letter 'E' which is not used in the word MATURITY.

2. Find out the one word among the options which can be formed by using the letters of the word REASONABLE.
(a) STONE *(b)* LONER *(c)* BRACE *(d)* OPERA
Ans. Option '*b*' alone is formed by using the letters in the word given. From other options letters 'T', 'C' and 'P' are new.

EXERCISE

Directions : *Find out the one word among the options which cannot be formed by using the letters of the word as given in each question.*

1. ROTATION
(a) TORN *(b)* NOTE
(c) TART *(d)* RAIN

2. PHILOSOPHY
(a) SOIL *(b)* SHIP
(c) SOLO *(d)* SPIN

3. SLAVATION
(a) SNORT *(b)* LATVIA
(c) SALIVA *(d)* AVAIL

4. ACADEMY
(a) DEMY *(b)* MACE
(c) DIRE *(d)* MADE

5. INCOGNITO
(a) GOING *(b)* INACTION
(c) IGNITION *(d)* TONGO

6. JUDICIARY
(a) INJURY *(b)* CADDY
(c) DICY *(d)* ACRID

7. DOCTRINE
(a) CRUST *(b)* DOCTOR
(c) TIRED *(d)* CREED

8. EDUCATED
(a) DATE *(b)* CUTE
(c) EAST *(d)* DUCT

9. INSUFFICIENT
(a) ENTICE *(b)* SCENT
(c) SUFFICE *(d)* THENCE

10. DECEMBER
(a) REDEEM *(b)* DECREE
(c) BRACED *(d)* MEMBER

11. FUGITIVE
(a) EXIT *(b)* FIVE
(c) GIVE *(d)* GIFT

12. CATASTROPHE
(a) TASTE *(b)* CHEAP
(c) POUCH *(d)* STARE

13. TORRENTIAL
(a) TRAIL *(b)* MENTAL
(c) LEARN *(d)* RETAIL

14. INFRASTRUCTURE
(a) RAPTURE *(b)* INSECURE
(c) CRAFTS *(d)* STRUCTURE

15. RECOMMEND
(a) MEND (b) ROME
(c) CANE (d) OMEN

16. MISCREANTS
(a) SCREAM (b) CRIME
(c) ASCENT (d) MIRAGE

17. CREDENTIAL
(a) CREATE (b) DENTAL
(c) TENDRIL (d) LOITER

18. MASTERPIECE
(a) MINCE (b) TRAMP
(c) PESTER (d) SPRITE

19. PERFECTIONIST
(a) OFTEN (b) CARTON
(c) STINT (d) ENTER

20. VAGABOND
(a) BOND (b) DONG
(c) VAIN (d) AVON

21. SUPERANNUATE
(a) NATURE (b) PRANT
(c) TRENDS (d) SENNATE

22. DIFFERENTIAL
(a) LITER (b) FARCE
(c) DRAIN (d) TIRED

23. BENEVOLENT
(a) BELT (b) OVAL
(c) EVEN (d) LOBE

24. WITHSTAND
(a) THIRD (b) THAWS
(c) STAND (d) STAIN

25. YEOMAN
(a) MANY (b) OMEN
(c) NAME (d) YAWN

26. DICTATORSHIP
(a) SHORT (b) CRASH
(c) TERSE (d) PORCH

27. RELUCTANT
(a) REGLANT (b) CULTURE
(c) TREAT (d) CREATE

28. TUBERCULOSIS
(a) TUMBLES (b) SUCROSE
(c) CLUSTER (d) ORBITS

29. JUXTAPOSE
(a) TAXES (b) PASTE
(c) TEASE (d) JOIST

30. MANIPULATION
(a) MANUAL (b) NATION
(c) IMPLANT (d) PANEL

31. BILLIONAIRE
(a) BLARE (b) BANGO
(c) BORNE (d) BRAIN

32. TENACIOUS
(a) ENACT (b) SCENT
(c) TRAIN (d) COAST

33. ANTIQUATED
(a) QUIET (b) ANTIQUE
(c) ACQUIT (d) EQUATE

34. INTERROGATE
(a) ORANGE (b) GREATER
(c) RINGER (d) TEASING

35. HABITATION
(a) HABIT (b) ACTION
(c) THAN (d) BOTH

36. AUTOMATICALLY
(a) CALAMITY (b) LACUNA
(c) TOMATO (d) MALTA

37. CARPENTER
(a) CARPET (b) PAINTER
(c) REPENT (d) NECTAR

38. MIRACULOUS
(a) LOCUS (b) SCAR
(c) SOLACE (d) MOLAR

39. PROGNOSTICATION
(a) RONTGEN (b) SPITOON
(c) ROGATION (d) START

40. TRANSLOCATION
(a) START (b) COAL
(c) TRACTOR (d) TALCUM

41. DISSEMINATION
(a) INDIA (b) NATIONS
(c) MENTION (d) ACTION

42. COMMENTATOR
(a) COMMON (b) MOMENT
(c) COSMOS (d) TART

43. PHARMACEUTICAL
(a) RHEUMATIC (b) CRITICAL
(c) PRACTICE (d) METRIC

44. CHOREOGRAPHY
(a) GEOGRAPHY
(b) GRAPH
(c) PHOTOGRAPHY
(d) OGRE

45. PARAPHERNALIA
(a) RENAL (b) PRAISE

(c) PENAL (d) PEAR

46. ADAPTABILITY
(a) ABILITY (b) DATA
(c) PALATE (d) PITY

47. COMPETITION
(a) TOTEM (b) POETIC
(c) COMPOSE (d) OPINE

48. OBSTETRICIAN
(a) SIREN (b) RETAIN
(c) TERMITE (d) SOBER

49. DEVELOPMENT
(a) PEDANT (b) ENVELOPE
(c) VOLTE (d) ELOPE

50. CARDIOGRAM
(a) AEROGRAM (b) RADIO
(c) DIAGRAM (d) CARGO

51. EQUIVOCATION
(a) VOCATION (b) LOCATION
(c) EQUATION (d) VATICAN

52. PORTFOLIO
(a) FORT (b) TROOP
(c) POLIO (d) FRAIL

53. APPORTIONMENT
(a) METEOR (b) APPOINT
(c) PROBATION (d) PEPPERMINT

54. HINDERLAND
(a) DANCER (b) HERALD
(c) HINDER (d) INLAND

55. PENTSTEMON
(a) STONE (b) TENET
(c) PISTON (d) MENSE

56. BOISTEROUS
(a) STEREO (b) SHOUT
(c) BOOSTER (d) TRESS

57. DISSOPPOINTMENT
(a) TENAMENT (b) OPPOSE
(c) OINTMENT (d) POSITION

58. TABERANACLE
(a) BRACE (b) CARNIVAL
(c) CATER (d) TRANCE

59. KALEIDOSCOPE
(a) CLASP (b) PRICK
(c) SCOOP (d) CLOCK

60. ELECTRIFYING
(a) FRYING (b) ENGINE
(c) ENIGMA (d) RECTIFY

61. BATHYGRAPHICAL
(a) PARAGRAPH (b) PHYLLARY
(c) TYPICAL (d) THEORETICAL

62. SUBORDINATE
(a) BOARD (b) SUBMIT
(c) URBANE (d) NATURE

63. GORGEOUS
(a) SOUR (b) ROAR
(c) URGE (d) EROS

64. ECONOMICALLY
(a) COMICAL (b) ECONOMY
(c) AMORAL (d) ALIMONY

65. HEMOGLOBIN
(a) NIMBLE (b) GLOBIN
(c) BELONG (d) MOVING

66. DOCUMENTATION
(a) ACUMEN (b) DONATE
(c) MENTAL (d) COUNT

67. WHOLESOME
(a) SHOVE (b) WHEEL
(c) LOOSE (d) HOLES

68. IMPORTANT
(a) TRUMP (b) IMPART
(c) PRINT (d) TRAIN

69. YIELDING
(a) GLIDE (b) INLAY
(c) YELL (d) DENY

70. PROPAGATE
(a) PRATE (b) PAGER
(c) GRAFT (d) AGATE

71. RATIONALLY
(a) LATER (b) RATION
(c) TRAIL (d) ORALLY

72. COMPROMISING
(a) GRAIN (b) COMING
(c) PRISM (d) SPOON

73. GRIEVANCE
(a) AVENGE (b) ENDURE
(c) GRIEVE (d) CAVERN

74. DEMONSTRATE
(a) STREAM (b) MODERN
(c) EASTER (d) RATTLE

75. INEXPENSIVE
(a) EXPENSE (b) NEXUS
(c) PENSIVE (d) VIXEN

Directions : *Find out the one word among the options which can be formed by using the letters of the word as given in each question.*

76. INVESTIGATE
(a) INVERT (b) GLIDE

(c) STING (d) ACTED

77. MAJORITY
(a) MORE (b) JURY
(c) READ (d) TRAY

78. WATERMELON
(a) MAKER (b) WRITE
(c) TOWER (d) NOVEL

79. PREDICTION
(a) DESIRE (b) CREDIT
(c) ACTION (d) PICKED

80. BARGAIN
(a) GRAIN (b) BARGE
(c) ANGRY (d) TRING

81. THERMOSTAT
(a) MOTHER (b) STAMEN
(c) THRUST (d) HOIST

82. LEARNED
(a) DREAM (b) CLEAR
(c) ELDER (d) DRAPE

83. ADVENTURE
(a) AWARE (b) EVENT
(c) TRUCE (d) DRIED

84. THANKSGIVING
(a) AVENGE (b) HAUNTS
(c) GRAINS (d) SAVING

85. NOCTURNAL
(a) CRUST (b) TRAIL
(c) CORAL (d) OCEAN

86. CHARMED
(a) HEAD (b) CHUM
(c) DECK (d) MORE

87. ULTIMATUM
(a) AUTUMN (b) LIMPID
(c) UTMOST (d) TUMULT

88. HARBINGER
(a) BIRTH (b) RANCH
(c) ABODE (d) GRAIN

89. OTHERWISE
(a) SHORT (b) WASTE
(c) HOVER (d) ITEMS

90. DERELICT
(a) TRACE (b) CREED
(c) LINER (d) ERODE

91. SINISTER
(a) TIMER (b) SISTER
(c) TEASE (d) STRAIN

92. WORKSHOP
(a) SHOCK (b) ROWER
(c) PORCH (d) WHOOP

93. DEVELOPING
(a) PLAIN (b) GREED
(c) DEVIL (d) VOICE

94. RESIDENTIAL
(a) GRIND (b) TRADE
(c) LOVER (d) STRAP

95. BLANDISHMENT
(a) BOARD (b) METAL
(c) SHAPE (d) CRASH

96. PAINSTAKER
(a) POKER (b) STALK
(c) TAKEN (d) PRIDE

97. BELLIGERENT
(a) GREEN (b) LEGAL
(c) BLOAT (d) INFER

98. UNDISCHARGED
(a) CHANGED (b) DISARMED
(c) GROUNDED (d) SHARPEN

99. LEVIGATE
(a) VEIN (b) GLAD
(c) EAST (d) GIVE

100. MELANCHOLY
(a) CHIME (b) MELON
(c) MADLY (d) CRANE

ANSWERS

1	2	3	4	5	6	7	8	9	10
(b)	(d)	(a)	(c)	(b)	(a)	(a)	(c)	(d)	(c)
11	**12**	**13**	**14**	**15**	**16**	**17**	**18**	**19**	**20**
(a)	(c)	(b)	(a)	(c)	(d)	(d)	(a)	(b)	(c)
21	**22**	**23**	**24**	**25**	**26**	**27**	**28**	**29**	**30**
(c)	(b)	(b)	(a)	(d)	(c)	(a)	(a)	(d)	(d)
31	**32**	**33**	**34**	**35**	**36**	**37**	**38**	**39**	**40**
(b)	(c)	(c)	(d)	(b)	(b)	(b)	(c)	(a)	(d)

41	42	43	44	45	46	47	48	49	50
(d)	(c)	(b)*	(c)	(b)	(c)	(c)	(c)	(a)	(a)
51	**52**	**53**	**54**	**55**	**56**	**57**	**58**	**59**	**60**
(b)	(d)	(c)	(a)	(c)	(b)	(a)	(b)	(b)	(c)
61	**62**	**63**	**64**	**65**	**66**	**67**	**68**	**69**	**70**
(d)	(b)	(b)	(c)	(d)	(c)	(a)	(a)	(b)	(c)
71	**72**	**73**	**74**	**75**	**76**	**77**	**78**	**79**	**80**
(a)	(a)	(b)	(d)	(b)	(c)	(d)	(c)	(b)	(a)
81	**82**	**83**	**84**	**85**	**86**	**87**	**88**	**89**	**90**
(a)	(c)	(b)	(d)	(c)	(a)	(d)	(d)	(a)	(b)
91	**92**	**93**	**94**	**95**	**96**	**97**	**98**	**99**	**100**
(b)	(d)	(c)	(b)	(b)	(c)	(a)	(a)	(d)	(b)

Note : *Ans. 43: The word CRITICAL is ruled out on the grounds that the given word has only one I.

SYMBOL SUBSTITUTION

Questions in these category are easy to attempt. Candidates must be quick in substituting symbols and calculations. The common pattern of questions asked are given below.

SOLVED EXAMPLES

1. If '+' stands for '×'; '×' stands for '÷'; '÷' stands for '–' and '–' stands for '+' then
   2 – 8 × 2 + 6 ÷ 7 = ?
   (*a*) 32 (*b*) 19 (*c*) 23 (*d*) 9 (*e*) 15
   Ans. (*b*) : After substituting the symbols in the given expression the new expression will be :
   2 + 8 ÷ 2 × 6 – 7
   The solving steps will be :
   2 + 4 × 6 – 7
   2 + 24 – 7
   26 – 7 = 19
2. If ▲ stands for '+'
   ■ stands for '–'
   ● stands for '÷'
   ✱ stands for '×' then
   13 ▲ 5 ✱ 20 ● 10 ■ 9 = ?
   (*a*) 26 (*b*) 37 (*c*) 14 (*d*) 55 (*e*) 20
   Ans. (*c*) : After substituting the symbols the new expression will be :
   13 + 5 × 20 ÷ 10 – 9
   The solving steps will be :
   13 + 5 × 2 – 9
   13 + 10 – 9
   23 – 9 = 14

There are questions wherein the candidates must be really quick with calculation because all the given options may be needed for getting the right answer.

3. What will be the correct mathematical signs that can be inserted in the following equations?
   25 . . . 5 . . . 8 . . . 60 = 100
   (*a*) – × + (*b*) ÷ – + (*c*) ÷ + – (*d*) ÷ × + (*e*) None of these
   Ans. (*d*) : The new equations according to the 4 options will be
   (*a*) 25 – 5 × 8 + 60 = 45 (*b*) 25 ÷ 5 – 8 + 60 = 57
   (*c*) 25 ÷ 5 + 8 – 60 = – 47 (*d*) 25 ÷ 5 × 8 + 60 = 100
   After quick calculations the answer option arrived at is '*d*'.
4. If '+' stands for subtraction,
   '÷' stands for addition,
   '–' stands for multiplication, and
   '×' stands for division,
   then which one of the following equations is correct?
   (*a*) 265 ÷ 11 + 2 – 14 = 22 (*b*) 2 + 14 – 4 × 11 = 16
   (*c*) 66 – 3 + 11 ÷ 12 = 199 (*d*) 46 + 10 ÷ 10 – 5 = 92

(*e*) None of these

Ans. (*c*) : After substituting the signs the result of the equations are :

(*a*) $265 + 11 - 2 \times 14 = 275$

(*b*) $2 - 14 \times 4 \div 11 = 78\frac{1}{11}$

(*c*) $66 \times 3 - 11 + 12 = 199$

(*d*) $46 - 10 + 10 \times 5 = 86$

It is clear that option '*c*' is the answer. (In such a case the candidate may not attempt the option '*d*')

In yet another type of questions the candidates are required to interchange signs or numbers in the given equations, which when made will make the equation correct.

5. Of the following question if the given interchange is made in sign, which of the alternatives will make the equation correct?

$16 - 8 \div 4 + 5 \times 2 = 8$

(*a*) × and – (*b*) × and ÷ (*c*) ÷ and + (*d*) – and ÷ (*e*) None of these

Ans. (*d*) : After interchanging the signs the result will be

(*a*) $16 \times 8 \div 4 + 5 - 2 = 32 + 5 - 2 = 35$

(*b*) $16 - 8 \times 4 + 5 \div 2$, (in this equation $5 \div 2$ gives the answer in fraction while the result 8 is an even number. No further calculations are necessary.)

(*c*) $16 - 8 + 4 \div 5 \times 2$, $4 \div 5$ is same as in (*b*)

(*d*) $16 \div 8 - 4 + 5 \times 2 = 2 - 4 + 10 = 8$

Therefore, option '*d*' is the correct answer.

6. If the given signs – and ×, and numbers 3 and 6 are interchanged, which of the following equations would be correct?

(*a*) $4 \times 3 - 6 = 19$ (*b*) $6 \times 1 - 3 = 12$ (*c*) $3 - 6 \times 8 = 10$ (*d*) $3 \times 6 - 18 = 24$

(*e*) $6 \times 5 - 3 = 12$

Ans. (*c*) : After interchanging the signs and numbers the equations will be

(*a*) $4 - 6 \times 3 = 14$ which is wrong (*b*) $3 - 1 \times 6 = 3$ which is wrong

(*c*) $6 \times 3 - 8 = 10$ which is correct (*d*) $6 - 3 \times 18 = 48$ which is wrong

(*e*) $3 - 5 \times 6 = 27$ which is wrong

(**Note :** Clearly, the answer is *c*. The candidate need not work out options *d* and *e* when it has been worked out that *c* is the answer.)

Certain symbols are substituted to form an order on which the options are based. The candidate has to select the option which follows the given order.

7. If ■ stands for >, ▲ stands for <, ϕ stands for =, and Ω stands for ≠ and given that A ϕ B, C ■ D, and D ▲ A, then

(*a*) C Ω A (*b*) B ■ D (*c*) B ▲ D (*d*) A ▲ D (*e*) None of these

Ans. (*b*) : What is given is A = B, C > D and D < A

So, A = B > D and C > D.

(*a*) C ≠ D cannot be depicted (*b*) B > D which is correct

(*c*) B < D which is wrong (*d*) A < D which is wrong

Option *b* clearly follows the given pattern between A, B, C and D.

EXERCISE

1. If "+" means "–"; "–" means "×"; "×" means "÷" and "÷" means "+", then $15 \times 5 \div 10 + 5 - 3 = ?$
   (a) 9.5 (b) 0
   (c) – 2 (d) 24
   (e) None of these
2. If "+" means "–"; "–" means "×"; "×" means "÷" and "÷" means "+", then $15 \times 3 \div 15 + 5 - 2 = ?$
   (a) 0 (b) 10
   (c) 20 (d) 6
   (e) None of these
3. If "+" means "÷"; "×" means "–"; "÷" means "+" and "–" means "×", then $16 \div 8 \times 6 - 2 + 12 = ?$
   (a) 22 (b) 24
   (c) 23 (d) 20
   (e) None of these
4. If "+" means "×"; "–" means "÷"; "÷" means "+" and "×" means "–", then what will be the value of $20 \div 40 - 4 \times 5 + 6 = ?$
   (a) 60 (b) 1.67
   (c) 150 (d) 0
   (e) None of these
5. If "+" means "×"; "–" means "÷"; "×" means "–" and "÷" means "+", then $5 + 8 - 4 \times 2 \div 9 = ?$
   (a) 15 (b) 13
   (c) 17 (d) 11
   (e) None of these
6. If × stand for addition, ÷ stands for subtraction, + stands for multiplication and – stands for division, then $(20 \times 6 \div 6 \times 4)$ is equal to
   (a) 5 (b) 24
   (c) 25 (d) 80
   (e) None of these
7. If "+" means "×"; "÷" means "–"; "×" means "÷" and "–" means "+", what will be the value of the following expression? $4 + 11 \div 5 - 50 = ?$
   (a) 79 (b) – 11
   (c) 91 (d) – 48.5
   (e) None of these
8. If P = 6, J = 4, L = 8, M = 24, then which of the given values can replace the question mark (?) in the following? $M \times J \div L + J = ?$
   (a) 8 (b) 36
   (c) 52 (d) 0
   (e) 16
9. If $A + B > C + D$, $B + E = 2C$ and $C + D > B + E$, it necessarily follows that
   (a) $A > C$ (b) $A + B > 2D$
   (c) $A + B > 2C$ (d) $A + B > 2E$
   (e) $D + B < 2C$
10. If $A + D > C + E$, $C + D = 2B$ and $B + E > C + D$, it necessarily follows that
    (a) $A + D > B + E$
    (b) $A + D > B + C$
    (c) $A + B > 2D$
    (d) $B + D > C + E$
    (e) $A + D < B + C$
11. If "+" means "÷"; "÷" means "–"; "–" means "×" and "×" means "+", then $10 \div 2 - 15 + 3 \times 5 = ?$
    (a) 10 (b) 15
    (c) 25 (d) 5
    (e) 0
12. If A stands for add, B for subtract, C for multiply and D for divide, then for what does 4A 3B 3A 2 stand?
    (a) 2 (b) 4
    (c) 6 (d) 8
    (e) 10
13. If × stands for addition, < for subtraction, + stands for division, > for multiplication, – stands for equal to, ÷ for greater than, and = stands for less than, state which of the following is true?
    (a) $5 \times 3 < 7 \div 8 + 4 \times 1$
    (b) $3 \times 4 > 2 - 9 + 3 < 3$
    (c) $5 > 2 + 2 = 10 < 4 \times 8$
    (d) $3 \times 2 < 4 \div 16 > 2 + 4$
    (e) None of the above
14. If × stands for add, y stands for subract, z stands for divide and p stands for multiply, then what is the the value of $(7 \text{ p } 3) \text{ y } 6 \times 5$?
    (a) 5 (b) 10

(c) 15 (d) 20
(e) 25

15. If → stands for subract, ← stands for add, ↑↑ stands for multiply, ↓↓ stands for divide, ↔ for greater than, ←↕→ stands for equal to, then which of the following alternatives is true?
(a) 4 ← 6 ↑↑ 2 ←↕→ 3 → 12 ← 12
(b) 10 ↓↓ 5 ↑↑ 5 ←↕→ 9 → 3 ← 4
(c) 15 ↑↑ 2 → 5 ←↕→ 12 ↓↓ 4 ← 3
(d) 13 ↓↓ 13 ← 1 ↔ 20 → 5 ↑↑ 2
(e) None of these

16. If "+" means "÷"; "÷" means "–"; "–"means "×" and "×" means "+", what will be the value of $8 + 2 \div 3 - 4 \times 6 = ?$
(a) – 2 (b) $-15\frac{1}{3}$
(c) 12 (d) 15
(e) None of these

17. If "+" means "÷"; "×" means "–"; "÷"means "×" and "–" means "+", what will be the value of the following expression?
$9 + 3 \div 4 - 8 \times 2 = ?$
(a) $6\frac{3}{4}$ (b) $-1\frac{3}{4}$
(c) $-6\frac{1}{4}$ (d) 18
(e) 24

18. If "–" means "÷"; "+" means "×"; "÷"means "–" and "×" means "+", then which of the following must be true?
(a) $1 \div 2 + 3 \times 6 - 8 = 12$
(b) $2 + 3 - 5 \times 8 \div 4 = 7$
(c) $5 + 6 \times 8 - 2 \div 3 = 31$
(d) $6 \div 1 + 2 - 8 \times 4 = 31$
(e) None of these

19. If "÷" means "+"; "+" means "×"; "–"means "÷" and "×" means "–", then
$5 + 8 - 4 \times 2 \div 9 = ?$
(a) 13 (b) 15
(c) 11 (d) 17
(e) None of these

20. If "+" means "minus"; "–" means "multiplied by"; "÷"means "plus" and "×" means "divided by" then
$10 \times 5 \div 3 - 2 + 3 = ?$
(a) 7 (b) $-2\frac{6}{16}$
(c) $17\frac{2}{3}$ (d) – 2
(e) None of these

21. If plus means divided by, divided by means minus, minus means multiplied by and multiplied by means plus, then
$12 + 6 \div 3 - 2 \times 8 = ?$
(a) 4 (b) 2
(c) – 2 (d) 8
(e) 6

22. What will be the correct mathematical signs that can be inserted in the following equation?
9 ... 8 ... 8 ... 4 ... 9 = 65
(a) – + × ÷ (b) ÷ × + –
(c) ÷ + × – (d) × + ÷ –
(e) + × ÷ –

23. If "÷" means "+"; "–" means "÷"; "×"means "–" and "+" means "×", then
$32 \div 8 - 4 \times 12 + 4 = ?$
(a) 40 (b) 1/12
(c) 16 (d) 12
(e) None of these

24. If "*x*" stands for "+"; "*y*" stands for "–"; "*z*"stands for "÷" and "*w*" stands for "×", then
$10w\,2x\,5y\,5 = ?$
(a) 15 (b) 12
(c) 20 (d) 10
(e) 25

25. If "–" stands for "×"; "×" stands for "+"; "+"stands for "÷" and "÷" stands for "–", then what will be the value of the following equation?
$8 - 4 + 16 \times 8 - 10 = ?$
(a) 54 (b) 82
(c) 15 (d) 10
(e) 110

26. If Δ denotes =; + denotes >, – denotes <, □ denotes ≠, × denotes ≯ and ÷ denotes ≮ then a + b – c denotes
(a) b Δ c □ a (b) b □ a ÷ c
(c) a ÷ b × c (d) b – a + c

(*e*) None of these

27. If '✱' denotes '×', 'Δ' denotes '÷', '□' denotes '–', '●' denotes '+', 'α' denotes '=' and 'β' denotes ≠, then which of the following euations is correct?

(*a*) 2 □ 10 ✱ 4 Δ 5 α 5 ● 12 Δ 6
(*b*) 27 Δ 9 ● 6 β 3 ✱ 6 □ 9
(*c*) 4 Δ 2 ✱ 0 α 7 Δ 1 ✱ 0
(*d*) 5 ● 6 Δ 3 □ 2 α 8 Δ 4 ✱ 3
(*e*) None of the above

28. If the given signs + and – are interchanged then which of the following equations will be correct?

(*a*) 2 + 7 – 8 = 3 (*b*) 3 – 1 + 4 = 2
(*c*) 9 + 3 – 5 = 7 (*d*) 6 + 3 – 8 = 5
(*e*) None of these

29. If 'A' stands for '×', 'B' stands for '–', 'C' stands for '+' and 'D' stands for '÷', what will be the result of the following expression?
8 B 3 C 10 A 2 D 5

(*a*) 7 (*b*) 1
(*c*) 9 (*d*) 13
(*e*) 11

30. If '×' means '+', '÷' means '–', '+' means '÷' and '–' means '×', then what will be the result of the following expression?
8 × 7 – 8 + 40 ÷ 2

(*a*) 4 (*b*) $6\frac{3}{7}$
(*c*) 13 (*d*) – 9
(*e*) $7\frac{2}{5}$

31. If plus means divided by, multiplied by means minus, divided by means multiplied by and minus means plus, then
18 + 3 ÷ 4 – 8 × 12 = ?

(*a*) $6\frac{1}{4}$ (*b*) 20
(*c*) $3\frac{1}{3}$ (*d*) $-6\frac{2}{3}$
(*e*) 10

32. If '–' means '×', '+' means '÷', '×' means '+' and '÷' means '–', then
8 + 6 ÷ 4 – 7 × 3 = ?

(*a*) $7\frac{1}{5}$ (*b*) 12
(*c*) $-11\frac{1}{2}$ (*d*) 14
(*e*) $-23\frac{2}{3}$

33. If A stands for '+', B stands for '–', C stands for '×', then 10 C 4 A 4 C 4 B 6 = ?

(*a*) 50 (*b*) 42
(*c*) 58 (*d*) 46
(*e*) 60

34. If ↓ stands for '÷', ↑ stands for '×', → stands for '+' and ← stands for '–', then
25 ↓ 5 → 3 ↑ 6 ← 8 = ?

(*a*) 9 (*b*) 12
(*c*) 16 (*d*) 15
(*e*) 23

35. If '+' means '×', '–' means '÷', '×' means '–' and '÷' means '+', then
9 + 8 ÷ 8 – 4 × 9 = ?

(*a*) 65 (*b*) 17
(*c*) 26 (*d*) 11
(*e*) 19

36. If '*a*' means '×', '*b*' means '÷', '*c*' means '+' and '*d*' means '–' then what will be the result of the following expression?
21 *c* 3 *d* 6 *a* 8 *b* 2

(*a*) 48 (*b*) 13
(*c*) 0 (*d*) 72
(*e*) 64

37. If '+' means '–', '–' means '×', '×' means '÷' and '÷' means '+', then
15 × 5 ÷ 10 + 5 – 3 = ?

(*a*) 4 (*b*) – 2
(*c*) – 8 (*d*) 10
(*e*) 16

38. Which of the following signs, if changed, will make the equation correct?
25 ÷ 5 + 17 × 2 – 6 = 10

(*a*) ÷ and – (*b*) + and –
(*c*) × and – (*d*) ÷ and +
(*e*) None of these

39. If Δ means >, □ means <, ϴ means =, and ✱ means ≠, and given that
B Δ D, D □ C, C Δ A and B ϴ A, then

(*a*) A Δ C (*b*) C □ A
(*c*) C ϴ A (*d*) B ✱ A
(*e*) None of these

40. If '+' means '÷', '÷' means '–', '×' means '+' and '–' means '×', then what will be the result of the following expression?

$12 + 6 \div 3 - 2 \times 8$

(*a*) 4 (*b*) 2
(*c*) 6 (*d*) 10
(*e*) 16

41. If '●' means '×', '■' means '+', '▲' means '÷', '>' means '=', '<' means ≠, ✱ means '>' and ♦ means '<', then which of the following equation is correct?

(*a*) 30 ▲ 10 ● 6 ♦ 8 ■ 7
(*b*) 5 ✱ 2 ■ 9 ▲ 3
(*c*) 9 ■ 25 ▲ 5 > 13
(*d*) 11 ● 5 ♦ 6 ● 3 ▲ 9 ■ 40
(*e*) None of these

42. If the + and × signs of the following equations are interchanged, which will be the correct equation?

(*a*) $7 \times 5 + 3 = 20$
(*b*) $4 + 9 \times 1 = 42$
(*c*) $6 \times 5 + 8 = 46$
(*d*) $2 + 11 \times 4 = 28$
(*e*) None of these

43. If '+' means '÷', '÷' means '+', '–' means '×' and '×' means '–', then

$3 + 6 - 2 \div 24 \times 6 = ?$

(*a*) 11 (*b*) 19
(*c*) 15 (*d*) 23
(*e*) None of these

44. If '–' means '×', '×' means '+', '+' means '÷' and '÷' means '–', then

$27 + 3 - 3 \times 11 \div 8 = ?$

(*a*) 18 (*b*) 30
(*c*) 27 (*d*) 42
(*e*) None of these

45. If 'a' stands for '÷', 'b' stands for '×', 'c' stands for '+' and 'd' stands for '–', then

5 c 20 a 4 b 2 d 10 = ?

(*a*) 5 (*b*) 10
(*c*) 15 (*d*) 20
(*e*) 25

46. If '✱' stands for '+', '■' stands for '×', '▲' stands for '–' and '●' stands for '÷', then

4 ■ 36 ● 6 ▲ 17 ✱ 8 = ?

(*a*) 3 (*b*) 17
(*c*) 11 (*d*) 15
(*e*) 21

47. If '+' stands for multiplication '×' stands for addition, '÷' stands for subtraction and '–' stands for division, then what will be the result of the following expression ?

$7 \times 4 \div 10 \times 2 + 5 = ?$

(*a*) 7 (*b*) 0
(*c*) 11 (*d*) 15
(*e*) None of these

48. If 'A' means '÷', 'B' means '+', 'C' means '×' and 'D' means '–', then

12 C 4 A 24 D 10 B 1 = ?

(*a*) $11\frac{1}{3}$ (*b*) 23
(*c*) -7 (*d*) $16\frac{4}{5}$
(*e*) $-6\frac{2}{5}$

49. If □ means >, Δ means <, ϕ means =, ‖ means ≠ and given that

A□C, BΔD and C□D, then

(*a*) B Δ C (*b*) C Δ A
(*c*) A Δ B (*d*) D ϕ C
(*e*) B ‖ C

50. If the signs '× and ÷' and numbers '2 and 4' are interchanged, then which of the following equation will be correct?

(*a*) $4 - 6 \times 3 + 1 \div 2 = 7$
(*b*) $2 \times 4 + 5 \div 1 - 6 = 3$
(*c*) $4 \div 3 - 8 + 16 \times 2 = 1$
(*d*) $5 \times 5 + 4 - 8 \div 2 = -29$
(*e*) None of these

EXPLANATORY ANSWERS

1. (*c*) : $15 \div 5 + 10 - 5 \times 3$
$3 + 10 - 15 = -2$

2. (*b*) : $15 \div 3 + 15 - 5 \times 2$
$5 + 15 - 10 = 10$

3. (*c*) : $16 + 8 - 6 \times 2 \div 12$
$16 + 8 - 1 = 23$

4. (*d*) : $20 + 40 \div 4 - 5 \times 6$
$20 + 10 - 30 = 0$

5. (c) : $5 \times 8 \div 4 - 2 + 9$
$10 - 2 + 9 = 17$

6. (b) : $20 + 6 - 6 + 4 = 24$

7. (e) : $4 \times 11 - 5 + 50$
$44 - 5 + 50 = 89$

8. (e) : $24 \times 4 \div 8 + 4$
$12 + 4 = 16$

9. (c) : A + B > C + D > B + E or 2 C
∴ A + B > 2C

10. (b) : 1. A + D > C + E
2. B + E > C + D or 2 B
Since, the relation between 1 and 2 is not clear it is however certain that A + D > B + C (combination with C is < A + D).

11. (d) : $10 - 2 \times 15 \div 3 + 5$
$10 - 10 + 5 = 5$

12. (c) : $4 + 3 - 3 + 2 = 6$

13. (c) : *(a)* $5 + 3 - 7 > 8 \div 4 + 1$
$1 > 3$
(b) $3 + 4 \times 2 = 9 \div 3 - 3$
$11 = 0$
(c) $5 \times 2 \div 2 < 10 - 4 + 8$
$5 < 14$
(d) $3 + 2 - 4 > 16 \times 2 \div 4$
$1 > 8$

14. (d) : $(7 \times 3) - 6 + 5$
$21 - 6 + 5 = 20$

15. (b) : *(a)* $4 + 6 \times 2 = 3 - 12 + 12$
$16 = 3$
(b) $10 \div 5 \times 5 = 9 - 3 + 4$
$10 = 10$
(c) $15 \times 2 - 5 = 12 \div 4 + 3$
$25 = 6$
(d) $13 \div 13 + 1 > 20 - 5 \times 2$
$2 > 10$

16. (a) : $8 \div 2 - 3 \times 4 + 6$
$4 - 12 + 6 = -2$

17. (d) : $9 \div 3 \times 4 + 8 - 2$
$12 + 8 - 2 = 18$

18. (c) : *(a)* $1 - 2 \times 3 + 6 \div 8 = 12$

$$\frac{-17}{4} = 12$$

(b) $2 \times 3 \div 5 + 8 - 4 = 7$

$$\frac{26}{5} = 7$$

(c) $5 \times 6 + 8 \div 2 - 3 = 31$
$31 = 31$
(d) $6 - 1 \times 2 \div 8 + 4 = 31$

$$\frac{-39}{4} = 31$$

19. (d) : $5 \times 8 \div 4 - 2 + 9$
$10 - 2 + 9 = 17$

20. (e) : $10 \div 5 + 3 \times 2 - 3$
$2 + 6 - 3 = 5$

21. (a) : $12 \div 6 - 3 \times 2 + 8$
$2 - 6 + 8 = 4$

22. (d) : *(a)* $9 - 8 + 8 \times 4 \div 9 = 65$
($8 \times 4 \div 9$ gives the result in fractions. So, there is no need for further calculation as the result 65 is a whole number.)
(b) $9 \div 8 \times 8 + 4 - 9 = 65$
$9 + 4 - 9$ *ie* $4 = 65$
(c) $9 \div 8 + 8 \times 4 - 9 = 65$
($9 \div 8$ gives the result in fraction)
(d) $9 \times 8 + 8 \div 4 - 9 = 65$
$72 + 2 - 9$ *ie* $65 = 65$
(e) $9 + 8 \times 8 \div 4 - 9$
$9 + 16 - 9$ *ie* $16 = 65$

23. (e) : $32 + 8 \div 4 - 12 \times 4$
$32 + 2 - 48 = -14$

24. (c) : $10 \times 2 + 5 - 5$
$20 + 5 - 5 = 20$

25. (b) : $8 \times 4 \div 16 + 8 \times 10$
$2 + 80 = 82$

26. (d) : What is given is a > b < c
The equations are :
(a) b = c ≠ a which is wrong
(b) b ≠ a < c which is wrong
(c) a ≮ b ≯ c which is wrong
(d) b < a > c which is correct
Therefore, *'d'* is the answer.

27. (c) : The solved equations will be :
(a) $2 - 10 \times 4 \div 5 = 5 + 12 \div 6$
$2 - 8 = 5 + 2$
$-6 = 7$ which is wrong
(b) $27 \div 9 + 6 \neq 3 \times 6 - 9$
$3 + 6 \neq 18 - 9$
$9 \neq 9$ which is wrong
(c) $4 \div 2 \times 0 = 7 \div 1 \times 0$
$2 \times 0 = 7 \times 0$
$0 = 0$ which is correct

(*d*) $5 + 6 \div 3 - 2 = 8 \div 4 \times 3$
$5 = 6$ which is wrong

28. (*a*) : After interchanging the signs the equation will be :
(*a*) $2 - 7 + 8 = 3$ which is correct
(*b*) $3 + 1 - 4 = 0$
(*c*) $9 - 3 + 5 = 11$
(*d*) $6 - 3 + 8 = 11$

29. (*c*) : $8 - 3 + 10 \times 2 \div 5$
$8 - 3 + 4 = 9$

30. (*e*) : $8 + 7 \times 8 \div 40 - 2$
$8 + \frac{7}{5} - 2$ *i.e.*, $\frac{37}{5}$ or $7\frac{2}{5}$

31. (*b*) : $18 \div 3 \times 4 + 8 - 12$
$24 + 8 - 12 = 20$

32. (*e*) : $8 \div 6 - 4 \times 7 + 3$
$\frac{4}{3} - 28 + 3$ *i.e.*, $-\frac{71}{3}$ or $-23\frac{2}{3}$

33. (*a*) : $10 \times 4 + 4 \times 4 - 6$
$40 + 16 - 6 = 50$

34. (*d*) : $25 \div 5 + 3 \times 6 - 8$
$5 + 18 - 8 = 15$

35. (*a*) : $9 \times 8 + 8 \div 4 - 9$
$72 + 2 - 9 = 65$

36. (*c*) : $21 + 3 - 6 \times 8 \div 2$
$21 + 3 - 24 = 0$

37. (*b*) : $15 \div 5 + 10 - 5 \times 3$
$3 + 10 - 15 = -2$

38. (*c*) : After changing the signs the equations will be :
(*a*) $25 - 5 + 17 \times 2 \div 6$
$25 - 5 + \frac{17}{3}$ (the answer will be in fractions whereas 10 is a whole number, so no further calculation)
(*b*) $25 \div 5 - 17 \times 2 + 6$
$5 - 34 + 6 = -23$ which is wrong
(*c*) $25 \div 5 + 17 - 2 \times 6$
$5 + 17 - 12 = 10$ which is correct
(*d*) $25 + 5 \div 17 \times 2 - 6$ ($5 \div 17$ gives the answer as in (*a*))

39. (*e*) : Given that $B > D$, $D < C$, $C > A$ and $B = A$ means $D < A = B < C$
(*a*) $A > C$
(*b*) $C < A$
(*c*) $C = A$
(*d*) $B \neq A$
None of the given options is correct.

40. (*a*) : $12 \div 6 - 3 \times 2 + 8$
$2 - 6 + 8 = 4$

41. (*e*) : The new equations will be :
(*a*) $30 \div 10 \times 6 < 8 + 7$
$18 < 15$ which is wrong
(*b*) $5 > 2 + 9 \div 3$
$5 > 5$ which is wrong
(*c*) $9 + 25 \div 5 = 13$
$14 = 13$ which is wrong
(*d*) $11 \times 5 < 6 \times 3 \div 9 + 40$
$55 < 42$ which is wrong

42. (*c*) : After interchanging the signs the equations are :
(*a*) $7 + 5 \times 3 = 22$ which is wrong
(*b*) $4 \times 9 + 1 = 37$ which is wrong
(*c*) $6 + 5 \times 8 = 46$ which is correct
(*d*) $2 \times 11 + 4 = 26$ which is wrong

43. (*b*) : $3 \div 6 \times 2 + 24 - 6$
$1 + 24 - 6 = 19$

44. (*b*) : $27 \div 3 \times 3 + 11 - 8$
$27 + 11 - 8 = 30$

45. (*a*) : $5 + 20 \div 4 \times 2 - 10$
$5 + 10 - 10 = 5$

46. (*d*) : $4 \times 36 \div 6 - 17 + 8$
$24 - 17 + 8 = 15$

47. (*c*) : $7 + 4 - 10 + 2 \times 5$
$7 + 4 - 10 + 10 = 11$

48. (*c*) : $12 \times 4 \div 24 - 10 + 1$
$2 - 10 + 1 = -7$

49. (*b*) : Given that $A > C$. $B < D$ and $C > D$ means $A > C > D$ and $B < D$
(*a*) $B > D$ which is wrong
(*b*) $C < A$ which is correct
(*c*) $A < B$ which cannot be decided
(*d*) $D \neq C$ which is wrong

50. (*d*) : After interchanging the signs and numbers the new equations will be :
(*a*) $2 - 6 \div 3 + 1 \times 4$
$2 - 2 + 4 = 4$ which is wrong
(*b*) $4 \div 2 + 5 \times 1 - 6$
$2 + 5 - 6 = 1$ which is wrong
(*c*) $2 \times 3 - 8 + 16 \div 4$
$6 - 8 + 4 = 2$ which is wrong
(*d*) $5 \div 5 + 2 - 8 \times 4$
$1 + 2 - 32 = -29$ which is correct

ARTIFICIAL VALUES AND MISSING NUMBERS

Playing with numbers and mathematical skills are needed to attempt these type of tests. The candidates have to work out the right combination of arithmetical symbols to arrive at the answer options which will take the place of the interrogation sign in the given questions.

SOLVED EXAMPLES

1. Select the right option which can be placed at the sign of interrogation?

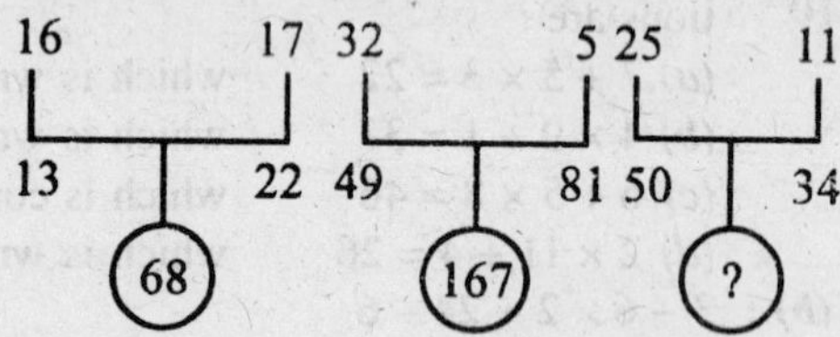

(*a*) 65 (*b*) 120 (*c*) 116 (*d*) 192

Ans. (*b*) : The number inside the circle is the sum of the other four numbers, *i.e.*,

16 + 17 + 13 + 22 = 68

32 + 5 + 49 + 81 = 167, similarly

25 + 11 + 50 + 34 = 120

2. Which one number can be placed at the sign of interrogation?

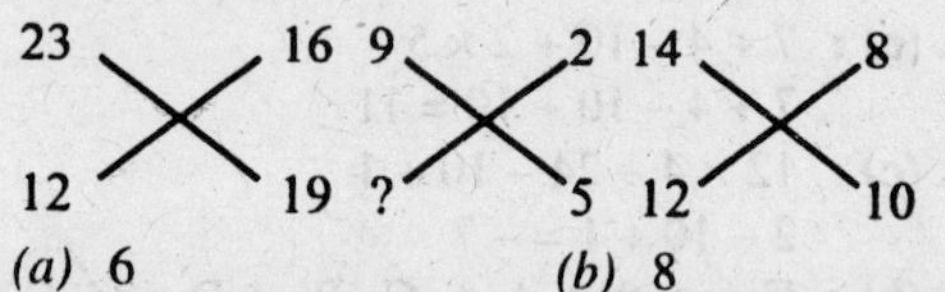

(*a*) 6 (*b*) 8 (*c*) 7 (*d*) 3

Ans. (*a*) : The difference between two opposite numbers is 4, *i.e.*,

23 – 19 = 4 and 16 – 12 = 4

14 – 10 = 4 and 12 – 8 = 4, similarly

9 – 5 = 4 and 6 – 2 = 4.

There are no definite rules to reach the right answer. Try solving the questions in the exercise given below to learn more about the different ways of getting the correct answer.

EXERCISE

Directions : *In each question given below which one number can be placed at the sign of interrogation?*

1.

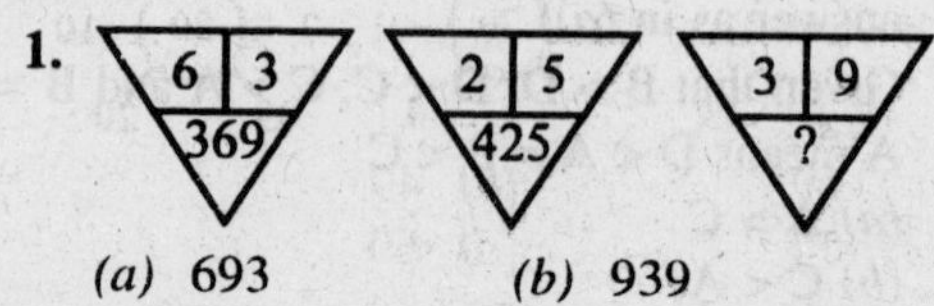

(*a*) 693 (*b*) 939

(*c*) 981 (*d*) 993

2.

(*a*) 68 (*b*) 100
(*c*) 72 (*d*) 81

3.

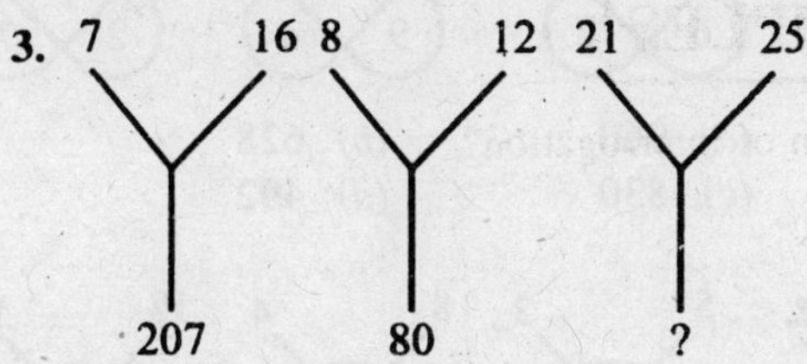

(*a*) 425 (*b*) 184
(*c*) 241 (*d*) 210

4.

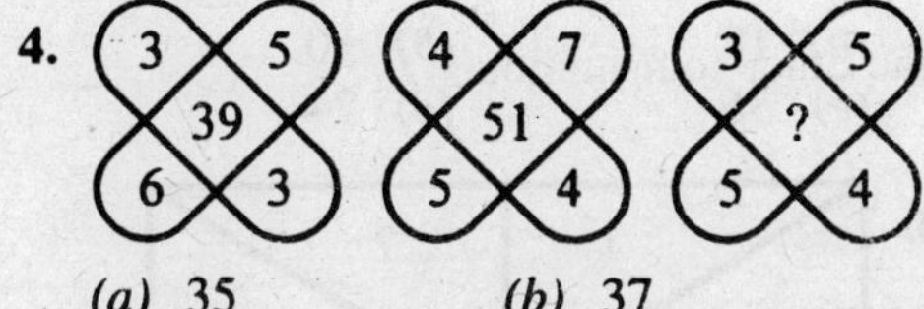

(*a*) 35 (*b*) 37
(*c*) 45 (*d*) 48

5.

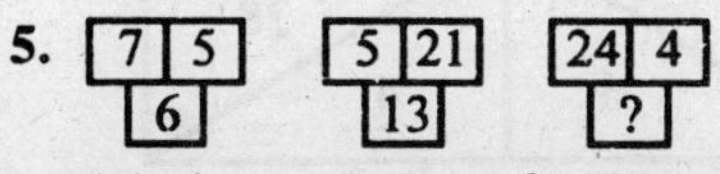

(*a*) 4 (*b*) 8
(*c*) 20 (*d*) 14

6.

14	9	4
12	7	2
10	5	0
16	11	?

(*a*) 9 (*b*) 6
(*c*) 3 (*d*) 7

7.

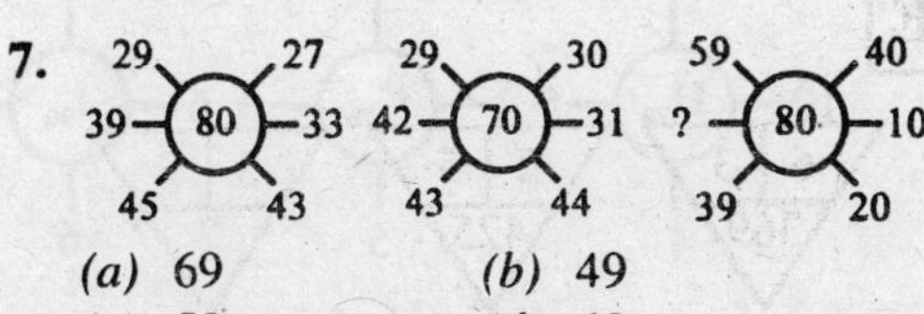

(*a*) 69 (*b*) 49
(*c*) 50 (*d*) 60

8.

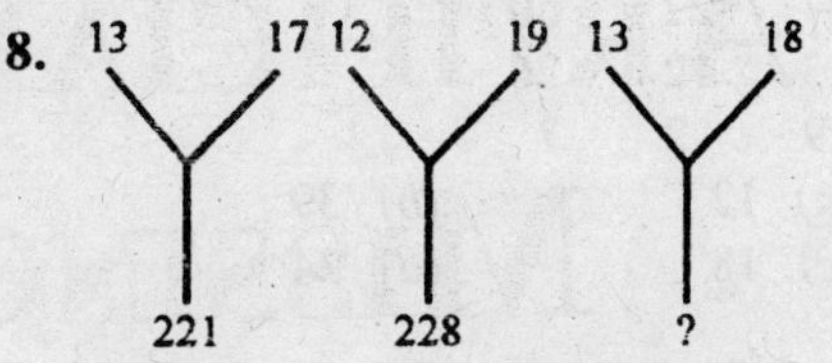

(*a*) 31 (*b*) 229
(*c*) 234 (*d*) 312

9.

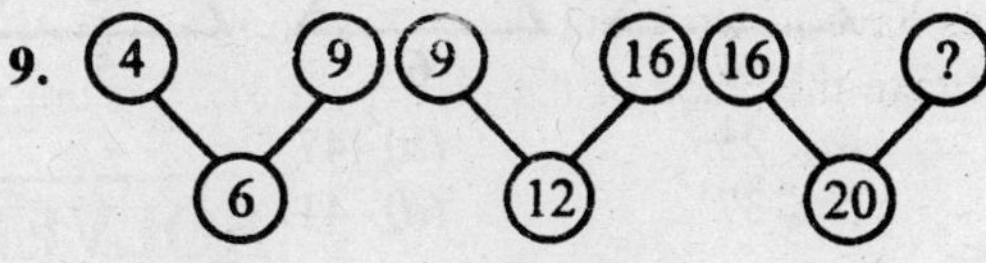

(*a*) 21 (*b*) 25
(*c*) 50 (*d*) 60

10.

51	(11)	61
64	(30)	32
35	(?)	43

(*a*) 25 (*b*) 27
(*c*) 32 (*d*) 37

11.

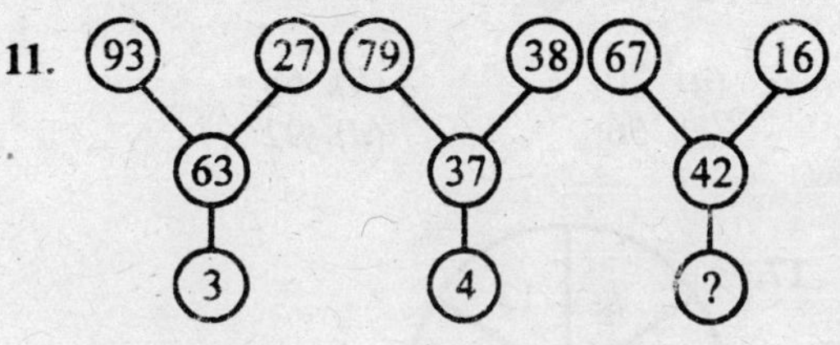

(*a*) 5 (*b*) 6
(*c*) 8 (*d*) 9

12.

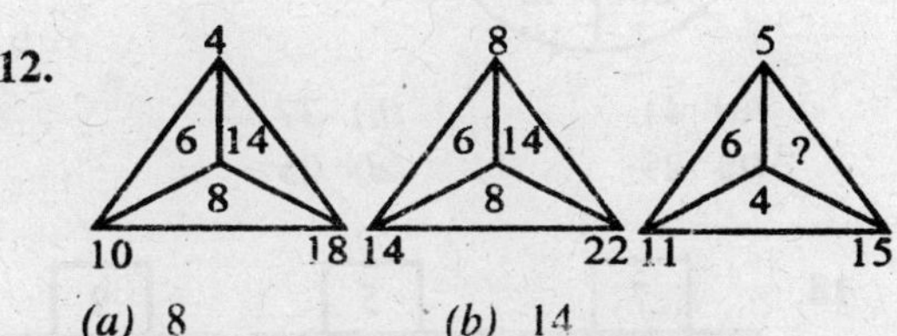

(*a*) 8 (*b*) 14
(*c*) 10 (*d*) 6

13.

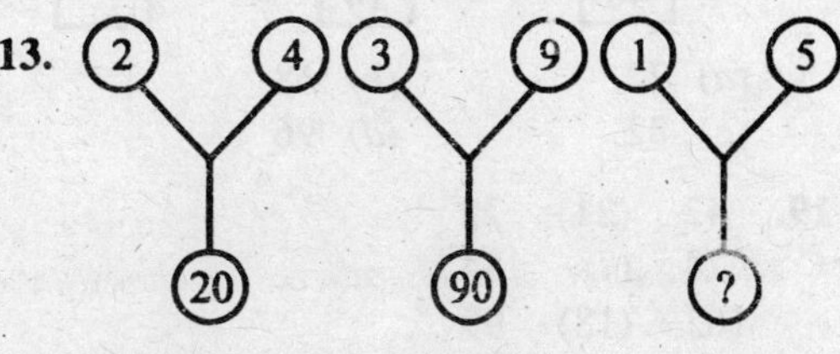

(*a*) 20 (*b*) 25
(*c*) 26 (*d*) 75

14. 27 22 50
13 12 26
9 2 ?
(*a*) 12 (*b*) 39
(*c*) 18 (*d*) 24

15.

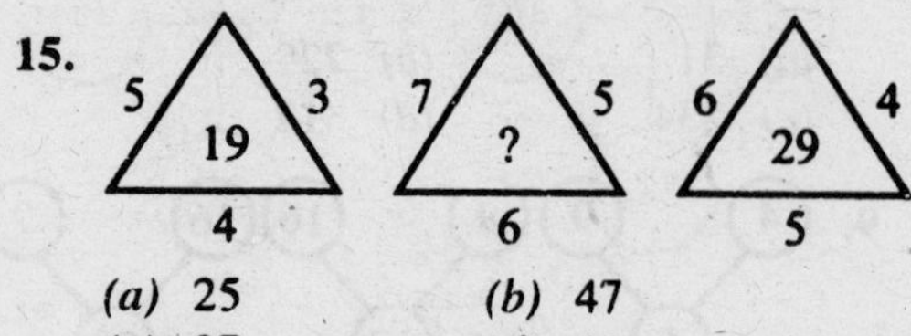

(*a*) 25 (*b*) 47
(*c*) 37 (*d*) 41

16.

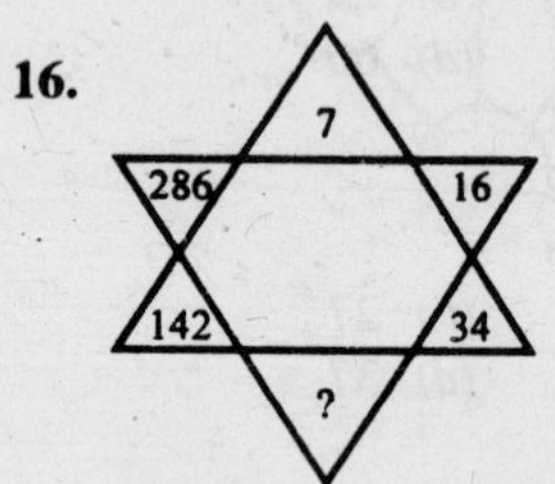

(*a*) 70 (*b*) 68
(*c*) 56 (*d*) 92

17.

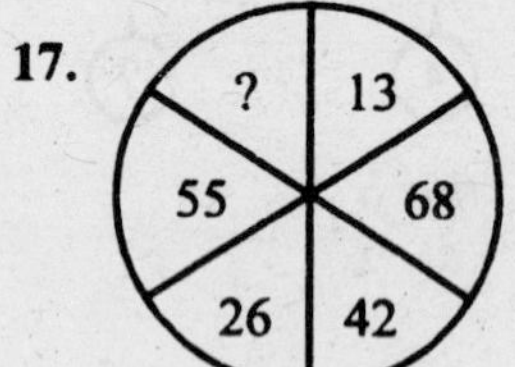

(*a*) 41 (*b*) 37
(*c*) 29 (*d*) 25

18.

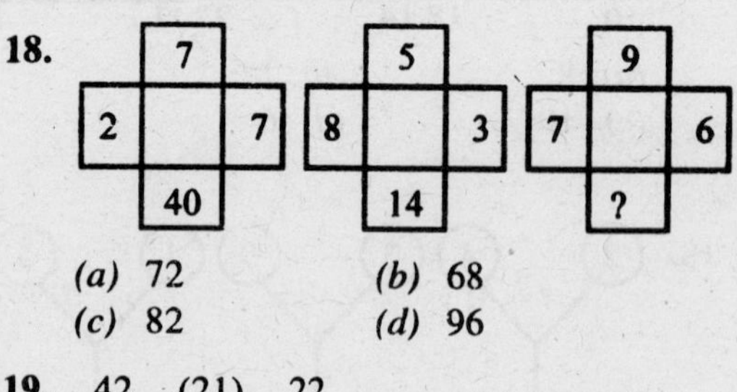

(*a*) 72 (*b*) 68
(*c*) 82 (*d*) 96

19. 42 (21) 22
78 (?) 84
162 (18) 99
(*a*) 12 (*b*) 13
(*c*) 60 (*d*) 72

20.

16 25 19
107 209 ?
7 10 20 4 2 17

(*a*) 68 (*b*) 93
(*c*) 175 (*d*) 217

21.

3 5 8 1 10 6
170 278 ?
6 2 9 4 2 7

(*a*) 960 (*b*) 628
(*c*) 830 (*d*) 492

22.

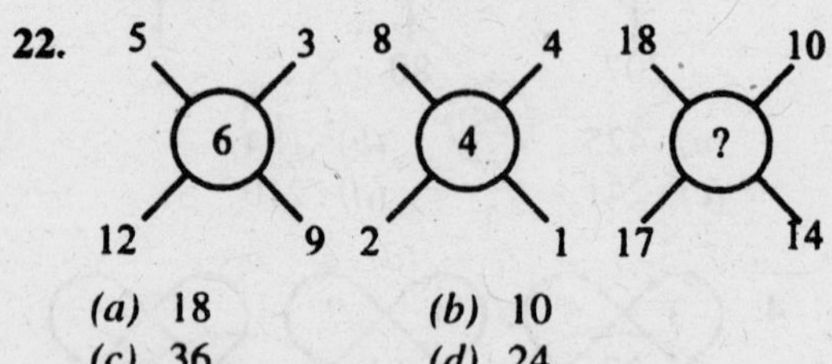

(*a*) 18 (*b*) 10
(*c*) 36 (*d*) 24

23.

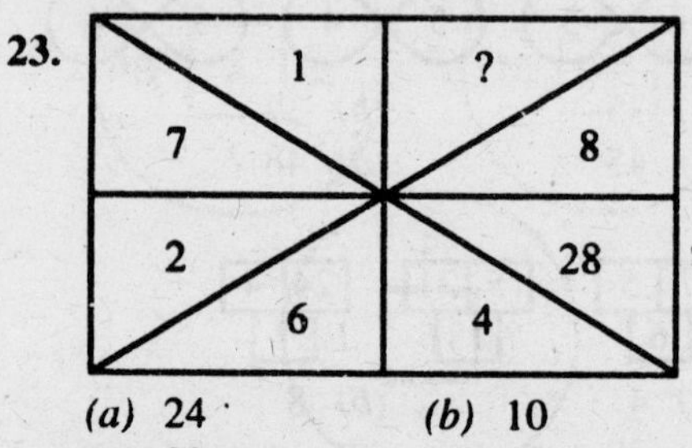

(*a*) 24 (*b*) 10
(*c*) 32 (*d*) 12

24. 6 (40) 4
3 (12) 3
7 (?) 2
(*a*) 51 (*b*) 36
(*c*) 22 (*d*) 4

25.

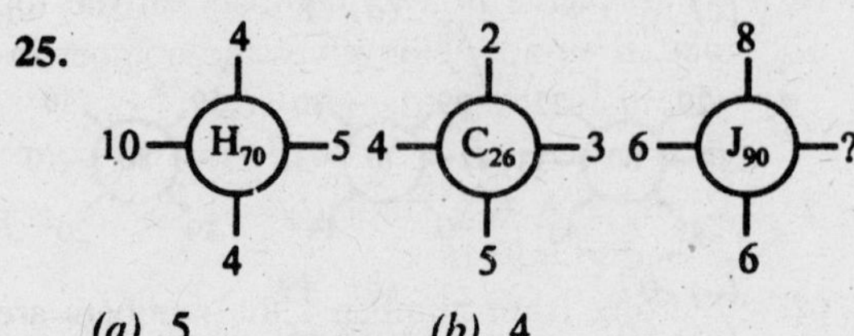

(*a*) 5 (*b*) 4
(*c*) 2 (*d*) 1

26.

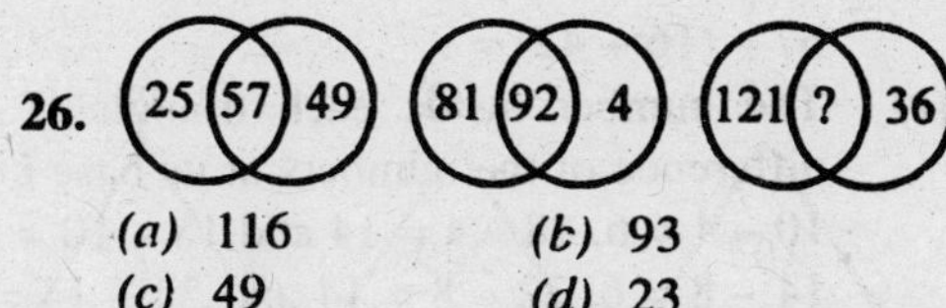

(*a*) 116 (*b*) 93
(*c*) 49 (*d*) 23

27.

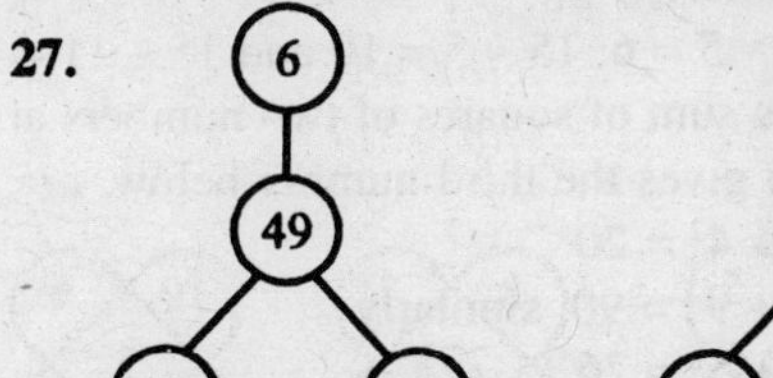

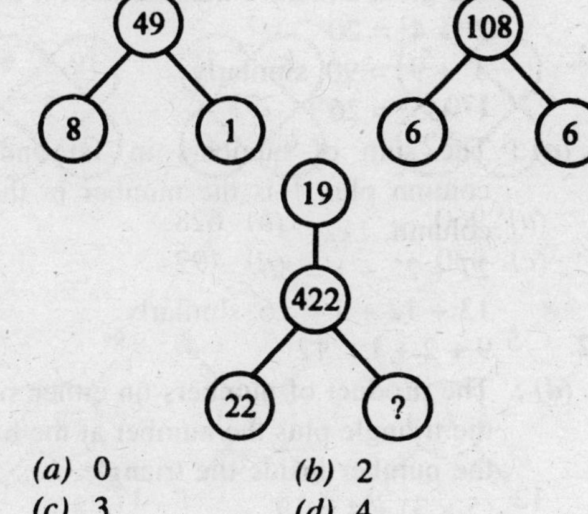

(*a*) 0 (*b*) 2
(*c*) 3 (*d*) 4

28.

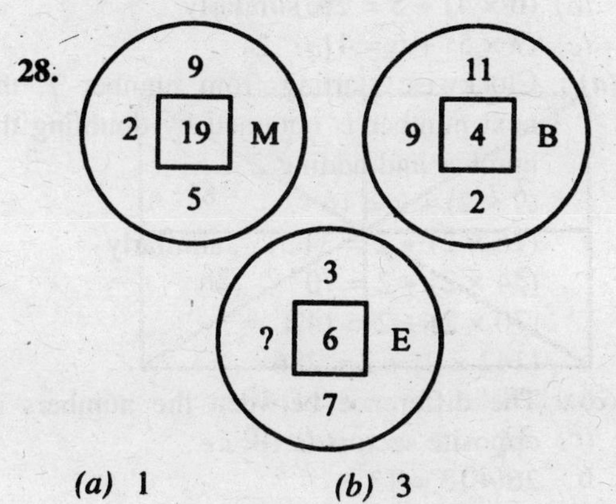

(*a*) 1 (*b*) 3
(*c*) 9 (*d*) 13

29.

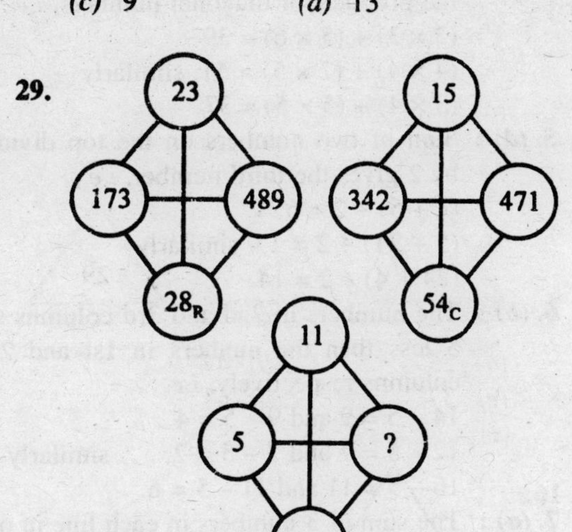

(*a*) 3 (*b*) 8
(*c*) 10 (*d*) 14

30.

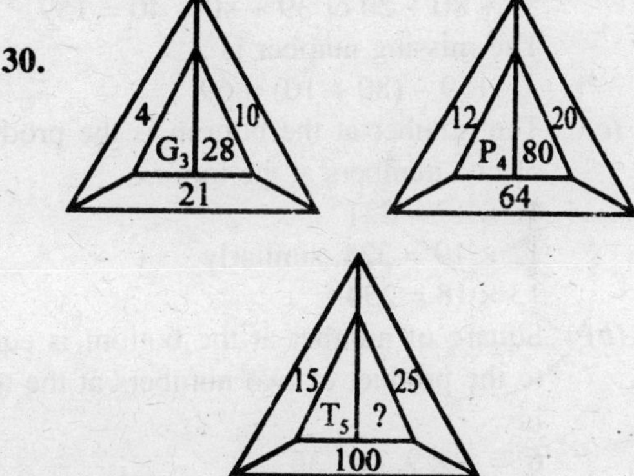

(*a*) 64 (*b*) 92
(*c*) 120 (*d*) 146

EXPLANATORY ANSWERS

1. (*c*) **:** The squares of two numbers on the top placed side by side gives the number inside the bottom triangle, *i.e.*,
6^2 and 3^2 = 369
2^2 and 5^2 = 425, similarly
3^2 and 9^2 = 981.

2. (*d*) **:** Starting from number 4 the numbers are the squares of numbers in natural order *i.e.*, $2^2 = 4$, $3^2 = 9$, $4^2 = 16$ . . . . . $9^2 = 81$

3. (*b*) **:** The number at the bottom is the difference of the squares of two numbers at the top, *i.e.*,
$16^2 - 7^2 = 256 - 49 = 207$
$12^2 - 8^2 = 144 - 64 = 80$, similarly
$25^2 - 21^2 = 625 - 441 = 184$

4. (*b*) **:** The number in the centre is the sum of

the products of diagonal numbers, *i.e.*,
(3 × 3) + (5 × 6) = 39
(4 × 4) + (7 × 5) = 51, similarly
(3 × 4) + (5 × 5) = 37

5. *(d)* : Sum of two numbers on the top divided by 2 gives the third number, *i.e.*,
(7 + 5) ÷ 2 = 6
(5 + 21) ÷ 2 = 13, similarly
(24 + 4) ÷ 2 = 14

6. *(b)* : The numbers in 2nd and 3rd columns are 5 less than the nunbers in 1st and 2nd columns respectively, *i.e.*,
14 – 5 = 9 and 9 – 5 = 4
12 – 5 = 7 and 7 – 5 = 2, . . . similarly
16 – 5 = 11 and 11 – 5 = 6.

7. *(a)* : The sum of 3 numbers in each line in one figure is same, *i.e.*,
29 + 80 + 43 or 39 + 80 + 33
or 45 + 80 + 27 = 152
29 + 70 + 44 or 42 + 70 + 31
or 43 + 70 + 30 = 143, similarly
59 + 80 + 20 or 39 + 80 + 40 = 159.
The missing number is :
159 – (80 + 10) = 69

8. *(c)* : The number at the bottom is the product of two numbers at the top, *i.e.*,
13 × 17 = 221
12 × 19 = 228, similarly
13 × 18 = 234

9. *(b)* : Square of number at the bottom is equal to the product of two numbers at the top, *i.e.*,
6^2 = 4 × 9, *i.e.*, 36
12^2 = 9 × 16, *i.e.*, 144, similarly
20^2 = 16 × ?, *i.e.*, 400. The missing number is 400 ÷ 16 = 25

10. *(b)* : The sum of the products of the digits of numbers in 1st and 3rd columns is the number in the 2nd column, *i.e.*,
(5 × 1) + (6 × 1) = 11
(6 × 4) + (3 × 2) = 30, similarly
(3 × 5) + (4 × 3) = 27

11. *(d)* : The sum of numbers on right and centre subtracted from the number on the left gives the number at the bottom, *i.e.*,
93 – (27 + 63) = 3
79 – (38 + 37) = 4, similarly
67 – (16 + 42) = 9

12. *(c)* : The number inside each triangle is the difference of the numbers at its base *i.e.*
10 – 4 = 6, 18 – 4 = 14 and 18 – 10 = 8
14 – 8 = 6, 22 – 8 = 14 and 22 – 14 = 8, similarly
11 – 5 = 6, 15 – 5 = 10 and 15 – 11 = 4.

13. *(c)* : The sum of squares of two numbers at the top gives the third number below, *i.e.*,
$2^2 + 4^2 = 20$
$3^2 + 9^2 = 90$, similarly
$1^2 + 5^2 = 26$

14. *(a)* : The sum of numbers in 1st and 2nd column plus 1 is the number in the 3rd column, *i.e.*,
27 + 22 + 1 = 50
13 + 12 + 1 = 26, similarly
9 + 2 + 1 = 12

15. *(d)* : The product of numbers on either side of the triangle plus the number at the base is the number inside the triangle, *i.e.*,
(5 × 3) + 4 = 19
(6 × 4) + 5 = 29, similarly
(7 × 5) + 6 = 41

16. *(a)* : Clockwise starting from number 7, the next number is obtained by doubling the number and adding 2, *i.e.*,
(7 × 2) + 2 = 16
(16 × 2) + 2 = 34 . . . , similarly
(34 × 2) + 2 = 70
(70 × 2) + 2 = 142
(142 × 2) + 2 = 286

17. *(c)* : The difference between the numbers in opposite sectors is 13, *i.e.*,
26 – 13 = 13
68 – 55 = 13, similarly
The missing number is 42 – 13 = 29
(42 + 13 = 55 is not given as option)

18. *(b)* : The number at the bottom is obtained by subtracting the sum of two numbers in the centre grid line from the square of the number at the top, *i.e.*,
7^2 – (2 + 7) = 40
5^2 – (8 + 3) = 14, similarly
9^2 – (7 + 6) = 68

19. *(b)* : The number inside the brackets is obtained by multiplying the number on the left by

2 and then dividing the product by the sum of digits of number on the right, *i.e.*,
(42 × 2) ÷ (2 + 2) = 21
(162 × 2) ÷ (9 + 9) = 18, similarly
(78 × 2) ÷ (8 + 4) = 13

20. *(a)* : Subtracting the sum of squares of two numbers at the base from the square of number at the apex gives the number inside the triangle, *i.e.*,
$16^2 - (7^2 + 10^2) = 107$
$25^2 - (20^2 + 4^2) = 209$, similarly
$19^2 - (2^2 + 17^2) = 68$

21. *(c)* : The number in the centre is the product of all the 4 numbers minus 10, *i.e.*,
(3 × 5 × 2 × 6) – 10 = 170
(8 × 1 × 4 × 9) – 10 = 278, similarly
(10 × 6 × 7 × 2) – 10 = 830

22. *(d)* : The number inside the circle is the product of difference of two numbers above and difference of two numbers below, *i.e.*,
(5 – 3) (12 – 9) = 6
(8 – 4) (2 – 1) = 4, similarly
(18 – 10) (17 – 14) = 24

23. *(a)* : Starting from number 1 anticlockwise the number in the diagonally opposite section is its multiplication by 4, *i.e.*,
1 × 4 = 4, 7 × 4 = 28, 2 × 4 = 8, similarly
6 × 4 = 24

24. *(a)* : Square of the number on the left plus the number on the right is the number within brackets, *i.e.*,
$6^2 + 4 = 40$
$3^2 + 3 = 12$, similarly
$7^2 + 2 = 51$

25. *(b)* : Letter H is 8th in order of alphabetical series. Taking the sum of numbers placed vertically outside the circle + 8; multiplying it by the number on the right; then subtracting from the product the number on the left, gives the number inside the circle, *i.e.*,
Step I → 4 + 8 + 4 = 16
Step II → 16 × 5 = 80
Step III → 80 – 10 = 70
Letter C is 3rd in order, so
Step I → 2 + 3 + 5 = 10
Step II → 10 × 3 = 30
Step III → 30 – 4 = 26
Similarly, J is 10th in order, so
Step I → 8 + 10 + 6 = 24
Step II → 24 × ?
Step III → (24 × ?) – 6 = 90
Simplifying the above equation :
24 × ? = 90 + 6, *i.e.*, 96
? = 96 ÷ 24 = 4

26. *(a)* : The digits in the centre are obtained from the root of numbers on both sides *i.e.*
$\sqrt{25} = 5$ and $\sqrt{49} = 7$
gives 57
$\sqrt{81} = 9$ and $\sqrt{4} = 2$ gives 92
Similarly
$\sqrt{121} = 11$ and $\sqrt{36} = 6$ gives 116

27. *(d)* : The number in the centre divided by the number on the top gives the quotient in the lower left circle and remainder on the lower right, *i.e.*,
6) 49 (8 Quotient
48
1 Remainder
17) 108 (6 Quotient
102
6 Remainder
Similarly,
19) 422 (22 Quotient
38
42
38
4 Remainder

28. *(b)* : Letter M is 13th in order of aphabetical series. So 13 (= M) × 2 (number on the opposite side) = 9 × 5 (product of numbers above and below the square) – 19 (number inside the square) *i.e.*
13 × 2 = (9 × 5) – 19
26 = (45 – 19)
26 = 26
Letter B is 2nd in order, so
2 × 9 = (11 × 2) – 4
18 = 22 – 4
18 = 18
Similarly, letter E is 5th in order
5 × ? = (3 × 7) – 6

$5 \times ? = 21 - 6$

$5 \times ? = 15$

$? = 15 \div 5 = 3$

29. (c) : Letter R is 18th in order of aphabetical series. So the product of vertically opposite numbers + 18 (= R) = the sum of two horizontally opposite numbers, *i.e.*,

$(28 \times 23) + 18 = 173 + 489$

$644 + 18 = 662$

$662 = 662$

Letter C is 3rd in order, so

$(54 \times 15) + 3 = 342 + 471$

$810 + 3 = 813$

$813 = 813$

Similarly, letter D is 4th in order

$(1 \times 11) + 4 = 5 + ?$

$11 + 4 = 5 + ?$

$15 = 5 + ?$ or $5 + ? = 15$

So, $? = 15 - 5 = 10$

30. (c) : Letter G is 7th in order of alphabetical series. Starting from left section of the big triangle the order is G – 3, *i.e.*, 7 – 3 = 4; G + 3, *i.e.*, 7 + 3 = 10 and G × 3, *i.e.*, 7 × 3 = 21. The number in the right section of inner triangle is the sum of outer numbers minus G, *i.e.*, (4 + 10 + 21) – 7 = 35 – 7 = 28

Letter P is 16th in order so

16 – 4 = 12; 16 + 4 = 20; 16 × 4 = 64; further

(12 + 20 + 64) – 16 = 96 – 16 = 80;

Similarly,

letter T is 20th in order so

20 – 5 = 15; 20 + 5 = 25; 20 × 5 = 100

further

(15 + 25 + 100) – 20 = 140 – 20 = 120

MATRICES

In these type of questions a set of numbers or letters are given in a figure which is divided into different cells. Some logic is applied to form a pattern in rows or columns. One of the cells is left empty. The candidates are required to analyse the logic and from the given options select one which will complete the given incomplete matrix.

SOLVED EXAMPLES

1. Which one number can be placed at the sign (?) of interrogation?

15	6	5
13	3	9
8	2	?
20	7	13

(a) 1 *(b)* 4 *(c)* 6 *(d)* 7

Ans. *(a)* : The pattern of logic is columnwise. The sum of numbers in first and second column equals the sum of numbers in third and fourth column, *i.e.*, 15 + 13 = 8 + 20, *i.e.*, 28 each.

So, 5 + 9 = 14 and 14 – 13 = 1

∴ 1 completes the matrix.

2. Complete the given matrix.

W	X	Y
F	G	H
A	B	

(a) K *(b)* M *(c)* C *(d)* N

Ans. *(c)* : The letters in each row are in continuous series, *i.e.*, WXY and FGH, So C will complete the series ABC.

In yet another form of matrix columns and rows are numbered and a letter from such matrices are represented first by its row and next by column. The candidate is required to identify the set for the word given.

3. Identify the set for the given word.

	0	1	2	3	4
0	A	B	C	D	K
1	D	K	A	C	E
2	C	E	D	K	A
3	K	A	C	E	D
4	E	D	K	A	C

	5	6	7	8	9
5	T	O	P	N	L
6	N	L	T	O	P
7	O	P	N	L	T
8	L	T	O	P	N
9	P	N	L	T	O

POND

(a) 76, 87, 65, 22 *(b)* 88, 99, 77, 33 *(c)* 57, 68, 89, 42 *(d)* 68, 99, 77, 33

Ans. *(a)* : Here 'P' is represented by row 7 and column 6
'O' by row 8 and column 7
'N' by row 6 and column 5, and
'D' by row 2 and column 2.

EXERCISE

Directions (Qs. 1 to 20) : *In each question given below which one number when placed at the sign of interrogation shall complete the number matrix.*

1.

4	5	6
2	3	7
1	8	3
21	98	?

(a) 16 *(b)* 73
(c) 76 *(d)* 94

2.

3	6	8
5	8	4
4	7	?

(a) 9 *(b)* 8
(c) 7 *(d)* 6

3.

1	4	9	?
1	2	3	4
2	4	6	?

(a) 16 and 8 *(b)* 25 and 5
(c) 36 and 4 *(d)* 49 and 7

4.

7	16	9
5	21	16
9	?	4

(a) 29 *(b)* 21
(c) 13 *(d)* 42

5.

6	6	8
5	7	5
4	3	?
120	126	320

(a) 12 *(b)* 16
(c) 8 *(d)* 4

6.

20	5	7	8
10	3	4	3
?	5	1	6
20	6	9	5

(a) 8 *(b)* 20

(c) 10 (d) 12

7.

7	49	7	98
9	81	9	162
6	36	6	72
5	25	5	?

(a) 50 (b) 40
(c) 60 (d) 80

8.

(2)	4	14
(3)	5	22
(?)	6	32

(a) 1 (b) 2
(c) 3 (d) 4

9.

6	40	4
3	12	3
7	?	2

(a) 4 (b) 51
(c) 36 (d) 22

10.

10	10	10	6
3	7	2	4
?	9	9	7
6	5	9	5

(a) 27 (b) 18
(c) 24 (d) 50

11.

2	?	6	7
5	8	2	4
8	6	4	1
5	9	2	3

(a) 6 (b) 2
(c) 4 (d) 7

12.

3	15	4
7	42	5
3	?	5

(a) 18 (b) 15
(c) 16 (d) 10

13.

65	82	96
21	?	71
44	19	25

(a) 43 (b) 39
(c) 63 (d) 48

14.

8	3	4
7	6	1
2	4	?
13	5	4

(a) 1 (b) 2
(c) 3 (d) 4

15.

18	24	32
12	14	16
3	?	4
72	112	128

(a) 5 (b) 4

(c) 3 (d) 2

16.

45	39	56
90	78	112
270	?	336
1080	936	1344

(a) 468 (b) 234
(c) 243 (d) 342

17.

7	4	5
8	7	6
3	3	?
29	19	31

(a) 4 (b) 3
(c) 6 (d) 5

18.

15	18	21
3	6	7
4	5	?
9	8	7

(a) 4 (b) 6
(c) 7 (d) 5

19.

10	4	10	9
6	8	3	2
7	5	?	1
9	7	8	10

(a) 5 (b) 4
(c) 6 (d) 2

20.

4	9	1	86
2	5	3	30
11	6	7	54
10	8	6	?

(a) 72 (b) 48
(c) 91 (d) 80

Directions (Qs. 21 to 30) : *In each question given below which letters when placed at the sign of interrogation shall complete the matrix?*

21.

J	M	?	T	X
O	L	H	E	A

(a) N (b) M
(c) Q (d) P

22.

A	E	D
H	J	B
C	?	N

(a) O (b) Q
(c) K (d) S

23.

A	M	B	N
R	C	S	D
E	U	F	?

(a) T (b) F
(c) V (d) R

24.

A	D	H
F	I	M
?	N	R

(a) P (b) N
(c) K (d) O

25.

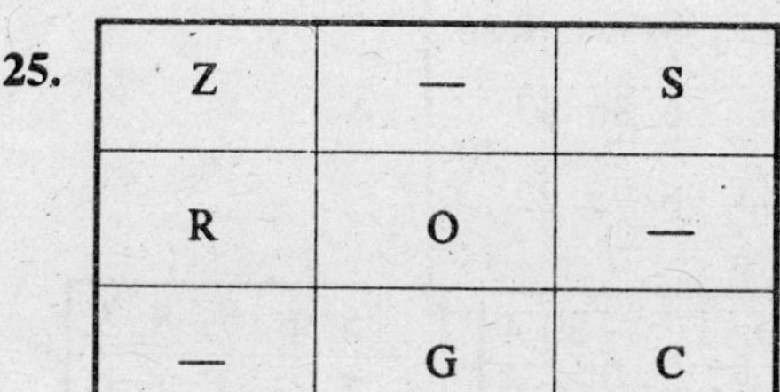

Z	—	S
R	O	—
—	G	C

(*a*) KWT (*b*) WKJ
(*c*) JKW (*d*) WJK

26.

H	K	Q
C	N	O
E	J	?

(*a*) L (*b*) N
(*c*) P (*d*) M

27.

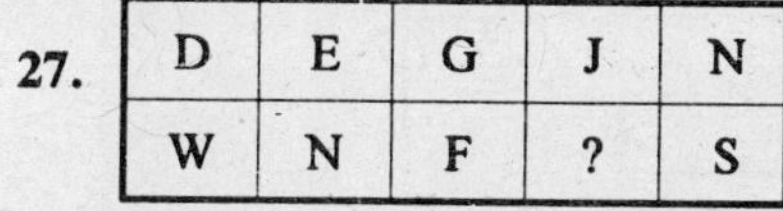

D	E	G	J	N
W	N	F	?	S

(*a*) T (*b*) Y
(*c*) Z (*d*) B

28.

H	N	Z
W	E	M
L	T	?

(*a*) V (*b*) J
(*c*) A (*d*) F

29.

J	B	M
N	F	Q
R	J	?

(*a*) U (*b*) P
(*c*) S (*d*) X

30.

X	B	F	J	?
T	P	L	H	D

(*a*) P (*b*) T
(*c*) N (*d*) M

Directions (Qs. 31 to 35) : *In questions given below, a word is represented by only one set of numbers as given in any one of the alternatives. The sets of numbers given in the alternatives are represented by two classes of alphabets as in the 2 matrices given below. The columns and rows of matrix I are numbered from 0 to 4 and that of matrix II from 5 to 9. A letter from these matrices can be represented first by its row and next by column number. Identify the set for the word given in each question.*

31.

	0	1	2	3	4
0	E	A	T	S	H
1	A	H	T	A	S
2	E	H	A	S	T
3	H	E	A	T	S
4	S	H	T	A	E

	5	6	7	8	9
5	O	R	K	L	P
6	L	P	O	R	K
7	O	K	R	P	L
8	P	R	K	L	O
9	R	L	K	O	P

REAP

(*a*) 56, 00, 22, 59
(*b*) 68, 21, 22, 86
(*c*) 96, 00, 01, 99
(*d*) 86, 34, 24, 69

32.

	0	1	2	3	4
0	C	A	F	E	D
1	C	D	A	E	D
2	D	E	C	F	E
3	A	D	D	D	C
4	D	C	A	C	A

	5	6	7	8	9
5	T	R	R	S	M
6	S	T	M	R	S
7	R	S	P	T	P
8	P	S	T	R	T
9	P	M	P	M	S

FARM

(*a*) 02, 30, 85, 65
(*b*) 20, 31, 76, 68
(*c*) 23, 12, 68, 96
(*d*) 44, 43, 87, 57

33.

	0	1	2	3	4
0	C	H	H	N	N
1	I	N	C	B	B
2	N	E	C	H	I
3	I	C	N	E	I
4	B	B	E	C	I

	5	6	7	8	9
5	Y	P	S	P	K
6	K	T	S	R	R
7	K	Y	R	Y	Y
8	P	R	K	P	R
9	S	Y	S	T	S

PREY

(*a*) 82, 76, 34, 77 (*b*) 80, 70, 43, 12
(*c*) 94, 87, 43, 56 (*d*) 88, 77, 33, 79

34.

	0	1	2	3	4
0	D	K	A	E	C
1	C	D	K	A	E
2	K	C	E	A	D
3	K	C	D	E	A
4	E	D	A	K	C

	5	6	7	8	9
5	P	L	O	T	N
6	T	P	N	L	O
7	P	N	T	O	L
8	O	N	T	P	L
9	L	O	P	N	T

COLD

(*a*) 10, 85, 79, 24
(*b*) 31, 99, 77, 22
(*c*) 30, 66, 86, 43
(*d*) 44, 96, 95, 22

35.

	0	1	2	3	4
0	M	M	R	M	R
1	O	F	R	F	N
2	R	N	O	R	O
3	F	O	F	M	O
4	F	M	R	R	F

	5	6	7	8	9
5	T	G	J	T	G
6	P	J	G	G	U
7	U	T	P	T	J
8	U	T	T	J	P
9	G	U	G	T	P

TURF

(*a*) 57,86, 44, 11
(*b*) 86, 75, 20, 32
(*c*) 77, 68, 41, 44
(*d*) 89, 97, 12, 30

EXPLANATORY ANSWERS

1. (*d*) : $4^2 + 2^2 + 1^2 = 21$, *i.e.*, $16 + 4 + 1 = 21$
$5^2 + 3^2 + 8^2 = 98$, *i.e.*, $25 + 9 + 64 = 98$
$6^2 + 7^2 + 3^2 = 36 + 49 + 9 = 94$

2. (*d*) : Sum of numbers in each row is 17, *i.e.*,
$3 + 6 + 8 = 17$
$5 + 8 + 4 = 17$
So, $17 - (4 + 7) = 6$

3. (*a*) : The root of number in first row is the number in the second row and this number multiplied by 2 is the number in the third row, *i.e.*,
$\sqrt{1} = 1$ and $1 \times 2 = 2$
$\sqrt{4} = 2$ and $2 \times 2 = 4$
$\sqrt{9} = 3$ and $3 \times 2 = 6$
So, square of 4, *i.e.*, 16 in the first row and 4×2, *i.e.*, 8 in the third row completes the matrix.

4. (*c*) :
$7 + 9 = 16$
$5 + 16 = 21$
$9 + 4 = 13$

5. (*c*) :
$6 \times 5 \times 4 = 120$
$6 \times 7 \times 3 = 126$
So, $320 \div (8 \times 5)$, *i.e.*, 8 in the third row completes the matrix.

6. (*d*) :
$5 + 7 + 8 = 20$
$3 + 4 + 3 = 10$
$5 + 1 + 6 = 12$
$6 + 9 + 5 = 20$

7. (*a*) :
$7 \times 7 = 49$ and $49 \times 2 = 98$
$9 \times 9 = 81$ and $81 \times 2 = 162$
$6 \times 6 = 36$ and $36 \times 2 = 72$
$5 \times 5 = 25$ and $25 \times 2 = 50$

8. (*d*) :
$2 \times 4 + 6 = 14$
$3 \times 5 + 7 = 22$
So, $(32 - 8) \div 6$, *i.e.*, 4 in the first column completes the matrix.

9. (*b*) :
$6^2 + 4 = 40$
$3^2 + 3 = 12$
$7^2 + 2 = 51$

10. (*c*) : The square of number in the last column and the sum of numbers in that row are

equal, *i.e.*,
$6^2 = 10 + 10 + 10 + 6$, *i.e.*, $36 = 36$
$4^2 = 3 + 7 + 2 + 4$, *i.e.*, $16 = 16$
$5^2 = 6 + 5 + 9 + 5$, *i.e.*, $25 = 25$
$7^2 = 49$ and so, $49 - (9 + 9 + 7)$, *i.e.*, 24 in the first column completes the matrix.

11. *(c)* : The sum of numbers in each row is 19, *i.e.*,

$5 + 8 + 2 + 4 = 19$
$8 + 6 + 4 + 1 = 19$
$5 + 9 + 2 + 3 = 19$

So, $19 - (2 + 6 + 7)$, *i.e.*, 4 in the second column completes the matrix.

12. *(a)* : $3 + (3 \times 4) = 15$
$7 + (7 \times 5) = 42$
$3 + (3 \times 5) = 18$

13. *(c)* : $65 - 44 = 21$
$82 - 19 = 63$
$96 - 25 = 71$

14. *(a)* : $8 + 7 - 2 = 13$
$3 + 6 - 4 = 5$

So, $4 - (4 + 1)$, *i.e.*, 1 completes the matrix.

15. *(c)* : $(18 \div 3)\ 12 = 72$
$(32 \div 4)\ 16 = 128$

So, $24 \div (112 \div 14) = 24 \div 8$, *i.e.*, 3 in the third row completes the matrix.

16. *(b)* : $45 \times 2 = 90$; $90 \times 3 = 270$ and $270 \times 4 = 1080$
$39 \times 2 = 78$; $78 \times 3 = 234$ and $234 \times 4 = 936$
$56 \times 2 = 112$; $112 \times 3 = 336$ and $336 \times 4 = 1344$

17. *(d)* : $(7 \times 3) + 8 = 29$
$(4 \times 3) + 7 = 19$

So, $(31 - 6) \div 5 = 25 \div 5$, *i.e.*, 5 in the third row completes the matrix.

18. *(a)* : $(15 \div 3) + 4 = 9$
$(18 \div 6) + 5 = 8$

So, $7 - (21 \div 7) = 7 - 3$, *i.e.*, 4 in the third row completes the matrix.

19. *(a)* : $(10 + 6) - 7 = 9$
$(4 + 8) - 5 = 7$
$(9 + 2) - 1 = 10$

So, $(10 + 3) - 8$, *i.e.*, 5 in the third row completes the matrix.

20. *(d)* : $4 + 9^2 + 1 = 86$
$2 + 5^2 + 3 = 30$
$11 + 6^2 + 7 = 54$
$10 + 8^2 + 6 = 80$

21. *(c)* : Clockwise the logic of skipping the letters is :

J M Q T X A E H L O
+2 +3 +2 +3 +2 +3 +2 +3 +2

22. *(b)* : The matrix is based on the position of the alphabet.

A (1) + D (4) = E (5)
H (8) + B (2) = J (10)
C (3) + N (14) = Q (17)

23. *(c)* : Alternate letters in each row are consecutive.

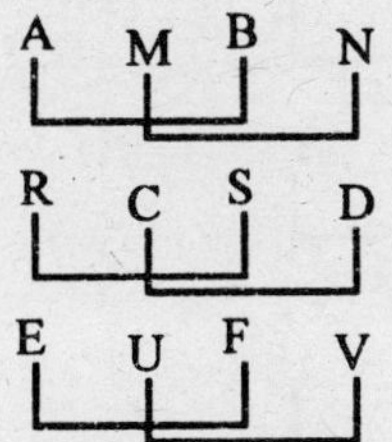

24. *(c)* : In each row the letters are moved + 3 and + 4 steps, *i.e.*,

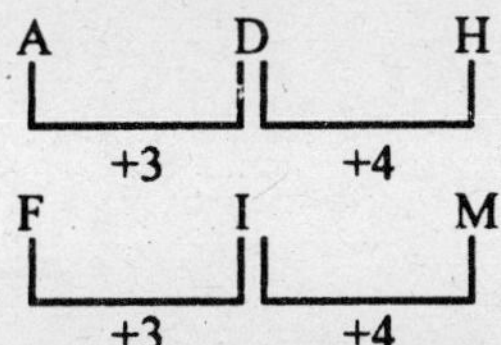

So, 'N' is moved 3 steps backward so that :

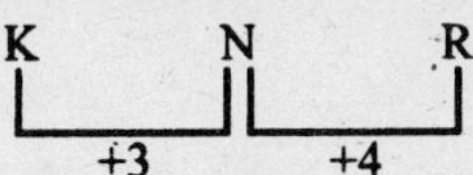

25. *(b)* : In each row the letters are moved – 3 and – 4 steps, *i.e.*,

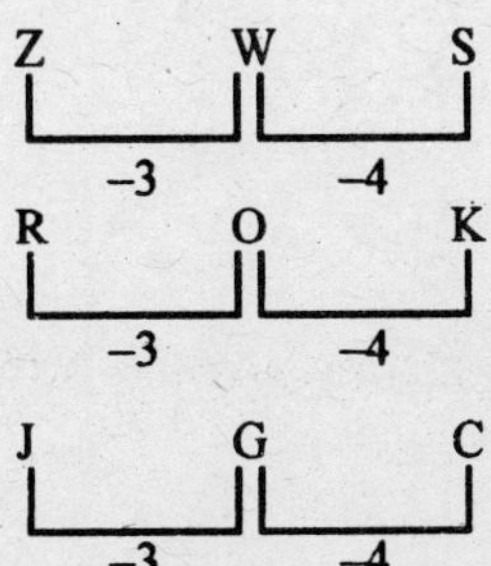

26. *(d)* : The matrix is based on position of alphabet.
Q (17) – H (8) + 2 = K (11)
O (15) – C (3) + 2 = N (14)
So, J (10) + E (5) – 2, *i.e.,* M (13) in the last column completes the series.

27. *(b)* : Clockwise the pattern is :

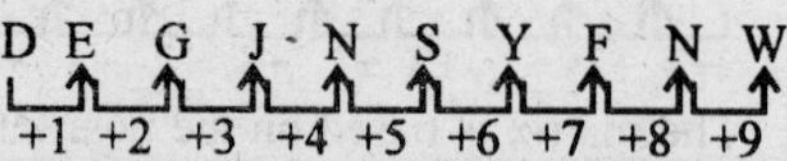

28. *(a)* : The letters in first row, second row and third row are formed by three, four and two straight lines respectively.

29. *(a)* : The letters in each column are moved four steps forward.

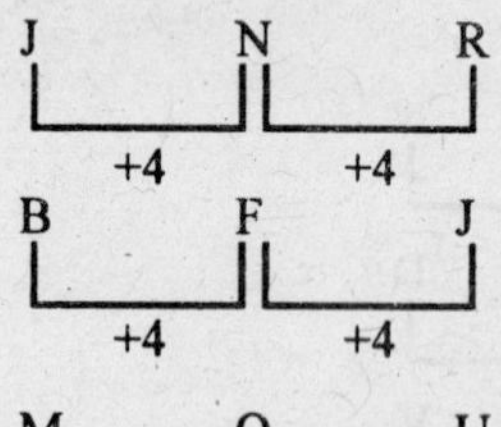

30. *(c)* : In first and second row the letters are moved four steps forward and four steps backward respectively in each cell.

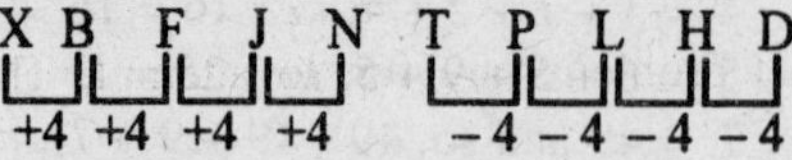

31. *(a)* : R is represented by row 5, column 6
E by row 0, column 0
A by row 2, column 2
P by row 5, column 9

32. *(c)* : F is represented by row 2, column 3
A by row 1, column 2
R by row 6, column 8
M by row 9, column 6

33. *(d)* : P is represented by row 8, column 8
R by row 7, column 7
E by row 3, column 3
Y by row 7, column 9

34. *(a)* : C is represented by row 1, column 0
O by row 8, column 5
L by row 7, column 9
D by row 2, column 4

35. *(b)* : T is represented by row 8, column 6
U by row 7, column 5
R by row 2, column 0
F by row 3, column 2

ALPHABET PROBLEMS

Alphabet problems are fun to attempt. They are based on alphabetical series in natural as well as reverse order.

Natural Order

A B C D E F G H I J K L M N O P Q R S T U V W X Y Z

Reverse Order

Z Y X W V U T S R Q P O N M L K J I H G F E D C B A

Note : The series starts from A on reaching Z and from Z on reaching A. Of these A E I O U are vowels and the rest are consonants.

SOLVED EXAMPLES

1. If the first ten letters of the following alphabet are written in the reverse order, which of the following letters will be the seventh to the left of the twelfth letter from the right end?

A B C D E F G H I J K L M N O P Q R S T U V W X Y Z

(a) H *(b)* C *(c)* I *(d)* B *(e)* None of these

Ans. *(b)* : The new series after reversing the first ten letters will be

JIHGFEDCBAKLMNOPQRSTUVWXYZ

7th 12th

12th letter from right end, counting from 'Z', will be 'O' and 7th letter to the left of 'O' is 'C'.

2. In the following list of letters, how many D's are followed by F, but not preceded by E?

X M N D F P R S T D D F O C E D F B T E D K

(a) 4 *(b)* 3 *(c)* 2 *(d)* 1 *(e)* None of these

Ans. *(c)* : D's followed by 'F' but not preceded by 'E' are :

X M N D F P R S T D D F O C E D F B T E D K

3. If the positions of the first and sixth letters of the world BENEFICIAL are interchanged; similarly the positions of the second and seventh are interchanged and so on, which letter will be third from the right end after rearrangement?

(a) E *(b)* N *(c)* C *(d)* F *(e)* None of these

Ans. *(b)* : The position of letters after interchanging the places of letters in word BENEFICIAL will be : ICIALBENEF

3rd letter from right end will be 'N'.

4. If it is possible to make a meaningful word with the second, the fifth, the tenth and the twelfth letters of the word METROPOLITAN, which of the following will be the third letter of that word? If no such word can be made, give 'X' as the answer and if more than one such word can be made, give 'M' as the answer.

(a) N *(b)* T *(c)* Q *(d)* X *(e)* M

Ans. *(e)* : The 2nd, 5th, 10th and 12th letters of the word METROPOLITAN are E, O, T and N. The words that can be made by using these four letters are : NOTE and TONE.

5. From the word "LAPAROSCOPY", how many independent meaningful English words can be made without changing the order of the letters and using each letter only once?

(a) 1 (b) 2 (c) 3 (d) 4 (e) More than 4

Ans. (b) : The words are : LAP and COPY.

6. Some letters are given in two diagrams. The letter given in the middle area can be used more than once, while each of the other letters can be used only once to form a meaningful word. The third letter of that meaningful word will be the answer. If no such meaningful word can be made, give 'X' as the answer and if more than one such meaningful word can be made given 'M' as the answer.

HV (E) BA

(a) H (b) A (c) E (d) X (e) M

Ans. (a) : The word formed is BEHAVE.

7. Letters of certain word has been rearranged and jumbled as CAPCET. Find that word and choose the last letter of this correct word.

(a) C (b) A (c) T (d) P (e) E

Ans. (c) : The word is ACCEPT.

8. How many pairs of letters are there in the word CARROT which have as many letters between them in the word as in the alphabet?

(a) One (b) Two (c) Three (d) Four (e) More than four

Ans. (a) : The pair of letters in the word having as many letters between them in the word as in the alphabet is

C A R R O T
S

R and T have 'O' in the word and 'S' in the alphabet.

EXERCISE

Directions : *The following questions are based on alphabet series in natural or reverse order and the combinations that can be made by changing the position of alphabet in given words.*

1. Which alphabet comes immediately before the sixth alphabet from the left extreme in alphabetical series?

(a) U (b) E
(c) F (d) V
(e) G

2. Which letter is midway between G and S?

(a) L (b) N
(c) M (d) No letter
(e) None of these

3. Which letter should be ninth letter to the left of ninth letter from the right if the first half of the alphabet is reversed?

(a) I (b) D
(c) F (d) E
(e) None of these

4. If the alphabet is in reverse order, which letter will be eighth letter to the left of the seventh letter counting from the right end?

(a) O (b) P
(c) N (d) Q
(e) None of these

5. What will be the fifth letter to the right of the thirteenth letter from the right?

(a) R (b) S
(c) I (d) O
(e) P

6. If the alphabet is written in reverse order, which willl be the sixth letter to the right of P?

(a) J (b) W
(c) K (d) V
(e) None of these

7. If the alphabet are divided in two equal

halves—from A to M and N to Z, which letter in the later half would be corresponding to letter J?
(*a*) W (*b*) Q
(*c*) V (*d*) R
(*e*) None of these

8. If the alphabet are written in the reverse order, which letter will be 12th to the left of the 16th letter from your left?
(*a*) X (*b*) W
(*c*) D (*d*) V
(*e*) None of these

9. If every alternate letter starting from B is deleted from the alphabet, which of the following will be the tenth letter from the right end?
(*a*) G (*b*) H
(*c*) Q (*d*) D
(*e*) None of these

10. Which letter is exactly midway between H and S?
(*a*) L (*b*) M
(*c*) N (*d*) K
(*e*) None of these

11. Starting from the fifth letter from the left, if twelve letters are written in reverse order, then which letter will be the seventh to the left of the fourteenth letter from the right?
(*a*) N (*b*) H
(*c*) L (*d*) O
(*e*) None of these

12. If every alternate letter starting from B is written in small letters, rest all are in capital letters, how will the month of 'September' be written?
(*a*) SEptEMbEr (*b*) sePTemBeR
(*c*) SEptembER (*d*) SEpteMbeR
(*e*) None of these

13. In the reverse alphabet series what letter will be second on the left of the central letter between J and T?
(*a*) P (*b*) N
(*c*) Q (*d*) No letter
(*e*) None of these

14. What letter will come in the centre of 19th letter from the left and 18th letter from the right?
(*a*) O (*b*) N
(*c*) L (*d*) M
(*e*) K

15. What will be the letter which is tenth on the right of eleventh letter from the left if the alphabet are written in reverse order?
(*a*) P (*b*) K
(*c*) F (*d*) U
(*e*) B

16. What letter will come in the centre of sixth letter from the right and thirteenth letter from the left?
(*a*) Q (*b*) R
(*c*) P (*d*) S
(*e*) T

17. If the vowels are removed from the alphabetical series, what will be the eighteenth letter to the left of twenty-first letter from the left in the reverse order?
(*a*) S (*b*) P
(*c*) R (*d*) X
(*e*) None of these

18. If the alphabetical series is reversed and every second letter is eliminated, what letter will come in the centre of the new series?
(*a*) M (*b*) O
(*c*) N (*d*) P
(*e*) R

19. In the new series obtained in the earlier question, what letter will be on the right of eleventh letter from the right?
(*a*) R (*b*) B
(*c*) O (*d*) H
(*e*) T

20. What letter will be third on the left of fifteenth letter on the right of K in the alphabet series?
(*a*) U (*b*) V
(*c*) W (*d*) T
(*e*) X

21. If every third letter in the series is eliminated, the number of vowels remaining in the new series will be :
(*a*) 1 (*b*) 2
(*c*) 3 (*d*) All 5
(*e*) None of these

22. What will be the eighth letter to the left of next letter of the letter twentieth from the left?

(a) K (b) P
(c) M (d) L
(e) R

23. What letter comes in the middle of sixteenth letter from the right and seventeenth letter from the left?

(a) L (b) N
(c) P (d) M
(e) O

24. If the alphabetical series is written in reverse order, what letters will come on either side of the seventh letter to the left of seventeenth letter from the right?

(a) X, Z (b) W, Y
(c) Y, W (d) Z, X
(e) None of the above

25. If the alphabetical series is written as AZ, BY, CX, DW and so on, then what will be the eleventh pair of letters?

(a) IR (b) LO
(c) JQ (d) KP
(e) None of the above

26. If in the word "DISTURBANCE", the first letter is interchanged with the last letter, the second letter is interchanged with the tenth letter and so on, which letter would come after the letter "T" in the newly formed word?

(a) I (b) U
(c) N (d) S
(e) T

27. If it is possible to make a meaningful word with the fourth, the seventh, the eleventh and the thirteenth letters of the word CATEGORISATION, which of the following will be the first letter of that word? If no such word can be made, give 'X' as the answer. If more than one such word can be made, give 'M' as the answer.

(a) R (b) T
(c) O (d) X
(e) M

28. How many pairs of letters are there in the word BUCKET which have as many letters between them in the word as in the alphabet?

(a) One (b) Two
(c) Three (d) Four
(e) More than four

29. If it is possible to make a meaningful word with the third, the fifth, the seventh and the tenth letters of the word PROJECTION, which of the following is the third letter of that word? If no such word can be made, give 'X' as the answer. If more than one such word can be made, give 'M' as the answer.

(a) T (b) N
(c) O (d) X
(e) M

30. If it is possible to make a meaningful word with the second, the fifth and the eighth letters of the word CARETAKER, which of the following will be the first letter of that word? If no such word can be made, give 'X' as the answer and if more than one such word can be made, give 'M' as the answer.

(a) T (b) E
(c) A (d) X
(e) M

31. If the position of the fifth and twelfth letters of the word GLORIFICATIONS is interchanged and likewise the position of the fourth and fourteenth letters, the third and tenth letters, the second and eleventh letters and the first and thirteenth letters are interchanged, which of the following will be twelfth letter from the right end?

(a) T (b) O
(c) R (d) I
(e) None of these

32. A meaningful word is made if we take the first, fourth, fifth, seventh, tenth, eleventh and the twelfth letters of the word "FELICITATIONS". Which of the following will be the fifth letter of that word from the right end of that word?

(a) T (b) C
(c) N (d) I
(e) None of these

33. If any two letters in the word PRISON have as many letters between them in the word as there are in the English alphabet, they form an alpha-pair. How many such alpha-pairs are there in the word PRISON?

(a) Nil (b) 1
(c) 2 (d) 3
(e) More than 3

34. If it is possible to make a meaningful word with the third, the sixth, the ninth and the eleventh letters of the word PRESENTATION, which letter will be third in that word? If more than one such words can be made, give 'M' as the answer. If no such word can be made, give 'X' as the answer.

(a) T (b) E
(c) M (d) N
(e) X

35. If it is possible to make a meaningful word with the fourth, the eighth and the tenth letters of the word COUNTERACT, which of the following will be the last letter of that word? If no such word can be made, give 'X' as answer. If more than one such word can be made, give 'M' as the answer.

(a) A (b) N
(c) T (d) X
(e) M

36. If it is possible to make a meaningful word out of the second, the fourth, the fifth and the eighth letters of the word 'ILLOGICAL' then which of the following will be the third letter of the so formed word? If more than one word can be formed then give 'X' as the answer. If no meaningful word can be formed then give 'Z' as the answer.

(a) O (b) A
(c) G (d) X
(e) Z

37. If two consecutive letters of the word BENEVOLENT are interchanged then what letter will come in the seventh place from the right?

(a) N (b) E
(c) L (d) V
(e) O

38. If a meaningful word can be made from the first, third, fifth and seventh letters of the word RECIPROCAL, what will be the last letter of the new word?

(a) R (b) A
(c) P (d) C
(e) No word can be made

39. On rearranging the jumbled spelling of the word SKARTINS, a language is obtained. What is the fifth letter from the right of the rearranged word?

(a) N (b) K
(c) R (d) S
(e) A

40. In the word 'BERATE' there are two letters which are as many letters apart as they are in alphabet. What is the last letter out of the two such letters?

(a) A (b) B
(c) E (d) R
(e) T

41. If the first and fourth letters, second and fifth letters and third and sixth letters of the word STUMPY are interchanged, what letters will enclose letter T?

(a) M, Y (b) U, P
(c) U, M (d) S, U
(e) Y, U

42. If the 1st, 3rd, 5th, 7th, 10th and 13th letters of the word "ENTERTAINMENT" are used to make a meaningful word, then what two letters will come in the centre?

(a) A M (b) T T
(c) R E (d) N A
(e) A T

43. In the word EXAMPLE there are two letters which are as many letters apart as they are in alphabet. What is the letter in the centre of two such letters in alphabetical series?

(a) C (b) N
(c) Q (d) Z
(e) E

44. On rearranging the jumbled spelling of the word GRUBY a sport is obtained. What is the letter in the centre?

(a) R (b) B
(c) G (d) U
(e) Y

45. If the word PALM is rearranged to form a new word, what will be the third letter from the left of the new word?

(a) M (b) L
(c) P (d) A
(e) No word can be made

46. If the alphabetical series is altered in this manner :
AB written as A, CD written as B, EF written as C and so on, then what will be the sixth letter from the right in the new series?
(a) E (b) H
(c) L (d) P
(e) I

47. If the letters 'VISERL' are rearranged to form a meaningful word, what will be the last letter of this word?
(a) E (b) R
(c) L (d) S
(e) V

48. If a meaningful word can be formed by using the second, fourth and fifth letters of the word ABATABLE, which letter will be in the middle? If more than one such word can be made give 'M' as the answer. If no such word can be made, give 'X' as the answer.
(a) T (b) B
(c) A (d) X
(e) M

49. If the letters 'CAPCET' are rearranged to form a meaningful word, what will be the third letter from the right?
(a) P (b) E
(c) C (d) T
(e) A

50. If the letters 'ILCEOP' are rearranged to form a meaningful word, what will be the fourth letter from the left?
(a) L (b) P
(c) O (d) I
(e) E

51. The letter given in the centre can be used more than once, while each other letter is to be used only once to form a meaningful word. The third letter of that meaningful word is the answer. If no such meaningful word can be made, give 'X' as the answer and if more than one such meaningfull word can be made, give 'M' as the answer.

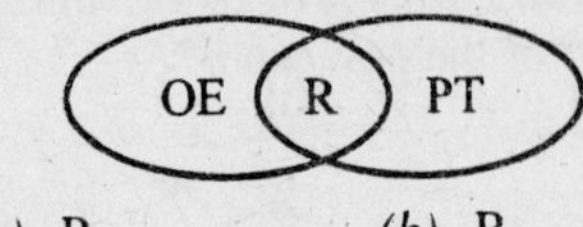

(a) P (b) R
(c) O (d) X
(e) M

52. Which is the middle letter between E and J?
(a) F (b) G
(c) H (d) I
(e) None of the above

53. What is the number of the different letters which occur in the word PANCHATANTRA?
(a) 9 (b) 6
(c) 7 (d) 11
(e) 12

54. Which of the following letter groups when read from backward consist of alphabet removed by two?
(a) NLJHF (b) VZXYW
(c) MJGDA (d) QSPRN
(e) None of the above

55. If the alphabet series is written in the manner AZBYCX . . . . and so on, what will be the fifth letter to the right of fifteenth letter from the left?
(a) P (b) J
(c) S (d) Q
(e) T

56. If every fourth letter of the alphabet series is selected and written in reverse order, what will be the fifth letter from the left?
(a) H (b) J
(c) P (d) R
(e) M

57. The letter in the centre can be used more than once, while each other letter is to be used only once to form a meaningful word. The fourth letter of that meaningful word is the answer. If no such meaningful word can be made give 'X' as the answer and if more than one such meaningful word can be made, give 'M' as the answer.

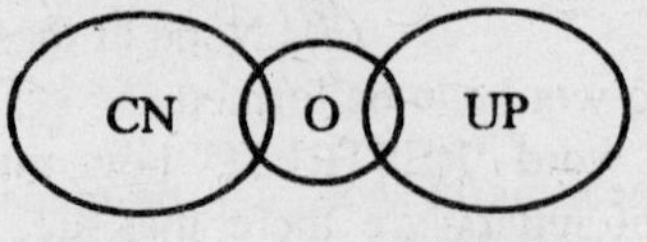

(a) O (b) U
(c) P (d) X
(e) M

58. If the letters of the word THORN are rearraged to form a direction, what will be the second letter from the right?

(a) T (b) N
(c) O (d) H
(e) No new word can be formed

59. In the word SEISMOGRAPH how many such pairs of letters are there that are as many letters apart as they are in the alphabet series?

(a) 1 (b) 2
(c) 3 (d) More than 3
(e) None of these

60. If a meaningful word can be formed by using the first, third, fifth, and seventh letters of the word INFORMAL, what will be the last letter?

(a) N (b) F
(c) M (d) R
(e) No new word can be made

61. Rearrange the letter AYDOT to form a meaningful word. The last letter of this word is the answer.

(a) A (b) T
(c) Y (d) D
(e) O

62. If a meaningful word can be formed by using the second, fourth, fifth and seventh letters of the word EASTERN, the last letter of this meaningful word is the answer. If no such meaningful word can be made give 'X' as the answer, and if more than one such meaningful word can be made give 'M' as the answer.

(a) A (b) T
(c) E (d) X
(e) M

63. If the letters 'ERVSECI' can be rearranged to form a meaningful word what will be the fifth letter from the right?

(a) R (b) V
(c) E (d) None of these
(e) No word can be formed

64. In the word 'RESTRICT' how many such pairs of letters are there that are as many letters apart as they are in the alphabet series?

(a) 1 (b) 2
(c) 3 (d) More than 3
(e) None of these

65. In the given chart the letter in the centre is to be used more than once, while other letters can be used only once to make a meaningful word. The second letter from right of this meaningful word is the answer. If no such meaningful word can be made give 'X' as the answer, and if more than one such meaningful word can be made, give 'M' as the answer.

INA (R) DOY

(a) A (b) R
(c) D (d) X
(e) M

66. Which letter is to the right of middle letter between F and R?

(a) L (b) G
(c) M (d) O
(e) H

67. If a meaningful word can be formed by using the first, third, fifth and sixth letters of the word AUTHORITY, the second letter from left of this meaningful word is the answer. If no such meaningful word can be made give 'X' as the answer, and if more than one such meaningful word can be made, give 'M' as the answer.

(a) H (b) U
(c) R (d) X
(e) M

68. If a meaningful word can be formed by using the second, fourth, fifth and seventh letters of the word INVESTIGATE, the third letter from left of this meaningful word is the answer. If no such meaningful word can be formed mark 'X' as the answer, and if more than one such meaningful word can be made, mark 'M' as the answer.

(a) E (b) I
(c) N (d) X
(e) M

69. How many such pairs of letters are there in the word PHILOSOPHER that are as many letters apart as they are in the alphabet series?

(a) 1 (b) 2

(c) 3 (d) More than 3
(e) None of these

70. How many X's are there in the following list of letters which are immediately preceded by P but not immediately followed by Q?
S P X Q R S R P X P R S X Q P X Q R P X S P R
(a) 1 (b) 2
(c) 3 (d) 4
(e) None of these

71. How many A's are there in the following list of letters which are not immediately preceded by C but immediately followed by B?
D C B A C B D D C A D B C A D B C A A B D C C D A B C
(a) 1 (b) 2
(c) 3 (d) 4
(e) None of these

72. The letter in the centre is to be used more than once while all other letters are to be used only once to form a meaningful word. The first letter of this meaningful word is the answer. If no such meaningful word can be made give 'X' as the answer, and if more than one such meaningful word can be made, give 'M' as the answer.

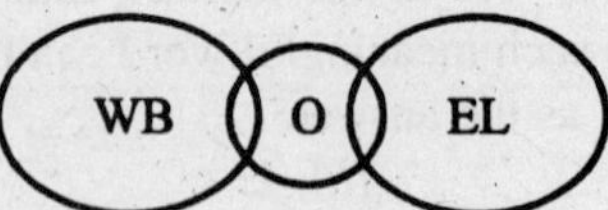

(a) L (b) E
(c) B (d) X
(e) M

73. How many P's are there in the following series which are immediately followed by W but not immediately preceded by K?
K P C W K P W N K G P W W P H K V P W Z P W
(a) 1 (b) 2
(c) 3 (d) 4
(e) None of these

74. How many pairs of letters are there in the word MOTHERLY which are as many letters apart in the word as they are in the alphabet series?
(a) 0 (b) 1
(c) 2 (d) 3
(e) More than 3

75. If a meaningful word can be formed by rearranging the letters WITST, the last letter of this meaningful word is the answer. If no such meaningful word can be formed mark 'X' as the answer, and if more than one such meaningful word can be made, mark 'M' as the answer.
(a) T (b) S
(c) W (d) X
(e) M

76. How many M's are there in this series which are immediately preceded by N and immediately followed by L?
N L M L N L N M L M N M L L M N L
(a) 1 (b) 2
(c) 3 (d) More than 3
(e) None of these

77. From the word INFATUATION how many independent meaningful English words can be made without changing the order of the letters and using each letter only once?
(a) 1 (b) 2
(c) 3 (d) 4
(e) More than 4

78. From the word HASTEN how many independent meaningful English words can be made without changing the order of the letters and using each letter only once?
(a) 1 (b) 2
(c) 3 (d) 4
(e) More than 4

79. From the word MATERIALISTIC how many independent meaningful words can be made without changing the order of the letters and using each letter only once?
(a) 1 (b) 2
(c) 3 (d) 4
(e) More than 4

80. From the word CATCHMENTAREA how many independent meaningful words can be made without changing the order of the letters and using each letter only once?
(a) 1 (b) 2
(c) 3 (d) 4
(e) More than 4

EXPLANATORY ANSWERS

1. (b) :

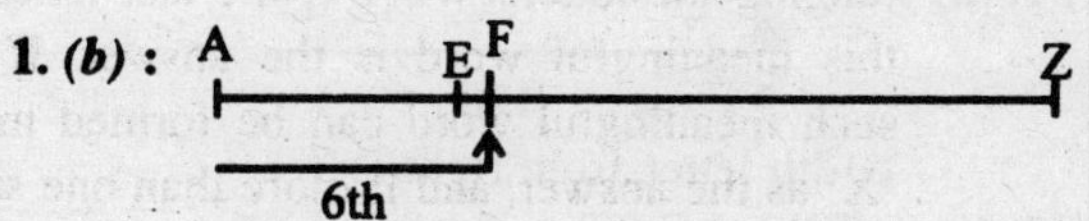

Sixth letter from left is 'F' and letter immediately before 'F' is 'E'.

2. (c) :

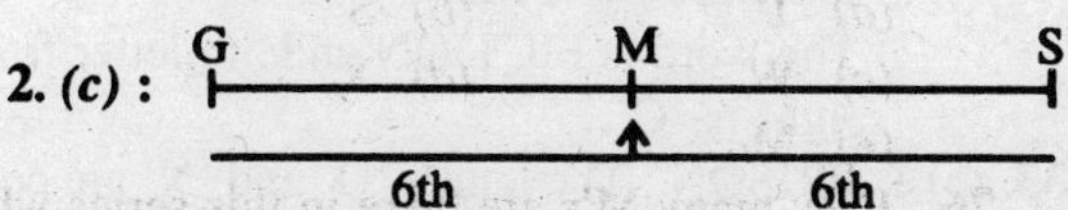

'M' is midway between G and S.

3. (d) : MLKJIGHFEDCBANOPQRSTUVWXYZ

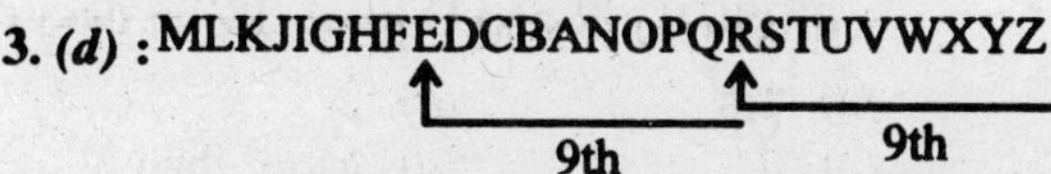

4. (a) : ZYXWVUTSRQPONMLKJIHGFEDCBA

5. (b) :

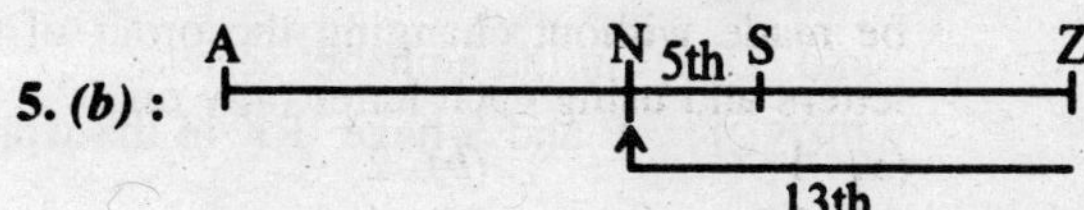

13th letter from right is 'N' and 5th letter to the right of 'N' is 'S'.

6. (a) :

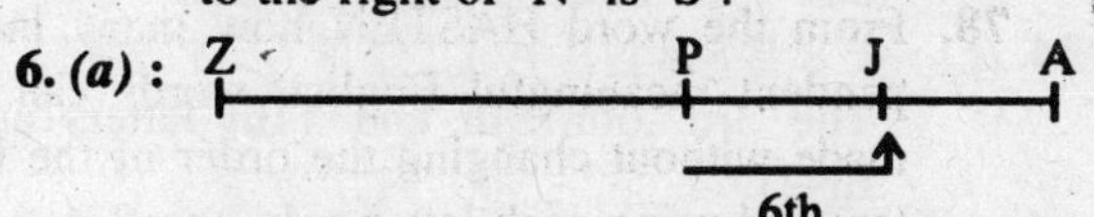

In reverse series the 6th letter to the right of 'P' is 'J'.

7. (a) : A B C D E F G H I J K L M
N O P Q R S T U V W X Y Z

8. (b) :

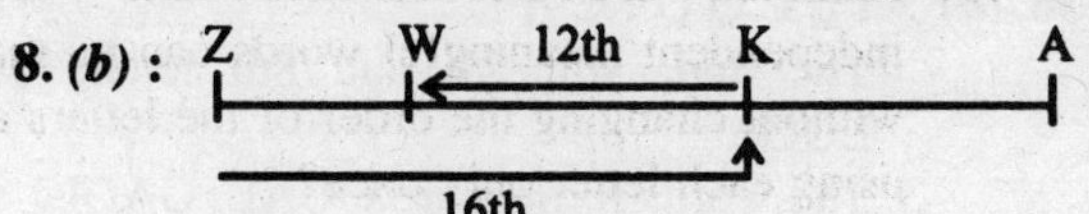

16th letter from left is 'K' and 12th letter to the left of 'K' is 'W'.

9. (a) : ACEGIKMOQSUWY

10th

10. (e) :

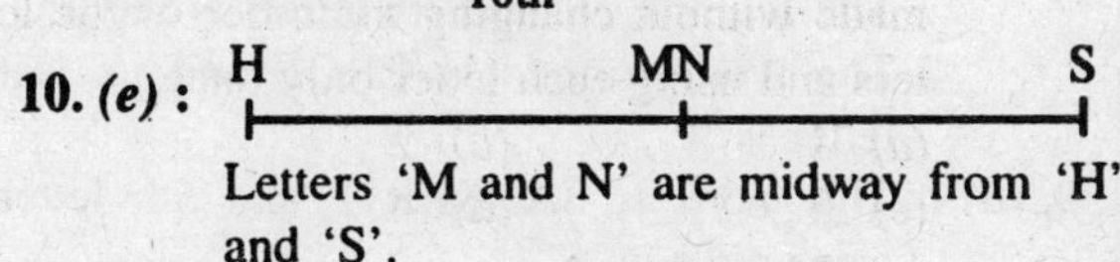

Letters 'M and N' are midway from 'H' and 'S'.

11. (d) : ABCDPONMLKJIHGFEQRSTUVWXYZ

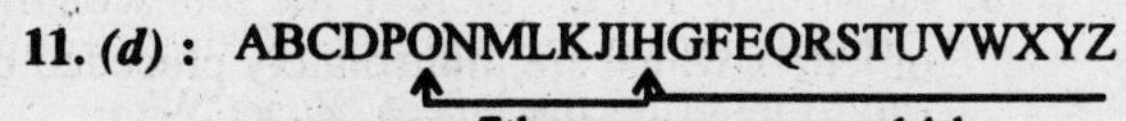

12. (a) : A b C d E f G h I j K l M n O p Q r S t U v W x Y z

2nd

13. (c) : T S R Q P O N M L K J

Central letter is 'O' and second letter on its left is Q.

14. (b) :

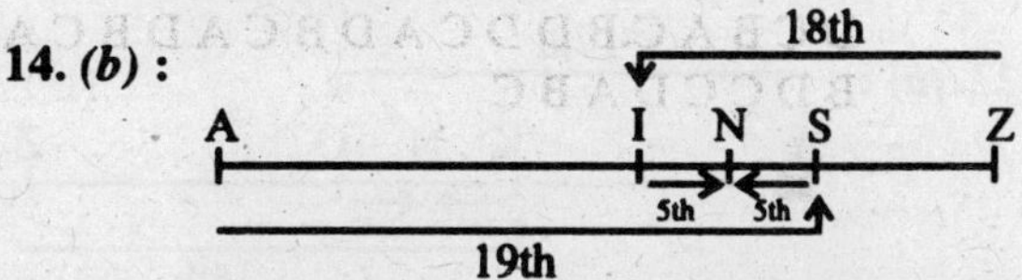

19th letter from left is 'S' and 18th letter from right is 'I'. The letter in the centre of 'I' and 'S' is 'N'.

15. (c) :

11th letter from left is 'P' and 10th letter of the right of 'P' is 'F'.

16. (a) :

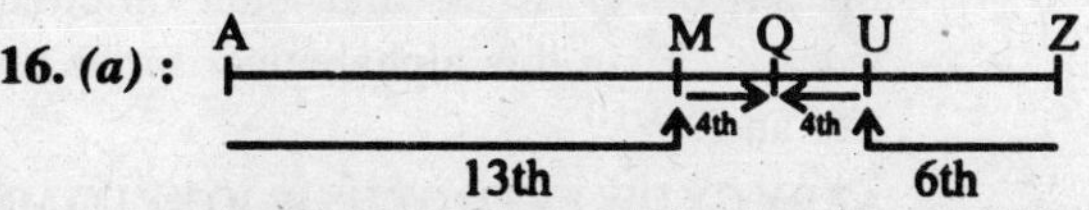

13th letter from left is 'M' and 6th letter from right is 'U'. The letter in the centre of 'M' and 'U' is 'Q'.

17. (d) : ZYXWVTSRQPNMLKJHGFDCB

1st 18th 21th

21st letter from left is 'B' and 18th letter to the left of 'B' is 'X'.

18. (c) : Z X V T R P N L J H F D B

7th 7th

19. (e) : Z X V T R P N L J H F D B

11th

11th letter from right is 'V' and letter on the right of 'V' is 'T'.

20. (c) : 

15th letter on the right of 'K' is 'Z' and third letter on the left of 'Z' is 'W'.

21. (b) : A B D E G H J K M N P Q S T V W Y Z

22. (c) : 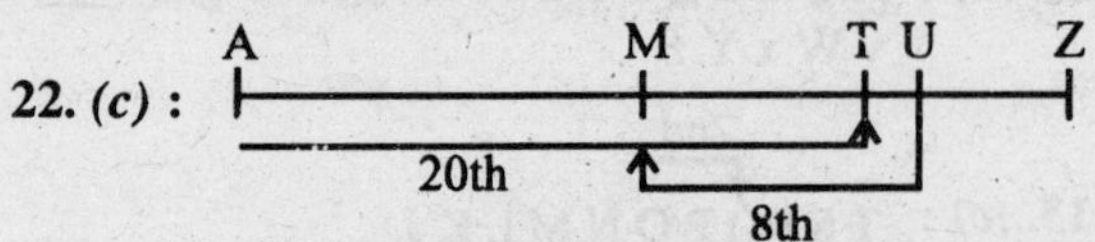

20th letter from left is 'T'. Letter next to 'T' is 'U'. 8th letter to the left of 'U' is 'M'.

23. (b) : 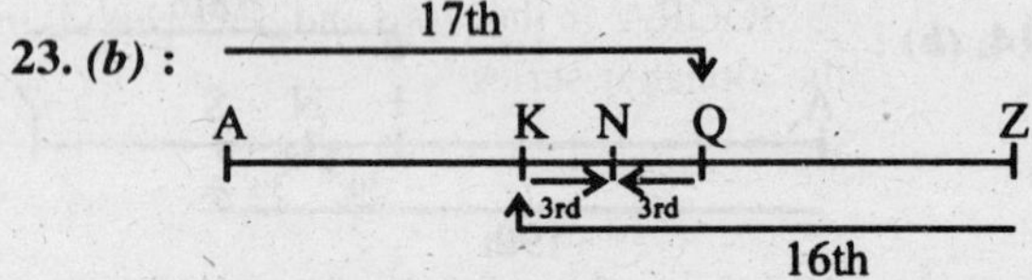

16th letter from right is 'K' and 17th letter from left is 'Q'. The letter in the middle of 'K' and 'Q' is 'N'.

24. (c) : 

17th letter from right is 'Q', 7th letter to the left of 'Q' is 'X' and letter on either side of 'X' in this alphabetical series are 'Y' and 'W'.

25 (d) : AZ BY CX DW EV FU GT HS IR JQ KP LO MN

11th

26. (d) : E C N A B R U T S I D

27. (e) : CATEGORISATION

The 4th, 7th, 11th and 13th letters are ERTO.

The words formed are TORE and ROTE.

28. (a) : BUCKET : C and E have K in the word

D

and D in the alphabetical series.

29. (e) : P R O J E C T I O N

The 3rd, 5th, 7th and 10th letters are OETN.

The words formed are TONE and NOTE.

30. (e) : C A R E T A K E R

The 2nd, 5th and 8th letters are ATE.

The words formed are ATE, EAT and TEA.

31. (a) : N I T S O F I C A O L I G R

12th

12th letter from right is T'.

32. (b) : F E L I C I T A T I O N S

The 1st, 4th, 5th, 7th, 10th, 11th and 12th lettes are FICTION.

The word is FICTION and 5th letter from right is 'C'.

33. (e) : PRISON : The letters 'O' and 'N' are continuous in the word and in alphabet series.

PRISON : R and O have 'IS' in the word

QP

and 'QP' in the alphabet series.

PRISON : R and N have 'ISO' in the word

QPO

and 'QPO' in the alphabet series.

PRISON : P and S have 'RI' in the word

QR

and 'QR' in the alphabet series.

34. (c) : P R E S E N T A T I O N

The 3rd, 6th, 9th and 11th letters are ENTO.

The words formed are NOTE and TONE.

35. (e) : C O U N T E R A C T

The 4th, 8th and 10th letters are NAT.

The words formed are TAN and ANT.

36. (d) : I L L O G I C A L

The 2nd, 4th, 5th and 8th letters are LOGA.

The words formed are GOAL, GAOL.

37. (a) : E B E N O V E L T N

7th

7th letter from right is 'N'.

38. (c) : R E C I P R O C A L

The 1st, 3rd, 5th and 7th letters are RCPO.

The word formed is CROP and its last letter is 'P'.

39. (d) : The word is SANSKRIT and 5th letter from right is 'S'.

40. (e) : BERATE : R and T have 'A' in the word and 'S' in the alphabet series. (S)
The last letter of this pair is 'T'.

41. (d) : M P Y S T U

42. (b) : E N T E R T A I N M E N T
The 1st, 3rd, 5th 7th, 10th and 13th letters are ETRAMT.
The word formed is MATTER.

43. (a) : EXAMPLE: A and E have 'MPL in the word and 'BCD' in the alphabet series. (BCD)
The letter in the centre is 'C'.

44. (c) : The sport is RUGBY. The letter in the centre is 'G'.

45. (a) : The word is LAMP and 3rd letter from left is 'M'.

46. (b) : A B C D E F G H I J K L M (6th)

47. (b) : The word is SILVER and the last letter is 'R'.

48. (e) : A B A T A B L E
The 2nd, 4th and 5th letters are BTA.
The words formed are : BAT. TAB.

49. (b) : The word is ACCEPT and the 3rd letter from right is 'E'.

50. (d) : The word is POLICE and the fourth letter from left is 'I'.

51. (e) : The words formed are REPORT and PORTER.

52. (e) : E F G H I J
Two letters 'GH' are in the middle of 'E' and 'J'.

53. (c) : P A N C H A T A N T R A
The different letters are P, A, N, C, H, T, R.

54. (c) : M J G D A
LK IH FE CB

55. (d) : AZBYCHDWEVFUGTHSIRJQKPLOMN
15th 5th
15th letter from left is 'H' and 5th letter to the right of 'H' is 'Q'.

56. (a) : X T P L H D.
5th

57. (c) : The word formed is COUPON and the fourth letter is 'P'.

58. (a) : The direction is NORTH and the second word from right is 'T'.

59. (b) : SEISMOGRAPH: R and P have 'A' in the word and 'Q' in the alphabet series. (Q)
SEISMOGRAPH: I and P have 'SMOGRA' in the word and 'JKLMNO' in the alphabet series. (JKLMNO)

60. (d) : I N F O R M A L
The 1st, 3rd, 5th and 7th letters are IFRA.
The word formed is FAIR; its last letter is 'R'.

61. (c) : The word is TODAY; its last letter is 'Y'.

62. (e) : E A S T E R N
The 2nd, 4th, 5th and 7th letters are ATEN.
The words formed are NEAT and TANE.

63. (a) : The word is SERVICE and fifth letter from right is 'R'.

64. (b) : R E S T R I C T : The letters 'S' and 'T' are continuous in the word and in alphabet series.
RESTRICT: E and I have 'STR' in the word and 'FGH' in the alphabet series. (FGH)

65. (d) : No word can be formed.

66. (c) : F G H I J K L M N O P Q R
6th 6th
The letter in the centre of F and R is 'L' and the letter to the right of 'L' is 'M'.

67. (d) : A U T H O R I T Y
1st, 3rd, 5th and 6th letters are ATOR.
No word can be formed.

68. (c) : I N V E S T I G A T E
The 2nd, 4th, 5th and 7th letters are NESI.
The word formed is SINE and the third letter from left is 'N'.

69. ***(c)*** **:** PHILOSOPHER : The letters 'O' and 'P' and 'H' and 'I' are continuous in the word and in alphabet series.
ONMLKJI
PHILOSOPHER : The letter 'P' and 'H' have 'HILOSOP' in the word and 'ONMLKJI' in the alphabet series.
MN
L and O have 'OS' in the word and 'MN' in the alphabet series.

70. ***(b)*** **:** SPXQRSRPXPRSXQPXQRPXSPR
1 2

71. ***(b)*** **:** D C B A C B D D C A D B C A D B C AAB D C C DABC
1 2

72. ***(e)*** **:** The words formed are BELOW, BOWEL and ELBOW.

73. ***(c)*** **:** KPCWKPWNKGPWWPHKVPW ZPW
1 2 3

74. ***(c)*** **:** MOTHERLY
NOPQ : M and R have 'OTHE' in the word 'NOPQ' in the alphabet series.
MOTHERLY
UVWX : T and Y have 'HERL' in the word and 'UVWX' in the alphabet series.

75. ***(a)*** **:** The word is TWIST, its last letter is 'T'.

76. ***(b)*** **:** N L M L N L N M L M N M L L M N L
1 2

77. ***(d)*** **:** The words formed are : IN, FAT, AT, ION.

78. ***(b)*** **:** The words formed are : HAS, TEN.

79. ***(b)*** **:** The words formed are : MATE, REALISTIC

80. ***(c)*** **:** The words formed are : CATCH, MEN, AREA.

INPUT INTERPRETATIONS

These type of logical interpretations are common in competitive examinations specially held for recruitment as officers in Banks. Candidates are required to clearly study the given data and information, understand the given pattern and then attempt questions following the data.

SOLVED EXAMPLE

Directions (Qs. 1 to 5) : *Study the following information to answer the given questions :*

A word rearrangement machine when given an input line of words, rearranges them, following a particular rule, in each step. The following is an illustration of input and the steps of rearrangement.

Input : Over you pat me crow easy to.

Steps :

(I) pat over you crow easy to me

(II) crow pat over you to me easy

(III) over crow pat to me easy you

(IV) to over crow pat easy you me, and so on.

As per the rule followed in the above steps, find out the appropriate step for the given input in the following questions.

1. If step V of an input is 'put down col in as much sa', what would be the VIIIth step?

(a) down in put much sa as col

(b) in put down col much sa as

(c) much in put down sa as col

(d) col put down as much sa in

(e) None of these

Ans. *(e)* : The steps followed are :

Step V : put down col in as much sa

Step VI : in put down col much sa as

Step VII : down in put much sa as col

Step VIII : much down in put as col sa

2. Input : but calm free are so not eat. Which of the following will be the IIIrd step for this input?

(a) so free but calm eat are not

(b) but calm are free not so eat

(c) are but calm free not eat so

(d) but so free eat are not calm

(e) None of these

Ans. *(d)* : The step followed are :

Input : but calm free are so not eat

Step I : free but calm so not eat are

Step II : so free but calm eat are not

Step III : but so free eat are not calm

3. Input : rim bye eat klin fe to low. Which of the following steps woulld be 'fe low rim to bye klin eat'?

(a) VIth *(b)* Vth *(c)* IVth *(d)* IIIrd

(e) None of these

Ans. *(b)* : The step followed are :

Input : rim bye eat klin fe to low

Step I : eat rim bye fe to low klin

Step II : fe eat rim bye low klin to
Step III : rim fe eat low klin to bye
Step IV : low rim fe eat to bye klin
Step V : fe low rim to bye klin eat

4. If step II of an input is 'ge su he for game free but', what would be the step VI?

(a) ge for but free he game su **(b)** for free ge game su he but
(c) free ge for but game su he **(d)** he ge su but game free for
(e) None of these

Ans. (e) : The step followed are :

Step II : ge su he for game free but
Step III : he ge su game free but for
Step IV : game he ge su but for free
Step V : ge game he but for free su
Step VI : but ge game he free su for

5. If step IV of an input is 'blue navy kit lime se get out', which of the following would definitely be the input?

(a) navy get lime out kit se blue **(b)** lime navy get kit se blue out
(c) lime blue navy kit get out se **(d)** kit blue navy, se get out lime
(e) None of these

Ans. (a) : The steps followed are :

Step IV : blue navy kit limc se get out
Step III : navy kit lime blue out se get
Step II : kit lime navy get blue out se
Step I : lime navy get kit se blue out
Input : navy get lime out kit se blue

EXERCISE

Directions (Qs. 1 to 6) : *Study the following information to answer the given questions :*

An electronic device when fed with the numbers, rearranges them in a particular order following certain rules. The following is a step-by-step process of rearrangement for the given input numbers—

Input :	85	16	36	04	19	97	63	09
Step I :	97	85	16	36	04	19	63	09
Step II :	97	85	63	16	36	04	19	09
Step III :	97	85	63	36	16	04	19	09
Step IV :	97	85	63	36	19	16	04	09
Step V :	97	85	63	36	19	16	09	04

(For the given input step V is also the last step.)

1. Which of the following will be the last step for the given input?

Input : 16 09 25 27 06 05

(a) I *(b)* II
(c) III *(d)* IV
(e) None of these

2. Which of the following will be the step II of the given input?

Input : 82 80 79 99 22 32 50

(a) 99 82 80 79 50 32 22
(b) 99 82 80 79 50 22 32
(c) 99 82 80 79 32 22 50
(d) 99 82 80 79 22 32 50
(e) None of these

3. Which of the following will be the step III for the given input?

Input : 09 25 16 30 32 19 17 06

(a) 32 25 09 16 30 19 17 06
(b) 32 30 25 09 16 19 17 06
(c) 32 30 09 25 16 19 17 06
(d) 32 09 25 16 30 19 17 06
(e) None of these

4. If the Step IV is as given below, which of the following was the input?

Step IV : 92 86 71 69 15 19 06 63 58

(a) 86 92 69 71 15 19 06 63 58

(*b*) 15 19 06 63 58 86 92 69 71
(*c*) 15 86 19 92 06 69 63 58 71
(*d*) Cannot be determined
(*e*) None of these

5. Which of the following will be the last step for the given input?
Input : 03 31 43 22 11 09
(*a*) IV (*b*) V
(*c*) VI (*d*) Can't be determined
(*e*) None of these

6. Which of the following will be the Vth step for the given input?
Input : 25 08 35 11 88 67 23
(*a*) 88 67 35 25 23 11 08
(*b*) 88 67 35 25 23 08 11
(*c*) 88 67 35 25 08 11 23
(*d*) 08 11 23 25 35 67 88
(*e*) None of these

Directions : (Qs. 7 to 10) : *Study the following information to answer the given questions :*

A word arrangement machine, when given an input line of words, rearranges them following a particular rule in each step. The following is an illustration of input and the steps of rearrangement:

Input : As if it on as Zoo figure Of in at
Step I : as As if it on Zoo figure Of in at
Step II : as As at if it on Zoo figure Of in
Step III : as As at figure if it on Zoo of in
Step IV : as As at figure if in it on Zoo Of
Step V : as As at figure if in it Of on Zoo
(and step V is the last step for this input.)

As per the rules followed in the above steps, find out in the given questions the appropriate step for the given input.

7. IV step was like this—
an apple at cot was red on one side
Which of the following will definitely be the input?
(*a*) apple at an cot was red on one side
(*b*) cot an at apple was red on one side
(*c*) was cot red an on at one apple side
(*d*) cannot be determined
(*e*) None of these

8. Input—Him and His either or her, which step will be the last step for this input?
(*a*) I (*b*) II
(*c*) III (*d*) IV
(*e*) V

9. Input—you are at fault on this, which of the following step would be—are at fault on you this?
(*a*) I (*b*) II
(*c*) III (*d*) IV
(*e*) V

10. Input—am ace all if Is
Which of the following will be the II step?
(*a*) all am ace if Is
(*b*) ace all am Is if
(*c*) ace all am if is
(*d*) Is if am ace all
(*e*) None of these

Directions (Qs. 11 to 15) : *Study the following information to answer the given questions :*

A word arrangement machine, when given an input line of words, rearranges them following a particular rule in each step. The following is an illustration of input and the steps of rearrangement.

Input : Go for to Though By easy To Access at
Step I : Access Go for to Though By easy To at
Step II : Access at Go for to Though by easy To
Step III : Access at By Go for to Though easy to
Step IV : Access at By easy Go for to Though To
Step V : Access at By easy for Go to Though To
Step VI : Access at By easy for Go Though to To
Step VII : Access at By easy for Go Though To to
(and Step VII is the last step for this input.)

As per the rules followed in the above steps, find out in the given questions the appropriate step for the given input.

11. Input : Over Go for through at one.
Which step number will be the last step of the above input?
(*a*) III (*b*) IV
(*c*) V (*d*) VII
(*e*) None of these

12. Input : Story for around on was He at.
Which of the following will be the IV step?
(*a*) around at He for story on was
(*b*) around at for He story on was
(*c*) around at for He on story was
(*d*) around at for He on was story
(*e*) None of these

13. Input : Together over series on feast the so.
Which of the following steps will be the last but one?
(*a*) II (*b*) III
(*c*) IV (*d*) V
(*e*) None of these

14. Input : every and peer to an for
Which of the following steps would be 'an and every for peer to'?
(*a*) II (*b*) IV
(*c*) V (*d*) III
(*e*) None of these

15. The step II of an input is as follows :
and Do pet to on that
Which of the following would definitely be the input?
(*a*) Do and pet on to that
(*b*) Do pet to and that on
(*c*) Do on pet to and that
(*d*) Cannot be determined
(*e*) None of these

Directions (Qs. 16 to 20) : *Study the following information carefullly and answer the questions given below :*

The admission ticket for an exhibition bears a password which is changed after every clock hour based on set of words chosen for each day. The following is an illustration of the code and steps of rearrangement for subsequent clock hours. The time is 9 a.m. to 3 p.m.

Day's first password :

First Batch : 9 a.m. to 10 a.m.
is not ready cloth simple harmony burning.
Second Batch : 10 a.m. to 11 a.m.
ready not is cloth burning harmony simple.
Third Batch : 11 a.m. to 12 noon
cloth is not ready simple harmony burning.
Fourth Batch : 12 noon to 1 p.m.
not is cloth ready burning harmony simple.
Fifth Batch : 1 p.m. to 2 p.m.
ready cloth is not simple harmony burning.

16. If the password for 11 a.m. to 12 noon was—"soap shy miss pen yet the she", what was the the password for the first batch?
(*a*) shy miss pen soap yet the she
(*b*) pen miss shy soap she the yet
(*c*) miss soap pen shy she the yet
(*d*) soap pen miss shy she the yet
(*e*) None of these

17. If the password for 6th batch, *i.e.,* 2 p.m. to 3 p.m. is—"are trap cut he but say lap", what will be the password for 2nd batch, *i.e.,*10–11 a.m.?
(*a*) are he cut trap lap say but
(*b*) cut he are trap but say lap
(*c*) he cut trap are lap say but
(*d*) trap are he cut lap say but
(*e*) None of these

18. If the password for the first batch was—"rate go long top we let have", which batch will have the password—"go rate top long have let we?"
(*a*) Second (*b*) Third
(*c*) Fourth (*d*) Fifth
(*e*) None of these

19. Day's first password—"camel road no toy say me not", what will be the password for fourth batch, *i.e.,* 12 noon to 1 p.m.?
(*a*) toy camel road no say me not
(*b*) toy no road camel not me say
(*c*) no road camel toy not me say
(*d*) road camel toy no not me say
(*e*) None of these

20. If the batch 2 of the day has following password—"came along net or else eky lot", what would be the password for batch 4, (*i.e.,* 12 noon to 1 p.m.)?
(*a*) along net or came else key lot
(*b*) or net along came lot key else
(*c*) came or net along lot key else
(*d*) net or came along else key lot
(*e*) None of these

Directions (Qs. 21 to 24) : *Study the following informatin to answer the given questions :*

There are five identical looking boxes having

different objects in it and every box has a label indicating their contents.

The following is the description of the contents and the label of each box . . .

Contents	*Label*
Two Pins	PP
Two Balls	BB
Two Clips	CC
One Pin and one Clip	PC
One Ball and one Clip	BC

Somebody has mischieviously inter-changed these lables in such a way that no box contains the label correctly explaining its content.

21. If the information is available that box PC does not contain either any Pin or any Clip and box PP does not contain any Pin and box CC contains one Clip and one Ball, which of the following will definitely be true if only one of the remaining boxes is opened?
(a) It will have atleast one Clip
(b) It will have atleast one Pin
(c) It will have two Pins
(d) It will have one Pin and one Clip
(e) None of these

22. If the box PP contained two Clips, the box CC atleast one Pin, which of the following will definitely be not true?
(a) The box PC contains two balls
(b) The box BB contains one Clip
(c) The box BC contains two Balls
(d) The box BC contains one Pin and one Clip
(e) The box BB contains one Ball and one Clip

23. If the first box opened contained label PP and second box opened contained label PC and out of the combined four items, one item was a Ball, which of the following will be definitely true?
(a) Other three items will not contain any Clip
(b) Other three items will contain atleast one Clip
(c) Other three item will not contain two Pins
(d) Other three items will not contain two Balls
(e) None of these

24. If the first box, containing the label BC was opened and it was found that one item is a Ball, which of he following would be definitely true?
(a) The other item will not be a Ball
(b) The other item will also be a Ball
(c) The other box with BB label will contain a Ball and a Clip
(d) The other item may either be a Ball or a Clip
(e) None of these

Directions (Qs. 25 to 29) : *Study the following information carefully and answer the questions given below :*

An export processing unit has a computerised machine which generates six codes to distinguish product of each of seven batches produced in a day. The machine is fed code for first batch of each day. Based on that, the machine generates 6 codes by rearrangement of words for subsequent batches. Following is an illustration of generation of codes for some batches of a day.

Day's first batch
—who nut cream page for table.

Day's second batch
—who for cream page nut table.

Day's third batch
—who for page cream nut table.

Day's fourth batch
—table for page cream nut who.

Day's fifth batch
—page table for nut who cream.

Day's sixth batch
—page who for nut table cream.

and so on till seventh batch. Next day based on the same rule, new set of words will be introduced as given above :

25. If the first batch code of a day is 'five gave it close to mine', which of the following will be the code for fourth batch?
(a) five to it close gave mine
(b) mine to close it gave five
(c) five to close it gave mine
(d) close five to gave mine it
(e) None of these

26. If the code of fifth batch of a day is 'same is tea at now then', which of the following

would definitely be the first code of that day?
(*a*) tea same is now then at
(*b*) same now tea at is then
(*c*) now at then same tea is
(*d*) now tea is same then at
(*e*) None of these

27. If the code of fourth batch is 'so when clean get lemon dust', which of the following would be the code for seventh batch?
(*a*) get dust lemon when so clean
(*b*) clean so when lemon dust get
(*c*) when get dust so clean lemon
(*d*) clean dust lemon when so get
(*e*) None of these

28. If the code of sixth batch of the day is 'very say could man on fire', which of the following batch codes would read as 'say could very fire man on'?
(*a*) Second (*b*) Third
(*c*) Fourth (*d*) Fifth
(*e*) None of these

29. If the seventh batch of the day is 'from door no leaf glass but', which of the following would be the first three words of the code of batch third of that day?
(*a*) door leaf from . . . .
(*b*) door leaf but . . . . .
(*c*) glass leaf from . . . . .
(*d*) but door no . . . . .
(*e*) None of these

Directions (Qs. 30 to 35) : *Study the following information to answer the given questions.*

A number sorting machine, when given an input of numbers, rearranges the numbers in a particular manner step by step as indicated below—till all the numbers are arranged in a particular order.

Input	29	2	15	5	20	11	50	105	28	19	30	140
Step I	2	29	15	5	20	11	50	105	28	19	30	140
Step II	2	140	15	5	20	11	50	105	28	19	30	29
Step III	2	140	5	15	20	11	50	105	28	19	30	29
Step IV	2	140	5	105	20	11	50	15	28	19	30	29
Step V	2	140	5	105	11	20	50	15	28	19	30	29
Step VI	2	140	5	105	11	50	20	15	28	19	30	29
Step VII	2	140	5	105	11	50	15	20	28	19	30	29
Step VIII	2	140	5	105	11	50	15	30	28	19	20	29
Step IX	2	140	5	105	11	50	15	30	19	28	20	29
Step X	2	140	5	105	11	50	15	30	19	29	20	28

(This is the final arrangement and Step X is the last step for the given input.)

30. Which of the following was the input of the following final output?
Final output :
16 159 19 160 40 161 80 162
(*a*) 19 16 159 40 162 80 160 161
(*b*) 162 16 40 19 161 159 80 160
(*c*) 80 159 19 16 40 160 162 161
(*d*) Cannot be determined
(*e*) None of these

31. Which of the following will be the Vth step for the following input?
Input :
15 19 90 3 50 16 4 99 91
(*a*) 3 99 4 91 50 16 90 19 15
(*b*) 3 99 4 91 15 16 90 19 50
(*c*) 3 99 4 91 15 90 16 19 50
(*d*) Cannot be determined
(*e*) None of these

32. Which of the following will be the IIIrd step for the following input?
Input :
20 10 50 55 40 19 12
(*a*) 10 55 50 20 40 19 12
(*b*) 10 20 50 55 40 19 12
(*c*) 10 55 12 40 20 19 50
(*d*) Cannot be determined
(*e*) None of these

33. Which of the following will be step II for the following input?
Input :
16 13 400 26 150 200 19
(*a*) 13 16 400 26 150 200 19
(*b*) 13 400 14 26 150 200 16
(*c*) 13 400 16 26 150 200 19
(*d*) Cannot be determined
(*e*) None of these

34. Which of the following will be first step for the following input?
Input :
100 500 2 400 20 3 800 1 999 666
(*a*) 1 500 2 400 20 3 800 100 999 666
(*b*) 2 500 100 400 20 3 800 1 100 666
(*c*) 999 500 2 400 20 3 800 1 100 666
(*d*) Cannot be determined
(*e*) None of these

35. How many steps would be required in get-

ting the final output for the following input?
Input : 10 4 1 9 8 12
(*a*) One (*b*) Two (*c*) Three (*d*) Four (*e*) None of these

EXPLANATORY ANSWERS

Qs. 1 to 6 : *Arrange the terms in descending order step-by-step as can be seen from the given table :*

1. (*b*) : Input : 16 09 25 27 06 05
Step I : 27 16 09 25 06 05
Step II : 27 25 16 09 06 05

2. (*b*) : Input : 82 80 79 99 22 32 50
Step I : 99 82 80 79 22 32 50
Step II : 99 82 80 79 50 22 32

3. (*b*) : Input : 09 25 16 30 32 19 17 06
Step I : 32 09 25 16 30 19 17 06
Step II : 32 30 09 25 16 19 17 06
Step III : 32 30 25 09 16 19 17 06

4. (*b*) : Input : 15 19 06 63 58 86 92 69 71
Step I : 92 15 19 06 63 58 86 69 71
Step II : 92 86 15 19 06 63 58 69 71
Step III : 92 86 71 15 19 06 63 58 69
Step IV : 92 86 71 69 15 19 06 63 58

5. (*b*) : Input : 03 31 43 22 11 09
Step I : 43 03 31 22 11 09
Step II : 43 31 03 22 11 09
Step III : 43 31 22 03 11 09
Step IV : 43 31 22 11 03 09
Step V : 43 31 22 11 09 03

6. (*a*) : Input : 25 08 35 11 88 67 23
Step I : 88 25 08 35 11 67 23
Step II : 88 67 25 08 35 11 23
Step III : 88 67 35 25 08 11 23
Step IV : 88 67 35 25 23 08 11
Step V : 88 67 35 25 23 11 08

Qs. 7 to 10 : *Arrange the terms in dictionary order step-by-step as can be seen from the given table :*

7. (*c*) : Input : was cot red an on at one apple side
Step III : an was cot red on at one apple side
Step II : an apple was cot red on at one side
Step III : an apple at was cot red on one side
Step IV : an apple at cot was red on one side

8. (*c*) : Input : Him and His either or her
Step I : and Him His either or her
Step II : and either Him His or her
Step III : and either her Him His or

9. (*d*) : Input : You are at fault on this
Step I : are you at fault on this
Step II : are at you fault on this
Step III : are at fault you on this
Step IV : are at fault on you this

10. (*c*) : Input : am ace all if Is
Step I : ace am all if Is
Step II : ace all am if Is

11. (*b*) : Words are written in dictionary order.
Input : Over Go for through at one
1st Step : at Over Go for through one
2nd Step : at For Over Go through one
3rd Step : at For Go Over through one
4th Step : at For go one Over through (Last Step)
4th step will be the last step.

12. (*b*) : Input : Story for around on was He at
1st Step : around Story for on was He at
2nd Step : around at Story for on was He
3rd Step : around at for Story on was He
4th Step : around at for He Story on was

13. (*d*) : Input : Together over series on feast the so
1st Step : feast Together over series on the so.
2nd Step : feast on Together over series the so
3rd Step : feast on over Together series the so
4th Step : feast on over series Together the so
5th Step : feast on over series so Together the
6th Step : feast on over series so the Together
(Last Step) : 6th step will be the last step.
5th step will be the last but one.

14. (*d*) : Input : every and peer to an for
1st Step : an every and peer to for
2nd Step : an and every peer to for
3rd Step : an and every for peer to

15. *(e)*

Qs. 16 to 20 : *These questions are based on certain rules, just identify the rules and relations in order to solve them. It is seen that :*

1. Out of seven words, the sixth word does not change at all. The fifth and the seventh word exchange their places alternately.

2. In the first four words, in the 2nd and 4th step the third word becomes the first word and the word preceding it follows it in the new sequence. But in the 3rd and 5th step 1st and 4th words and 2nd and 3rd words interchange their position.

1st Batch : is not ready cloth simple harmony burning.

According to law in the 2nd step the third word ('ready' should become the first word and 'not' the second word in the new sequence). The fifth and seventh word should interchange their position. Thus the second sequence should be "ready not is cloth burning harmony simple".

Whereas in the third sequence the words (1 and 4 and 2 and 3 should interchange their position as well as 5th and 7th word should interchange).

The third sequence should thus be :

cloth is not ready simple harmony burning.

Both of these correlate with the sequences given. Based on these the questions can be easily solved.

16. *(a)* **17.** *(a)* **18.** *(c)* **19.** *(d)* **20.** *(a)*

21. *(b)* : PC is labelled as BB
PP is labelled as CC
CC is labelled as BC

22. *(c)* : PP is labelled as CC
CC is labelled as PP
BB is labelled as BC
PC is labelled as BB
BC is labelled as PC

23. *(e)*

24. *(b)* : BC is labelled as BB

Qs. 25 to 29 : The operations are as follows :

Ist batch → IInd batch : 2nd and 5th words are interchanged.

IInd Batch → IIIrd Batch : 3rd and 4th words are interchanged.

IIIrd Batch → IVth Batch : 1st and 6th words are interchanged.

IVth Batch → Vth Batch : 1st, 2nd, 3rd, 4th, 5th, 6th words become 2nd, 3rd, 1st, 6th, 4th, 5th respectively.

Vth Batch → VIth Batch : 2nd and 5th words are interchanged [Same as (1)].

VIth Batch → VIIth Batch : 3rd and 4th words are interchanged [Same as (2)].

25. *(b)* : I Batch → five gave it close to mine
II Batch → five to it close gave mine
III Batch → five to close it gave mine
IV Batch → mine to close it gave five

26. *(c)* : V Batch → same is tea at now then
IV Batch → is tea same then at now
III Batch → now tea same then at is
II Batch → now tea then same at is
I Batch → now at then same tea is

27. *(d)* : VI Batch → so when clean get lemon dust
V Batch → clean so when lemon dust get
VI Batch → clean dust when lemon so get
VII Batch→clean dust lemon when so get

28. *(b)* : VI Batch → very say could man on fire
V Batch → very on could man say fire
IV Batch → on could very fire man say
III Batch → say could very fire man on

29. *(a)* : VII Batch→from door no leaf glass but
VI Batch → from door leaf no glass but
V Batch → from glass leaf no door but
IV Batch → glass leaf from but no door
III Batch → door leaf from but no glass

30. *(e)* : The input is likely to be :
162 16 80 19 159 40 161 160

31. *(b)* :

Input :	15	19	90	3	50	16	4	99	91
Step I :	3	19	90	15	50	16	4	99	91
Step II :	3	99	90	15	50	16	4	19	91
Step III :	3	99	4	15	50	16	90	19	91
Step IV :	3	99	4	91	50	16	90	19	15
Step V :	3	99	4	91	15	16	90	19	50

32. *(e)* :

Input :	20	10	50	55	40	19	12
Step I :	10	20	50	55	40	19	12
Step II :	10	55	50	20	40	19	12
Step III :	10	55	12	20	40	19	50

33. *(c)* :

Input :	16	13	400	26	150	200	19
Step I :	13	16	400	26	150	200	19
Step II :	13	400	16	26	150	200	19

34. *(a)* :

Input :	100	500	2	400	20	3	800	1	999	666
Step I :	1	500	2	400	20	3	800	100	999	666

35. *(d)* :

Input :	10	4	1	9	8	12
Step I :	1	4	10	9	8	12
Step II :	1	12	10	9	8	4
Step III :	1	12	4	9	8	10
Step IV :	1	12	4	10	8	9

BEST REASON AND COMMON SENSE

These type of questions are framed to test the candidate's awareness of daily experiences and knowledge of various subjects. The candidate has to select from the given options, the one that goes best with the given statement.

SOLVED EXAMPLES

1. A song always has :
(a) meaning *(b)* lyrics *(c)* rhyme *(d)* music

Ans. *(b)* : In a song, the most important are the lyrics. Without lyrics there can be no song and hence no meaning or rhyme or even music.

2. In summer, people wear light coloured clothes because :
(a) they want to look smart
(b) light colours are safe against excess heat
(c) dark coloured clothes are not available
(d) the sun rays cannot tan the skin

Ans. *(b)* : Light colours absorb less heat and thus keep away excess heat.

3. Teachers must have a thorough knowledge of the subject they teach because :
(a) they can boast about their learning
(b) they can get a good job
(c) the students will listen to them carefully
(d) they will be able to solve the questions of their students

Ans. *(b)* : Only if the teachers are skilled can they get a good job. If they don't get a job they cannot teach the students.

EXERCISE

Directions : *In each of the questions given below, there are five options. Find out the one that is correct in verification of the given statement.*

1. A mirror always :
(a) refracts *(b)* reveals the truth
(c) distorts *(d)* reflects

2. While riding a horse downhill, a person must :
(a) bend to his left
(b) bend his body backwards
(c) bend to his right
(d) bend his body in front

3. I am walking towards North. I will see the sun :
(a) rising on my left
(b) setting on my right
(c) rising on my right
(d) in front of me

4. Deserts always have :
(a) dry weather *(b)* camel
(c) sand *(d)* storms

5. A hospital always has :
(a) emergency *(b)* nurses
(c) laboratories *(d)* doctors

6. The most essential thing for a driver is :
(a) his uniform *(b)* his wallet
(c) his duty *(d)* his eyesight

7. Sound travels .... light.
(a) slower than (b) as slow as
(c) faster than (d) as fast as

8. What is always associated with a tree?
(a) roots (b) branches
(c) flowers (d) leaves

9. The diagonals of a parallelogram are perpendicular. This figure is a :
(a) quadrilateral (b) square
(c) rectangle (d) rhombus

10. Escalators help in :
(a) vertical movement only
(b) horizontal movement only
(c) vertical and horizontal movements
(d) circular movement only

11. Blood is formed in the human adult by :
(a) bone marrow (b) liver
(c) heart (d) lungs

12. Man who wears spectacles when working with a microscope, should :
(a) keep on wearing the spectacles
(b) take off the spectacles
(c) wearing or taking off the spectacles make no difference
(d) not use the microscope at all

13. The pitch of the voice of women in general is :
(a) higher than that of men
(b) much lower than that of men
(c) same as men
(d) cannot be compared

14. Gas used for refrigeration is :
(a) chlorine (b) ammonia
(c) oxygen (d) helium

15. Which of the following is an explosive?
(a) RDX (b) TNT
(c) Picric acid (d) All of the above

16. A figure is a circle which :
(a) is divided into four equal parts
(b) has two right angles
(c) has a large area
(d) has no angles

17. Electricians wear rubber gloves because :
(a) they keep their hands soft
(b) they are bad conductors of electricity
(c) they are cheaper than other gloves
(d) it is fashionable for them to do so

18. Those working in laboratories must wear aprons because :
(a) they are a part of the uniform
(b) aprons keep their dresses safe
(c) only scholars wear aprons
(d) aprons are made of colourful dress material

19. Platinum is costlier than silver because it is :
(a) rarely found
(b) whiter than silver
(c) more in demand
(d) lighter than silver

20. Traffic signals are necessary at all cross roads because :
(a) they add colour to the black roads
(b) they are the indications of being on crossroads
(c) they help in regulating the traffic
(d) traffic policemen are not on duty during night time

21. Children must read more and more books because :
(a) they are being collected in school library
(b) teachers insist on reading them
(c) they are helpful in increasing the knowledge
(d) the reading habit will give less time for watching television

22. It is necessary to exercise in the morning because :
(a) it keeps our body fit
(b) it is easier to pass the time if one wakes up very early
(c) it is a good habit
(d) many people are illiterate and they cannot read the morning newspaper

23. Women wear jewellery because :
(a) they want to flaunt their riches
(b) they cannot keep the ornaments at home where no one is there in their absence
(c) men like women who wear jewellery
(d) they want to look beautiful

24. Every nation must maintain a strong army because :
(a) many people can be employed
(b) it is essential for the nation's defence

(*c*) it helps in maintaining law and order in the country
(*d*) it will control the terrorist activities

25. Person sitting next to me is my best friend because :
(*a*) he takes me out for a movie every week
(*b*) he stood by me during my difficult times
(*c*) he is praised by one and all
(*d*) he helps me with my studies

26. Poking of the fire brightens it because :
(*a*) unburnt parts catch fire
(*b*) it scatters sparks in all direction
(*c*) it allows in more air
(*d*) the burnt particles move away

27. Rubber soles are used in shoes because :
(*a*) they are porous than leather
(*b*) they are cheaper
(*c*) they are durable
(*d*) they can be mended easily

28. Sea-water tastes saltish because :
(*a*) salt is deposited in the sea by rivers
(*b*) water bodies secrete salt
(*c*) of the presence of salt rocks at the sea bed
(*d*) sea weeds produce salt

29. Privatisation is advocated because :
(*a*) Government requires funds to bridge deficits in the budget
(*b*) Public sector undertaking's performance has been poor
(*c*) of the shift in philosophy of the public sector's role
(*d*) Government and public sector cannot merge their functionings

30. Breathing gets difficult at greater heights because :
(*a*) of the lack of oxygen at higher places
(*b*) the person is tired by the time he reaches his destination
(*c*) the person is suffering from asthma
(*d*) the air of places at greater heights is polluted

31. It is easier to walk on road than on hardened ice because :
(*a*) people are accustomed to walking on road
(*b*) traffic on roads is regulated
(*c*) the shoe companies are not efficient in making shoes fit for walking on ice
(*d*) there is less friction on ice

32. A clown always acts funny because :
(*a*) he is paid only if he acts thus
(*b*) he is not suitable for serious performances
(*c*) it is his job to make others laugh
(*d*) his mind is full of pranks

33. It is necessary for every company to advertise its products because :
(*a*) advertising is an effective way of boosting the sale of their products
(*b*) every big company advertises its products
(*c*) it provides employment to many models
(*d*) it is officially recommended by the company's financial department

34. A person's blood pressure is normally lower in the morning because :
(*a*) he has had a good sound sleep
(*b*) the person ate a light dinner and slept early
(*c*) it is a natural biological rhythm
(*d*) all of the above

35. Parents give pocket–money to their children because :
(*a*) they have extra money in hand
(*b*) they want their children to know the value of money
(*c*) they want their children to be spendthrift
(*d*) they do not want their children to feel inferior to their friends belonging to richer families

36. Preservation of oil is necessary because :
(*a*) the government has passed such law
(*b*) the gulf countries are gradually refusing to export oil
(*c*) the oil preserved for longer period of time has more properties
(*d*) improper use will exhaust the resources

37. All industrial units should be away from the residential units because :
(*a*) the workers will go home for lunch and

work will suffer
(b) industry's expansion projects can be easily carried out
(c) the smoke emitted from industries is harmful
(d) the town-planners are more concerned about their rules of designing

38. The Selection Board call the candidates for the interview because :
(a) they want to see the candidate's physical appearance
(b) it is then easier to decide which candidate is fit for the job
(c) the members of the Selection Board have no other work during office hours
(d) none of the above

39. Smoking near a leaking gas cylinder is dangerous because :
(a) the gas may catch fire and cylinder may burst
(b) the warning sign on the cylinder says so
(c) the person who is smoking may get burns in his mouth
(d) all gas cylinders have oxygen in them

40. People send New Year cards to their friends and relatives because :
(a) it is coustomary
(b) people don't have time to write letters
(c) they want to wish their loved ones every happiness and prospertiy
(d) it is easier and cheaper to wish all the friends and relatives by sending cards

ANSWERS

1	2	3	4	5	6	7	8	9	10
(d)	(b)	(c)	(c)	(d)	(d)	(a)	(a)	(d)	(c)
11	**12**	**13**	**14**	**15**	**16**	**17**	**18**	**19**	**20**
(a)	(c)	(a)	(b)	(d)	(d)	(b)	(b)	(a)	(c)
21	**22**	**23**	**24**	**25**	**26**	**27**	**28**	**29**	**30**
(c)	(a)	(d)	(b)	(b)	(c)	(a)	(a)	(b)	(a)
31	**32**	**33**	**34**	**35**	**36**	**37**	**38**	**39**	**40**
(d)	(c)	(a)	(c)	(b)	(d)	(c)	(b)	(a)	(c)

SITUATION REACTION

This type of test includes questions wherein the candidate must use common sense in a logical, prompt and correct manner. In question based on spot reaction, some event is mentioned followed by options which reveal possible instant reactions related to the event. The candidate's action depends on experience of unforeseen events. From the suggested alternatives, he has to select the most suitable action he will possibly take on the spot of the event.

SOLVED EXAMPLE

1. While going to the office, you see a child being hit by a speeding car. The most immediate thing you would do is :
   (*a*) chase the car on your scooter
   (*b*) ignore and pass by
   (*c*) render first aid to the child
   (*d*) inform at the nearest police station about the accident

   Ans. (*c*) : The most important step is to save the child.

Note : There is no limit to the variations in such type of questions. The questions are given in this chapter only for an idea.

EXERCISE

Directions : *Each of the following questions is followed by four alternatives. Select the most appropriate answer that shall suggest your immediate action.*

1. In the examination hall, you find that your question paper is too tough to be answered satisfactorily by you. The best thing you can do is:
   (*a*) try cheating from your neighbouring candidate.
   (*b*) leave the paper and walk out.
   (*c*) try attempting those questions first of which you know something.
   (*d*) complain to the examiner about the toughness of the question paper.
2. Your best friend is annoyed with you for certain reasons. You will :
   (*a*) try your best to reason out your friend's annoyance.
   (*b*) go out and make new friends.
   (*c*) show indifference.
   (*d*) remind the friend of your good friendship.
3. You were invited to a party, but on the day of the party you are informed that the party has been cancelled. You will :
   (*a*) try to find out the reason for its cancellation.
   (*b*) decide that you will never go to that place ever again.
   (*c*) not discuss the matter with anyone.
   (*d*) hold the party at your place instead.
4. You find that the cooking gas cylinder is leaking. The first thing you would do is :
   (*a*) switch off the light.
   (*b*) close the knob of the cylinder.
   (*c*) call the fire brigade for help.
   (*d*) alert all the members at home.
5. While returning home from a far away place you find that your pocket has been picked. You will :
   (*a*) try to hitch-hike till home.
   (*b*) hire a taxi and pay on reaching home.
   (*c*) go to the nearest police station and lodge a FIR.

(d) call home and ask someone to pick you from the place you make the phone call.

6. Your friend has not invited you to his marriage party, will you :
   (a) ignore the whole affair?
   (b) send him your best wishes?
   (c) attend the ceremony?
   (d) hold it against him?
7. You are interviewed for a new job. Which of the following questions is most important to you?
   (a) Remuneration you will be paid.
   (b) Opportunities for promotion.
   (c) Scope to develop your ideas and use them to improve the working of the organisation.
   (d) All the above are equally important.
8. You are walking down the street and suddenly you see two hundred–rupee notes on the pavement. What action will you take?
   (a) Give the money to beggar.
   (b) Pocket it yourself.
   (c) Deposit it in the nearest police station.
   (d) Leave it where it is.
9. You have made some silly mistakes which have been pointed out to you. Will you :
   (a) get angry?
   (b) feel miserable?
   (c) feel thankful?
   (d) laugh it away?
10. You are in a bus. The bus reaches your stop but still you have not purchased the ticket because of heavy rush. What will you do?
   (a) Hand the money to someone sitting nearby to give it to the conductor.
   (b) Jump out quickly to avoid embarassment.
   (c) Give the money to the driver.
   (d) Call the conductor, give him the money and get the ticket.

ANSWERS

1	2	3	4	5	6	7	8	9	10
(c)	(a)	(a)	(b)	(b)	(b)	(d)	(c)	(c)	(d)

ASSERTION AND REASON

Questions of this pattern are based on facts and are given to judge the candidate's general knowledge and intelligence along with his ability to reason out correctly. In this test two statements labelled as Assertion (A) and the other lebelled as Reason (R) are given. In the context of these two statements the candidate has to choose the correct option from the given options. These type of questions are usually asked in competitive examinations conducted by Union Public Service Commission.

SOLVED EXAMPLES

Directions : *In the context of the given statements which one of the following is correct?*

(*a*) Both A and R are true and R is the correct explanation of A.
(*b*) Both A and R are true but R is not the correct explanation of A.
(*c*) A is true but R is false.
(*d*) A is false but R is true.

1. **Assertion (A)** : Transformer is useful for stepping up or stepping down voltages.
   Reason (R) : Transformer is a device used in DC circuits.
   Ans. (*c*) : In the above two statements A is true but R is false.
2. **Assertion (A)** : A beaker filled with water at 4°C overflows if the temperature is decreased or increased.
   Reason (R) : Density of water is maximum at 4°C.
   Ans. (*a*) : Both the given statements are true and clearly, R explains A.
3. **Assertion (A)** : The emergence of economic globalism does not imply the decline of socialist ideology.
   Reason (R) : The ideology of socialism believes in universalism and globalism.
   Ans. (*d*) : Decline of socialist ideology implies the emergence of economic globalism and so A is false. R however, truely expresses the ideology of socialism.
4. **Assertion (A)** : CFC production is detrimental to Ozone layer.
   Reason (R) : Amount of CFC produced in India in one year is approximately equivalent to that produced by the entire world in a day or two.
   Ans. (*b*) : Both the given statements state true facts but R is not the right explanation for A. The amount of CFC (Chloro-fluoro-carbon) produced in the whole world at large is detrimental to the Ozone layer.

EXERCISE

Directions : *In each question given below there are two statements labelled as Assertion (A) and the other labelled as Reason (R). Of these statements which one of the following is correct?*

(*a*) Both A and R are true and R is the correct explanation of A.
(*b*) Both A and R are true but R is not the correct explanation of A.
(*c*) A is true but R is false.
(*d*) A is false but R is true.

1. **Assertion (A) :** Eggs of mosquitoes being very light in weight, float on water and water bodies.
   Reason (R) : Surface tension of water balances the weight of eggs.
2. **Assertion (A) :** Gun powder is an example

of a mixture.

Reason (R) : The components of gun powder are not present in a fixed ratio.

3. **Assertion (A) :** In cold wintry nights, the valleys in high mountainous areas are colder than the higher slopes.

Reason (R) : The cold, moist heavy air descends down the slopes of the mountain.

4. **Assertion (A) :** The sponsor and the most prominent figure of the Chisti order of Sufis in India is Khwaja Moinuddin Chisti.

Reason (R) : The Chisti order takes its name from a village Chisti in Ajmer.

5. **Assertion (A) :** The reservation of thirty–three percent of seats for women in Parliament and State legislature does not require constitutional amendment.

Reason (R) : Political parties contesting elections can allocate thirty-three percent of seats they contest to women candidates without any constitutional amendment.

6. **Assertion (A) :** Comets always have their tails away from the Sun.

Reason (R) : Solar winds drive the gaseous tail away from the Sun as the comet approaches the Sun.

7. **Assertion (A) :** Human figure was the pivot of the sculpture of the Gupta period.

Reason (R) : In the Gupta period, the artists lost interest in nature.

8. **Assertion (A) :** Diamond and graphite are allotropic forms of carbon.

Reason (R) : Diamond and graphite have different types of bonding between the carbon atoms.

9. **Assertion (A) :** The percentage share of tea exports from India has been declining considerably.

Reason (R) : There has been a substantial increase in the consumption of other beverages in the importing countries.

10. **Assertion (A) :** Oxides of nitrogen illustrate the law of multiple proportions.

Reason (R) : Nitrogen forms five oxides. The weight of Oxygen combining with a fixed weight of Nitrogen is in the simple ratio 1 : 2 : 3 : 4 : 5.

11. **Assertion (A) :** Areas near the equator receive rainfall throughout the year.

Reason (R) : High temperatures and high humidity cause conventional rain in most afternoons near the equator.

12. **Assertion (A) :** Classical Sanskrit literature reached the pinnacle of its glory during the time of Kalidas.

Reason (R) : The Gupta period is the classical period of Sanskrit literature.

13. **Assertion (A) :** The British sovereignty continued to exist in free India.

Reason (R) : The British sovereign appointed the last Governer–General of free India.

14. **Assertion (A) :** Water is highly polar in character.

Reason (R) : There is extensive association in water molecule due to hydrogen bonding.

15. **Assertion (A) :** $K_2Cr_2O_7$ is reduced.

Reason (R) : Oxidation number of chromium is decreased.

The above statements relate to this reaction

$$K_2Cr_2O_7 + 7H_2SO_4 + 6FeSO_4 \rightarrow K_2SO_4 + Cr_2(SO_4)_3 + 3Fe_2(SO_4)_3 + 7H_2O$$

16. **Assertion (A) :** Photorespiration causes a high loss of photosynthetically fixed carbon dioxide without producing energy-rich compounds.

Reason (R) : Photorespiration takes place under anaerobic conditions.

17. **Assertion (A) :** Wilful disobedience or/non–compliance of court orders and use of derogatory language about judicial behaviour amounts to contempt of court.

Reason (R) : Judicial activism cannot be practised without arming the judiciary with punitive powers to punish contemptuous behaviour.

18. **Assertion (A) :** Phenolphthalein indicator is not suitable in the titration of weak base and strong acid.

Reason (R) : Phenolphthalein works in the pH range 8.3 to 10 only whereas the titration of weak base and strong acid requires a pH range of 6 to 3.

19. **Assertion (A) :** An important policy instrument of economic liberalisation is reduction in import duties on capital goods.

Reason (R) : Reduction in import duties would help the local enterpreneurs to improve technology to face the global markets.

20. Assertion (A) : The word 'minority' is not defined in the Constitution of India.
Reason (R) : The Minorities Commission is not a constitutional body.

21. Assertion (A) : Though India's national income has gone up several fold since 1947, there has been no marked improvement in the per capita income level.
Reason (R) : Sizeable proportion of the population of India is still living below the poverty line.

22. Assertion (A) : Sterilised milk usually spoils upon long exposure to air.
Reason (R) : Air supplies necessary oxygen to spoilage organisms present in milk.

23. Assertion (A) : Mangroves are very specialised forest ecosystems of tropical and sub–tropical regions bordering certain sea coasts.
Reason (R) : They stabilise the shoreline and act as bullwark against encroachments by sea.

24. Assertion (A) : The Constitution of India provides for the appointment of a Governer for a State for a period of five years.
Reason (R) : The Governer holds office during the pleasure of the President.

25. Assertion (A) : Vitamin B complex is taken along with antibiotics to protect the intestinal flora of E coli bacteria.
Reason (R) : Antibiotics kill bacteria in the body.

26. Assertion (A) : In developed nations agricultural production has increased.
Reason (R) : Percentage of population engaged in agriculture has increased.

27. Assertion (A) : Quit India Movement marked the culmination of Indian National Movement.
Reason (R) : After the Quit India Movement it was a matter of time and finding suitable mechanism for transfer of power.

28. Assertion (A) : India is the largest producer of steel in the world.
Reason (R) : India has huge reserves of iron ore.

29. Assertion (A) : The pattern of consumption of goods and services varies from one country to another.
Reason (R) : The population varies from one country to another.

30. Assertion (A) : Sound waves cannot be polarized.
Reason (R) : Sound waves can be longitudinal or transverse.

31. Assertion (A) : The material used for suspension of coil in a moving coil galvanometer is phosphor bronze.
Reason (R) : Phosphor bronze have very high rigidity.

32. Assertion (A) : If the budget presented to the Rajya Sabha is not passed within the stipulated period the budget proposals are not affected.
Reason (R) : In financial matters the Lok Sabha is more powerful than the Rajya Sabha.

33. Assertion (A) : The desert soils in India are poor in mineral nutrients and infertile.
Reason (R) : The dearth of rainfall and humus do not allow good soil formation.

34. Assertion (A) : The solar eclipse occurs twice during a month but is not always observed.
Reason (R) : The solar eclipse occurs on the days of the new moon.

35. Assertion (A) : The process of nuclear fusion produces more energy than nuclear fission.
Reason (R) : Nuclear fission is an exothermic process.

36. Assertion (A) : In High Fidelity radio broadcasts, frequency modulation (FM) is preferred over amplitude modulation (AM) for transmission purposes.
Reason (R) : Atmospheric disturbances affect the amplitude of the transmitted broadcast signals.

37. Assertion (A) : Radio carbon dating is a precise method of determining the age of ancient objects.
Reason (R) : Once an object dies, the amount of radioactive carbon present in it decreases with time following a definite law.

38. Assertion (A) : The magnification provided

by common laboratory microscopes is less than 1000.

Reason (R) : The diameter of the pupil of human eye is about 2.5 mm.

39. Assertion (A) : A diamond sparkles more than a glass imitation cut to the same shape.

Reason (R) : The refractive index of diamond is less than that of glass.

40. Assertion (A) : If the physical state of a conductor remains unchanged, the voltage between its ends is proportional to current flowing in it.

Reason (R) : When a potential difference is maintained across the ends of a conductor, a force eE acts on free electrons inside the conductor where e is electronic charge and E is the intensity of the electric field and the electron moves freely under the influence of the force.

41. Assertion (A) : While taking a sharp turn at a high speed a truckload of fodder overturns more frequently than a truckload of iron beams.

Reason (R) : The centre of gravity of a truck carrying fodder is lowered on the vertical line though its CG, falls outside the base on a sharp turn, while for a truck carrying iron beams this does not happen.

42. Assertion (A) : It is easy to drive a sharp needle through a piece of cloth or cardboard than to drive a blunt nail through the same materials.

Reason (R) : The radius of the tip of a sharp needle is much smaller than the radius of the tip of a blunt nail.

43. Assertion (A) : Water is a good solvent for many salts.

Reason (R) : The dielectric constant of water is high.

44. Assertion (A) : Air passengers sometimes feel pain in the ears when the plane rapidly loses height.

Reason (R) : Atmospheric pressure is lower at lower altitudes.

45. Assertion (A) : A dentist uses a concave mirror to examine a small cavity.

Reason (R) : A concave mirror forms real images for all positions of an object.

46. Assertion (A) : If a conductor is required to store electrical charge, its shape is spherical and radius large. If it is required to discharge electrical energy, it is made pointed and narrow.

Reason (R) : Intensity of electric field on the surface of a charged conductor is inversely proportional to its radius of curvature at that point.

47. Assertion (A) : Sweden, Canada, Finland and Norway are the world's leading exporters of wood pulp.

Reason (R) : The coniferous woods are preferred for the manufacture of pulp.

48. Assertion (A) : The vaccine enables the body to build up its own antibodies.

Reason (R) : Active immunity can be acquired only by injecting dead or weakened germs into the body.

49. Assertion (A) : Vegetation is the index of climate.

Reason (R) : Rainfall and temperature predominantly affect the type of vegetation.

50. Assertion (A) : Jharkhand Mukti Morcha is recognised as a 'state party'.

Reason (R) : Jharkhand Mukti Morcha is recognised in four states.

51. Assertion (A) : The presence of oxygen is necessary for a given gas to become inflammable.

Reason (R) : Oxygen is inflammable.

52. Assertion (A) : The Britishers referred to Bal Gangadhar Tilak as "the Father of the Indian Unrest".

Reason (R) : Bal Gangadhar Tilak was the first to demand freedom as his birth right.

53. Assertion (A) : When the price of X rises the quantity demanded of Y increases.

Reason (R) : X and Y are substitutes.

54. Assertion (A) : A gas-filled balloon stops rising after it has attained a certain height in the sky.

Reason (R) : At the highest point, the density of air is such that the buoyant force on the balloon just equals its weight.

55. Assertion (A) : Obesity is not a problem for

a sportsman even though his diet contains more carbohydrates and fats than an average man.

Reason (R) : A sportsman is able to spend more calories through strenuous exercise.

56. Assertion (A) : The growth of rice plant is better when it is cultivated along with blue-green algae.

Reason (R) : Blue-green algae increases the soil fertility through nitrogen fixation.

57. Assertion (A) : On December 21, the sun is overhead at the Tropic of Capricorn.

Reason (R) : December 21 is the date of vernal equinox.

58. Assertion (A) : Birds do not lay eggs by millions as some of the lower animals do.

Reason (R) : Survival rate is much higher because of the parental care.

59. Assertion (A) : Robert Clive defeated Siraj-ud-Daullah in the battle of Plassey.

Reason (R) : Clive's army was superior and it followed superior military tactics.

60. Assertion (A) : The entire west coast of the United States has Mediterranean type of climate.

Reason (R) : This region gets winter rainfall from 'westerlies' winds.

61. Assertion (A) : Glass tumbler breaks in winter when hot water is poured in it.

Reason (R) : Hot water expands the outer surface of the glass.

62. Assertion (A) : Now-a-days DDT has lost its use as an insecticide.

Reason (R) : DDT is harmful to man.

63. Assertion (A) : A hydrogen-filled balloon stops rising after it has attained a certain height in the sky.

Reason (R) : The atmospheric pressure decreases with height and becomes zero when maximum height is attained.

64. Assertion (A) : Carbondioxide is prepared by burning carbon or by the reaction between a carbonate and an acid or by the decomposition of limestone.

Reason (R) : In all these methods of preparation of CO_2, the elements of carbon and oxygen are available in the fixed ratio of 4 : 8.

65. Assertion (A) : Cotton is grown in alluvial soils.

Reason (R) : Alluvial soils are very fertile.

66. Assertion (A) : The biological processes of growth, development and differentiation enable the plants and animals to enter the functional state of life.

Reason (R) : Various biological and environmental factors regulate the state of life.

67. Assertion (A) : In the early Vedic period, the Aryans built their civilization in Sapta Sandhava.

Reason (R) : Among the Aryan tribes, the Koyas and Gonds were the most important.

68. Assertion (A) : In the recent past, Dada Saheb Phalke award has been given to Raj Kapoor and Ashok Kumar.

Reason (R) : This award is given every year to the best actor in Hindi films.

69. Assertion (A) : Deficiency of iodine in diet may produce Myxoedema, a symptom of hypothyroidism.

Reason (R) : Deficiency of iodine reduces the secretion of thyrotropic hormone.

70. Assertion (A) : Khilaft Movement was launched in India to drive out the British from India.

Reason (R) : After the World War I, the British rule in India become more repressive.

71. Assertion (A) : When a copper wire is placed in a solution of silver nitrate, silver is deposited on it.

Reason (R) : The oxidation potential of copper is lower than that of silver.

72. Assertion (A) : There was a general tendency among the Chola kings to change the then existing names of all the places situated within their territory and call them after the names of Chola kings.

Reason (R) : This was to mark out the places by their very names as belonging to the Cholas.

73. Assertion (A) : The morphology of chromosomes is best studied during the metaphase or anaphase of mitotic division.

Reason (R) : The chromosomes attain maximum contraction during the metaphase and anaphase of mitotic division.

74. Assertion (A) : Buddhism became very popular in India during the life time of its founder.
Reason (R) : Buddha preached in the language of the people and did not harp on the caste system.

75. Assertion (A) : Natural selection maintains and propagates the beneficial genes while limiting harmful ones in particular environment.
Reason (R) : There are genes which are responsible for the production of beneficial characters while others are harmful.

76. Assertion (A) : Heating vegetable oils with caustic soda gives soap and glycerine.
Reason (R) : Vegetable oils contains salts of fatty acids.

77. Assertion (A) : An adiabatic expansion is always accompanied by a drop in temperature.
Reason (R) : When a system is undergoing adiabatic expansion, the internal energy of the system is used for doing work in expansion.

78. Assertion (A) : The electric current flowing through a wire deflects a magnetic needle placed in its neighbourhood in such a way that the needle assumes a position perpendicular to the plane passing through the wire and through the centre of the needle.
Reason (R) : An electric current is a stream of moving charges which create a magnetic field whose direction is at right angles to the direction of the current.

79. Assertion (A) : In summer, when a piece of metal is touched it feels hotter than when a piece of wood is touched.
Reason (R) : Metal is better conductor of heat than wood.

80. Assertion (A) : The First War of Independence in 1857 failed to secure freedom from the British Government.
Reason (R) : The leadership of Bahadur Shah Zafar did not have popular support and most of the Indian rulers of important States shied away from the struggle.

81. Assertion (A) : Indian Federation can be best termed as "Centralised Federation".
Reason (R) : If a state law has received prior assent of the President, then what will prevail over the Parilamentary law.

82. Assertion (A) : A mixture of ethyl alcohol and water can be completely separated into its compounds.
Reason (R) : Water boils at 100°C and ethyl alcohol at 80°C.

83. Assertion (A) : The shape of soap bubble is spherical.
Reason (R) : The bubble has a maximum surface area.

84. Assertion (A) : The Savannahs having scattered trees amidst grasses are called parklands.
Reason (R) : The Savannahs occur between temperate deciduous and coniferous forests.

85. Assertion (A) : India has a parliamentary system of Government.
Reason (R) : Indian Parliament is bicameral.

86. Assertion (A) : Moon cannot be used as a satellite for communication.
Reason (R) : Moon does not move in the equatorial plane of the earth.

87. Assertion (A) : Mercury is used in clinical thermometer for measuring body temperatures.
Reason (R) : Mercury shines and is easily observable.

88. Assertion (A) : Absolute humidity generally declines from the equator towards the poles.
Reason (R) : On a hot summer day air can hold much more moisture than it would on a cold winter day.

89. Assertion (A) : If there is an explosion on the surface of the moon, no one will ever hear it.
Reason (R) : The moon is as yet uninhabited.

90. Assertion (A) : Fishes can easily cut their way through the water.
Reason (R) : The body of the fish is streamlined.

EXPLANATORY ANSWERS

1. *(a)* : Both the statements and reason are true and R explains the assertion.

2. *(c)* : A is true but R is false because ordinary black gunpowder consists of KNO_3, charcoal and sulphur which is about 75%, 15% and 10% respectively.

3. *(a)* : Both A and R are true and R explains the climate of cold wintry night in A.

4. *(b)* : Both A and R are true but R is not the explanation of A.

5. *(d)* : In our country reservation of seats for any category in Parliament/State legislature requires the passing of the amendment to the Indian Constitution, for the candidates belonging to any category. So, A is false but R is true.

6. *(a)* : Both A and R are correct and R is the correct explanation of A.

7. *(c)* : Statement A is true but the artists in Gupta period never lost interest in nature though the pivot of sculpture were human figures. So, Statement R is false.

8. *(a)* : Both statements are true and the type of bonding explains why diamond & graphite are allotropic forms of carbon.

9. *(c)* : Statement A is true but R is based on assumption and therefore it is false.

10. *(a)* : Both the statements are correct and R is the correct explanation of A.

11. *(a)* : Both the statements state facts and clearly R is the correct explanation of A.

12. *(a)* : Both the statements are true and it was during the Gupta period that Sanskrit literature flourished. It was also the time when Kalidas wrote his works.

13. *(d)* : The British Sovereign did appoint the last Governer–General of free India but British Sovereignty ended after India attained Independence. So, Statement A is false and R is true.

14. *(b)* : Both the statements are true but they are independent in expression.

15. *(a)* : On the basis of the reaction both statements are true and R is the correct explanation of A.

16. *(c)* : A is true but R is false.

17. *(b)* : Both the statements are correct but R is not the explanation of A.

18. *(a)* : Both the statements are correct and R clearly explains A.

19. *(a)* : Both the statements are true and R is the correct explanation of A.

20. *(b)* : Both the statements are true but R is not related to A.

21. *(b)* : Both the statements are true but they are independent expressions.

22. *(a)* : Both the statements are true and R clearly explains A.

23. *(a)* : Both the statements are true and R is the correct reason for A.

24. *(b)* : Both the statements are true but independent expressions.

25. *(b)* : Both the statements are correct but R does not explain A.

26. *(c)* : Statement A is true but R which is based on assumption, is not true.

27. *(d)* : Statement A is false but R is true.

28. *(d)* : India has huge reserves of iron ore but it is not the largest producer of steel in the world.

29. *(b)* : Both the statements are true but R is not the correct explanation of A.

30. *(b)* : Both the statements are true but R is not the explanation of A.

31. *(b)* : Both the statements are true but expression in R is not the explanation of A.

32. *(d)* : Time period affects the budget proposals. So, statement A is false, but R is true.

33. *(a)* : Both the statements are true and clearly, R explains A.

34. *(d)* : Statement A is not true and statement R is true.

35. *(d)* : Statement A is false but R is true.

36. *(a)* : Both the statements are true and clearly R explains A.

37. *(a)* : Both the statements are true and R is the correct reason for A.

38. *(a)* : Both the statements are true and R is the

explanation of A. When seen by the human eye through the microscope, the magnification is less than 1000.

39. *(c)* : Statement A is true but R is false because refractive index of diamond is more than that of glass.

40. *(b)* : Both the statements are true but R does not explain A.

41. *(a)* : Both the statements are true and R clearly explains A.

42. *(a)* : Both the statements are true and R is the correct reason for A.

43. *(a)* : Both the statements are true and the dielectric constant of water makes it a good solvent for many salts.

44. *(a)* : Both the statements are true and R is the correct explanation of A.

45. *(c)* : Statement A is true but R is false because a concave mirror forms virtual images for all portions of an object.

46. *(c)* : Statement A is true but R is false.

47. *(a)* : Both the statements are true and R is the correct explanation of A.

48. *(b)* : Both the statements are true but R is independent of A.

49. *(a)* : Both the statements are true and R explains A.

50. *(c)* : Statement A is a fact but R is a false statement.

51. *(c)* : Statement A is true but R is a wrong statement because oxygen is not inflammable.

52. *(b)* : Both the statements are true and are independent expressions.

53. *(a)* : Both the statements are true and R clearly explains A. When the price of one item is increased the demand for its equivalent item which is low in cost is also increased.

54. *(a)* : A gas-filled balloon only reaches a certain height. Statement A is true and R clearly explains A.

55. *(d)* : Obesity is a problem for a sportsman. Statement A is false but R is a true expression.

56. *(a)* : Both the statements are true and R clearly explains A.

57. *(c)* : Statement A is factually wrong but R is true.

58. *(b)* : Both the statements are true and they are independent expressions.

59. *(a)* : Both the statements are true and R is the correct explanation of A.

60. *(d)* : Statement A is false and R is true.

61. *(c)* : Statement A is true but R is false because the inner surface expands while the outer suface which is constant with the cold atmosphere does not break.

62. *(b)* : Both the statements are true because insects have become immune to DDT and DDT is harmful to human beings. However, both the statements are not related.

63. *(d)* : Statement A is not true because the hydrogen-filled balloon keeps gaining height. Statement R is true.

64. *(a)* : Both the statements are true and R clearly explains A.

65. *(d)* : Statement A is false because cotton is grown in black soil, however, statement R is true.

66. *(a)* : Both the statements are true and R explains A.

67. *(c)* : Statement A is historically wrong but R is true.

68. *(c)* : Statement A is factually wrong but R is true.

69. *(a)* : Both the statements are true and R is the correct explanation of A.

70. *(c)* : Statement A is true but R is false.

71. *(a)* : Both the statements are true and R is the correct explanation of A because the oxidation potential of copper is lower than that of silver, the silver is deposited on the copper when its wire is placed in silver nitrate solution

72. *(d)* : Statement A is false, however, R is true.

73. *(c)* : Statement A is true, but R is false.

74. *(a)* : Both the statements are true and R is the correct explanation of A.

75. *(a)* : Both the statements are true and R explains A.

76. *(c)* : Statements A is true, however R is false because vegetable oils are triestus of glycerol.

77. *(a)* : Both the statements are true and R clearly explains A.

78. *(d)* : Statement A is false but R is true.

79. *(a)* : Both the statements are true and R is the correct explanation of A.

80. *(c)* : Statement A is true but R is factually wrong.

81. *(b)* : Both the statements are true but they are not related.

82. *(d)* : Statement A is false but R is true.

83. *(b)* : Both the statements are true and they are independent expressions.

84. *(c)* : Statement A is not true but R is true.

85. *(b)* : Both the statements are true and they are independent expressions.

86. *(a)* : Both the statements are true and R is the correct explanation of A.

87. *(a)* : Both the statements are true and R clearly explains A.

88. *(a)* : Both the statements are true and R clearly explains A.

89. *(b)* : Both the statements are true and they are independent expressions.

90. *(a)* : Both the statements are true and R is the correct explanation of A.

DECISION MAKING

In this type of tests certain categories of information are given followed by certain criteria. Further, the candidates are given a few cause that needs to be analysed. They are required to take the right decision, from the given options, after comparing the information in each case with the given information and criteria.

SOLVED EXAMPLES

Directions : *Read the following information carefully to answer the questions given below :*

Following are the criteria for appointing persons for the post of Technical Officers in an organisation. The candidate must—

(i) have passed XII Std. examination with at least aggregate percentage of 60 in Physics, Chemistry and Mathematics.
(ii) be a graduate in engineering discipline with at least 60 per cent marks.
(iii) have passed the written examination.
(iv) have passed group discussion and interview with at least 50 per cent marks.
(v) not be more than 22 years as on July 15, 1998.

In the case of a candidate who satisfies all other criteria except at—

(a) (i) above in terms of percentage of marks but has secured 90 per cent marks in graduation, may be appointed.
(b) (v) above but is a post graduate in engineering, is to be referred to Director–Personnel.
(c) (ii) above but has appeared in the final degree examination, may be provisionally appointed.

Based on these criteria and information provided below, decide the course of action in each case. You are not to assume anything. If the data provided is not adequate to decide the given course of action, your answer will be 'data inadequate'. These cases are given to you as on 1. 6. 1998.

1. Ashok Taneja has secured 90 per cent aggregate marks in Physics, Chemistry and Mathematics in XII Std. He is yet to get the result of the final degree examination in Electronics. He has passed the written examination and has secured 60 per cent marks both in group discussion and interview. He was born on July 19, 1976.

(a) Data inadequate *(b)* Do not appoint
(c) Refer to Director–Personnel *(d)* Appoint
(e) Appoint provisionally

Ans. *(e)* : Criterion *(ii)* is not satisfied but criterion *(c)* gives the decision.

2. Priya Mirchandani has secured 70 per cent aggregate marks in Physics, Chemistry and Mathematics in XII Std. and 80 per cent in graduation in Metallurgy and 50 per cent in post graduation. She was born on February 25, 1976. She has passed the written examination and has secured 55 per cent marks both in group discussion and interview.

(a) Appoint provisionally *(b)* Do not appoint
(c) Refer to Director–Personnel *(d)* Appoint
(e) Data inadequate

Ans. *(c)* : Criterion *(v)* is not satisfied but criterion *(b)* gives the decision.

3. Samir Gupta was born on 19th March, 1975. He has secured 60 per cent marks in both graduation and post graduation in Civil Engineering. He has passed in the written examination and has secured 60 per cent marks both in group discussion and interview.

(*a*) Refer to Director–Personnel (*b*) Do not appoint
(*c*) Appoint provisionally (*d*) Data inadequate
(*e*) Appoint

Ans. ***(d)*** **:** Criterion (*i*) is not given and criterion (*v*) is not satisfied.

4. Sandip Malhotra has appeared in the final degree examination in Mechanical Engineering. He has secured 70 per cent aggregate marks in Physics, Chemistry and Mathematics in XII Std. He has passed the written examination and has secured 75 per cent marks in both group discussion and interview. He was born on April 15, 1976.

(*a*) Do not appoint (*b*) Refer to Director–Personnel
(*c*) Appoint provisionally (*d*) Appoint
(*e*) Data inadequate

Ans. ***(a)*** **:** Both criterion (*v*) and criterion (*b*) are not satisfied.

5. Seema Malhotra has secured 60 per cent marks in graduation in Chemical Engineering and 70 per cent aggregate marks in Physics, Chemistry and Mathematics in XII Std. She will be 23 years old on August 10, 1999. She has passed the written examination and has secured 55 per cent marks both in group discussion and interview.

(*a*) Data inadequate (*b*) Appoint Provisionally
(*c*) Appoint (*d*) Do not appoint
(*e*) Refer to Director–Personnel

Ans. ***(c)*** **:** All criteria are satisfied.

EXERCISE

Directions (Qs. 1 to 5) : *Read the following information carefully and answer the questions given below it. Following are the criteria for admitting a student in the first year engineering course in a college.*

The student must—

(*i*) have passed XII standard examination in science with at least 80% marks.

(*ii*) not be more than 20 years old as on 1. 8. 1998.

(*iii*) have secured at least 90 marks in the entrance test out of a total of 150 marks.

(*iv*) be able to pay Rs. 15,000 as tuition fees for the first semester and Rs. 5,000 admission charges at the time of taking admission.

In the case of a candidate, who satisfies all other criteria except at—

(*a*) (*iv*) above but can pay at least 60% of the stipulated fees, the case may be referred to the Admission Committee.

(*b*) (*iii*) above but has secured more than 95% marks in the XIIth standard examination, the case may be referred to Chairman–Admissions.

You are given the following cases as on 1. 8. 1998. Depending upon the information provided in each case and based on the criteria mentioned above, recommend your decision. You are not to assume anything. If the information provided is not adequate to take a decision, mark 'Data inadequate' as the answer.

1. Subodh Mohaptara was 19 years old as on 20th December, 1997. He has secured 98% marks in XIIth standard examination with science and 80 marks in the entrance test. He can pay the requisite tuition fees and admission charges.

(*a*) Admit
(*b*) Refer to Admission Committee
(*c*) Data inadequate
(*d*) Do not admit
(*e*) Refer to Chairman–Admissions

2. Reema Jaiswal was born on 20th July, 1978. She has secured 85% and 75% marks in XIIth standard with science and entrance test respectively. She can pay the requisite tuition fees and admission charges.

(*a*) Refer to Chairman–Admission

(b) Refer to Admission Committee
(c) Data inadequate
(d) Do not admit
(e) Admit

3. Ashok Dubey was born on 27th November, 1978. He has secured 90% marks in the XIIth standard examination with science and 95 marks in the entrance test. He can pay Rs. 10,000 tuition fees and Rs. 3,500 admission charges.
(a) Admit
(b) Data inadequate
(c) Refer to Admission Committee
(d) Do not admit
(e) Refer to Chairman–Admissions

4. Sudha Mirchandani has secured 95% marks in XIIth standard science stream and 70% marks in the entrance test. She can pay only 65% of the requisite tuition fees and admission charges.
(a) Do not admit
(b) Admit
(c) Data inadequate
(d) Refer to Chairman–Admissions
(e) Refer to Admission Committee

5. Salil Malhotra was born on 25th September in 1979. He has secured 85% and 95% marks in the XIIth standard examination in science stream and entrance test respectively. He can pay the requisite tuition fees and admission charges.
(a) Admit
(b) Do not admit
(c) Refer to Chairman–Admissions
(d) Refer to Admission Committee
(e) Data inadequate

Directions (Qs. 6 to 12) : *Read the following information to answer the given questions :*

Following are the criteria for selecting candidates for Research Fellowship :
The candidate must—
(i) be a post–graduate with minimum of 65% marks.
(ii) not be more than 30 years as on 15. 10. 1993.
(iii) have at least 3 years research experience.
(iv) have diploma in Statistics.
(v) have secured at least 50% marks in the entrance test.
(vi) have finalised the topic for research.

However, in case a candidate who fulfills all other criteria except
(a) (iii) above, but has M. Phil degree, should be referred to Dean.
(b) (iv) above, should be referred to Chairman.
(c) (i) above, but has at least 55% marks in post–graduation and 65% in the entrance test, should be given fellowship.
(d) (v) above, but has at lest 45% marks, should be wait–listed.

Based on these criteria and information provided below, decide the course of action in each case. You are not to assume anything. If the data provided is not adequate to decide the given course of action, your answer will be "data inadequate". These cases are given to you as on 15. 10. 1993.

6. 26 years old, Mamta Deo is a post graduate with 58%. She has got four years' research experience and has finalised topic for research. She got 70% marks in diploma in Statistics and 54% marks in the entrance examination.
(a) Fellowship not to be granted
(b) Refer to Dean
(c) Refer to Chairman
(d) Grant Fellowship
(e) Data inadequate

7. Shushila Nair has 65% marks in her post–graduation and is M. Phil. She has 5 years research experience. She has secured 65% in the entrance test and has finalised the research topic. Her date of birth is 11. 8. 65.
(a) Grant fellowship
(b) Wait–list
(c) Refer to Dean
(d) Refer to Chairman
(e) Data inadequate

8. Ameer Khan has got 58% in the entrance test. He has 68% in his post-graduation and 55% in M. Phil. He has got diploma in Statistics and has also finalised the topic for research.
(a) Grant Fellowship

(*b*) Refer to Dean
(*c*) Refer to Chairman
(*d*) Wait-list
(*e*) Data inadequate

9. 28 years old Neetu Singh is M. Phil with 60% marks. She has secured 70% marks in entrance examination and has finalised the topic for research. She has also got diploma in Statistics.
(*a*) Grant Fellowship
(*b*) Fellowship not to be granted
(*c*) Refer to Chairman
(*d*) Refer to Dean
(*e*) Data inadequate

10. Sadhana Suman has got diploma in Statistics with 60% marks and post-graduation with 56% marks. Her date of birth is 12. 12. 1968. She has got one year research experience and is still doing her M. Phil. She has secured 65% marks in entrance exam and has also finalised the research topic.
(*a*) Grant Fellowship
(*b*) Fellowship not to be granted
(*c*) Refer to Dean
(*d*) Data inadequate
(*e*) Wait-list

11. Amar Sikka is 28 years old and has got 65% marks in post-graduation and 60% marks in M. Phil. He has got 65% marks in entrance examination and has finalised the topic for research. He also has a diploma in Statistics.
(*a*) Grant Fellowship
(*b*) Fellowship not to be granted
(*c*) Refer to Dean
(*d*) Refer to Chairman
(*e*) Data inadequate

12. Madan Paul has got 5 years' research experience and has finalised the research topic. He has got 56% marks in post-graduation. His date of birth is 15. 2. 1966. He has also got diploma in Statistics. He got 70% marks in the entrance test.
(*a*) Grant Fellowship
(*b*) Fellowship not to be granted
(*c*) Refer to Dean
(*d*) Data inadequate
(*e*) None of these

Directions (Qs. 13 to 19) : *Read the following information to answer the given questions :*

Following are the conditions for selecting candidates for Research Fellowship :

The candidate must—
(*i*) be a post-graduate with minimum of 60% marks.
(*ii*) not be more than 30 years as on 1. 9. 1993.
(*iii*) have at least 3 years' research experience.
(*iv*) have diploma in statistics.
(*v*) have secured at least 55% marks in the entrance test.
(*iv*) have finalised the topic for research.

However, in the case of a candidate who fulfills all other criteria except—
(*a*) (*iii*) above but has M. Phil degree, should be given fellowship.
(*b*) (*iv*) above should be referred to Dean.
(*c*) (*i*) above but has atleast 55% marks in post–graduation, should be wait-listed.
(*d*) (*v*) above but has atleast 50% marks, should be referred to Chairman.

Based on these criteria and information provided below, decide the course of action in each case. You are not to assume anything. If the data provided is not adequate to decide the given course of action, your answer will be "data inadequate". These cases are given to you as on 1. 9. 1993.

13. Vijay Gupta is 24 years old and has got 58% marks in the entrance examination. He has secured 63% marks in his post-graduation and 55% marks in M. Phil. He has got diploma in Statistics and has also finalised the topic for research.
(*a*) Grant Fellowship
(*b*) Refer to Dean
(*c*) Refer to Chairman
(*d*) Wait-list
(*e*) Data inadequate

14. Ajoy Dwivedi has secured 65% marks in the post-graduation and has secured 5 years research experience. He has secured 65% marks in the entrance test and has finalised the research topic. His date of birth is 11. 8. 1965.
(*a*) Grant Fellowship
(*b*) Wait-list
(*c*) Refer to Dean

(d) Data inadequate
(e) None of these

15. Madan Soren has got diploma in Statistics with 60% marks and post-graduation with 56% marks. His date of birth is 12. 12. 1968. He has got 1 year research experience and is still doing his M. Phil. He has secured 60% marks in the entrance exam and has also finalised the research topic.
(a) Grant fellowship
(b) Fellowship not to be granted
(c) Refer to Dean
(d) Data inadequate
(e) Wait-list

16. 26 years old Mamta Kulkarni is M. Phil with 60% marks. She has secured 70% marks in the entrance examination and has finalised the topic for research. She has also got diploma in Statistics.
(a) Grant Fellowship
(b) Fellowship not to be granted
(c) Refer to Chairman
(d) Refer to Dean
(e) Data inadequate

17. Chander Manoj has got 5 years' research experience and has finalised the research topic. He has got 56% marks in post-graduation and 60% marks in the entrance test. His date of birth is 15. 2. 1966. He has also got diploma in Statistics.
(a) Grant Fellowship
(b) Fellowship not to be granted
(c) Refer to Dean
(d) Data inadequate
(e) None of these

18. Raman Hooda is 28 years old and has got 65% marks in Post-graduation and 60% marks in M. Phil. He has got 65% marks in the entrance examination and has finalised the topic for research. He also has a diploma in Statistics.
(a) Grant Fellowship
(b) Fellowship not to be granted
(c) Refer to Dean
(d) Refer to Chairman
(e) Data inadequate

19. 26 years old Janaki Deo is a post-graduate with 58% marks. She has got four years research experience and has finalised the topic for research. She got 70% marks in the diploma in Statistics and 54% marks in the entrance examination.
(a) Fellowship not to be granted
(b) Refer to Dean
(c) Refer to Chairman
(d) Grant Fellowship
(e) Data inadequate

Directions (Qs. 20 to 27) : *Read the following information carefully and answer the questions given below :*

Following are the criteria of promotion from Junior Officer's Cadre to Senior Officer's Cadre in an organisation :

The candidate must—
(a) have completed atleast 5 years in the organisation.
(b) have secured 65% marks in the written test for promotion.
(c) have secured 60% marks in the Group Discussion.
(d) have secured 70% marks in the interview.
(e) have good record of his work performance.
(f) have good communication skill and get along well with his colleagues.
(g) not be more than 40 years and less than 30 years as on 1. 9. 93.
(h) have good academic record with an average of at least 65% marks.

However, in the case of a candidate who—
(i) satisfies all other conditions except (d) above but has secured 75% marks in the written test and 65% marks in he Group Discussion, the case is to be referred to the General Manager (Personnel)–GM(P) for the decision.
(j) satisfies all other criteria except (h) above but has secured an average of more than 60% marks, the case is to be referred to the Managing Director (MD) of the organisation.

Now read the information provided in the case of each candidate in each of the questions given below and decide on the basis of the information provided and based on the above conditions, which of the courses of action you would suggest. These cases are given as on 5. 9. 1993. (Remember you are not to assume anything which is not provided in the question). If complete information is not provided, the answer would be Data inadequate.

20. 38 years old Rajesh has secured 65% marks in the written test for promotion, 73% marks in interview and 62% marks in Group Discussion. He has good record of his work performance, good communication skills and gets along well with his colleagues. He has good academic record with an average of 61% marks and has completed 7 years in the organisation.
(*a*) Refer to GM(P)
(*b*) Refer to MD
(*c*) Promote
(*d*) Do not promote
(*e*) Data inadequate

21. 34 years old Sudha has secured 60% marks in the written test for promotion, 72% marks in inteview and 69% marks in Group discussion. She has good communication skill and gets along well with her colleagues. Her record of work performance is good and she has completed 6½ years in the organisation.
(*a*) Refer to MD
(*b*) Do not promote
(*c*) Refer to GM(P)
(*d*) Promote
(*e*) Data inadequate

22. Surekha has secured 70% marks in written test for promotion, 69% marks in Group Discussion and 72% marks in the interview. She has a good academic record with an average of 67% marks. She has good record of work performance and gets along well with her colleagues. She has good communication skill and has completed 7 years in the organisation.
(*a*) Do not promote
(*b*) Promote
(*c*) Refer to GM(P)
(*d*) Refer to MD
(*e*) Data inadequate

23. 39 years old Pawan has secured 66% marks in written promotion test and has a good academic record with an average of 62% marks. He has secured 65% marks in Group Discussion and 72% marks in interview. He has good record of his work performance, communication skill and gets along well with his colleagues. He has completed 6 years in the organisation.
(*a*) Do not promote
(*b*) Refer to MD
(*c*) Refer to GM(P)
(*d*) Promote
(*e*) Data inadequate

24. 34 years old Sudhir has secured 76% marks in the written test for promotion, 66% marks in Group Discussion and 67% marks in interview. He has good academic record with an average of 68% marks, good communication skill and gets along well with his colleagues. His work performance is good and he has completed 6 years in the organisation.
(*a*) Promote
(*b*) Refer to MD
(*c*) Refer to GM(P)
(*d*) Do not promote
(*e*) Data anadequate

25. 32 years old Manjula has good academic record with an average of 66% marks. She has secured 67% marks in Group Discussion, 75% marks in interview and 60% marks in written test for promotion. She has good communication skill and gets along well with her colleagues. She has good record of her work performance and has completed 7 years in the organisation.
(*a*) Do not promote
(*b*) Refer to MD
(*c*) Promote
(*d*) Refer to GM(P)
(*e*) Data inadequate

26. 31 years old Krishna secured 65% marks in written test for promotion, 72% marks in interview and 62% marks in Group Discussion. He has good academic record with an average of 67% marks and good communication skill. He has completed 9 years in the organisation. He gets easily annoyed and irritated with his colleagues and his record of work performance since the last two years is just average.

(a) Promote (b) Refer to GM(P)
(c) Refer to MD (d) Do not promote
(e) Data inadequate

27. 33 years old Neelima has secured 63% marks in Group Discussion, 71% marks in interview and 66% marks in written test for promotion. She hase good academic record with an average of 68% marks and has good communication skill. She gets along well with her colleagues and has good record of her work performance. She has completed 6 years in the organisation.

(a) Refer to GM(P)
(b) Do not promote
(c) Promote
(d) Refer to MD
(e) Data inadequate

Directions (Qs. 28 to 35) : *Read the following information carefully and answer the questions based on the given information. Following are the criteria for admitting a student in Medical course.*

The student must—

(a) have passed XIIth Std. Science examination with Biology amd have secured at least 60% marks.
(b) be of 18 years of age as on September 1, 1994.
(c) have obtained 70% marks in the entrance test.
(d) be able to pay Rs. 20,000 at the time of admission.

In the case of a candidate, who satisfies all other criteria except at—

I. (c) above, but has obtained 90% marks in the XIIth Std. Science examination, should be referred to the Principle.

II. (d) above, but can pay Rs. 10,000 at the time of admission, can be provisionally admitted.

You are given the following cases as on September 1, 1994. Depending upon the information provided in each case and based on the criteria mentioned above, recommend your decision. You are not to assume anything. Give answer

(a) if the students is to be admitted:
(b) if the student is not to be admitted;
(c) if the student is to be referred to the principle;
(d) if the student is to be admitted provisionally, and give answer;
(e) if the data are inadequate.

28. Mahesh Sagar has secured 75% marks in the entrance test and can pay admission fee of Rs. 15,000 at the time of admission. He has secured 60% marks in the XIIth Std. Science examination with Biology.

29. Sunil Agarwal has passed XIIth Std. Science examination with Biology and secured 95% marks. His date of birth is July 15, 1976. He has obtained 60% marks in the entrance test. He can pay the fee of Rs. 20,000 at the time of admission.

30. Jayaesh Ozha was 17 years old as on 11th September, 1993. He has secured 90% marks in his XIIth Std. Science examination with Biology. He has secured 75% marks in the entrance test and can pay the admission fee of Rs. 20,000.

31. Pramod Lohia was born on 5th April, 1973. He has secured 80% marks in the XIIth Std. Science examination with Biology and can pay admission fee of Rs. 20,000. He has secured 85% marks in the entrance test.

32. Usha Jethmalani has secured 68% marks in her XIIth Std. Examination in Science with Biology and has secured 75% marks in the entrance test. She was born on 20th October, 1975. She can pay the admission fee of Rs. 20,000.

33. Sudha Malhotra has secured 70% marks in the entrance test and 60% marks in her XIIth Std. Science Examinaion with Biology. She can pay the admission fee of Rs. 20,000 and was born on 7th November, 1978.

34. Rajesh Gupta has secured 90% marks in the XIIth Std. Science Examination with Biology and 60% marks in the entrance test. He was born on 3rd Obtober, 1973. He can pay the admission fee of Rs. 20,000.

35. Prasad Mehra was born on 4th July, 1976. He has secured 80% marks in the entrance test. He has secured 85% marks in the XIIth Std. Science Examination with Biology. He can pay the admission fee of Rs. 15,000.

Directions (Qs. 36 to 45) : *Study the following information to answer the questions.*

The following are the criteria for organising the Training Programme of an Institute, in different Hotels.

To organise the programme in Hotel Taj, the following criteria must be fulfilled :

(i) The Programme Coordinator should be of the rank of Deputy Director or Joint Director.

(ii) The Programme should be in one of these areas—HRD, Advertising, Computers or Statistics.

(iii) The duration of the Programme should not be more than seven days.

(iv) The fee per participant should not be less than Rs. 5,000/-

(v) The number of participants should be at least 50.

If all the other criteria are fulfilled except—

(a) the duration of the course is more than seven days—the programme is to be organised in Hotel Ritz.

(b) the Programme Coordinator is of the rank of Assistant Director, but the fee per participant is more than Rs. 7,000, the Programme will be organised in Taj.

(c) the number of participants being less than 50 but more than 30, the Programme will be organised in Hotel Sideways.

(d) the fee, per participant is less than Rs. 5000 but more than Rs. 3,500, the Programme should be organised in Hotel Sansy.

(e) the Programme is in other than the areas mentioned in *(ii)* above, but the Programme Coordinator is of Joint Director level, the Programme should be organised in Hotel Sideways.

Based on the above criteria and the information provided in each question, decide about the appropriate course of action. You are not to assume anything. If some information is not available to decide the course of action, the answer would be "data inadequate".

Give answer

(a) if the Programme is to be organised in Hotel Taj;

(b) if the Programme is to be organised in Hotel Sideways;

(c) if the Programme is to be organised in Hotel Ritz;

(d) if the Programme is to be organise in Hotel Sansy; and

(e) if the data are inadequate.

36. Prof. V. D. Dixit, Assistant Director, has offered four days' programme for 60 participants in the area of HRD. The fee per participant is Rs. 8,000.

37. Dr. Ashwani Dolke, Joint Director is organising five days' programme on Research Methodology. The total number of participants are 60 and the fee per participant is Rs. 7,000.

38. Dr. (Mrs.) Saroj Rao, Deputy Director of the institute wants to organise a programme for 55 candidates with a fee of Rs. 6,000 per participant. The duration of the course is four days and it is in the area of computers.

39. A Training Programme on Advertising is to be organised for 45 participants.The fee per participant is Rs. 6,000 and the duration of the course is six days.

40. A Training Programme on Statistics is proposed by the Deputy Director with Rs. 3,30,000 fee for 50 participants. The duration will be 8 days.

41. A five days' Training Programme by Joint Director is to be organised in the field of Statistics. The total fee for the Programme is Rs. 2,10,000 for 50 participants.

42. Nikhil Mukesh, Joint Director, is an expert on Computers. He is offering five days' programme on Mathematics for 60 participants. The fee per participant is Rs. 5,300.

43. A five days' Training Programme for 55 participants is to be organised by Shri Jacob Singh, Assistant Director. The fee per participant is Rs. 8,000.

44. Dr. Narayan Shiva, Deputy Director is offering a Programme on HRD with a total fee of Rs. 1,92,500 at the rate of Rs. 5,500 per participant. The duration of the course is five days.

45. Mrs. Shiela D'souza, Deputy Director has

submitted a proposal to organise four days' Programme on Computers. The fee per participant would be Rs. 4,000 for 60 participants.

Directions (Qs. 46 to 55) : *Study the following information carefully and answer the questions given below it :*

Following are the criteria for allotment of residential accomodation by an organisation to its employees. The employee must—

(a) have completed at least 10 years in this unit of the organisation but of which at least 4 years in the supervisory cadre.

(b) not have more than five members in the family.

(c) have at least 5 years of service remaining, the retirement age being 58 years.

(d) not have his/her own house.

(e) not be staying in a house owned by his/her spouse.

In the case of an employee who—

I. satisfies all other criteria except at *(a)* above and joined the organisation as a manager, should be referred to the Director–Finance.

II. satisfies all other criteria except at *(c)* above and at present working as a Senior Manager, is to be referred to the Managing–Director.

III. has been transferred from another city, the condition *(a)* may be waived.

Based on the above criteria and on the basis of the information provided in case of each employee in each of the following questions, you have to decide whether or not, accommodation is to be provided or the case is to be referred to higher authority. Please note that that you are not to assume anything in the case of any of the employees. All the cases are presented before you on 31st July, 1992.

Mark answer *(a)* if the employee is to be provided with accommodation.

Mark answer *(b)* if the employee is not to be provided with accommodation.

Mark answer *(c)* if the complete information as regards all the above criteria are not provided in the question.

Mark answer *(d)* if the case is to be referred to the Director–Finance.

Mark answer *(e)* if the case is to be referred to the Managing Director.

46. Hemant Adhikari has joined the organisation four years back as an Officer. He stays with his wife and two children. Neither he nor his wife owns a house.

47. Medha Pradhan has joined the organisation in 1975 when she was twenty-eight years old as an Officer. She is unmarried and stays with her mother in a rented house. She does not own a house.

48. Geeta Gokhale has been working in the organisation for the last ten years, out of which five years as an Officer. Her date of birth is 8th June 1940. She stays with her husband and three children. Neither she nor her husband owns a house.

49. Vipin Ghade has recently been transferred from another office and was 53 years old as on 8th February, 1992. He has been working in the organisation for the last twenty years out of which ten years as a Manager. There are four members in his family. Neither he nor his wife owns a house.

50. Ashok Patkar has joined the organisation as a Manager in 1986 and was 30 years old as on 15th August, 1989. He has four members in his family. Neither he nor his wife owns a house.

51. Vikas Kulkarni was 52 years old as on 5th May, 1990. He has been working in the organisation for the last eight years out of which five years as an officer. He stays with his wife and one son. Neither he nor his wife owns a house.

52. Shirish Apte is a Senior Manager for the last four years and has been working in the organisation for the last twelve years. He has three members including himself in the family. Neither he nor his wife owns a house. He will be retiring from the organisation in 1998.

53. Sudha Karkare was promoted as a Supervisor five years back after joining the organisation in 1979 as a clerk. She stays with her husband and two children in a rented house and she does not own any house. She was 42 years old as on 23rd April, 1991.

54. Kubal Das stays with his wife and three children. He has been working in the organisation for the last twelve years out of which five years as a Manager. His date of birth is 2nd July 1945.

55. Satish Aggrawal has been working in this unit for the last 15 years and has one son and two daughters along with his wife in the family. Neither he nor his wife owns a house. His date of birth is 20th January, 1950.

Directions (Qs. 56 to 63) : *Read the following information carefully and answer the questions given below :*

Following are the conditions for drawing a list of suitable candidates to be called for interview after a written test for recruitment is conducted for supervisory level persons for a reputed company providing software and services.

The candidate must—

(a) be holding a degree in basic science with 60% or above or engineering degree with 45% and above marks.

(b) have passed the written examination with 65% or above marks.

(c) be in the age group of 24 years to 30 years as on 1. 4. 1997.

(d) have experience in a computer company for a minimum period of 3 years after having obtained diploma in computer with 60% or above marks.

(e) be presently drawing a monthly salary of Rs. 8,000 and above.

In case of the applicant, who satisfies all other criteria except—

(I) at *(a)* above, be referred to the Manager (Recruitment).

(II) at *(b)* above but has obtained more than 75% marks in M.Sc. or Engineering degree, be referred to the Assistant General Manager (A.G.M.).

(III) at *(c)* above, be referred to the General Manager (G.M.).

Based on these criteria and information provided below, decide the course of action in each case. You are not to assume anything. If the data provided is not adequate to decide the given course of action, your answer will be "Data inadequate". The cases are given to you as on 1. 4. 1997.

56. Bimbadevi, aged 27 years, is a graduate in Science with diploma in computers and has been working for the last three and half years in a computer firm. Her present monthly salary is Rs. 10,500. She has passed her graduation, diploma and witten examination with 55%, 70% and 68% marks respectively.

(a) Do not call for interview
(b) Refer to G.M.
(c) Refer to Manager (Recruitment)
(d) Data inadequate
(e) Call for interview

57. Kasam Bhure did his B. Sc. with 70% marks followed by diploma in computers with 69% marks. He is employed from June 1993 in a computer firm with a salary of Rs. 9,700. He was born in Octorber 1973. He has passed the written examination with 72% marks.

(a) Call for interview
(b) Refer to Manager (Recruitment)
(c) Data inadequate
(d) Refer to G.M.
(e) Do not call for interview

58. Kamalnath has been working in computer company for the last 6 years after completing his diploma in computers with 62% marks. He has passed his Engineering degree and written examination with 55% and 68% marks respectively. He has completed 28 years of age in September 1995.

(a) Data inadequate
(b) Do not call for interview
(c) Call for interview
(d) Refer to G.M.
(e) Refer to A.G.M.

59. Niranjan Singh did his diploma in Computers at the age of 22 years after completing his B.Sc. Immediately after completing his dimploma, he got job in a computer company and is employed for the last four years with a salary of Rs. 10,500. He has got more than 65% marks in all the examinations including the written examination.

(a) Data inadequate
(b) Refer to Manager (Recruitment)
(c) Do not call for interview

(d) Refer to A.G.M.
(e) Call for interview

60. Deepa Sahi is working in supervisory capacity for the last 4 years in a computer company after having completed her Engineering degree with 55% and diploma in computers with 70% marks. She has secured 72% marks in the written examination. Her date of birth is 15 January, 1967 and her present salary is Rs. 10,000.
(a) Data inadequate
(b) Call for interview
(c) Do not call for interview
(d) Refer to Manager (Recruitment)
(e) Refer to G.M.

61. Mina Khan completed her B.Sc. at the age of 21 years, completed her one year's diploma in computers immediately and got a job from June 1994. She draws a monthly salary of Rs. 11,000. She has cleared all her examinations including written examination with a minimum of 68% marks.
(a) Refer to G.M.
(b) Refer to A.G.M.
(c) Refer to Manager (Recruitment)
(d) Do not call for interview
(e) Data inadequate

62. Jemi Desouza, born on 12. 2. 1968, is employed in a computer company for the last five years and is presently drawing a monthly salary of Rs. 9,500. He has successfully completed his degree in Engineering with 64% marks, diploma in computers and written examination with 65% and 60% marks respectively.
(a) Do not call for interview
(b) Call for interview
(c) Data inadequate
(d) Refer to G.M.
(e) Refer to Manager (Recruitment)

63. Anand Gupta has done his Master's degree in Science and then completed his diploma in Computers with 64% marks from a reputed institute. For the last 4 years, he has been working in a computer company. His age is 27 years and his present salary is Rs. 8,500. He obtained 68% marks in the written examination.
(a) Refer to Manager
(b) Data inadequate
(c) Call for interview
(d) Do not call for interview
(e) Refer to A.G.M.

Directions (Qs. 64 to 70) : *Trinity Health Club gives 40 per cent concession in monthly fees to those who satisfy anyone of the following criteria :*

(i) All children in the age group of 5 to 12 years who come from low income group and produce income and birth certificates.
(ii) All girls/women up to 25 years of age who represent their school or college in sports and games.
(iii) Unemployed married women in the age group of 35 to 50 years.
(iv) Senior citizens of age 50 years and above.
(v) All physically handicapped persons who produce relevent medical certificates.
(vi) All people who donate blood once a year or social workers/volunteers of registered social/cultural organisations.
(vii) Servicemen/Ex-Servicemen of Police/Defence Forces.
(viii) Sons and daughters of donors/founder members of the Trinity Health Club.

Decide in each of the following whether the person is 'eligible', find out the category/ies which is/are applicable to him/her for taking this decision and indicate your answer accordingly. The number indicated in the brackets in the choice indicates the category/ies mentioned above. Do not assume any information which is not given.

64. Bela, a 9 year old school girl and daughter of a merchant, has participated in dance and music competitions. Her father, who is 55 years old, has given large donations for organising blood camps. Her father is one of the founders of Trinity Club.
(a) Eligible under *(i)* only
(b) Eligible under *(i)*, *(ii)*, *(iv)* and *(viii)*
(c) Eligible under *(ii)* and *(viii)* only
(d) Eligible under *(i)*, *(ii)* and *(vi)* only
(e) Not eligible

65. Nina Gupta, a college-going married unemployed woman of 22 years, arranges donations for physically handicapped students. She has represented her school at the State-level elocution competition.

(*a*) Eligible under *(viii)* only
(*b*) Not Eligible
(*c*) Eligible under *(ii)* only
(*d*) Eligible under *(ii)*, *(iii)* only
(*e*) Eligible under *(ii)*, *(iii)*, *(vii)* and *(viii)*

66. Mridula is a young married and employed lady police officer. Her husband is a captain in the army. She is a sportswoman and represents police forces in national level competitions. She occasionally donates blood for her sick mother who is 55 years old.

(*a*) Eligible under *(vii)* only
(*b*) Eligible under *(ii)* and *(iii)* only
(*c*) Not eligible
(*d*) Eligible under *(ii)*, *(iii)* and *(iv)* only
(*e*) Eligible under *(vi)* and *(vii)* only

67. Mrs. Ratna, wife of Major Ravi Singh, is active in evening parties and clubs. She encourages people to donate to the Trinity club. She is 32 years old and unemployed.

(*a*) Not eligible
(*b*) Eligible under *(iii)* only
(*c*) Eligible under *(viii)* only
(*d*) Eligible under *(vii)* only
(*e*) Eligible under *(iii)*, *(vi)*, *(vii)* and *(viii)*

68. Mr. Rane established a registered trust for social work after his retirement from army at the age of 48 years. Since then he has been actively carrying out social work for the last eight years. His son is the founder member of "Trinty".

(*a*) Eligible under *(iv)* only
(*b*) Not eligible
(*c*) Eligible under *(iv)* and *(vi)* only
(*d*) Eligible under *(iv)*, *(vi)* and *(vii)*
(*e*) Eligible under *(iv)*, *(vi)*, *(vii)* and *(viii)*

69. Rita is an 11 years old school girl who can produce her birth certificate. Her parents are senior citizens and regular blood donors. Though a medically–certified physically handicapped person, she represents her school in national competition for the physically handicapped.

(*a*) Eligible under *(i)*, *(ii)* and *(iv)*
(*b*) Eligible under *(ii)* and *(v)* only
(*c*) Not eligible
(*d*) Eligible under *(iv)* and *(v)* only
(*e*) Eligible under *(i)*, *(ii)* and *(vi)* only

70. Dipti who represents her school in Badminton is the 14–year old daughter of physically handicapped parents having very low income. Her mother aged 40 years is unemployed. She has birth certificate and low income group certificate.

(*a*) Eligible under *(i)* only
(*b*) Eligible under *(ii)* only
(*c*) Eligible under *(i)*, *(ii)* and *(v)*
(*d*) Eligible under *(i)*, *(ii)*, *(iii)*, *(v)* only
(*e*) Not eligible

Directions (Qs. 71 to 80) : *A reputed educational foundation is to select meritorious graduate students for the award of scholarships for higher studies abroad who fulfill the following criteria :*

(i) Age : More than 20 years but less than 25 years, as on 1. 4. 1997.
(ii) Minimum Percentage of marks : B. Sc.–60% or BA–50% or B. Com–55%.
(iii) Prizes/awards : Should have won at least one either in Essay, Debate or Sports.
(iv) Annual Family Income : Not to be more than Rs. 1,00,000.
(v) Domicile : Must be staying in India for the last 15 years or above, as on 1. 4. 1997.

Concessions : One has to fulfill the above conditions. However, certain concessions are available to the following categories :

(*a*) Wards of Farmers—relaxation in the maximum age limit upto five years.
(*b*) SC/ST applicants—relaxation in marks upto 5%.

Consideration :

(*c*) Not fulfilling criterion *(iii)* above—the case may be referred to the Secretary of the Foundation.
(*d*) Not fulfilling criterion *(iv)* above—the case may be referred to the Chairman of the Foundation.

You have to study the information provided for a candidate in each of the following questions and decide the course of action.

Give answer—

(a) If the candidate is to be selected.

(b) If the candidate is to be selected under any concession.

(c) If the case is to be referred to the Secretary.

(d) If the case is to be referred to the Chairman, and

(e) If the candidatc is not to be selected.

Note : The candidate is to be considered "Not to be selected", if any required information (creteria *i* to *v*) is not provided.

71. Hailing from a poor scheduled tribe family living near Rourkela since 1949, 21 year old Ratan got his B. A. degree with 46% marks. His father, a school teacher and sole earner in the family has a monthly income of Rs. 4,200. Ratan won the first prize in a District Level Essay competition.

72. Family of 22 year old Antony is settled at Cochin since 1969. He has 59% marks in B. A. and had won a gold medal in the All India Lions Club Essay Comeption. His father—a farmer— has an annual income of Rs. 79,000.

73. Yogesh, who will be 23 years old on 1. 1. 1999, passed B. Com. with 51 per cent marks. His father, a Government employee, has been working at Srinagar since 1979 whose present monthly salary is Rs. 8,200. Yogesh got the 3rd prize in the State Essay Championship.

74. Twenty-three years old Mandakini has 58% marks in B.Com. and had won the 1st prize in her final year Debate Competition. Her annual family income is about Rs. 1.25 lakh. Her father is settled in Shillong for the last 21 years.

75. Mahasweta was born on 4. 3. 1979 and recently passed B. Sc. with 63% marks. Her father, a lecturer at a Junior College at Ranchi since 1978, has an annual family income of Rs. 82,000. She won a third prize in the State Athletic Championship.

76. Irfan, son of a Foreman in Indonesia, came to India with his family in 1970 and since then settled at Aligarh. He got a first prize in an International Debate Competition. He is a graduate in science with 69% marks. His annual family income is Rs. 96,000.

77. 24 years old Jagdeep has 57% marks in B. Com. and has bagged the first prize in College Music Competition. His father, an industrial workman and sole earner in the family, has a monthly income of Rs. 7,800 and is settled in Nasik since 1958.

78. 26 years old Rukmini has been staying with her father at Chandbali village in Tripura since her birth. Her father, a farmer, has an annual income of Rs. 78,000. She obtained 59% marks in B. Com. and had won a prize in College Sports Competition.

79. Born on 21. 2. 1976, Rachna completed her B. Sc. in March 1996. Her father is a farmer settled in Madhya Pradesh for the last 32 years. She is a State Champion in Badminton. Her annual family income is Rs. 91,000.

80. Chelaram, son of a farmer who has been staying in Haryana for the last five decades, passed B.A. with 51% marks. He has got a second prize in the District Level Weightlifting Championship. His date of Birth is 3. 9. 1974 and his father's annual income is Rs. 83,000.

EXPLANATORY ANSWERS

1. ***(e)*** **:** Criterion *(iii)* is not satisfied but Criterion *(b)* gives the decision.

2. ***(d)*** **:** Both Criterion *(iii)* and Criterion *(b)* are not satisfied.

3. ***(c)*** **:** Criterion *(iv)* is not satisfied but Criterion *(a)* gives the decision.

4. ***(c)*** **:** Criterion *(ii)* is not given.

5. ***(a)***

6. ***(a)*** **:** Both Criterion *(i)* and Criterion *(c)* are not satisfied.

7. ***(d)*** **:** Criterion *(iv)* is not given but Criterion *(b)* gives the decision.

8. ***(e)*** **:** Both Criteria *(ii)* and *(iii)* are not given and Criterion *(a)* alone cannot give the decision.

9. ***(e)*** **:** Both Criterion *(i)* and Criterion *(iii)* are not given and criterion *(a)* alone cannot give the decision.

10. *(b)* : Both Criterion *(iii)* and Criterion *(a)* are not satisfied.

11. *(c)* : Criterion *(iii)* is not satisfied but Criterion *(a)* gives the decision.

12. *(a)* : Criterion *(i)* is not satisfied but Criterion *(c)* gives the decision.

13. *(a)* : Criterion *(iii)* is not satisfied but Criterion *(a)* gives the decision.

14. *(c)* : Criterion *(iv)* is not satisfied but Criterion *(b)* gives the decision.

15. *(b)* : Both Criterion *(iii)* and Criterion *(a)* are not satisfied.

16. *(e)* : Criterion *(i)* is not given and Criterion *(c)* is not satisfied.

17. *(e)* : Criterion *(i)* is not satisfied but Criterion *(c)* gives the decision of "wait–list." This option is not given.

18. *(a)* : Criterion *(iii)* is not satisfied but Criterion *(a)* gives the decision.

19. *(a)* : Both Criterion *(i)* and Criterion *(iii)* are not satisfied, Criterion *(c)* and Criterion *(d)* gives different decisions.

20. *(b)* : Criterion *(h)* is not satisfied but Criterion *(j)* gives the decision.

21. *(b)* : Criterion *(b)* is not satisfied.

22. *(e)* : Criterion *(g)* is not given.

23. *(b)* : Criterion *(h)* is not satisfied but Criterion *(j)* gives the desicion.

24. *(c)* : Criterion *(d)* is not satisfied but Criterion *(i)* gives the decision.

25. *(a)* : Criterion *(b)* is not satisfied.

26. *(d)* : Both Criterion *(e)* and Criterion *(f)* are not satisfied.

27. *(c)*

28. *(e)* : Criterion *(a)* is not given.

29. *(c)* : Criterion *(c)* is not satisfied but Criterion *(I)* gives the decision.

30. *(b)* : Criterion *(b)* is not satisfied.

31. *(a)* **32. *(a)***

33. *(b)* : Criterion *(b)* is not satisfied.

34. *(c)* : Criterion *(c)* is not satisfied but Criterion *(I)* gives the decision.

35. *(d)* : Criterion *(d)* is not satisfied but Criterion *(II)* gives the decision.

36. *(a)* : Criterion *(i)* is not satisfied but Criterion *(b)* gives the decision.

37. *(b)* : Criterion *(ii)* is not satisfied but Criterion *(e)* gives the decision.

38. *(a)*

39. *(e)* : Criterion *(i)* is not given.

40. *(c)* : Criterion *(iii)* is not satisfied but Criterion *(a)* gives the decision.

41. *(d)* : Criterion *(iv)* is not satisfied but Criterion *(d)* gives the decision.

42. *(b)* : Criterion *(ii)* is not satisfied but Criterion *(e)* gives the decision.

43. *(e)* : Criterion *(ii)* is not given.

44. *(b)* : Criterion *(v)* is not satisfied but Criterion *(c)* gives the decision (No. of participants is 1, 92, 500 ÷ 5,500, *i.e.*, 35)

45. *(d)* : Category *(iv)* is not satisfied but category *(d)* gives the decision.

46. *(c)* : Criterion *(c)* is not given and Criterion *(a)* is not satisfied.

47. *(a)* **48. *(a)***

49. *(b)* : Both Criterion *(c)* and Criterion *(II)* are not satisfied.

50. *(a)*

51. *(b)* : Both Criterion *(a)* and Criterion *(c)* are not satisfied.

52. *(e)* : Criterion *(c)* is not satisfied but Criterion *(II)* gives the decision.

53. *(a)*

54. *(c)* : Criterion *(d)* is not given.

55. *(c)* : Criterion *(a)* is not given.

56. *(c)* : Criterion *(a)* is not satisfied but Criterion *(I)* gives the decision.

57. *(d)* : Criterion *(c)* is not satisfied but Criterion *(III)* gives the decision.

58. *(a)* : Criterion *(e)* is not given.

59. *(e)*

60. *(e)* : Criterion *(c)* is not satisfied but Criterion *(III)* gives the decision.

61. *(d)* : Both Criterion *(a)* and Criterion *(d)* are not satisfied and Criterion *(I)* alone cannot give the decision.

62. *(a)* : Both Criterion *(b)* and Criterion *(II)* are not satisfied.

63. *(b)* : Neither Criterion *(a)* nor Criterion *(II)* is given.

64. *(c)* : Both Criterion *(ii)* and Criterion *(viii)* are satisfied.

65. *(c)* : Only Criterion *(ii)* is satisfied.
66. *(e)* : Both Criteria *(vi)* and *(vii)* are satisfied.
67. *(a)* : None of the Criterion is satisfied.
68. *(d)* : Criteria *(iv), (vi)* and *(vii)* are satisfied.
69. *(b)* : Both Criterion *(ii)* and Criterion *(v)* are satisfied.
70. *(b)* : Only Criterion *(ii)* is satisfied.
71. *(b)* : Criterion *(ii)* is not satisfied but Criterion *(b)* gives the decision.
72. *(a)*
73. *(e)* : Criterion *(ii)* is not satisfied and Criterion *(b)* is not given.
74. *(d)* : Criterion *(iv)* is not satisfied but Criterion *(d)* gives the decision.
75. *(e)* : Criterion *(i)* is not satisfied.
76. *(e)* : Criterion *(i)* is not given.
77. *(a)*
78. *(b)* : Criterion *(i)* is not satsified but Criterion *(a)* gives the decision.
79. *(e)* : Criterion *(ii)* is not given and so, remain unsatisfied.
80. *(a)*

LOGICAL DIAGRAMS

In these type of questions, a set of five different figures is given as options. Each figure represents a logical pattern of certain groups of related words wherein each word represents a class. One has to identify the most appropriate logical figure for the set of words given. Some of the relationships represented by these diagrams are given below. Understand the relationship patterns and then attempt the exercise following the explanation.

SOLVED EXAMPLES

1. The given classes have nothing in common.
Example : Milk, Eggs.

2. The given classes have something in common, but neither of them is completely contained in the other.
Example : Colour, Red

3. Of the two given classes, one is wholly contained in the other, but not vice–versa.
Example : Fruits, Apples

4. Same logic as figure 2.
Example : Tall, Men, Educated

5. Of the three given classes, one is completely contained in the other and not vice–versa while the third class has nothing in common with either of the two classes.
Example : Water, Solids, Liquids

6. Two classes are wholly contained in the third class, but not vice–versa, also the two contained classes have nothing in common.
Example : Punjab, Agra, India

7.  **Two classes are wholly contained in the third class, but not vice–versa, and the two contained classes also have something in common though neither class is wholly contained in the other.**

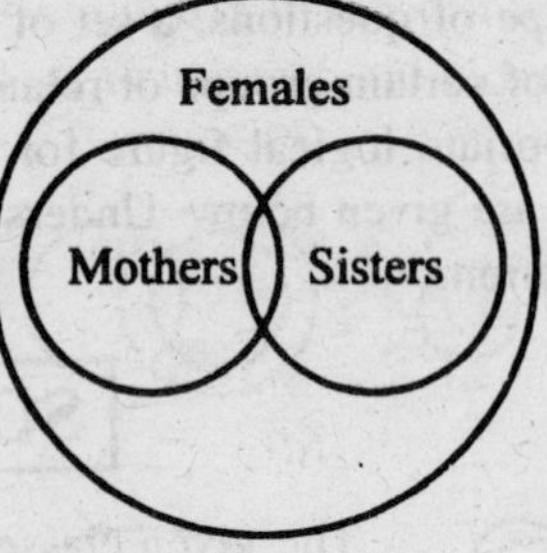

Example : Mothers, Sisters, Females

8.  **The first class is contained wholly in the other two classes, but not vice–versa. The second is wholly contained in the third and partially in the first. A part of third class is contained in the second of which some is contained in the first.**

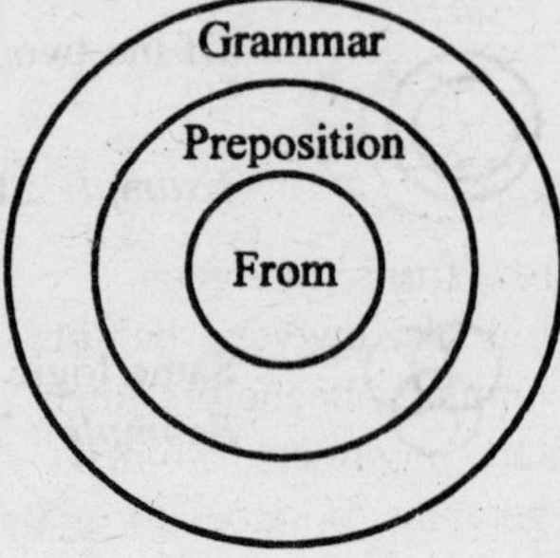

Example : Preposition, From, Grammer.

9. 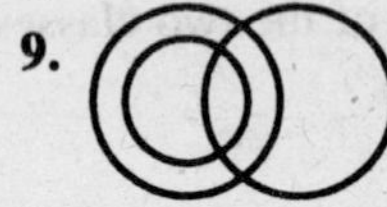 **First class is wholly contained in the second and not vice–versa. The third class is partially contained in the other two classes.**

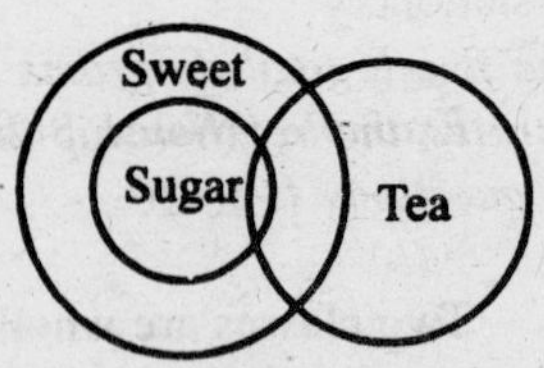

Example : Sugar, Sweet, Tea

Note : Some people drink tea without Sugar.

10.  The first and second class have some part in common, and so have the second and third class, but the first and the third class have nothing in common.

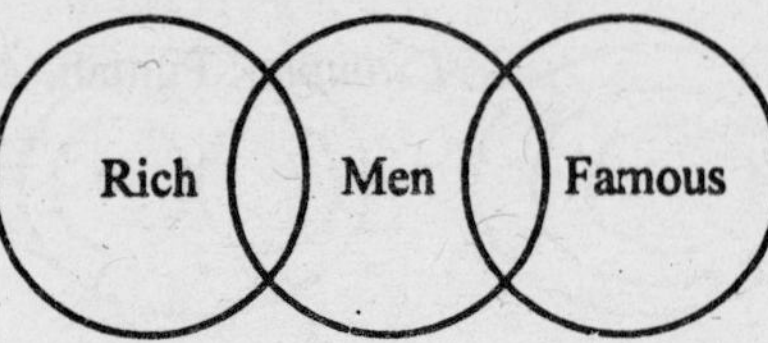

Example : Rich, Men, Famous.

EXERCISE

Directions : *From the five logical Diagrams, select one which best illustrates the relationship among three given classes in the questions 1 to 10.*

(a) *(b)*

(c) *(d)*

(e)

1. Birds, fruits, mangoes
2. Criminals, lawyers, bandits
3. Swimmers, bachelors, men
4. Smart, engineers, women
5. Vegetables, potatoes, brinjals
6. Grapes, sweet, fruit
7. Doctors, architects, humans
8. Scholars, people, Indians
9. Children, naughty, studious
10. Pens, pencils, stationery

Directions : *From the five logical diagrams select one which best illustrates the relationship among three given classes in questions 11 to 20.*

(a) *(b)*

(c) *(d)*

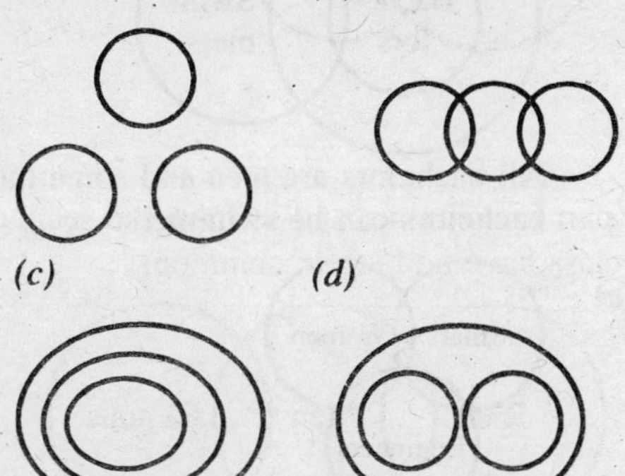

(e)

11. Ink, crayons, red
12. Canines, dogs, pups
13. Table, chair, stool
14. Ripe, mangoes, basket
15. Scholars, studious, illiterates
16. Cars, ships, means of conveyance
17. Age, number, thirteen
18. Country, state, continent
19. Father, parent, mother
20. Iron, metal, mercury

Directions : *From the five logical diagrams select one which best illustrates the relationship among three given classes in the questions 21 to 30.*

(a) *(b)*

(c) *(d)*

(e)

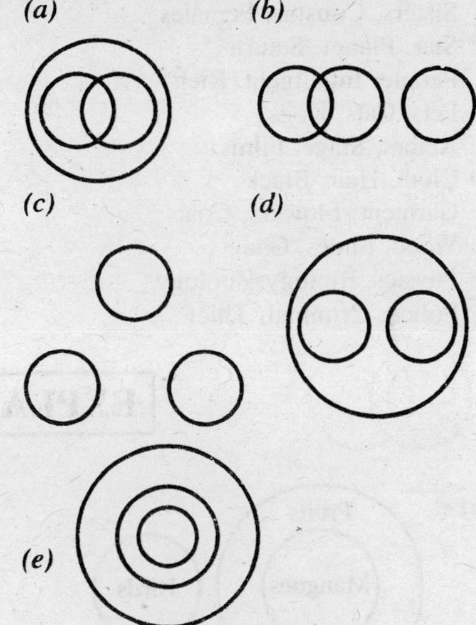

21. Lizards, Reptiles, Crocodiles
22. Whales, Tortoise, Fishes
23. Birds, Crows, Parrots
24. Sisters, Women, Mothers
25. Plants, Scientists, Men
26. Novels, Album, English
27. Sentences, Words, Paragraph
28. Beef, Mutton, Flesh
29. Principal, Student, Parent
30. Lily, Rose, Flower.

Directions : *From the five logical diagrams select one which best illustrates the relationship among three given classes in the questions 31 to 40.*

(a) (b)

(c) (d)

(e)

31. Sisters, Cousins, Females
32. Star, Planet, Saturn
33. People, Intelligent, Rich
34. Pets, Cats, Dogs
35. Actors, Stage, Films
36. Cloth, Hair, Black
37. Garment, Flowers, Coats
38. Wood, Shoes, Chair
39. Physics, Biology, Zoology
40. Police, Criminal, Thief

Directions : *From the five logical diagrams select one which best illustrates the relationship among three given classes in the questions 41 to 50.*

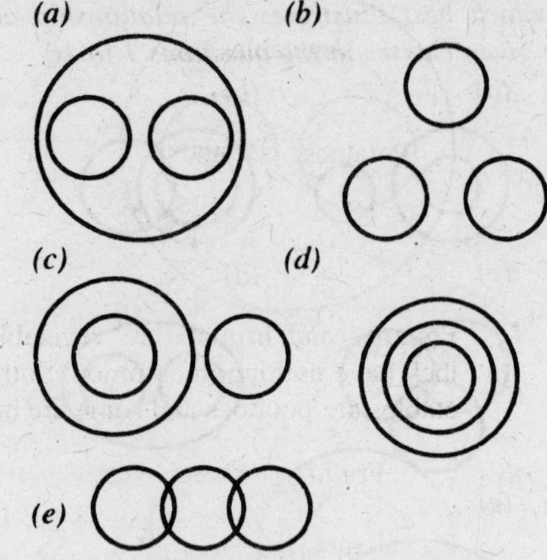

41. Country, Nepal, India
42. Body, Blood, Veins
43. Chess, Games, Hockey
44. Tractor, Aircraft, Cart
45. Oriental, Continental, Mughlai
46. Delhi, Lucknow, Uttar Pradesh
47. Russian, People, German
48. Days, Months, Years
49. Stamp, Pen, Chalk
50. Marble, Animal, Goat

EXPLANATORY ANSWERS

1. *(a)* :

Fruits
Mangoes
Birds

All mangoes are fruits, but neither fruits, nor mangoes can be birds.

2. *(a)* :

Criminals
Bandits
Law-yers

All bandits are criminal, but neither criminals nor bandits can be lawyers.

3. *(b)* :

Men
Bache-lors
Swim-mers

All bachelors are men and some men and bachelors can be swimmers.

4. *(c)* :

Smart
Women
Engineers

Some women can be smart and some

women can be engineers and vice–versa. Some engineers can be women and some engineers can be smart and vice–versa.

5. *(d)* :

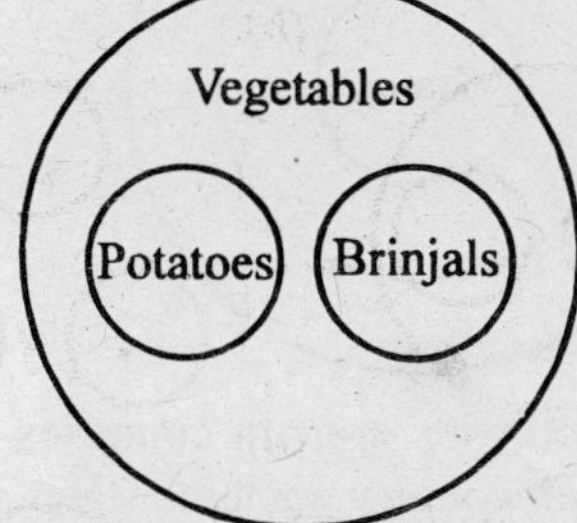

Potatoes and brinjals are vegetables but they have nothing in common. Some vegetables are potatoes and some are brinjals.

6. *(b)* :

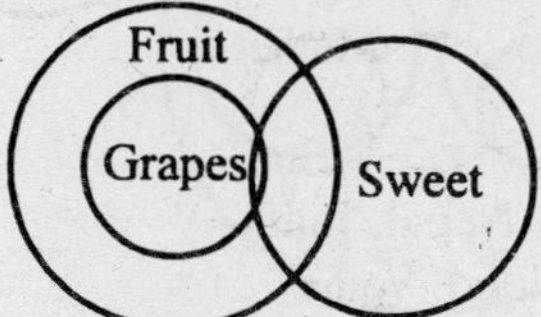

Some grapes are sweet and all grapes are fruit. But not all that is sweet is fruit.

7. *(d)* :

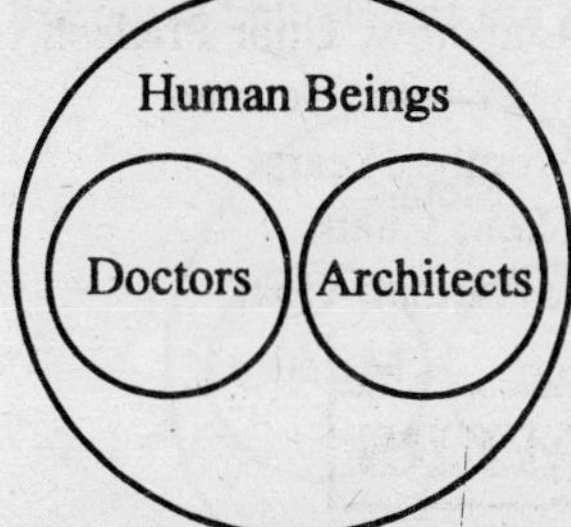

Doctors and architects are two separate classes, but all doctors and architects are humans and some humans are either doctors or architects.

8. *(e)* :

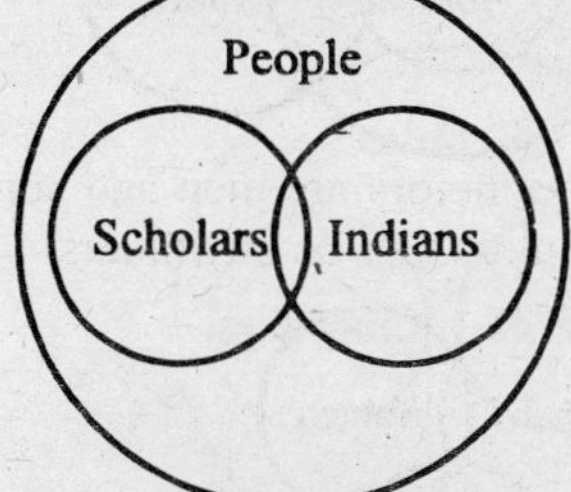

Some Indians can be scholars and some scholars can be Indians. All scholars and Indians are people.

9. *(c)* :

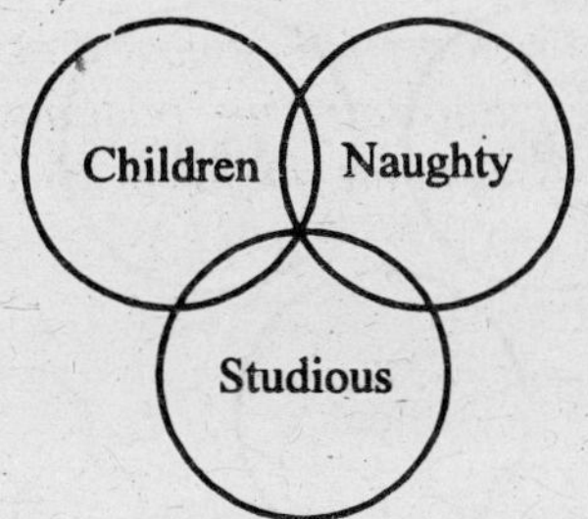

Some children can be naughty and some can be studious, some studious can be children and some naughty. Some naughty can be studious and some children.

10. *(d)* :

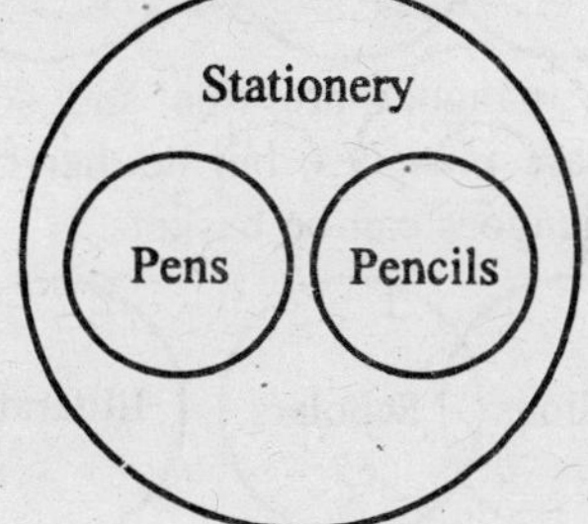

Pens and pencils both are items of stationery and some stationery is pens and pencils, but pens and pencils are two separate classes.

11. *(b)* :

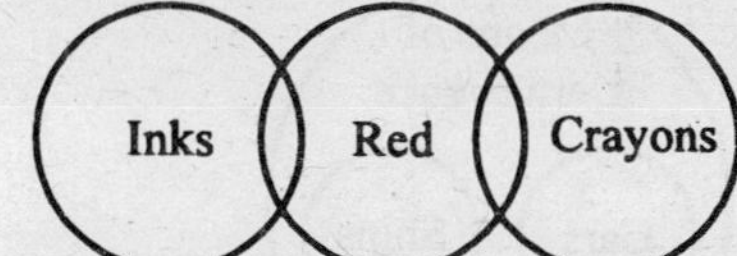

Some ink and some crayons can be red and some red units can be inks and crayons, but ink and crayon have nothing in common.

12. *(c)* :

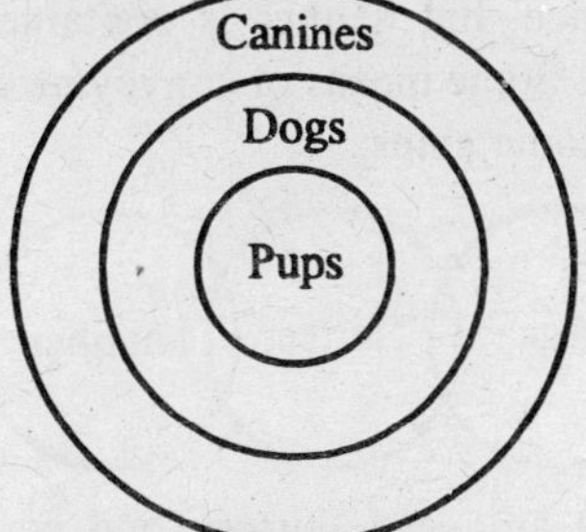

All pups are dogs and all dogs are canines. Some canines are dogs, of which some are pups.

13. (a) :

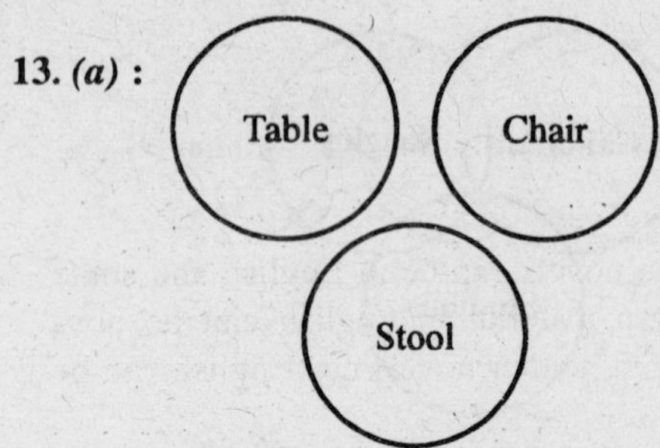

All three are different classes.

14. (e) :

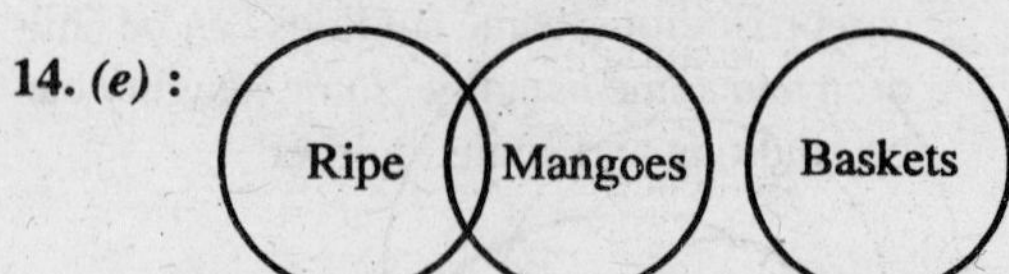

Some mangoes are ripe and some ripe units are mangoes, but neither ripe units nor mangoes can be baskets.

15. (e) :

Some studious can be scholars and some scholars can be studious, but neither studious nor scholars can be illiterates.

16. (d) :

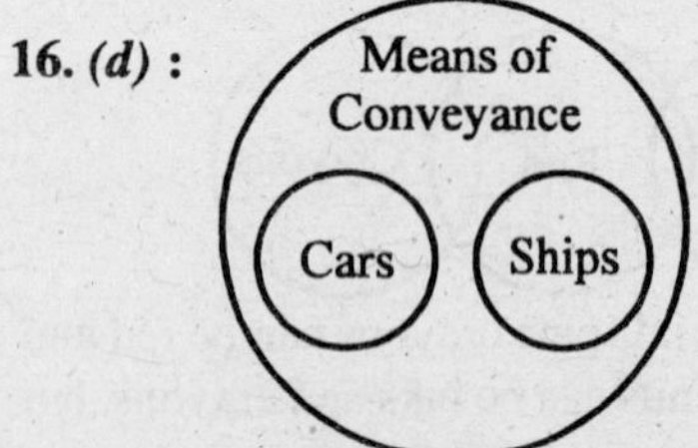

All cars and all ships are means of conveyance, but neither is contained in the other. Some means of conveyance are cars and some ships.

17. (b) :

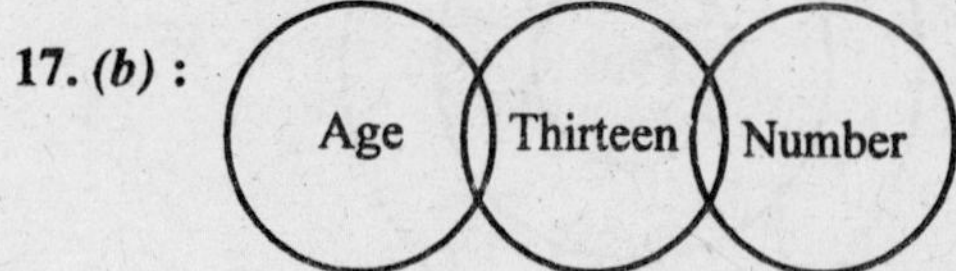

Some are aged thirteen and some numbers are thirteen. Some thirteen units are numbers and some ages. Age and number have nothing in common.

18. (c) :

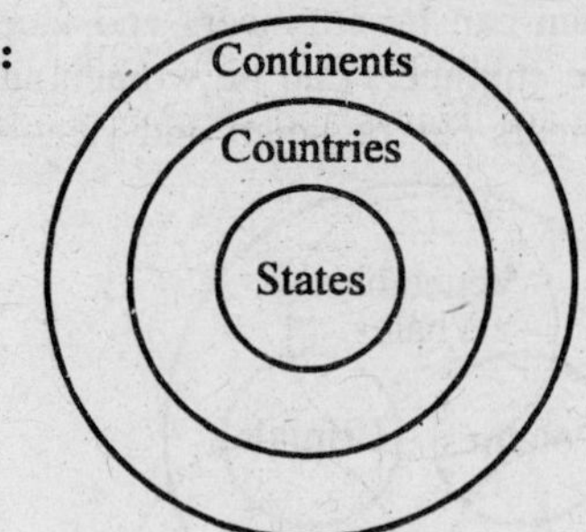

All continents contain countries within it and each country contains states within it.

19. (d) :

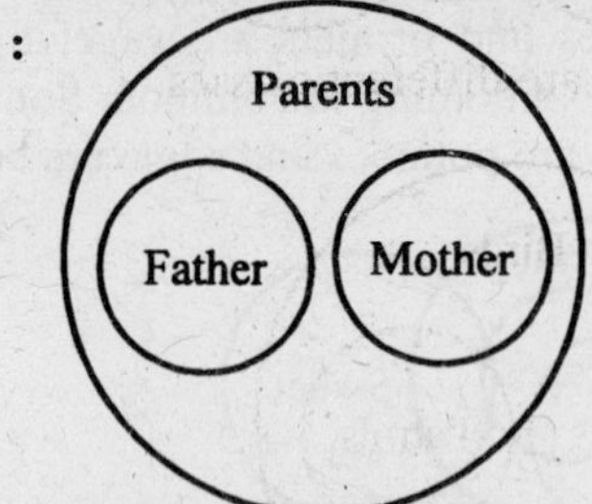

All fathers and mothers are parents, but they are two separate classes. Some of the parents are fathers and some are mothers.

20. (d) :

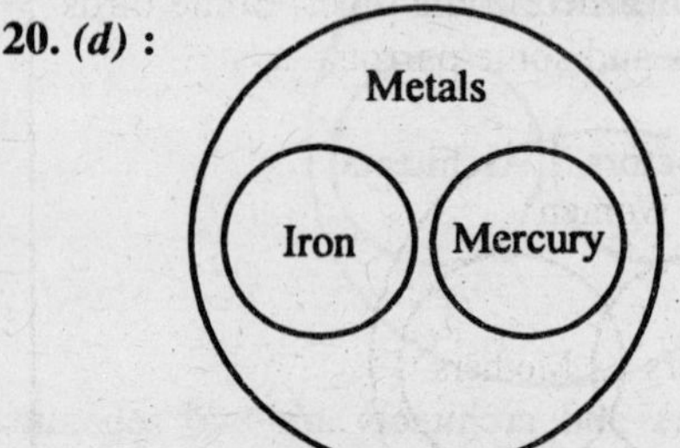

Iron and mercury are metals, but they have nothing in common. Some metals are iron and some mercury.

21. (d) :

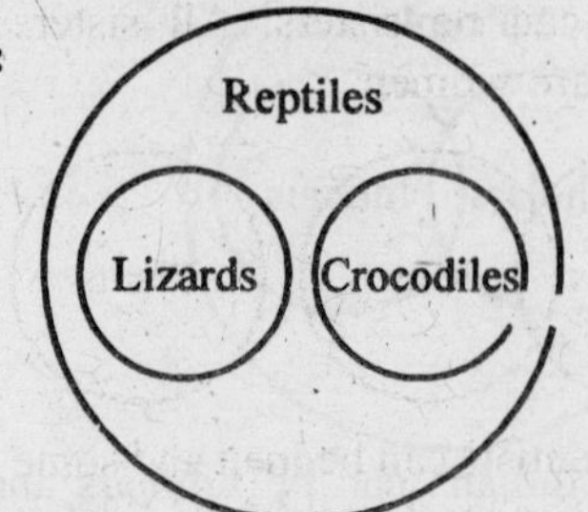

All lizards and crocodiles are reptiles, but

neither is contained in the other. Some reptiles are lizards and some crocodiles.

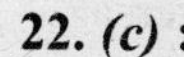

22. *(c)* :

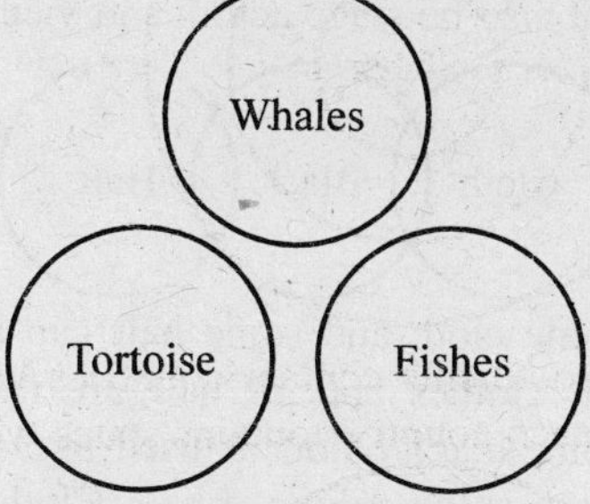

All three are different classes.

23. *(d)* :

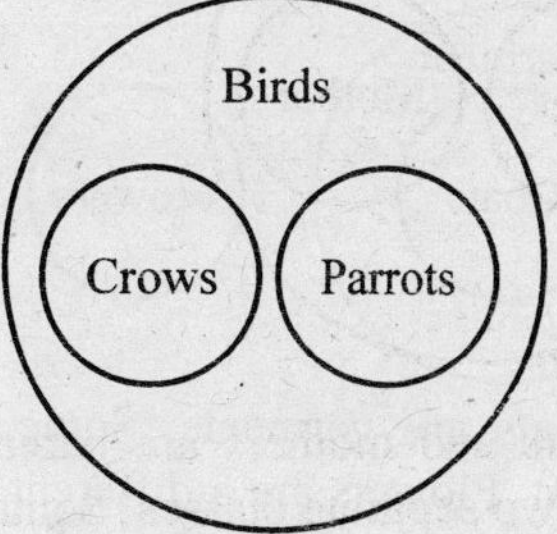

All crows and parrots are birds but neither is contained in the other. Some birds are crows and some parrots.

24. *(a)* :

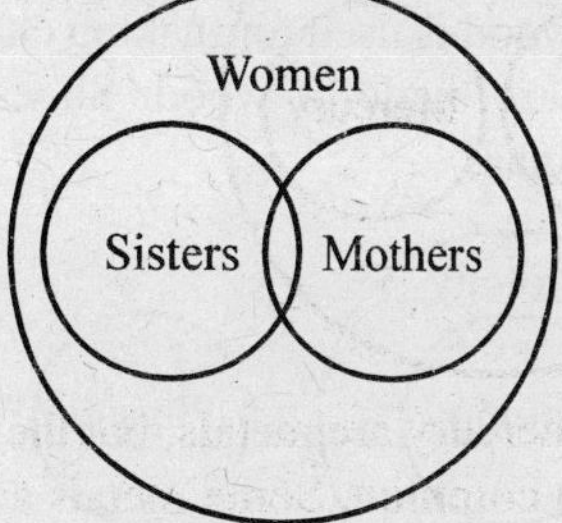

Some sisters can be mothers and some mothers can be sisters. All sisters and mothers are women.

25. *(b)* :

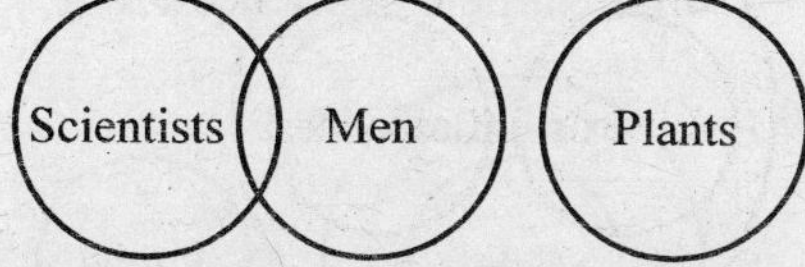

Some scientists can be men and some men can be scientists, but neither scientists nor men can be plants.

26. *(b)* :

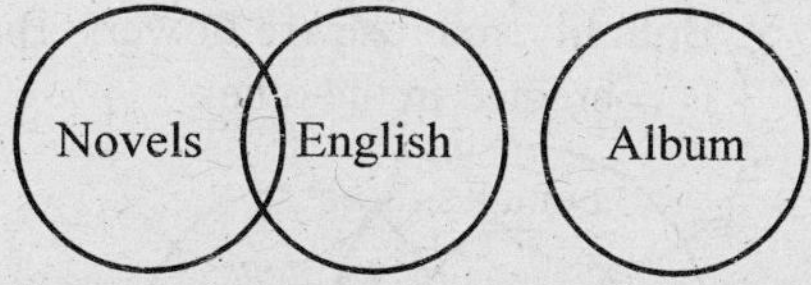

Some novels can be in English and some written material in English can be novels, but neither novels nor English can be album.

27. *(e)* :

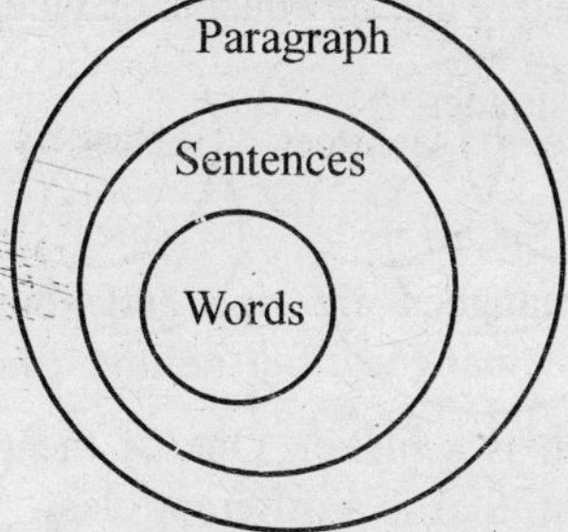

All paragraphs contain sentences within it and all sentences contain words within it.

28. *(d)* :

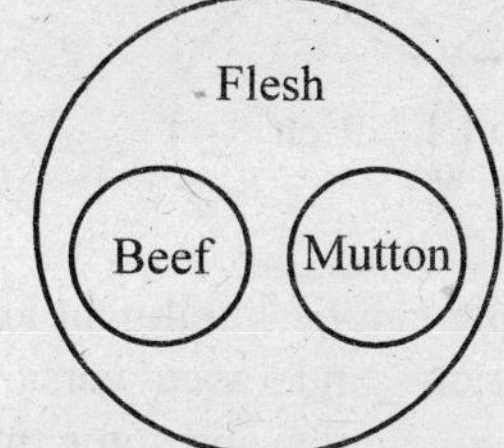

All beef and mutton are flesh of some animals. Some flesh is beef and some mutton.

29. *(b)* :

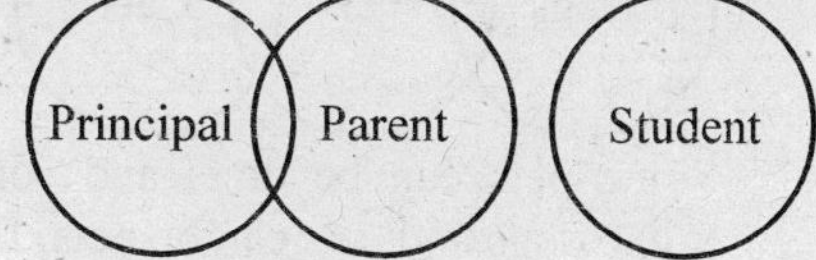

A Principal can be a parent and parent can be a principal. A student is a different class.

30. *(d)* :

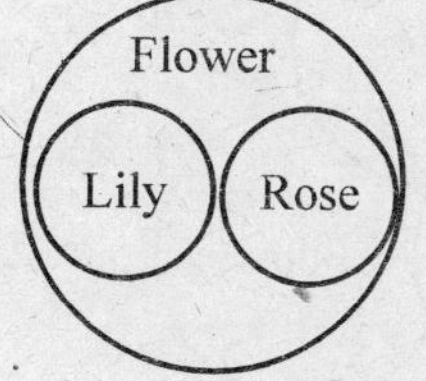

Both lily and rose are flowers. But neither is contained in the other.

31. ***(a)*** **:**

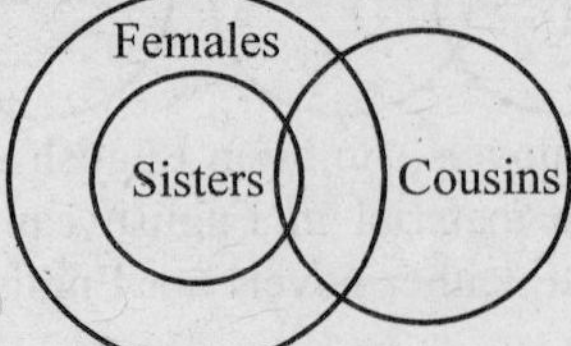

All sisters are females. Some females who are sisters can be cousins or vice–versa.

32. ***(e)*** **:**

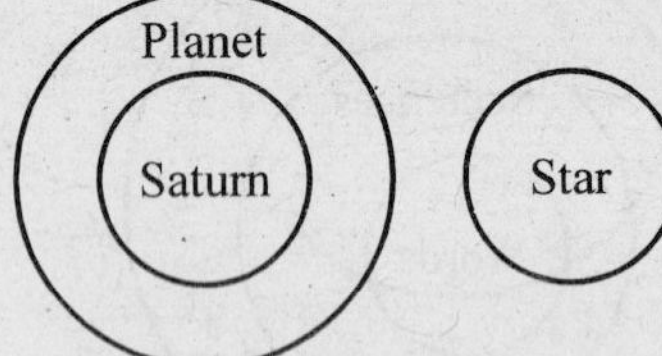

Saturn is a planet. One of the planets is Saturn. Star is a different class.

33. ***(b)*** **:**

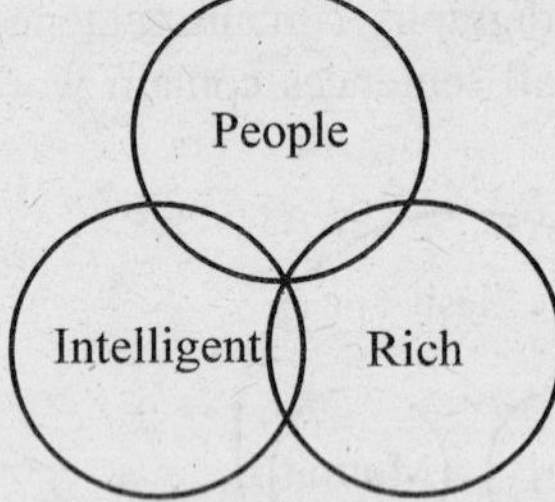

Some people can be intelligent and some can be rich and vice–versa. Some intelligent can be rich and some intelligent beings can be people and vice versa.

34. ***(c)*** **:**

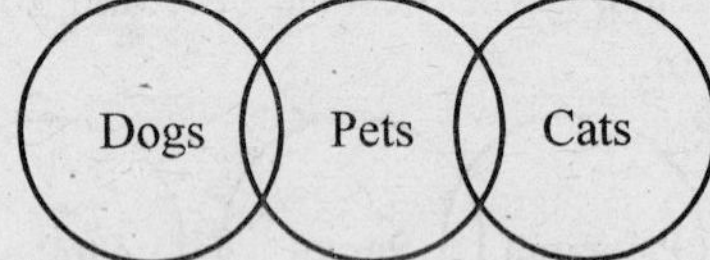

Some pets can be dogs and some cats. Some dogs and cats can be pets. Dogs and cats are different classes.

35. ***(b)*** **:**

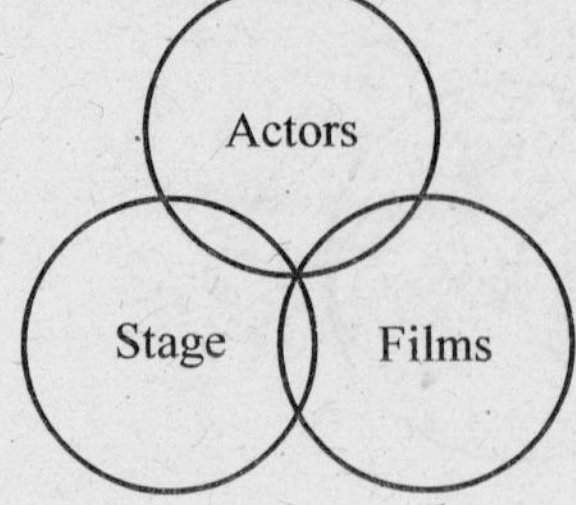

Some actors can be stage actors and some film actors and vice-versa. Some people working in films can be actors and some can also be stage actors and vice-versa.

36. ***(c)*** **:**

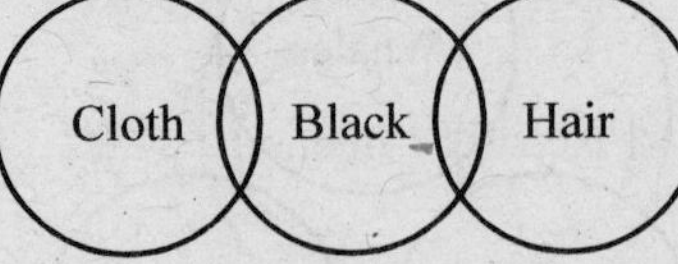

Some cloth and some hair can be black. (all clothes and all hair are not black). Some black colour is used in clothes and some is the colour of hair. Cloth and hair are different classes.

37. ***(e)*** **:**

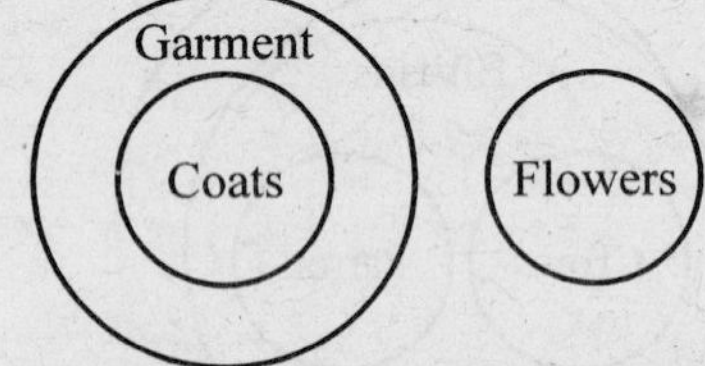

All coats are garments. Some garments are coat. Flowers are a different class.

38. ***(d)*** **:**

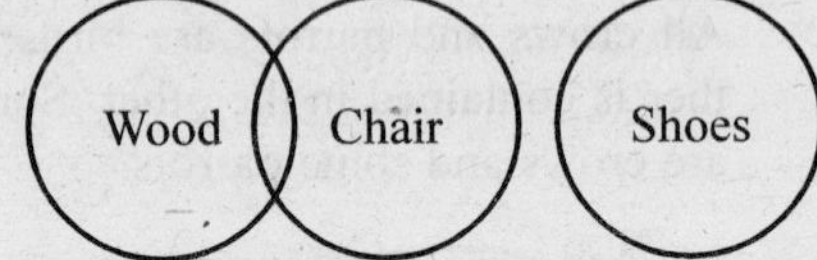

Some wood is used for making chair. Some chairs are made of wood. Shoes are different class.

39. ***(e)*** **:**

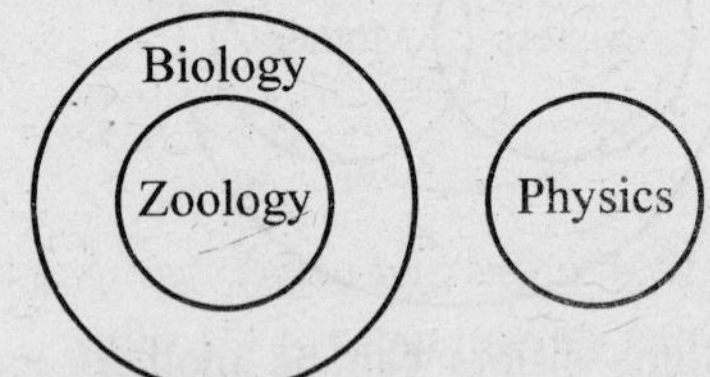

Zoology is a part of Biology. Biology contains the study Zoology. Physics is a different field of sciences.

40. ***(e)*** **:**

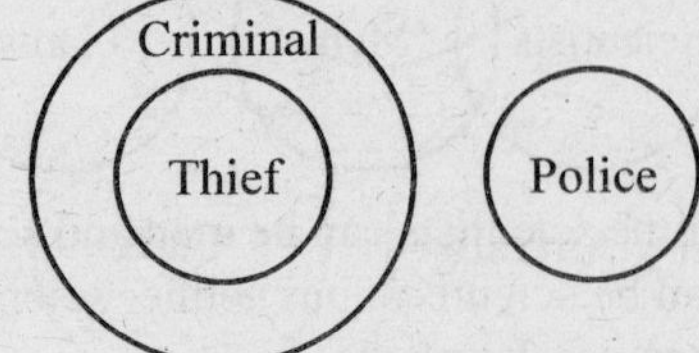

Thief is a criminal. Some criminals can

be thieves. Police is a different class.

41. *(a)* :

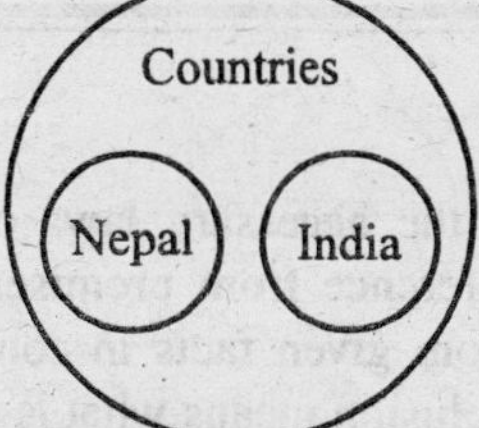

Nepal and India are countries but neither is contained in the other.

42. *(d)* :

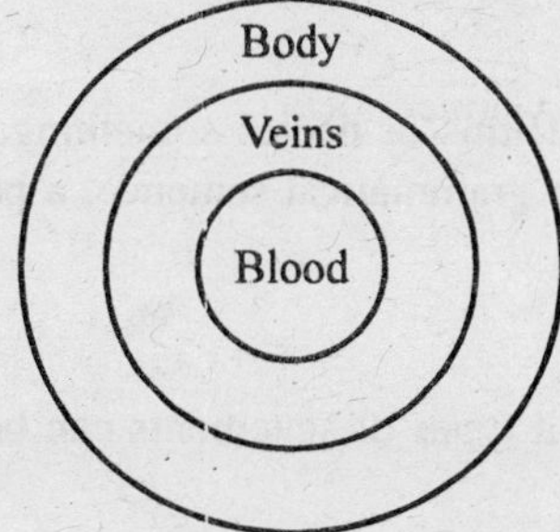

Body contains veins within it and all veins contain blood within it.

43. *(a)* :

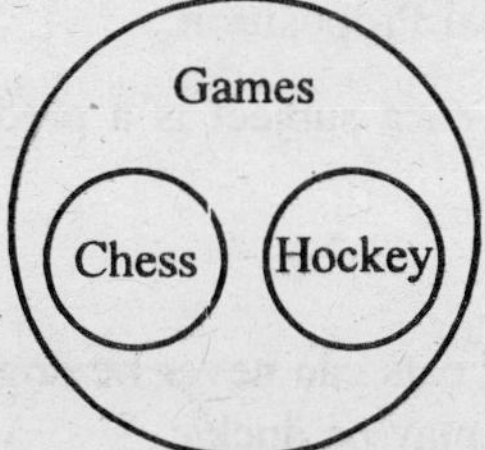

Both chess and hockey are games but neither is contained in the other.

44. *(b)* :

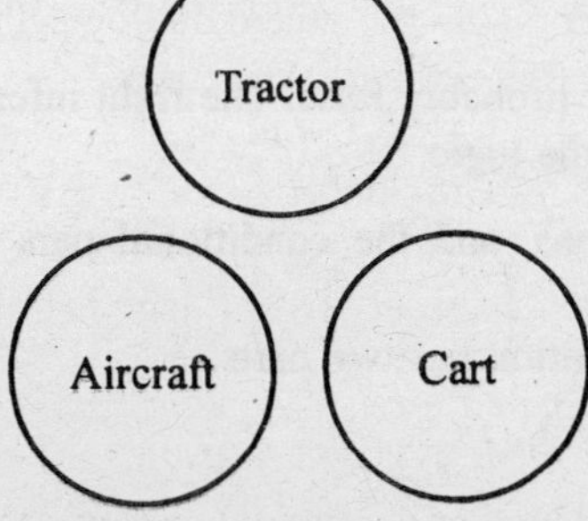

All three are different classes.

45. *(b)* :

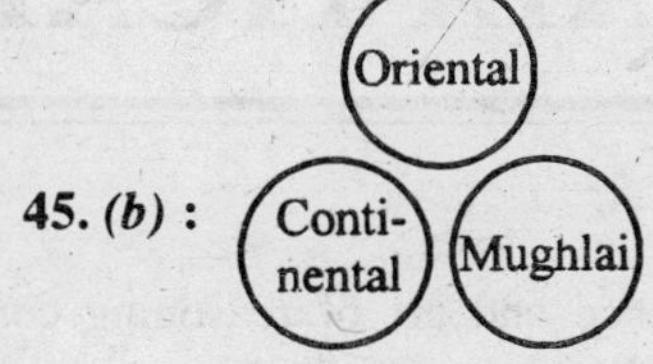

All three are different classes.

46. *(c)* :

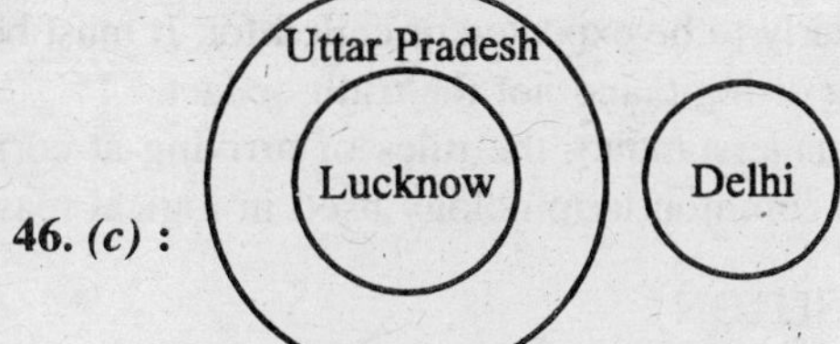

Lucknow is in Uttar Pradesh. One of the part of Uttar Pradesh is Lucknow. Delhi is a different /separate place.

47. *(e)* :

Some Russian and some German can be people. Some people can be Russian and some German. Russian and German are separate classes.

48. *(d)* :

Years have months contained within it and months have days contained within it.

49. *(b)* :

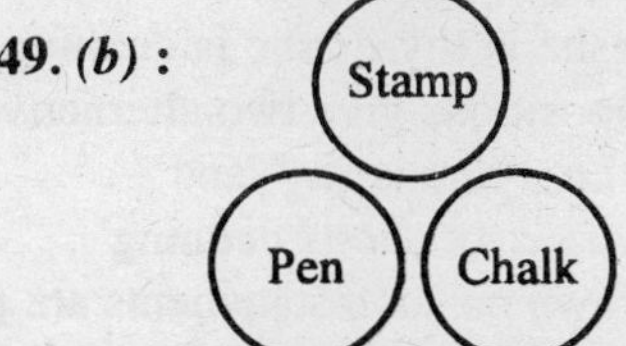

All three are different classes.

50. *(c)* :

Goat is an animal. Some animals are goats. Marble is a different class.

ANALYTICAL REASONING

LOGIC

Logic is the science and art of reasoning correctly, the science of the necessary laws of thought. *Reasoning* is the mind's power of drawing conclusions and deducing inference from premises. And so, *Logical Reasoning* implies the process of drawing logical conclusions from given facts in conformity to what is fairly to be expected or called for. It must be noted that logical conclusion means what is derived by reasoning or logic and not the truth or fact.

For understanding the rules of arriving at correct inferences or conclusions, it is necessary to understand the common terminology used in logical reasoning.

PROPOSITION

The logical proposition is an expression or a statement which affirms or denies something, so that it can be characterised as true or false, valid or invalid. Like any other grammatical sentence, a proposition has a subject, a predicate and a copula connecting the two.

Example : Kings are mortals.

Here *Kings* is the subject, *mortal* is predicate and *are* is copula.

A proposition is a statement used in logical reasoning, but not all types of statements can be used for the purpose of logical arguments.

Examples : 1. Oh ! there she is.
2. Where have you been ?

Sentences or statements that are exclamatory or interrogative in nature are not taken as logical propositions. Mainly, the propositions can be classified into four categories *(a)* Categorical Proposition; *(b)* Disjunctive Proposition; *(c)* Hypothetical Proposition; and *(d)* Relational Proposition.

***(a)* Categorical Proposition :** Emphasises what is and what is not, *i.e.*, a subject is a predicate or is not predicate.

Example : I. All cats are dogs.
II. No hens are ducks.

Logically speaking, all cats must be dogs irrespective of the truth that cats can never be dogs. So, also in second sentence, no hens are ducks leaves no argument that some hens may be ducks.

***(b)* Disjunctive Proposition :** Leave every scope of confusion as they have either—or—in them.

Example : Either she is shy or she is cunning.

These type of propositions give two alternatives.

I. antecedent, *i.e.*, 'She is shy' and
II. consequent, *i.e.*, 'or she is cunning'

The inferences drawn on such statements are probably true or probably false. The right inference often depends on one's own ability to sense and analyse the validity of the logic.

***(c)* Hypothetical Proposition :** Correspond to the conditions, and the conditional part starts with words such as 'if'.

Example : If I am late, I will miss the train. Here also, proposition has two parts.

I. antecedent—if I am late, and
II. consequent—'I will miss the train.

***(d)* Relational Proposition :** Denote the relation between the subject and the predicate. The relation can be (I) symmetrical, (II) non–symmetrical, or (III) asymmetrical

Example : I. She is as tall as Pinki.

II. Jai is wiser than Roy.

III. Tim is brother of Ria.

For the validity of drawing inference in an argument the propositions are also classified on the basis of quality; as Affirmative (Positive) or Negative, and Quantity; as Universal or Particular. Universal as well as particular propositions can be both Affirmative or Negative.

In order to understand this classification, four categories have been made:

***(a)* Universal Affirmative—'A' Proposition :**

Only subjective term is distributed:

Example : I. All men are strong.

II. All birds have beaks.

In the above statements, subject is 'All men' and 'All birds'.

***(b)* Universal Negative—'E' Proposition :**

Both subjective and predicative terms are distributed.

Example : I. No man is perfect.

II. No fools are wise.

In the above statements, the distributed term is 'No', 'No one'. When no man is perfect, then one who is perfect cannot be man. Similarly, when no fools are wise, then one who is wise cannot be a fool.

***(c)* Particular Affirmative—'I' Proposition :**

Neither of the terms is distributed.

Example : I. Some children are very naughty.

II. Some politicians are dishonest.

In the above statements, the distributed term is not particular; *i.e.,* 'Some'. When some children are naughty, then some of those who are naughty may be children. Similarly, when some politicians are dishonest, then some dishonest men may be politicians. There is no defined certainty. However, statements with 'some' and no negative sign are particular affirmatives.

***(d)* Particular Negative :—'O' Proposition :**

Here the predicative term is distributed. 'Some' used with a negative sign is a particular negative proposition.

Example : I. Some students are not intelligent.

II. All animals are not pets.

In the statement 'All animals' may mislead it to be a Universal Negative but 'All' with 'not' is a Particular Negative. However, words such as 'some' 'mostly' 'all but one' etc. are Particular Propostions.

Premise

Premise is a proposition stated or assumed for after–reasoning especially one of the two propositions in a syllogism, from which the inference is drawn. Of the two statements, the first is major premise and the second is minor premise.

Example : I. All dogs are hens. (major premise)

II. All pups are dogs. (minor premise)

Inference : All pups are hens. Based on the two premises, the inference is drawn.

Term

Term is a word used in a specially understood or defined source which may be subject or predicate of a proposition. The terms in the major premise are called major terms and that in the minor premise are called minor terms. The middle term occurs in both the premise.

In the above example, dogs, hens and pups are three terms used. Of these 'hens' is the major term, 'pups' is the minor term and 'dogs' is the connecting or the middle term.

Inference

Inference is the logical conclusion drawn from given premise. This iogical deduction follows necessarily from the reasoning of given premises and not of the truth.

Logical Diagram

Logical Diagram is figurative representation of the proposition.

Example : All men are mortals.
All kings are men.

Inference : All kings are mortals. Based on the given statements, the logical diagram will be :

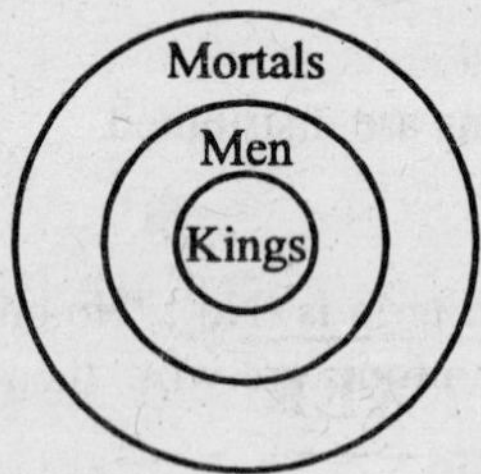

On analysing the diagram, it is clear that all kings are men and all men are mortals. Therefore, the inference drawn, all kings are mortals, is correct.

Example : No cows are birds.
No hens are cows.

Inference : No birds are cows.
No cows are hens.

The diagrammatic representation will be :

Birds, hens and cows are three separate terms and there is no middle term. As such, both the inference drawn are correct.

Example : Some pens are blue.
Some chalks are blue.

Inference : Some chalks are pens.

The figurative presentation of the above statements will be :

If there are more than three terms, no inference can be drawn. 'Blue' in both the propositions is not the same thing. So, there are four terms. The inference drawn is incorrect.

There are different types of logical reasoning depending on the type of propositions or the conclusions/ inferences following the propositions.

PART - I

VALIDITY OF CONCLUSION

Syllogism is a logical argument in three propositions, two premises and a conclusion that follows necessarily from them. The conclusion is Valid or Invalid.

Example : All women are mothers.
All girls are women.

Inference : All girls are mothers.

If the two premises are drawn, the logical diagram will be :

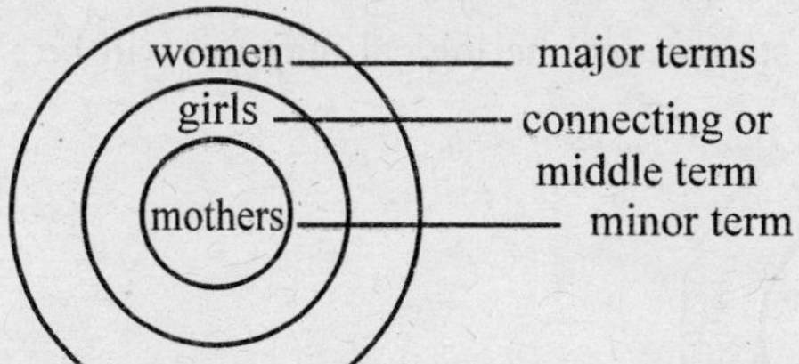

So, the given conclusion or inference is valid.

Such problems on syllogism can be solved mentally with a little bit of intelligence and common sense.

EXERCISE

Directions : *In the following statements, state if the inference drawn (the third statement) is valid or invalid.*

1. Some tables are chairs.
   Some stools are chairs.
   Some tables are stools.
2. All elephants are huge.
   No tigers are huge.
   No tigers are elephants.
3. All parrots are birds.
   All birds are kites.
   All parrots are kites.
4. No grapes are roses.
   All guards are grapes.
   All guards are roses.
5. No dates are figs.
   No figs are rum.
   Some dates are rum.

EXPLANATORY ANSWERS

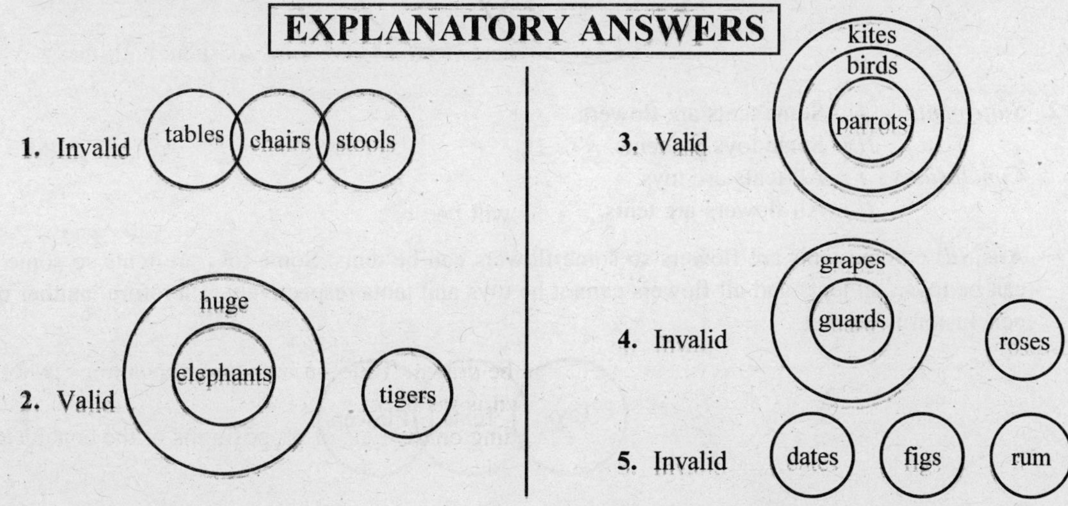

PART - II

SYLLOGISM

In this reasoning pattern the two premises are followed by two conclusions drawn from them. Five options *(a)*, *(b)*, *(c)*, *(d)* and *(e)* are given as answers. Based on the two statements the candidate has to select the right option as answer.

SOLVED EXAMPLES

In the questions below the answer is given as :

(a) if only conclusion I follows.

(b) if only conclusion II follows.

(c) if either I or II follows.

(d) if neither I nor II follows, and

(e) if both I and II follows.

1. *Statements* *I :* All officers are lazy.
II : Some men are officers.

Conclusions *I :* All lazy are men.
II : Some men are lazy.

Ans. *(b)* : When all officers are lazy and some men are officers then some men must be lazy. Therefore, conclusion II is correct.

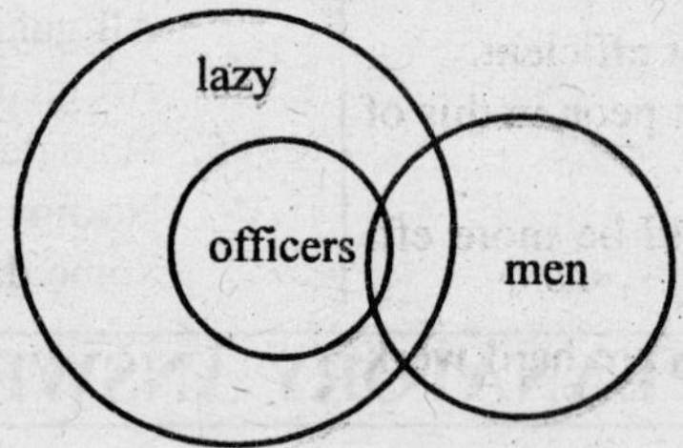

2. *Statements* *I :* Some tents are flowers.
II : Some toys are tents.

Conclusions *I :* All tents are toys.
II : All flowers are tents.

Ans. *(d)* : Some tents are flowers so some flowers can be tents. Some toys are tents so some tents can be toys. All tents and all flowers cannot be toys and tents respectively. Therefore, neither of the conclusion is correct.

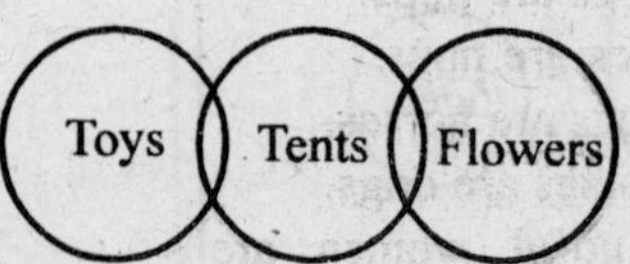

EXERCISE

Directions : *In each question below are given two statements followed by two conclusions numbered I and II. You have to take the two given statements to be true even if they seem to be at variance from commonly known facts and then decide which of the given conclusions logically follows from the two given statements, disregarding commonly known facts. Read both the statements and—*

Give answer (a) if only conclusion I follows; give answer (b) if only conclusion II follows; give answer (c) if either I or II follows; give answer (d) if neither I nor II follows and give answer (e) if both I and II follows.

1. *Statements I :* All tomatoes are red.
II : All grapes are tomatoes.
Conclusions I : All grapes are red.
II : Some tomatoes are grapes.

2. *Statements I :* All painters are smilling.
II : Some authors are painters.
Conclusions I : All smiling authors are painters.
II : Some authors are smiling.

3. *Statements I :* All peons in this office are efficient.
II : Ramu is not efficient.
Conclusions I : Ramu is not peon in this office.
II : Ramu should be more efficient.

4. *Statements I :* All weavers are hard working.
II : No hard working men are foolish.
Conclusions I : No weavers are foolish.
II : Some foolish are weavers.

5. *Statements I :* All fishes are cars.
II : All cars are vegetables.
Conclusions I : Some vegetables are cars.
II : Some vegetables are fishes.

6. *Statements I :* Some dogs are pups.
II : All horses are pups.
Conclusions I : Some dogs are horses.
II : Some horses are dogs.

7. *Statements I :* All beautiful women are mothers.
II : All mothers are understanding.
Conclusions I : All beautiful women are understanding.
II : All mothers are beautiful women.

8. *Statements I :* Some toys are tables.
II : No table is black.
Conclusions I : Some toys are black.
II : Some toys are not black.

9. *Statements I :* All rivers are mountains.
II : Some rivers are deserts.
Conclusions I : Some mountains are deserts.
II : Some deserts are not mountains.

10. *Statements I :* All men are horses.
II : All horses are elephants.
Conclusions I : All men are elephants.
II : All elephants are men.

11. *Statements I :* All talented persons are trustworthy.
II : Some trustworthy are musicians.
Conclusions I : All talented persons are musicians.
II : Some musicians are not talented person.

12. *Statements I :* Alcoholic drinks are injurious to health.
II : All old women drink whisky.
Conclusions I : All old women have poor health.
II : All young women are in good health.

13. *Statements I :* All students are employed.
II : No employed are babies.
Conclusions I : No students are babies.
II : Some employed are students.

14. *Statements I :* Some engineers are teachers.

II : Some engineers are efficient.

Conclusions I : Some teachers are efficient.

II : All efficient are engineers.

15. *Statements* I : Some foods are sweet.

II : Some foods are sour.

Conclusions I : All foods are either sweet or sour.

II : Some sweet are sour.

16. *Statements* I : All hair are black.

II : Some black are long.

Conclusions I : Some hair are long.

II : No hair is long.

17. *Statements* I : All dogs are monkeys.

II : No monkey is a cat.

Conclusions I : No dog is a cat.

II : No cat is a dog.

18. *Statements* I : Some phones are watches.

II : All watches are guns.

Conclusions I : All guns are watches.

II : Some guns are phones.

19. *Statements* I : All umbrellas are aeroplanes.

II : Some aeroplanes are birds.

Conclusions I : Some umbrellas are birds.

II : Some birds are umbrellas.

20. *Statements* I : Some clips are pins.

II : Some pins are staples.

Conclusions I : Some pins are clips.

II : Some staples are pins.

21. *Statements* I : All puppets are dolls.

II : All dolls are toys.

Conclusions I : Some toys are puppets.

II : All toys are puppets.

22. *Statements* I : Some fat are thin.

II : No thin is tall.

Conclusions I : Some fat are tall.

II : Some fat are not tall.

23. *Statements* I : Some doors are windows.

II : Some windows are pencils.

Conclusions I : All doors are pencils.

II : Some pencils are doors.

24. *Statements* I : Some boys are tables.

II : Some tables are chairs.

Conclusions I : Some boys are chairs.

II : Some chairs are boys.

25. *Statements* I : All dogs are jackals.

II : Some jackals are crows.

Conclusions I : Some dogs are crows.

II : All dogs are crows.

26. *Statements* I : All trees are parrots.

II : No parrots is cat.

Conclusions I : No tree is cat.

II : Some cats are trees.

27. *Statements* I : Some pens are hammers.

II : All hammers are nails.

Conclusions I : Some nails are pens.

II : Some nails are hammers.

28. *Statements* I : All cars are cats.

II : All fans are cats.

Conclusions I : All cars are fans.

II : Some fans are cars.

29. *Statements* I : Many scooters are trucks.

II : All trucks are trains.

Conclusions I : Some scooters are trains..

II : No truck is a scooter.

30. *Statements* I : All trees are corns.

II : All corns are bad.

Conclusions I : All trees are bad.

II : Some bad are trees.

31. *Statements* I : All sharks are ferocious.

II : No ferocious is harmful.

Conclusions I : Some sharks are harmful.

II : Some ferocious are not sharks.

32. *Statements* I : All men are good-looking.

II : Some men are teachers.

Conclusions I : Some teachers are good-looking.

II : Some good-looking are not men.

33. *Statements* I : Some doctors are institutes.

II : Some croocks are institutes.

Conclusions I : All institutes are doctors.

II : Some institutes are crooks.

34. *Statements* I : All pilots are experts.

II : All authors are pilots.

Conclusions I : All authors are experts.

II : No expert is a author.

35. *Statements* I : Some sweets are candies.

II : No candy is sour.

Conclusions I : No sour is candy.

II : Some candies are sweets.

36. *Statements* I : No buses are trucks.

II : No trucks are cars.
Conclusions I : Some trucks are buses.
II : No cars are buses.

37. *Statements I* : All players are tall.
II : Rohan is a player.
Conclusions I : All tall are players.
II : Rohan is tall.

38. *Statements I* : Some grapes are nuts.
II : Some nuts are fruits.
Conclusions I : Some grapes are fruits.
II : Some grapes are not fruits.

39. *Statements I* : Some magazines are texts.
II : All texts are editors.
Conclusions I : Some texts are magazines..
II : Some editors are magazines.

40. *Statements I* : All bottles are boxes.
II : Some boxes are trunks.
Conclusions I : All trunks are bottles.
II : Some boxes are bottles.

41. *Statements I* : All workers are on strike.
II : All employees are on strike.
Conclusions I : All those who are on strike are workers.
II : All those who are on strike are employees.

42. *Statements I* : All ants are hardworking.
II : Some ants are lazy.
Conclusions I : All lazy are hardworking.
II : All hardworking are lazy.

43. *Statements I* : Some pets are dogs.
II : Some dogs are puppies.
Conclusions I : No dogs are pets.
II : No puppies are dogs.

44. *Statements I* : All green is black.
II : All black is red.
Conclusions I : All red is green.
II : Some black is green.

45. *Statements I* : No clock is correct.
II : All watches are correct.
Conclusions I : No clock is a watch.
II : Some correct are clocks.

46. *Statements I* : Some artworks are paintings.
II : All paintings are masterpieces.
Conclusions I : All masterpieces are paintings.
II : Some masterpieces are artworks.

47. *Statements I* : Some men are genius.
II : No brother is genius.
Conclusions I : Some brothers are men.
II : Some brothers are not men.

48. *Statements I* : All pants are skirts.
II : No shirt is a skirt.
Conclusions I : Some skirts are pants.
II : All shirts are pants.

49. *Statements I* : All planes are tyres.
II : All tyres are engines.
Conclusions I : No engine is a plane.
II : No tyre is a plane.

50. *Statements I* : Some cartoons are funny.
II : Some cartoons are silly.
Conclusions I : All funny are cartoons.
II : Some silly are cartoons.

EXPLANATORY ANSWERS

1. *(e)* : When all tomatoes are red and all grapes are tomatoes, then all grapes are also red. When all grapes are tomatoes, then some tomatoes must be grapes. Therefore, both conclusions I and II are correct.

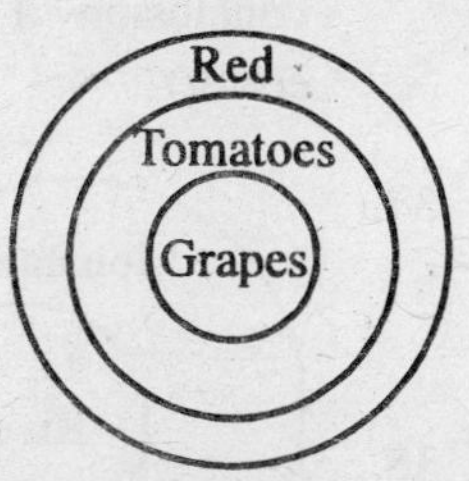

2. *(b)* : When all painters are smiling and some authors are painters, then some authors are smiling. Therefore, only conclusion II is correct.

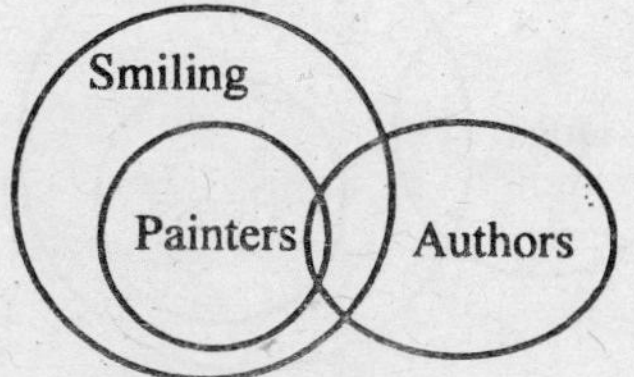

3. *(a)* : When all the peons of the office are efficient, then Ramu cannot be a peon in this office. Therefore, only conclusion I is correct.

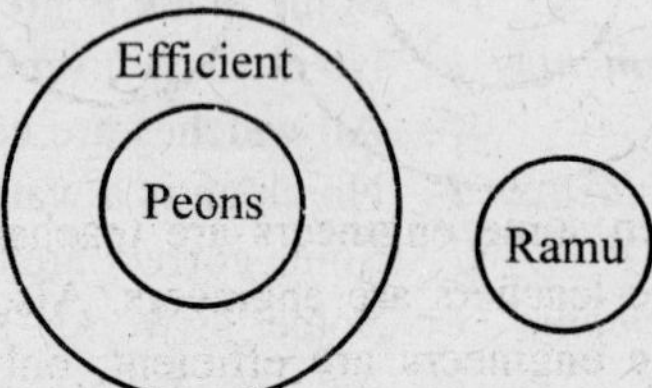

4. *(a)* : When all weavers are hardworking and no hardworking men are foolish, then no weavers are foolish. Therefore, only conclusion I is correct.

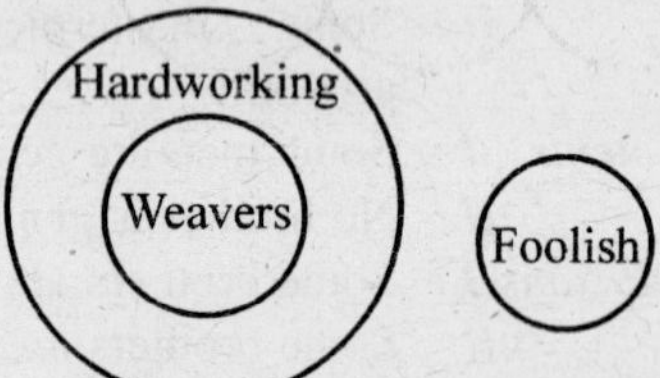

5. *(e)* : When all fishes are cars and all cars are vegetables, then all fishes will naturally be vegetables. This means that some vegetables are fishes. And when all cars are vegetables, then some vegetables will be cars naturally. Therefore, both the conclusions I and II are correct.

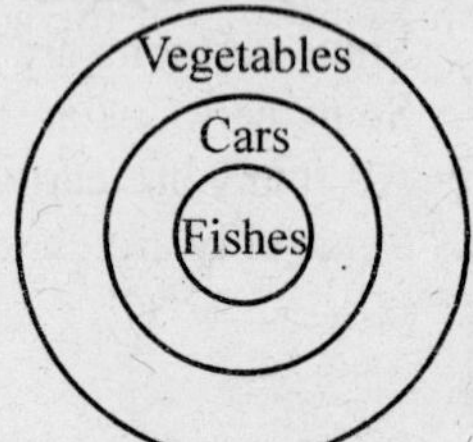

6. *(d)* : No relationship can be established between the two statements. Therefore, neither conclusion I nor conclusion II is correct.

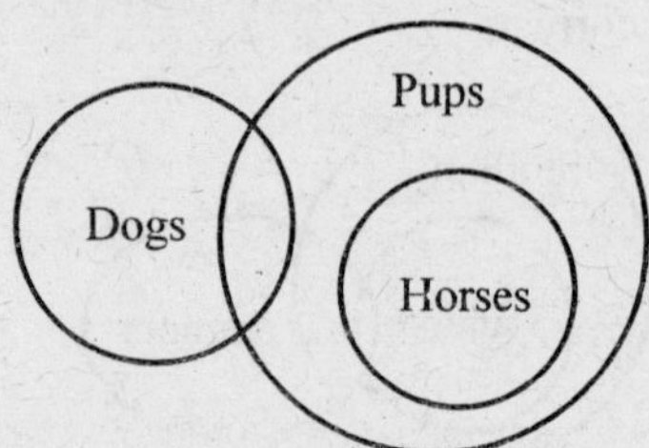

7. *(a)* : When all beautiful women are mothers and all mothers are understanding, then naturally all beautiful women are understanding. All mothers need not be beautiful women. Therefore, only conclusion I is correct.

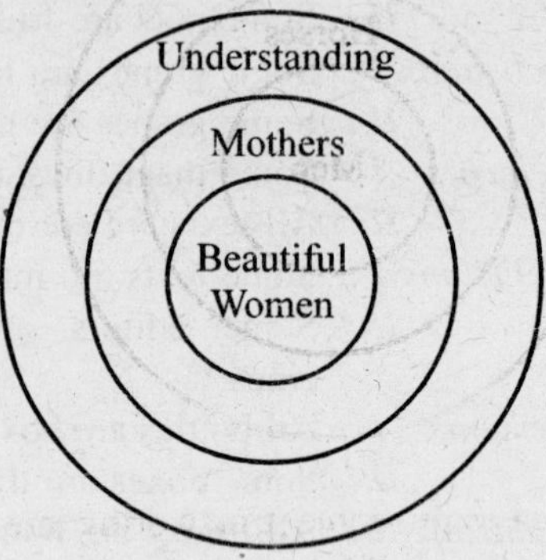

8. *(b)* :. When some toys are tables and no table is black, then it is indicated that some toys can not be black. Therefore, conclusion II is correct.

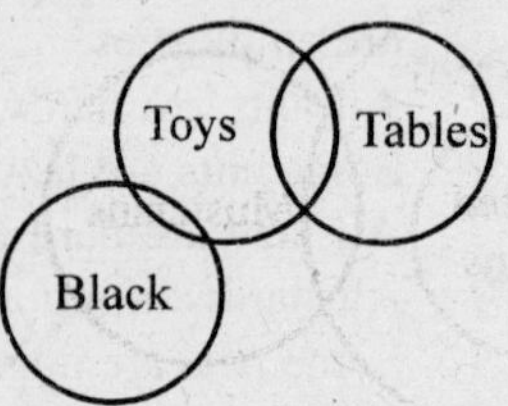

9. *(e)* : When all rivers are mountains and some rivers are deserts, then some deserts cannot be mountains and also, some mountains need not be deserts. Therefore, both conclusion I and conclusion II are correct.

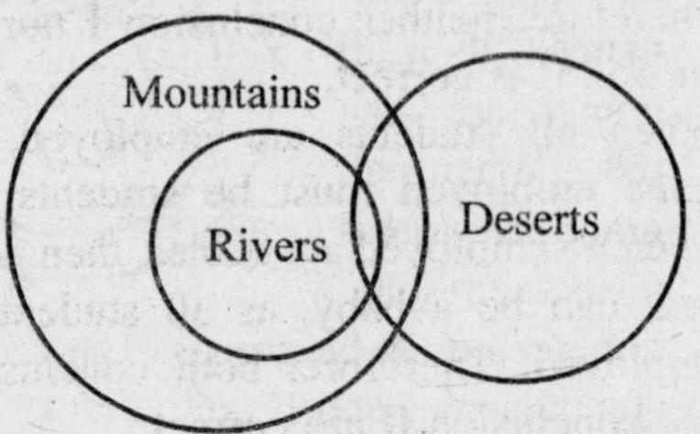

10. (a) : When all men are horses and all horses are elephants then, naturally all men are elephants, but all elephants need not be men. Therefore, only conclusion I is correct.

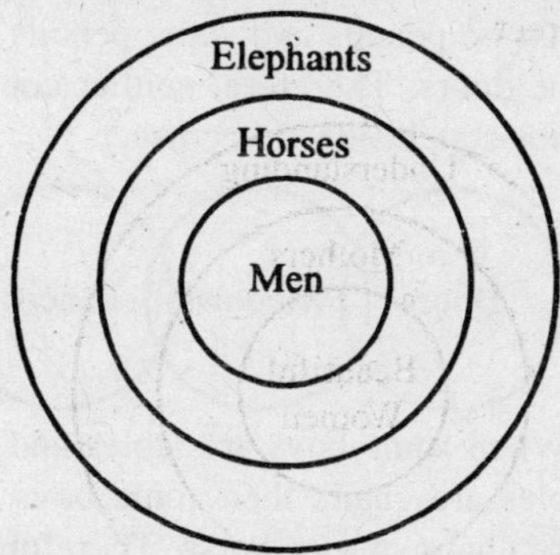

11. (b) : When only some trustworthy are musicians, then all talented persons cannot be musicians. In the same logical way, when some trustworthy are musicians, then some musicians are not talented. Therefore, only conclusin II is correct.

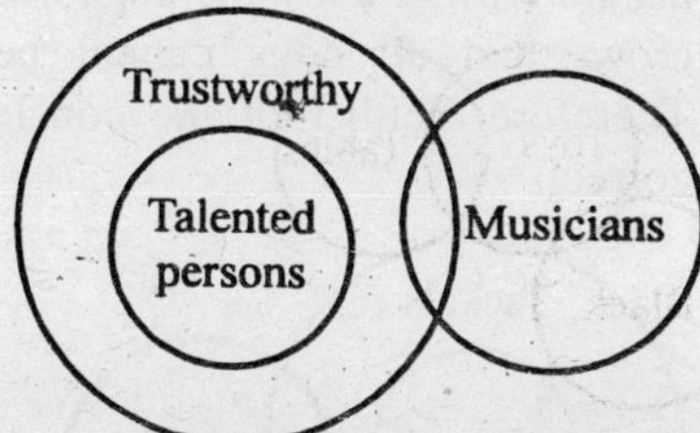

12. (d) : Even though alcoholic drinks are injurious to health and all old women drink whisky, which is an alcoholic drink, it does not necessarily mean that all old women must have poor health and that all young women are in good health, because they do not take alcoholic drinks. Therefore, neither conclusion I nor conclusion II is correct.

13. (e) : When all students are employed, then some employed must be students. And when no employed are babies, then no student can be a baby, as all students are employed. Therefore, both conclusion I and conclusion II are correct.

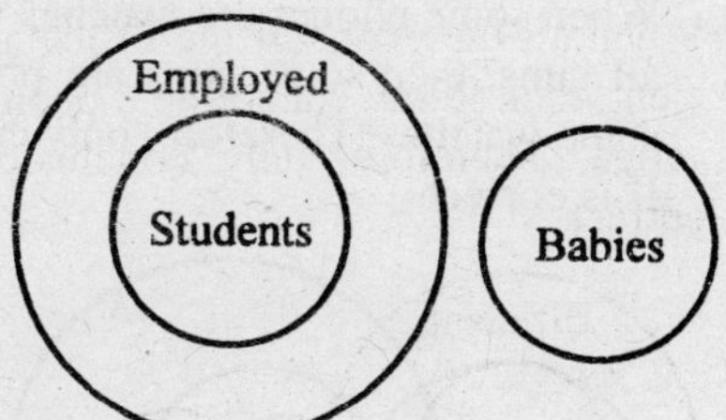

14. (d) : When some engineers are teachers, then some teachers are engineers. Also, when some engineers are efficient, only some efficient are engineers. Thererfore, both the conclusions are incorrect.

15. (d) : When some foods are sweet and some foods are sour, then all foods are not necessarily sweet or sour and what is sweet need not be sour. Therefore, neither of the conclusions is correct.

16. (d) : When all hair are black and some black are long, then it is not for certain that some hair are long or no hair is long. Some hair that are black may or may not be long. Therefore, neither of the conclusions is correct.

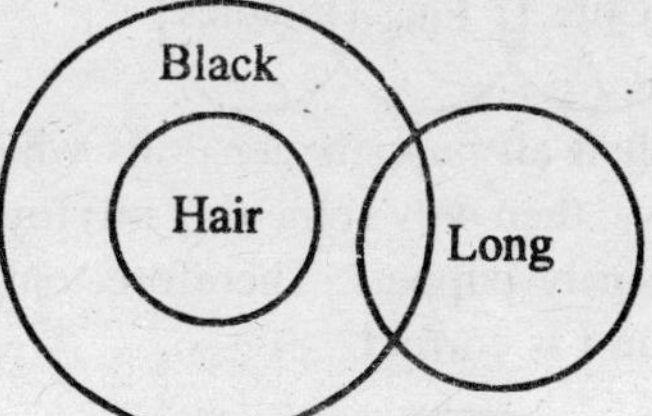

17. (e) : No relationship is established between the two statements. So both the conclusions are correct.

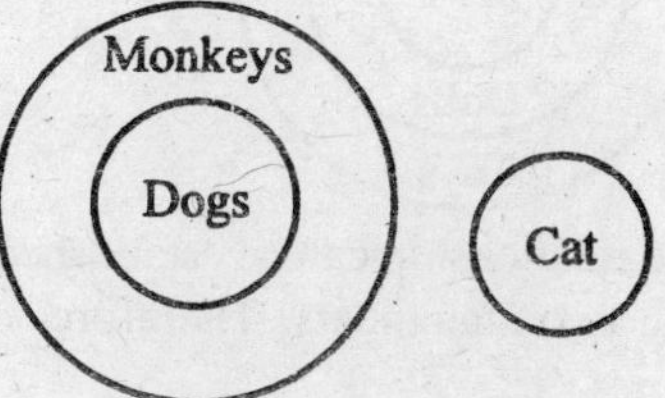

18. (b) : When some phones are watches which are all guns, then some guns are phones and some watches. Therefore, only conclusion II is correct.

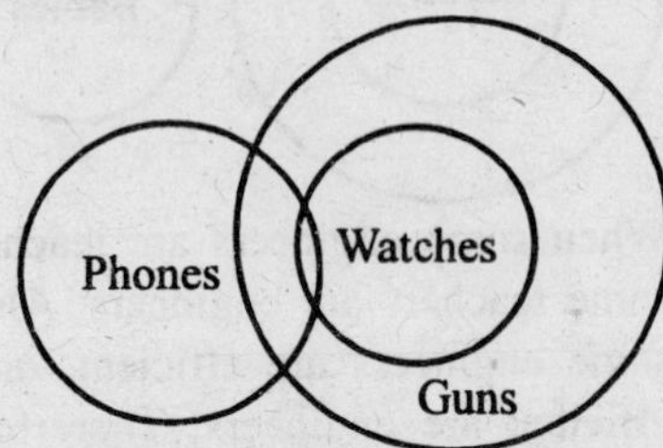

19. (d) : All umbrellas are aeroplanes and some aeroplanes are birds, then the umbrellas are not necessarily birds or vice versa. Therefore, neither conclusion I nor conclusion II is correct.

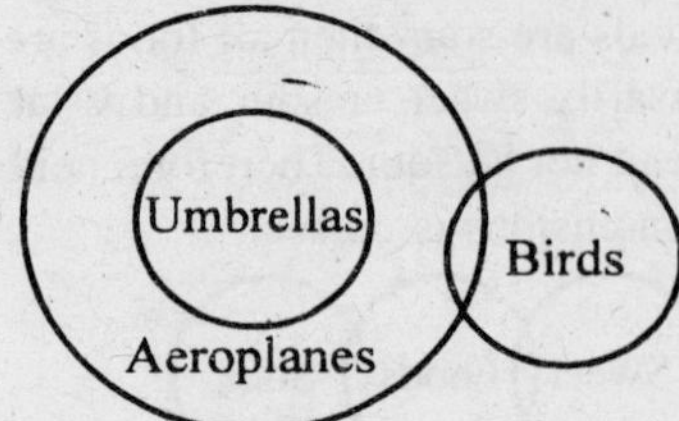

20. (e) : If some clips are pins, then some pins are necessarily clips and when some pins are staples, then some staples are necessarily pins. Therefore, both conclusions I and II are correct.

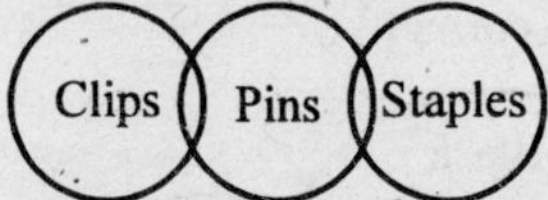

21. (a) : When all puppets are dolls which are all toys, then only some (not all) toys are necessarily puppets. Therefore, only conclusion I is correct.

22. (b) : No relationship can be established between the two statements. Therefore, only conclusion II is correct.

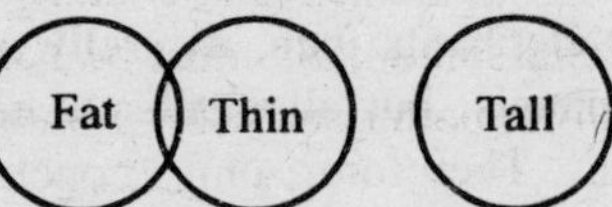

23. (d) : When some doors are windows and some windows are pencils then all doors cannot be pencils and some pencils need not be doors. Therefore, neither conclusion I nor conclusion II is correct.

24. (d) : When some boys are tables and some tables are chairs then some boys need not be chairs or vice versa. Therefore, neither of the conclusions is correct.

25. (d) : When all dogs are jackals and some jackals are crows then some dogs need not be crows and all dogs cannot be crows. Therefore, neither of the conclusions is correct.

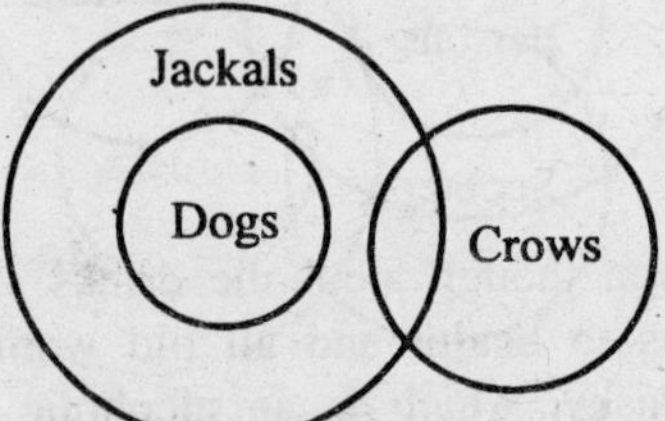

26. (a): When all trees are parrots and no parrot is cat then no tree is a cat and some cats cannot be trees. Therefore, only conclusion I is correct.

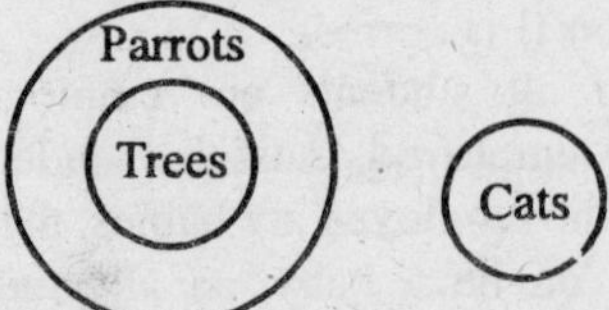

27. (e) : When some pens are hammers which are

all nails then some nails must be pens and some nails must be hammers. Therefore, both conclusion I and II are correct.

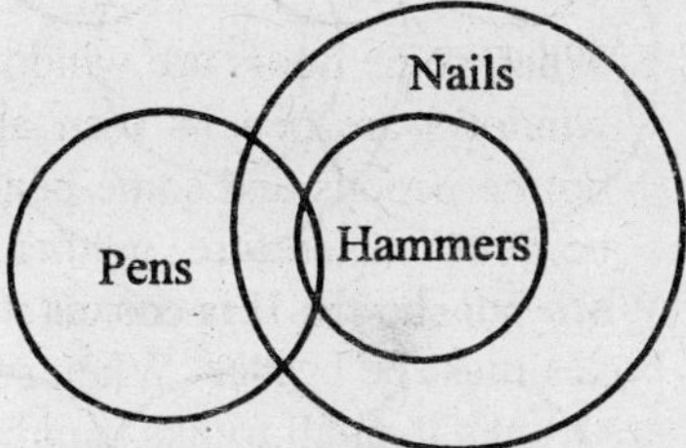

28. *(d)* : All cars and fans are cats but cars cannot be fans and vice versa. Therefore, neither of the conclusions is correct.

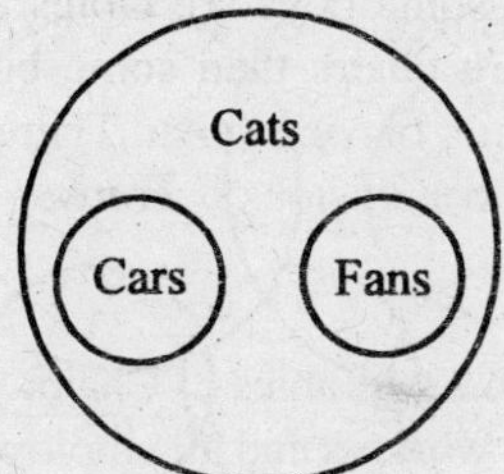

29. *(a)* : When many scooters are trucks which are all trains, then some scooters must be trains and some trucks must be scooters. Therefore, only conclusion I is correct.

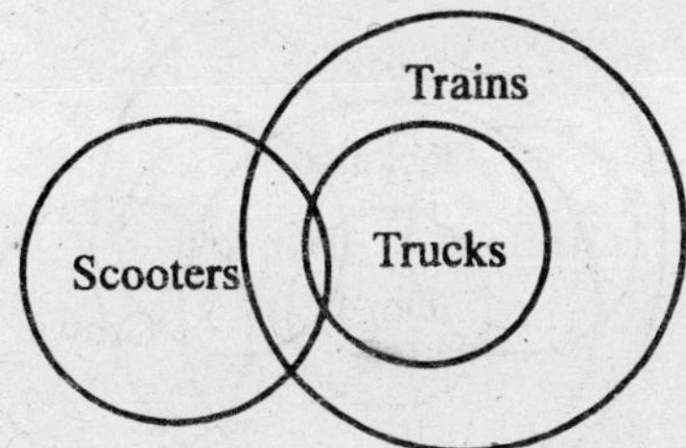

30. *(e)* : When all trees are corns which are all bad, then all trees must be bad and some bad must be trees. Therefore, both conclusion I and conclusion II are correct.

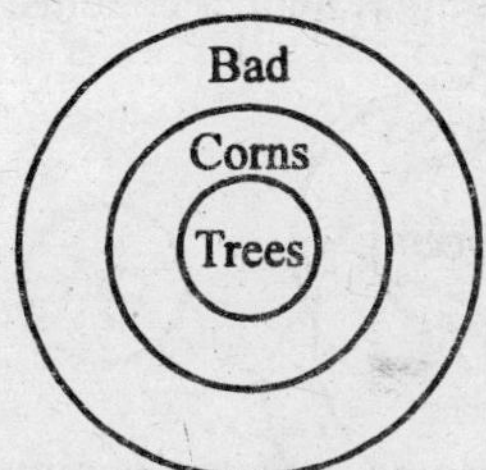

31. *(b)* : There is no relationship between the two statements. When all sharks are ferocious then some ferocious are sharks and some are not. When no ferocious is harmful then all sharks that are ferocious cannot be harmful. Therefore, only conclusion II is correct.

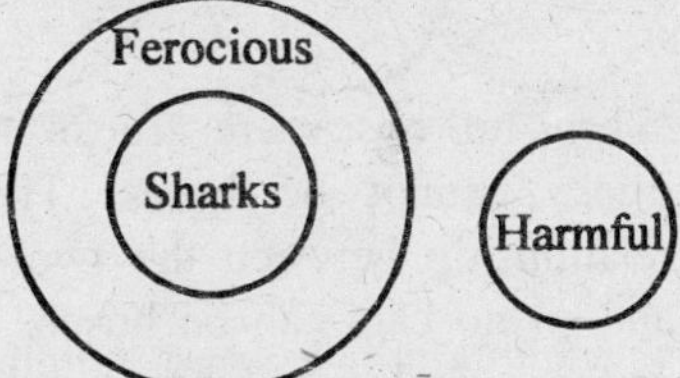

32. *(e)* : When some men are teachers but all men are goodlooking, then some teachers must be goodlooking and some goodlooking must be men. Therefore, both conclusion I and conclusion II are correct.

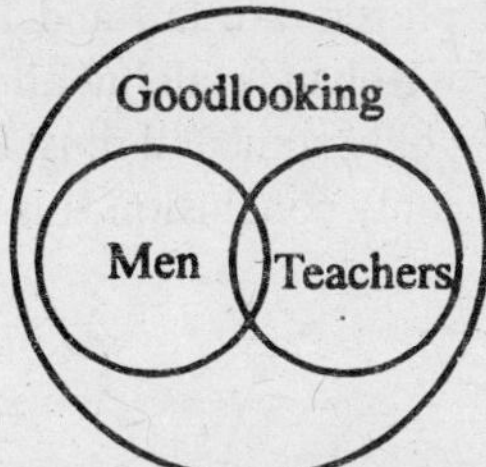

33. *(b)* : When some doctors and some crooks are institutes then all institutes cannot be doctors or crooks. However, some institutes must be doctors or crooks. Therefore, only conclusion II is correct.

34. *(a)* : When all authors are pilots who are all experts then all authors must be pilots and some experts must be authors. Therefore, only conclusion I is correct.

35. *(e)* : When no candy is sour then no sour can

be candy. When some sweets are candies then some candies must be sweets. Therefore, both conclusion I and conclusion II are correct.

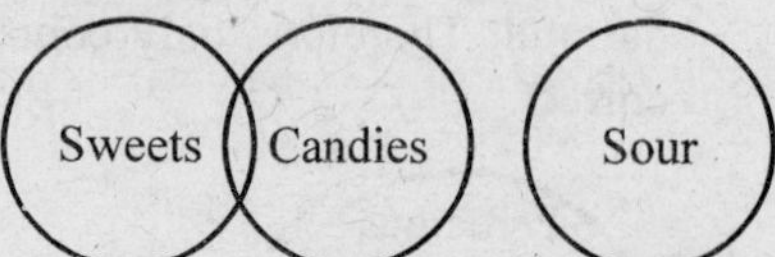

36. *(d)* : When no buses are trucks then some trucks cannot be buses. There is no relationship between the two statements and so no cars can be buses. Therefore, neither conclusion I nor conclusion II is correct.

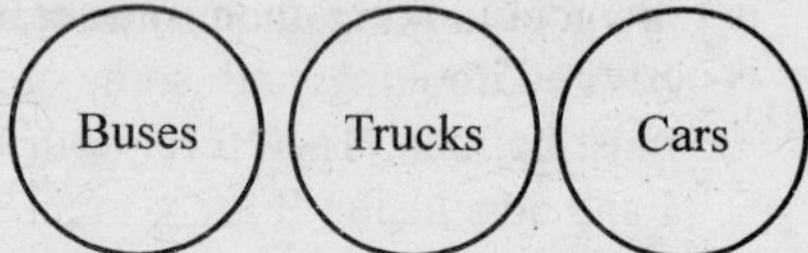

37. *(b)* : When all players are tall and Rohan is a player, then Rohan is tall but all tall cannot be players, only some tall must be players. Therefore, only conclusion II is correct.

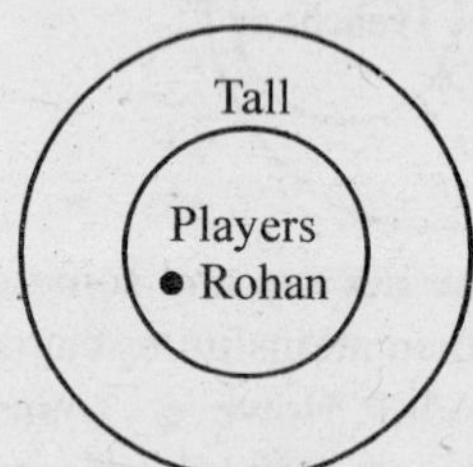

38. *(c)* : Some grapes are nuts so some nuts must be grapes and some nuts that are not grapes may or may not be fruits. Some nuts are fruits and some fruits which are not nuts may or may not be grapes. Therefore, either conclusion I or conclusion II may be correct.

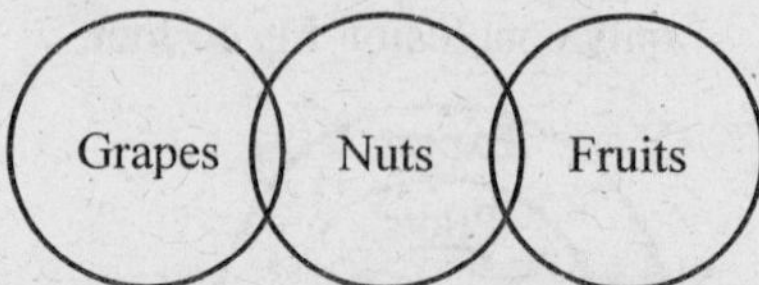

39. *(e)* : When some magazines are texts then some texts must be magazines. When all texts are editors then some editors must necessarily be magazines. Therefore, both the conclusions are correct.

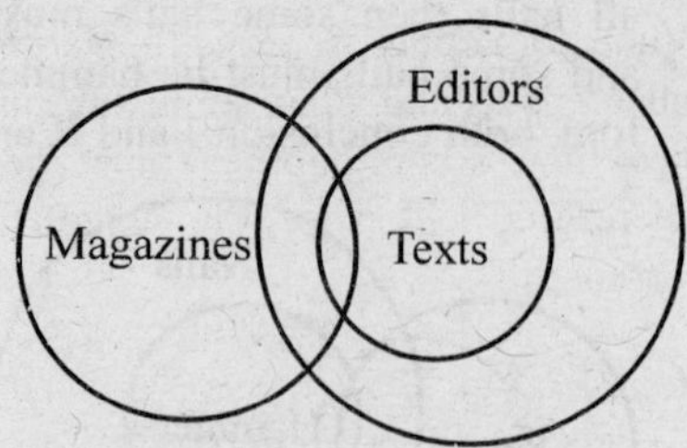

40. *(b)* : When all bottles are boxes then some boxes must be bottles. When some boxes are trunks then all trunks cannot be boxes or bottles. Therefore, only conclusion II is correct.

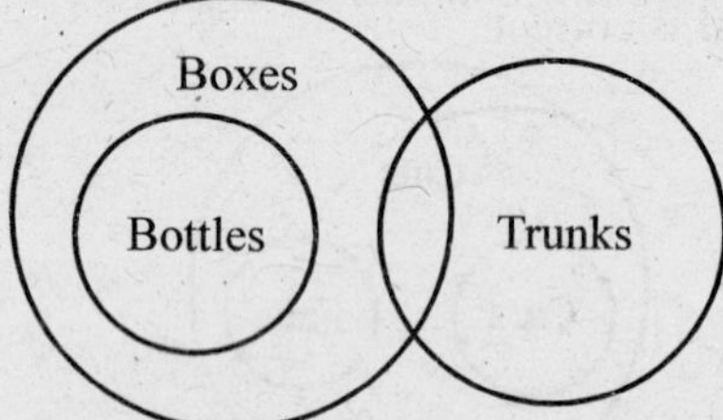

41. *(d)* : When all workers and all employees are on strike, then all those who are on strike cannot be one of the two, *i.e.* only workers or only employees. Therefore, neither conclusion I nor conclusion II is correct.

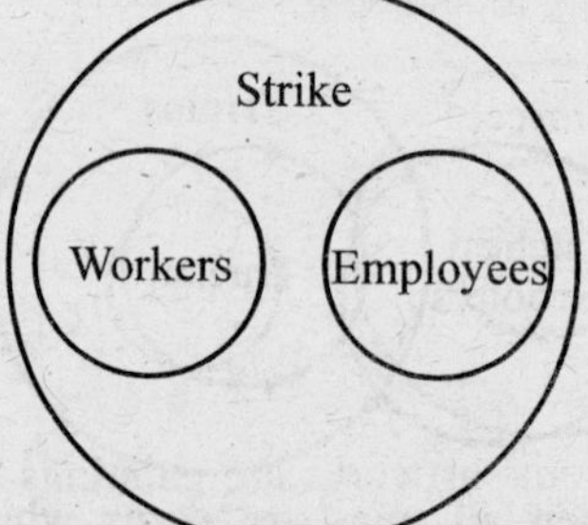

42. *(d)* : When all ants are hardworking and some ants are lazy, then some lazy must be hardworking but all hardworking cannot be lazy. Therefore, neither conclusion I nor II are correct.

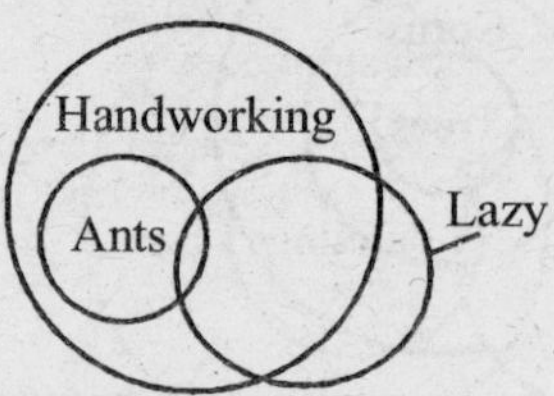

43. ***(d)*** **:** When some pets are dogs then some dogs must be pets and when some dogs are puppies then some puppies must be dogs. Therefore neither of the conclusions is correct.

44. ***(b)*** **:** When all green is black then some black must be green. When all green is black which is all red, then some (not all) red must be green. Therefore, only conclusion II is correct.

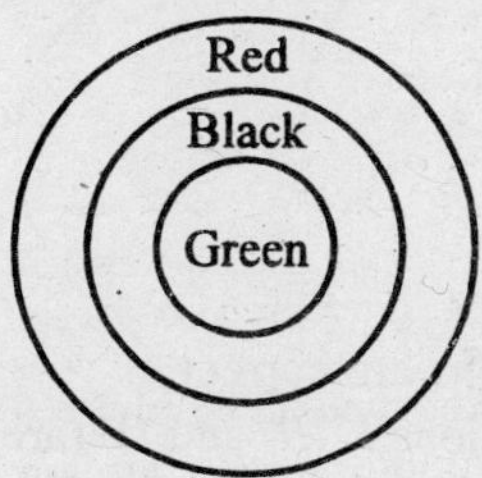

45. ***(a)*** **:** When all watches are correct and no clock is correct, then some correct cannot be clock and no clock can be a watch. Therefore, only conclusion I is correct.

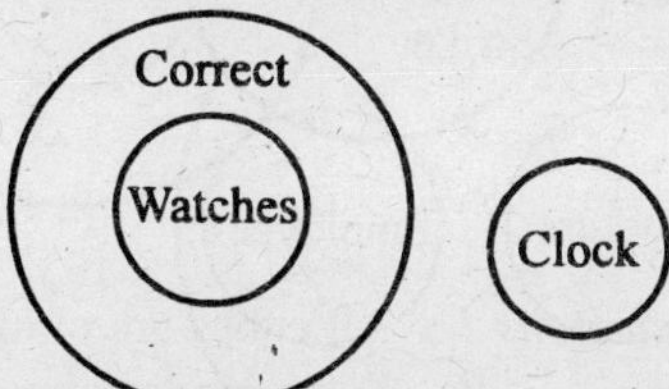

46. ***(b)*** **:** When some artworks are paintings which are all masterpieces, then some masterpieces must be artwork. When all paintings are masterpieces then some (not all) masterpieces must be paintings. Therefore, only conclusion II is correct.

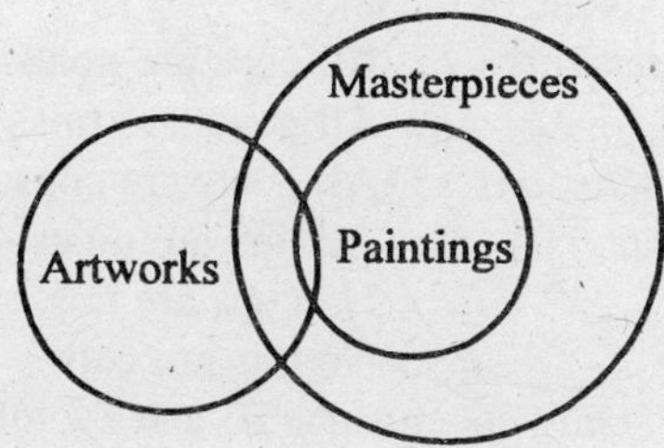

47. ***(c)*** **:** Some men are genius and no brother is a genius. Some men who are not genius may or may not be brothers, *i.e.* some brothers may or may not be men. Therefore, either conclusion I or conclusion II is correct.

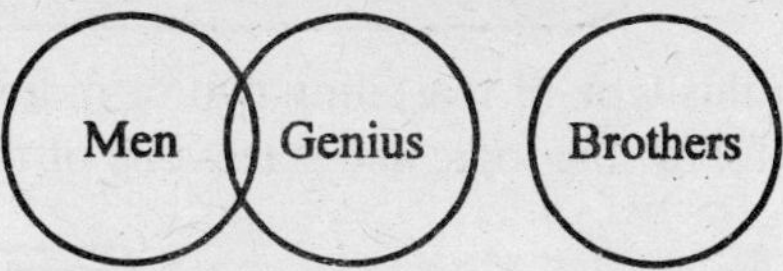

48. ***(a)*** **:** When all pants are skirts then some skirts must be pants. When no shirt is a skirt and all pants are skirts, then shirts cannot be pants. Therefore, only conclusion I is correct.

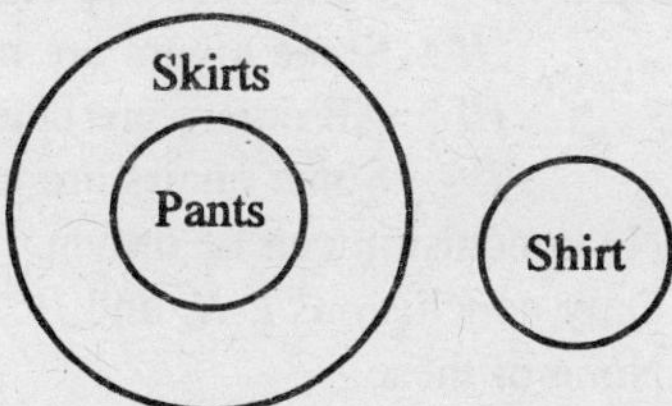

49. ***(d)*** **:** When all planes are tyres then some tyres must be planes. When all planes are tyres which are all engines then some engines must be planes. Therefore, neither conclusion I nor conclusion II is correct.

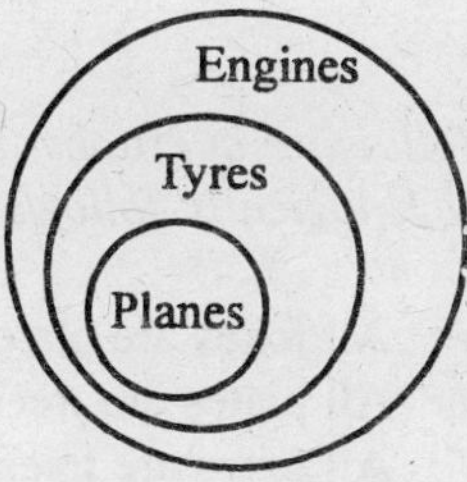

50. ***(b)*** **:** When some cartoons are funny then some (not all) funny must be cartoons. When some cartoons are silly, then some silly must be cartoons. Therefore, only conclusion II is correct.

PART - III

DRAWING MULTIPLE CONCLUSIONS

In this type of reasoning two or more than two conclusions are inferred based on two statements. One has to follow the logic and select one of the options as the right choice.

SOLVED EXAMPLE

From the given options (*a*), (*b*), (*c*), (*d*) and (*e*) select the set of conclusion which logically follows from the given statements.

Statements *I* : Some men are chairs.
II : All chairs are cigars.
Conclusions *I* : Some men are cigars.
II : Some cigars are men.
III : All cigars are chairs.
IV : Some chairs are men.

(*a*) No conclusion can be drawn.
(*b*) All conclusions are correct.
(*c*) Only conclusions *I, II,* and *IV* (are correct).
(*d*) Only conclusions *I, III,* and *IV* (are correct).
(*e*) None of these.

Ans. (*c*) **:** When some men are chairs and all chairs are cigars, then naturally some men are cigars and vice versa. Some cigars will have to be men. And when some men are chairs, then some chairs will have to be men. Therefore, conclusions I, II and IV are correct.

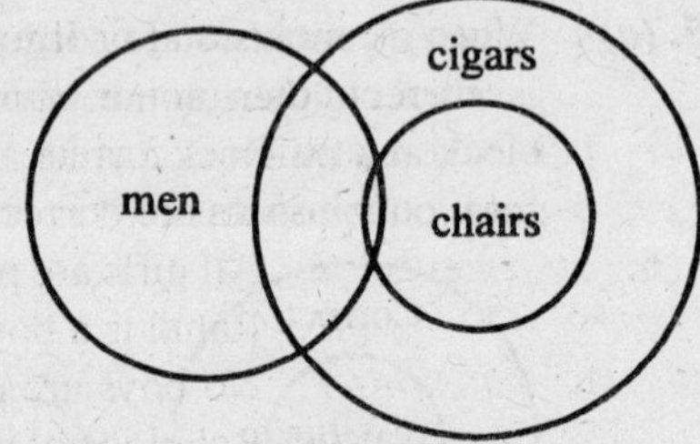

EXERCISE

Directions : *In the following questions, select the set of conclusion which logically follows from the given statements.*

1. *Statements* *I* : All foxes are plates.
II : All plates are trees.
Conclusions *I* : All foxes are trees.
II : All trees are foxes.
III : Some trees are foxes.
IV : Some trees are plates.
(*a*) All conclusions are correct.
(*b*) Only conclusions *I, III,* and *IV* follow.
(*c*) Only conclusions *II, III,* and *IV* follow.
(*d*) Only conclusions *I* and *IV* follow.
(*e*) None of the above.

2. *Statements* *I* : Some cubes are squares.
II : All squares are circles.
Conclusions *I* : All cubes are circles.
II : Some circles are cubes.
III : Some circles are squares.
IV : All squares are cubes.
(*a*) Only conclusion I follows.
(*b*) Only conclusion I, II and III follow.
(*c*) All conclusions are correct.
(*d*) Only conclusions II and III follow.
(*e*) None of the above.

3. *Statements* *I* : All cups are goats.
II : All goats are tins.
Conclusions *I* : All goats are cups.
II : All tins are goats.
III : No cups are tins.
IV : No tins are cups.
(*a*) Only conclusions III and IV follow.

(*b*) Only conclusios I and II follow.
(*c*) Only conclusions I, II and III follow.
(*d*) All conclusions are correct.
(*e*) None of the above.

4. *Statements* *I*: All bombs are bags.
II: Some bags are jets.
Conclusions *I*: All bombs are jets.
II: All jets are bombs.
III: Some jets are bombs.
IV: Some bombs are jets.
(*a*) Only conclusion III follows.
(*b*) Only conclusions I and II follow.
(*c*) All conclusions are correct.
(*d*) Only conclusions III and IV follow.
(*e*) None of these.

5. *Statements* *I*: Some thorns are jackets.
II: Some jackets are boats.
Conclusions *I*: No thorns are boats.
II: All jackets are boats.
III: Some boats are thorns.
IV: No jackets are thorns.
(*a*) Either conclusion I or IV follows.
(*b*) Either conclusion I or II follows.
(*c*) Either conclusion I or III follows.
(*d*) No conclusion is correct.
(*e*) All conclusions are correct.

6. *Statements* *I*: All girls are pens.
II: Rahul is a boy.
Conclusions *I*: No boys are pens.
II: Rahul is not a pen.
III: Some pens are girls.
(*a*) Only conclusions II and III follow.
(*b*) Only conclusion III follows.
(*c*) All conclusions are correct.
(*d*) Only conclusions I and III follow.
(*e*) None of the above.

7. *Statements* *I*: No men are cows.
II: All cows are windows.
Conclusions *I*: No cows are men.
II: No men are windows.
III: Some windows are cows.
IV: Some cows are men.
(*a*) Only conclusions I and IV follow.
(*b*) Only conclusions II, III and IV follow.
(*c*) Only conclusions I and III follow.
(*d*) All conclusions are correct.
(*e*) None of the above.

8. *Statements* *I*: Some tigers are lizards.
II: All lizards are turtles.
Conclusions *I*: All tigers are turtles.
II: All turtles are tigers.
(*a*) Only conclusion I follows.
(*b*) Only conclusion II follows.
(*c*) Both conclusions are correct.
(*d*) Data is insufficient.
(*e*) None of the above.

9. *Statements* *I*: All that is black is red.
II: Coal is black.
Conclusions *I*: Coal is red.
II: Coal is not red.
III: All that is red is black.
(*a*) Only conclusions I and II follow.
(*b*) Only conclusions II and III follow.
(*c*) Only conclusion I follows.
(*d*) All conclusions follow.
(*e*) None of these.

10. *Statements* *I*: All penguins are peacocks.
II: All peacocks are farmers.
Conclusions *I*: Some farmers are penguins.
II: All penguins are farmers.
III: Some peacocks are penguins.
(*a*) Only conclusions I and II follow.
(*b*) Only conclusions II and III follow.
(*c*) Data is insufficient.
(*d*) All conclusions are correct.
(*e*) None of the above.

11. *Statements* *I*: No chair is tree.
II: All trees are trains.
Conclusions *I*: No chair is train.
II: No train is chair.
III: Some trains are trees.
IV: No train is tree.
(*a*) Only IV follows.
(*b*) Only III and IV follow.
(*c*) Only I and II follow.
(*d*) Only II and III follow.
(*e*) None of these.

12. *Statements* *I*: Some men are goats.
II: All goats are jackals.
Conclusions *I*: Some men are jackals.
II: Some jackals are men.
III: All jackals are goats.
IV: Some goats are men.
(*a*) Only I & II follow.

(b) Only III and IV follow.
(c) Only IV follows.
(d) All follow.
(e) None of these.

13. *Statements* *I*: Some pens are knives.
II: Some knives are horses.
Conclusions I: Some knives are pens.
II: Some pens are horses.
III: Some horses are pens.
IV: Some horses are knives.
(a) Only II and III follow.
(b) Only I and IV follow.
(c) Only IV follows.
(d) Only I follows.
(e) None follows.

14. *Statements* *I*: Some typists are stenographers.
II: Some stenographers are boys.
Conclusions I: All boys are stenographers.
II: All boys are typists.
III: Some typists are boys.
IV: No typist is a boy.
(a) Only I follows.
(b) Only II and III follow.
(c) Only either I or III follows.
(d) Only either I cr IV follows.
(e) Only either III or IV follows.

15. *Statements* *I*: All teachers are students.
II: Some students are girls.
Conclusions I: All teachers are girls.
II: Some girls are teachers.
III: Some girls are students.
IV: All students are teachers.
(a) Only I follows.
(b) Only I, II and III follow.
(c) Only III follows.
(d) Only II and III follow.
(e) None of the above.

16. *Statements* *I*: All green are blue.
II: All blue are white.
Conclusions I: Some blue are green.
II: Some white are green.
III: Some green are not white.
IV: All white are blue.
(a) Only I and II follow.
(b) Only II and III follow.
(c) Only I and III follow.
(d) Only I and IV follow.
(e) All follow.

17. *Statements* *I*: All doors are cots.
II: Some cots are erasers.
Conclusions I: Some doors are erasers.
II: All cots are doors.
III: Some cots are doors.
IV: Some erasers are doors.
(a) Only III and IV follow.
(b) Only I and II follow.
(c) Only III follows.
(d) All follow.
(e) None of these.

18. *Statements* *I*: All buses are roads.
II: All roads are rivers.
Conclusions I: All buses are rivers.
II: Some roads are buses.
III: Some rivers are roads.
IV: Some rivers are buses.
(a) None follows.
(b) Only I and II follow.
(c) Only II, III and IV follow.
(d) Only I, II and III follow.
(e) All follow.

19. *Statements* *I*: Some bags are pockets.
II: No pocket is a pouch.
Conclusions I: No bag is a pouch.
II: Some bags are not pouches.
III: Some pockets are bags.
IV: No pocket is a bag.
(a) Only either I or IV follow.
(b) Only II and III follow.
(c) Only I and III follow.
(d) All follow.
(e) None follows.

20. *Statements* *I*: Some soaps are clean.
II: All clean are wet.
Conclusions I: Some clean are soaps.
II: No clean is a soap.
III: Some wet are soaps.
IV: All wet are soaps.
(a) Only I follows.
(b) Only either I or II follows.
(c) Only either III or IV follows.
(d) Only I and III follow.
(e) None of the above.

21. *Statements* *I*: No parrot is crow.
II: All crows are bats.
Conclusions *I*: Some bats are parrots.
II: All bats are parrots.
III: Some bats are crows.
IV: Some bats are not crows.
(*a*) Only III and IV follow.
(*b*) Only I, II, and III follow.
(*c*) Only II, III and IV follow.
(*d*) None follows.
(*e*) Only I and II follow.

22. *Statements* *I*: All stars are planets.
II: All planets are trees.
Conclusions *I*: All planets are stars.
II: All stars are trees.
III: All trees are planets.
IV: Some trees are stars.
(*a*) Only II, III and IV follow.
(*b*) Only I and III follow.
(*c*) None follows.
(*d*) All follow.
(*e*) Only II and IV follow.

23. *Statements* *I*: All soaps are detergents.
II: All detergents are powders.
Conclusions *I*: All soaps are powders.
II: Some detergents are soaps.
III: Some powders are soaps.
IV: Some powders are detergents.
(*a*) Only I follows.
(*b*) Only II and IV follow.
(*c*) Only III and IV follow.
(*d*) All follow.
(*e*) None follows.

24. *Statements* *I*: Some chairs are shoes.
II: Some shoes are sticks.
Conclusions *I*: Some chairs are sticks.
II: No shoe is stick.
III: All sticks are shoes.
IV: All shoes are chairs.
(*a*) Only either I or III follows.
(*b*) Only either II or IV follows.
(*c*) Only I may follow.
(*d*) Only either I and II follows.
(*e*) Only either III or IV follows.

25. *Statements* *I*: All buses are dogs.
II: Some dogs are horses.
Conclusions *I*: Some horses are dogs.
II: Some dogs are buses.
III: Some dogs are not horses.
IV: Some horses are not dogs.
(*a*) Only I and II follow.
(*b*) Only II, III and IV follow.
(*c*) Only III and IV follow.
(*d*) Only I, II and III follow.
(*e*) None follows.

26. *Statements* *I*: Some doors are mangoes.
II: All mangoes are bananas.
Conclusions *I*: All bananas are mangoes.
II: All doors are bananas.
III: Some doors are bananas.
IV: Some mangoes are not doors.
(*a*) Only I and II follow.
(*b*) None follows.
(*c*) All follow.
(*d*) Only II and III follow.
(*e*) Only III and IV follow.

27. *Statements* *I*: Some chairs are windows.
II: No window is sky.
Conclusions *I*: No window is chair.
II: No chair is window.
III: Some windows are skies.
IV: Some chairs are skies.
(*a*) Only either III or IV follows.
(*b*) Only either II or III follows.
(*c*) Only either II or IV follows.
(*d*) None follows.
(*e*) Only I and IV follow.

28. *Statements* *I*: All cats are tigers.
II: Some tigers are lions.
Conclusions *I*: All cats are lions.
II: All lions are cats.
III: Some lions are cats.
IV: Some cats are not lions.
(*a*) Only I follow.
(*b*) All follow.
(*c*) Only I and II follow.
(*d*) Only III and IV follow.
(*e*) None of these.

29. *Statements* *I*: No fruit is tree.
II: All trees are stones.
Conclusions *I*: No stone is fruit.
II: No tree is fruit.

III: Some stones are trees.
IV: Some stones are fruits.
(a) Only II and III follow.
(b) Only either I or IV and II and III follow.
(c) Only either I or III and IV follow.
(d) Only I or III follows.
(e) None of these.

30. *Statements* *I*: All cups are plates.
II: All plates are tables.
Conclusions *I*: All cups are tables.
II: All tables are cups.
III: Some tables are cups.
IV: Some tables are plates.
(a) All follow.
(b) Only I, III and IV follow.
(c) Only II, III and IV follow.
(d) Only I and IV follow.
(e) None of these.

31. *Statements* *I*: Some pencils are papers.
II: Some papers are boxes.
Conclusions *I*: Some pencils are boxes.
II: Some boxes are pencils.
III: Some boxes are papers.
IV: Some papers are pencils.
(a) Only I and II follow.
(b) All follow.
(c) Only III and IV follow.
(d) None follows.
(e) None of these.

32. *Statements* *I*: All buses are trees.
II: Some trees are buses.
Conclusions *I*: All buses are windows.
II: Some buses are windows.
III: Some windows are buses.
IV: Some trees are buses.
(a) None follows.
(b) Only II, III and IV follow.
(c) Only I, II and III follow.
(d) Only III follows.
(e) Only II and III follow.

33. *Statements* *I*: Some dogs are doors.
II: All doors are bats.
Conclusions *I*: Some dogs are bats.
II: All dogs are bats.
III: Some bats are dogs.
IV: All bats are dogs.
(a) All follow.
(b) None follows.
(c) Only II and IV follow.
(d) Only I and III follow.
(e) None of these.

34. *Statements* *I*: Some dogs are doors.
II: All doors are chairs.
Conclusions *I*: Some dogs are chairs.
II: Some chairs are dogs.
III: All chairs are dogs.
IV: Some doors are dogs.
(a) None follows.
(b) All follow.
(c) Only I, II and IV follow.
(d) Only I, III and IV follow.
(e) None of these.

35. *Statements* *I*: Some parrots are monkeys.
II: Some monkeys are jackals.
Conclusions *I*: Some parrots are jackals.
II: Some jackals are parrots.
III: Some jackals are monkeys.
IV: Some monkeys are parrots.
(a) All follow.
(b) Only I and III follow.
(c) Only II and IV follow.
(d) Only I and II follow.
(e) None of these.

36. *Statements* *I*: All parrots are koels.
II: No koel is goat.
Conclusions *I*: No parrot is goat.
II: Some parrots are goats.
III: All koels are parrots.
IV: Some goats are parrots.
(a) Only I follows.
(b) Only III follows.
(c) Only II and III follow.
(d) None follows.
(e) None of these.

37. *Statements* *I*: Some shirts are tables.
II: No table is chair.
Conclusions *I*: No shirt is chair.
II: Some tables are shirts.
III: No chair is shirt.
IV: Some chairs are shirts.
(a) All follow.
(b) Only II follows.
(c) Only II and IV follow.
(d) Only III follows.
(e) None of these.

38. *Statements* *I*: All tigers are jackals.
II: All jackals are horses.
Conclusions *I*: All jackals are tigers.
II: All horses are jackals.
III: No tiger is horse.
IV: No horse is tiger.
(*a*) Only III and IV follow.
(*b*) Only I and II follow.
(*c*) Only I, II and III follow.
(*d*) All follow.
(*e*) None follows.

39. *Statements* *I*: All cows are hens.
II: All cats are hens.
Conclusions *I*: All hens are cows.
II: All hens are cats.
III: Some hens are cows.
IV: Some hens are cats.
(*a*) Only I and II follow.
(*b*) Only III follows.
(*c*) Only IV follows.
(*d*) Only III and IV follow.
(*e*) None of the above.

40. *Statements* *I*: All bags are chalks.
II: All chalks are bottles.
Conclusions *I*: Some bottles are bags.
II: All bags are bottles.
III: All bottles are bags.
IV: Some chalks are not bags.
(*a*) Only I, III and IV follow.
(*b*) Only II, III and IV follow.
(*c*) None of these.
(*d*) Only I, II and IV follow.
(*e*) All follow.

41. *Statements* *I*: Some frogs are bricks.
II: All bricks are cakes.
Conclusions *I*: Some cakes are not frogs.
II: Some cakes are frogs.
III: No cake is frog.
IV: All frogs are cakes.
(*a*) Only I and II follow.
(*b*) All follow.
(*c*) None follows.
(*d*) Only II, III and IV follow.
(*e*) Only I, II and IV follow.

42. *Statements* *I*: Some cars are scooters.
II: No scooter is a cycle.
Conclusions *I*: No car is cycle.
II: No scooter is car.
III: Some cars are cycles.
IV: Some scooters are cars.
(*a*) All follow.
(*b*) None follows.
(*c*) Only I and III follow.
(*d*) Only I, II and IV follow.
(*e*) Only IV follows.

43. *Statements* *I*: No educationists are researchers.
II: All researchers are teachers.
Conclusions *I*: No teacher is researcher.
II: No teacher is educationist.
III: All researchers are teachers.
IV: Some teachers are researchers.
(*a*) None follows.
(*b*) All follow.
(*c*) Either I or III follows.
(*d*) Only II follows.
(*e*) Only III and IV follow.

44. *Statements* *I*: All phones are scales.
II: All scales are calculators.
Conclusions *I*: All calculators are scales.
II: All scales are phones.
III: All phones are calculators.
IV: Some calculators are phones.
(*a*) None follows.
(*b*) Only I and II follow.
(*c*) All follow.
(*d*) Only III and IV follow.
(*e*) Only II follows.

45. *Statements* *I*: Some tables are TVs.
II: Some TVs are radios.
Conclusions *I*: Some tables are radios.
II: Some radios are tables.
III: All radios are TVs.
IV: All TVs are tables.
(*a*) None follows.
(*b*) Only II and IV follow.
(*c*) Only I and III follow.
(*d*) All follow.
(*e*) Only IV follows.

46. *Statements* *I* : Some caps are tanks.
II : Some tanks are bulbs.
Conclusions *I* : Some tanks are caps.
II : Some bulbs are tanks.
III : Some caps are bulbs.
IV : No bulb is cap.
(a) Only I, II and III follow.
(b) Only I, II and IV follow.
(c) Only I, II and either III or IV follow.
(d) None of these.
(e) All follow.

47. *Statements* *I* : All crystals are magnets.
II : Some magnets are chocolates.
Conclusions *I* : Some magnets are crystals.
II : Some chocolates are not magnets.
III : No chocolate is crystal.
IV : All magnets are crystals.
(a) Only I, II and IV follow.
(b) Only I, II and III follow.
(c) None of these.
(d) All of these.
(e) Only II and III follow.

48. *Statements* *I* : No boat is shop.
II : All shops are guns.
Conclusions *I* : All boats are guns.
II : No boat is gun.
III : Some guns are shops.
IV : All guns are shops.
(a) Only either I or II follows.
(b) Only I follows.
(c) Only II follows.
(d) Only III and IV follow.
(e) None of these.

49. *Statements* *I* : Some pens are books.
II : Some books are pencils.
Conclusions *I* : Some pens are pencils.
II : Some pencils are pens.
III : All pencils are books.
IV : All books are pens.
(a) All follow.
(b) None follows.
(c) Only I and III follow.
(d) Only II and IV follow.
(e) Only I follows.

50. *Statements* *I* : All researchers are psychologists.
II : Some psychologists are scientists.
Conclusions *I* : All researchers are scientists.
II : Some researchers are scientists.
III : Some scientists are psychologists.
IV : Some psychologists are researchers.
(a) None follows.
(b) Only III and IV follow.
(c) All follow.
(d) Only III follows.
(e) Only II and IV follow.

EXPLANATORY ANSWERS

1. ***(b)*** :

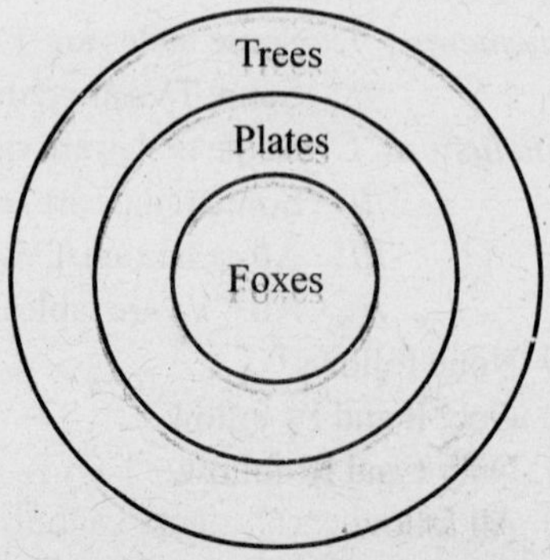

Trees
Plates
Foxes

When all foxes are plates and all plates are trees, then naturally all foxes will be trees and some trees will then have to be foxes. And when all plates are trees then some trees will have to be plates. Therefore, only conclusions I, III and IV are correct.

2. ***(d)*** : When it is given that some cubes are squares and all squares are circles, then some cubes will naturally be circles, though all cubes cannot be circles. When some cubes are circles, then some circles will have to be cubes. And when all squares are circles, then some circles will have to be squares. As per given statement II, all squares are circles. Therefore all squares cannot be cubes. As such only conclusions II and III are correct.

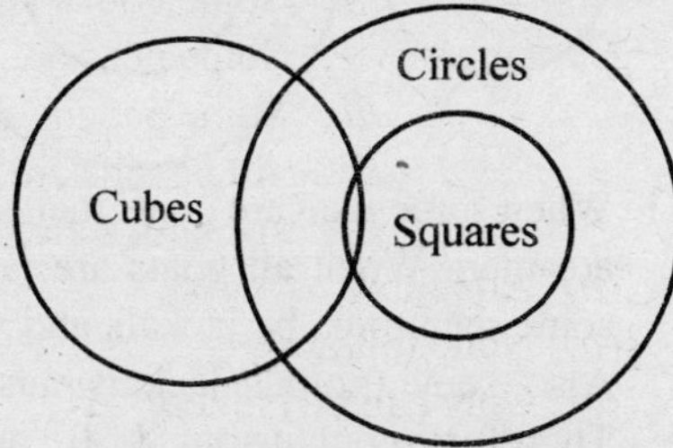

3. *(e)* : When all cups are goats, then only some goats can be cups. When all goats are tins, then only some tins can be goats. When all cups are goats and all goats are tins, then naturally all cups are tins and some tins must be cups. Therefore, all the conclusions are incorrect.

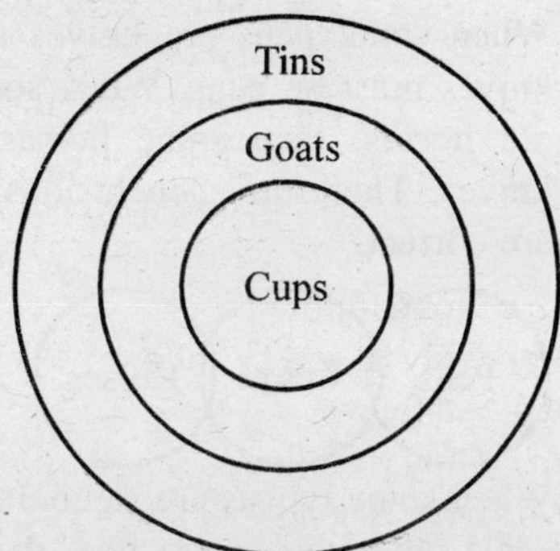

4. *(e)* : When all bombs are bags and some bags are jets then all bombs cannot be jets. 'Some bags' indicate that there is no chance of some bombs being jets, or some jets being bombs. Further all jets cannot be bombs. Therefore, all conclusions are incorrect.

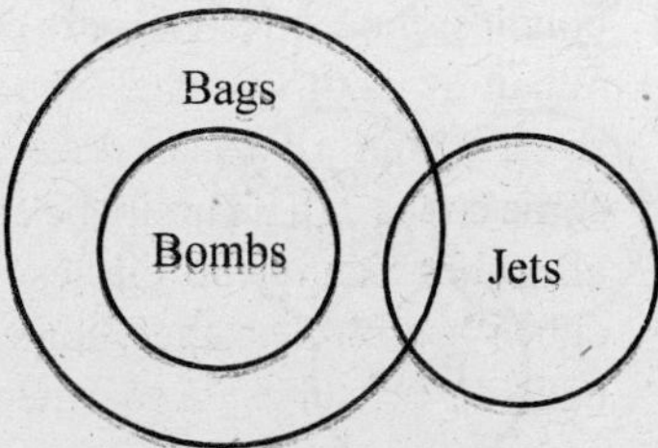

5. *(d)* : When some thorns are jackets and some jackets are boats, then some thorns may be boats but some boats cannot be thorns. As per Statement I, some thorns are jackets, some jackets need to be thorns. When Statement II conveys that some jackets are boats, then it is clear that all jackets cannot be boats. Therefore, no particular given conclusion can be drawn from the given statements.

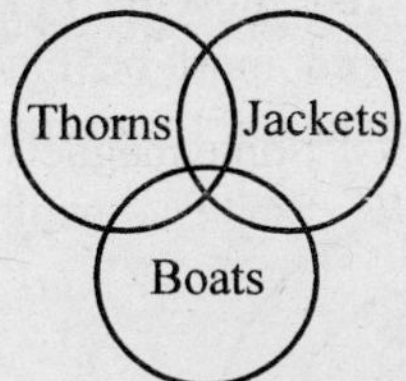

6. *(b)* : When all girls are pens then,
(i) some pens must be girls

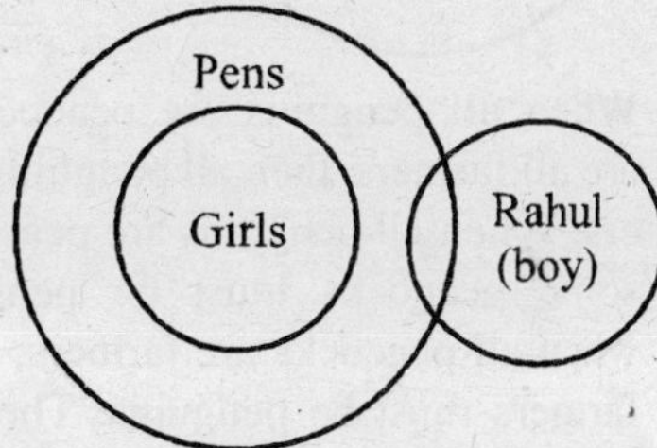

7. *(c)* : No men are cows and all cows are windows. When no men are cows, then cows cannot be men. When all cows are windows, then some windows must be cows.

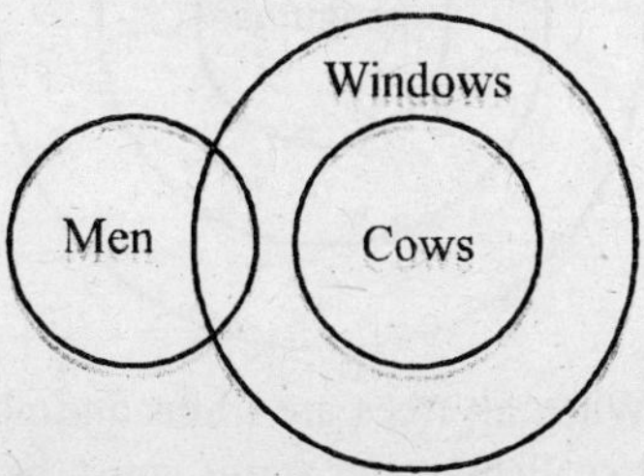

8. *(e)* : When some tigers are lizards, which are all turtles, then all tigers cannot be turtles or vice–versa.

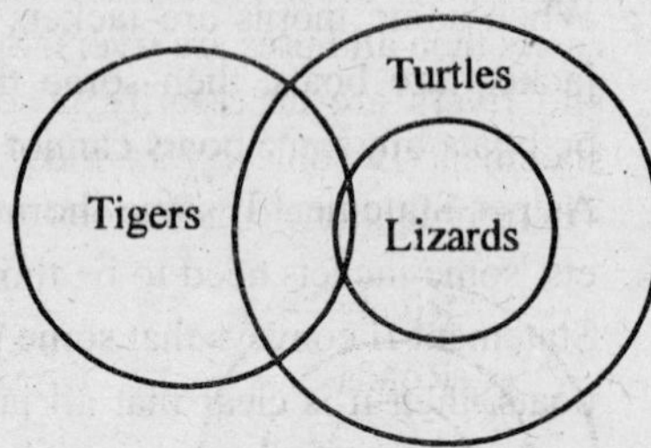

9. (c) : When all, that is black, is red and when coal is black, then coal is red. When all that is black is red, then it is not necessary that all red must be black, though some that is red must be black. Therefore, only conclusion I is correct.

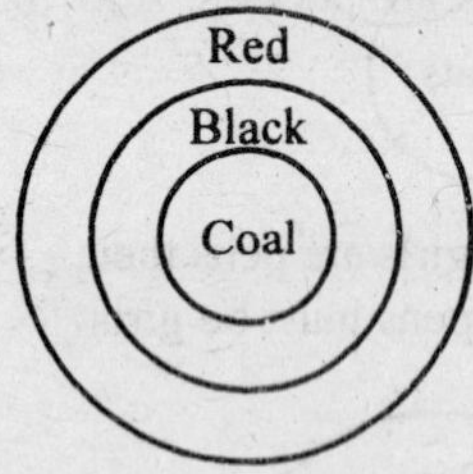

10. (d) : When all penguins are peacocks, which are all farmers, then all penguins are farmers. When all penguins are peacocks, then some peacocks must be penguins and when all peacocks are farmers, then some farmers must be penguins. Therefore, all conclusions are correct.

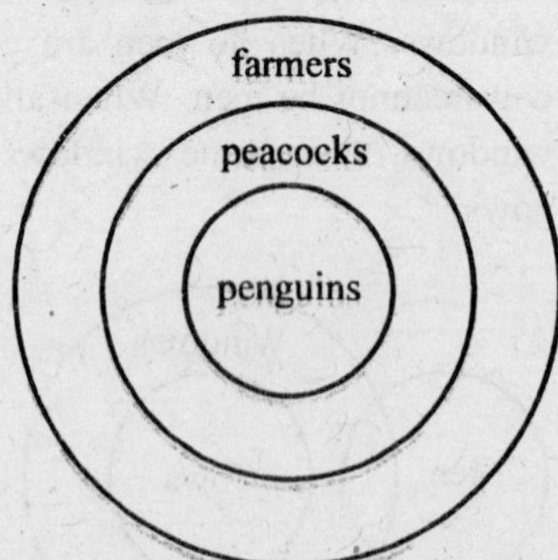

11. (e) : When all trees are trains and no chair is a tree then some trains must be trees. No chair is train and vice versa cannot be established for certain. Therefore, only conlcusion III is correct.

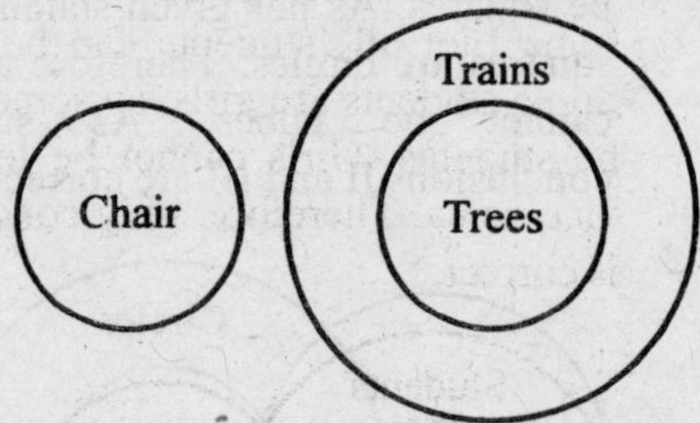

12. (e) : When some men are goats then some goats are men. When all goats are jackals then some men must be jackals and vice versa. Also, some (not all) jackals must be goats. Therefore conclusions I, II, and IV are correct.

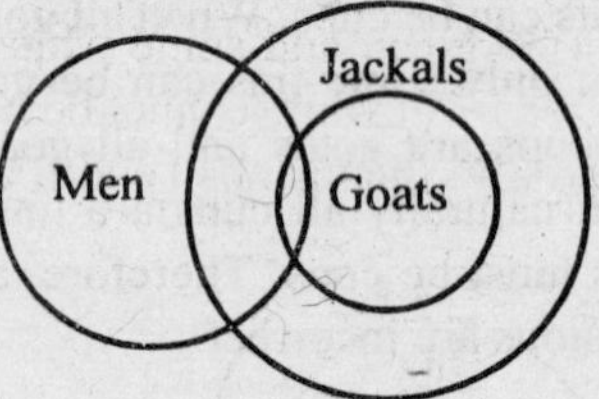

13. (b) : When some pens are knives then some knives must be pens. When some knives are horses, then some horses must be knives. Therefore, conclusions I and IV are correct.

14. (e) : When some typists are stenographers and some stenographers are boys then all boys cannot be stenographers or typists. However, some typists who are not stenographers may not be boys. Therefore, either conclusion III or IV is correct.

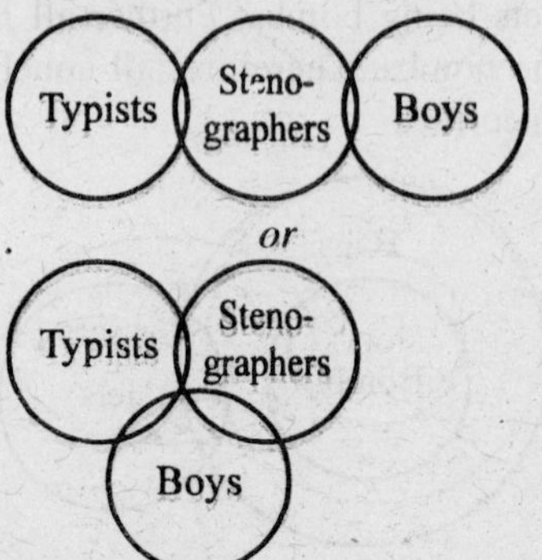

15. *(c)* : When all teachers are students then only some (not all) students can be teachers. Some students are girls, so some girls can be students. Girls cannot be teachers or vice versa. Therefore, only conclusion III is correct.

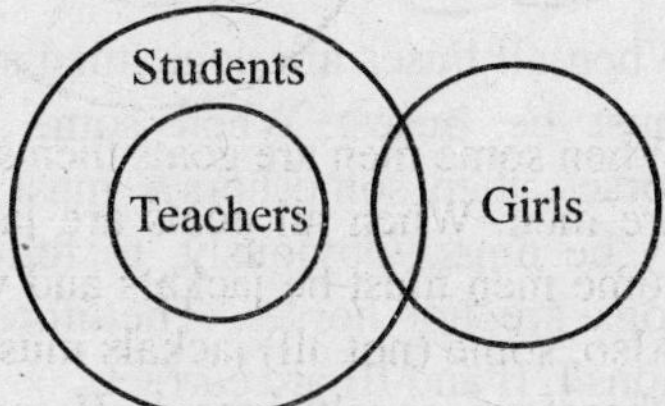

16. *(a)* : When all green are blue and all blue are white, then all green is white. Some blue must be green and some white must also be green. All white cannot be blue. Therefore, only conclusions I and II are correct.

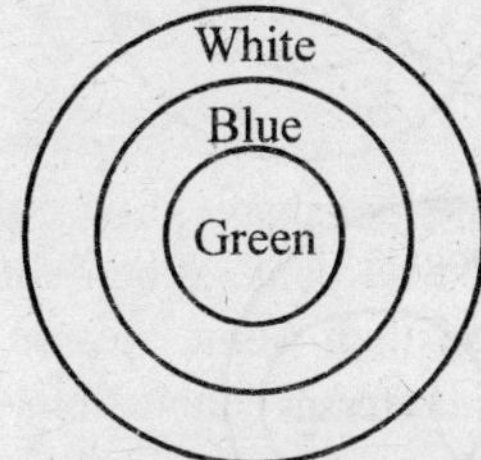

17. *(c)* : When all doors are cots then some cots (not all) can be doors. When some cots are erasers then some doors may or may not be erasers or vice versa. Therefore, only conclusion III is correct.

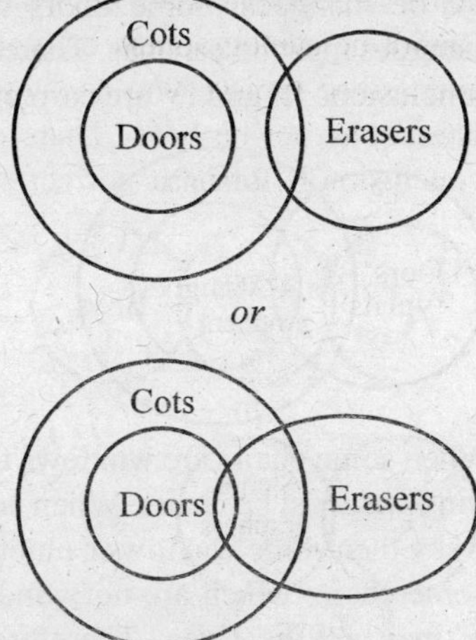

18. *(e)* : When all buses are roads and all roads are rivers then all buses are rivers. Some roads and rivers are necessarily buses. As per statement II some rivers must be roads. Therefore, all the conclusions are correct.

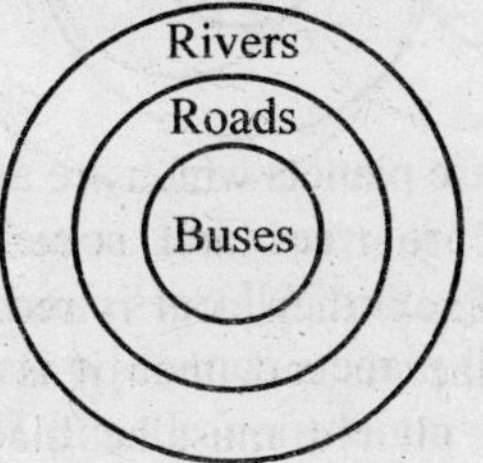

19. *(b)* : Some bags are pockets, so some pockets must be bags. No pocket is a pouch. When some bags are pockets, some bag can not be pouch. Therefore, only conclusions II and III are correct.

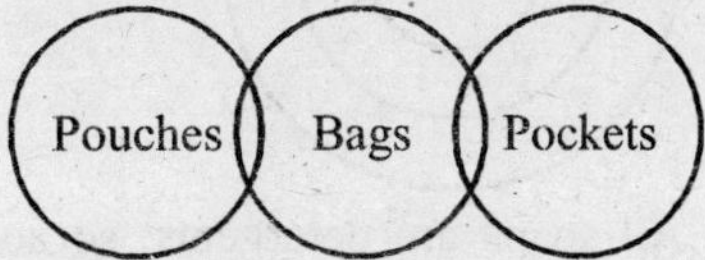

20. *(d)* : When all soaps are clean, some clean must be soaps. When all clean are wet, then some (not all) wet must be clean. Therefore only conclusions I and III follow.

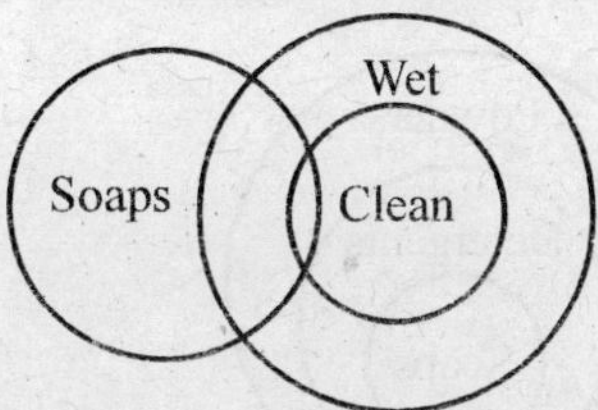

21. *(a)* : When all crows are bats, then some bats are crows and some are not. Bats may or may not be parrots and vice versa. Therefore, only conclusions III and IV are correct.

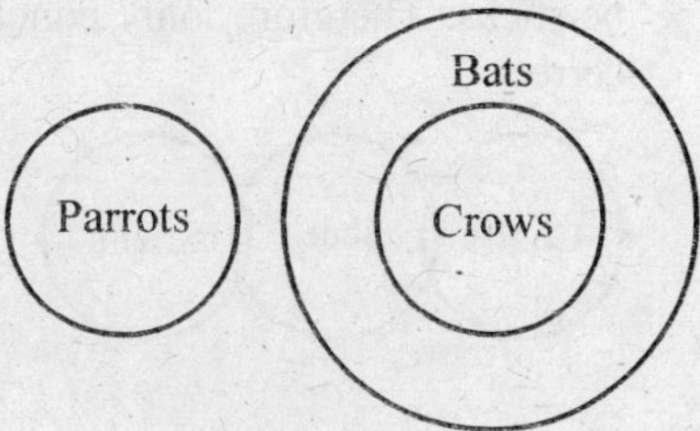

or

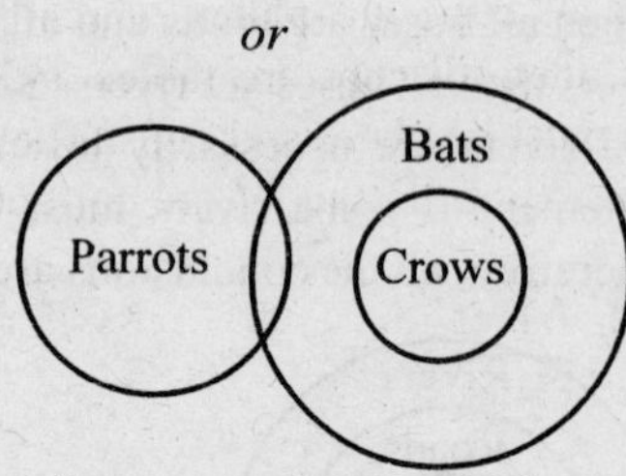

22. *(e)* **:** All stars are planets which are all trees, so, all stars are trees and some trees are necessarily stars. All trees cannot be planets and all planets cannot be stars. Therefore, only conclusions II and IV are correct.

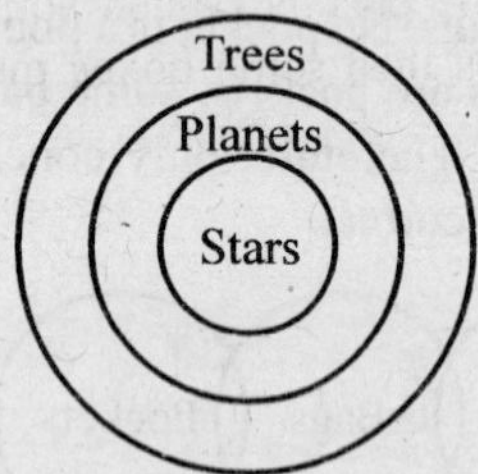

23. *(d)* **:** All soaps are detergents, so some detergents are soaps. All detergents are powders, so some powders are detergents. Also all soaps are powders and thence some powders must be soaps. Therefore, all the conclusions are correct.

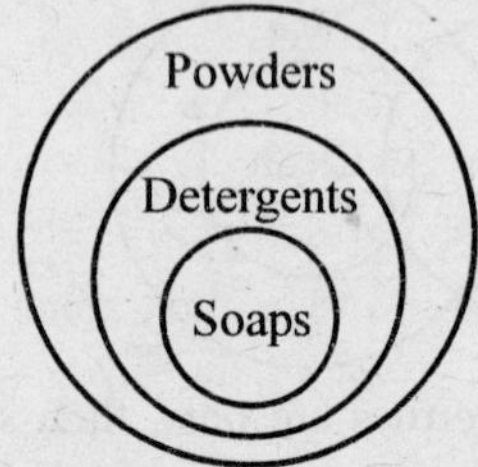

24. *(c)* **:** When some chairs are shoes, all shoes cannot be chairs. When some shoes are sticks, all sticks cannot be shoes. Some chairs which are not shoes may or may not be sticks. Therefore, only conclusion I is correct.

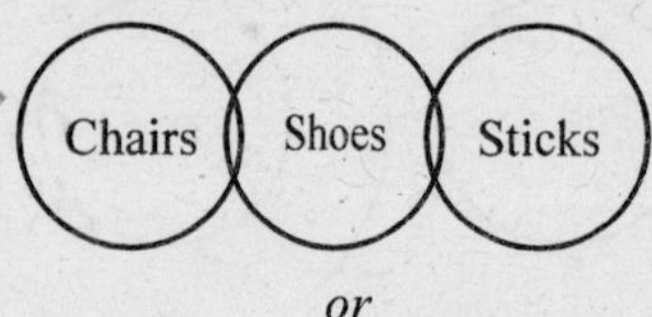

or

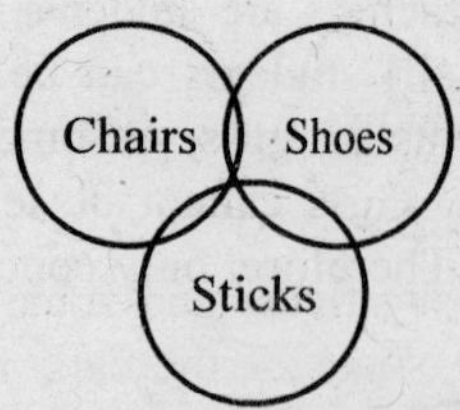

25. *(d)* **:** When all buses are dogs, then some dogs must be buses. When some dogs are horses, then some horses must necessarily be dogs. Obviously, to follow, some dogs are not horses. Therefore, conclusions I, II and III are correct.

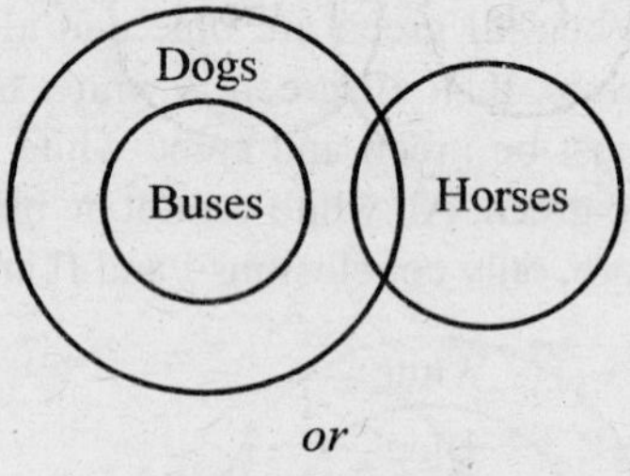

or

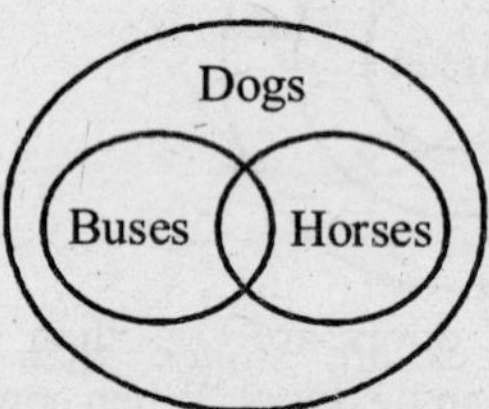

26. *(e)* **:** When some doors are mangoes, then some mangoes are and some are not doors. All mangoes are bananas, so all bananas cannot be mangoes. Some doors which are mangoes must be bananas. Therefore, only conclusions III and IV are correct.

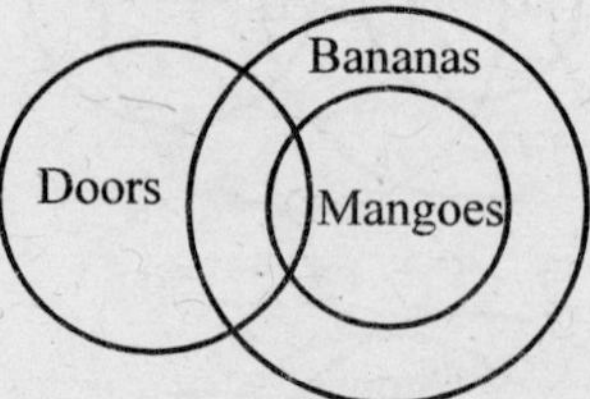

27. *(d)* **:** When some chairs are windows then some windows must be chairs. When no window is sky then some windows cannot be skies. Some chairs which are not windows may or may not be skies. Therefore, all the conclusions are incorrect.

28. *(e)* : When all cats are tigers and some tigers are lions, then some of the cats may or may not be lions and vice versa. Therefore, either conclusion III or conclusion IV is correct.

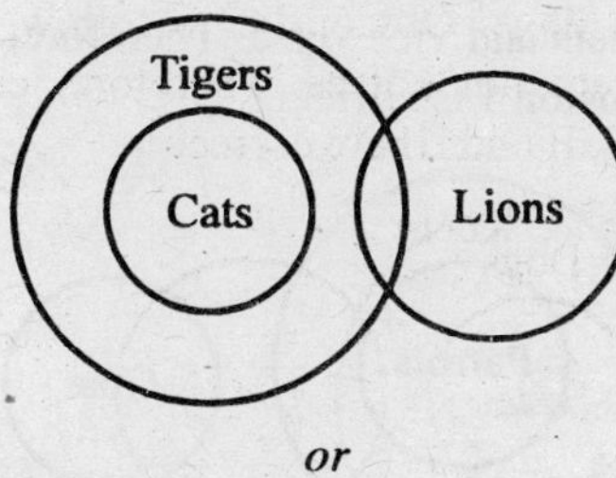

or

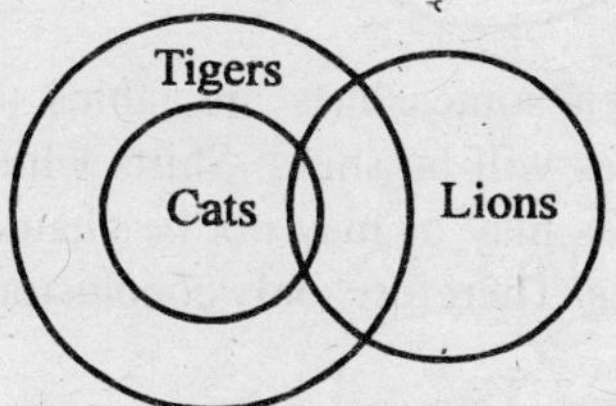

29. *(b)* : When no fruit is tree, then no tree is fruit. When all trees are stones, then some stones must be trees. Stones which are not trees may or may not be fruits and vice versa. Therefore, either conclusions I or IV and conclusions II and III are correct.

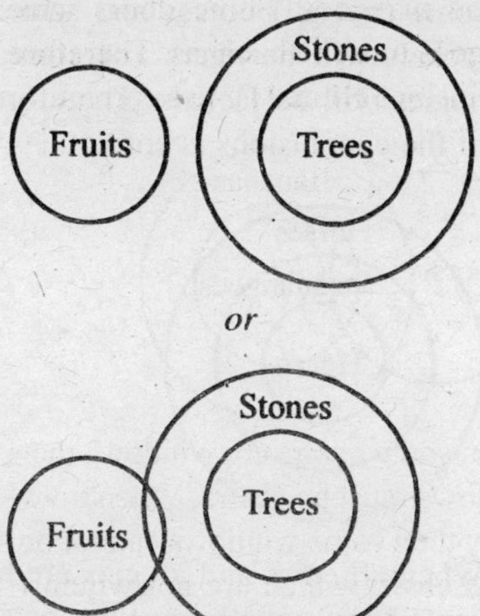

30. *(b)* : When all cups are plates which are all tables, then all cups are tables and some tables must be plates and cups. Therefore, conclusions I, III and IV are correct.

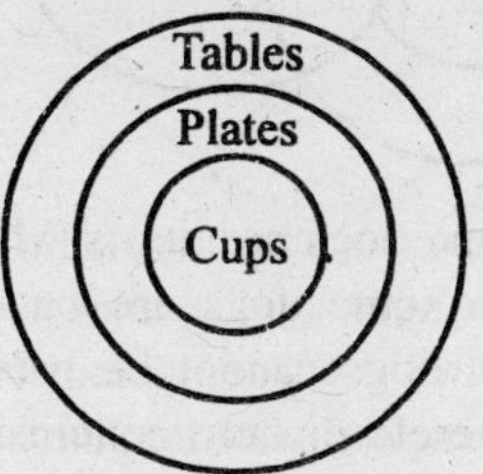

31. *(c)* : When some pencils are papers then some papers must be pencils. When some papers are boxes then some boxes must be papers. Pencils which are not papers may or may not be boxes and boxes which are not papers may or may not be pencils. Therefore, only conclusions III and IV are correct.

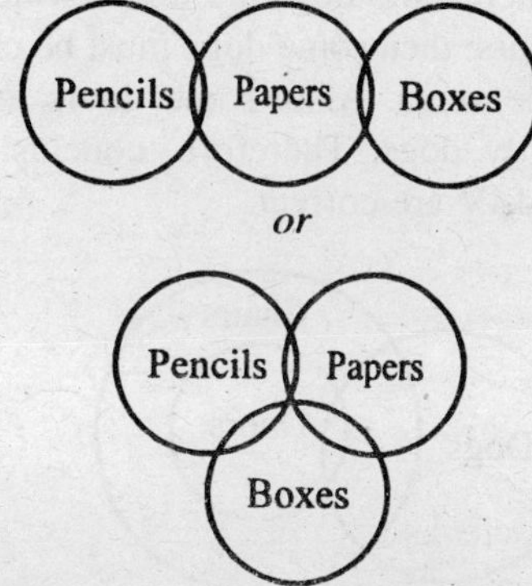

32. *(b)* : When all buses are trees then some trees must be buses. Some of the buses which are trees may be windows and some windows will be buses. So, from the given options, conclusions II, III and IV are correct.

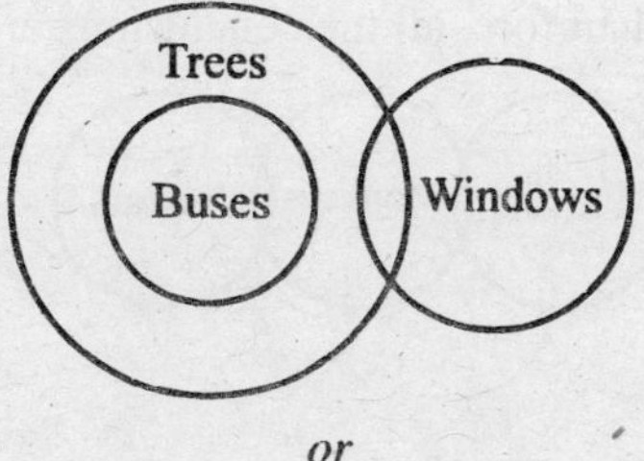

or

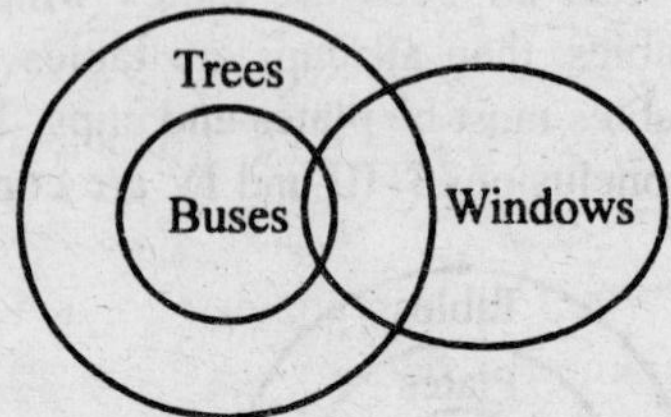

33. ***(d)*** **:** When some dogs are doors which are all bats, then some dogs are bats and vice versa. All dogs cannot be bats and vice versa. Therefore, only conclusions I and III are correct.

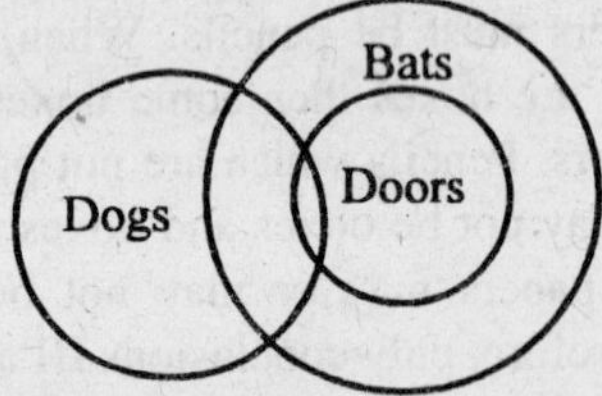

34. ***(c)*** **:** When some dogs are doors which are all chairs, then some dogs must be chairs and vice versa. Also, some doors are necessarily dogs. Therefore, conclusions I, II and IV are correct.

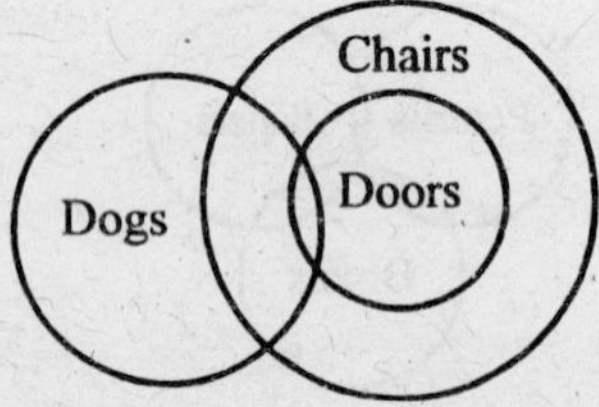

35. ***(a)*** **:** Some parrots are monkeys, so some monkeys must be parrots, and some parrots which are not monkeys may be jackals. Some monkeys are jackals, so some jackals must be monkeys, and some monkeys which are not jackals may be parrots. Therefore, all the conclusions are correct.

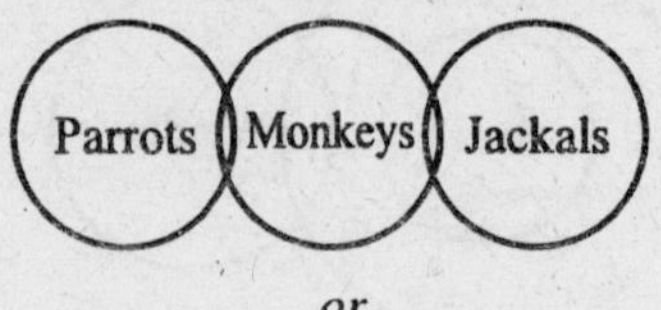

or

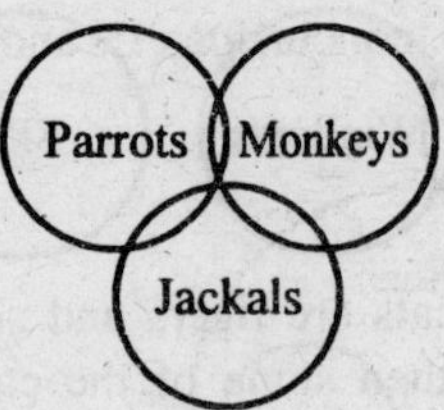

36. ***(a)*** **:** When all parrots are koels, then some koels can be parrots. When no koel is goat then all parrots that are koels cannot be goats and vice versa. Therefore, only conclusion I is correct.

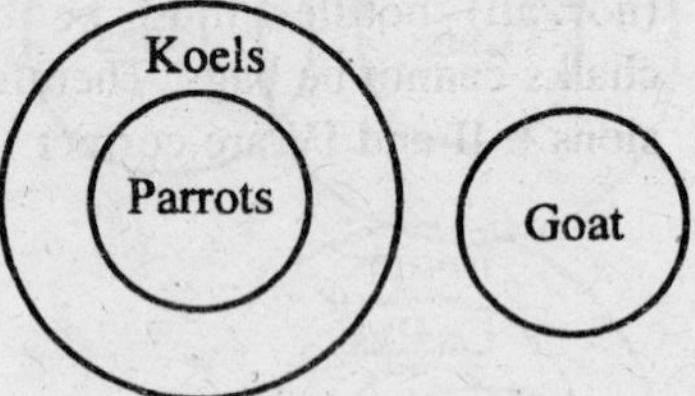

37. ***(b)*** **:** When some shirts are tables then some tables will be shirts. Shirts which are not tables may or may not be chairs and vice versa. Therefore, only conclusion II is correct.

38. ***(e)*** **:** When all tigers are jackals and all jackals are horses, then all tigers will be horses; some (not all) horses and some (not all) jackals will be tigers and some (not all) horses will be jackals. Therefore, neither of the conclusions is correct.

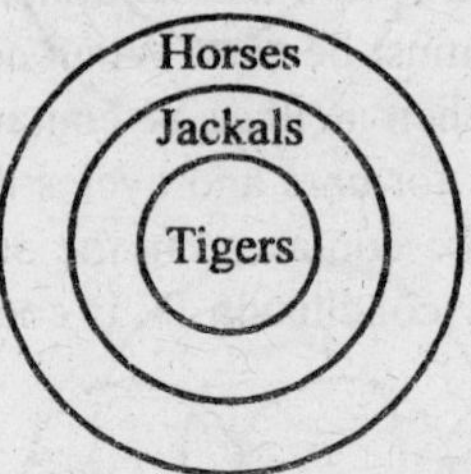

39. ***(d)*** **:** When all cows and all cats are hens, then some hens (not all) must be cows and cats.

Therefore, conclusions III and IV are correct.

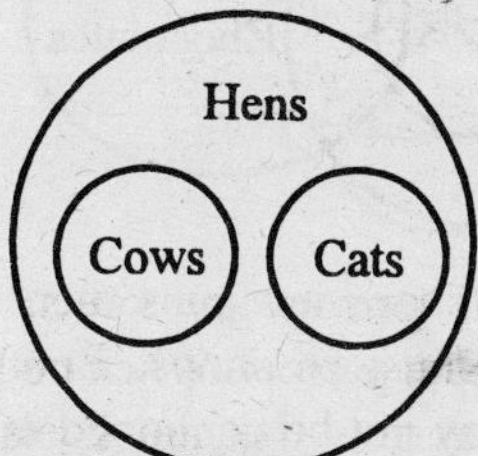

40. *(d)* : When all bags are chalks which are all bottles, then all bags are bottles and some (not all) bottlles must be bags. Some chalks cannot be bags. Therefore, conclusions I, II and IV are correct.

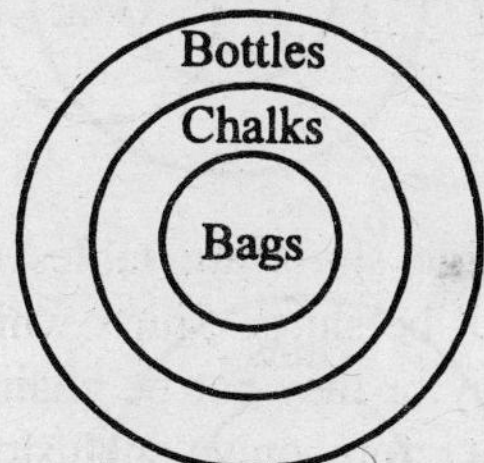

41. *(a)* : When some frogs are bricks which are all cakes then some frogs must be cakes and vice versa. Also some cakes are not frogs, and all frogs cannot be cakes. Therefore, conclusions I and II are correct.

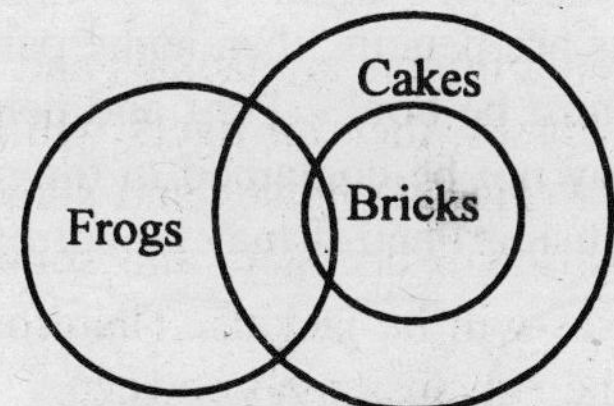

42. *(e)* : When some cars are scooters, then some scooters must be cars. When no scooter is a cycle then neither is contained in the other. As for cars and cycles they may or may not be contained in the other. Therefore, only conclusion IV is correct.

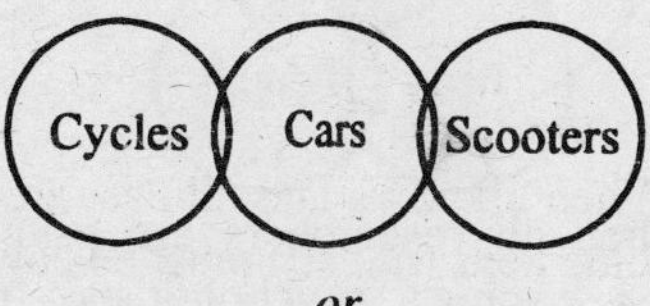

or

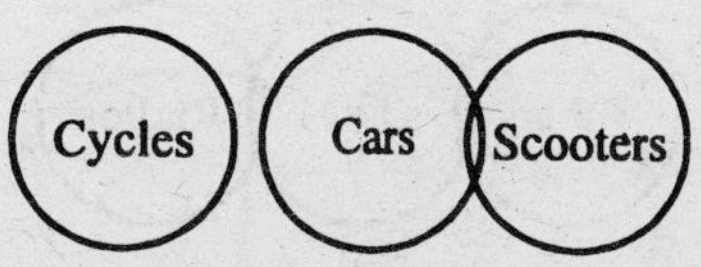

43. *(e)* : When all researchers are teachers, then some teachers must be researchers. Educationists and teachers may or may not be contained in the other. Therefore, only conclusions III and IV follow.

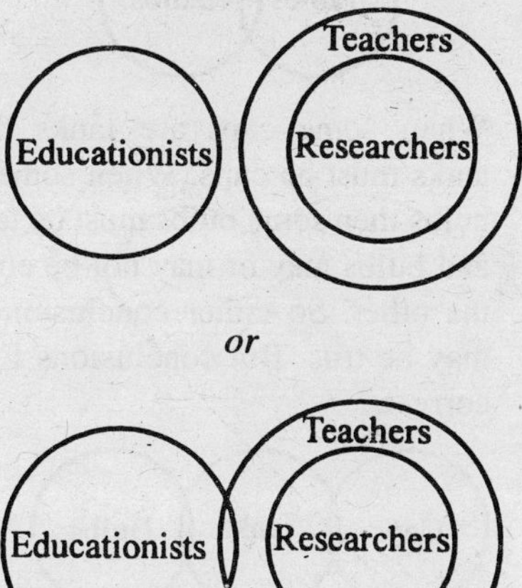

44. *(d)* : When all phones are scales which are all calculators, then all phones are calculators and some calculators must be phones. All calculators and scales cannot be phones. Some scales must be phones. Therefore, only conclusions III and IV are correct.

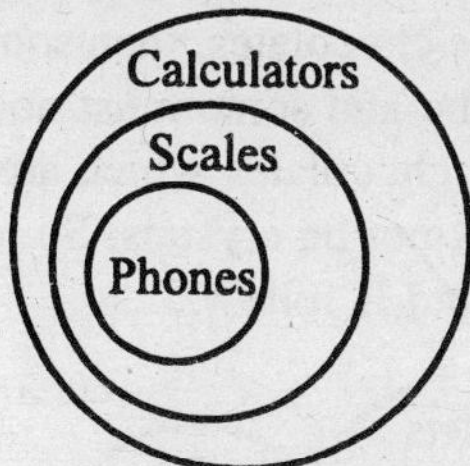

45. *(a)* : When some tables are TVs then only some TVs must be tables. When some TVs are radios then only some radios must be TVs. Tables and Radios may or may not be contained in the other. Therefore, neither of the conclusion is correct.

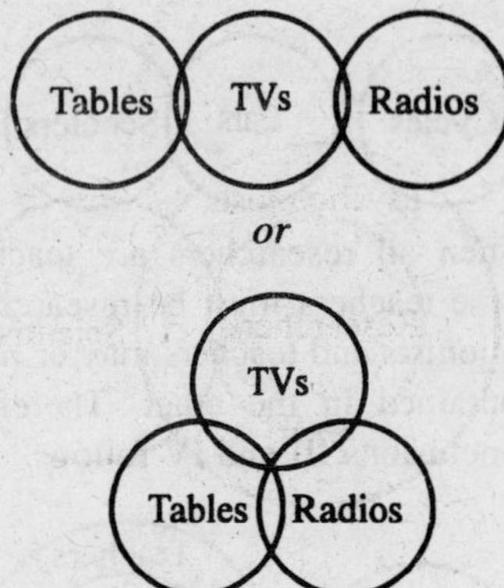

46. (c) : When some caps are tanks then some tanks must be caps. When some tanks are bulbs then some bulbs must be tanks. Caps and bulbs may or may not be contained in the other. So either conclusion III or IV may be true. But conclusions I and II are correct.

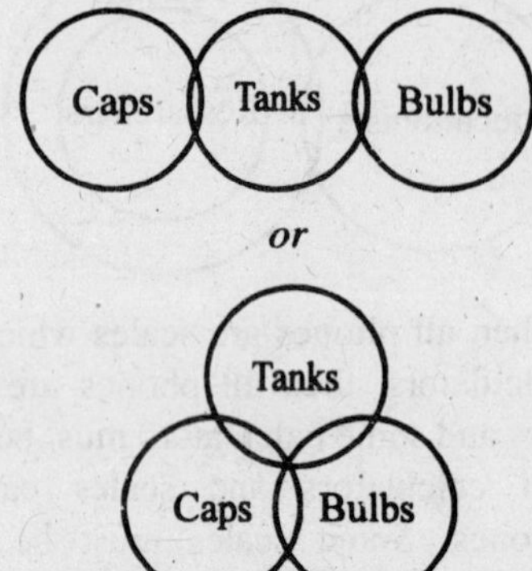

47. (c) : When all crystals are magnets then some magnets must be crystals. When some magnets are chocolates, then some chocolates must be and some must not be magnets. Some chocolates which are magnets may or may not be crystals. So, only conclusions I and II follow.

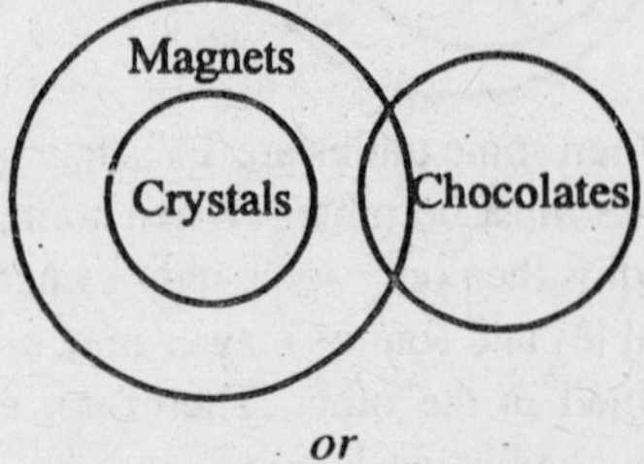

or

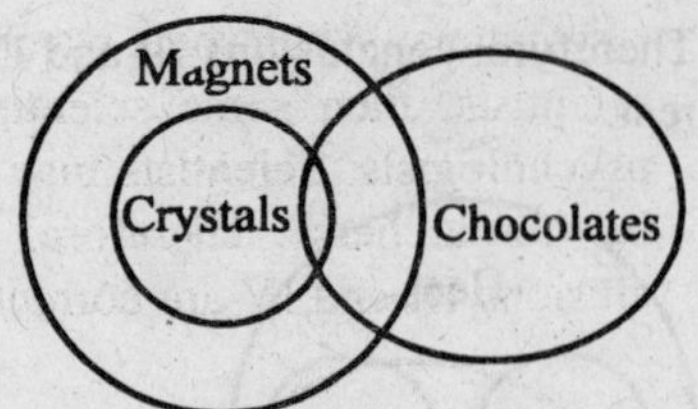

48. (e) : When all shops are guns then some (not all) guns must be shops. Boat and guns may or may not be contained in the other. So, either conclusion I or II may be true. But conclusion III is correct.

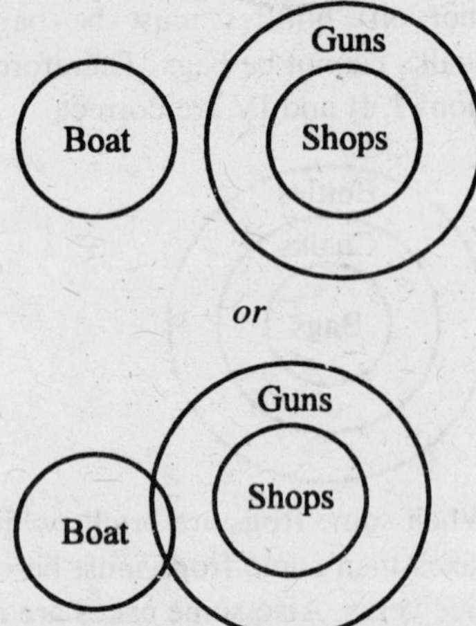

49. (b) : When some pens are books, then some books (not all) must be pens. When some books are pencils, then some pencils (not all) must be books. Pens and pencils may or may not be contained in the other. So, conclusion I and II may be correct.

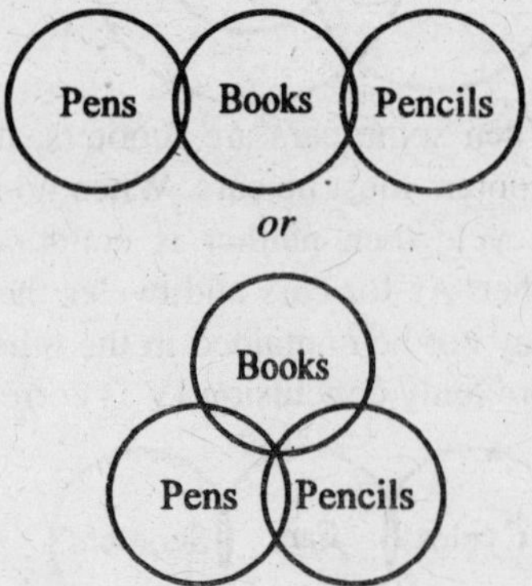

50. (b) : When all researchers are psychologists, then some psychologists must be researchers. When some psychologists are scientists, then some scientists must be psychologists. Scientists may or may not be researchers. Therefore, only conclusions III and IV are correct.

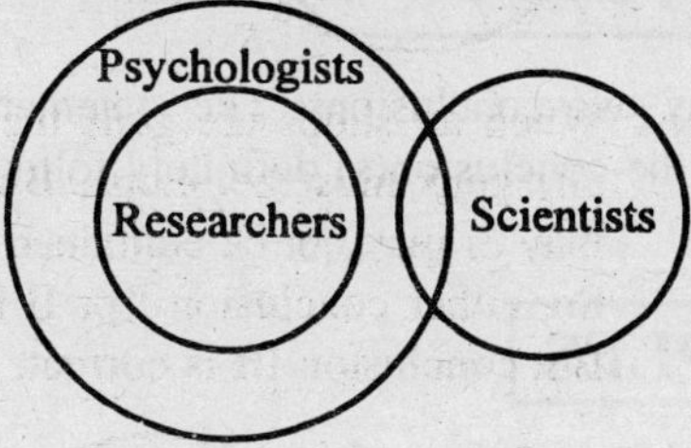

or

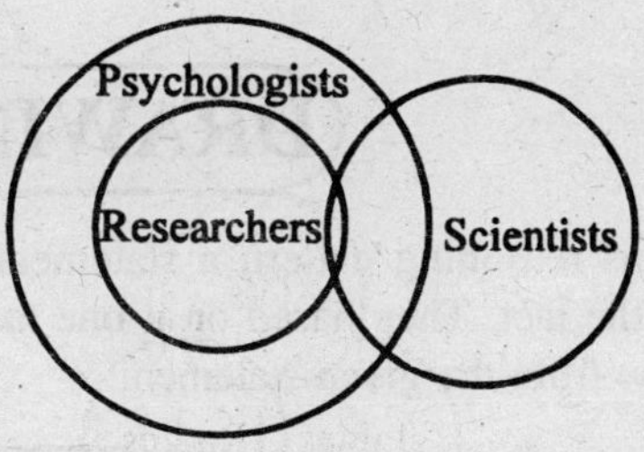

PART - IV

DRAWING CONCLUSIONS

In this reasoning pattern a statement is given followed by two conclusions. The statement is to be taken as the fact. Then based on it one has to decide which of the conclusion(s) definitely follows or does not follow from the given statement.

SOLVED EXAMPLES

In the questions below the answer is given as:

(a) if only conclusion I follows,
(b) if only conclusion II follows,
(c) if either conclusion I or II follows,
(d) if neither conclusion I nor II follows, or
(e) if conclusions I and II both follow.

1. *Statement* : It is said that teachers should not go on strike. Why should they not? Strike is an inherent right.

Conclusions I : Teachers cannot get justice unless they go on strike.

II : Every teacher should go on strike.

Ans. ***(a)*** **:** Only conclusion I follows from the given statements, *i.e.,* as an inherent right the teachers can get justice in appropriate cases if they go on strike. Conclusion II does not follow.

2. *Statement* : The government of country 'X' has recently announced several concessions and offered attractive package tours for foreign visitors.

Conclusions I : Now, more numbers of foreign tourists will visit the country.

II : The government of country 'X' seems to be serious in attracting foreign tourists.

Ans. ***(e)*** **:** Concessions and attractive package tours will encourage tourists and country 'X' has taken the step only because it seems to be serious about foreign visitors. So both conclusion I and conclusion II follow from the given statement.

EXERCISE

Directions : *In the following questions, each question has a statement followed by two conclusions. Taking the statement to be true, decide which of the given conclusions definitely follows from the given statement. Indicate your answer as (a) if only I follows; (b) if only II follows; (c) either I or II follows; (d) if neither I nor II follows; and (e) if both I and II follow.*

1. *Statement* : The Principal humiliated the teacher in the presence of students.

Conclusions I : The Principal did not like the teacher.

II : The teacher was not popular amongst his students.

2. *Statement* : Good health is dependent on right eating habits. Most of the people do not follow any rule regarding eating.

Conclusions I : Most of the people have poor health.

II : People are ignorant of proper eating habits.

3. *Statement* : Until our country achieves

economic equality and political freedom, democracy would be meaningless.

Conclusions I : Political freedom and democracy go hand in hand.

II : Economic equality leads to real political freedom and democracy.

4. *Statement* : Black cloud follows thunder. Rains follow thunder.

Conclusions I : Thunder is the cause of rain.

II : Black cloud is the cause of thunder.

5. *Statement* : Practice is better than precept. Most doctors are heavy smokers.

Conclusions I : Most doctors cannot advise people not to smoke.

II : Doctors do not regard smoking as injurious.

6. *Statement* : Workers feel highly motivated when they get sense of involvement by participating in the management of companies.

Conclusions I : Workers should be motivated to produce more.

II : Workers should be allowed to participate in the management of companies.

7. *Statement* : Industrial revolution which first of all started in Europe has brought about modern age.

Conclusions I : Disparity between rich and poor results in revolution.

II : Revolution overhauls society.

8. *Statement* : America's defence secretary reiterated that they would continue to supply arms to Pakistan.

Conclusions I : Pakistan is incapable of manufacturing arms.

II : It would ensure peace in the region.

9. *Statement* : Poor people are more trustworthy as compared to the rich. They can do wonders if they are taken into confidence.

Conclusions I : Poor people are wonderful people.

II : By and large rich people are not trustworthy.

10. *Statement* : Government has spoiled many top ranking financial institutions by appointing bureaucrats as Directors of these institutions.

Conclusions I : Government should appoint Directors of the financial institutes taking into consideration the expertise of the person in the area of finance.

II : The Director of the financial institute should have expertise commensurate with the financial work carried out by the institute.

11. *Statement* : The Constitutional amendment carried out just last month prohibits the employment of child labour in any organisation.

Conclusions I : The employers must now abide by this amendment to the Constitution.

II : Children below 14 years will now be engaged in acquiring education.

12. *Statement* : People who speak too much against the dowry are those who had taken it themselves.

Conclusions I : It is easier said than done.

II : People have double standards.

13. *Statement* : Vegetable prices are soaring in the market.

Conclusions I : Vegetables are becoming a rare commodity.

II : People cannot eat vegetables.

14. *Statement* : As far as the rate of literacy is concerned, there is hardly any difference between the States of Kerala and West Bengal, but one is ahead of the other in respect of the percentage of population unemployed.

Conclusions I : Unemployment is more in Kerala than in West Bengal.

II : West Bengal has higher unemployment than Kerala.

15. *Statement* : He tirelessly argues for the replacement of the present system of allocating work to the teaching staff in the department by another system which will give the teachers higher job satisfaction.

Conclusions I : No system is free from problems and therefore there should be no system.

II : Any system you may evolve but it should give higher job satisfaction to the teachers.

16. *Statement* : The unequal allocation of funds by the Government for literacy and employment generation programmes stands out clearly when we analyse the attitude of government towards these two areas.

Conclusions I : Government has more favourable attitude towards literacy programmes than employment generation programmes.

II : Government has more favourable attitude towards employment generation programmes than literacy programmes.

17. *Statement* : Amul chocolates sold enough in comparison to all other chocolate brands in India.

Conclusions I : No other chocolate is sold in India.

II : The selling data of every chocolate brand is available in India.

18. *Statement* : Wearing Khadi is not only good for our health but also for our nation.

Conclusions I : Economy of India also depends upon Khadi sector.

II : It is difficult to maintain Khadi clothes.

19. *Statement* : Ideas given by our ancestors that were once discarded as uneconomical and unviable, turn out to be as functional and inevitable in present cicumstances.

Conclusions I : In ancient period ideas were considered either completely functional or totally infeasible.

II : Ideas cannot change from time to time.

20. *Statement* : The Supreme Court gave a judgement that the maintenance of old age parents is the responsibility of the married girls, if they do not have brothers.

Conclusions I : Constitution is always interpreted to help oppressed people out.

II : Before the Supreme Court gave its verdict, a married girl must have denied to pay for the maintenance of her parents.

21. *Statement* : Rapid growth presupposes efficiency which in turn requires a meritocracy, which runs counter to the principle of representation.

Conclusions I : Meritorious persons yield

better results.

II : Rapid growth and the demand for representation are not complimentary.

22. *Statement* : The average number of students per teacher is 50 in urban areas, whereas, it is 60 in rural areas. The national average is 55.

Conclusions I : The student–teacher ratio in the rural areas is higher than in the urban areas.

II : More students study with the same teacher in the rural areas as compared to those in the urban areas.

23. *Statement* : The rise of the Japanese economy has triggered a revolution in the recent past as a result of their dedication and commitment.

Conclusions I : Revolution leads to economic prosperity.

II : Hard work and sincerity result in economic prosperity.

24. *Statement* : Power consumption in every family has been doubled during the last five years.

Conclusions I : There is a lot of development in the society.

II : Power rates have become cheaper.

25. *Statement* : The knowledge of content does not matter much, what matters is whether you can orally express it or not.

Conclusions I : Art of delivery and knowledge of content are not necessarily interdependent.

II : Oral expression is an acquired skill.

26. *Statement* : Skyscrapers are coming up with a high speed in cosmopolitan cities.

Conclusions I : There is a vertical growth in cosmopoliltan cities.

II : There is a lot of speed pressure in cosmopolitan cities.

27. *Statement* : Now more and more mothers have developed positive attitude towards breast feeding.

Conclusions I : Mothers had wrong notions about breast feeding.

II : Breast feeding is proved good for mother and child both.

28. *Statement* : Of the ten fishermen caught in the seastorm, nine managed to return to the shore. Parveen has not yet returned after four days.

Conclusions I : Parveen got killed in the storm.

II : Parveen has survived the storm.

29. *Statement* : Now you don't need an import licence to own a VCR.

Conclusions I : VCRs are now manufactured indigenously.

II : VCRs are now freely permitted to be imported.

30. *Statement* : Use of cosmetics is hazardous.

Conclusions I : Cosmetics have got side effects.

II : Cosmetics are expensive.

31. *Statement* : The interview panel may select a candidate who neither possesses the desired qualifications nor the values and attributes.

Conclusions I : The inclusion of specialists on the interview panel does not guarantee that the selection will be proper.

II : The interview test has certain limitations in the matter of selection of candidates.

32. *Statement* : Although the education system has progressed from the point of view of the number of schools, most of them are ill-equipped and have not achieved excellence in imparting education.

Conclusions I : In future, we should provide good teachers and equipment to these schools.

II : We need not open any more schools in the future.

33. *Statement* : Nation 'X' faced growing international opposition for its decision to explode eight nuclear weapons at its test site.

Conclusions I : The citizens of the nation favoured the decision.

II : Some powerful countries do not want other nations to become as powerful as they are.

34. *Statement* : The Chief Minister asserted that his government will make full efforts for the upliftment of farmers and rural poor people.

Conclusions I : Previous governments have not made serious efforts for uplifting these people.

II : This government will not make full efforts for upliftment of urban poor.

35. *Statement* : State government has agreed in principle to sanction more number of posts of primary school teachers in rural and urban areas to reduce the teacher–student ratio.

Conclusions I : Student–teacher ratio in urban areas is higher than that of rural areas.

II : Student–teacher ratio in rural areas is higher than that of urban areas.

36. *Statement* : One research study reveals that childrens' personality can't be understood without a detailed study about their home environment.

Conclusions I : Teachers' as well as parents' role is equally important for the betterment of the child.

II : Schools are ignoring the importance of home atmosphere.

37. *Statement* : In India, more emphasis should be placed on areas such as agriculture, engineering and technology instead of basic and pure sciences.

Conclusions I : India has achieved sufficient progress in basic and pure sciences.

II : In the past, the productivity factor in our economy was neglected.

38. *Statement* : Multinational fast food chains have reached India with great difficulty, but the farmers' associations are not ready to accept them.

Conclusions I : Farmers' associations are opposing modernisation.

II : Farmers' associations do not wish to enter into competition with the multinationals.

39. *Statement* : In direct distribution, the company can find out the problems of consumers and get an opportunity to solve them. The consumer thus becomes a devoted buyer.

Conclusions I : Responsible companies take the advantages of direct distribution.

II : Direct distribution is the only key to success in business.

40. *Statement* : A large majority of the work force in India is unorganised. Most of them earn either the minimum or uncertain wages while others are engaged in sundry jobs.

Conclusions I : The workers in the organised sector get better facilities and stay longer in their jobs.

II : Some workers in the unorganised sector of the work force have a regular and fixed income.

41. *Statement* : The General Manager asked four managers to either submit their resignations by the next day or face termination orders from service. Three of them had submitted their resignations by that evening.

Conclusions I : The next day, the remaining manager would also resign.

II : The General Manager would terminate his services the next day.

42. *Statement* : Company X has a record of manufacturing cameras of quality and the latest design so that you do not spoil even a single shot irrespective of the weather conditions.

Conclusions I : No other company except X is reputed in the camera industry.

II : Anyone can take an acceptable shot with camera X.

43. *Statement* : The best evidence of India's glorious past is the growing popularity of *Ayurvedic* medicines in the West.

Conclusions I : Ayurvedic medicines are not popular in India.

II : Allopathic medicines are more popular in India.

44. *Statement* : From the next academic year, students will have the option of dropping Mathematics and Science for their school leaving certificate examination.

Conclusions I : Students who are weak in Science and Mathematics will be benefitted.

II : Earlier students did not have the choice of continuing their education without taking these subjects.

45. *Statement* : Good voice is a natural gift but one has to keep practising to improve and excel well in the field of music.

Conclusions I : Natural gifts need nurturing and care.

II : Even though your voice is not good, one can keep practising.

46. *Statement* : This world is neither good not evil; each man manufactures a world for himself.

Conclusions I : Some people find this world quite good.

II : Some people find this quite bad.

47. *Statement* : The Prime Minister emphatically stated that his government will make every possible effort for the unliftment of poor farmers and farmhands.

Conclusions I : Except poor farmers and farmhands, all others have got benefits of fruits of development.

II : No serious efforts have been made in the past for upliftment of any section of the society.

48. *Statement* : The party president has directed that no member of the party will give press briefing or interviews to government and private T.V. channels about the discussion in scheduled meeting of the party.

Conclusions I : Party members will observe

this directive of the president.

II : The general public will not come to know about the happenings in the scheduled meeting of the party.

49. *Statement* : While presenting a stage show recently, the famous actor declared that he has a practice of either taking full payment or none for his stage show.

Conclusions I : The actor has taken full payment for his recent stage show.

II : The actor did not take any money for his recent stage show.

50. *Statement* : The national norm is 100 beds per thousand population but in this State, 150 beds per thousand are available in the hospitals.

Conclusions I : Our national norm is appropriate.

II : The State's health system is taking adequate care in this regard.

EXPLANATORY ANSWERS

1. *(a)* : Only conclusion I follows. Conclusion II is not confirmed by the given statement.

2. *(a)* : Conclusion I definitely follows. Conclusion II is not confirmed by the given statement.

3. *(b)* : Only conclusion II follows. Conclusion I cannot be drawn from the given statement.

4. *(b)* : Only conclusion II follows. Conclusion I is wrong as rains are the cause of thunder.

5. *(e)* : Both conclusion I and conclusion II follow from the statements as the doctors who are heavy smokers indicate that they do not regard smoking as injurious and thus, cannot advise people not to smoke.

6. *(e)* : Both conclusions I and II follow from the statement as involvement of workers boosts production and benefits the companies.

7. *(b)* : Only conclusion II follows. Conclusion I is not related the statement.

8. *(d)* : Neither conclusion I nor conclusion II follows. Both the conclusions are unrelated to the statement.

9. *(b)* : Only conclusion II follows. Conclusion I is not related to the statement.

10. *(e)* : Both conclusion I and conclusion II follow.

11. *(a)* : Only conclusion I follows. Conclusion II is not related to the statement.

12. *(e)* : Both conclusion I and conclusion II follow as people who talk too much often do not practise what they say.

13. *(d)* : Neither conclusion I nor conclusion II is confirmed by the statement.

14. *(d)* : Neither conclusion I nor conclusion II follows as the precentage of unemployment in each state is not mentioned.

15. *(b)* : Only conclusion II follows. Conclusion I runs counter to the statement as a system is necessary.

16. *(d)* : Neither conclusion I nor conclusion II is confirmed by the statement.

17. *(b)* : Only conclusion II follows as the data of every chocolate brand shows the comparision of Amul chocolates with other brands. Coclusion I is not confirmed by the statement.

18. *(a)* : Only conclusion I follows. Conclusion II is not related to the statement.

19. *(d)* : Neither conclusion I, nor conclusion II follows; both the conclusions are unrelated.

20. *(b)* : Only conclusion II follows, because the Supreme Court judgement must have come in such a case and not in vaccum.

21. *(e)* : Both conclusion I and conclusion II follow as the statement presupposes better results with merit and contradiction between merit and representation.

22. *(b)* : The conclusion I runs counter to the facts mentioned in the statement. Only conclusion II follows.

23. *(b)* : The conclusion I is not confirmed by the statement. Only conclusion II follows.

24. *(d)* : Neither conclusion I nor conclusion II definitely follows from the statement.

25. *(a)* : Only conclusion I follows. Conclusion II is not related to the statement.

26. *(e)* : Appearance of skycrapers in cosmopolitan cities is the manifestation of space pressure in vertical growth. Thus both conclusion I and II follow.

27. *(e)* : Both conclusion I and conclusion II follow.

28. *(c)* : It is not certian if Parveen is killed in the storm or has survived the storm. Thus, either conclusion I or conclusion II follows from the statement.

29. *(b)* : Conclusion II alone follows from the statement. Conclusion I relates the indigenous production of VCRs. It is not related to the statement.

30. *(a)* : Only conclusion I follows definitely from the statement. Conclusion II is not related to the statement.

31. *(e)* : Both conclusion I and conclusion II follow considering the decision of the interview pannel.

32. *(a)* : Only conclusion I follows. Conclusion II is not related to the statement.

33. *(d)* : Neither conclusion I nor conclusion II can be drawn from the given statement.

34. *(d)* : Nothing is said about the previous governments or that the urban poor will be ignored. So, neither conclusion I nor conclusion II follows.

35. *(d)* : Figures of student-teacher relation in urban and rural areas is not given. So, neither conclusion I nor conclusion II follows.

36. *(a)* : Conclusion I definitely follows from the statement. Conclusion II is not confirmed.

37. *(b)* : Emphasis is the need of the time. Only conclusion II follows.

38. *(b)* : Conclusion I is generalised. Only conclusion II follows.

39. *(a)* : Only conclusion I follows. Conclusion II is assumed from the statement.

40. *(b)* : Conclusion I is not confirmed but conclusion II follows.

41. *(c)* : Either conclusion I or conclusion II follows. Either the General Manager will take action or the managers will resign.

42. *(b)* : Conclusion II definitely follows from the given statement. Facts of other companies are not given.

43. *(d)* : The statement indicates that Ayurvedic medicines were popular even in the past, and nothing is said about allopathic medicines. So, neither conclusion I nor conclusion II follows.

44. *(e)* : Both conclusion I and conclusion II definitely follow from the given statement.

45. *(a)* : The statement is about 'natural gifts'. So only conclusion I follows.

46. *(e)* : Both conclusion I and conclusion II follow.

47. *(d)* : The statement does not clarify that all others were benefitted or no efforts were made, earlier. So, neither conclusion I nor conclusion II follows.

48. *(e)* : Both conclusion I and conclusion II follow from the given statement.

49. *(c)* : The statement suggests that the actor either takes full payments or none. So, either conclusion I or conclusion II necessarily follows.

50. *(b)* : Conclusion I is not confirmed by the statement. Conclusion II follows from the statement as the state norms provide more beds than the national norms.

PART - V

DRAWING SYMBOLIC CONCLUSIONS

This type of reasoning pattern is a new concept in competitive examinations. Instead of sentences mathematical expressions are used. After understanding the symbols and their meanings one has to attempt the questions and select the best conclusion(s) which follows from the groups of given statements.

SOLVED EXAMPLES

Directions (Qs. 1 to 5) : *In the following questions, the symbols @, $\underset{=}{@}$, =, * and $\underset{=}{*}$ are used with the following meanings :*

'P @ Q' means 'P is greater than Q'

'P $\underset{=}{@}$ Q' means 'P is either greater than or equal to Q'

'P = Q' means 'P is equal to Q'

'P * Q' means 'P is smaller than Q'

'P $\underset{=}{*}$ Q' means 'P is either smaller than or equal to Q'

Now in each of the following questions, assuming the given statements to be true, it is to be found that which of the two conclusions I and II given below them is/are definitely true?

Answer is given as—

(*a*) If only conclusion I is true;
(*b*) If only conclusion II is true;
(*c*) If either I or II is true;
(*d*) If neither I nor II is true;
(*e*) If both I and II are true.

1. *Statement* : D @ F, F = S, S $\underset{=}{*}$ M
Conclusions : *I.* D @ M *II.* F @ M
Ans. (*d*) : Given : $D > F, F = S, S \leq M$
$\therefore F \leq M$
Neither of the conclusions is true.

2. *Statement* : P @ T, M $\underset{=}{*}$ K, T = K
Conclusions : *I.* T @ M *II.* T = M
Ans. (*c*) : $P > T, M \leq K, T = K$
$\therefore T \geq M \Rightarrow$ Either conclusion I or II is true.

3. *Statement* : J = V, V * N, R $\underset{=}{*}$ J
Conclusions : *I.* R * N *II.* J $\underset{=}{@}$ N
Ans. (*a*) : Given : $J = V, V < N, R \leq J$
$\Rightarrow J < N, R \leq J$
$\therefore R < N \Rightarrow$ Conclusion I is true.

4. *Statement* : S * M, M @ L, L $\underset{=}{@}$ Z

Conclusions : *I.* S = Z *II.* $S \overset{*}{=} L$

Ans. *(d)* : Given S < M, M > L, L ≥ Z

Both conclusions I and II are not true.

5. *Statement* : L $\underset{=}{@}$ U, C * L, C @ B

Conclusions : *I.* U = C *II.* L @ B

Ans. *(b)* : Given : L ≥ U, C < L, C > B

⇒ L > C > B ⇒ L > B

Conclusion II is true.

EXERCISE

Now in each of the following questions assuming the given statements to be true, find which of the two conclusions I and II given below them is/are definitely true?

Give answer—

(a) if only conclusion I is true.
(b) if only conclusion II is true.
(c) if either I or II is true.
(d) if neither I nor II is true.
(e) if both I and II are true.

Directions (Qs. 1 to 5) : *In the following questions, the symbols* ⊕, $\underline{\oplus}$, =, @ *and* $\underline{@}$ *are used with the following meanings :*

P ⊕ Q means P is greater than Q.

P $\underline{\oplus}$ Q means P is either greater than or equal to Q.

P = Q means P is equal to Q.

P @ Q means P is smaller than Q.

P $\underline{@}$ Q means P is either smaller than or equal to Q.

1. *Statements* : P = M, K @ P, S ⊕ K
Conclusions : *I.* S ⊕ M *II.* S @ M

2. *Statements* : T $\underline{\oplus}$ J, F ⊕ T, J ⊕ O
Conclusions : *I.* F ⊕ J *II.* O @ T

3. *Statements* : E $\underline{@}$ G, H $\underline{\oplus}$ D, E @ D
Conclusions : *I.* H ⊕ E *II.* D ⊕ G

4. *Statements* : T = U, R $\underline{@}$ P, P $\underline{@}$ T
Conclusions : *I.* R = U *II.* R @ U

5. *Statements* : L $\underline{\oplus}$ B, N $\underline{@}$ C, B @ N
Conclusions : *I.* L ⊕ N *II.* C ⊕ B

Directions (Qs. 6 to 10) : *In the following questions the symbol* @, $\underline{@}$, =, © *and* $\underline{©}$ *are used with the following meanings :*

P @ Q means P is greater than Q.

P $\underline{@}$ Q means P is either greater than or equal to Q.

P = Q means P is equal to Q.

P © Q means P is smaller than Q.

P $\underline{©}$ Q means P is either smaller than or equal to Q.

6. *Statements* : H $\underline{@}$ G, D @ E, H = E
Conclusions : *I.* D @ H *II.* G © D

7. *Statements* : L $\underline{@}$ N, J $\underline{©}$ P, P $\underline{@}$ L
Conclusions : *I.* J = L *II.* P = N

8. *Statements* : B @ V, K © C, C $\underline{©}$ B
Conclusions : *I.* V @ C *II.* B @ K

9. *Statements* : K @ T, S = K, T $\underline{©}$ R
Conclusions : *I.* S @ R *II.* T = R

10. *Statements* : U = M, P $\underline{@}$ U, M $\underline{@}$ B
Conclusions : *I.* P = B *II.* P @ B

Directions (Qs. 11 to 15) : *In the following questions, the symbols* *, $\overset{*}{=}$, =, @ *and* $\underset{=}{@}$ *are used with the following meanings :*

A * B means A is greater than B,

A $\overset{*}{=}$ B means A is either greater than or equal to B.

A = B means A is equal to B.

A @ B means A is smaller than B and

A $\underset{=}{@}$ B means A is either smaller than or equal to B.

11. *Statements* : T $\overset{*}{=}$ P, P @ S, P = M
Conclusions : *I.* S * M *II.* T @ S

12. *Statements* : R $\underset{=}{@}$ M, M * P, R $\overset{*}{=}$ L
Conclusions : *I.* M = L *II.* P = L

13. *Statements* : M = T, T $\underset{=}{@}$ Z, S * M
Conclusions : *I.* Z * M *II.* Z = M

14. *Statements* : L @ C, C * Z, Z $\underset{=}{@}$ F
Conclusions : *I.* C * F *II.* F = C

15. *Statements* : Z @ B, N $\overset{*}{=}$ S, B @ N
Conclusions : *I.* B = Z *II.* S $\underset{=}{@}$ B

Directions (Qs. 16 to 20) : *In the following question the symbol @, $\underset{=}{@}$, =, □ and $\underline{\square}$ used with the following meanings :*

P @ Q means P is greater than Q.

P $\underset{=}{@}$ Q means P is either greater than or equal to Q.

P = Q means P is equal to Q.

P □ Q means P is smaller than Q.

P $\underline{\square}$ Q means P is either smaller than or equal to Q.

16. *Statements* : H @ W, W $\underline{\square}$ S, M @ S
Conclusions : *I.* M = H *II.* M @ H

17. *Statements* : M @ N, N $\underline{\square}$ T, T = P
Conclusions : *I.* P @ N *II.* P = N

18. *Statements* : M = N, N @ B, B □ P
Conclusions : *I.* P = N *II.* B □ M

19. *Statements* : P $\underline{\square}$ Q, Q $\underline{\square}$ R, T $\underline{\square}$ Q
Conclusions : *I.* R @ T *II.* R @ P

20. *Statements* : G $\underline{\square}$ S, F @ S, T □ G
Conclusions : *I.* F @ T *II.* T = S

Directions (Qs. 21 to 25) : *In the following questions, the symbols #, %, @, © and δ are used with the following meanings illustrated:*

'P % Q' means 'P is not greater than Q'.

'P δ Q' means 'P is not smaller than Q'

'P © Q' means 'P is neither equal to nor smaller than Q'.

'P @ Q' means 'P is neither smaller than nor greater than Q'.

In each questions, three statements showing relationships have been given, which are followed by three conclusions I, II & III. Assuming that the given statements are true, find out which conclusion(s) is/are definitely true.

21. *Statements* : M © K, K δ T, T © J
Conclusions : *I.* J # K, *II.* T # M,
III. M # J
(*a*) None is true
(*b*) Only I is true
(*c*) Only II is true
(*d*) Only III is true
(*e*) Only II and III are true

22. *Statements* : J δ H, H @ B, B % N
Conclusions : *I.* N δ H, *II.* N @ J,
III. J δ B
(*a*) Only I and II are true
(*b*) Only II and III are true
(*c*) Only I and III are true
(*d*) All are true
(*e*) None of these

23. *Statements* : B # T, T © K, K % M
Conclusions : *I.* K # B, *II.* M # T,
III. B # M
(*a*) Only I is true
(*b*) Only II is true
(*c*) Only III is true
(*d*) Only II and III are true
(*e*) None of these

24. *Statements* : D % F, F δ K, K @ R
Conclusions : *I.* R % F, *II.* R % D,
III. R @ D
(*a*) Only I is true
(*b*) Only II is true
(*c*) Only III is true
(*d*) Only I and II are true
(*e*) None of these

25. *Statements* : W © M, M % F, D # F
Conclusions : *I.* D # M, *II.* W © F,
III. W © D
(*a*) Only I is true
(*b*) Only I and II are true
(*c*) Only II and III are true
(*d*) Only I and III are true
(*e*) All are true

Directions (Qs. 26 to 30) : *In the following questions the symbols, +, →, @, ⇒ and = are used with the following meanings :*

+ means *greater than*

→ means either greater than or equal to

@ means smaller than

⇒ mean smaller than or equal to and

= means equal to.

26. *Statements* : Z @ P, T = M, M → Z
Conclusions : *I.* M + Z *II.* T + P

27. *Statements* : B ⇒ P, C + N, P = N
Conclusions : *I.* P @ C *II.* C + B

28. *Statements* : M ⇒ N, L + N, M = P
Conclusions : *I.* N = P *II.* N @ P

29. *Statements* : A ⇒ C, M ⇒ F, C + F
Conclusions : *I.* M = A *II.* C + M

30. *Statements* : K @ P, Z + K, K → M
Conclusions : *I.* Z = M *II.* Z + M

Directions (Qs. 31 to 35) : *In the following questions, the symbols ©, *, = @, ← are used as follows :*

A © B means A is greater than B.
A * B means A is either greater than or equal to B.
A = B means A is equal to B.
A @ B means A is smaller than B.
A ← B means A is either smaller than or equal to B.

31. *Statements* : P @ Q, Q © K, K @ M
Conclusions : *I.* M = Q *II.* M © Q

32. *Statements* : P * F, M ← F, F © N
Conclusions : *I.* M = P *II.* M @ P

33. *Statements* : Q @ R, R @ M, M © D
Conclusions : *I.* D © R *II.* D © Q

34. *Statements* : M @ K, K © R, R © P
Conclusions : *I.* P @ K *II.* P @ M

35. *Statements* : T © M, M = P, P © R
Conclusions : *I.* P @ T *II.* T © R

EXPLANATORY ANSWERS

1. *(d)* : $P = M, K < P, S > K$
$\Rightarrow K < M, K < S$

2. *(e)* : $T \geq J, F > T, J > O$
$\Rightarrow F > J > O$
$\Rightarrow F > J \;\&\; O < J$
$\Rightarrow T \geq J > O$
$\Rightarrow T > O$

3. *(a)* : $E \leq G, H \geq D; E < D$
$\Rightarrow H > E$

4. *(c)* : $T = U, R \leq P, P \leq T$
$\Rightarrow R \leq U$

5. *(b)* : $L \geq B, N \leq C, B < N$
$\Rightarrow B < C \Rightarrow C > B \Rightarrow$ II

6. *(e)* : $H \geq G, D > E, H = E$
$\Rightarrow D > H,$
$\Rightarrow H \geq G, E \geq G$
$\Rightarrow D > G \Rightarrow G < D$

7. *(d)* : $L \geq N, J \leq P, P \geq L$
Hence, both conclusions are false.

8. *(b)* : $B > V, K < C, C \leq B$
$\therefore K < C, C \leq B \Rightarrow K < B$
$\Rightarrow B > K \Rightarrow$ Conclusion II is true.

9. *(d)* : $K > T, S = K, T \leq R$
from these relations both conclusions are false.

10. *(c)* : $U = M, P \geq U, M \geq B$
$\Rightarrow P \geq M, M \geq B \Rightarrow P \geq B$
$\Rightarrow$ Either conclusion I or II is true.

11. *(a)* : $T \geq P, P < S, P = M$
$\therefore S > M$

12. *(d)* : $R \leq M, M > P, R \geq L$
$\therefore L \leq R \leq M$

13. *(c)* : $M = T, T \leq Z, S > M$
If $T = Z$, then $Z = M$
If $T < Z$, then $Z > M$

14. *(d)* : $L < C, C > Z, Z \leq F$
Hence, both conclusions are false.

15. *(d)* : $Z < B, N \geq S, B < N$
Hence, both conclusions are false.

16. *(d)* : $H > W, W \leq S, M > S$
$\Rightarrow H > W, S \geq W, M > S$
$\Rightarrow H > W, M > S, S \geq W$
No relationship can be established between M and H.

17. *(c)* : $M > N, N \leq T, T = P$
$\Rightarrow M > N, T \geq N, T = P$
$T = P \geq N$

18. *(b)* : $M = N, N > B, B < P$
$\Rightarrow M = N > B$
$\& P > B$

19. *(d)* : $P \leq Q, Q \leq R, T \leq Q$
$\Rightarrow P \leq Q \leq R, T \leq Q \leq R$
I. $R > T$ may/may not be true.
II. $R > P$ may/may not be true.

20. (a) : $G \le S, F > S, T < G$
$\Rightarrow F > S \ge G > T$
I. $F > T$ is true.
II. $T = S$ is not true.

21. (a) : $M © K \Rightarrow M < K$
$K \delta T \Rightarrow K \ge T$
$T © J \Rightarrow T < J$
I. $J \# K \Rightarrow J > K$ (false)
II. $T \# M \Rightarrow T > M$ (false)
III. $M \# J \Rightarrow M > J$ (false)

22. (c) : $J \delta H \Rightarrow J \ge H$
$H @ B \Rightarrow H = B$
$B \% N \Rightarrow B \le N$
$\Rightarrow J \ge H = B \le N$
I. $N \delta H \Rightarrow N \ge H$ (true)
II. $N @ J \Rightarrow N = J$ (false)
III. $J \delta B \Rightarrow J \ge B$ (true)

23. (b) : $B \# T \Rightarrow B > T$
$T © K \Rightarrow T < K$
$K \% M \Rightarrow K \le M$
$B > T < K \le M$
I. $K \# B \Rightarrow K > B$ (false)
II. $M \# T \Rightarrow M > T$ (true)
III. $B \# M \Rightarrow B > M$ (false)

24. (a) : $D \% F \Rightarrow D \le F$
$F \delta K \Rightarrow F \ge K$
$K @ R \Rightarrow K = R$
$\Rightarrow D \le F \ge K = R$
I. $R \% F \Rightarrow R \le F$ (true)
II. $R \% D \Rightarrow R \le D$ (false)
III. $R @ D \Rightarrow R = D$ (false)

25. (e) : $W © M \Rightarrow W < M$
$M \% F \Rightarrow M \le F$
$D \# F \Rightarrow D > F$
$\Rightarrow W < M \le F < D$
I. $D \# M \Rightarrow D > M$ (true)
II. $W © F \Rightarrow W < F$ (true)
III. $W © D \Rightarrow W < D$ (true)

26. (d) : $Z < P, T = M, M \ge Z$
So, $M \ge Z$, or $T \ge Z$ and $P > Z$
As $M \ge Z$, it cannot be said that $M > Z$ is valid. As there is no relationship between T and P, it cannot be said whether $T > P$ or not. So, neither I nor II is true.

27. (e) : $B \le P, C > N, P = N$
From statements (1), (2), (3)
$\Rightarrow C > N \ge B$ or $C > B$ (Conclusion II)
From statements (2) and (3) $\Rightarrow C > P$
or, $P < C$ (Conclusion I)

28. (d) : $M \le N, L > N, M = P$
From the three statements $\Rightarrow P \le N < L$.
Or $P \le N$. Thus neither I nor II, *i.e.*, $P = N$ or $P > N$ should be correct.

29. (b) : $A \le C, M \le F, C > F$
From statements (2) and (3)
$\Rightarrow C > F \ge M$ and $C \ge A$
Thus only (II) is correct.

30. (b) : $K < P, Z > K, K \ge M$
From statements (2) and (3) $\Rightarrow Z > K \ge M$ and $P > K$ (from statement I)
$Z > K \ge M \Rightarrow Z > M$
As $Z > M$, it cannot be equal to M.
Thus II is valid.

31. (d) : $P @ Q \Rightarrow P < Q$
$Q © K \Rightarrow Q > K$
$K @ M \Rightarrow K < M$

32. (c) : $P * F \Rightarrow P \ge F$
$M \leftarrow F \Rightarrow M \le F$
$F © N \Rightarrow F > N$
from statements (1) and (2),
$P \ge F \ge M$
$\Rightarrow P > M$ or $P = M$

33. (d) : $Q @ R \Rightarrow Q < R$
$R @ M \Rightarrow R < M$
$M © D \Rightarrow M > D$

34. (a) : $M @ K \Rightarrow M < K$
$K © R \Rightarrow K > R$
$R © P \Rightarrow R > P$
$\therefore K > M$ and $K > P$
i.e., $P < K$, *i.e.*, $P @ K$

35. (e) : $T © M \Rightarrow T > M, M = P$
$P © R \Rightarrow P > R$
$\therefore T > P > R \Rightarrow T > R \Rightarrow T © R$
Also $T > M \Rightarrow P < T \Rightarrow P @ T$

PART - VI

DRAWING ASSUMPTIONS

In this type of reasoning a statement is given and assumptions are drawn from it. An assumption is something assumed, supposed and taken for granted. The implicity of the two assumptions is in question. The implication means the hidden meaning, something which is derived from and as such based upon the statement.

SOLVED EXAMPLES

In the questions below the answer is given as :

(a) If only assumption I is implicit.
(b) If only assumption II is implicit.
(c) If either I or II is implicit.
(d) If neither I nor II is implicit.
(e) If both I and II are implicit.

1. *Statement* : The integrated steel plants in India would no longer have to depend on imports for continuous casting refractories.

Assumptions I : Continuous casting refractories are needed by India.

II : Continuous casting refractories are in demand.

Ans. ***(e)*** **:** Both assumption I and II are implicit in the statement. According to the statement India is self–sufficient in continuous casting refractories and as such needed in the country. Continuous casting refractories are in demand as they are needed in integrated steel plants.

2. *Statement* : Education and social change are complementary; and leads to a steady loss of tradition on people's mind.

Assumptions I : There is a direct relationship between education and social change and decline of tradition on people's mind.

II : Traditions can make priceless contribution to society.

Ans. ***(a)*** **:** Only assumption I is implicit in the given statement. Assumption II is a generalised conclusion.

EXERCISE

Directions : *In each question below is given a statement followed by two assumptions numbered I and II. An assumption is something supposed or taken for granted. You have to consider the statement and the following assumptions and decide which of the assumptions is implicit in the statement. Give answer—*

(a) If assumption I is implicit.
(b) If assumption II is implicit.
(c) If either I or II is implicit.
(d) If neither I nor II is implicit.
(e) If both I and II are implicit.

1. *Statement* : Apart from the entertainment value of television, its educational value cannot be ignored.

Assumptions I : People take the television to be means of entertainment only.

II : The educational value of television is not realised properly.

2. *Statement* : Ten candidates who were on the waiting list could finally be admitted to the course.

Assumptions I : Wait-listed candidates get admission with difficulty.

II : A large number of candidates were on the waiting list.

3. *Statement* : In Mumbai, railway trains are indispensable for people in the suburbs to reach their places of work on time.

Assumptions I : Railway trains are the only mode of transport available in the suburbs of Mumbai.

II : Only railway trains run punctually.

4. *Statement* : The mangoes are too cheap to be good.

Assumptions I : When the mango crop is abundant, the prices go down.

II : The lower the selling price, the inferior is the quality of the commodity.

5. *Statement* : Of all the newspapers published in Delhi, 'The Time and Space' has the largest number of readers.

Assumptions I : Volume of readership of all the newspapers in Delhi is known.

II : No newspaper in Delhi other than 'The Time and Space' has large readership.

6. *Statement* : 'Smoking Prohibited'. A notice in a railway compartment.

Assumptions I : Some persons like to smoke in the compartment.

II : Some persons smoke in the compartment.

7. *Statement* : A friend in need is a friend indeed.

Assumptions I : Relatives are of no help in difficult circumstances.

II : Taking help from a friend is desirable.

8. *Statement* : When in Chennai, stay at Hotel 'X' for comfort and good service, because my best friend has recommended it.

Assumptions I : My best friend is trustworthy.

II : Comfort and good service cannot be expected from all hotels.

9. *Statement* : A friend in need is a friend indeed.

Assumptions I : A person needs help from others on certain occasions.

II : A friend is expected to help when needed.

10. *Statement* : 'Smoking Prohibited.' A notice in a railway compartment.

Assumptions I : Generally, people expect a notice.

II : Smoking is injurious to health.

11. *Statement* : If you have the expertise, we have the job for you.

Assumptions I : You have the expertise.

II : We need a person with expertise.

12. *Statement* : Government has permitted private doctors to increase their fees.

Assumptions I : Private doctors are in financial difficulties.

II : Government doctors do not need to increase fees.

13. *Statement* : Opening a post office in Khabli is wasteful.

Assumptions I : Inhabitants of Khabli never need post office.

II : There is an adequate number of post offices in Khabli.

14. *Statement* : Buy shack—the TV with ten year's gaurantée.

Assumptions I : People are attracted by longer period of guarantee.

II : People want to buy TVs.

15. *Statement* : Crime will be severely punished.

Assumptions I : Fear of punishment will reduce crime.

II : Criminals are afraid of punishment.

16. *Statement* : A system of moral values is indispensable to group living.

Assumptions I : No society can survive without a moral order.

II : A congenial atmosphere is to be created both at home and school to make the child feel morally secure.

17. *Statement* : Only when human civilization reaches perfection, one could expect many people to use leisure intelligently.

Assumptions I : As civilization progresses, there will be more leisure for more number of people.

II : Most people would prefer being told what to do.

18. *Statement* : If he is a sincere worker, he will soon get a raise.

Assumptions I : He is a sincere worker.

II : The sincerity in job pays.

19. *Statement* : Educational and economic advancement leads to a steady loss of the hold of religion on people's mind.

Assumptions I : There is direct relation between economic progress & decline of religion.

II : Religion can make priceless contribution to society.

20. *Statement* : Go by aeroplane to reach Bangalore from Mumbai quickly.

Assumptions I : Mumbai and Bangalore are connected by aeroplane service.

II : There is no other means of going from Mumbai to Bangalore.

21. *Statement* : I have written several letters to the Branch Manager regarding my account in the bank but did not receive any reply so for.

Assumptions I : Branch Manager is expected to read letters received from the customer.

II : Branch Manager is expected to reply to the letters received from the customer.

22. *Statement* : Shri Roy, retired IAS official, has taken over as the new Director of the All India Nuclear Research Institute. It is now expected that the administration of the institute will improve.

Assumptions I : The Institute had no Director before Shri Roy.

II : Director is supposed to look after the administration of the Institute.

23. *Statement* : The cotton crop continues to be poor even after the introduction of improved variety of cotton seeds.

Assumptions I : The yield of cotton was expected to increase after introduction of improved variety of seeds.

II : The yield of cotton was adequate before the introduction of new variety of seeds.

24. *Statement* : No budgetary provision for the purpose of appointing additional faculty would be made in the context of institute's changed financial priorities.

Assumptions I : Appointment of faculty requires funds.

II : There are areas other than appointment of faculty which require more financial attention.

25. *Statement* : The office building needs repairing just as urgently as it needs internal as well as external painting.

Assumptions I : Efficiency of people working in the office cannot be improved unless office building is repaired.

II : Repairing and painting of office building require funds.

26. *Statement* : All the employees are notified that the organisation will provide transport facilities at half cost from the nearby railway station to the office except those who have been provided with travelling allowances.

Assumptions I : Most of the employees will travel by the office transport.

II : Those who are provided with travelling allowance will not read such notice.

27. *Statement* : Incentives must be given to strengthen the motivation of the employees.

Assumptions I : Incentives are expected to motivate the employees.

II : Employees at present are not motivated.

28. *Statement* : Despite heavy rains traffic has not been disturbed.

Assumptions I : Rains do not affect traffic movement.

II : Adequate precautions were taken for traffic management during rainy season.

29. *Statement* : Interview conducted for selecting people for jobs should measure personality characteristics of candidates.

Assumptions I : Performance on the job depends on personality characteristics.

II : Personality characteristics can be measured in interview.

30. *Statement* : An opportunity to carry out reforms in elections to the Parliament and State Legislatures has been lost when we rejected most of the recommendations of Goswami Committee for partisan reasons.

Assumptions I : Goswami Committee made certain good recommendations to improve the existing election system.

II : Most of the decisions in our country are taken with partisan considerations.

31. *Statement* : Many historians have done more harm than good by distorting truth.

Assumptions I : People believe what is reported by the historians.

II : Historians are seldom expected to depict the truth.

32. *Statement* : In order to achieve optimum industrial growth, the State Government should provide the necessary infrastructural facilities to the entrepreneurs.

Assumptions I : The entrepreneurs are in need of infrastructural facilities.

II : The State Government has failed to provide such facilities in the past.

33. *Statement* : The civic authority appealed to the people for reduction in usage of water as there may be an acute shortage during the coming weeks.

Assumptions I : There will be no rain in recent future.

II : The people are ready to follow the advice of the civic authority.

34. *Statement* : Prabhat purchased a book for giving as a present to his friend on his birthday.

Assumptions I : Prabhat will be invited by his friend on his birthday.

II : Prabhat's friend may not have this particular book.

35. *Statement* : The government, through a notification has banned smoking in public places.

Assumptions I : People should abide by the notification.

II : The message in the notification will reach general public.

36. *Statement* : It is not always true that adoption of sophisticated technology increases production efficiency..

Assumptions I : Adoption of sophisticated technology is not a difficult thing to achieve.

II : Production and efficiency can be increased by getting rid of sophisticated technology.

37. *Statement* : Government should deploy army to rehabilitate the people displaced due to earthquake.

Assumptions I : Army should be entrusted with activities other than war to give them enough exposure.

II : Rehabilitation of earthquake victims is obligatory for the Government.

38. *Statement* : "Wanted a two bedroom–hall–kitchen flat in the college area"—an advertisement.

Assumptions I : Landlords generally respond to such advertisements.

II : Flats may be available in the college area.

39. *Statement* : The president of the club informed its members that to run the club efficiently, there is an urgent need to raise its resources by voluntary contribution.

Assumptions I : The president's message will be accepted by the members.

II : The members are capable of making voluntary contributions.

40. *Statement* : If you do not get desired response to your fund-raising campaign through the routine advertisements, appeal to the public's regional sentiments.

Assumptions I : People in general nurture regional sentiments.

II : Nobody bothers to read advertisements in the newspapers.

41. *Statement* : "You take care yourself we will take care of your money, save with us—an advertisement from a Bank.

Assumptions I : People read advertisements.

II : Catchy slogans appeal to people.

42. *Statement* : Increase the rate, if you want to save the company.

Assumptions I : The company is in trouble.

II : The product wll be sold with increased rate.

43. *Statement* : "Do not lean out of the moving trains"—A warning.

Assumptions I : Such warning will have some effect.

II : Leaning out from a moving train is more dangerous than from a moving bus.

44. *Statement* : Bajaj is the only moped which you would purchase when you are ready to.

Assumptions I : Bajaj is an excellent moped.

II : People go in for an excellent moped.

45. *Statement* : If you are a graphic artist, we have a challenging job for you.

Assumptions I : You are a graphic artist.

II : We need a graphic artist.

46. *Statement* : Use 'Z' tubes which have 10 years longer life to any other.

Assumptions I : People prefer only those tubes which are durable.

II : Other tubes are not durable.

47. *Statement* : You know that your suit is excellent when people ask about your tailor who tailored the suit.

Assumptions I : People do not ask about your tailor if your suit is not good.

II : People want to know the criterion of an excellent suit.

48. *Statement* : The successful man has the ability to judge himself correctly.

Assumptions I : To judge others is of no use to a successful man.

II : The successful man cannot make a wrong judgement.

49. *Statement* : In Calcutta, railway trains are indispensable for people in the suburbs to reach their places of work in time.

Assumptions I : Only railway trains run punctually.

II : Railway trains are the only mode of transport available in the suburbs of Calcutta.

50. *Statement* : Everybody loves reading 'Novels'.

Assumptions I : Novels are only for reading.

II : No body loves reading of any other material.

EXPLANATORY ANSWERS

1. *(e)* : Both assumptions I and II are implicit.

2. *(a)* : Assumption II is not implicit in the statement. Only assumption I is implicit.

3. *(d)* : Neither assumption I nor assumption II is implicit in the statement.

4. *(b)* : Assumption I is not implicit in the statement, because it states the principle of supply and prices. Only assumption II is implicit which states the principle of price-quality parity.

5. *(a)* : Assumption I is implicit in the statement because the largest readership may be established only if the volume of readership of all the newspapers is known.

6. *(b)* : Assumption II suggests that some persons smoke in the compartment. 'Smoking Prohibited' is the notice for those persons.

7. *(d)* : The statement highlights the criterion of a true friend.

8. *(e)* : Both assumptions I and II are implicit because *(i)* the advice is from a trustworthy best friend, and *(ii)* all hotels cannot provide comfort and good service.

9. *(b)* : Only assumption II is implicit because only a true friend helps in need.

10. *(d)* : None of the assumptions is implicit. The statement does not imply that people expect a notice or smoking is injurious to health.

11. *(b)* : Only assumption II is implicit.

12. *(d)* : None of the assumptions is implicit. Permitting the private doctors to increase their fees may be due to many factors, and not necessarily the financial difficulty of the doctors.

13. *(e)* : Both the assumption I and assumption II are implicit.

14. *(a)* : Only assumption I is implicit. A longer period of guarantee is naturally an attraction.

15. *(e)* : Both the assumptions are implicit.

16. *(a)* : Assumption II is not related to group living or society.

17. *(e)* : Both assumptions I and II are implicit because they relate to civilization having made progress.

18. *(b)* : Sincerity in job pays is clearly implicit in the statement.

19. *(a)* : Assumption I is clearly implicit in the statement as with economic progress people pay better attention to religion.

20. *(a)* : Only assumption I is implicit. One can

not go to Bangalore from Mumbai unless there is an air service connecting the two cities. Assumption II is not implicit because other means of transport between the two cities may take longer time.

21. ***(e)*** **:** Both assumptions I and II are implicit as the correspondence is directed to the Branch Manager.

22. ***(b)*** **:** Assumption II is implicit. Assumption I is not implicit as Shri Roy has taken over the post as the new Director.

23. ***(a)*** **:** Only assumption I is implicit. Assumption II runs counter to the fact in given statement.

24. ***(e)*** **:** Both assumptions I and II are implicit.

25. ***(d)*** **:** Neither assumption I nor assumption II is implicit in the statement.

26. ***(d)*** **:** Neither assumption I nor assumption II is implicit in the statement.

27. ***(e)*** **:** Both assumptions I and II are implicit.

28. ***(b)*** **:** Assumption I is not implicit as rains do affect traffic movement. Only assumption II is implicit in the statement.

29. ***(e)*** **:** Both assumptions I and II are implicit as performance and personality characteristics are taken into consideration in an interview.

30. ***(a)*** **:** Only assumption I is implicit. Assumption II is not related to the statement.

31. ***(a)*** **:** Only assumption I is implicit as historians have made people believe in what they have written. Assumption II is not implicit in the statement.

32. ***(e)*** **:** Both assumptions I and II are implicit in the statement.

33. ***(b)*** **:** Only assumption II is implicit. Assumption II is not related to the statement.

34. ***(e)*** **:** Both assumptions I and II are implicit. Prabhat bought a book which his friend does not have and he shall give it to his friend when invited to the party.

35. ***(e)*** **:** Both assumptions I and II are implicit as the message must reach the people who should then abide by it.

36. ***(d)*** **:** Neither assumption I nor assumption II is implicit. Both assumptions reflect ideas different from what is given in the statement.

37. ***(b)*** **:** Assumption I is not implicit as the statement is the need of urgency and the action of the government to help the earthquake victims. Only assumption II is implicit.

38. ***(e)*** **:** Both assumption I and assumption II are implicit in the statement as landlords often watch out for such advertisement to rent their property and also there is a demand for flats is college area.

39. ***(b)*** **:** Assumption I is not drawn from the statement. Assumption II is implicit as efficient members are capable and can make voluntary contributions to the club.

40. ***(a)*** **:** Assumption I is implicit in the statement. Assumption II is not implicit as certain people do read such advertisements.

41. ***(e)*** **:** Both assumptions I and II are implicit. People read advertisements, and catchy slogans attract people.

42. ***(a)*** **:** Only assumption I is implicit. Company is in trouble and so the rate should be increased. Nothing is said about the selling of product.

43. ***(a)*** **:** Only assumption I is implicit. Warnings always have some effect. The comparison of danger is baseless.

44. ***(e)*** **:** Both assumption I and assumption II are implicit. The statement conveys that Bajaj is an excellent product and people go in for excellent products.

45. ***(b)*** **:** Only assumption II is implicit in the statement. Assumption I is doubtful because statement is conditional.

46. ***(e)*****:** Both assumption I and assumption II are implicit. The degree of comparison 'longer life' is indicative of the fact that other tubes are not durable and people prefer better quality products.

47. ***(b)*** **:** Only assumption II is implicit. Perfection or excellence arouses curiosity.

48. ***(e)*** **:** Both assumption I and assumption II are implicit. 'Judge himself correctly' emphasises the implicity of the assumptions.

49. ***(a)*** **:** Only assumption I is implicit because of the word 'indispensable'. Assumption II is in no way implicit in the statement.

50. ***(e)*** **:** Both assumption I and assumption II are implicit in the statement.

PART - VII

DRAWING MULTIPLE ASSUMPTIONS

In this type of reasoning the implicity of three assumptions based on the statement is in question. From the given options the candidate has to find the set of assumptions which are implicit in the statement.

SOLVED EXAMPLE

Statement : "You should not drink whisky. You must take care of your health," A tells his friend B.

Assumptions I : A knows about the ill-effects of whisky.

II : Whisky is not good for health.

III : Whisky is intoxicating.

(*a*) I and III are implict.

(*b*) Only II is implicit.

(*c*) II and III are implicit.

(*d*) I and II are implicit.

(*e*) All are implicit.

Ans. (*d*) : Assumption I and II are obvious and implicit in the statement. Nothing is said about the intoxicating effect of whisky. So assumption III is not implicit.

EXERCISE

Directions : *In each question below is given a statement followed by three assumptions number I, II and III. An assumption is something supposed or taken for granted. You have to consider the statement along with the assumptions and decide which of the assumptions is implicit in the statement. Then decide which of the alternatives is the correct answer.*

1. *Statement :*

"Use Riya Cold Cream for fair complexion"—an advertisement.

Assumptions :

I. People like to use cream for fair complexion.

II. People are easily fooled.

III. People respond to advertisements.

(*a*) Only I is implicit.

(*b*) Only II is implicit.

(*c*) Only I and III are implicit.

(*d*) Only I and II are implicit.

(*e*) All are implicit.

2. *Statement :*

"Slogans against smoking in office should be put on the notice board"—an employee in an office suggests.

Assumptions :

I. The employee felt that his suggestion will be considered.

II. People smoke in the office.

III. Some people will stop smoking after reading the slogans.

(*a*) Only I is implicit.

(*b*) Only I and II are implicit.

(*c*) Only II and III are implicit.

(*d*) None is implicit.

(*e*) All are implicit.

3. *Statement :*

"I want to present him a book on techniques of yoga on his birthday"—A tells B.

Assumptions :

I. A and B will be invited for the birthday celebrations.

II. The person to whom the book is to be presented, is not keeping good health.

III. Book is the best gift for birthdays.

(*a*) Only I and II are implicit.
(*b*) Only II and III are implicit.
(*c*) Only I and III are implicit.
(*d*) None is implicit.
(*e*) All are implicit.

4. *Statement :*

Keeping in view the financial constraint, the management institution has decided to charge at the time of providing employment in various organisations, a placement fee of Rs. 25000 from the organisation in which the student will be provided the employment.

Assumptions :

I. It will help in increasing the demand of the students belonging to the management institution.

II. The amount collected in this way will be purposeful.

III. It may be possible that the organisation providing employment may select less number of students in future.

(*a*) None follows.
(*b*) Only II and III follow.
(*c*) Only I follows.
(*d*) Only I and II follow.
(*e*) None of these.

5. *Statement :*

In order to reduce the gap between income and expenditure the company has decided to increase the price of its product from next month.

Assumptions :

I. The rate will remain more or less same after the increase.

II. The expenditure will more or less remain same in near future.

III. The rival companies will also increase the price of the similar product.

(*a*) All are implicit.
(*b*) Only II and III are implicit.
(*c*) Only I and II are implicit.
(*d*) Only III is implicit.
(*e*) None of these.

6. *Statement :*

The professor announced in the class that the next periodical examination will be held on 15th of the next month.

Assumptions :

I. All the students may appear in the examination.

II. The college will remain open on 15th of the next month.

III. The students can study till 15th of the next month to pass the examination.

(*a*) Only II and III are implicit.
(*b*) Only II is implicit.
(*c*) Only I and II are implicit.
(*d*) Only III is implicit.
(*e*) None of these.

7. *Statement :*

"We must introduce objective type tests to improve our examinations for admission to MBA"–The Chairman of the Admission Committe tells the Committee.

Assumptions :

I. The admission at present is directly through the interviews.

II. The Admission Committee is desirous of improving the admission examinations.

III. The Chairman himself is an MBA.

(*a*) Only I is implicit.
(*b*) Only II is implicit.
(*c*) Only I and II are implicit.
(*d*) Only I and III are implicit.
(*e*) None is implicit.

8. *Statement :*

"Since no university has responded to our proposal, we shall not depute any faculty member for the course this year"–A notice in a department.

Assumptions :

I. The proposal has been received by the universities.

II. The proposal had also indicated financial provisions.

III. The proposal was not received by the universities.

(*a*) Only I is implicit.

(*b*) Only III is implicit.
(*c*) Only either I or III is implicit.
(*d*) None is implicit.
(*e*) All are implicit.

9. *Statement :*
"Wanted a two-bedroom flat in the court area for immediate possession"—advertisement.
Assumptions :
I. Flats are available in court area.
II. Some people will respond to the advertisement.
III. It is a practice to give such an advertisement.
(*a*) None is implicit.
(*b*) Only I and II are implicit.
(*c*) Only II is implicit.
(*d*) All are implicit.
(*e*) None of these.

10. *Statement :*
A group of friends decided to go for a picnic to Avon during the next holiday season to avoid crowd of people.
Assumptions:
I. Generally many people do not go to Avon.
II. People prefer other spots to Avon.
III. Many people do not know about Avon.
(*a*) All are implicit.
(*b*) Only II is implicit.
(*c*) Only I and II are implict.
(*d*) None is implicit.
(*e*) None of these.

11. *Statement :*
"Buy 'Y' T.V. for better sound quality"–an advertisement.
Assumptions:
I. 'Y' T.V. is the only T.V. in the market.
II. 'Y' T.V. is the costliest.
III. People generaly ignore such advertisements.
(*a*) Only I is implicit.
(*b*) Only II is implicit.
(*c*) Only III implicit.
(*d*) All are implicit.
(*e*) None is implicit.

12. *Statement :*
"Look at her audacity. Madhu has not replied to my letter"—A tells B.
Assumptions :
I. Madhu received his letter.
II. Madhu did not receive his letter.
III. The letter was sent by post.
(*a*) Only I is implicit.
(*b*) Only II is implicit.
(*c*) Only III is implicit.
(*d*) All are implicit.
(*e*) None is implicit.

13. *Statement :*
"Put a notice on the Board that all the employees should come on time to office."—An officer tells his assistant.
Assumptions :
I. All the employees come late.
II. Employees read such notice on the Board.
III. Employees will follow the instructions.
(*a*) Only I and II are implicit.
(*b*) Only III is implicit.
(*c*) Only I and III are implicit.
(*d*) Only II and III are implicit.
(*e*) All are implicit.

14. *Statement :*
The telephone company informed the subscribers through a notification that those who do not pay their bills by the due date will be charged penalty for every defaulting day.
Assumptions :
I. Majority of the people may pay their bills by the due date to avoid penalty.
II. The money collected as penalty may set off the losses due to delayed payment.
III. People generally pay heed to such notices.
(*a*) None is implicit.
(*b*) Only II and III are implicit.
(*c*) Only I and II are implicit.
(*d*) All are implicit.
(*e*) None of these.

15. *Statement :*
Considering the tickets sold during the last seven days, the circus authorities decided to continue the show for another fortnight which includes two weekends.

Assumptions :

I. People may not turn up on weekdays.

II. The average number of people who will be visiting circus will more or less be same as that of the last seven days.

III. There may not be enough response at other places.

(a) None is implicit.
(b) Only II is implicit.
(c) Both I and II are implicit.
(d) All are implicit.
(e) None of these.

16. *Statement :*

"If you want best training in computers, join our classes"–an advertisement.

Assumptions:

I. People want training related with computers.

II. People read advertisements.

III. People want quality training.

(a) Only I and II are implicit.
(b) Only III is implicit.
(c) Only I and III are implicit.
(d) Only II and III are implicit.
(e) All are implicit.

17. *Statement :*

The national air carrier has decided to start a weekly air service from town 'A' to town 'B'.

Assumptions :

I. There will be enough passengers to make the operation economically viable.

II. Other carriers may not start such service.

III. The people staying around these towns can afford the cost of air travel.

(a) All are implicit.
(b) Only I is implicit.
(c) Both II and III are implicit.
(d) Both I and II are implicit.
(e) None of these.

18. *Statement :*

Prabodh wrote a second letter to his mother after a month as he did not receive any reply to the first letter.

Assumptions :

I. Prabhodh's mother did not receive the letter.

II. The letter generally reaches within a fortnight.

III. His mother promptly sends reply to his letters.

(a) Only II and III are implicit.
(b) Only III is implicit.
(c) None is implicit.
(d) Only I and II are implicit.
(e) None of these.

19. *Statement :*

The school authority decided to open a summer school this year in the schoo. compound for the students in the age range of 7–14 years.

Assumptions :

I. All the students will attend the summer school.

II. All the parents will prefer to remain in city than going out of town for enabling their children to attend the summer school.

III. Those who cannot afford to go out of station will send their children to summer school.

(a) Only II implicit.
(b) Only II and III are implicit.
(c) None is implicit.
(d) All are implicit.
(e) Only III is implicit.

20. *Statement :*

In view of the recent spurt in sugar prices in the open market the government has asked the dealers to release vast quantity of imported sugar in the open market.

Assumptions :

I. The dealers will follow the government directive.

II. The sugar prices will come down.

III. The price of indigenous sugar will remain unchanged.

(a) None is implicit.
(b) Only I and II are implicit.
(c) Only I and III are implicit.
(d) All are implicit.
(e) Only II and III are implicit.

21. *Statement :*

"X–Chocolate is ideal as a gift for someone

you love"—an advertisement.

Assumptions :

I. People generally give gifts to loved ones.

II. Such advertisements generally influence people.

III. Chocolate can be considered as a gift item.

(a) Only I and II are implicit.

(b) Only I and III are implicit.

(c) All are implicit.

(d) Only II and III are implicit.

(e) None of these.

22. *Statement :*

Prakash decided to get the railway reservation in May for the journey he wants to make in July, to Chennai.

Assumptions :

I. The railways issues reservations two months in advance.

II. There are more than one train to Chennai.

III. There will be vacancy in the desired class.

(a) Only II and III are implicit.

(b) Only I is implicit.

(c) All are implicit.

(d) Only I and III are implicit.

(e) None of these.

23. *Statement :*

To improve the employment situation in India, there is a need to recast the present educational system towards implementation of scientific discoveries in daily life.

Assumptions :

I. The students after completing such education may be able to earn their livelihood.

II. This may bring meaning of education in the minds of the youth.

III. The state may earn more revenue as more and more people will engage themselves in self employment.

(a) Only I and II are implicit.

(b) Only III is implicit.

(c) Only I and III are implicit.

(d) None is implicit.

(e) None of these.

24. *Statement :*

To increase profit, the oil exporting countries decided to reduce the production of crude by 5 million barrels per day.

Assumptions :

I. The price of crude may increase due to less production.

II. The demand of crude may remain same in future.

III. Other countries may continue buying crude from these countries.

(a) All are implict.

(b) Only II and III are implicit.

(c) Only I and II are implicit.

(d) None is implicit.

(e) None of these.

25. *Statement :*

The state electricity board has sent a notice to all the consumers that if the bill amount is paid by 10th of the due month a rebate of 2% will be offered; however, if the bill for two consecutive months is not paid a penalty of 3% will be levied on the consumer.

Assumptions :

I. The consumers may be motivated to pay the bill before 10th of the due month.

II. The consumers will avoid being defaulters in future.

III. The content of the notice will be received seriously by the consumers.

(a) All are implicit.

(b) Only III is implicit.

(c) Only I and II are implicit.

(d) Only II and III are implicit.

(e) None of these.

26. *Statement :*

"Fly with us and experience the pleasure of flying"—an advertisement by an airlines.

Assumptions :

I. More passengers may be attracted to travel by the airline after reading the advertisement.

II. People generally may prefer an enjoyable flight.

III. Other airlines may not be offering the same facilities.

(a) None is implicit.

(b) Only II is implicit.

(c) Only II and III are implicit.

(*d*) Only I is implicit.
(*e*) None of these.

27. *Statement :*
"We do not want you to see our product on newspaper, visit our shop to get a full view"—an advertisement.
Assumptions :
I. People generally decide to purchase any product after seeing the name in the advertisement.
II. Uncommon appeal may attract the customers.
III. People may come to see the product.
(*a*) All are implicit.
(*b*) None is implicit.
(*c*) Only II and III are implicit.
(*d*) Only I and II are implicit.
(*e*) None of these.

28. *Statement :*
The Reserve Bank of India has directed the banks to refuse fresh loans to the defaulters.
Assumptions :
I. The banks may still give loans to the defaulters.
II. The defaulters may repay the earlier loan to get fresh loan.
III. The banks may recover the bad loans through such harsh measures.
(*a*) All are implicit.
(*b*) None is implicit.
(*c*) Both II and III are implicit.
(*d*) Both I and II are implicit.
(*e*) None of these.

29. *Statement :*
During pre-harvest kharif season, the government has decided to release vast quantity of foodgrains from FCI.
Assumptions :
I. There may be a shortage of foodgrains in the market during this season.
II. The kharif crop may be able to replenish the stock of FCI.
III. There may be a demand from the farmers to procure kharif crop immediately after harvest.
(*a*) None is implicit.
(*b*) Only I and II are implicit.
(*c*) Only II and III are implicit.
(*d*) All are implicit.
(*e*) None of these.

30. *Statement :*
"As our business is expanding, we need to appoint more staff"—Owner of a company informs his staff.
Assumptions :
I. The present staff is not competent.
II. More staff will further expand the business.
III. Suitable persons are to be taken as posts will be available.
(*a*) Only I is implicit.
(*b*) Only II is implicit.
(*c*) Only III is implicit.
(*d*) All are implicit.
(*e*) None is implicit.

EXPLANATORY ANSWERS

1. (*c*) : The advertisement itself denotes that people like to use cream for fair complexion and they do respond to advertisements. Advertisements are for awareness of the product not for fooling people.

2. (*e*) : Suggestion for putting up the notice is made because some people must be smoking in office. Notice board is read by people in office and some may stop smoking after reading the slogans.

3. (*c*) : According to A presents are best gifts for birthdays and when A has bought the book he expects to be invited for the birthday celebration. Nothing is mentioned about health of the birthday person.

4. (*b*) : The amount collected will lessen the financial constraint and there is every possibility for selecting less number of students because of the fee charged.

5. (*e*) : The increased amount is not mentioned and nothing is said about the rival companies. As the rates are increased to meet the expenditure, the latter may remain same. Only assumption II is implicit.

6. *(d)* : The students have the time to study till 15th of the next month. All students may or may not appear in the examination and the announcement does not inform anything about the college being open till the mentioned date.

7. *(b)* : Assumption II is obvious from the statement. Nothing is mentioned about the interviews or the qualification of the Chairman of the Admission Committee.

8. *(d)* : The universities have or have not received the proposal is a matter of doubt and the matter of the proposal is not mentioned.

9. *(c)* : It is a fact that people do read advertisement and some of them will respond to them. Availability of the flat in court area is doubtful and it is a matter of need, not practice, to give such an advertisement.

10. *(a)* : The friends decided to go to Avon in order to avoid crowd. This means that many people do not know about Avon (as known places attract crowds) and that is why they do not go there. People prefer known places instead of Avon.

11. *(e)* : The degree of comparison 'better sound' indicates there are other T.V.s also. Nothing is mentioned about the price of the T.V. in advertisement or its rivals. Advertisements enhancing the quality of any product are not ignored by the people.

12. *(c)* : Madhu received the letter or not is doubtful. As A is expecting a reply, he had certainly sent the letter.

13. *(d)* : Notice boards are read by the employees and the instructions in the notice are meant to be followed. However, all the employees cannot come late to office.

14. *(e)* : After receiving the notification people will pay heed to the notice and make payments on time to avoid penalty. Nothing is said about the utility of money collected as penalty. Therefore, assumptions I and III are implicit.

15. *(b)* : The circus show is continued for another fortnight because the people visiting the circus are expected to be more or less same as in the earlier days. People turn up every day and the response at other places cannot be assumed.

16. *(e)* : Advertisement is given because people who want quality training related with computers will read such advertisements.

17. *(a)* : The reason for starting the service is that there are enough passengers. Other carriers may not start the service as national air carrier has taken the decision to do it. Now people staying in towns A and B can afford the air travel as weekly services may have some benefits for the passengers.

18. *(a)* : Prabodh's mother received the letter or not is doubtful. Before writing the second letter Prabodh had waited for 15 days to receive the reply knowing that his mother gives a prompt reply.

19. *(c)* : The assumptions are not related to the statements.

20. *(b)* : The dealers have to follow the government directives and when vast quantity of sugar is released in the market, its prices will come down.

21. *(c)* : The advertisement indicates that people do consider chocolates as gift item for loved ones and so X–chocolate can be that ideal gift. Such advertisements usually influence people.

22. *(b)* : Prakash is making reservations for July in May. This means that railway reservations are made two months in advance. Assumption II and III are not related to the statement.

23. *(a)* : Change in the educational system may help students to earn their livelihood after completing such education. Scope of self-employment will be more and this may benefit the state revenue. Assumption III is irrelevant.

24. *(a)* : Production is reduced when demand is also less but as the company has to make profits, the price may increase. Countries, which do not have oil may still continue to buy the product from the oil exporting countries.

25. ***(a)*** **:** People react seriously to such notices and pay the bill by the due date in order to avoid being defaulters.

26. ***(c)*** **:** After reading the advertisement people may travel by this airline as they prefer an enjoyable flight. Other airlines may or may not be offering the same facilities. Therefore assumption I and II are implicit.

27. ***(c)*** **:** People are aware of the product when they do not decide to buy it just by name. Such advertisements which have a different appeal attract the people and they may go to the shop for more information.

28. ***(a)*** **:** The Reserve Bank of India knows about the defaulters and that some banks may be deceived by the tricks of repaying earlier loans in order to get more loans. By taking this step the banks may recover the earlier bad loans.

29. ***(d)*** **:** The decision of the Government implies the chances of shortage. There is possibility that the crop yield will replenish the used stock and also the demand after the harvest may be immediate.

30. ***(c)*** **:** Expansion in business may create new posts and suitable persons are needed to fill these posts. The competency of the present staff has nothing to do with appointments. Assumption II is senseless as per the information.

PART - VIII

DISTINGUISHING ARGUMENTS

In this type of reasoning one has to decide upon the forcefulness of an argument. One should keep in mind that the argument should not be *(i)* an assumption; *(ii)* generalised (it should be specific); *(iii)* ambiguous; *(iv)* hidden as an implication; *(v)* an example or quotation. Also, the argument should be factually correct and in conformity with the prevailing ideas of truth.

In making decisions about important questions, it is desirable to be able to distinguish between 'strong' arguments and 'weak' arguments so far as they relate to the questions. 'Strong' arguments must be both important and directly related to the question. 'Weak' arguments may not be directly related to the question and may be of minor importance or may be related to the trivial aspect of the question.

SOLVED EXAMPLES

In the questions below, the answer is given as :

(a) If only argument I is strong.
(b) If only argument II is strong.
(c) If either I or II is strong.
(d) If neither I nor II is strong.
(e) If both I and II are strong.

1. Should students union in universities be abolished?
Arguments :
I. Yes ! Students can pay full attention to their career development.
II. No ! All the great leaders had been students' union leaders.
Ans. ***(a)*** **:** Union activities burn away a lot of precious time which the student can otherwise utilise, for studies. And history confirms that all great leaders had not been students' union leaders.
So, only argument I is strong.

2. Should military education be made compulsory in our country?
Arguments :
I. No. It is against the policy of non-violence.
II. Yes. Every citizen should protect his country.
Ans. ***(b)*** **:** Argument I indicates that the person who is in military service practices non-violence, which is wrong. Argument II is directly related to the statement.

EXERCISE

Directions : *Each question below is followed by two arguments numbered I and II. You have to decide which of the given arguments is a 'strong' argument and which is a 'weak' argument. Give answer :*

(a) If only argument I is strong.
(b) If only argument II is strong.
(c) If either I or II is strong.
(d) If neither I nor II is strong.
(e) If both I and II are strong.

1. Should higher education be restricted only to the most deserving ones?
Arguments :
I. No, it is against the principle of democracy.
II. Yes, only deserving people are entitled

in this country.

2. Should strikes in the field of education be banned?
Arguments :
I. Yes, it is against professional ethics.
II. Yes, it affects the students adversely.

3. Should young entrepreneurs be employed?
Arguments :
I. Yes, that will help in industrial development of the country.
II. Yes, that will reduce the burden on the employment market.

4. Guides published by private agencies should be banned.
Arguments :
I. Yes, because only then the students will start reading textbooks.
II. No, because these are of immense help to the weak students in the eleventh hour.

5. Should India manufacture atom bombs?
Arguments :
I. Yes, it is imperative to protect the sovereignty and integrity of the country.
II. No, this will create imbalance in the power of nations in this region.

6. Should open book systems be introduced in examinations?
Arguments :
I. Yes, because it will avoid mass copying.
II. No, because then all students will get 100% marks.

7. Should smoking be prohibited?
Arguments :
I. Yes, it is wrong to smoke away millions of good money.
II. No, it will throw thousands of workers in the tobacco industry out of employment.

8. Should there be a uniform syllabus for all universities in India?
Arguments :
I. Yes, why not?
II. No, in a vast country like India, variation is necessary to suit local needs.

9. Should religion be banned?
Arguments :
I. Yes, it develops fanaticism in people.
II. No, religion binds people together.

10. Should educated people work in villages?
Arguments :
I. Yes, because they can revolutionize agriculture and revamp rural atmosphere.
II. No, the educated should be employed in cities.

11. Should there be complete ban on strike by Government employees in India?
Arguments :
I. Yes, this is the only way to teach discipline to the employees.
II. No, this deprives the citizens of their democratic rights.

12. Should India have no military force at all?
Arguments :
I. No, other countries in the world do not believe in non-violence.
II. Yes, many Indians believe in non-violence.

13. Should India encourage exports when most things are insufficient for internal use itself?
Arguments :
I. Yes, we have to earn foreign exchange to pay for our imports.
II. No, even selective encouragement would lead to shortages.

14. Should total ban be put on trapping wild animals?
Arguments :
I. Yes, trappers are making a lot of money.
II. No, ban on hunting and trapping are not effective.

15. Should fashionable dresses be banned?
Arguments :
I. Yes, fashions keep changing and hence consumption of cloth increases.
II. No, fashionable clothes are a person's self-expression and therefore his/her fundamental right.

16. Should luxury hotels be banned in India?
Arguments :
I. Yes, they are places from where international criminals operate.
II. No, affluent foreign tourists will have no place to stay.

17. Should cutting of trees be banned altogether?
Arguments :
I. Yes, it is very necessary to do so to restore ecological balance.
II. No, a total ban would harm timber based industries.

18. Should education upto graduation be made compulsory for all?
Arguments :
I. Yes, it is very desirable.
II. No, what is the use?

19. Should telecasting feature films be stopped?
Arguments :
I. Yes, young children are misguided by the feature films.
II. No, this is the only way to educate the masses.

20. Should taxes on colour television be further increased?
Arguments :
I. Yes, colour television is a luxury item and only rich people buy them.
II. No, television are bought by the poor too.

21. Should voting age in India be lowered to 16?
Arguments :
I. Yes, why should it not be so in India when in some other countries the voting age is 16 ?
II. No, it will be foolish to do so when even the marriage age for boys is 21.

22. Should religion be taught in our schools?
Arguments :
I. Yes, do the parents not wish to develop their wards into mature individuals?
II. No, how can one dream of such a step when we want the young generation to fulfill its role.

23. Should family planning be made compulsory in India?
Arguments :
I. Yes, looking at the miserable conditions in India, there is no other go.
II. No, in India there are people of various religions and family planning is against the tenets of some of the religions.

24. Should correspondence courses at university level in India be discontinued?
Arguments :
I. Yes, only interactoin between teachers and students and among students while learning helps total development of personality at the University level.
II. No, such a step of discontinuation is the craze of the elite, who have no knowledge of what is meant by poverty.

25. Should hunting be banned?
Arguments :
I. Yes, it has been proved to be a definite environmental hazard.
II. No, what will hunters do?

26. Should those who receive dowry, despite the law prohibiting it, be punished?
Arguments :
I. Yes, because those who violate the law must be punished.
II. No, dowry system is firmly rooted in the society since time immemorial.

27. Should religion be taught in our schools?
Arguments :
I. No, ours is a Secular State.
II. Yes, teaching religion helps inculcate moral values among children.

28. Should octroi be abolished?
Arguments :
I. Yes, it will eliminate an important source of corruption.
II. No, it would adversely affect government revenue.

29. Should promotion of personnel in an organisation be made only on the basis of seniority?
Arguments :
I. Yes, otherwise senior persons will become disinterested in their work.
II. No, it does injustice to the really deserving persons.

30. Should colleges be given the status of a University?
Arguments :
I. Yes, managements of colleges will appreciate it.
II. No, colleges even in Western countries have not yet been given such a status.

31. Should workers be allowed to participate in the management of factories?

Arguments :

I. Yes, it is one of the demands of workers.

II. No, the management will oppose this idea.

32. Should competitive examinations for electing candidates for jobs consist of objective tests only?

Arguments :

I. Yes, the assessment of objective tests is reliable.

II. No, the number of questions to be answered in the objective tests is always very large.

33. Should military training be made compulsory for all?

Arguments :

I. Yes, it is very desirable.

II. No, what is the use?

34. Should India stop nuclear programme?

Arguments :

I. Yes, China desires so.

II. No, the nation must always remain up-to-date in its defence preparedness.

35. Should killing of wild animals be banned altogether?

Arguments :

I. Yes, it is very necessary to restore ecological balance.

II. No, a total ban would harm the leather industry.

36. Are modern girls really against dowry?

Arguments :

I. Yes, they want to end the age-old atrocities caused by dowry.

II. No, they think dowry is their lawful right and a means to their status in society.

37. Can all scientists be good singers?

Arguments :

I. Yes, because musical notes are scientifically based.

II. No, because good singers are gifted with an inborn talent for singing.

38. Inter-caste marriages will lead to National Integration.

Arguments :

I. Yes, this will lead to intermingling of various castes and thus casteism will disappear.

II. This will lead to a lot of male-adjustment of married couples, especially when the rituals and dogmas of different castes differ a good deal.

39. Simple living and high thinking is a good principle of life.

Arguments :

I. This makes one a great person.

II. All great men follow this principle.

40. Should number of public holidays be reduced?

Arguments :

I. No, there is going to be hue and cry.

II. Yes, it must be done as early as possible.

41. Should all the schools be made co-educational?

Arguments :

I. Yes, otherwise how else do we promote education of girl child. More girls should be enrolled in the co-educational schools.

II. No, in a conservative society like ours, parents have many reservations against co-education and it may hamper education of girls.

42. Should tabloids be banned?

Arguments :

I. No, how can such a stupid thing be ever even thought of.

II. Yes, no problem. We have many good newspapers.

43. Should students have their union?

Arguments :

I. Yes, because they shall fight for the cause of the students.

II. No, because it gives a chance to the politicians to play their dirty game through the unions.

44. Should wild life be protected?

Arguments :

I. Yes, otherwise some species could disappear.

II. No, the wild beasts are a menace to the neighbouring villages, so they should be destroyed.

45. Should Government stop spending huge amounts of money on international sports?

Arguments :

I. Yes, this money can be utilised for the upliftment of the poor.

II. No, sportspersons will be frustrated and will not get international exposure.

46. Should all the transport corporations be handed over to the private organisations?

Arguments :

I. Yes, there will be significant change in the quality and punctuality of services.

II. No, there would not be job secuity for the employees at all the levels.

47. Sanskrit should become the national language of the country.

Arguments :

I. It is our cultural heritage.

II. It is understood by all the Indians.

48. Economics has been called the 'dismal science', because :

Arguments :

I. Economics is not a science.

II. Political economists have been predicting that ever increasing population will ultimately lead to catastrophic conditions.

49. Should violence be depicted in films?

Arguments :

I. Yes, because it makes the films very interesting and useful.

II. No, because this spreads violence.

50. India is a poor country and therefore should not try to spend too much moeny on launching of rockets and satellites.

Arguments :

I. Yes, launching them successfully does not in any way help the country.

II. It drains away the meagre resources of the country.

EXPLANATORY ANSWERS

1. *(a)* : In a democracy, every person has equal rights, so argument I is strong.

2. *(b)* : Argument II is directly related to the statement. Argument I is weak because strike is a big power used by employees for their defence.

3. *(e)* : Both argument I and argument II are strong and directly related to the statement.

4. *(b)* : Argument I is based on assumption but argument II follows the statement because guides are helpful for short-time preparation.

5. *(a)* : Argument I is strong because it is directly related to the statement and argument II is weak as it is based on assumption.

6. *(d)* : Both argument I and argment II are based on assumption.

7. *(d)* : Argument I is ambiguous and argument II is based on assumption.

8. *(b)* : Argument I is the implication of the statement but considering the diversity factor in India, assumption II is strong.

9. *(b)* : Only argument II is strong. Religion does not develop fanaticism, but it will be misused by the people.

10. *(a)* : Argument I is strong as education would not be wasted by doing working in village, but it will be used for all round development.

11. *(b)* : Argument I is based on assumption and argument II is important and directly related to the statement.

12. *(d)* : Neither argument I nor argument II is strong as both are based on assumptions.

13. *(a)* : Argument II is based on assumption but argument I is strong.

14. *(d)* : Neither argument I nor argument II is strong.

15. *(b)* : Nothing is important about the 'consumption of clothes' in the statement. However, argument II is important and strong because the manner of dressing is a persons's own choice.

16. *(b)* : Argument I is not strong. Argument II is related to the statement.

17. ***(e)*** **:** Both argument I and argument II are strong and directly related to the statement.

18. ***(d)*** **:** Argument I means that all students want to be graduates, which is wrong, and argument II is pessimistic approach. As such, neither argument I nor argument II is strong.

19. ***(d)*** **:** Neither argument I nor argument II is strong. Argument I is not strong because films also educate masses. Argument II is weak because films are not the only way to educate the masses.

20. ***(d)*** **:** Neither argument I nor argument II is strong. Television which is a means of entertainment is bought by those who can afford it, and not only by the rich people. A really poor person cannot afford to buy a television not even at the present price.

21. ***(d)*** **:** Neither the argument I nor argument II is strong. It is no sound argument that other countries have done so. Similarly, marriage age is not directly related to age of voting.

22. ***(d)*** **:** Neither of the arguments is strong because maturity and playing a successful role has no connection with teaching of religion in our schools.

23. ***(a)*****:** Only argument I is strong. Planning is necessary to avoid chaos.

24. ***(a)*** **:** If the objective of education is total development of personality, then argument I is sound.

25. ***(a)*** **:** Only argument I is strong. Hunting has only been a pleasurable sport. Hunters can do something better.

26. ***(a)*** **:** Only argument I is strong. Social evils must be uprooted and not carried on.

27. ***(a)*** **:** Only argument I is strong. Teaching religion may lead to communal differences and disparities.

28. ***(e)*** **:** Both argument I and argument II are strong. On one hand the illegal method of collecting octroi will be checked, but on the other the Government will suffer revenue losses.

29. ***(e)*** **:** Both argument I and argument II are equally forceful. Senior persons look forward to promotions. Also, a not so good senior may be an obstacle in the path of prosperity of a really deserving person.

30. ***(d)*** **:** Neither argument I nor argument II is strong. The management may not be capable to keeping up the status. Rules in western countries do not apply in Indian education system as compulsory.

31. ***(d)*** **:** Neither argument I nor argument II is strong. Management is the sole decider of the actions to be taken.

32. ***(e)*** **:** Both argument I and argument II are strong. The number of questions in such tests is always large but it also shows the candidate's indepth knowledge of the subject.

33. ***(d)*** **:** Neither argument I nor argument II is strong.

34. ***(b)*** **:** Argument II is strong, because national defence preparedness is vital for our country.

35. ***(e)*** **:** Both the arguments I and II are strong. Such a step would restore ecological balance but it would harm the leather industry.

36. ***(e)*** **:** In our society today though there are girls who want to end the system, they even consider it as their lawful right. So, both the arguments are strong.

37. ***(b)*** **:** Scientifically based musical notes does not mean that scientists can be good singers. Singing is a talent. Only argument II is strong.

38. ***(c)*** **:** The two arguments are contrary to each other. So, either of the two arguments can be strong.

39. ***(e)*** **:** Both argument I and argument II are strong.

40. ***(d)*** **:** Neither the issue of holidays raise a hue and cry, nor the necessity of urgency makes sense. So, neither argument I nor argument II is strong.

41. ***(b)*** **:** Making schools co-educational is not the solution for promoting education of girl child. Argument II is strong as what is said is very likely to happen.

42. ***(d)*** **:** Neither argument I nor argument II is strong.

43. ***(e)*** **:** Both argument I and argument II are strong.

44. ***(a)*** **:** What is once destroyed cannot be recovered and wild life species must be protected. Only argument I is strong. Wild life can be protected in zoos or safaris. So, argument II is weak.

45. ***(b)*** **:** Upliftment of the poor has its own government quota. On the other hand facilities must be provided to able sportsmen. So, only argument II is strong.

46. ***(e)*** **:** Competition is more among private organisations as they seek efficiency. So, both argument I and argument II are strong.

47. ***(e)*** **:** Both argument I and argument II are strong.

48. ***(b)*** **:** Argument I is wrong. Argument II is strong.

49. ***(c)*** **:** Violence is the base of action films but on the other hand this also harms immature minds. So, either argument I or argument II is strong.

50. ***(e)*** **:** For a country like India rocket launching costs a lot as it drains away the resources. So, both argument I and argument II are strong.

PART - IX

DRAWING INFERENCE

Questions on this type of reasoning have become quite common in competitive examinations. In this test, instead of a statement or proposition, a passage is given which is a congregation of many propositions coupled with arguments. Some inferences are given followed by the passage. The candidate has to decide whether the given inference follows, or does not follow in the light of the given passage.

SOLVED EXAMPLES

Given below are two passages followed by possible inferences which can be drawn from the facts stated in the passage. Each inference is examined separately in the context of the passage to decide upon its degree of truth or falsity. The answers are marked . . . .

(a) if the inference is "definitely true", *i.e.,* it properly follows from the statement of facts given.

(b) if the inference is "probably true," though not "definitely true" in the light of the facts given.

(c) if the "data are inadequate", *i.e.*, from the facts given you cannot say whether the inference is likely to be true or false.

(d) if the inference is "probably false", *i.e.*, though not "definitely false" in the light of the facts given.

(e) if the inference is "definitely false", *i.e.*, cannot possibly be drawn from the facts given or it contradicts the given facts.

PASSAGE I

The serious accident, in which a person was run over by a car yesterday, has again focussed attention on the most unsatisfactory state of street lighting. No one expects side roads to be provided with the same standard of lightings as a main road, but unless the council is prepared to make good its promise as regards road lighting, it will only be a question of time before there are further and perhaps fatal accidents.

1. The accident that occurred was fatal.

Ans. ***(e)*** **:** This conclusion cannot be drawn from the facts given.

2. Several accidents have so far taken place because of unsatisfactory lightings.

Ans. ***(a)*** **:** Mark the words 'again focussed attention on the most . . . lighting'.

3. There will not be a single accident on road if they are satisfactorily illuminated.

Ans. ***(c)*** **:** Data are insufficient. This statement is not confirmed by the paragraph.

4. It seems that the council has promised to improve the state of lighting on side roads.

Ans. ***(a)*** **:** Mark the words "the council is prepared to make good its promise as regards the road lighting."

5. The accident occurred at night.

Ans. ***(a)*** **:** It must be night because the passage deals with unsatisfactory state of street lighting.

PASSAGE II

Gujarat has hardly 8.5 per cent of its total area under forest. Of this, a considerable portion is covered by wild grass and marshes. Denuded of thick forests, fauna have disappeared from many places. Mandvi, for instance, had its share of fauna once. The state government has imposed a total ban on cutting of trees for five years from this year. The imminent destruction of over 40,000 hectares of forest land by the Narmada project has led to nation–wide strong protest.

6. A dam on the Narmada river is planned.

Ans. ***(b)*** **:** Narmada project is a planned one.

7. Once there was thick forest in Mandvi.

Ans. ***(a)*** **:** Mandvi had its share of fauna once.

8. Gujarat Government is quite conscious of the need of conservation of forests.

Ans. ***(a)*** **:** Gujarat Government has imposed ban on cutting of trees.

9. There is thick forest in 8.5 per cent of the total area of Gujarat.

Ans. ***(e)*** **:** Considerable portion of 8.5 per cent is covered under grass and marshes.

10. Gujarat is the first State in India to impose a total ban on cutting of trees.

Ans. ***(c)*** **:** Nowhere in the paragraph has it been hinted that Gujarat is the first State in India to impose a ban on cutting of trees.

Now, note that if the inference is drawn directly from the passage it is 'Definitely True'. If the inference is not definitely true but on some assumptions it can be true then it is 'Probably True'. If no conclusion can be drawn from the passage then the 'Data are inadequate.' If the inference cannot be directely related with the passage but on certain assumptions, it is found to be universally false then it is 'Probably False'. Lastly, if the inference is not directly related to the pasage then it is 'Definitely False.'

EXERCISE

Directions : *Below are given some passages followed by several possible inferences which can be drawn from the facts stated in each passage. You have to examine each inference separately in the context of the passage and decide upon its degree of truth or falsity.*

Mark Answers	If you think...
(a) "Definitely True"	the inference properly follows from the statement of facts given.
(b) "Probably True"	the inference may be true in the light of the facts given but not definitely true.
(c) "Data Inadequate"	from the facts given it cannot be said whether the inference is likely to be true or false.
(d) "Probably False"	the inference is probably false in the light of the facts given though not definitely false.
(e) "Definitely False"	the inference cannot possibly be drawn from the facts given or it contradicts the given facts.

PASSAGE 1

Indian granite industry is in peril in the absence of a uniform policy from the state governments, despite the thrust given by liberalisation policies of the union government. Compared to the remarkable progress in the field during the last three years, the absence of matching policies by state governments had put granite quarry owners and others involved in the industry on the verge of collapse in the international market. The policies differed from state to state, had created problems as far as loyalty, dead rent and duration of lease were concerned.

1. Each state having granite quarry has set up its own rules which are contrary to the interest of the industry.

2. Till three years ago, granite production in India was not profitable.

3. The granite production is largely controlled by individuals.

4. The granite produced in India does not match with the quality of international level.

5. The union government's liberalisation policy became applicable to granite industry only during the last three years.

PASSAGE 2

Steel production has always been burdened with costs much higher than in comparable plants overseas. On the one hand custom duty on almost all steel imports has been reduced, on the other excise duty has been raised. Domestic steel products are now uncompetitive which in turn has led to the demand that both the custom and excise rates should be reviewed to prevent sickness in the industry.

6. The steel industry in general is making losses as a fall out of the government policy.

7. The cost of production of steel in other countries is less than that in India.

8. India can compete with the foreign countries in regard to the price of steel with a favourable government policy.

9. Foreign steel has become cheaper comparative to domestic steel.

10. The government is considering lowering of excise duty on steel products.

PASSAGE 3

The annual domestic consumption of plastics in India is expected to grow between 2.5 and 3 million tonnes by the end of the Ist half of this century from the current level of about one million tonnes. The global consumption of plastics now stands at 100 million tonnes. To sustain the present growth pattern, India would need two additional polymer plants of 1,000 tonnes every year till the turn of the Ist half of this century. Entrepreneurs should now think in lines of globalisation and promote projects of international capacity and they would have to look at technology transfer as well as upgradation and strategic and creative alliances.

11. The total domestic consumption of plastics in India is about one per cent of the global consumption.

12. At present India does not import plastics.

13. India lacks in technological capabilities in producing plastics.

14. There is an expected growth of about .2 per cent in the plastic consumption every year.

15. Potentially India can be one of the major players in the production of plastics in the international market.

PASSAGE 4

The smaller pesticide formulation units in India operate under heavy constraints such as obsolete technology, small scale of operation and dependence on larger units for raw materials. In view of the loss of expensive material by the smaller units, it is important to either eliminate or reduce losses to the extent possible through innovative and sustainable waste minimisation techniques. Operating profit margins of the units are very low and small adverse conditions land these companies in trouble. Maximum losses suffered by these units are through poor house keeping, sub-optional operating practices, and lack of proper opportunities for recycling waste.

16. Smaller units should be operationally self–sufficient so as to minimise losses.

17. Recycling of wastes through modern techniques can set off large part of the losses incurred by the smaller units.

18. Pesticide units should necessarily be on a large scale to make them economically viable.

19. Lack of funds compels smaller units to ignore house keeping.

20. Waste management process in India needs modernisation.

PASSAGE 5

More than a decade of erosion in budgetory support from the Union government, has seriously affected Indian Railways' capacity to finance its plan expenditures. The situation has come to pass where the railways must now think of innovative ways to get longer mileage from its investments. Significantly the resource crunch has had grievous impact on the railways. As a result, it will not be in a position to acquire necessary equipments and this will seriously affect the railways' capacity to serve the needs of the economy in future.

21. During the current plan period the railways will not be able to expand its network.

22. The fiscal position of railways in the earlier plan period was better than the current plan period.

23. Railways had so far believed in traditional ways in generating income.

24. Government has shifted its priority from railways to other areas.

25. The Union Government has reduced drastically the budgetory support to railways during the last decade.

PASSAGE 6

As in the case of absolute number of illiterates, the actual number of illiterate females is also increasing with time and faster than the number of male illiterates. More so in the backward states, in the rural areas, and among scheduled castes and scheduled tribes.

The correlation between female illiteracy and infant mortality is equally clear. It is found that mortality was highest in the case of illiterate mothers both in urban and rural areas but much higher in the latter.

26. The illitercy rate is higher among females as compared to that of males.

27. In terms of absolute numbers there are more male illiterates than female illiterates.

28. Infant mortality is correlated more with male than female illiteracy.

29. Infant mortality rate is almost same in urban and rural areas.

30. In backward states, the population of scheduled castes and scheduled tribes is more than that in other states.

PASSAGE 7

A worrying feature of Indian urbanisation has been its tendency to increase pressure on the inner cities. The first results of the 1991 census suggest that the density of population in urban areas is within manageable limits, with most cities, including Greater Mumbai, being well below the 23,000 per square kilometre mark set by Calcutta. But within several of the older cities the walled areas have high densities which exert pressure on the outdated amenities in these areas, a pressure that is accentuated by the poor maintenance of housing as well as other assets in the inner cities. The inner cities were designed for a pattern of urban life far removed from what exists today. The makers of narrow winding lanes could hardly have anticipated modern transportation.

31. The rate of growth in density of population in the inner cities has been more than that in surroundings areas.

32. The increase in density of population in urban areas has outgrown the increase in amenities.

33. At the time of planning the cities in the past, the use of bigger roads was envisaged by the planners.

34. The density of population in the inner city of Greater Mumbai is the highest in India.

35. The pace of Indian urbanisation is much slower by international standards.

PASSAGE 8

A survey in India indicated that in the core section of the companies, which were analysed, the compensation package for executives was divided into several fringe benefit groups. The number of items included in it rose as one ascended the management hierarchy. In many companies, provision was made for transportation and medical and housing assistance. A few companies also provided for children's education or permitted family allowance. Some of them have now adopted a specialised approach called the "cafetaria approach" in salary fixation. What is sought here is that the benefits must meet an executive's needs. Therefore, an apppropriate selection has to be made of the benefits in terms of his needs after consulting him. Thus, this approach would individualise the system as the final choice is left to the executive concerned.

36. Now-a-days most of the companies in India are designing their compensation packages on the lines of such packages offered by the companies in foreign countries.

37. While designing the compensation package for executives, certain companies try to establish a match between needs and benefits.

38. The survey conducted in India for compensation package included employee working at different levels, including executives.

39. Fringe benefits offered by many companies take care of most of the basic physiological needs of the executives.

40. There is a standard universal compensation package for executives in most companies.

PASSAGE 9

One-third population of the country being below poverty line, it is unavoidable that since independence, dominance of Government sponsored programmes have been evident—objective of each of those was to improve the lot of all the poor people. However, success of such programmes have been limited. Even being the excellent desired effect of these programmes, these could never avoid the clutches of bureaucracy. Resulting this that the benefits of the government sponsored programmes could not ultimately reach those people for whom primarily these programmes were prepared.

41. Bureaucracy has proved to be a speed-breaker in the implementation of welfare programmes.

42. The targeted group has substantially benefitted from the achievements of the programmes.

43. Government had no sponsored programmes for the welfare of the poor in the pre-independence era.

44. The rich became more richer in pre-independence era.

45. The Government has never cared for the welfare of the poor.

PASSAGE 10

Post-harvest management of fruits and vegetables is vital in quality exports. At present, a wide variety of techniques of post-harvest management are available in India. However, an inadequacy is felt in respect of certain fruits. Cases where the production cost is high, poor post-harvest management will render export business non-viable.

46. All the techniques of post-harvest management are indigenous.

47. India has effective post-harvest management techniques for those fruits which are costly to produce.

48. Quantity of exports of fruits is more than that of vegetables.

49. India exports quality fruits.

50. Post-harvest management of vegetables is more crucial than that of fruits.

PASSAGE 11

"Though, the state cultivates only 3.2 lakh tonnes of mangoes, they are of premium quality. And with mangoes becoming second most consumed fruit in the world after grapes, the government has been trying exporting it through sea route which is cheaper. An experiment which was done in this regard last year has proved successul."

51. The state also cultivates a large number of medium quality mangoes.

52. Quality of mangoes is an important factor in exports.

53. The state also exports good quality grapes.

54. There are some problems in exporting the mangoes through sea route.

55. Most of the other exports are through sea route, which is cheaper.

PASSAGE 12

Doordarshan has undoubtedly helped popularise Yoga among the people, especially city-dwellers. But performing various '*asanas*' without adequate instructions could be hazardous, according to a renowned 'Yoga expert' who has conducted hundreds of yoga *shivirs* (camps). He says several people who tried to learn yoga through the programme of Doordarshan have come to him complaining of pain in different parts of their body. He explains that the *asanas* involve a complicated but scientific technique of breathing which controls the flow of oxygen in various parts of the body under calculated stress.

56. TV programmes on Yoga have successfully replaced personal guidance by 'Yoga experts'.

57. Yoga exercises *(asanas)* are quite safe for any person.

58. Many TV viewers of Yoga programmes are unable to master the scientific technique of breathing while performing '*asanas*'.

59. Uncontrolled flow of oxygen in parts of the body causes pain in those parts.

60. Quite a large number of 'Yoga expert' are available.

PASSAGE 13

When I look back on the process of history, when I survey the genesis of America, I see this written over every page that the nations are renewed from the bottom, not from the top, that the genius which springs up from the ranks of the unknown men is the genius which renews the youth and the energy of the people.

(Woodrow Wilson, U. S. President)

61. Most of the leaders today were common unknown men.

62. People belonging to the ranks of the unknown lot have no genius among them.

63. Nations are not renewed from the top.

64. President Woodrow Wilson was a scholar of history.

65. No leader was ever born in the top class.

PASSAGE 14

The healthy growth of tractor industry in India is mainly determined by positive agricultural growth, good crop and unsaturated market. The growth in the last three years has been between 15 to 20 per cent. In the current year, a growth of around 10 per cent is projected.

In the northern market particularly including States producing wheat like Punjab and Haryana, the sales have reduced because of high level of market penetration. But in western and southern States, markets have lower market penetration. Besides, now high horsepower (H. P.) tractors (30 to 45 H. P.) which are useful for rice fields are more in demand than less than the 25 H. P. tractors.

66. The factors which determine growth of tractor industry in India are entirely different from the western countries.

67. In the current year, the projected trend in sale of tractors indicates higher growth in agriculture and higher yield of crops.

68. The companies who have been producing only low horsepower tractors may face financial problems.

69. The tractor manufacturers need to concentrate in western and southern States to boost their sales.

70. The market for tractors in European countries has reached the stage of saturation.

PASSAGE 15

Urban lifestyles, fast foods, changing diet patterns, lack of exercise, obesity and smoking are responsible for increase in the incidence of diabetes, heart attacks and cancer. Research has also shown that modern cooking oils have an unhealthy ratio of harmful fatty acids to essential fatty acids which contribute to free radical attacks and increase insulin resistance.

Ghee, coconut oil and mustard oil have a healthy ratio of fatty acids. Their use in rural India, coupled with a traditional high fibre diet and physical exercise, probably account for the lower incidence of diabetes and heart attacks in the rural population, the study reveals.

71. Urban health conscious people can stop using modern cooking oils and reduce chances of occurrence of these diseases.

72. Only cooking oil is responsible for rise in the incidences of diseases like heart attacks, cancer, etc.

73. The increase in diseases like diabetes, heart attacks, etc. is controllable by taking proper measures.

74. Rural people should not migrate to urban cities if they value their health.

75. Most of the rural population is healthy and free of diseases.

PASSAGE 16

Education in the human values means an inculcation of truth, right action, peace, love and non-violence. These values, in turn, train and develop in a balanced manner the body, intellect, mind and heart. It is useless to saturate the minds of students with notions that they easily forget. Only by educating them to learn their deepest and innate qualities will we give them the capacity to give to their lives the right meaning.

76. Education in human values has been introduced in many schools.

77. Mind has a specific capacity to learn.

78. The parent's role is most crucial in imparting good values.

79. There is need to re-orient our educational system.

80. Human values cannot be inculcated through education.

PASSAGE 17

The most empirical argument in favour of prayer is that it relieves the mind of tension, which is the natural concomitant of a life of hurry and worry. It neutralises mental repressions and purifies the subconscious. It releases an extra amount of hope and energy and thus enables a person to face life squarely. Life is not all sweetness, enjoyment and success; it is drudgery, pain and failure, too.

81. There are some arguments for the benefits of prayer, which can be tested.

82. Prayer, by direct miracles, removes hurdles and difficulties from our lives.

83. Prayer is an important part of all religions.

84. People are interested in finding out effects of prayer.

85. Subconsciousness plays no role in our lives.

PASSAGE 18

In 1994–95 India consumed 65.3 million tonnes (mt) of petro products, out of which consumptions of diesel was 28.3 million tonnes. The annual increase in diesel consumption from 1990–91 has been 8.5 per cent as against 4.7 per cent for all petro products.

As per 1993–94 data, 11 per cent of diesel consumption is by industry, plantation etc. Eight per cent by road transport, 5.5 per cent by the railways and 75 per cent by unspecified users. The consumption by farmers for tractors and irrigation pumps has been roughly 5.7 million tonnes valued at about Rs. 5,500 crores. The agricultural produce in 1994–95 valued at Rs. 2,23,076 crores.

The consumption of diesel in 1995–96 is estimated at 32 million tonnes whereas consumption of petrol accounts for 14 per cent of diesel consumption.

86. The consumpton of petrol by farmers for agricultural purpose is approximately 50 percent less than use of diesel.

87. The consumption of petrol for 1995–96 can be estimated to be in the range of 14 million tonnes.

88. One rupee increase in diesel price will generate as much revenue as roughly seven rupee increase in petrol price.

89. The percentage increase in the consumption of diesel in India is equal to that of all petro products.

90. If the cost of diesel is increased along with small matching increase in procurement price, the farmer may be marginally affected.

PASSAGE 19

Indian rice exporters might face tough competition in the international market, allege exporters. International demand for Indian rice surfaced either due to its low prices or due to the crop failure in other competitive countries. However, our competitors are having a good crop of rice this year and which indeed sounds as a threat for India, they pointed out. The leading producing countries like Thailand, Vietnam, Myanmar, U.S.A. and Pakistan are bringing down their prices at par with Indian prices. Internationally, these countries have reduced their prices by $50 per ton in lower grades, coming almost at par with Indian prices. Indian rice is currently quoting between $260 and $265 per ton. However, in high grade the differential still remains high, therefore, India can expect to be competitive in high grades provided the quality and deliveries are ensured on time. Pakistan is our main competitor and it has reduced its price by 15 per cent coming almost in line with the Indian price. The very fact that international players have started reducing their prices is a signal for Indian exporters to gear up for 1999–2000.

91. Indian crops were most inferior in quality than the leading rice producing countries.

92. India should increase production of rice by 15% to gear up for 1999–2000.

93. To remain in the international market, India should reduce its price.

94. India has no potential threat in the international market for exporting of rice.

95. Quality and delivery of goods on time are the two main components for being in the forefront.

PASSAGE 20

Of the roughly 4,40,000 children who currenly languish in America's foster-care system, 20,000 are available for adoption, most of them are older children between the ages of 6 and 12. Among the adoptable children, 44 per cent are white and 43 per cent are black. But 67 per cent of all families waiting to adopt are white, and many of them are eager to take a black child. The hurdles, however, are often formidable. Though only three US States—Arkansas, California and Minnesota—have laws promoting race matching in adoptions, 40 other favour the practice.

96. Two-third of the white families are waiting to adopt a black child.

97. Among the adoptable children at least 10 percent are neither black nor white.

98. Children beyond 12 years of age are less suitable for adoption.

99. Majority of the US States have laws that discourage the practice of adoption.

100. White children are being preferred for adoption by majority of black families.

EXPLANATORY ANSWERS

1. ***(a)*** **:** The policies differed from state to state.

2. ***(c)*** **:** Remarkable progress during the last three years is mentioned in the paragraph but nothing suggests that the production was not profitable.

3. ***(a)*** **:** There is absence of a uniform policy from the state Governments.

4. ***(c)*** **:** According to the paragraph, absence of matching policies had put the quarry owners and others involved in the industry on the verge of collapse in the international market. Nothing is mentioned about the granite quality produced in India or of the international level.

5. ***(e)*** **:** The inference does not relate to the facts given in the statement.

6. ***(d)*** **:** Government policy alone may not be responsible for the losses. Cost or quality factor may also be responsible.

7. ***(c)*** **:** The paragraph mentions that steel production in India has always been burdened with costs much higher than in comparable plants overseas. But nowhere in the paragraph it is mentioned that the cost of production of steel is less in other countries.

8. ***(a)*** **:** If the government reviews its policy, India can definitely compete with the foreign countries in regard to the steel price.

9. ***(a)*** **:** Customs duty on almost all steel products has been reduced.

10. ***(b)*** **:** There is a demand that both the customs and excise rates should be reviewed.

11. ***(a)*** **:** The global consumption of plastics is 100 million tonnes and current level of consumption in India is 1 million tonnes.

12. ***(c)*** **:** The paragraph does not mention about the import or export of plastics.

13. ***(a)*** **:** Entrepreneurs would have to look at technology transfer as well as upgradation and strategic and creative alliances.

14. ***(a)*** **:** The expected growth by end of the Ist half of this century is between 2.5 and 3 million tonnes. India needs 2 additional polymer plants of 1,000 tonnes per year.

15. ***(a)*** **:** By thinking in lines of globalisation and promoting projects of international capacity India can be one of the major players in the production of plastics in the international market.

16. ***(d)*** **:** Nowhere in the paragraph it is stated that the losses of the smaller units can be minimised if they are made operationally self–sufficient.

17. ***(a)*** **:** Lack of proper opportunities for recycling waste is one of the reasons for maximum losses suffered by smaller units.

18. ***(c)*** **:** The paragraph is about the problems and losses of smaller units. Comparatively, larger units must be facing lesser problems and losses.

19. ***(e)*** **:** Low profit margins and adverse conditions compels smaller units to ignore house keeping.

20. ***(a)*** **:** To prevent or eliminate the loss of expensive material by the smaller unit waste management process in India needs modernisation.

21. (a) : Due to low budget the railways cannot acquire necessary equipments.

22. (a) : Earlier, there was no need to think of innovative ways.

23. (a) : Railway budget of the Union Government had supported the Indian Railways for more than a decade.

24. (b) : Erosion in budgetary support from the Union Government is probably true if the Government has shifted its priority to other areas.

25. (a) : There has been a grievous impact on the railways.

26. (a) : The actual number of illiterate females is also increasing with time and faster than the number of male illiterates.

27. (c) : The passage tells about the increase in number of male and female illiterates but mentions nothing about the present ratio of illiterate males and females.

28. (e) : Infant mortality is correlated with female illiteracy.

29. (e) : Mortality is highest in the case of illiterate mothers in rural areas.

30. (c) : The population figures are not mentioned in the passage.

31. (b) : Urbanisation has increased pressure on the inner cities. Probably, the rate of growth in density of population is more in inner cities.

32. (a) : This inference is directly drawn from the passage.

33. (e) : The makers of narrow winding lanes could hardly have anticipated modern transportations.

34. (e) : The density of population in urban areas is within manageable limits, with most cities, including Greater Mumbai. So, the density of population in the inner city of Greater Mumbai is not the highest.

35. (c) : Nothing is mentioned in the passage about the international urbanisation standards.

36. (c) : Nowhere in the passage has been mentioned anything about the packages offered by the companies in foreign countries.

37. (a) : Companies are trying to provide transportation, medical and housing assistance, children's education etc.

38. (e) : The survey was conducted only for executives.

39. (a) : The compensation package is made in terms of the need of the executive after consulting him.

40. (e) : The number of items in the compensation package rose as the executive ascended the management hierarchy.

41. (a) : Even being the excellent desired effect of these programmes, these could never avoid the clutches of bureaucracy.

42. (e) : Benefits of the govenment sponsored programmes could not reach those poeple for whom primarily the programmmes were prepared.

43. (c) : Nothing is mentioned in the passage about such sponsored programmes in the pre–Independence era.

44. (c) : The passage narrates nothing about the pre-Independence era.

45. (e) : The objective of Government-sponsored programmes was to improve the lot of all the poor people.

46. (c) : All the techniques of poor harvest management are not discussed in the passage.

47. (a) : Cases where production cost is high, poor harvest management will render export business non-viable.

48. (c) : Quantity of exports of fruits and vegetables is not mentioned in the passage.

49. (b) : The passage states that post-harvest management of fruits and vegetables is vital in quality exports. Probably, India is exporting quality fruits because a wide variety of post-harvest management techniques are available in India.

50. (d) : Inadequacy in respect of certain fruits does not confirm that pre-harvest management of vegetables is more crucial than that of fruits.

51. (e) : The state cultivates only premium quality mangoes.

52. (a) : Only because the quality of mangoes is good, the government has been trying to export them.

53. (c) : Nowhere in the passage it is mentioned

that the state also exports good quality grapes.

54. ***(e)*** **:** The government experiment to export mangoes through sea route proved successful.

55. ***(b)*** **:** Exporting mangoes through sea route is cheaper so there is a probability that most of other exports are also through sea route.

56. ***(e)*** **:** Many people who tried to learn yoga without the guidance of an expert have complaints of pains in various parts of their body.

57. ***(e)*** **:** The *asanas* are safe only if conducted under proper guidance of expert.

58. ***(a)*** **:** The inference is true as the passage refers to complaints by many who tried to master the technique without personal guidance.

59. ***(c)*** **:** It is not supported by facts outlawed in the passage.

60. ***(c)*** **:** The passage does not support this fact.

61. ***(e)*** **:** Common unknown men of past cannot be leaders today. They should be genius to be known and remembered.

62. ***(c)*** **:** The paragraph does not confirm this inference.

63. ***(a)*** **:** The nations are renewed from the bottom.

64. ***(b)*** **:** Woodrow Wilson's words are marked down in history and from what he has said it is likely that he was a scholar of history.

65. ***(d)*** **:** It is not true that those who are leaders are born in a particular class. Some leaders even belong to top class. But considering what Woodrow Wilson said, "the nations are renewed from the bottom, not from the top", it is probable that the inference is false.

66. ***(c)*** **:** Nothing is mentioned in the passage about the tractor industry in western countries.

67. ***(c)*** **:** This inference is not supported by the facts laid down in the passage.

68. ***(b)*** **:** As high horsepower tractors are more in demand the companies producing only low horsepower tractors will probably face financial problems.

69. ***(b)*** **:** Because of the lower level of market penetration in western and southern states the companies may have a better chance to boost the sales of their tractors which are useful for rice fields.

70. ***(c)*** **:** There is no mention of European countries in the passage.

71. ***(a)*** **:** The inference is true as the health conscious people living in urban areas can be easily made aware of harms caused by modern cooking oils through various media.

72. ***(c)*** **:** This inference is not confirmed by the facts given in the passage.

73. ***(a)*** **:** By taking proper measures like intake of fibre diet, physical exercise etc. increase in diseases can be controlled.

74. ***(c)*** **:** There is no such account in the passage that confirms this inference.

75. ***(a)*** **:** This inference is directly drawn from the passage.

76. ***(c)*** **:** There is no mention in the passage about such education being introduced in schools.

77. ***(a)*** **:** It is useless to saturate the minds of students with notions that they easily forget.

78. ***(c)*** **:** Anything regarding importance of parent's role in particular in imparting good values is not mentioned in the passage.

79. ***(a)*** **:** A re-oriented educational system will educate the students to learn their deepest and innate qualities and give them the capacity to give their lives the right meaning.

80. ***(d)*** **:** The inference cannot be definitely false but in certain cases it may not be false.

81. ***(a)*** **:** Prayer relieves the mind of tension.

82. ***(e)*** **:** Prayer is no miracle. It releases an extra amount of hope and energy and enables a person to face life squarely.

83. ***(b)*** **:** The inference by itself is true but only a probability is reflected in the passage.

84. ***(c)*** **:** Nowhere in the passage is mentioned about the people's interest.

85. ***(e)*** **:** Subconciousness definitely plays a role in our lives and this is why the passage mentions the role of prayer in purifying the subconscious.

86. ***(c)*** **:** The amount of consumption of petrol by farmers is not mentioned in the passage.

87. (e) : The consumption of petrol is 14% of diesel *i.e.*, (14 ÷ 100) × 32 = 4.48 or 4.5% million tonnes.

88. (a) : The consumption of diesel is more than consumption of petrol. It is mentioned in the passage that consumption of petrol was 14% that of diesel. The ratio of consumption is 32 : 4.5 *i.e.*, about 7 : 1.

89. (e) : The percentage increase in the consumption of diesel was 8.5% as against 4.7% for all petro products.

90. (c) : The data given in the passage does not confirm this inference.

91. (e) : In high grade of rice, the differential still remains high—confirms the high quality of Indian rice.

92. (e) : India should also reduce the prices in competition with other countries.

93. (a) : The very fact that the international players have started reducing their prices is a signal for Indian exporters to reduce its price as well.

94. (b) : Other competitive countries are having a good crop of rice and are trying to get at par with Indian prices, which may pose a threat.

95. (a) : India can expect to be competitve in high grades provided the quality and deliveries are ensured on time.

96. (c) : Information about the white families wanting to adopt a black child is not given in the passage.

97. (a) : 44% are white, 43% are black, so at least 10% (exactly 13% according to passage) are neither black nor white.

98. (c) : Nothing is mentioned in the passage about children beyond 12 years.

99. (e) : Majority of the state laws favour the practice, only three states discourage it.

100. (c) : There is no mention in the passage about white children being preferred by black families.

PART - X

COURSE OF ACTION

In these type of questions a situation is presented and some courses of action are suggested in the context of that situation. The candidates are required to determine which course of action follows immediately from the given statement without letting their own perception influence the decision.

SOLVED EXAMPLES

In each question below a statement is followed by two courses of action numbered I and II. A course of action is a step or administrative decision to be taken for improvement, follow-up or further action in regard to the problem, policy etc. on the basis of the information given in the statement. Everything in the statement is assumed to be true and then it is decided as to which of the two given suggested courses of action logically follows for pursuing.

The answer is given as—

(*a*) If only I follows
(*b*) If only II follows
(*c*) If either I or II follows
(*d*) If neither I nor II follows, or
(*e*) If both I and II follow.

1. *Statement* :

Some blunders were detected in the Accounts Section of an organisation.

Courses of action :

I. An efficient team of auditors should be appointed to check the accounts.

II. A show-cause notice should be issued to all those employees who were involved in the irregularity.

Ans. *(e)* : According to the statement some blunders have been found. So, course of action I follows. It should also be made clear if the blunders were done on purpose or were just careless mistakes. So, course of action II also follows.

2. *Statement:*

The Minister said that the teachers are still not familiarised with the need, importance and meaning of population education in the higher education system. They are not even clearly aware about their role and responsibilities in the population education programme.

Courses of Action :

I. Population Education Programme should be included in the college curriculum.

II. Orientation programme should be conducted for teachers on population education.

Ans. *(b)* : When the teachers are still not aware of the need, importance and meaning of Population Education in the higher education system and their own role and responsibilities, it cannot be included in the college curriculum. So, course of action I does not follow. But, to make the teachers familiar with the concepts of this programme an orientation programme should be conducted. So, course of action II follows.

EXERCISE

Directions (Qs. 1 to 20) : *In each question below is given a statement followed by two courses of action numbered I and II. A course of action is a step or administrative decision to be taken for improvement, follow-up or further action in regard to the problems, policy, etc. on the basis of the information given in the statement. You have to assume everything in the statement to be true, then decide which of the given suggested courses of action logically follows for pursuing.*

Give answer (a) if only I follows; give answer (b) if only II follows; give answer (c) if either I or II follows; give answer (d) if neither I nor II follows and give answer (e) if both I and II follow.

1. *Statement :*
Although the Indian economy is still heavily dependent on agriculture, its share in global agriculturai trade is less than the share of agricultural exports to total exports.
Courses of Action :
(i) Efforts should be made to increase our agricultural production.
(ii) The exports of non-agricultural commodities should be reduced.

2. *Statement :*
About 30 to 40 per cent of children who are enrolled, do not attend school on any given day.
Courses of Action :
(i) More schools should be started.
(ii) Reasons for this absenteeism should be found out.

3. *Statement :*
Certain mining industries in Gujarat may come to a standstill because of the notification issued by the Ministry of Environment and Forest banning mining operations and industries alike within 25 kms of National Park, the bird sanctuary and reserve forest areas.
Courses of Action :
(i) The Ministry should be asked to immediately withdraw the notification.
(ii) The Government should make efforts to shift the parks, sanctuaries and reserve forests to other non-mining areas.

4. *Statement :*
The Indian electronic component industry venturing into the West European markets faces tough competition from the Japanese.
Courses of Action :
(i) India should search for other international markets for its products.
(ii) India should improve the quality of the electronic components to compete with the Japanese in capturing these markets.

5. *Statement :*
Air export volumes have increased substantially over the past decade causing backlogs and difficulties for air cargo agents because of increased demand for space and service.
Courses of Action :
(i) Airlines and air cargo agents should jointly work out a solution to combat the problem.
(ii) The reasons for the increase in the volume of air export should be found out.

6. *Statement :*
The world conference on 'Education of All' took place in Thailand in 1990. Widely attended conference endorsed the Framework for Action for Meeting the Basic Learning Needs of all Children.
Courses of Action :
(i) India should suitably implement the Action points of this conference.
(ii) India should also immediately organise this type of conference.

7. *Statement :*
Huge amount of resources are required to develop tourist places in a country like India which is endowed with vast coastal lines, rivers, forests, temples, etc.
Courses of Action :
(i) More tourist-resorts along the coastal line only should be started.
(ii) The tourist-potential of India should be exploited.

8. *Statement :*
Financial stringency prevented the Manipur

Government from paying salaries to its employees since April this year.... a report in December.

Courses of Action :

(*i*) The Manipur Government should immediately curtail the staff strength at least by 30 per cent.

(*ii*) The Manipur Government should reduce wasteful expenditure and arrange to pay the salaries of its employees.

9. *Statement :*

Reports of steep and continued decline in the inflows into the Gobindsagar reservoir of the Bhakra Dam, coupled with a depleted stock of steam coal with the thermal power plants in the north, may lead to a serious power crisis in the region.

Courses of Action :

(*i*) The supply of steam coal to the thermal power plants needs to be immediately stepped up by the Government.

(*ii*) The Government should set up hydraulic power plants on other rivers in the region.

10. *Statement :*

The police department has come under a cloud with recent revelations that at least two senior police officials are suspected to have been involved in the illegal sale of a large quantity of weapons from the State police armoury.

Courses of Action :

(*i*) A thorough investigation should be ordered by the State Government to bring out all those who are involved into the illegal sale of arms.

(*ii*) State police armoury should be kept under Central Government's control.

11. *Statement :*

Assembly and Parliamentary elections should be held simultaneously.

Courses of Action :

(*i*) The Constitution should be amended for this purpose.

(*ii*) The President should be given responsibility for deciding it.

12. *Statement :*

Express Highways are essential for rapid transportation via roads.

Courses of Action :

(*i*) Tenders for Express Highways should be issued soon.

(*ii*) Only Express Highways should be built from now on for the rapid development of the country.

13. *Statement :*

The production of silk in State 'X' has come down drastically due to loopholes in implementation of sericulture development programme despite availability of funds.

Courses of Action :

(*i*) Government of State 'X' should immediately study the loopholes and take corrective action to plug the loopholes.

(*ii*) The silk producers of State 'X' must be given technical help for this year.

14. *Statement :*

In order to speed up the work of assessment of papers of H.S.C. Examination, the examination board in State 'X' has decided to appoint temporary and inexperienced teachers of Junior Colleges as examiners.

Courses of Action :

(*i*) Many of the teachers should be given higher compensation as they are putting hard efforts in spite of lack of knowledge and expertise.

(*ii*) These teachers need to be given proper orientation by experienced examiners and centralised assessment may be made under supervision of moderators.

15. *Statement :*

If the retired Professors of the same Institutes are also invited to deliberate on re-structuring of the organisation, their contribution may be beneficial to the Institute.

Courses of Action :

(*i*) Management may seek opinion of the employees before calling retired Professors.

(*ii*) Management should involve experienced people for the systematic re-structuring of the organisation.

16. *Statement :*

Experts Committee on Industrial Relations

has revealed in their recent report that not only the internal problems of the organisations were successfully managed through quality circles but also employees' motivation level was increased significantly.

Courses of Action :

(i) Organisations should organise orientation programmes for their employees on quality circles.

(ii) Employees should be encouraged to join quality circle programmes.

17. *Statement :*

Monsoons may fail this year as its parameters are not giving consistent results.

Courses of Action :

(i) A more detailed study regarding the parameters of efficiency should be taken up.

(ii) Water conservation methods should be strictly implemented from now onwards.

18. *Statement :*

Researchers are feeling agitated as libraries are not equipped to provide the right information to the right users at the right time in the required format. Even the users are not aware about the various services available for them.

Courses of Action :

(i) All the information available in the libraries should be computerised to provide faster services to the users.

(ii) Library staff should be trained in computer operations.

19. *Statement :*

One of the problems facing the food processing industry is the irregular supply of raw material. The producers of raw materials are not getting a reasonable price.

Courses of Action :

(i) The government should regulate the supply of raw material to other industries also.

(ii) The government should announce an attractive package to ensure regular supply of raw material for food processing industry.

20. *Statement :*

India's performance in the last Olympic Games was very poor. Not even a single medal could be bagged by the players. Government had spent Rs. 5 crores in training and deputing a team of players to participate in the Olympic Games.

Courses of Action :

(i) India should stop sending players to the future Olympic games.

(ii) Government should immediately set up an inquiry commission to find out the reasons for India's dismal performance.

Directions (Qs. 21 to 40) : *In each question below is given a statement followed by three courses of action numbered I, II and III. Assume everything in the statement to be true then dicide which of the given options suggests the logical answer.*

21. *Statement :*

India's pre-eminent position in the world black pepper production and trade is in danger as some of the countries which recently started production of this 'King of the spices' crop from Indian root stocks, are faring better by adopting modern cultivation practices.

Courses of Action :

(i) India should immediately stop supplying root stocks of black pepper to other countries.

(ii) India should adopt modern technology for cultivating black pepper to compete in the international market.

(iii) India should reduce the price of its black pepper to remain competitive in the world market.

(a) All follow.
(b) Only II follows.
(c) Only I follows.
(d) Only III follows.
(e) None of these.

22. *Statement :*

A large number of tribal inhabitants are found to have been suffering from various diseases due to exposure to radioactive waste near the Uranium mine.

Courses of Action :

(i) The Government should immediately close down the mine.

(ii) The Government should immediately

take steps to save local people from exposure to radioactive waste.

(iii) The tribals should be rehabilitated at a safer place.

(a) Only II and III follow.
(b) Only I and II follow.
(c) Only I and III follow.
(d) Only III follows.
(e) None of these.

23. *Statement :*

A blast was triggered off injuring many when the night shift workers at an ordnance factory were handling 'fox signalling explosive'.

Courses of Action :

(i) The factory management should train its staff as regards the safety aspects of handling such explosive material.

(ii) The services of the supervisor in-charge of the night shift should be terminated.

(iii) The factory should immediately stop carrying out such exercises at night.

(a) None follows.
(b) All follow.
(c) Only I follows.
(d) Only I and II follow.
(e) None of these.

24. *Statement :*

There was a spurt in criminal activities in the city during the recent festival season.

Courses of Action :

(i) The police should immediately investigate into the causes of this increase.

(ii) In future the police should take adequate precaution to avoid recurrence of such situation during festival season.

(iii) The known criminals should be arrested before any such season.

(a) None follows.
(b) All follow.
(c) Only II and III follow.
(d) Only I and II follow.
(e) None of these.

25. *Statement :*

The weather bureau has through a recent bulletin forecast heavy rainfall during the next week which may cause waterlogging in several parts of the city.

Courses of Action :

(i) The bulletin should be given wide publicity through the mass media.

(ii) The civic authority should keep in readiness the pumping system for removal of water from these parts.

(iii) The people should be advised to stay indoors during the period.

(a) All follow.
(b) Only II and III follow.
(c) Only II follows.
(d) Only I and II follow.
(e) None follows.

26. *Statement :*

A major rail accident involving a mail train was averted due to the presence of mind of one signal man at a wayside cabin.

Courses of Action :

(i) The railway track for at least 50 km should be cleared of any traffic ahead of all the mail trains.

(ii) The railway signalling systems should immediately be made automatic.

(iii) The signal man should be rewarded so as to encourage others.

(a) All follow.
(b) None follows.
(c) Only I and II follow.
(d) Only II and III follow.
(e) None of these.

27. *Statement :*

In one of the worst accidents in railway level crossing fifty people died when a bus carrying them collided on to a running train.

Courses of Action :

(i) The train driver should immediately be suspended.

(ii) The driver of the bus should be tried in court for negligence on his part.

(iii) The railway authority should be asked to man all its level crossings.

(a) None follows.
(b) Only III follows.
(c) Only I and II follow.
(d) Only II and III follow.
(e) None of these.

28. *Statement :*

A mass mortality of shrimps in ponds on entire Andhra Coast has recently been reported due to the presence of a virus.

Courses of Action :

(i) The water of the ponds affected should immediately be treated for identifying the nature of the virus.

(ii) The catching of shrimps from the ponds should temporarily be stopped.

(iii) The fisherman should be asked to watch for the onset of such phenomenon in future.

(*a*) All follow.
(*b*) Only I and II follow.
(*c*) Only II and III follow.
(*d*) Only I follows.
(*e*) None of these.

29. *Statement :*

Faced with a serious resource crunch and a depressing overall economic scenario, Orissa is unlikely to achieve the targetted percent compound annual growth rate during the 8th plan.

Courses of Action :

(i) The target growth should be reduced for the next plan.

(ii) The reasons for the failure should be studied.

(iii) Orissa's performance should be compared with that of other states.

(*a*) Only I follows.
(*b*) Only I and III follow.
(*c*) Only II and III follow.
(*d*) Neither follows.
(*e*) All follow.

30. *Statement :*

The army has been alerted in the district following floods triggered by incessant rains.

Courses of Action :

(i) Relief to flood affected people should be arranged.

(ii) Supply of food articles should be arranged.

(iii) Adequate medical facilities should be arranged.

(*a*) Only I follows.
(*b*) Only II follows.
(*c*) Only I and III follow.
(*d*) None follows.
(*e*) All follow.

31. *Statement :*

If the faculty members also join the strike, there is going to be a serious problem.

Courses of Action :

(i) The faculty members should be persuaded not to go on strike.

(ii) Those faculty members who join the strike should be suspended.

(iii) The management should not worry about such small things.

(*a*) Only I follows.
(*b*) Only I and II follow.
(*c*) Only II and III follow.
(*d*) None follows.
(*e*) All follow.

32. *Statement :*

The world will have to feed more than 10 billion people in the next century of whom half will be in Asia and will eat rice as their staple.

Courses of Action :

(i) More funds should immediately be allocated for rice research to help ensure adequate supplies.

(ii) The people in Asia should be encouraged to change their food habit.

(iii) The rice should be grown in countries outside Asia to meet the demand.

(*a*) Only I and II follow.
(*b*) Only II and III follow.
(*c*) Only I and III follow.
(*d*) All follow.
(*e*) None of these.

33. *Statement :*

Higher disposal costs encourage those who produce waste to look for cheaper ways to get rid of it.

Courses of Action :

(i) The disposal costs should be made higher.

(ii) The disposal costs should be brought down.

(iii) A committee should be set up to study

the details in this respect.
(*a*) Only I follows.
(*b*) Only II follows.
(*c*) Either I or II follows.
(*d*) Only II and III follow.
(*e*) All follow.

34. *Statement :*
Over 27,000 bonded labourers indentified and freed are still awaiting rehabilitation.
Courses of Action :
(*i*) More cases of bonded labourers should be identified.
(*ii*) Till the proper rehabilitation facilities are available, the bonded labourers should not be freed.
(*iii*) The impediments in the way of speedy and proper rehabilitation of bonded labourers should be removed.
(*a*) Only I follows.
(*b*) Only II follows.
(*c*) Only III follows.
(*d*) Only II and III follow.
(*e*) None follows.

35. *Statement :*
Lack of coordination between the University, its colleges and various authorities has resulted in students ousted from one college seeking migration to another.
Courses of Action :
(*i*) If a student is ousted from a college, the information should be sent to all the other colleges of the University.
(*ii*) The admissions to all the colleges of the University should he handled by the University directly.
(*iii*) A separate section should be made for taking strict action against students indulging in anti-social activities.
(*a*) Only I follows.
(*b*) Only II follows.
(*c*) Only III follows.
(*d*) Only I and III follow.
(*e*) Only II and III follow.

36. *Statement :*
The Institute has fixed for the investors a validity period of one year for transfer forms for some of its listed schemes.
Courses of Action :
(*i*) The Institute should consult investors before fixing the duration of validity period.
(*ii*) The investors should be duly informed about the validity period.
(*iii*) List of schemes covered under this validity period should be communicated.
(*a*) All follow.
(*b*) Only I and II follow.
(*c*) Only I and III follow.
(*d*) Only III follows.
(*e*) Only II and III follow.

37. *Statement :*
In the Teacher's Day function, Shri Sharma, a State awardee and a retired principal, had questioned the celebration of Teacher's Day in 'today's materialistic world'.
Courses of Action :
(*i*) The expenditure on Teacher's Day celebration should be reduced.
(*ii*) More funds should be allocated for the celebration of Teacher's Day.
(*iii*) The role and responsibilities of teachers should be seen in today's perspective.
(*a*) All follow.
(*b*) None follows.
(*c*) Either I or II follows.
(*d*) Only III follows.
(*e*) Only II and III follow.

38. *Statement:*
In the city, over 75 per cent of the people are living in slums and sub-standard houses which is a reflection on the housing and urban development policies of the Government.
Courses of Action :
(*i*) There should be a separate department looking after housing and urban development.
(*ii*) The policies in regard to urban housing should be reviewed.
(*iii*) The policies regarding rural housing should also be reviewed so that such problems could be avoided in rural areas.
(*a*) Only I follows.
(*b*) Only II follows.
(*c*) Only II and III follow.
(*d*) Either II or III follows.

(*e*) Only I and II follow.

39. *Statement :*

Cholera broke out recently in parts of the city killing a large number of people and affecting hundreds of households.

Courses of Action :

(*i*) An enquiry should be initiated to identify the cause of the catastrophe.

(*ii*) The civic administration should make the general public aware of, through mass media, the preventive measures to be adopted in such a situation.

(*iii*) The para-military forces should be called in to help the civic administration.

(*a*) None follows.

(*b*) Only II follows.

(*c*) Both I and II follow.

(*d*) All follow.

(*e*) None of these.

40. *Statement :*

According to the officials, paucity of funds with the organisation has led to the pathetic condition of this brilliant architectural structure.

Courses of Action :

(*i*) A new architectural structure for the building should be designed.

(*ii*) The reasons for the poor condition of the structure should be found out.

(*iii*) Grant should be given to improve the condition of the structure.

(*a*) Only I follows.

(*b*) Only II follows.

(*c*) Only III follows.

(*d*) Only II and III follow.

(*e*) Only I and III follow.

EXPLANATORY ANSWERS

1. (*d*) : India's share in global agricultural trade is less than the share of agricultural exports to total exports. Therefore, there is no necessity of increasing the agricultural production. Reducing the exports of non-agricultural commodity will not affect the share of agricultural exports. So, neither course of action follows.

2. (*d*) : About 30 to 40 per cent of enrolled children do not attend schools. Therefore, the decision to start more schools is pointless. The statement does not mention that a particular group of children do not attend schools. This means the percentage of absent children comprises of various children who are absent at different times. There cannot be specific reasons for this absenteeism. So, neither course of action follows.

3. (*d*) : The department cannot withdraw the notification because environment pollution must be checked around the game sanctuary and reserve forest areas. Further, it is coherent to shift the mining industries. So, neither course of action follows.

4. (*e*) : In the face of tough competition from the Japanese, India should either improve the quality of electronic components to capture the market or search for other international markets where Japanese have not captured the market. So, both the course of action follow.

5. (*a*) : The reasons for the increase in the volume of air exports according to the statement is, increase in demand for space and service. Therefore, the airlines and air cargo agents should jointly work out a solution to combat the problem. So, only course of action I follows.

6. (*e*) : In a country like India where illiteracy rate is still high, such conferences should be organised and India must suitably implement the action points of the "Education for All" conference. So, both the courses of action follow.

7. (*b*) : Considering the amount of resources required to develop tourist resorts in India it is necessary to exploit the tourist potential. So, only course of action II follows.

8. (*b*) : Curtailing the staff strength would only hinder the work. Instead, the government can reduce wasteful expenditure and arrange to pay the salaries of its employees. So, only course of action II follows.

9. (*a*) : To check the spurt of serious power crisis in the region, the government should immediately step up the supply of steam coal to the thermal power plant. Setting up of hydraulic power plants is an entirely new proposal. So, only course of action I follows.

10. (*a*) : It is unlikely that the Central Government should keep a check an every state police armoury. But, a thorough investigation can bring out the culprits and the police department can continue to function with the force of efficient police officers. So, only course of action I follows.

11. (c) : If the Assembly and Parliamentary elections are held simultaneously, it will save a lot of time and finances. But this is possible only if the Constitution is amended for this purpose. If the Constitution cannot be amended, the President should be given the responsibility for deciding it. So, either courses of action follows.

12. (d) : Express highways are essential for rapid transportation via roads but other ways of rapid transportation are also available. These highways require exorbitant expenditure and it is not possible to build only such highways for a country's rapid development. So, neither course of action follows.

13. (*a*) : Course of action I is an instant response to the given statement. Any technical help is useless in presence of loopholes. So, only course of action I follows.

14. (*b*) : Inexperienced teachers must be given proper orientation so that they assess the papers rightly. Compensation is a reward for efficient work and not just hard work. So, only course of action II follows.

15. (b) : Retired professors are expected to be more experienced than the present employees. The management should consider their opinion for the re-structuring of the organisation. So, only course of action II follows.

16. (*e*) : Orientation programmes bring forth the internal problems of an organisation which can then be solved and also, the employees get motivated to come forward. So, both the courses of action follow.

17. (*e*) : If the parameters are faulty, they should be corrected and conservation is necessary for the prevention of resources for future. So, both the courses of action follow.

18. (*e*) : In order to maintain a systematic function libraries should be computerised and library staff should be trained in computer operations. So, both the courses of action follow.

19. (*b*) : At present the food processing industry needs the attention of the Government and not other industries. A regular supply of raw material can resolve the problem. So, only course of action II follows.

20. (*b*) : Poor performance can be improved if the reasons are apparent. Stepping out of such games is an immature decision. So, only course of action II follows.

21. (*b*) : Major threat to India is from countries adopting modern cultivation practices. If India also adopts the modern cultivation technology it can compete in the international market. Stopping the supply or reducing the prices is no solution for competing in the world market. So, only course of action II follows.

22. (*a*) : As Uranium is useful, its mine should not be closed. But the government must take steps to save the local people and rehabilitate them at safer places. So, courses of action II and III follow.

23. (*c*) : In order to avoid such accidents the staff should be trained. Supervisor incharge cannot be blamed for the inexperienced act of a worker and one accident is no reason enough to put an end to exercises in the ordnance factory.

24. (*b*) : The criminal activities must be immediately investigated. Known criminals must be arrested precautionarily so that such activities do not recur during the festival season. So, all the courses of action follow.

25. (e) : A week's rainfall is no cause for panic. Waterlogging will clear off after the rain stops and people cannot be advised to shirk their work or routine because of the

26. (e) : The statement mentions the alert mind of the signal man at a wayside cabin. When no accident had occurred, neither course of action follows.

27. (d) : Following the accident, the main step is the driver's arrest and trial in court. Suspending the driver is like leaving him unpunished and manning all railway crossing can be too costly. So, in lieu of the statement, so course of action II and III follows.

28. (*d*) : In order to save the shrimps immediate action is required to identify and treat the virus. While this is being done catching of shrimps will also stop and the fisherman will become aware of such situations in future. So, only course of action I immediately follows the statement.

29. (c) : Reducing the target growth is not the solution. The reasons for the failure should be studied and also the state's performance should be compared with that of other states, may be it is not only Orissa but other states as well which are affected. So, courses of action II and III follow.

30. (e) : Areas affected by floods need attention. As known, Army services can easily provide relief, supply food articles and arrange medical facilities for the flood affected people. So, all the courses of action follow.

31. (a) : The faculty members have not yet joined the strike. They can be persuaded not to go on strike, as strike is a matter of concern for the management. If the faculty members do not join, there is no need for their suspension. So, only course of action I follows.

32. (a) : In the next century 5 billion people will be in Asia and rice will be their staple food. So funds should be immediately allocated for rice research to help ensure adequate supplies. On the other hand the Asians should be encouraged to change their food habit. If rice is grown outside Asia also then people with other food habits will face a problem. So, courses of action I and II follow.

33. (d) : Disposal costs is already high, it should be brought down and a committee should be set up to study the details. So, only courses of action II and III follow.

34. (c) : Bonded labour must be freed but when a large number of such freed labour is still awaiting rehabilitation, more cases can be identified later. The process of rehabilitation should be made easy. So, only course of action III follows.

35. (a) : Information about the ousted student must be sent to other colleges of the university. Whosoever is the Admissions Authority should know about this student and there is no need for any special section to deal with students indulging in anti-social activities. So, only course of action I follows.

36. (e) : The Institute by itself has the authority to take decisions. However, the investors should be duly informed about the schemes and validity period. So, courses of action II and III follow.

37. (d) : The question put up by Shri Sharma on the Teacher's Day Function could be asking about the teacher's role and responsibilities. Questions regarding the expenditures and funds cannot be sensibly asked about during a function. So, only course of action III follows.

38. (e) : Considering the problem stated in the city, there is a need for reviewing the policies and a separate department can efficiently look after the housing and urban development. Rural housing problems are not mentioned in the statement. So, courses of action I and II follow.

39. (d) : The cause of the catastrophe must be known and the people made aware of the preventive measures. Services of para-military forces will be needed to help the civic administration deal with the situation. So, all the courses of action follow.

40. (c) : Immediate steps should be taken to improve the structure. Reason for the poor condition of the structure is lack of funds so grants should be given. Any brilliant architectural structure should be maintained if it is possible to do so and not scraped up for any new structure. So, only course of action III follows.

PART - XI

STATEMENT SUFFICIENCY

A systematic approach is needed to attempt questions of this pattern. In these type of tests the candidate has to analyse the given data and decide if he can get the answer to the given question using the given data.

SOLVED EXAMPLES

Each of the question below consists of a question and two statements numbered I and II given below it. After reading both the statements it has to be decided whether the data provided in the statements are sufficient to answer the question. The answer is given as (*a*) if the data in statement I alone are sufficient to answer the question, while the data in statement II alone are not sufficient to answer the question; (*b*) if the data in statement II alone are sufficient to answer the question, while the data in statement I alone are not sufficient to answer the question; (*c*) if the data either in statement I alone or in statement II alone are sufficient to answer the question; (*d*) if the data even in both the statements I and II together are not sufficient to answer the question; and (*e*) if the data given in both the statements I and II together are necessary to answer the question.

1. *Question :* How old is Gopal?

Statements : I. Gopal is eight years older than his brother.

II. Gopal's mother, who is 35 years older than his brother, was born in 1942.

Ans. (*d*) : Gopal is eight years older than his brother and Gopal's mother is 35 years older than Gopal's brother but Gopal's brother's age is not mentioned and Gopal's age cannot be determined. So, the data even in both the statements I and II together are not sufficient to answer the given question.

2. *Question :* Does drinking coffee lead to headache?

Statement : I. Over-stimulation of pancreas leads to headache.

II. Coffee contains caffeine which excessively stimulates pancreas.

Ans. (*e*) : According to the given statements coffee content caffeine excessively stimulates pancreas which leads to headache. This answer to the given question is derived from both the statements. So, the data given in both the statements I and II together are necessary to answer the question.

EXERCISE

Directions : *Each of the questions below consist of a question and two statements numbered I and II given below it. You have to decide whether data provided in the statements are sufficient to answer the question. Read both the statements and give answer—*

(*a*) if the data in statement I alone are sufficient to answer the question, while the data in statement II alone are not sufficient to answer the question.

(*b*) if the data in statement II alone are sufficient to answer the question, while the data in statement I alone are not sufficient to answer the question.

(*c*) if the data either in statement I or in statement II alone are sufficient to answer the question.

(*d*) If the data even in both statements I and II together are not sufficient to answer the question and

(*e*) if the data in both statements I and II together are necessary to answer the question.

1. Who is father of Kamal?

I. Kamal and Navin are brothers.

II. Navin's mother is wife of Ashok's brother.

2. How many sons does Suresh have?
   I. Kamal and Suhas are children of Mala.
   II. Mala is married to Suresh.
3. In a certain code '1 3' means 'stop smoking' and '5 9' means 'injurious habit'. What is the meaning of '9' and '5' respectively in that code?
   I. '1 5 7' means 'stop bad habit'.
   II. '8 3 9' means 'smoking is injurious'.
4. Which day of November is Narayan's birthday this year?
   I. His birthday is after 8th but before 11th.
   II. His birthday is on Tuesday.
5. Rakesh's monthly salary is Rs. 4,000. What is Anil's monthly salary?
   I. Anil gets Rs. 500 more than the average salary of his and Rakesh's.
   II. Average of Rakesh's and Anil's salary is Rs. 4,500.
6. On which day of the week did Atul reach Mumbai?
   I. Atul's brother reached Mumbai one day earlier to Atul.
   II. Atul's mother reached Mumbai on Thursday which was two days later than the arrival of his brother.
7. How many children in a room are boys?
   I. 50% of the children are in white dress.
   II. Only boys are in white dress.
8. Among four friends A, B, C and D, who is the heaviest?
   I. B is heavier than A, but lighter than D.
   II. C is lighter than B.
9. How many cups of tea did Mohan take yesterday in office (Presume that he paid for the tea taken by him)?
   I. He paid Rs. 15 for the day for tea and snacks.
   II. Tea in his office costs Re 1 per cup.
10. Who among Sheela, Nupur, Mohini and Chanda is tallest?
    I. Sheela is taller than Mohini.
    II. Chanda is taller than Nupur.
11. The area of a playground is 484 sq. metres. What is its perimeter?
    I. It costs Rs. 912 to put a fence around the playground.
    II. The playground is a perfect square.
12. How many students in a class play hockey?
    I. Two-thirds of the students play hockey while all the remaining 21 students play chess.
    II. All the 42 students in the class who are above 16, play hockey.
13. Who is the heaviest among Amol, Prabhu, Narayan and Navin?
    I. Amol and Prabhu are of the same weight.
    II. Prabhu weighs more than Narayan, but less than Navin.
14. How many daughters does 'L' have?
    I. R's father has three daughters.
    II. 'T' is R's sister and daughter of L.
15. Who is the brother of C?
    I. D is the daughter of M.
    II. M is the father of C.
16. Who is the father of M?
    I. A and B are brothers.
    II. B's wife is sister of M's wife.
17. How many students in a class play football?
    I. Forty boys play football.
    II. There are forty boys and thirty girls in the class.
18. What is Shubha's date of birth?
    I. On 21st September, 1994, Shubha completes 15 years, 3 months and 5 days.
    II. Shubha's brother who is exactly two years younger to her, was born on June 16, 1981.
19. In a certain code language, 'pe nop can' means 'we like roses'. Which word means 'roses'?
    I. 'nop te cap' means 'we are honest'.
    II. 'pe me say' means 'they like flowers'.
20. Rajiv's rank is 17th in his class. What is his rank from the last?
    I. There are 70 students in his class.
    II. Abhijit who ranks 20th in Rajiv's class is 51st from the last.
21. A library contains only English, Hindi and Telugu novels. How many Telugu novels are there in the library?
    I. Of the one thousand novels in the library, fifty per cent novels are in English and Hindi.

II. The number of Hindi novels is double the number of English novels.

22. 'You must renew your driving licence within ten days from the date of expiry'. What is the exact date before which the licence must be renewed?

I. The statement was uttered on 17th February.

II. It was a leap year.

23. How many sons does D have?

I. A's father has three children.

II. B is A's brother and son of D.

24. Whether Nishant is entitled to free studentship?

I. The school offers free studentship to those who are under 12 years of age and have secured 60 per cent marks in the last final examination.

II. Nishant has secured 85 per cent marks in the last final examination.

25. How is 'beautiful' coded in a code?

I. '6 5 9' means 'good green leaf' in that code.

II. '9 3 5' means 'beautiful green leaf' in that code.

26. Who among R, T, M, K and P is the tallest?

I. T and K are shorter than P.

II. M is taller than P but shorter than R.

27. How many sisters does P have?

I. R and T have two sisters M and Q.

II. P is brother of T.

28. How is M related to P?

I. J has two sons of which one is P.

II. M's sister is sister of P's mother.

29. Ramesh, Nanda and Rohit together wanted to meet on Wednesday afternoon between 12.00 Noon to 5.00 p.m. At what time can they meet?

I. Ramesh has his tuitions between 12.00 Noon to 5.00 p.m. every day except on Wednesday and Saturday.

II. Nanda goes to swimming between 2.00 p.m. to 4.00 p.m. on all days except Sunday and Rohit attends craft class between 3.00 p.m. to 5.00 p.m. on all days except Thursday.

30. Who among P, Q, R and S is the shortest?

I. L is not as tall as P or R but is taller than S and Q, Q being shorter than R.

II. S is shorter than R who is shorter than P who is taller than Q.

31. Out of the books A, B and C, which book was read by Mohin today?

I. Book 'C' was taken by Mohin's friend yesterday evening and he will return it only by tomorrow.

II. Book 'A' was read by Mohin yesterday night.

32. How much amount Chandramauli required to pay for the new car in the buy-back scheme?

I. The cost of the new car was three-times the cost price of his old car.

II. His old car was valued at Rs. 25,000 under buy-back scheme.

33. How many New Year's greeting cards were sold this year in your shop?

I. Last year 2935 cards were sold.

II. The number of cards sold this year was 1.2 times that of last year.

34. What is the exact duration of this course?

I. It has three semesters but there is internship in-between second and third semester.

II. Duration of the internship varies as per the report of the professor.

35. Among E, F, G, H and I, who is in the middle while standing in a row?

I. F, who is 4th from the right end, is immediately to the left of G.

II. H, who is not the neighbour of E & F, is to the immediate left of I who is at the right end.

36. How 'K' is related to 'T'?

I. 'K' is nephew of 'P' who is mother of 'M' who is sister of 'T'.

II. 'T's uncle is 'J' who is father of 'B' who is brother of 'K'.

37. What does 'se' mean in a code language?

I. 'ram ish bu' means 'you are right' in that code language.

II. 'se tho ish' means 'right and true' in that code language.

38. Among P, Q, R and T, who stood first in the examination?

I. 'Q' was immediately followed by 'P' but no one was after 'P'.

II. 'R' was ahead of 'Q' but could not score as much as 'T'.

39. How many students in the class did not qualify?

I. 3/4th of the girls and 2/3rd of the boys in a class of 50 students, having boys and girls in the ratio of 3 : 2, qualified.

II. Number of girls qualified is 5 more than the number of boys failed in a class of 50, where number of boys is 30.

40. At what time did Suresh leave his home for office?

I. Suresh received a phone call at 9.15 a.m. at his home.

II. Suresh's car reached office at 10.15 a.m., 45 minutes after he left his residence.

41. What is the area of this plot?

I. The perimeter of the plot is 208 metres.

II. The length is more than the breadth by 4 metres.

42. How many flats are there in this housing complex ?

I. Each wing has 16 flats which is incidentally equal to the number of total buildings.

II. Each building has 4 wings, A, B, C, D.

43. How many gift boxes were sold on Monday?

I. It was 10 per cent more than the boxes sold on the earlier day, *i.e.* Sunday.

II. Every third visitor to the shop purchased a box and 1500 visitors were there on Sunday.

44. Ramesh, Rohit and Anwar, in what proportion you would distribute profit among three of you?

I. Ramesh gets two-fifth of the profit.

II. Rohit and Anwar have made 75 per cent of the total investment.

45. The cost of the kit is solely based on number of leaves. The kit has how many leaves?

I. The cost of the kit of medium size is Rs. 850.

II. The small size kit contains 55 leaves.

46. What is the distance between A and B?

I. Journey between A and B can be performed by rail.

II. Railway time-table gives the distance of rail journey.

47. How many doctors are practicing in this town?

I. There is one doctor per seven hundred residents.

II. There are 16 wards in this town with each ward having one doctor.

48. On which day the flat was purchased by Mohan in 1996?

I. Certainly before 18th December, 1996 but definitely not before 15th December, 1996.

II. Certainly after 16th December, 1996 but not later than 19th December, 1996.

49. How many candidates were selected for the course?

I. The course authorities had decided to admit 35 per cent of the candidates for the course.

II. Three hundred candidates had taken application forms from the Institute.

50. It is 8.00 p.m. When can Harish get next bus for Belapur from Panvel?

I. Buses for Belapur leave after every 30 minutes, till 10 p.m.

II. Fifteen minutes ago one bus has left for Belapur.

EXPLANATORY ANSWERS

1. (*e*) : According to the statements the mother of Kamal and Naveen is the wife of Ashok's brother. This means that Ashok's brother is the father of Kamal. So, both the statements together are necessary to answer the question.

2. (*d*) : It is clear from the two statements that Suresh has two children Kamal and Suhas but the sex of either child is not known. So, even both the statements together are not sufficient to answer the question.

3. (*c*) : According to statement I '157' means 'stop bad habit'. Code '59' means 'injurious habit'. Here code '5' and 'habit' are common and then '9' is the code for 'injurious'. According to statement II '839' means 'smoking is injurious'. Code '59' means 'injurious habit'. Here code '9' and 'injurious' are common and then '5' is the code for 'habit'. So, either of the statements alone is sufficient to answer the question.

4. (*d*) : Which of the dates fall on Tuesday is not clear from the statements. So, the data even in both statements I and II together are not sufficient to answer the question.

5. (*c*) : According to statement I Anil's salary is Rs. 500/- more than his and, Rakesh's average salary *i.e.* 4000 + 500 = Rs. 4500. According to statement II average salary of Rakesh and Anil is Rs. 4.500, which means Anil's monthly salary is Rs. 4, 500. So, either of the statement alone is sufficient to answer the question.

6. (*e*) : Atul's mother reached Mumbai on Thursday and his brother had reached two days earlier, *i.e.,* on Tuesday. Atul's brother reached Mumbai one day earlier to Atul. This means that Atul reached Mumbai on Wednesday. So, both the statements together are necessary to answer the question.

7. (*d*) : The percentage of boys who are all in white dress is 50% but the number of boys in the room cannot be calculated. So, even both the statements together are not sufficient to answer the question.

8. (*e*) : According to both the statements the descending order of friends is D>B>A/C. Here D is the heaviest. So, both the statements together are necessary to answer the question.

9. (*d*) : Payment of Rs. 15 is made for tea and snacks together. So, even both the statements together are not sufficient to answer the question.

10. (*d*) : The two statements are not related and so, even together they are not sufficient to answer the question.

11. (*b*) : Area of the playground is 484 sq. metres. As per statement II the playground is a square. So, Area of a square is $a^2 = 484$ sq. metres. The side of this square $a = \sqrt{484}$ *i.e.* 22 metres. Perimeter of a square is $4a$ *i.e.* $22 \times 4 = 88$ metres.
So, data in statement II alone is sufficient to answer the question.

12. (*c*) : If the total number of students is 'x' then according to statement I

$$x - 2/3x = 21$$
$$3x - 2x = 63$$
$$\therefore \quad x = 63$$

The total number of students who play hockey is 63 – 21 = 42.
According to statement II 42 students play hockey. So, either of the statements alone is sufficient to answer the question.

13. (*e*) : According to both the statements the descending order will be Navin > Prabhu and Amol > Narayan. Here Navin is the heaviest. So, both the statements together are necessary to answer the question.

14. (*e*) : R's father has three daughters. 'R' is definitely one of them. 'T' is R's sister and daughter of 'L'. So, 'L' is the wife of R's father and has three daughters. So, both the statements together are necessary to answer the question.

15. (*d*) : According to the statements M is the father of D and C and D is the sister of C. So, even both the statements together are not sufficient to answer the question.

16. (*d*) : The statements do not mention anything about M's father. So, both the statements together are not sufficient to answer the question.

17. (*a*) : According to statement I 40 boys play football. Statement II only specifies the number of boys and girls in the class. So data in number of statement I alone is sufficient to answer the question.

18. (*c*) : According to statement I Shubha's date

of birth is 21st September 1994 less 15 years, 3 months and 5 days, *i.e.* 16th June 1979.

According to statement II Shubha's date of birth is June 16, 1981 less two years *i.e* June 16, 1979. So, either of the statements alone is sufficient to answer the question.

19. (*e*) : 'pe nop can' means 'we like roses'. According to statement I 'nop te cap' means 'we are honest'. Here, code 'nop' and 'we' are common. According to statement II 'pe me say' means 'they like flowers'. Here code 'pe' and 'like' are common. Now from the given code 'pe nop can', 'nop' means 'we', 'pe' means 'like' and 'can' means 'roses'. So, both the statements together are necessary to answer the question.

20. (*c*) : According to statement I there are 70 students in the class. If Rajiv's rank is 17th in his class then his rank from the last is (70 – 17) + 1 *i.e.* 54th.

According to statement II Abhijit ranks 20th in Rajiv's class and is 51st from the last. The total number of students in the class is (20 + 51) – 1 *i.e.* 70. Now, Rajiv's rank from last will be (70 – 17) + 1 *i.e.* 54th.

So, either of the statements alone is sufficient to answer the question.

21. (*a*) : According to Statement I 50 per cent of 1,000 novels in the library are in English and Hindi, *i.e.* 500 novels. The remaining 500 novels are in Telugu. In statement II the total number of novels is not given. So, data in statement I alone is sufficient to answer the question.

22. (*d*) : The information given in the statements does not relate to the question. So, even both the statements together are not sufficient to answer the question.

23. (*d*) : A's father has three children. 'A' is definitely one of them. 'B' is A's brother and son of D. So, D is the mother of three children. 'B' is a son but the sex of two other children is not given. So, even both the statements together are not sufficient to answer the question.

24. (*d*) : Statement I mentions the requirements for entitlement of free studentship. Statement II does not mention Nishant's age. So, even both the statements together are not sufficient to answer the question.

25. (*e*) : '659' means 'gold green leaf' and '935' means 'beautiful green leaf'. Here '95' which is common means 'green leaf' which is also common. Now, code '3' means 'beautiful'. So, both the statements together are necessary to answer the question.

26. (*e*) : According to both the statements the ascending order will be T/K<P<M<R. Here, R is the tallest. So, both the statements together are necessary to answer the question.

27. (*d*) : Sex of 'R' and 'T' is not known. So, even both the statements together are not sufficient to answer the question.

28. (*d*) : Statement I is not related to the question. According to statement II P's mother is the sister of M but as sex of M is not known, the relation of M with P cannot be determined. So, even both the statements together are not sufficient to answer the question.

29. (*e*) : Ramesh has his tuitions between 12 noon to 5 p.m. Nanda goes to swimming between 2 p.m. to 4 p.m. Rohit attends craft classes between 3 p.m. to 5 p.m. As Ramesh is free on Wednesday, all can meet on this day between 12 noon to 2 p.m. So, both the statements together are necessary to answer the question.

30. (*d*) : According to both the statements the ascending order will be P<R<L<Q/S. Either Q or S can be the shortest. So, even both the statements together are not sufficient to answer the question.

31. (*e*) : Book C will be returned tomorrow by Mohin's friend. Book A was read yesterday night by Mohin. Book B was read by Mohin today. So, both the statements together are necessary to answer the question.

32. (*e*) : The old car was valued at Rs. 25,000 under buy-back scheme. The cost of new car is 25000 × 3 = Rs. 75,000. The amount Chandramauli was required to pay for the new car is 75,000 – 25,000 *i.e.* Rs. 50,000. So, both the statements together are necessary to answer the question.

33. (*e*) : The number of cards sold this year are 2935 × 1.2 = 3558. So, both the statements together are necessary to answer the question.

34. (*d*) : Definite duration of internship is not known so, even both the statements together are not sufficient to answer the question.

35. (*e*) : According to both the statements the standing order is E, F, G, H, I. Here, G is standing in the middle. So, both the statements together are necessary to answer the question.

36. (*c*) : According to statement I 'P' is the mother of 'M' and 'T' and 'K' who is the nephew (brother's or sister's son) of 'P' is the cousin of 'T'. According to statement II 'J' is the uncle of 'T' and father of 'B' and 'K' who are both cousins of 'T'. So, either of the statements alone is sufficient to answer the question.

37. (*d*) : 'ram ish bu' means 'you are right' and 'se tho ish' means 'right and true'. Here 'ish' which is common means 'right' which is also common. Now it is not possible to determine which word from 'and true' is meant by code 'se'. So, even both the statements together are not sufficient to answer the question.

38. (*e*) : According to both the statements the standing in order of merit is T, R, Q, P. Here T stood first in the examination. So, both the statements together are necessary to answer the question.

39. (a) : According to statement I number of boys in the class is 30 and that of girls is 20. The number of boys who qualified is 2/3rd of 30, *i.e.*, 20. The number of girls who qualified is 3/4th of 20, *i.e.*, 15. Of 50 students who did not qualify are 50 – (20 + 15), *i.e.*, 15. In statement II the number of boys who did not qualify is not given and hence further calculations are not possible. So data in statement I alone is sufficient to answer the question.

40. (*b*) : Statement I is not related to the question. According to statement II the time when Suresh had left his home for office is 10:15 a.m. less 45 minutes *i.e.* 9:30 a.m. So, only statement II alone is sufficient to answer the question.

41. (*e*) : According to both the statements the perimeter of the plot is 208 metres

and 2 (B + B + 4) = 208
i.e. 2B + 2B = 208 – 8
4B = 200
B = 50
Now, 2 (B + L) = 208
i.e. 2 (50 + L) = 208
2 L = 208 – 100
L = 108/2 = 54

∴ The area of the plot is L × B *i.e.* 54 × 50 = 2700 sq metres.

So, both the statements together are necessary to answer the question.

42. (*e*) : According to both the statements each building has 4 wings, each wing has 16 flats and there are 16 buildings. The total number of flats will be 4 × 16 × 16 = 1024. So, both the statements together are necessary to answer the question.

43. (e) : According to both the statements the number of boxes purchased on Sunday was 1500/3, *i.e.* 500 boxes and the number of boxes purchased on Monday was 10% more than the boxes sold on Sunday, *i.e.* 500 + (500 × 10/100) *i.e.* = 550 boxes. So, both the statements together are necessary to answer the question.

44. (d) : The statements give incomplete information. So even both the statements together are not sufficient to answer the question.

45. (*d*) : The number of leaves of medium size kit or the cost of small size kit is not known. So, even both the statements together are not sufficient to answer the question.

46. (*b*) : Statement I is not related to the question

and statement II is the appropriate answer. So, data in statement II alone is sufficient to answer the question.

47. (*b*) : Statement I mentions only the ratio between doctor and residents. According to statement II there are 16 wards and each ward has a doctor. This means 16 doctors are practising in the town. So, data in statement II alone is sufficient to answer the question.

48. (e) : According to statement I the flat was purchased between 15th and 18th December and according to statement II between 16th and 19th December. It is definite that Mohan purchased the flat on 17th December 1996. So, both the statements together are necessary to answer the question.

49. (*d*) : The number of candidates who submitted the forms is not known so, even both the statements together are not sufficient to answer the question.

50. (*e*) : According to both the statements the bus left 15 minutes before 8 p.m., *i.e.*, at 7:45 p.m. and Harish can get the next bus for Belapur at 30 minutes after 7:45 p.m., *i.e.* at 8:15 p.m. So, both the statements together are necessary to answer the question.

PART - XII

INFERAL CONCLUSIONS

In this type of reasoning a statement is followed by inferences drawn from it. From these inferences only one definitely follows which is the hidden proposition of the sentence and it is the right answer to the question.

SOLVED EXAMPLE

1. Ability is poor man's wealth. This means :

(*a*) A poor man has the ability to earn wealth.

(*b*) A wealthy man is always able.

(*c*) A poor man can earn wealth if he has ability.

(*d*) A poor man is always able.

Ans. (c) : 'Ability is poor man's wealth'. Therefore the inference 'poor man can earn wealth if he has ability' definitely follows from the statement.

EXERCISE

Directions : *In each question one or more statements are given followed by various inferential conclusions. The inferential conclusion which can be drawn, without assuming anything in addition to the information given, is the correct answer.*

1. Unless you have atleast two years work experience, you stand limited chance to be selected for the job. This is reflected in the selections of about last eight years.

(*a*) Minimum stipulation of two years' work experience is made very clear to everybody aspiring for the job.

(*b*) Most applicants have much more than two years' work experience.

(*c*) Prior work experience is considered an important advantage in performing the job.

(*d*) If you have more than two years' work experience, you are bound to be selected.

(*e*) There is no minimum educational qualification stipulated for the job.

2. Some students, who get only average marks in school, become highly successful later in their profession though these are only exceptions.

(*a*) There is no link whatsoever between academic performance and success in the profession.

(*b*) There are other exceptions also— like good school performance but utter failure otherwise.

(*c*) Only those who perform well in school are given good jobs.

(*d*) Some students under-perform during school years.

(*e*) Usually low performers but who studied in good schools perform well in their profession.

3. Various offices of an organisation are usually connected by an internal telephone system called INTERCOM.

(*a*) PBX is manually operated and controlled by an operator.

(*b*) A good internal communication system is essential for dealing with inter-departmental business.

(*c*) Communication made over the intercom can be kept secret.

(*d*) A maximum of 10 pins can be connected together in the intercom between a distance of 3000 meters.
(*e*) Every organisation has the means to offer such services to its employees.

4. High rate of population growth is linked closely with the fact of dwindling area under forest cover.
(*a*) Forests are inimical to human growth.
(*b*) There is less danger to human population from wild animals.
(*c*) Decreasing space of forest cover acts as incentive for humans to reproduce at a faster rate.
(*d*) Population growth leads to demand for more land.
(*e*) The statement is based on statistics provided by the government records.

5. Word Processors are screen-based systems in which the typed matter is displayed on a screen.
(*a*) The text can be stored on hard disc, floppy disc for subsequent amendment or printing.
(*b*) It is manually and electrically operated.
(*c*) Editing is possible by inserting new material or deleting unwanted material.
(*d*) It holds data in memory for future use.
(*e*) Even children can operate the computer system.

6. The least technological development in the field of copying is photo-copying system.
(*a*) It does not have capacity to reduce or enlarge the script of photograph.
(*b*) It is an electrically-operated machine which produces an image of the original copy.
(*c*) Every copy produced looks as original, impressive and attractive.
(*d*) It is fast, easy to operate and cheaper and elegant in producing copies.
(*e*) All important documents of the agencies and organisations can be saved.

7. The population of big cities is increasing day by day but the civic amenities and support services are the same and not expanding.
(*a*) Birth rate is higher in cities as compared to villages.
(*b*) The cities are dying.
(*c*) If civic services are improved, the rate of population growth would further increase.
(*d*) More and more people are using services which have limited capacity.
(*e*) Newcomers are not given access to most of the services, that is how they are surviving without expanding services.

8. Women being poorly educated, 33 per cent reservation for women in legislative bodies will mean rule by the poorly educated over the educated people.
(*a*) Uneducated women are elected by uneducated women.
(*b*) 33 per cent of the elected women will be uneducated.
(*c*) The number of uneducated persons in the legislative bodies will rise significantly.
(*d*) Educated persons will loose voice in the legislature.
(*e*) There is a need for women upliftment.

9. Fax machine uses telephone to transmit any form of written or printed matter, diagrams, photographs from one location to another.
(*a*) It is a method of editing, amending and printing of any document.
(*b*) Equipments have to be on both receiving and sending ends.
(*c*) This machine is known as Fascimile Telegraphy.
(*d*) It can send copy of document to long distances by combining the speed of telephone with the reproduction facility of the office copier.
(*e*) None of the above.

10. Many types of calculators are used in offices for calculations, day to day billing, accounting etc.
(*a*) Calculator can be used for arithmetical processes.
(*b*) Electronic calculator can be used for multiple functions.
(*c*) It can be used for making payments to a large number of people.

(*d*) It enables you to add, subtract, multiply, divide, calculate percentage and square roots.
(*e*) Calculator have now become a necessity.

11. Most of the people convey that they get bright and excellent ideas in the early morning hours.
(*a*) Ideas come only in the early morning hours.
(*b*) Chances of getting bright ideas at night are less.
(*c*) People are not able to express clearly how they get ideas.
(*d*) After sound sleep of two hours mind becomes fresh.
(*e*) Unless the ideas are bright, it does not serve any purpose.

12. The average age of both men and women in India has gone up considerably over the last 70 years.
(*a*) Rekha would probably live longer than her grandmother.
(*b*) There is a wider difference between the average age of men and women.
(*c*) There seems to be a small difference between the average age of men and women.
(*d*) Drugs to increase longevity have been found.
(*e*) The average age of marriage has also gone up over the years.

13. Population explosion in India is due to high rate of illiteracy in the rural areas.
(*a*) Illiterates in urban areas practice family planning.
(*b*) Urban areas have very small percentage of the total population.
(*c*) Rural areas contribute significantly to population growth.
(*d*) Urban people are all literates.
(*e*) Rural people are highly educated.

14. Computer is a device which automatically accepts data, processes in a sequence and supply the results.
(*a*) A Computer has five main parts—input, output, storage, calculating and control.
(*b*) The exact photographs and pictures can be drawn with the help of this device.
(*c*) The physical parts such as the keyboard, the central processing unit and the printer are known as HARDWARE.
(*d*) The programmes and data are called SOFTWARE.
(*e*) All computer programmes are its software.

15. E-mail is the quickest means of communication in printed form.
(*a*) The message is produced at both the sending and receiving installations.
(*b*) In big cities telegram, connected with teleprinter service are transmitted.
(*c*) Incoming messages are typed automatically at the receiving end.
(*d*) The outgoing messages are sent through telephone.
(*e*) Messages are sent from one computer to another with the help of modem, over the telephone lines.

ANSWERS

1	2	3	4	5	6	7	8	9	10
(*c*)	(*d*)	(*c*)	(*d*)	(*b*)	(*a*)	(*d*)	(*d*)	(*a*)	(*c*)
11	**12**	**13**	**14**	**15**					
(*b*)	(*a*)	(*c*)	(*b*)	(*e*)					

VENN DIAGRAMS

In these type of questions diagrammatic representation presents a logical illustration of particular class or statements based on which the questions are asked. A clear view of the diagram makes the concepts clear for attempting such questions.

SOLVED EXAMPLES

1. Children

1

2 4

3

7

5 6

Studious

Naughty

Study the above diagram and specify the region representing children who are naughty as well as studious.

(*a*) 3 and 6 (*b*) 2 and 4 (*c*) only 3 (*d*) only 4 (*e*) only 1

Ans. (*c*) : The explanation depicting children who are naughty as well as studious will be :

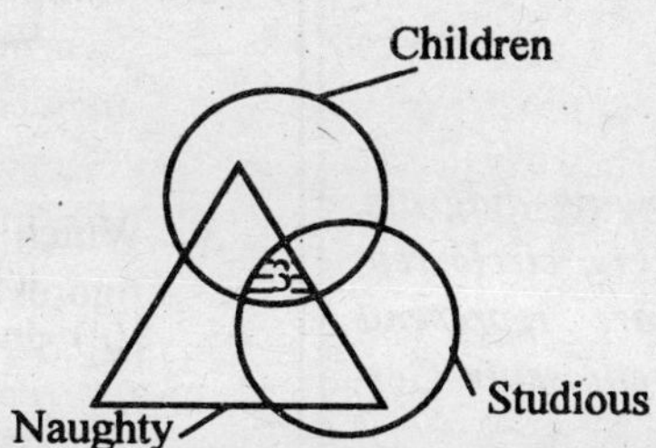

It is now clear that only region 3 represents all the three classes.

2. In the following diagram, rectangle represents women, triangle represents Sub-Inspectors of police and circle represents graduates. Which numbered area represents women graduate Sub-Inspectors of police?

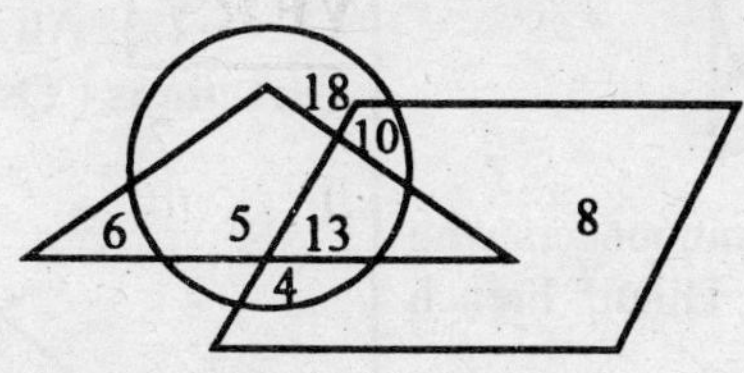

(*a*) 10 (*b*) 5 (*c*) 8 (*d*) 3 (*e*) 13

Ans. (*e*) : The explanation of the figure will be :

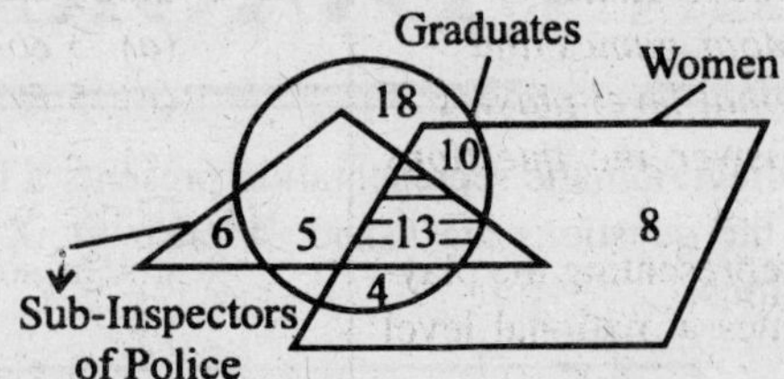

It is clear that region 13 represents women who are graduates and Sub-Inspectors of Police.

EXERCISE

1. What is the number which is common to only two geometrical figures?

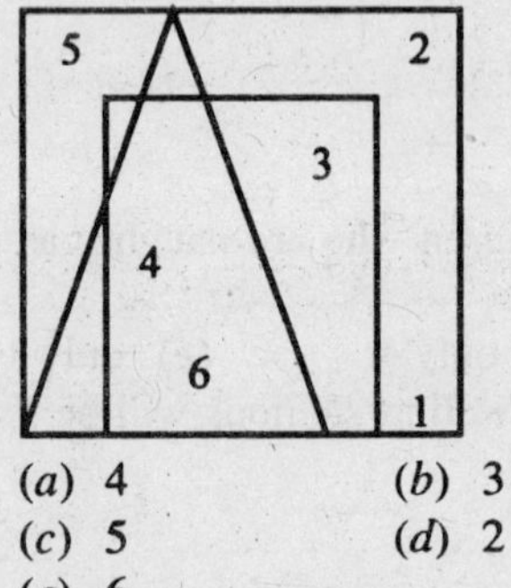

(*a*) 4 (*b*) 3
(*c*) 5 (*d*) 2
(*e*) 6

Directions (Qs. 2–3) : *In the following diagram, rectangle represents Hindi Announcers, circle represents English Announcers, square represents French Announcers, and triangle represents German Announcers.*

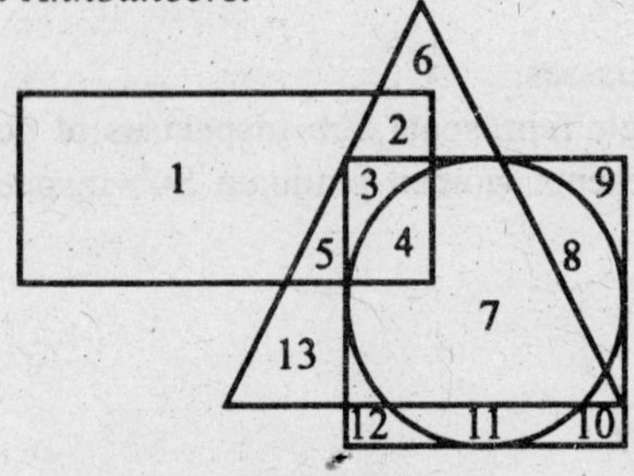

2. Which area represents those announcers who can present programmes in Hindi, French and German only?
(*a*) 1 (*b*) 2
(*c*) 3 (*d*) 4
(*e*) 5

3 Which area represents those announcers who can present programmes in French and English only?
(*a*) 7 (*b*) 9
(*c*) 11 (*d*) 13
(*e*) 6

Directions (Qs. 4-5) : *Study the diagram to answer questions 4 and 5.*

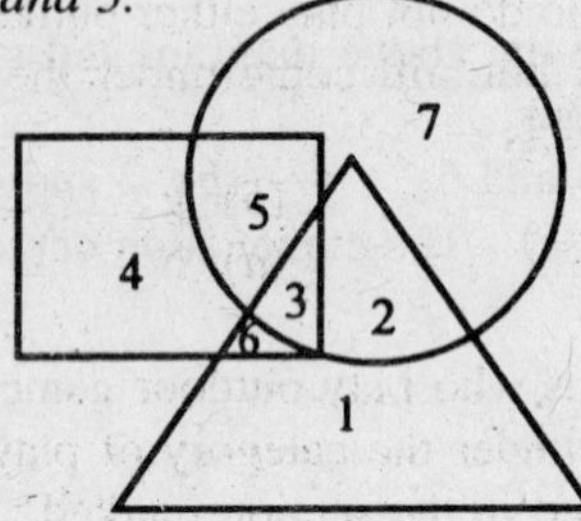

4. Which number is in all the geometrical figures?
(*a*) 5 (*b*) 6
(*c*) 2 (*d*) 3
(*e*) 4

5. Number 6 is in :
(*a*) Rectangle and triangle
(*b*) Circle and traingle
(*c*) Rectangle and circle
(*d*) Rectangle only
(*e*) All figures

Directions (Qs. 6 to 9) : *In the following diagram*

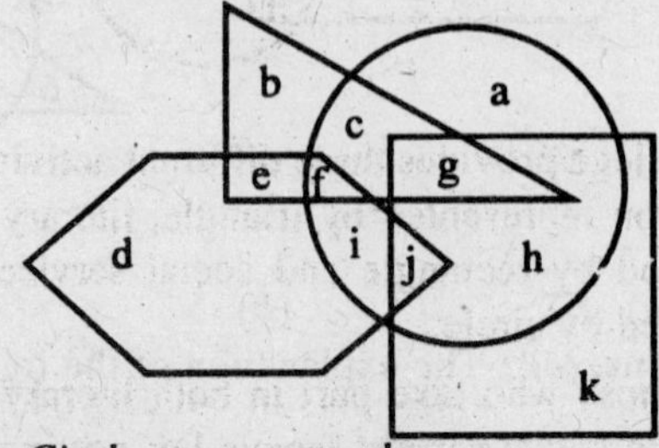

The Circle represents players

The Triangle represents outdoor games
The Hexagon represents indoor games and
The Square represents national level players
Study the diagram and answer the questions given below :

6. The letter in the section representing the players who play indoor games at national level is :
(*a*) f (*b*) i
(*c*) j (*d*) g
(*e*) h

7. The letter representing the section of outdoor as well as indoor game players who do not play at the national level is :
(*a*) c (*b*) f
(*c*) e (*d*) i
(*e*) k

8. The section representing national level players who do not play either outdoor or indoor games but still come under the category of players is :
(*a*) k (*b*) g
(*c*) c (*d*) h
(*e*) a

9. Persons who play outdoor games but do not come under the category of players are represented in the section marked :
(*a*) b (*b*) c
(*c*) a (*d*) d
(*e*) e

Directions (Qs. 10 to 13) : *Study the diagram given below.*

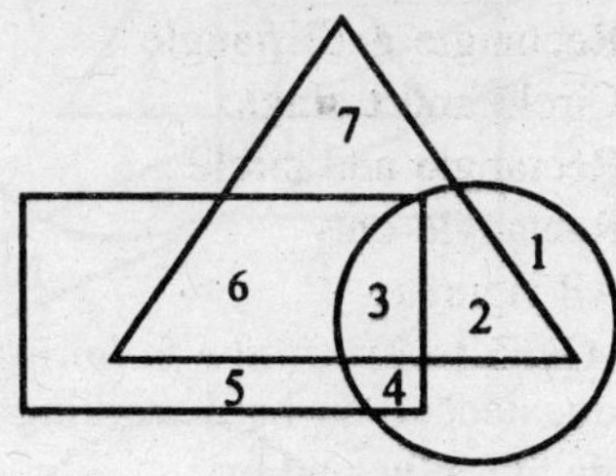

A college provides three different activities, students union represented by triangle, literary society represented by rectangle and social service league represented by circle.

10. Those who take part in both literary society and social service league but not in students union are represented by :
(*a*) 3 & 4 (*b*) 5 & 6
(*c*) 5 & 1 (*d*) 4
(*e*) 2

11. Those who take part in students union but not in social service league are represented by :
(*a*) 2 & 7 (*b*) 6 & 7
(*c*) 6 (*d*) 7
(*e*) 3

12. Those students who are members of literary society only and not of any other activity are represented by :
(*a*) 2 (*b*) 5
(*c*) 3 & 4 (*d*) 3
(*e*) 4 & 6

13. Those students who are members of all three groups are represented by :
(*a*) 2 (*b*) 3
(*c*) 4 (*d*) 6
(*e*) 7

Directions (Qs. 14 to 18) : *The questions below are based on this figure.*

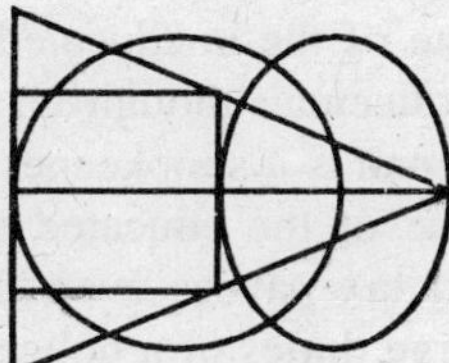

The figure above represents a set of persons : the triangle represents educated persons, the square represents policemen, the circle represents road tax payers and the ellipse represents shopkeepers.

14. According to the given figure we can say that :
(*a*) Some of the road tax payee policemen are shopkeepers too.
(*b*) Some of the educated shopkeepers pay road tax.
(*c*) Some of the road tax payee shopkeepers are policemen too.
(*d*) Some of the uneducated policemen pay road tax.
(*e*) None of the above.

15. Looking at the given figure we can say that :
(*a*) Some persons who are neither shopkeepers nor policemen are educated.
(*b*) Some persons who are either shopkeep-

ers or policemen pay road tax, though uneducated.

(*c*) Some persons who are either shopkeepers or policemen pay road tax and are also educated.

(*d*) All the above statements are correct.

(*e*) None of the above.

16. According to the figure we can say that :

(*a*) Policemen do not pay road tax.

(*b*) Shopkeepers do not pay road tax.

(*c*) Some shopkeepers are educated.

(*d*) Some policemen are shopkeepers.

(*e*) None of the above.

17. Loooking at the figure it can be concluded that :

(*a*) All educated shopkeepers pay road tax.

(*b*) All road tax paying policemen are educated.

(*c*) All educated policemen pay road tax.

(*d*) All road tax paying shopkeepers are educated.

(*e*) None of the above.

18. On the basis of this figure it can be concluded that :

(*a*) None of the uneducated shopkeepers is a policeman though an uneducated policeman is a shopkeeper.

(*b*) Some of the educated shopkeepers are road tax payees even though they discharge duties of a policeman.

(*c*) Some of the educated policemen who pay road tax are sharing profits with uneducated shopkeepers.

(*d*) None of the educated shopkeepers is a policman nor an educated policeman a shopkeeper.

(*e*) All the above statements are correct.

Directions (Qs. 19 to 22) : *These questions are based on the following diagram :*

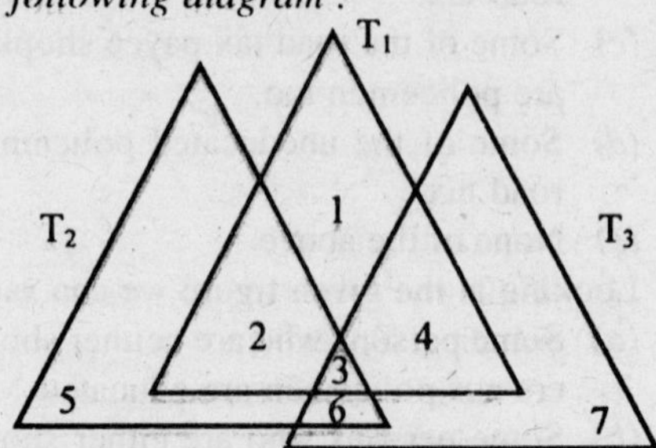

T_1 represents Indians; T_2 represents teachers, and T_3 represents scholars.

19. The section representing Indians, who are scholars, but not teachers is :

(*a*) 2 (*b*) 3

(*c*) 5 (*d*) 6

(*e*) 4

20. The section representing teachers and scholars, who are not Indians is :

(*a*) 6 (*b*) 5

(*c*) 3 (*d*) 4

(*e*) 7

21. The section of scholars, who are neither Indians nor teachers is :

(*a*) 2 (*b*) 7

(*c*) 4 (*d*) 5

(*e*) 6

22. The section representing neither scholars nor teachers, but only Indians is :

(*a*) 4 (*b*) 3

(*c*) 2 (*d*) 1

(*e*) 5

Directions (Qs. 23 to 28) : *In the diagram given below, the circle stands for 'educated', square for 'hard-working', triangle for 'urban people' and rectangle for 'honest'. The different regions of the diagram are numbered from 1 to 12. Study the diagram carefully and answer the questions.*

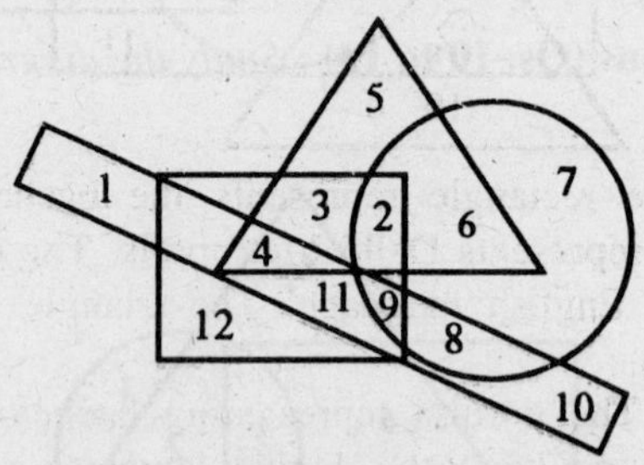

23. Uneducated urban hard-working and honest people are indicated by :

(*a*) 3 (*b*) 11

(*c*) 9 (*d*) 4

(*e*) 2

24. Non-urban educated people who are neither hard-working nor honest are indicated by :

(*a*) 5 (*b*) 7

(*c*) 10 (*d*) 11

(*e*) 4

25. Urban educated people who are neither honest nor hard-working are indicated by :

(*a*) 9 (*b*) 11
(*c*) 4 (*d*) 5
(*e*) 6

26. Non-urban people, who are honest, educated and hard-working are indicated by :

(*a*) 11 (*b*) 10
(*c*) 8 (*d*) 9
(*e*) 2

27. Educated, hard-working and urban people are indicated by :

(*a*) 7 (*b*) 2
(*c*) 3 (*d*) 4
(*e*) 5

28. Urban people who are hard-working and uneducated, but not honest are indicated by :

(*a*) 6 (*b*) 2
(*c*) 3 (*d*) 4
(*e*) 10

Directions (Qs. 29 to 33) : *On the basis of the following diagram answer questions 29 to 33.*

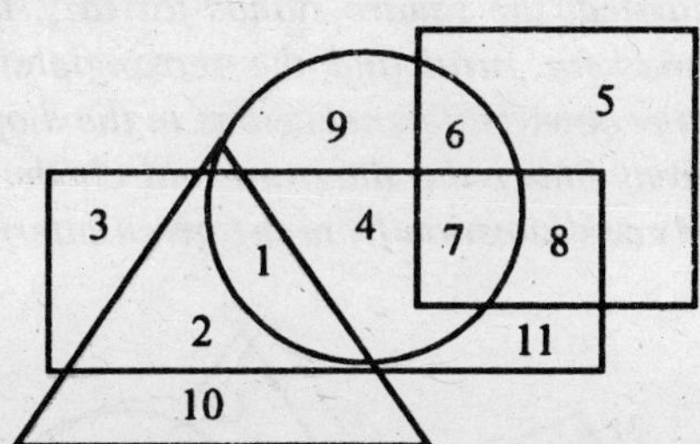

The rectangle represents the bachelors. The square represents Delhi Metropolis. The circle represents English language. The triangle represents tourists.

29. The portion representing bachelor tourists, who know the English language is :

(*a*) 2 (*b*) 1
(*c*) 7 (*d*) 4
(*e*) 9

30. The portion representing bachelors who are in Delhi and do not know the English language is :

(*a*) 6 (*b*) 7
(*c*) 8 (*d*) 9
(*e*) 5

31. Which of the following is true?

(*a*) Some of the tourists are staying in Delhi Metropolis.
(*b*) No person in Delhi Metropolis knows English.
(*c*) English is spoken by a few tourists and some persons in Delhi.
(*d*) None of the above statements is true.
(*e*) All the above statements are true.

32. Tourists, who are bachelors and do not know the English language is represented by the section marked :

(*a*) 1 (*b*) 3
(*c*) 4 (*d*) 10
(*e*) 2

33. Which of the following is not true?

(*a*) No tourist is in Delhi.
(*b*) Some bachelors do not know the English language but they are in Delhi.
(*c*) Some English-speaking persons are neither tourists nor are they are in Delhi.
(*d*) All the above statements are true.
(*e*) None of the above statements is true.

Directions (Qs. 34 to 38) : *In the following diagram, the circle represents College Professors, the triangle stands for Surgical Specialists, and Medical Specialists are represented by the rectangle. Answer the following questions based on the diagram.*

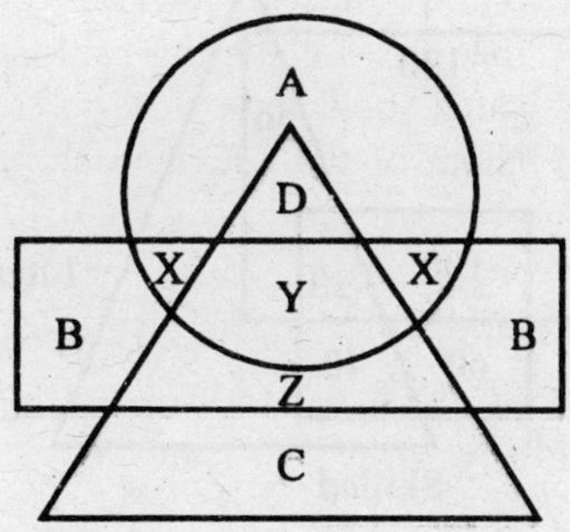

34. 'C' represents :

(*a*) Surgical Specialists.
(*b*) Medical and Surgical Specialists.
(*c*) College Professors.
(*d*) Medical Specialists.
(*e*) College Professors and Medicals Specialists.

35. 'B' represents :
(*a*) Medical specialists who are neither professors nor surgical specialists.
(*b*) Professors who are not medical specialists.
(*c*) Professors who are not surgical specialists.
(*d*) Professors who are neither medical nor surgical specialists.
(*e*) None of these.

36. College professors who are also surgical specialists are represented by:
(*a*) A (*b*) B
(*c*) C (*d*) D
(*e*) X

37. College professors who are also medical specialists are represented by :
(*a*) A (*b*) X
(*c*) Y (*d*) Z
(*e*) C

38. Surgical specialists who are also medical specialists but not professors, are represented by :
(*a*) X (*b*) B
(*c*) Z (*d*) C
(*e*) Y

Directions (Qs. 39 to 44) : *Study the figure and answer questions given below :*

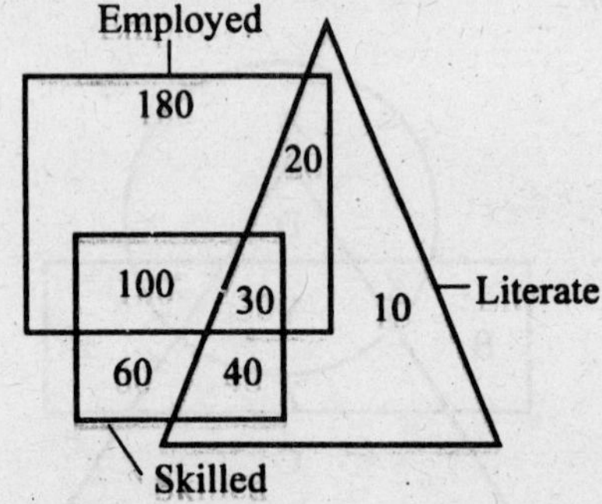

39. Number of persons who are illiterate but skilled are :
(*a*) 100 (*b*) 60
(*c*) 160 (*d*) 90
(*e*) 120

40. Number of persons who are employed, literate and skilled are :
(*a*) 20 (*b*) 30
(*c*) 40 (*d*) 70
(*e*) 100

41. Number of persons who are unemployed but literate are :
(*a*) 10 (*b*) 40
(*c*) 50 (*d*) 60
(*e*) 110

42. Number of persons who are unskilled but employed are :
(*a*) 120 (*b*) 130
(*c*) 140 (*d*) 200
(*e*) 150

43. Number of persons who are skilled are :
(*a*) 100 (*b*) 130
(*c*) 140 (*d*) 90
(*e*) 230

44. Number of persons who are employed but neither literate nor skilled is :
(*a*) 180 (*b*) 100
(*c*) 20 (*d*) 30
(*e*) 130

Directions (Qs. 45 to 49) : *The questions are based on the following diagram in which the circle stands for educated, the square stands for lazy, the triangle stands for rural and the rectangle stands for corrupt people. Different regions in the diagram are numbered. Study the diagram and choose the answer of each question from the given alternatives.*

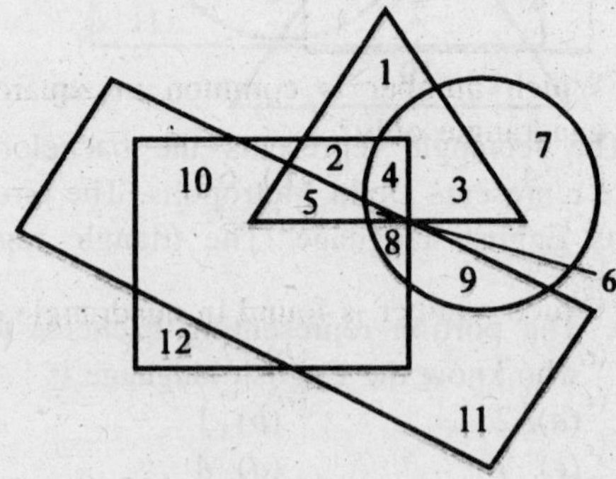

45. Non-educated rural people who are lazy but not corrupt are indicated by :
(*a*) 1 (*b*) 2
(*c*) 5 (*d*) 4
(*e*) 6

46. Lazy educated people who are rural but not

corrupt are indicated by :
(*a*) 3 (*b*) 4
(*c*) 2 (*d*) 6
(*e*) 8

47. Non-rural educated people who are corrupt but not lazy are indicated by :
(*a*) 9 (*b*) 8
(*c*) 10 (*d*) 6
(*e*) 12

48. Non-rural uneducated people who are not corrupt but lazy are indicated by :
(*a*) 8 (*b*) 10
(*c*) 11 (*d*) 12
(*e*) 9

49. Non-corrupt educated people who are rural but not lazy are indicated by :
(*a*) 1 (*b*) 2
(*c*) 7 (*d*) 3
(*e*) 4

Directions (Qs. 50 to 54) : *Study the following diagram and answer questions 50 to 54.*

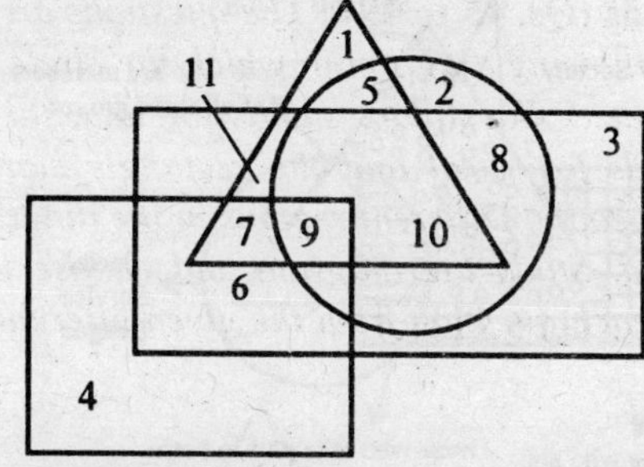

50. Which number is common in square and quadrangle only?
(*a*) 4 (*b*) 6
(*c*) 7 (*d*) 9
(*e*) 11

51. Which number is found in quadrangle only?
(*a*) 6 (*b*) 7
(*c*) 3 (*d*) 9
(*e*) 2

52. Which number is found in circle only?
(*a*) 5 (*b*) 4
(*c*) 10 (*d*) 8
(*e*) 2

53. Which number is common in circle and triangle ?
(*a*) 10 (*b*) 2
(*c*) 1 (*d*) 5
(*e*) 6

54. Which number is common in all the geometrical figures?
(*a*) 9 (*b*) 10
(*c*) 7 (*d*) 5
(*e*) 1

Directions (Qs. 55 to 60) : *Refer to the given diagram and answer these questions :*

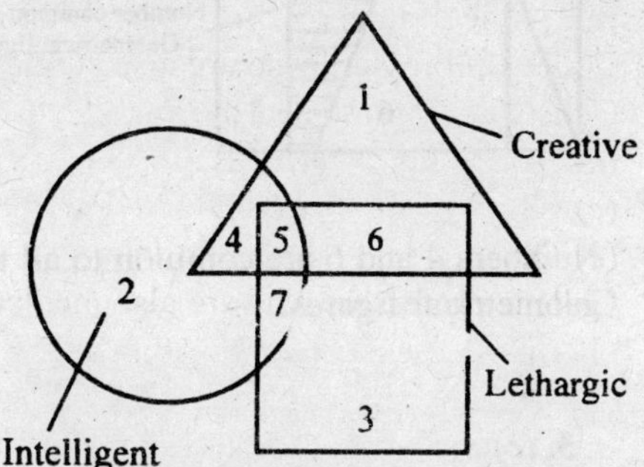

55. Who are intelligent as well as creative persons ?
(*a*) 1 (*b*) 2
(*c*) 4 (*d*) 6
(*e*) 7

56. Who are creative but lethargic persons?
(*a*) 1 (*b*) 3
(*c*) 5 (*d*) 6
(*e*) 4

57. Who are lethargic but neither intelligent nor creative persons?
(*a*) 3 (*b*) 3 & 6
(*c*) 6 (*d*) 1, 3 & 6
(*e*) 5 & 6

58. Who are intelligent but lethargic persons?
(*a*) 4 (*b*) 5
(*c*) 6 (*d*) 3
(*e*) 7

59. Who are intelligent and lethargic but creative persons?
(*a*) 1, 4 & 5 (*b*) 5, 6 & 7
(*c*) 5 (*d*) 7
(*e*) None of them

60. Who are intelligent but neither lethargic nor creative persons?
(*a*) 4 (*b*) 2
(*c*) 5 (*d*) 6
(*e*) 7

EXPLANATORY ANSWERS

1. *(b)* :

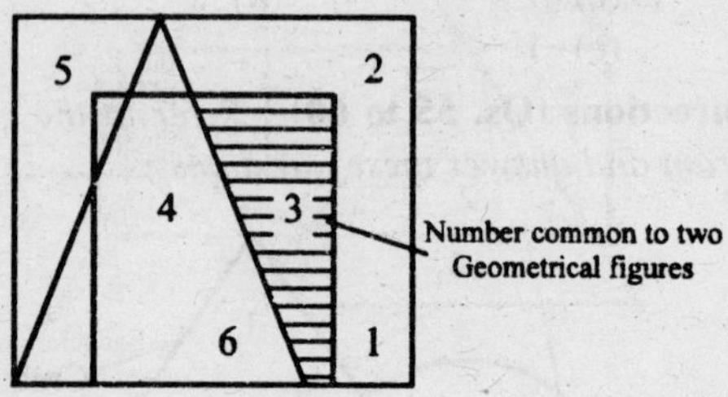

Note : Numbers 4 and 6 are common to all three geometrical figures.

2. *(c)*, **3.** *(c)* :

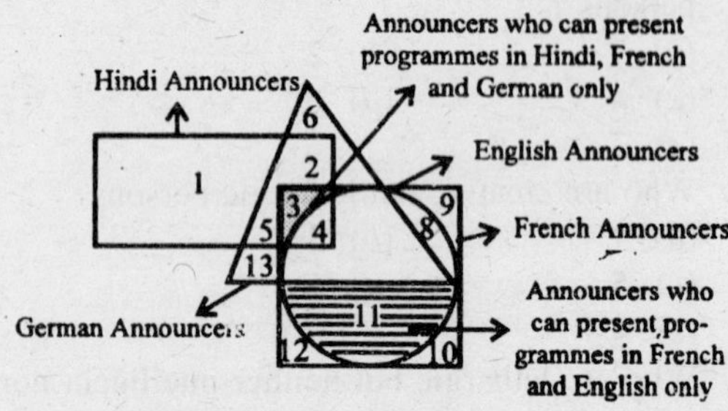

4. *(d)*, **5.** *(a)* :

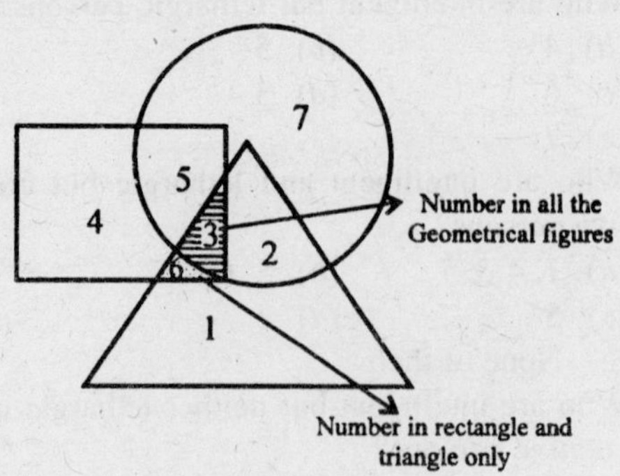

6. *(c)*, **7.** *(b)*, **8.** *(d)*, **9.** *(a)* :

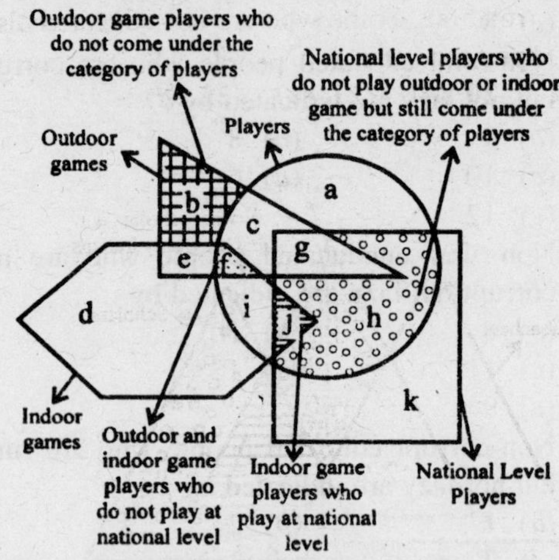

10. *(d)*, **11.** *(b)*, **12.** *(b)*, **13.** *(b)* :

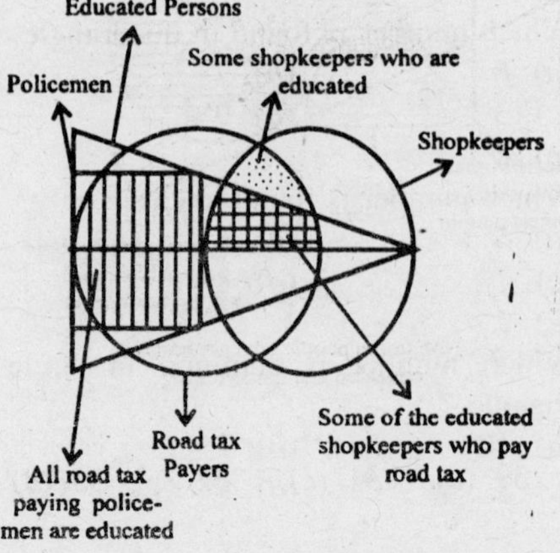

14. *(b)*, **15.** *(d)*, **16.** *(c)*, **17.** *(b)*, **18.** *(d)* :

Note : Policemen and shopkeepers are entirely independent of each other. Some of both the categories above are educated and pay road tax. Some who are not-educated also pay road tax.

19. *(e)*, **20.** *(a)*, **21.** *(b)*, **22.** *(d)* :

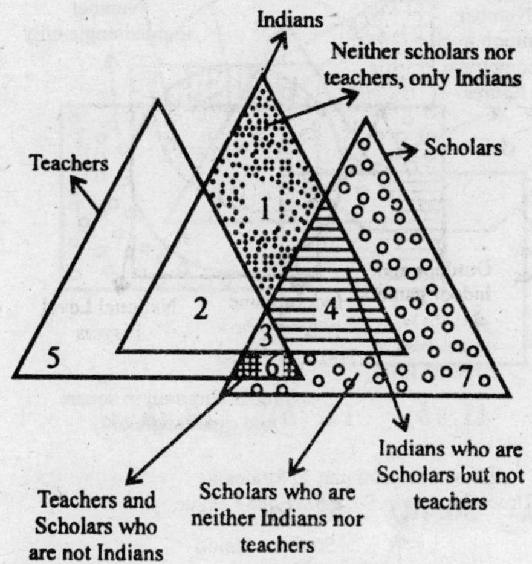

23. *(d)*, **24.** *(b)*, **25.** *(e)*,
26. *(d)*, **27.** *(b)*, **28.** *(c)* :

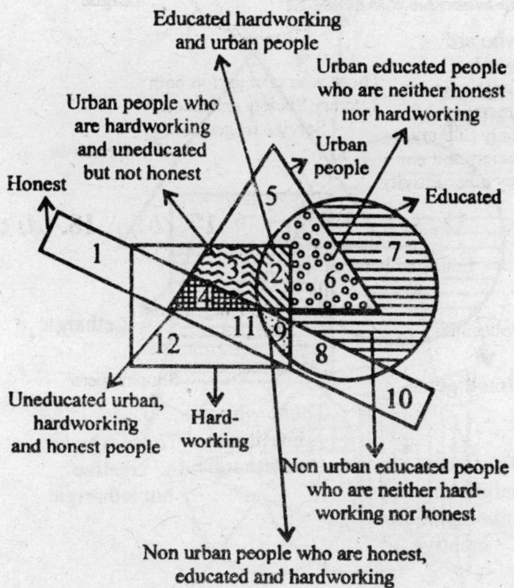

29. *(b)*, **30.** *(c)*, **31.** *(c)*, **32.** *(e)*, **33.** *(d)* :

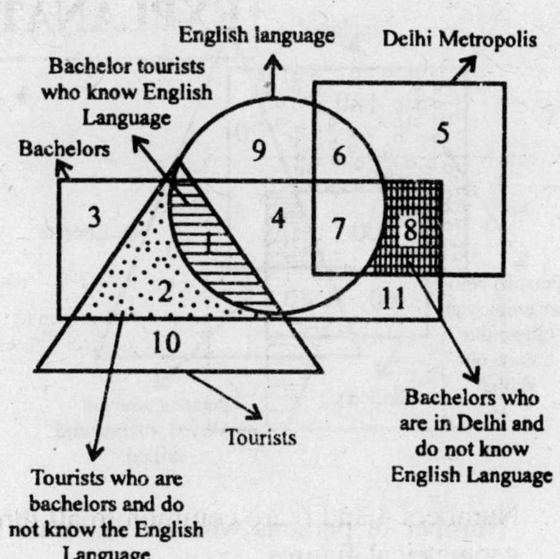

Note : There is no tourist in Delhi Metropolis. Sections 1, 6 and 7 support answer 31. Sections 9 and 4 support option C in answer 33.

34. *(a)*, **35.** *(a)*, **36.** *(d)*,

37. *(b)*, **38.** *(c)* :

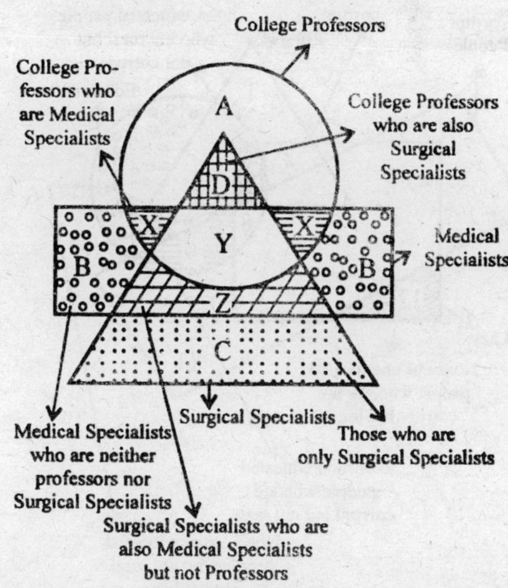

39. *(c)*, **40.** *(b)*, **41.** *(c)*,

42. *(d)*, **43.** *(e)*, **44.** *(a)* :

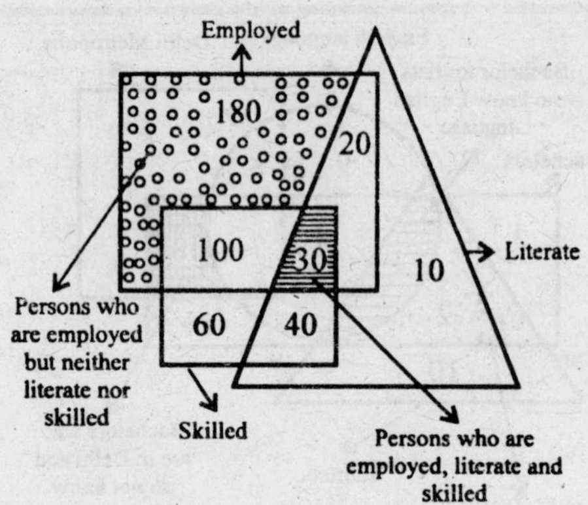

Number of persons who are illiterate but skilled = 100 + 60 = 160

Number of persons who are unemployed but literate = 40 + 10 = 50

Number of persons who are unskilled but employed = 180 + 20 = 200

Number of persons who are skilled = 100 + 30 + 60 + 40 = 230

45. *(b)*, **46.** *(b)*, **47.** *(a)*, **48.** *(d)*, **49.** *(c)* :

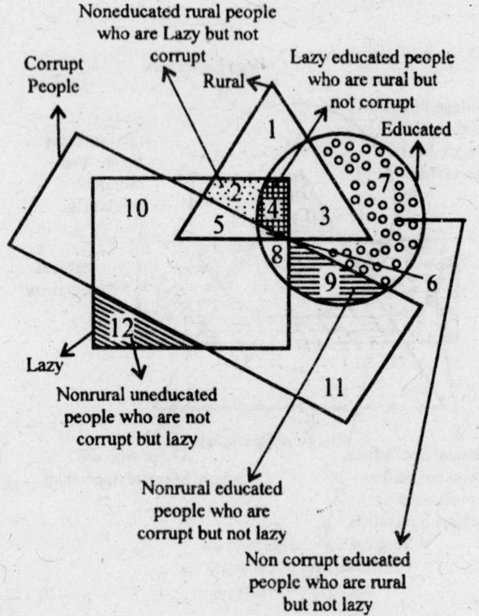

50. *(b)*, **51.** *(c)*, **52.** *(e)*, **53.** *(d)*, **54.** *(a)* :

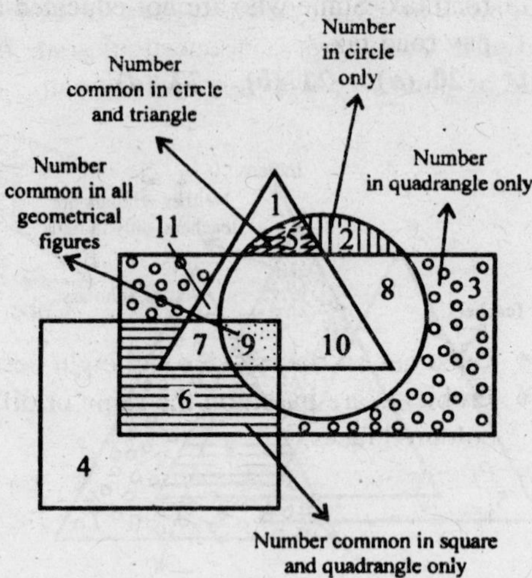

55. *(c)*, **56.** *(d)*, **57.** *(a)*,

58. *(e)*, **59.** *(c)*, **60.** *(b)* :

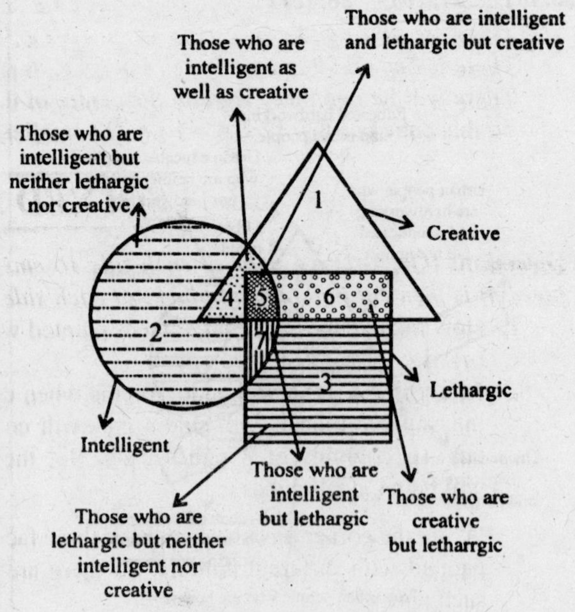

Cubes and Dices

The questions related to problems on cubes and dices are aimed to check the imaginative power of the candidate. The candidate must have the ability to visualise quickly in three-dimensional object for what is asked of it. To attempt such questions some basic facts should be kept in mind and the visualisation ability should be combined with fast and accurate calculations.

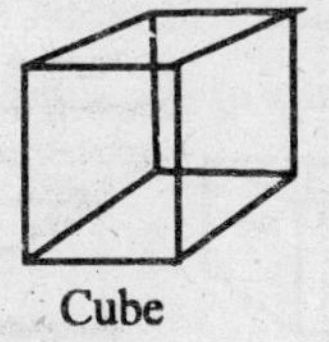

Cube

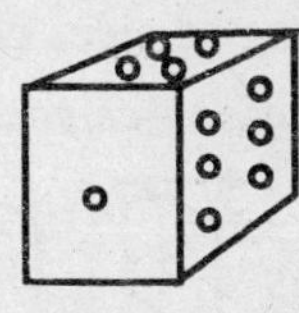

Dice

- Cube has six faces/sides and eight corners.
- Problems are based on the same or different coloured faces.
- Problems are based on cutting the squares into specified number of smaller equal parts.

- Dice has six faces/sides.
- Problems are based only on the value occurring on the six faces.

Diagrammatically, the explanation of a cube which is painted green on all sides can be understood easily taking one side of the cube.

a	b	a
b	c	b
a	b	a

This cube is divided into $3 \times 3 \times 3 = 27$ equal small cubes.
There are four corner pieces 'a'. so 4×2 *i.e.*, 8 pieces will be painted on 3 sides.
There are four middle pieces 'b', so 4×3 *i.e.*, 12 pieces will be painted on 2 sides
There is one middle piece 'c', so 1×6 *i.e.*, 6 pieces will be painted only on 1 side.
There will be one piece right in the centre of this cube *i.e.*, piece will not have paint at all.
So this cube has $8 + 12 + 6 + 1$ *i.e.*, 27 smaller cubes.

SOLVED EXAMPLES

Directions (Qs. 1–2) : *A cube of each side 16 cms, is painted orange, red and black on pairs of opposite faces. It is then cut into cubical blocks of each side 4 cms.*

1. How many cubes have three faces painted with different colours?

(*a*) 4 (*b*) 8 (*c*) 12 (*d*) 16

Ans. (*b*) : A cube with side 16 cms when cut into cubical blocks with side 4 cms will contain 16 columns of 4 cubes each. So, there will be 64 small cubes.

'a' are the corner pieces which have three faces painted with different colours, So there are 8 such cubes.

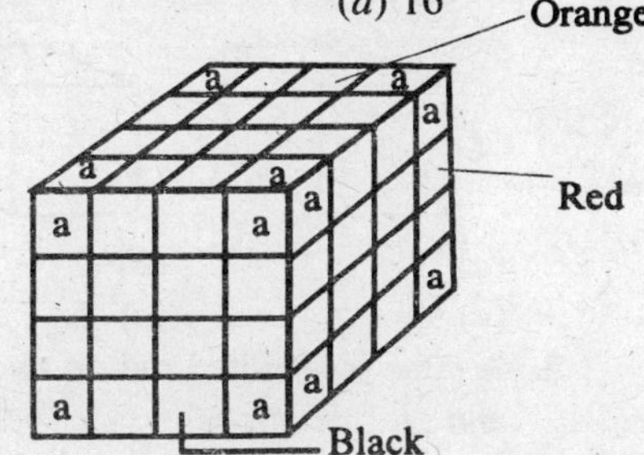

2. How many cubes have no face painted?
(*a*) 6 (*b*) 11 (*c*) 8 (*d*) 12

Ans. (*c*) : Diagrammatically, the explanation taking one side of the cube will be :

a	b	b	a
b	c	c	b
b	c	c	b
a	b	b	a

a = There are 4 × 2 *i.e.,* 8 cubes with 3 sides painted.
b = There are 8 × 3 *i.e.,* 24 cubes with 2 sides painted.
c = There are 4 × 6 *i.e.,* 24 cubes with 1 side painted.
There are total 64 cubes.
So, the number of cubes having no sides painted will be 64 – (8 + 24 + 24) *i.e.* 8 cubes.

Directions (Qs. 3–4) : *Given below are three positions of the same dice having numbers 1 to 6.*

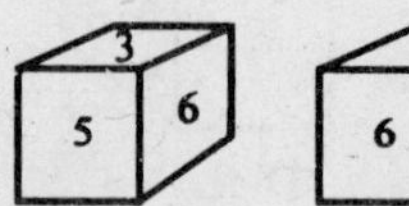

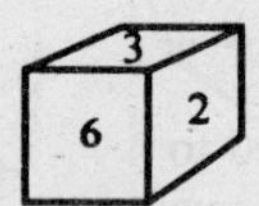

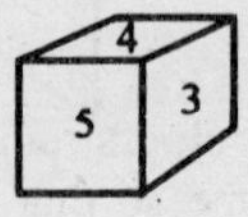

3. Which number occurs on the face opposite of face 5?
(*a*) 1 (*b*) 2 (*c*) 3 (*d*) 6

Ans. (*b*) : Numbers adjacent to 5 are 3, 6, and 4.
Number on face opposite of face 3 will be 1 and number on face opposite of face 5 will be 2.

4. The face on the bottom in the second dice has the number :
(*a*) 5 (*b*) 4
(*c*) 1 (*d*) Cannot be determined

Ans. (*c*) : Numbers on the sides of the dice are 5, 6, 2 and 4. Now, as the number on top face is 3, the number on the face on the bottom will be 1.

EXERCISE

1. Two positions of a dice are shown below. When there are two circles at the bottom, the number of circles at the top will be :

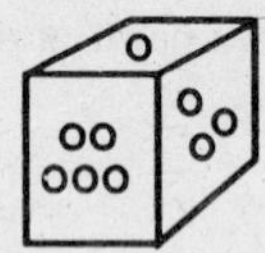
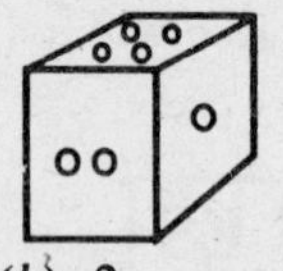

(*a*) 5 (*b*) 2
(*c*) 3 (*d*) 6

2. Two positions of a dice are shown below. When 4 is at the bottom, what number will be on the top?

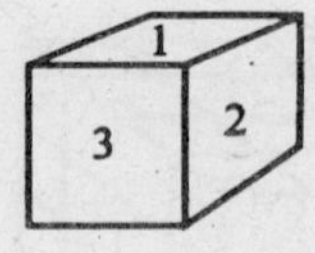

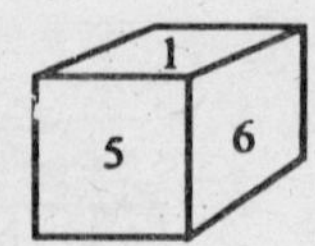

(*a*) 1 (*b*) 2
(*c*) 5 (*d*) 6

3. A cube is painted red on two adjacent faces and on one opposite face, yellow on two adjacent faces and green on the remaining face. It is then cut into 64 equal cubes. How many cubes have only one red and one green face?
(*a*) 4 (*b*) 8
(*c*) 12 (*d*) 16

4. Two positions of a dice with 1 to 6 dots on its sides are shown below. If the dice is resting on the side with three dots, what will be the number of dots on the side at the top?

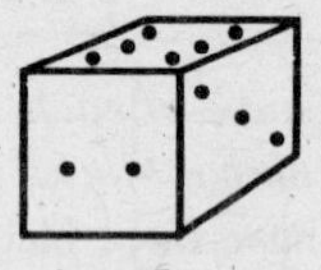
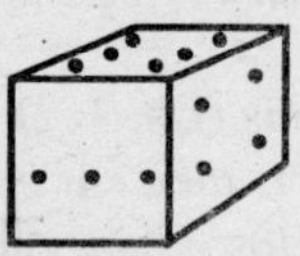

(*a*) 1 or 5 (*b*) 2
(*c*) 3 (*d*) 5

5. A cube, on whose sides letters have been written, is shown below in different positions as can be seen from different directions. Find the missing letter?

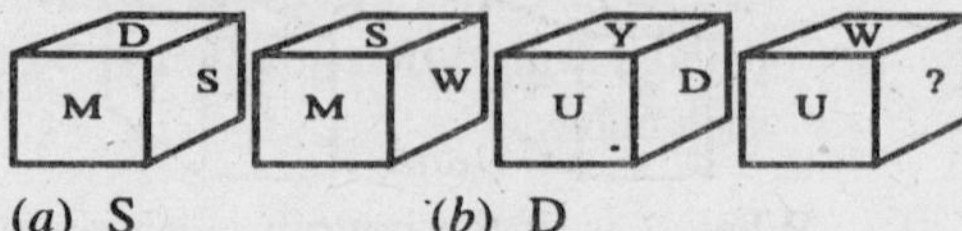

(*a*) S (*b*) D
(*c*) Y (*d*) W

6. If the total number of dots on opposite faces of a cubical block is always 7, find the figure which is correct?

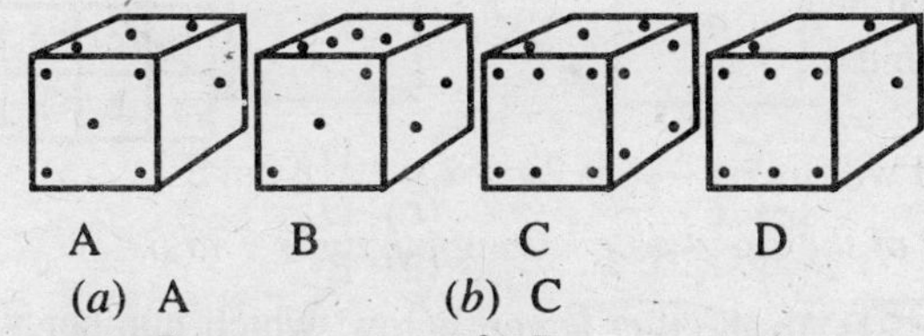

(*a*) A (*b*) C
(*c*) D (*d*) B

7. The minimum number of colours required to paint all the sides of a cube so that no two adjacent faces may have the same colour, is :

(*a*) 6 (*b*) 4
(*c*) 3 (*d*) 2

8. In a dice a, b, c and d, are written on the adjacent faces, in a clockwise order and e and f at the top and bottom. When c is at the top, what will be at the bottom?

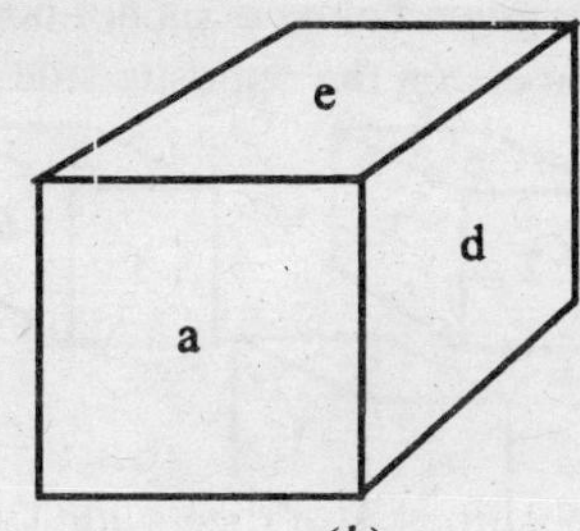

(*a*) a (*b*) c
(*c*) e (*d*) b

9. The number of cubes arranged one over the other in this figure will be :

(*a*) 8 (*b*) 6
(*c*) 5 (*d*) 10

10. Two positions of a block are shown below. 5 and 6 are on opposite faces.

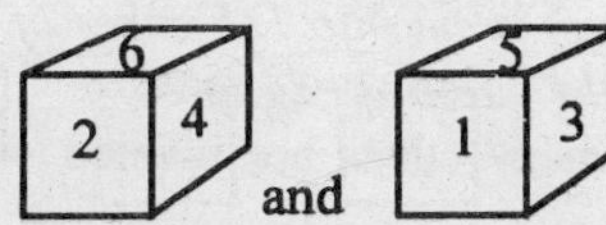

When 2 is at the bottom, what number will be at the top?

(*a*) 1 (*b*) 3
(*c*) 4 (*d*) 5

11. Two positions of a dice are given below. When 1 is at the top, which number will be at the bottom?

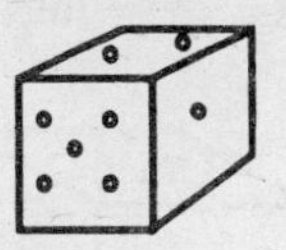 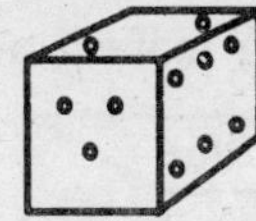

(*a*) 3 (*b*) 6
(*c*) 2 (*d*) 1

12. Two positions of a dice are shown below. When 2 is at the bottom, which number will be at the top?

 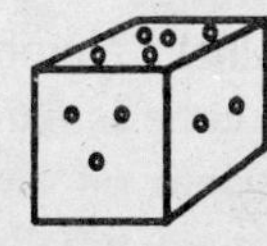

(*a*) 1 (*b*) 2
(*c*) 3 (*d*) 4

13. Study the three dices given below. What number will be opposite to the side bearing number 2?

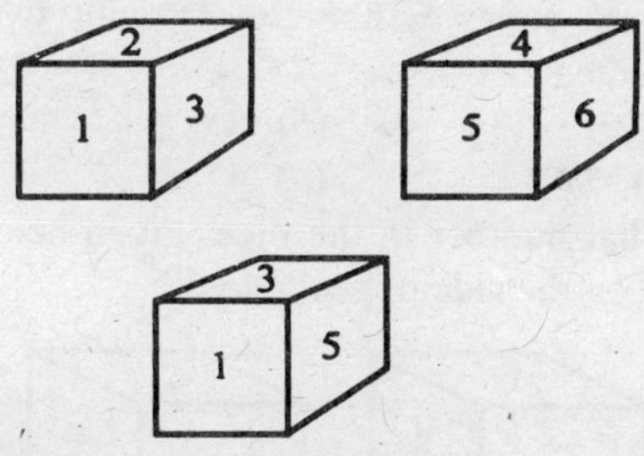

(*a*) 4 (*b*) 3
(*c*) 6 (*d*) 5

14. The sides of a cube are painted in different colours. Black side is opposite to red. White side is between black and red. Green side is adjacent to grey and blue side is adjacent to green. What colour will be on the side opposite to the white side of the cube?

(*a*) Blue (*b*) Green
(*c*) Grey (*d*) Data is insufficient

15. A cube is painted black on two adjacent faces and on one opposite face, red on two opposite faces and green on the remaining face. If it is cut into 64 equal cubes, then how many cubes will have only one black coloured face?

(*a*) 32 (*b*) 16
(*c*) 12 (*d*) 8

16. Six sides of a cube are coloured in the following manner

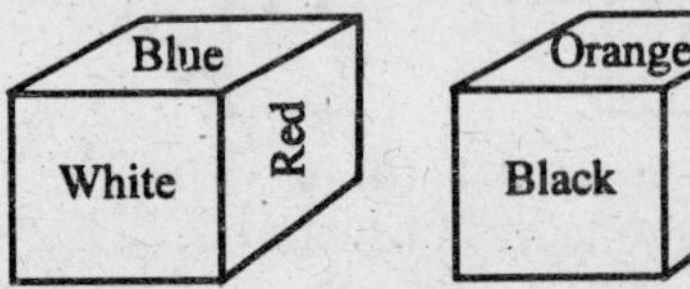

If blue and orange are opposite and red is on the top, which colour will be at the bottom?

(*a*) Orange (*b*) Purple
(*c*) Black (*d*) Yellow

17. A toy cube is painted orange on all sides. It is cut into 64 smaller cubes of equal size. How many smaller cubes are not painted at all?

(*a*) 4 (*b*) 8
(*c*) 16 (*d*) 20

18. A six centimetre cube is painted green on all sides. It is cut into two centimetre cubes. How many cubes will be there with two sides painted ?

(*a*) 12 (*b*) 8
(*c*) 24 (*d*) 4

19. What number in the dice, given below, will be on the side opposite to 6?

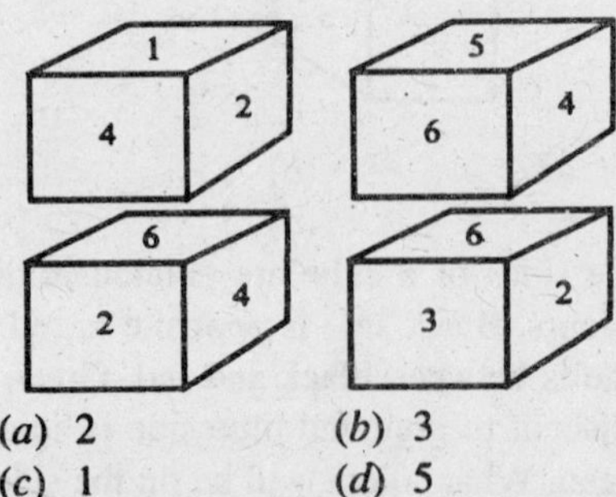

(*a*) 2 (*b*) 3
(*c*) 1 (*d*) 5

20. If the numbers on the opposite sides of the cube total as 7, which one of the following dices is definitely defective?

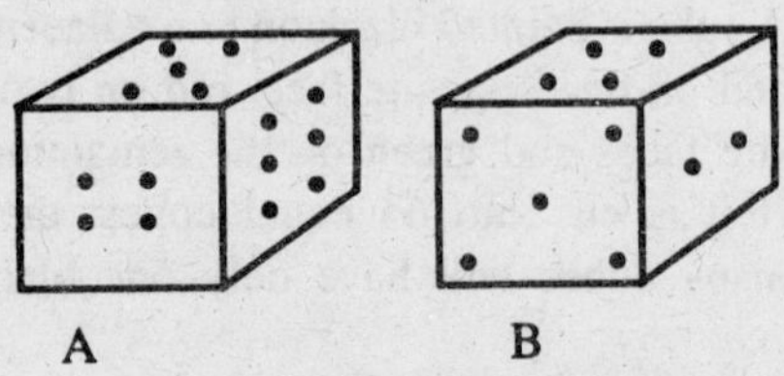

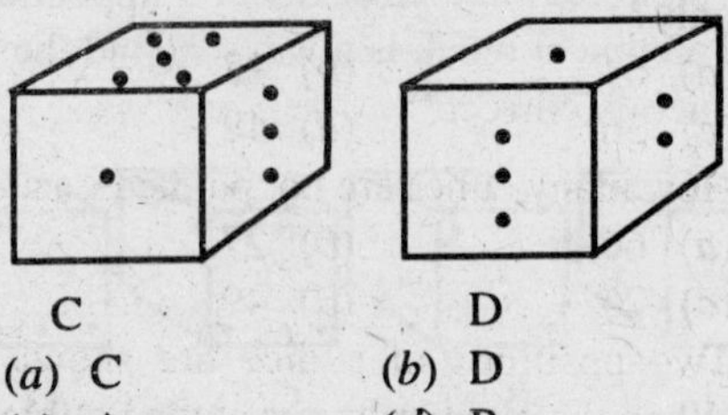

(*a*) C (*b*) D
(*c*) A (*d*) B

21. In the dice given below, which number will be on the top if 2 is at the bottom?

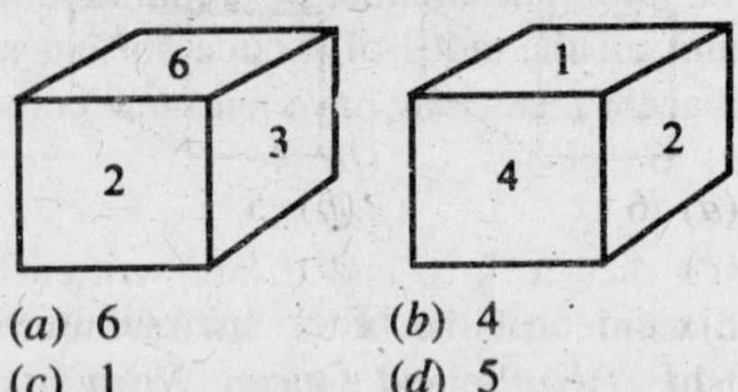

(*a*) 6 (*b*) 4
(*c*) 1 (*d*) 5

22. Which of the following pairs of numbers of the dice given below does not correctly give the numbers on the opposite side?

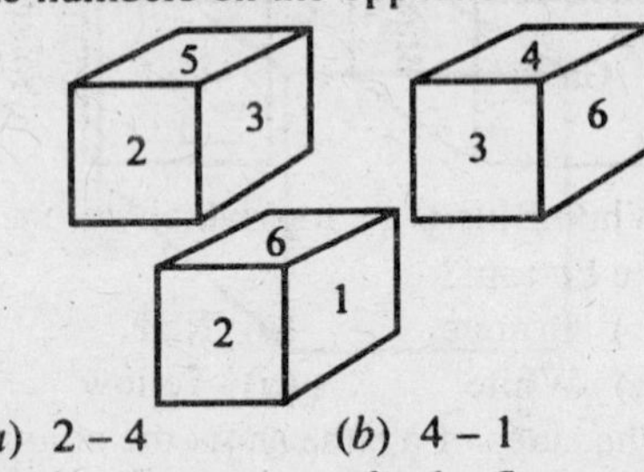

(*a*) 2 – 4 (*b*) 4 – 1
(*c*) 3 – 1 (*d*) 6 – 5

23. What will be the number of dots on the top of the following dice, if it is placed as in the second figure?

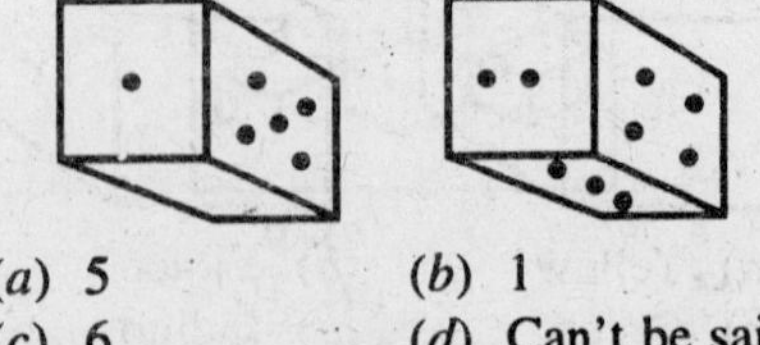

(*a*) 5 (*b*) 1
(*c*) 6 (*d*) Can't be said

Directions (Qs. 24 to 26) : *A cube, painted white on all the faces, is cut into 125 cubes of equal size. Now answer the questions 24 to 26.*

24. How many cubes are painted on one face only?

(*a*) 54 (*b*) 8
(*c*) 16 (*d*) 27

25. How many cubes are painted on two sides

only?

(*a*) 64 (*b*) 12

(*c*) 36 (*d*) 48

26. How many cubes are not painted on any face?

(*a*) 66 (*b*) 27

(*c*) 25 (*d*) 49

27. Two positions of a dice are shown below. When the number four is at the bottom, which number will be at the top?

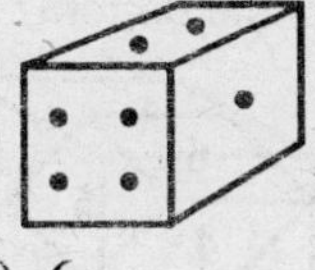

(*a*) 6 (*b*) 5

(*c*) 4 (*d*) 3

28. Six sides of the block are coloured Green, Blue, Red, Yellow, Orange, White in the following manner :

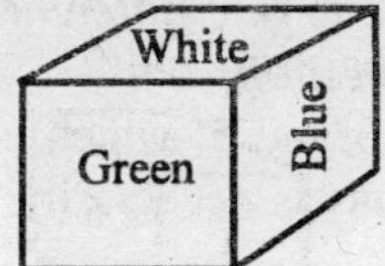

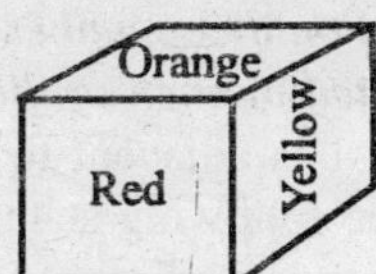

When Blue is on top, which colour will be at the bottom?

(*a*) Orange (*b*) Red

(*c*) White (*d*) Yellow

29. The sides of a cube show the colours of rainbow. Two positions of the cube are shown below. Which of the colours of rainbow is left out?

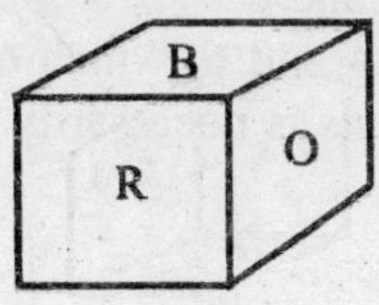

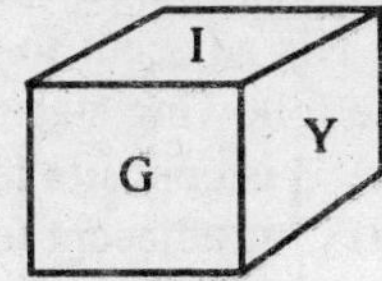

(*a*) Yellow (*b*) Violet

(*c*) Green (*d*) Indigo

Directions (Qs. 30-31) : *A die is thrown 4 times and its four different positions are given below :*

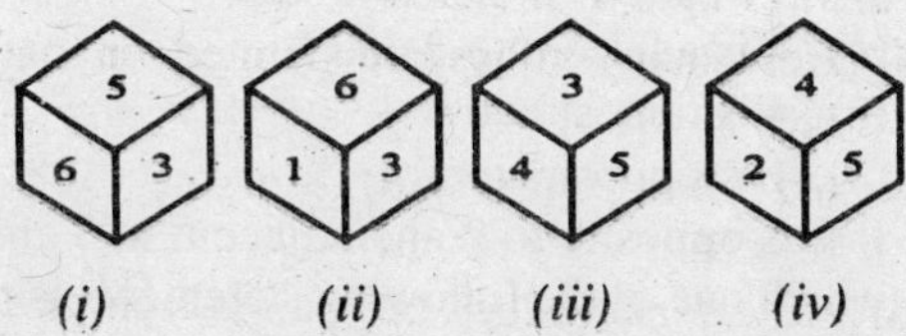

(*i*) (*ii*) (*iii*) (*iv*)

30. Find the number on the face opposite the face showing 3.

(*a*) 2 (*b*) 1

(*c*) 5 (*d*) 4

31. Find the number on the face opposite the face showing 6.

(*a*) 5 (*b*) 3

(*c*) 4 (*d*) 1

32. Observe the dots on a dice (one to six dots) in the following figures. How many dots are contained on the face opposite to that containing four dots?

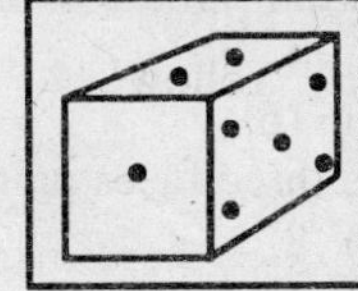
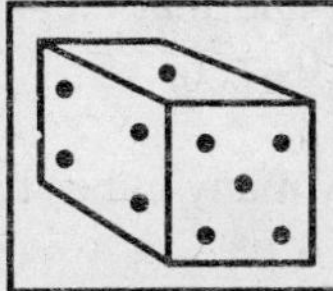

(*a*) 3 (*b*) 5

(*c*) 2 (*d*) 6

33. Two positions of a dice are shown below :

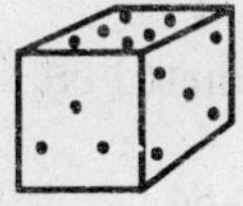

When three is at the bottom, what number will be at the top?

(*a*) 5 (*b*) 4

(*c*) 1 (*d*) 2

34. Four positions of a dice are shown below :

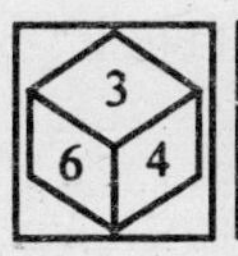

Identify the number at the bottom when top is 2.

(*a*) 6 (*b*) 4

(*c*) 3 (*d*) 1

Directions (Qs. 35–36) : *Three positions of a dice are given. Find out the number of the face with question mark.*

35.

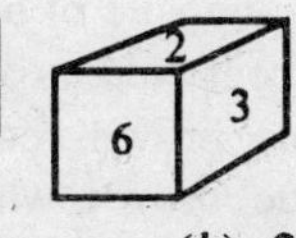

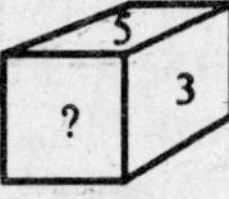

(*a*) 1 (*b*) 2

(*c*) 4 (*d*) 6

36. 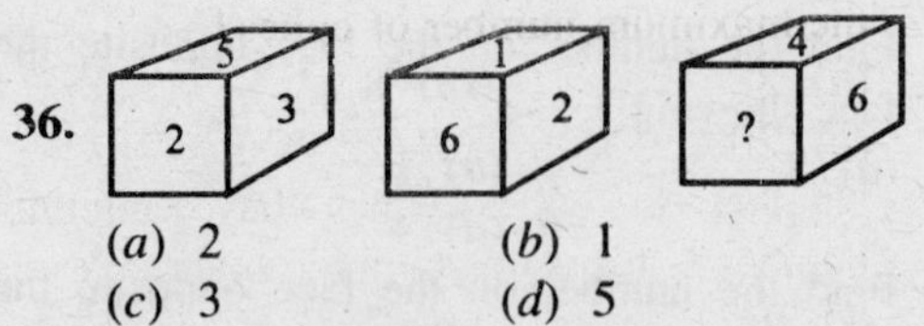

(*a*) 2 (*b*) 1
(*c*) 3 (*d*) 5

Directions (Qs. 37 to 40) : *The questions are based on the following statement :*

A cube is painted red on two adjacent faces, yellow on two opposite faces and green on the remaining faces. It is cut into 64 smaller cubes of equal size.

37. How many cubes are painted on two faces only and that too with the same colour?
(*a*) 0 (*b*) 4
(*c*) 8 (*d*) 16

38. How many cubes have three faces painted?
(*a*) 4 (*b*) 8
(*c*) 16 (*d*) 32

39. How many cubes are painted on one face only and are yellow?
(*a*) 32 (*b*) 16
(*c*) 8 (*d*) 4

40. How many cubes are painted on all faces?
(*a*) 0 (*b*) 4
(*c*) 8 (*d*) 64

Directions (Qs. 41 to 43) : *Study the information given below :*

The six faces of a cube are coloured black, brown, green, red, white and blue.
(i) Red is opposite of black
(ii) Green is between red and black
(iii) Blue is adjacent to white
(iv) Brown is adjacent to blue
(v) Red is at the bottom

41. Which colour is opposite of brown?
(*a*) White (*b*) Red
(*c*) Green (*d*) Blue

42. Which of the following can be deduced from (i) and (v)?
(*a*) Black is on the top
(*b*) Blue is on the top
(*c*) Brown is on the top
(*d*) Brown is opposite of black

43. The four adjacent colours are :
(*a*) black, blue, brown, red
(*b*) black, blue, brown, white
(*c*) black, blue, red, white
(*d*) black, blue, red, white

Directions (Qs. 44–45) : *In each of the following questions, a dice has been marked with some letters or numerals and placed in three different positions as shown in the figure.*

44. 

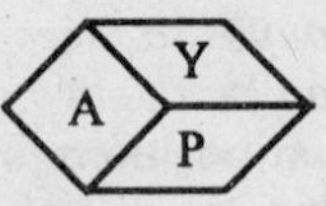

Which letter is opposite to L?
(*a*) A (*b*) P
(*c*) M (*d*) X

45. 

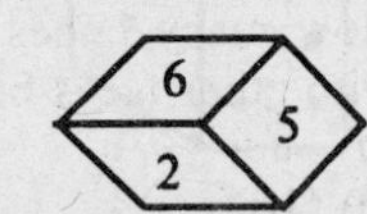

Which numeral is opposite to 4?
(*a*) 1 (*b*) 2
(*c*) 5 (*d*) 6

Directions (Qs. 46 to 50) : *The following questions are based on dice numbered 1 to 6 in different ways as indicated in each of the questions.*

46. If 1 is adjacent to 2, 3 and 5, which one of the following statements is necessarily true?
(*a*) 1 is adjacent to 4
(*b*) 1 is adjacent to 6
(*c*) 2 is adjacent to 5
(*d*) 4 is adjacent to 6

47. If 1 is opposite to 5 and 2 is opposite to 3 then :
(*a*) 4 is adjacent to 5 and 6
(*b*) 6 is adjacent to 3 and 4
(*c*) 2 is adjacent to 4 and 6
(*d*) 4 is adjacent to 3 and 6

48. If 1 is adjacent to 2, 4 and 6, which one of the following statements is necessarily true?
(*a*) 3 is opposite to 5
(*b*) 3 is adjacent to 5
(*c*) 1 is adjacent to 3
(*d*) 2 is opposite to 6

49. If 2 is opposite to 3 and adjacent to 4 and 6, which one of the following statements is necessarily true?
(*a*) 1 is adjacent to 2 and 3
(*b*) 4 is adjacent to 2 and 6
(*c*) 4 is opposite to 6
(*d*) 1 is opposite to 5

50. If 1 is opposite to 2 and adjacent to 3 and 4, which one of the following statements is nec-

essarily true?
(*a*) 3 is opposite to 5
(*b*) 4 is opposite to 6
(*c*) 3 is opposite to 4
(*d*) 2 is opposite to 6

Directions (Qs. 51 to 55) : *A cube is coloured red on two opposite faces, blue on two adjacent faces and yellow on the two remaining faces. It is then cut into two halves along the plane parallel to the red faces. One piece is then cut into four equal cubes and the other one into 32 equal cubes.*

Now answer the following questions based on the above :

51. How many cubes have each a yellow face with other faces blank?
(*a*) 4 (*b*) 14
(*c*) 16 (*d*) 17

52. How many cubes have at least one blue face?
(*a*) 4 (*b*) 14
(*c*) 16 (*d*) 17

53. How many cubes do not have any coloured face?
(*a*) 0 (*b*) 2
(*c*) 4 (*d*) 8

54. How many cubes do not have any red face?
(*a*) 8 (*b*) 16
(*c*) 20 (*d*) 24

55. How many cubes have at least two coloured face?
(*a*) 20 (*b*) 24
(*c*) 28 (*d*) 32

Directions (Qs. 56 to 61) : *In the figure given below there are 27 cubes. Answer the questions that follow :*

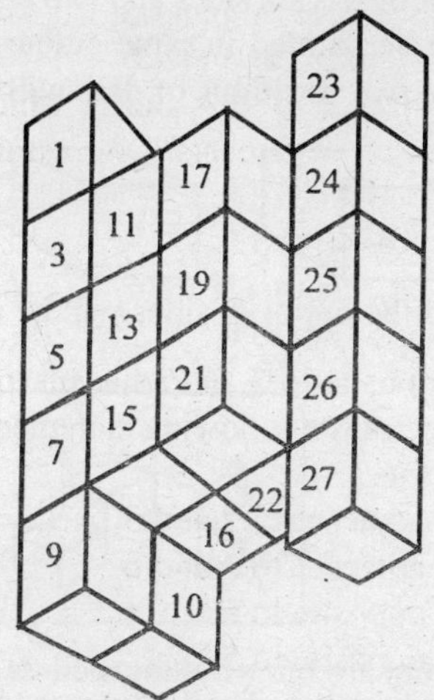

56. Which of the cubes 3, 8, 20 or 27 touches the maximum number of cubes?
(*a*) 3 (*b*) 8
(*c*) 20 (*d*) 27

57. Number of cubes which have minimum number of faces touching the other cubes is :
(*a*) 1 (*b*) 2
(*c*) 4 (*d*) 6

58. Number of cubes which have maximum number of faces touching the other cubes is :
(*a*) 1 (*b*) 2
(*c*) 3 (*d*) 4

59. What cube is hidden under the cube 19?
(*a*) 18 (*b*) 20
(*c*) 24 (*d*) 25

60. Which of the cubes 7, 21, 22 or 23 touches minimum number of cubes?
(*a*) 7 (*b*) 21
(*c*) 22 (*d*) 23

61. Which of the cubes 6, 13, 19 or 25 touches maximum number of cubes?
(*a*) 6 (*b*) 13
(*c*) 19 (*d*) 25

Directions (Qs. 62 to 64) : *In each question below a dice has been marked with some letters or numerals and placed in three different positions. Answer the questions that follow :*

62. Which letter is opposite to Q?

(*a*) P (*b*) R
(*c*) S (*d*) T

63. Which letter/numeral is opposite to 3?

(*a*) 2 (*b*) A
(*c*) B (*d*) C

64. If one of the 3 visible faces of the cube is hidden, which letter is opposite to O?

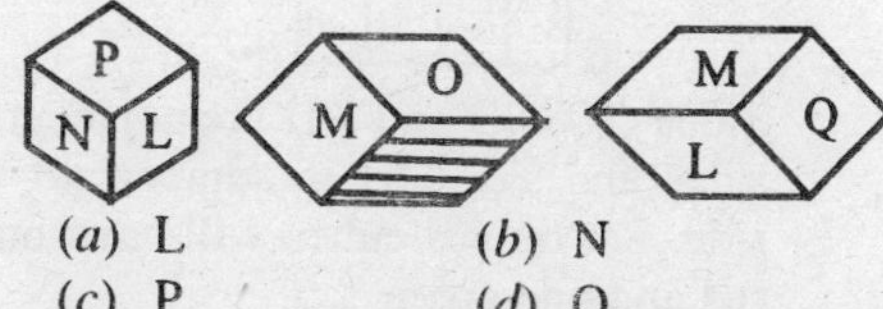

(*a*) L (*b*) N
(*c*) P (*d*) Q

Directions (Qs. 65 to 67) : *Given below are the three positions of the same dice. Answer the questions that follow :*

65. What is the number on the face opposite of face 2?
(*a*) 1
(*b*) 6
(*c*) 5
(*d*) Cannot be determined

66. In the third position of the dice which number lies on the face on the bottom?
(*a*) 2 (*b*) 3
(*c*) 4 (*d*) None of these

67. When value 5 is on the face on the top, which value lies on the face on the bottom?
(*a*) 3 (*b*) 4
(*c*) 1 (*d*) 2

Directions (Qs. 68 to 70) : *A solid cube with each side 3 cm has been painted red, blue and green on pairs of opposite faces. It is then cut into small cubes with each side 1 cm. Answer the questions that follow :*

68. How many cubes have one face painted red and one face painted green?
(*a*) 12 (*b*) 8
(*c*) 6 (*d*) 14

69. How many cubes have only one face painted?
(*a*) 6 (*b*) 4
(*c*) 12 (*d*) 9

70. How many cubes are painted blue on one face and either red or green on another face?
(*a*) 4 (*b*) 6
(*c*) 8 (*d*) 12

EXPLANATORY ANSWERS

1. (*a*) : After observing the views of the same dice, the faces that can be clearly understood to be the opposites are :
2 — 5, 4 — 3 and 1— 6.

2. (*a*) : In the given dice, the numbers adjacent to 1 are 3, 2, 5 and 6. So, the numbers on the opposite faces will be 1 and 4.

3. (*b*) :

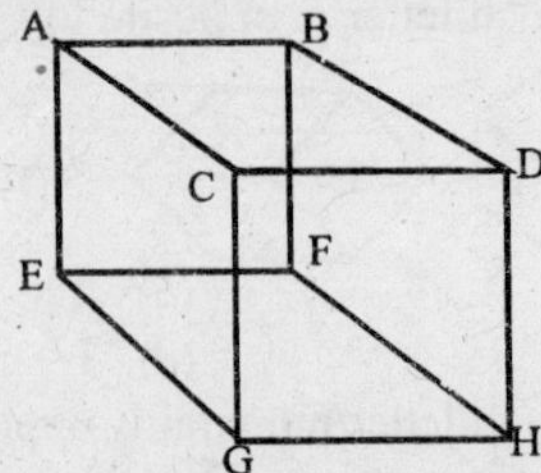

The red sides are EGAC, ABCD and BDFH.
The yellow sides are ABEF and EFGH
The green side is CDGH.

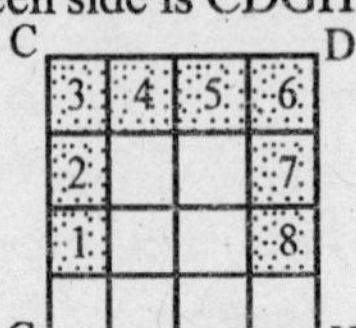

Sides GC, CD and DH are adjacent to red sides and side GH is adjacent to yellow side. So, only 8 cubes will have one side red and one green.

4. (*a*) : It is, however, clear that the number on the face opposite 2 dots is the face with 4 dots. But it is not clear if the number 1 or 5 is on face opposite the face 3. The answer is either 1 or 5.

5. (*c*) : The letters on the top and bottom sides are W and D respectively and the letters on the sides are U, Y, M and S clockwise.

6. (*a*) : In this cubical block the number of dots on opposite faces will be 1—6, 3—4 and 5—2.

7. (*c*) : A cube has six sides and two opposite sides can be painted in same colour.

8. (*a*) : The two positions of dice will be :

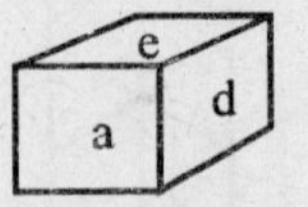

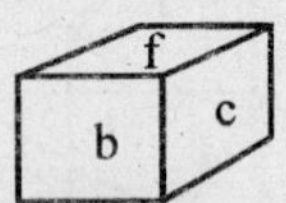

and the opposite sides will be a—c, b—d.

9. (*d*) :

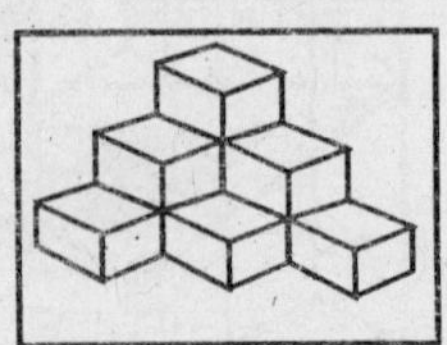

There are three columns containing 1 cube

each. There are two columns containing 2 cubes each. There is one column containing 3 cubes. So, the total number of cubes is : $(3 \times 1) + (2 \times 2) + (1 \times 3)$ *i.e.*, $3 + 4 + 3 = 10$.

10. (*b*) : When 5 and 6 are on opposite faces then the numbers on opposite faces will be 4—1 and 2—3. So, if 2 is at the bottom, 3 will be at the top.

11. (*b*) : After observing the two views of the same dice, the faces that can be clearly understood to be the opposites are : 1—6, 2—4 and 3—5. So, when 1 is at the top, 6 will be at the bottom.

12. (*d*) : The sides which are clearly understood to be the opposites are 1—3, 2—4 and 5—6. So, when 2 is at the bottom, 4 will be at the top.

13. (*d*) : The numbers on the sides opposite to each other are 1 and 4; 2 and 5; 3 and 6.

14. (*b*) :

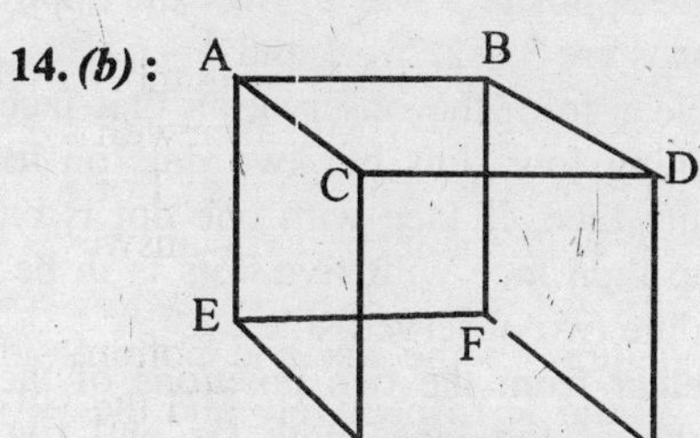

Side ABCD is red; and EFGH is black. If ACEG is white; and CDGH is grey; then adjacent to it BDFH can be green; and ABEF is orange. Then the colour of the side opposite to white side of the cube (ACEG) will be green (BDFH).

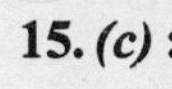

15. (*c*) :

Three faces of the cube are painted black and the rest are in different colours. If this cube is cut into 64 equal cubes, then only the 4 cubes in centre of one face will come out with only one black coloured face. So, the total number of one black coloured face small cubes will be $4 \times 3 = 12$.

16. (*d*) :

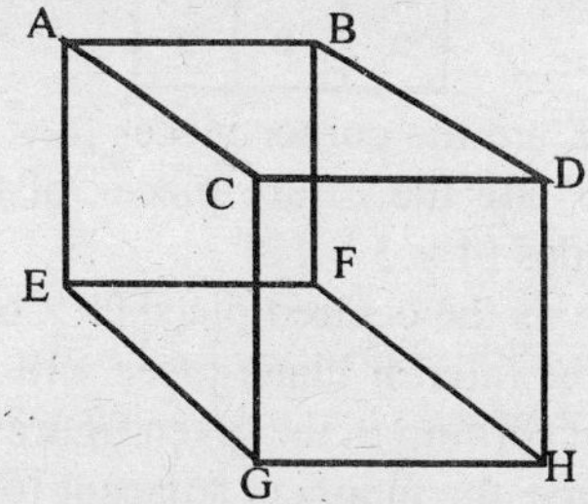

If side ABCD is red; then ABEF will be white; and ACEG will be blue. If side BDFH is orange (opposite to blue); then CDGH will be black; and EFGH will be yellow (opposite to red and at the bottom).

17. (*b*) : The smaller 64 pieces will be cut in the manner that :

1. 8 pieces will be painted on 3 sides,
2. 24 pieces on 2 sides.
3. 24 pieces on 1 side, and
4. 8 will not have paint at all.

Diagrammatically, the explanation taking one side of the cube will be :

a	b	b	a
b	c	c	b
b	c	c	b
a	b	b	a

1. 'a' are the corner pieces $[4 \times 2 = 8]$
2. 'b' are the centre pieces of the cornered sides $[8 \times 3 = 24]$
3. 'c' are the centre pieces $[4 \times 6 = 24]$
4. Remaining interior pieces $= 64 - (8 + 24 + 24)$ $= 64 - 56 = 8$.

18. (*a*) : The smaller 27 pieces of the cube will be cut in the manner that :

1. 8 pieces will be painted on 3 sides,
2. 12 pieces on 2 sides,
3. 6 pieces on 1 side, and
4. 1 piece will not have paint at all.

Diagrammatically, the explanation taking

one side of the cube will be :

a	b	a
b	c	b
a	b	a

1. 'a' are the corner pieces [4 × 2 = 8]
2. 'b' are the centre pieces of the cornered sides [4 × 3 = 12]
3. 'c' is the centred piece [1 × 6 = 6]
4. The interior blank piece will be only 1.

19. (*c*) : According to the given figures of the same dice, the numbers adjacent to 6 are 5, 4, 2 and 3. So, the number opposite to the side 6 will be 1.

20. (*d*) : 5 and 2 are on adjacent sides instead of being on the opposite side.

21. (*d*) : In the given dice, the numbers adjacent to 2 are 6, 3, 1 and 4. The only number that can be opposite to the side 2 is 5.

22. (*b*) : After observing the views of the same dice, the sides that can be clearly understood to be the opposites are : 2 – 4, 3 – 1 and 5 – 6.

23. (*c*) : The numbers adjacent to 2 are 1, 5, 3 and 4. So, the number of dots opposite to the side with 2 dots will be 6.

24. (*a*), 25 (*c*), 26. (*b*) :
The smaller 125 pieces of the cube will be cut in the manner—

1. 8 pieces will be painted on 3 faces.
2. 36 pieces on 2 faces.
3. 54 pieces on 1 face only.
4. 27 pieces will not have paint at all.
Diagrammatically, the explanation taking one side of the cube will be :

a	b	b	b	a
b	c	c	c	b
b	c	c	c	b
b	c	c	c	b
a	b	b	b	a

1. 'a' are the corner pieces [4 × 2 = 8]
2. 'b' are the centre pieces of the cornered sides [12 × 3 = 36]
3. 'c' are the centred pieces [9 × 6 = 54]
4. The interior blank pieces will be 27.

27. (*d*) : The sides of the dice which are clearly understood to be the opposites are : 1 – 6, 2 – 5 and 3 – 4. So, when 4 is at the bottom, 3 will be at the top.

28. (*d*) : The coloured sides of the block which are clearly understood to be the opposites are: White – Orange, Blue – Yellow and Green – Red. So, when blue is on the top, yellow will be at the bottom.

29. (*b*) : The rainbow colours are VIBGYOR. Only V, *i.e.*, violet is left out.

30. (*a*) : From figures (i), (ii) and (iii) it is clear that the faces adjacent to 3 have numbers 6, 5, 1 and 4. So, the number on face opposite of face 3 will be 2.

31. (*c*) : From figures (i), (iii) and (iv) it is clear that the faces adjacent to 5 have numbers 6, 3, 4 and 2. So the number on face opposite of face 5 is 1. In earlier question the face apposite 3 was 2. Now the opposite faces are 3 – 2, 5 – 1 and 4 – 6.

32. (*c*) : It is clear from the observation that face containing four dots has two dots on its opposite face. If face with one dot is on the top then face with five dots is in between the two observed sides.

33. (*d*) : It is clear from the two positions of the dice that if the faces with six and five dots are on side, then faces with three and two dots are on the opposite. So, if three is at the bottom, 2 will be on the top.

34. (*b*) : After observing the views of the same dice, it can be clearly understood that :
(*i*) the sides adjacent to 1 are 5, 4, 6 and 2. So, side opposite 1 is 3.
(*ii*) the sides adjacent to 5 are 3, 4, 1, 2. So, side opposite 5 is 6.
(*iii*) the sides adjacent to 4 are 3, 6, 5 and 1. So, side opposite 4 is 2.
So, when number on the top is 2, bottom number will be 4.

35. (*b*) : The numbers 1, 2, 3 and 4 on the dice are written on adjacent faces while 5 and 6 are on opposite faces. Here, considering the adjacent order of the numbers, 2 will come on the face with question mark. If the number on the top was 6, then number 4 will come on the face with question mark.

36. (*b*) : Numbers adjacent to 2 are : 5, 3, 1 and 6. So 2 and 4 are on opposite faces. 5 and 3 are adjacent numbers if 2 is at the bottom. So, 1 and 6 will be adjacent when 4 is on the top.

37. (*b*), 38. (*b*), 39. (*c*), 40. (*a*) :

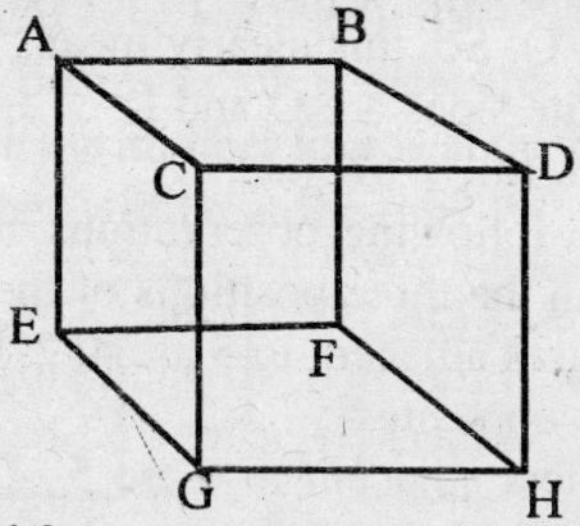

Red faces are ABCD and ABEF
Yellow faces are ACEG and BDFH
Green faces are EFGH and CDGH.

Note that Red and Green colours are on two adjacent faces. So, 2 corner cubical pieces of Red and 2 of Green (*i.e.* total 4 cubes) will be painted on two faces only and that too with the same colour.

All the corners pieces of the cube will have three faces painted. *i.e.*, 8 cubes.

Yellow sides are on the opposites. Diagrammatically, the explanation taking one side will be :

a	b	b	a
b	c	c	b
b	c	c	b
a	b	b	a

'c' are the centered pieces and are painted on one face only in yellow. So, 4 × 2 (sides) *i.e.* 8 cubes will have one side painted and in yellow.

Also, note that when a painted cube is cut into smaller cubes like this, not all pieces are coloured. The maximum number of sides painted in a small cube will be 3. No cube will be painted on all faces.

41. (*a*), 42. (*a*), 43. (*d*) :

According to the given information the two positions of the cube will be :

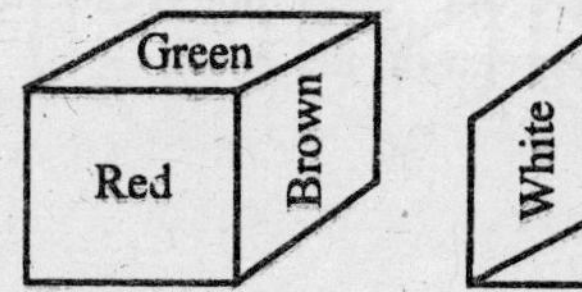

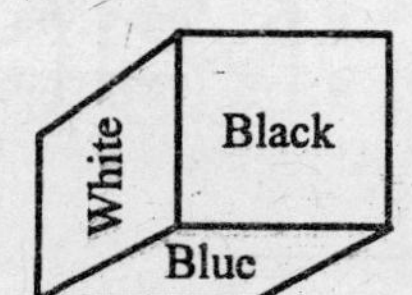

The whole cube will be :

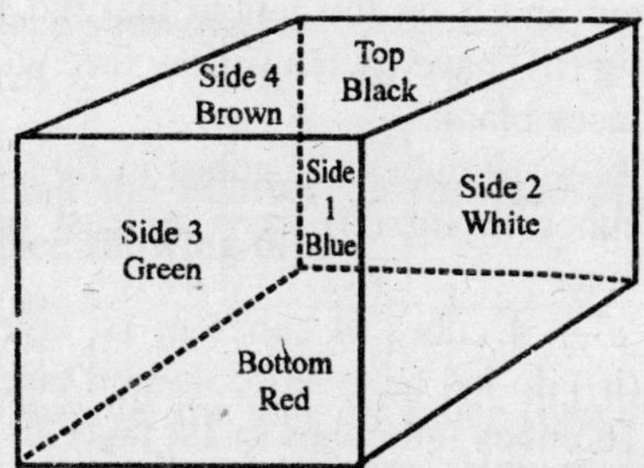

The colours on opposite faces will be : Red—Black, Green—Blue and Brown—White.

44. (*a*) : It is clear from the positions of the dice that letters adjacent to A are X, M, Y and P. So, the opposite letters are A and L.

45. (*d*) : It is clear from the positions of the dice that letters adjacent to 3 are 1, 6, 5, 4. So, the number opposite 3 is 2. Also, the numbers adjacent to 6 are 1, 3, 2, 5. So, the number opposite 6 is 4. Clearly, the opposite numbers are now 3—2, 6—4 and 1—5.

46. (*d*), 47. (*c*), 48. (*b*), 49. (*a*), 50. (*d*)
51. (*a*), 52. (*d*), 53. (*c*), 54. (*b*), 55. (*a*) :

The whole cube is :

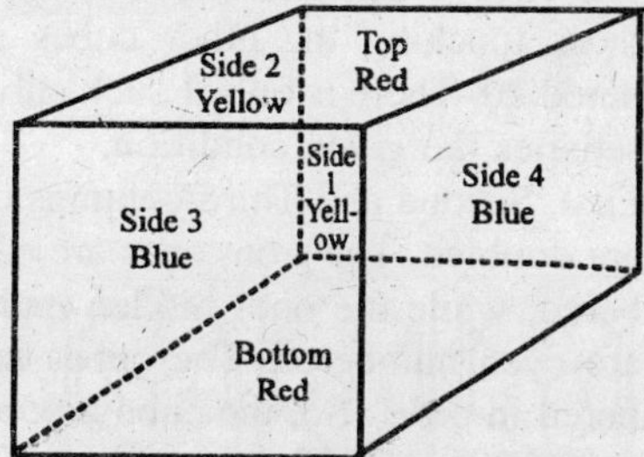

(*i*) Piece cut into 4 parts with Bottom Red.

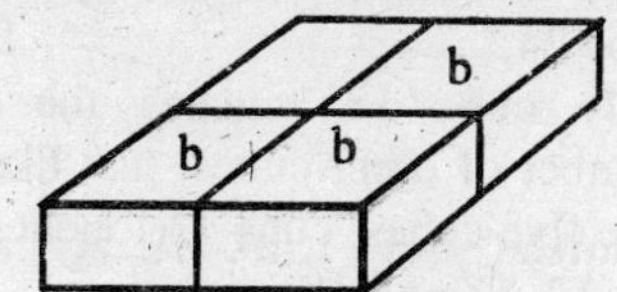

(*ii*) Piece cut into 32 parts with Top Red.

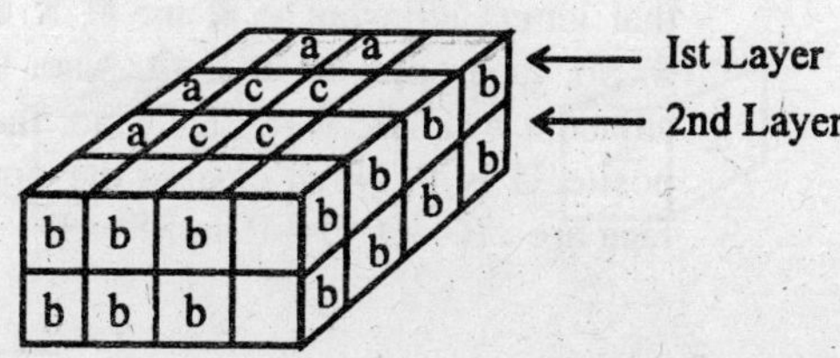

* 'a'— 4 cubes (two middle cubes in the top and 2 on the left in the 2nd layer in fig (ii)) have each a yellow face with other faces blank.
* 'b'— 17 cubes (14 cubes in fig (ii) and 3 cubes in fig (i)) have at least one blue face.
* 'c'— 4 cubes (4 cubes in 1st layer in fig (ii)) do not have any coloured face.
* 16 cubes (all cubes in 1st layer in fig (ii)) do not have any red face.
* 20 cubes (4 cubes in fig (i); 8 cornered cubes in both layers in fig (ii) and 8 middle cubes in 2nd layer in fig (ii)) have at least two coloured faces.

56. (*c*), **57.** (*b*), **58.** (*a*),
59. (*b*), **60.** (*d*), **61.** (*b*) :

* The sides of cube numbered 20 touches five other cubes, *i.e.*, the maximum number of cubes. The five cubes are : 14, 18, 19, 22 and 25.
* The cubes having the minimum number of faces touching other cubes are only touching one cube. These are numbered 23 and 27.
* The cube which has maximum number of faces touching the other cubes is numbered 20. There is only 1 such cube which satisfies the given condition.
* First, Second and Third columns of cubes are doubled. The front ones are odd numbered, while the ones hidden under them are even numbered. The cubes are numbered in order. So, the cube hidden under cube 19 is cube 20.
* Cube 23 touches only 1 other cube, *i.e.* cube 24.
* Only cube 13 touches the maximum number of other cubes, just like cube 20. The five cubes, cube 13 touches are — 5, 11, 12, 15 and 19.

62. (*b*) : It is clear from the positions of the dice that letters adjacent to R are P, T, U and S. So, face opposite R is Q. Also, letters adjacent to U are R, S, T, Q. So, face opposite U is P. Now, clearly the opposite face are : R—Q, U—P and S—T.

63. (*d*) : After observing the views of the same dice the sides that can be clearly understood to be the opposites are : 1—8, A—2 and C—3.

64. (*a*) : It is clear from the given positions of the dice that letters adjacent to L are P, N, M and Q. So, this clearly means that the opposite sides are O and L.

65. (*b*), **66.** (*c*), **67.** (*a*) :
The following observations can be made from the three positions of the same dice.
(i) Letters adjacent to 5 are 4, 2, 6 and 1. So, 3 is opposite 5.
(ii) Letters adjacent to 6 are 5, 4, 1 and necessarily 4. So, 2 is opposite 6.
(iii) When opposite numbers are 3—5 and 2—6 then 1 and 4 must be opposites.

68. (*a*), **69.** (*a*), **70.** (*c*) :
The whole cube is :

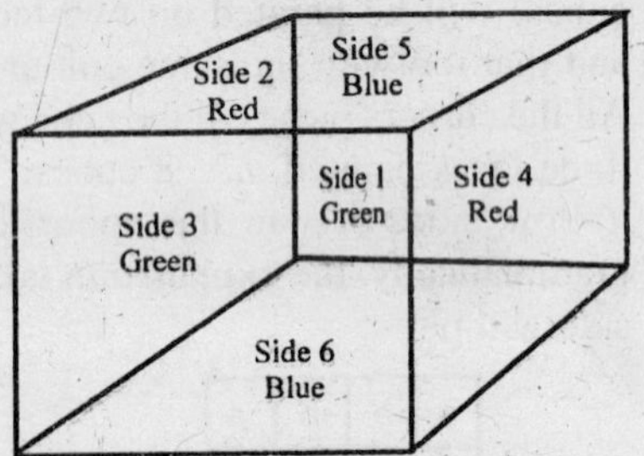

The divided cube is :

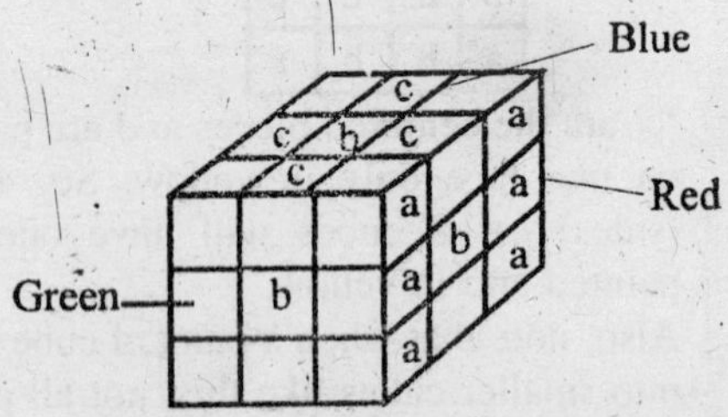

'a'— 12 cubes (6 each on opposite sides) have one face painted red and the other painted green.
'b'— 6 cubes (1 on each side) have only one face painted).
'c'— 8 cubes (4 each on opposite side) have one face painted blue and either red or green on the other.